1995 CLEVELAND INDIANS
THE SLEEPING GIANT AWAKES

EDITED BY JOSEPH WANCHO

ASSOCIATE EDITORS: RICK HUHN, LEN LEVIN, AND BILL NOWLIN

Society for American Baseball Research, Inc.
Phoenix, AZ

1995 Cleveland Indians
The Sleeping Giant Awakes

Edited by Joseph Wancho
Associate Editors: Rick Huhn, Len Levin, and Bill Nowlin

Copyright © 2019 Society for American Baseball Research, Inc.
All rights reserved. Reproduction in whole or in part without permission is prohibited.
ISBN 978-1-943816-95-8
(Ebook ISBN 978-1-943816-94-1)

Book design: Rachael Sullivan
Society for American Baseball Research
Cronkite School at ASU
555 N. Central Ave. #416
Phoenix, AZ 85004
Phone: (602) 496-1460
Web: www.sabr.org
Facebook: Society for American Baseball Research
Twitter: @SABR

All photographs throughout this book are courtesy of the National Baseball Hall of Fame, except for the following:

Tom Hamilton, courtesy of the Cleveland Indians.
Jack Corrigan: 297
Chuck Guerrieri: 41, 119, 191, 235, 260, and 325.
Larry Phillips: 246.
Lou Boyd: 383, 384.
Bill Gagliano: 365, 369, 374, 375, 385, 388.

CONTENTS

Introduction — Joseph Wancho.......5
The Fans of the 1995 Cleveland Indians — John McMurray.......7

THE PLAYERS

Sandy Alomar Jr. — Joseph Wancho.......12
Ruben Amaro — Rory Costello.......17
Paul Assenmacher — Nick Waddell.......24
Carlos Baerga — Joseph Wancho.......29
David Bell — Philip A. Cola.......34
Albert Belle — Tom Wancho.......41
Bud Black — Nick Waddell.......46
Jeromy Burnitz — Kelly Boyer Sagert......50
Mark Clark — Bob LeMoine.......55
Dennis Cook — Alan Cohen.......62
Alan Embree — Bill Nowlin.......68
Alvaro Espinoza — Gregg Omoth.......74
John Farrell — Bill Nowlin.......78
Brian Giles — Mark Hodermarsky....84
Jason Grimsley — Chip Greene.......88
Orel Hershiser — Joseph Wancho.......95
Ken Hill — Gregory H. Wolf.......99
Wayne Kirby — Ed Gruver.......106
Jesse Levis — Chip Greene.......110
Kenny Lofton — Richard Bogovich......117
Albie Lopez — Harry Schoger.......122
Dennis Martinez — Rory Costello.......127
Jose Mesa — Joseph Wancho.......136
Eddie Murray — Alan Cohen.......142
Charles Nagy — Steve West.......151
Chad Ogea — David Skelton.......156
Gregg Olson — Wynn Montgomery...162
Tony Pena — Blake Sherry.......170
Herbert Perry — Jay Hurd.......175
Eric Plunk — Ted Leavengood........179
Jim Poole — Chip Greene.......182
Manny Ramirez — Bill Nowlin.......189
Billy Ripken — Jimmy Keenan.......196
Joe Roa — Clayton Trutor.......201
Paul Shuey — Charles Faber.......205
Paul Sorrento — Alan Cohen.......208
Julian Tavarez — Paul Hofmann.......214
Jim Thome — Joseph Wancho.......221
Eddie Tucker — Richard Cuicchi.......227
Omar Vizquel — Augusto Cardenas.....232
Dave Winfield — Doug Skipper.......241

THE COACHING STAFF

Mike Hargrove — Gregory H. Wolf.....257
Buddy Bell — Joseph Wancho........264
Luis Isaac — Richard Bogovich.....270
Charlie Manuel — Andy Sturgill.........276
Dave Nelson — Rick Schabowski....281
Jeff Newman — Gary Livacari.........286
Mark Wiley — Joel Rippel.........290

THE BROADCASTERS

Jack Corrigan — Joseph Wancho.......297
Tom Hamilton — Kelly Boyer Sagert....302
Mike Hegan — Joseph Wancho.......307
Rick Manning — Kelly Boyer Sagert....312

Herb Score   Joseph Wancho.........315

THE FRONT OFFICE

Richard Jacobs   Clayton Trutor.........325
John Hart   Rick Balazs.........330
Dan O'Dowd   Christopher Williamson.......338

THE BALLPARK

Jacobs Field   Stephanie Liscio.........345

SELECTED GAMES

May 7, 1995   Richard Cuicchi.........352
June 4, 1995   Joseph Wancho.........355
June 5, 1995   Gregory H. Wolf.........357
June 30, 1995   Joseph Wancho.........359
July 21, 1995   Richard Cuicchi.........361
September 8, 1995   Joseph Wancho.........363
September 13, 1995   Gregory H. Wolf.........365

OTHER FEATURES

1995 American League Division Series
                 Mark S. Sternman.........369
1995 American League Championship Series
                 Steve West.........374
1995 World Series   Jeanne M. Mallett.........383
1995 Cleveland Indians By the Numbers
                 Dan Fields.........395

Acknowledgments.........404

Contributors.........406

INTRODUCTION

JOSEPH WANCHO

At approximately 10:00 P.M. EDT on September 8, 1995, a popup by Baltimore's Jeff Huson nestled into the glove of third baseman Jim Thome for the final out of a 3-2 Indians win. The victory set off a celebration not seen in Cleveland in 41 years. THE CLEVELAND INDIANS WERE HEADED TO THE POSTSEASON!

The long-awaited celebration in Cleveland was not much of a surprise. The Indians ran away from the pack in the American League's Central Division, leading Kansas City by 21½ games heading into the month of September. Still, at the moment the horsehide was secured by Thome, you could not blame Cleveland fans if they were checking the sky above Jacobs Field to see if pigs had taken flight or consulting the weather report to see if hell had indeed frozen over.

Not since the 1954 World Series, when Cleveland was swept by the New York Giants in four games, had "Indians Fever" spread through the city like a pandemic. There had been some glimpses of hope, but they were few and far between. The Indians finished in second place, five games behind Chicago, in 1959. In the 35 seasons that followed, the Tribe finished .500 or above in seven of those years. Two of the seven seasons were partial seasons due to players strikes.

Cleveland sportswriter Terry Pluto wrote a book in 1994 that describes this period of Indians baseball. The book, *The Curse of Rocky Colavito: A Loving Look at a Thirty-Year Slump*, traces the trials and tribulations of a franchise and its general place of ignominy from the time Colavito was traded to Detroit on April 17, 1960, through 1993. For Tribe fans, you had to laugh at the insanity of it all, or you would just cry at the memories and anecdotes as written by Pluto.

But the light was shining brightly at the end of the tunnel. Fortunately, it was not an oncoming train but instead the bright lights of a new baseball-only stadium. The Indians moved across downtown from their dreary home at Cleveland Stadium to the shiny, open-air Jacobs Field. The Indians posted a 66-47 record in 1994, finishing one game behind the White Sox in the newly formed Central Division. The season came to a crashing halt due to a players strike on August 12 and once again Cleveland fans were left with an empty season. But there was hope on the horizon. Yes sir, there was real, honest-to-goodness, not-just-BS-hope.

The Tribe has had wonderful success in their new ballpark, which is turning 25 years old in 2019. The Indians have been to the postseason 11 times through 2018 and that is no small feat for a club branded with the tag "mid-market team." The Indians ruled Cleveland from 1994 through 2001, winning two pennants and five playoff appearances. The Cleveland Browns had left town and were now putting down roots in Baltimore. The Cleveland Cavaliers, while competitive, were usually ousted in the first round of the playoffs. The Indians were the best ticket in town and 455 straight sellouts from June 12, 1995, to April 2, 2001, are a testament to their popularity.

While the Indians have made it to the brink of baseball nirvana, losing in Game Seven of two World Series (1997, 2016), it is the 1995 team that fans fondly remember the most.

Perhaps this is due to that team's being the first to break through and make it to the postseason. Maybe it's because of the different characters and personalities who made up that team. Maybe it is because they had an All-Star seemingly at every position.

As you leaf through the following pages, you will be transported back in time to 1995. The biographies of all the players, coaches, and broadcasters bring back that glorious time once again for Tribe fans. The manuscript is also sprinkled with personal perspectives, as well as game stories from key matchups during the 1995 season.

Gabe Paul served as the Indians general manager from 1961 through 1973. He also was the team president from 1978 through 1984. Paul once said that as far as the Indians are concerned, the city of Cleveland is a "sleeping giant." If you put a winning product on the field, the sleeping giant will awake. In 1995, Paul's point was made loud and clear: The Sleeping Giant Awoke.

Terry Pluto wrote a sequel to his previous book, *Reverse the Curse: How the Indians Became the Best Team in Baseball.* Tribe fans liked the outcome of this book much better.

- Joseph Wancho

THE FANS OF THE 1995 CLEVELAND INDIANS

BY JOHN MCMURRAY

That the Cleveland Indians established a single-season team attendance record in 1995 is no surprise, given the Indians' dominance over other American League teams.[1] Yet it was the fervor and passion of those fans and their deep connection to the 1995 team that anyone who was in Cleveland at the time recalls more than two decades later.

Cleveland has had a long history of supporting its local teams, especially when their fortunes turn for the better. Fans routinely filled the Richfield Coliseum to see the Cleveland Cavaliers during the 1976 "Miracle of Richfield," the first season the Cavaliers won the division title. In 1980, after more than a decade of lackluster finishes, the "Kardiac Kids" Cleveland Browns sold out Municipal Stadium week after week. The resurgent Indians, who did not finish above fourth place between 1968 and 1993, certainly fit the mold of a team that Clevelanders would show up to support, as they had just turned a significant corner. At the same time, Cleveland's diehard baseball fans were guaranteed to be in attendance, regardless.

Still, the 1995 Indians offered something more. Fans could see from early in that season that this team was a championship-caliber club. Yet, by playing winning baseball in a new ballpark in a new location during the middle of the city's renaissance, the 1995 Indians experience was something that no Cleveland team had offered before or since. The 2,842,745 fans who came to Jacobs Field that season – the second-best attendance in the American League – saw young and fearless team in a ballpark that was a marked departure from drab Municipal Stadium. The entire experience was new. With the Indians seemingly capable of winning every game, a sense of electricity flowed through the stadium stands from the game's start to finish. The Indians were a phenomenon, and the fans served as a driving source of energy.

Starting in 1994, when the Indians consistently played competitive baseball in their first season in Jacobs Field, the vibe surrounding Cleveland baseball appeared to change dramatically. As of Opening Day in 1994, the Indians had already sold as many tickets for that season as they had for all of 1993, and, as Richard Justice wrote after the first game, fans in attendance at the 1994 home opener "had seen what they'd come for: the rebirth of baseball in Cleveland and in a sense, the rebirth of Cleveland."[2]

Fans' attachment to the new-look Cleveland Indians began to build throughout 1994. An Associated Press article from June of that year spoke of how fans "are pouring out in record numbers" to see the team and that "merchandise sales have risen considerably." David Nolan, president of the Cleveland Convention and Visitors Bureau, attributed a surge in hotel occupancy to the team's strong performance, claiming that "it's 6 to 8 percent higher than projected for occupied rooms. That's also how it is for food and beverage sales all across downtown."[3] That Cleveland might have made the World Series in 1994 had it not been for the players strike scrubbing that year's postseason only whetted local fans' appetites for 1995. If other cities' interest in baseball waned after the strike, Cleveland's surged.

The fan experience at Jacobs Field also made an extraordinary difference. Gone were the obstructed views and seats that felt miles from the action, replaced by a setting that brought fans close to the field and part of a collective experience. For the first time, "charm" was a word used to describe Cleveland's ballpark, and, as Ed Sherman said, "[c]hanging addresses from Cleveland Stadium – depressing redefined – to Jacobs Field is like moving from Siberia to Maui."[4] No longer were fans sitting widely apart from one another, as they often did across the cavernous old stadium; to the contrary, they sat clustered together – and were hopping to buy seats for games in July when they went on sale before Christmas.

But it was the way the team won that kept fans' rapt attention. For decades, Indians teams seldom had more than one legitimate power hitter. Suddenly they had a roster where anyone in the starting lineup was capable of hitting home runs, and lofty ones at that. These new players also did it with a swagger befitting the mid-1970s New York Yankees. If Albert Belle was this team's Reggie Jackson or Jim Thome its George Brett, fans' perspective on the entire franchise changed, as team followers – almost unfathomably – came to view the Cleveland Indians as the favorites in any game they played. It was winning combined with pageantry and showmanship. Even when Cleveland hitters swung and missed, they swung big. As a result, being at Jacobs Field to see it in person became essential.

Then there were the comeback wins. None in the regular season was more emblematic of this team's potential in 1995 than the June 4 victory, capped by Paul Sorrento's two-out ninth-inning home run to win the game, when the team had fallen behind 8-0 against the Toronto Blue Jays. The record 455-game sellout streak that began in Cleveland in 1995 stemmed from this team having a late-inning magic that no other Cleveland baseball team has had before or since. If the boxes behind home plate and adjacent to the dugouts at Jacobs Field did indeed cost $100,000 per season, somehow it was worth it in order to see 40 years of pedestrian baseball turned around so authoritatively and decisively, usually with a home run that seemed to say *take that!*

In 1995 Cleveland fans wore their team's apparel proudly. The more of it, it seemed, the better. After noting that the Indians had spent "40 years wandering in baseball's barren land," Murray Chass quoted fan Shirley Klein, who said that season: "You can't go anywhere without seeing Indians shirts and hats. I walk in the morning and people toot their horns because I wear an Indians shirt."[5] By the middle of 1995, one estimate had 27,000 Indians caps and a comparable number of T-shirts sold in the team's store at the ballpark by early July 1995.[6]

Indeed, the transition was as complete as it was unexpected: The Cleveland Indians in 1995 had become a point of civic pride. Alan Sudimack, a local marketing vice president, said in September 1995: "I'm so proud of this city right now that if a member of the Indians ran over me in his car, I'd jump up and say, 'I'm sorry, did I scratch the paint?'"[7]

Ira Berkow described how Gary Goldwasser, a local attorney, changed from his suit and glasses into his Cleveland gear, "transformed from a mild-mannered lawyer into, well, Superfan!" Goldwasser, Berkow noted, "is not alone and won't be alone." Rather "all over town, citizens have been performing similar rituals." For his part, Goldwasser said: "Everybody in this city hangs on every game. All we do is talk about the Indians. … My wife, Lois, who's never had much interest in baseball, can now tell you the averages of all the players. It's like that in family after family here."[8]

Fans who couldn't get tickets to games were connected to the team through the radio broadcasts. Tom Hamilton, a relative newcomer to the team's broadcasts, with his anticipatory home-run calls, made fans feel like they were at the park. At the same time, announcer Herb Score was a connection both to Cleveland's winning teams of the mid- to late 1950s, of which he was a member, and to its many losing teams, which he covered for more than 30 years as an announcer. Their complementary styles worked, and fans bonded with Herb and Tom, who connected them with this once-in-a-generation ballclub.

As much as fans flocked to Jacobs Field to see winning baseball for the first time in generations, they came also to see a unique team chemistry. The 1995 Cleveland Indians were a tight-knit baseball team whose confidence and belief it in itself connected the fan base.

Other Cleveland baseball teams have made it to the World Series more recently, but fans of the 1995 team remember this team the most fondly. Beyond the 1995 team making it to the World Series for the first time since 1954, but it was also a team that had an unmistakable *je ne sais quoi*. And a big part of the experience was sharing it with fans – young and old, longtime and new – who experienced the joy of Cleveland baseball with an enthusiasm and passion that may not be equaled until a Cleveland team one day does win the World Series.

NOTES

1. With thanks to the Giamatti Research Center at the Baseball Hall of Fame, which provided clippings of articles used in this chapter. See baseball-reference.com/teams/CLE/attend.shtml for Indians attendance figures.

2. Richard Justice, "New Stadium, New Day for Cleveland," *Washington Post*, April 5, 1994: C3.

3. Associated Press, "Cleveland Rocks as Indians Roll in New Ballpark: Team's Got AL's Best Record, Fans Have Reasons to Show Up," *Washington Post*, June 25, 1994: D-1A.

4. Ed Sherman, "Is This Heaven? No, It's Cleveland … Cleveland? Believe It," *Chicago Tribune*, April 27, 1994: E10.

5. Murray Chass, "Indians' Lost Years Took Their Toll on Faithful," *New York Times*, September 10, 1995: S9.

6. Ira Berkow, "Indians and Fans Help Revive a Sick Game," *New York Times*, July 5, 1995: B7.

7. Iver Peterson, " 'Mistake by the Lake' Wakes Up, Roaring: Cleveland Finds That Winning Feeling," *New York Times*, September 10, 1995: 18.

8. Berkow.

THE PLAYERS

SANDY ALOMAR JR.

BY JOSEPH WANCHO

Jacobs Field in Cleveland was the site for major-league Baseball's 68th All-Star Game on July 8, 1997. A sold-out crowd of 44,916 turned out for the midsummer classic as it returned to the shores of Lake Erie for the first time since 1981. The host Indians ended the first half of the season on a positive note, sweeping Kansas City in a three-game set. They held a 3½-game lead over second-place Chicago at the break.

One of the reasons for the Tribe's success was the unlikely power coming from the bat of Sandy Alomar Jr. The veteran backstop started the season in fine fashion, as he slugged a home run in five consecutive games from April 4-8. His 11 home runs at the break matched his season total of the season before and were just three short of his career-high 14 homers in 1994. "I'm in a zone," said Alomar. "Everything looks like a beach ball."[1]

But it was more than the long ball that Alomar was contributing to the team's fortunes. He owned the second-longest hitting streak in franchise history, 30 games (from May 25 through July 6). The streak, in which Alomar batted .429, was second only to Nap Lajoie's 31-game streak in 1906. "It's been a remarkable run for him," said the Twins' Paul Molitor. "To be able to have the mind-set to call a game (as catcher) and still be able to do that. ..."[2]

For the All-Stars on July 8, pitching was the name of the game. The teams battled to a 1-1 tie through the top of the seventh inning. Each team scored its tally on a home run. Edgar Martinez, who was the first designated hitter elected to the All-Star Game, socked a 2-and-2 offering from Greg Maddux into the left-field plaza in the bottom of the second frame. In the top of the seventh, Braves catcher Javy Lopez led off with a solo shot off the Royals' Jose Rosado.

Jim Thome led off the bottom of the seventh inning by grounding out. Bernie Williams walked and with two outs took second base on a wild pitch by the Giants' Shawn Estes. Alomar, who had replaced Ivan Rodriguez in the bottom of the sixth inning, stepped to the plate. "When Sandy went to the plate, Paul O'Neill turned to me and said, 'If all things were fair, Sandy would hit a homer and win the ballgame,'" said Indians manager Mike Hargrove, one of manager Joe Torre's coaches for the game.[3] Sandy sent a 2-and-2 pitch from Estes on a line into the left-field bleachers. "I felt like I was flying," said Alomar. "I've never run the bases so fast on a home run."[4]

The 3-1 AL advantage stood up, as the junior circuit snapped a three-game losing streak. The NL was held to three hits. Alomar became the first Indian to homer in the All-Star Game since Rocky Colavito in 1959. Alomar was voted the game's MVP, the first Indian to be so honored and the first player ever to win the award in his home ballpark. "This is a dream I don't want to wake up from," said Alomar. "You probably only get one chance to play an All-Star Game in your home stadium."[5]

"It was another of those storybook things," said Torre. "I had one last fall [the 1996 World Series], and now this. I was happy for Sandy to win it in his own park."[6]

Santos (Velazquez) Alomar was born on June 18, 1966, in Salinas, Puerto Rico. He was the middle child (older sister Sandia, younger brother Roberto) born to Santos and Maria Alomar. Sandy Sr. suited up for six different teams over a 15-year career in the major leagues. He had a career batting average of .245. He was mainly a second baseman, although he also saw time at shortstop. After his playing days, Alomar coached 15 years on the big-league level. In addition to his time in the major leagues, Sandy Sr. also managed the Puerto Rican National Team.

The elder Alomar did not push his sons into baseball. "The only influence is from them seeing me play," he said.[7] The life of a ballplayer means a lot of travel and time away from the family. Sandy Sr. credited his wife, Maria, with raising their three children, saying, "She deserves more credit than me. I was a ballplayer and couldn't be around that much. She stayed home and raised those kids. That's why they're the kind of people they are."[8]

Roberto Alomar took to baseball right away. He had the natural ability to play the game and at age 7 he made Sandy's little league team for 9-to-12-year-olds. But for Sandy, he had other interests to keep him busy. "Sandy left the game at age 12 and got into dirt-bike riding and karate," said his father. "He was doing dangerous things, more or less. He said the only way he could find excitement in baseball was to become a catcher."[9]

Young Sandy took to catching and was signed as an amateur free agent on October 21, 1983, by the San Diego Padres. After graduating from Luis Munoz Rivera High School in Salinas, Alomar began his journey to the major leagues. It was a long climb indeed. At first, the going was rough for the young catcher, who hit a combined .221 through his first three years in the minor leagues. But like most talented players, Alomar put in the work and by 1987 he blossomed into a coveted prospect in the Padres chain. It became a family affair of sorts, as Roberto joined his older brother on multiple minor-league squads. Sandy Sr. joined San Diego manager Steve Boros' coaching staff in 1986.

In 1988 Alomar was named co-Minor League Player of the Year by *The Sporting News* (with Gary Sheffield of Denver). Alomar, who was the catcher for the Las Vegas Stars of the Pacific Coast League, batted .297 and had career highs in home runs (16) and RBIs (71). "I didn't expect to hit like that," said Alomar. "As the season started, I struggled a little bit, but then I started swinging harder and pulling the ball more and hitting more home runs."[10]

It was reported that 22 of the other 25 major-league clubs were interested in acquiring Alomar. The Padres already had their catcher of the future in Benito Santiago. The time looked right to possibly trade their star prospect and get plenty in return. While Santiago was the National League Rookie of the Year in 1987, Roberto was promoted to the Padres in 1988 and became their starting second baseman. Sandy was frustrated, feeling there was nothing more he could do on the minor-league level. Rumors persisted that he would be traded, or that Santiago might be moved. One rumor had Alomar headed to Atlanta for All-Star Dale Murphy. "Every organization in the league would love to have a Sandy Alomar," said Atlanta general manager Bobby Cox.[11]

But no deal was ever made and Alomar returned to Las Vegas in 1989. He started the season poorly, batting .242 up to June 5, and then he became a man possessed, batting .351 the rest of the way. For the season, Alomar batted .306, with 13 home runs and 101 RBIs. He showed value behind the plate as well, fielding his position at a .984 clip, and throwing out 34 percent of would-be basestealers (25 of 74). He was once again honored by *The Sporting News* and *Baseball America* as the Minor League Player of the Year. "It means a lot to me," said Alomar of the award. "The way I felt, I was so frustrated. I figured there was no way I'd win it again."[12]

When the Cleveland Indians front office offered slugging outfielder Joe Carter a multiyear deal at the end of the 1989 season, Carter said, "No thanks." He could be a free agent at the end of the 1990 season, and was looking forward to leaving Cleveland, and getting a fresh start – not to mention snagging a boatload of cash. Alomar, who was getting frustrated with his situation in San Diego, was just hoping for a chance to play in the big leagues. After all, he had accomplished all he could in the minors, and it really did not matter to him whose uniform he was wearing. On December 6, 1989, at the annual winter meetings, Cleveland GM Hank Peters and San Diego GM Jack McKeon hammered out a deal that sent Carter to the Padres and Alomar, infielder Carlos Baerga, and outfielder Chris James to Cleveland.

Alomar was penciled in as the starting catcher as soon as the ink was dry on the trade. He did not disappoint. Cleveland manager John McNamara praised his young backstop in all facets of his game. "To me, he's very, very impressive at blocking balls," said McNamara. "He does it even when there's no need, when nobody is on base. Sandy's been taught well. He's absorbed the teaching, put it to good use.

"Sandy is hitting for a better average than I expected at this stage of his career. He's adjusted very well to major-league pitching. I never had any doubt about his catching, but you just never know about his hitting."[13]

McNamara was not the only person to notice the outstanding play of his prized rookie. All of baseball took notice when Alomar was voted the starting catcher for the American League in the All-Star Game. He was the first rookie catcher ever to start in an All-Star Game. The game would be extra-special, as Roberto, then with San Diego, was also named an All-Star and Sandy Sr. would also join his sons as a coach for the NL at Wrigley Field for the midsummer classic.

Sandy's season was capped off with his being the unanimous choice for the AL Rookie of the Year. "This award means more to me than the All-Star Game," said Alomar. "You have a lot of chances to be in the All-Star Game, but you've only got one chance to win this award. I was supposed to be Rookie of the Year, and that made it tough. I was traded for Joe Carter, and that made it tough. But the manager and the rest of the guys on the team really helped me."[14] Alomar was the fourth Indian to win the award. He was also awarded a Gold Glove for excellence in fielding his position. He was the first Indian to be so recognized since Rick Manning in 1976.

Alomar was instantly a fan favorite among Indians fans. However, the injuries began to pile up beginning in 1991, his second season. Though Alomar was selected to start the All-Star Game in both 1991 and 1992, he was dealing with myriad setbacks that included back surgery, injuries to his right rotator cuff, his right hip flexor, his right knee (two, caused by sliding), and the webbing between the fingers on his right hand (also twice). The 132 games Alomar played in his rookie year were the most of his career.

The Indians moved across downtown to their new ballpark, Jacobs Field, for the 1994 season. Alomar, despite missing time on the disabled list with the torn webbing on his right hand, was putting together a wonderful season, batting .288 with 14 home runs and 43 RBIs, when the players' strike on August 11 led to the remainder of the season being canceled.

Perhaps because Alomar suffered so many injuries, Cleveland signed Tony Peña before the 1994 season. For the next three seasons, the veteran provided solid leadership and was a reliable substitute for Alomar. It was a great free-agent signing for the Indians, as Alomar was recuperating from knee surgery and did not return to the active roster until June 29, 1995. Still, he batted .300 in 54 starts at catcher that season. The Indians, who sported one of the most potent lineups in baseball, moved Alomar to the bottom of their lineup. "I think Sandy can still hit

10 to 15 homers this year," said manager Mike Hargrove. "He has that kind of power. The thing that is really impressive is the way he's accepted hitting ninth. The number 9 hitter is usually the weakest hitter in the lineup, but that's not the case with this team."[15]

The Indians returned to the postseason for the first time in 41 years, winning their division by 30 games. They marched through the American League playoffs before losing to Atlanta in the World Series.

The Indians won the AL Central from 1995 to 1999. In 1997 they advanced to the World Series again, only to lose to Florida in seven games. Alomar's power surge in 1997 continued in the postseason, as he hit two home runs in the ALDS, one in the ALCS, and two in the World Series.

In 1999 Alomar was reunited with brother Roberto, who signed a free-agent contract with Cleveland. Together with Omar Vizquel, they formed one of the better middle-infield defenses in the big leagues. But Sandy missed most of the season after surgery on his left knee (he started 35 games), and in 2000 he split time with Einar Diaz at catcher. That season he batted .289 and drove in 42 runs.

But the end of an era was near as Alomar and the Indians were unable to negotiate a contract after the 2000 season. Alomar, ever the classy player, took the "life goes on" route and signed with the Chicago White Sox. He split time with Mark Johnson at catcher.

But the White Sox were just as interested in Alomar's ability to teach their young receivers and work with their green pitching staff. He was traded to Colorado in 2002, but returned to the South Side for the 2003 and 2004 seasons. "I got kind of teary-eyed when he got traded," said pitcher Mark Buerhle. "I'm still learning (from him). I'm out there thinking, 'I'm going to throw this pitch,' and he puts something else down. I'm not going to shake him off because he's been around the league a long time."[16]

The White Sox made it clear that they wanted Alomar to work with Miguel Olivo, a catching prospect for whom the front office had high hopes.

In 2003 Sandy was reunited again with Roberto, who by this time in his career was serving as a utility player for Chicago.

Alomar spent the remaining years as a backup catcher with Texas (2005), the Los Angeles Dodgers and the White Sox (2006), and the New York Mets (2007). He retired with a .273 batting average in a 20-year career. He hit 112 home runs and 249 doubles, and drove in 588 runs. He threw out just over 30 percent of baserunners, and fielded at a .991 clip at catcher for his career.

Alomar stayed with the Mets as a catching instructor in 2008 and 2009. Manny Acta was hired to replace Eric Wedge as Cleveland's manager in 2010. Acta offered Alomar a job as his first-base coach. "I jumped at it," said Alomar. "For me, it was coming home. No place in baseball means as much to me as Cleveland."[17]

Acta was fired near the end of the 2012 season. Alomar was named interim manager, and looked to be the favorite until Terry Francona's name was thrown into the mix of candidates. "I knew they'd hire him if he wanted the job," said Alomar. "I don't blame them. I understand. He's won two World Series. He's a heck of a guy."[18]

As of 2016, Alomar was Francona's first-base coach. Francona, who played for the Indians in 1988, was a teammate of Alomar's in winter ball with Ponce in the Puerto Rico League. When the Indians acquired Alomar in 1989, Francona gushed at the young man's ability. "He's the best catcher I've ever played with," said Francona. "He's better than Gary Carter when Carter was good. Sandy might not drive in 100 runs like Carter did in his prime, but overall he's a better ballplayer. He's the best defensive catcher I've ever seen. His arm is almost incredible."[19]

When Francona insisted that Sandy Alomar be a part of his staff, he knew exactly what he was getting. Even way back when.

NOTES

1. Bill Livingston, "Sweet Sandy! AL Triumphs on Alomar Blast," *Cleveland Plain Dealer*, July 9, 1997: 1A.

2. Mel Antonen, "Sandy Alomar's Streak Hits 30," *USA Today*, July 7, 1997: 1C.

3. Paul Hoynes, "Sandy Steals the Show; Alomar's Home Run Lifts AL," *Cleveland Plain Dealer*, July 9, 1997: 1D.

4. Ibid.

5. Ibid.

6. "Sweet Sandy."

7. Chuck Johnson, "Alomar Sons Deepen Roots in Baseball," *USA Today*, July 13, 1990: 2C.

8. Ibid.

9. Ibid.

10. "Big League Awards in the Minors," *The Sporting News*, December 5, 1988: 46.

11. Barry Bloom, "Alomar Hopes That His 'First' Won't Last," *The Sporting News*, December 4, 1989: 52.

12. Ibid.

13. Sheldon Ocker, "Alomar More Than Lives Up to Hype," *The Sporting News*, July 2, 1990: 12.

14. Paul Hoynes, "It's Unanimous! Indians Catcher Alomar Is Rookie of the Year," *Cleveland Plain Dealer*, November 8, 1990: 1F.

15. Paul Hoynes, "Deep Thunder Alomar Homers Twice at Bottom of Order," *Cleveland Plain Dealer*, July 21, 1995: 1D.

16. Nancy Armour (Associated Press), "Sandy Ready to Teach," *Elyria (Ohio) Chronicle-Telegram*, March 3, 2003: C4.

17. Terry Pluto, "Playing, Coaching for Tribe 'Paradise,'" *Cleveland Plain Dealer*, April 3, 2013: C3.

18. Ibid.

19. "Alomar Draws Praise From Former Mate," *The Sporting News*, March 19, 1990: 30.

RUBEN AMARO JR.

BY RORY COSTELLO

"I take a great deal of pride in my background and my heritage."[1]

That was Ruben Amaro Jr. in 2011, on being a third-generation Latino baseball man. Yet he has often spoken the same way about his maternal side. Altogether, his background is unique in major-league history: Cuban-Mexican/Jewish-American.

From this start, a unique career path has also unfolded. The switch-hitting outfielder played in the majors from 1991 through 1998, but he had to struggle to stay there. His only full seasons in "The Show" were his last two. After his playing career ended, Amaro stepped directly into the front office. He spent 10 years as assistant general manager of the Philadelphia Phillies, and he then served as their GM from November 2008 through early September 2015. After that he made an unusual transition back to the field, joining the Boston Red Sox as a coach in October 2015.

Ruben Amaro Jr. has another distinction. He has been to the World Series as a batboy (with the Phillies in 1980), as a player (with the Cleveland Indians in 1995), and as an executive (with the Phillies in 2008 and 2009).

As an Amaro family motto says, "Baseball is our way of life."[2] It started with Santos Amaro (1908-2001), who had a long and distinguished career in Cuba and Mexico. Except for racial barriers, the Amaros could have been the first family to send three generations of players to the big leagues.[3] Ruben Amaro Sr., a smooth-fielding shortstop, played in the majors from 1958 through 1969. He went on to serve the Phillies and other organizations for decades in many capacities.

Santos Amaro's father came to Cuba from Portugal and his mother was the child of Abencerraje Moors from Africa. Like many Cubans, Santos was a coffee-colored man. While playing in Mexico in 1929, he met a fair-skinned Mexican woman of Spanish descent named Josefina Mora, who was a baseball player too. They married in 1930, and Ruben Sr. was born in Nuevo Laredo, Mexico in 1936.

While he was playing with the Phillies, Ruben Sr. met Judith Herman at the gourmet cheese shop that Judy's mother ran in Philadelphia's Reading Terminal Market.[4] In 2008 Judy also said, "My sister Marlene taught English to Pancho Herrera and Tony Taylor [two other members of the Phillies then]. Ruben would drive them to our house for the lessons."[5]

Ruben Sr. and Judy married in December 1961. They had one other child. David Amaro, born in 1962, was drafted in the 24th round by the Chicago Cubs in 1984. He played that summer in short-season Class-A ball and eight games in the Mexican League in 1985, but an injured wrist curtailed his career. Ruben Jr. was born in Philadelphia on February 12, 1965.

Ruben Amaro Sr.'s pro career lasted until 1971, when Ruben Jr. was 6. "I can't remember seeing my father play," he said in 1992, "and that's too bad."[6] However, age 6 did provide his earliest memories of the regal and quiet Santos Amaro. The family took Christmas vacations in Veracruz, Mexico, where Santos and Josefina lived. "Buelo" (short for *Abuelo*, Spanish for grandfather) was then in his 60s, but he still had the habit of taking 10-mile walks. "As a six-year-old, that was astonishing to me," said Ruben Jr. in 2013. "I asked my father, 'What does he do on those walks?' And my dad said, 'He thinks.'"[7] That influence was deep.

"When I was little, I wanted to be a doctor or veterinarian," Amaro said in 2010. "Soccer was actually my first love."[8] He was good enough to get an offer to attend high school in Germany for a year and a half, to be assessed as a pro soccer prospect there. However, that nation still held unhappy associations for his Jewish mother, so he did not go.[9]

On the other side of Amaro's religious heritage, Ruben Sr. was a devout Catholic. Ruben Jr. said, "We had a very diversified family. We did Passover, Yom Kippur, Chanukah. We were exposed to both faiths pretty equally." Though he never had a bar mitzvah, he recalled, "I had a lot of friends who were bar mitzvahed and went to a lot of them."[10]

Education was extremely important to both Ruben Sr. (something that came from Santos) and Judy Amaro. They sent Ruben Jr. to Frankford Friends, a small private elementary school where his mother later taught Spanish, and then William Penn Charter School in Philadelphia, a private academy founded in 1689. A couple of years ahead of him at Penn Charter was pitcher Mark Gubicza, who went on to a 14-year career in the majors.

In 1980 the Phillies became World Series champions. Ruben Sr. was the team's first-base coach, and Ruben Jr. was one of the batboys. It was an important formative experience. He later said, "Baseball is such an intricate game, a thinking game. I was 15, and I was watching Pete Rose, Steve Carlton, Larry Bowa, Manny Trillo, Bob Boone. Did I say Mike Schmidt? Most of them are Hall of Famers, or close to it. I learned from all of them."[11]

Amaro remained a Phillies batboy through 1983, though he missed the World Series that fall because he had started at Stanford University. After winning All-City honors in both baseball (first-team second baseman) and soccer (second team), and doing well academically, he had offers from other high-quality schools, including Duke, Vanderbilt, and Princeton. He chose Stanford because the school's respected baseball coach, Mark Marquess, knew the Amaro family history and thought Ruben could help his team, although the young man was still undersized then. Amaro accepted the offer, even though there was neither a scholarship nor guaranteed playing time.[12]

Amaro became a four-year letter winner with Stanford. Marquess moved him from the infield to the outfield as a sophomore. During his senior year, as the leadoff man, he hit .344 with 38 stolen bases.[13] The team also had star pitcher Jack McDowell, another major leaguer to be in Ed Sprague Jr., and future NFL defensive back Toi Cook. Stanford won the College World Series for the first time in its history in June 1987.

Just a few days before, the California Angels had made Amaro their 11th-round pick in the amateur draft. A couple of weeks later, after graduating from college with a degree in human biology, he signed and began his minor-league career. The bonus the Angels offered was small – just $1,500 – and he turned to his father for advice. Ruben Sr. said, "It's not going to get any better. Sign it, get in your car and start driving."[14]

It took Amaro four years to climb the ladder to the majors. He didn't have power – he never had more than nine home runs in a season at any level – but he did hit for high average in the minors. In 1989, which he spent in Class-A and

Double-A ball, he hit .368 overall. He followed that up with a mark of .317 in 1990, earning promotion to Triple-A.

During the winter of 1989-90, Amaro played winter ball for the first time. He went to Venezuela, joining Águilas del Zulia, a team that his father served in various roles for more than 20 years. He went back for six more winter seasons, as late as 1997-98, all but one of them with Zulia. For much of that time, Ruben Sr. was the manager. Overall, in 219 games in the Venezuelan league, Ruben Jr. hit .281 with 5 homers and 83 RBIs.

Amaro also met his first wife, Virginia Machado, in Venezuela. They married on December 6, 1996, and had two daughters, Andrea and Sophia (the union ended in divorce). In another interesting twist, Virginia's aunt is Lilia Machado, who became Ruben Amaro Sr.'s second wife. The Machado family owns and operates the Zulia club. Ruben Sr. and Lilia's two sons, Luis Alfredo and Rubén Andrés, also became ballplayers. Luis played short-season Class-A ball for the Phillies in 2011. Before marrying Lilia and after separating from Judy, Ruben Sr. had a daughter named Alayna from a relationship with Mary Beth Allio. Ruben Jr. is close with all three of his half-siblings.

Amaro remained at Edmonton in 1991 and hit .326. He got his first brief call-up to the majors in June 1991, after Junior Felix went on the 15-day disabled list. He made his debut on June 8 at Anaheim Stadium, pinch-running for designated hitter Dave Parker. Amaro represented the tying run with nobody out, but after advancing on a sacrifice, he had to stop at third base after freezing instinctively on a liner back through the box. Tigers closer Mike Henneman then got out of the jam with a double-play ball. A few days later, Amaro was sent back to Edmonton.

The Angels recalled him that September, and he appeared in nine more games, starting three in left field and two at second base. The 1991 season was the only time he ever played the latter position in the majors. Aside from two very brief appearances at first base in 1996 and 1997, he was exclusively an outfielder. (He also got 11 at-bats as a DH during his two years with the Indians.)

On December 8, 1991, California traded pitcher Kyle Abbott and Amaro to the Phillies in return for Von Hayes. *The Sporting News* called the deal "The Steal of the Winter." Hayes was washed up – "Wow, I didn't think we could even get one player for Von," said Lenny Dykstra[15] – and was finished after 1992. However, Abbott, who was viewed as a top pitching prospect, was awful with Philadelphia in 1992. He got back to the majors just briefly in 1995 and 1996. Modest as it was, Amaro's career lasted the longest of the three players involved.

Amaro was stunned by the news of the trade. He said, "I thought, 'Wow, some of those fans are difficult.' But then I realized these are knowledgeable fans. They love players who bust their butts, like Len Dykstra and John Kruk. I'm very competitive. I fit in that mold."[16]

As it turned out, though, Dykstra, Kruk, et al. gave the college boy a hard time. "Some of that I brought on myself," Amaro later admitted. "Just by being an arrogant little toad. Oh yeah. I think I was limited enough talentwise that I had to fake myself into thinking I was better than I was. I kind of rubbed some of the guys the wrong way, but I got straightened out. They made sure of that."[17]

Amaro spent most of the 1992 season with the Phillies. In the season's second game, at Veterans Stadium, he sparked an 11-3 rout of the Chicago Cubs. He was filling in for Dykstra, whose wrist had been broken by a Greg Maddux pitch on Opening Day. The new leadoff man was 3-for-4 with two doubles and his first of 16 home runs in the majors. It drew a standing ovation from the crowd. "In my wildest dreams, I didn't think of this," Amaro said. "Not in a million years. One thing just fell in place after the other. I'm in shock."[18]

In fact, Amaro went deep three times in just five days from April 8-12. His modest response was, "Mistake pitches. I've never tried to hit a home run in my life. I was as surprised as anybody."[19] As the *Philadelphia Inquirer* later put it, though, that one spectacular week was followed by long periods of frustration.[20] He suffered some severe slumps, and in late July – hitting just .199 – he was optioned to Triple-A Scranton/Wilkes-Barre. "After some early success, I just took myself out of my game," he said. "I started to try to outthink the pitchers instead of just going up there and swinging the bat. They gave me five or six opportunities to earn a starting job, and I didn't. I don't have anybody to blame but myself."[21]

The demotion lasted just a few weeks, though. Overall in Philadelphia that year, Amaro got into 126 games, starting 87 of them, and made 427 plate appearances. All were major-league career highs for him. He was the team's primary right fielder that year, though he also got plenty of action in left and center. By season's end his average had picked up a bit, to .219. The substantial playing time was also a big reason why he reached big-league bests in homers (seven) and RBIs (34).

In reality, however, manager Jim Fregosi "liked Amaro as a fifth outfielder, [but] instead was forced to play him as a regular for much of that last-place season."[22] That winter the Phillies loaded up with three free-agent outfielders: Pete Incaviglia, Milt Thompson, and Jim Eisenreich.

Amaro played just 25 games for the Phillies in 1993. He was with the big club for roughly a month, from mid-June through mid-July; he returned in September. Philadelphia won the National League pennant that season, but Amaro was left off the postseason roster in favor of Tony Longmire. He wasn't even allowed to dress for the playoffs and World Series.[23] On November 2 he was traded to Cleveland for reliever Heathcliff Slocumb.

He'd hoped for more from the change of scenery, but Amaro didn't play much as an Indian either. In 1994 he was called up from Triple-A Charlotte in late May but got just 25 plate appearances in 26 games before the players' strike ended the season in August. In 1995 he shuttled between the new top affiliate, Buffalo, and Cleveland. In fact, he was sent outright to Buffalo in May; his contract was purchased once more when Eddie Murray went on the DL in July. In his scattered stints with the Indians that year, Amaro got into 28 games and hit .200-1-7 in 68 plate appearances.

Nonetheless, after Cleveland won the AL Central Division, Amaro stayed with the team in the postseason. He and Dave Winfield were the two position players "on the bubble" as the roster was determined. Both were eligible because they had been on the disabled list at the end of August. Winfield was nearly 44 by then and exclusively a DH. He'd been bothered by a sore shoulder for much of the year and was not swinging the bat well. Amaro, who could run and play defense, was the more useful man to have on the bench.

Amaro did not appear against Boston as Cleveland swept the AL Division Series. In the AL Championship Series, against Seattle, he appeared in three games as a pinch-runner. As the Indians clinched the pennant in Game Six, he contributed. It was a tight 1-0 game starting the top of the eighth, but catcher Tony Peña hit a leadoff double. Amaro ran for Peña and got a good jump on Kenny Lofton's well-placed bunt. A few pitches later, he scored on a passed ball; right behind him, boldly exploiting the same misplay, was Lofton. Cleveland added another run to ice a 4-0 win.

As the Tribe advanced to the World Series, it was significant for the Amaro family. Ruben Sr. had been a member of the 1964 Phillies, infamous for their collapse down the stretch, and even being a coach for the 1980 champions did not make up for that lost opportunity to play in the fall classic. Ruben Jr. hadn't been born yet – in fact, his mother was expecting him at the time – but he certainly knew what had happened. The memory of his own missed opportunity in 1993 was also not distant.

In the Series itself, Amaro made two brief appearances. In Game Two at Atlanta, he batted for Julian Tavarez to lead off the top of the ninth, but Mark Wohlers struck him out and went on to close out the Braves' 4-3 win. In the concluding Game Six, Amaro entered in the seventh inning, replacing right fielder Manny Ramirez in a double switch – a strategy on which manager Mike Hargrove was second-guessed.[24] Amaro grounded out against Tom Glavine to end the top of the eighth, and again no balls were hit his way when Atlanta batted. Wohlers then nailed down the 1-0 win – and the title – for the Braves.

Not long after the Series ended, on November 9, Cleveland waived Amaro. He signed a minor-league deal with the Toronto Blue Jays in January 1996. To start the 1996 season, Amaro was with Syracuse, the Jays' top farm club. In early May, however, he was released.

As he said later that year, Amaro then made his own break. He called Phillies general manager Lee Thomas and asked if Thomas had anything for him. Thomas said he'd have to get back to Amaro, but fortune smiled when outfielder Lee Tinsley went on the DL with a strained rib cage. Thomas and assistant GM Ed Wade called Amaro and said they had a job – not just at Triple-A Scranton/Wilkes-Barre, but in the majors. Amaro said, "Oh, that's great. I'll have my agent call you." Thomas responded that if the agent had to call, then not to come. Amaro said, "I'll be there in three hours."[25]

Although he was sent down to Scranton/Wilkes-Barre after several days, he returned in early July and never played another day in the minors. He spent the remainder of his career, which lasted through 1998, as a reserve with the Phillies. He got into 270 games, starting 49 of them, and made 447 plate appearances. He was used a lot as a pinch-hitter and performed pretty well in that role, going 35-for-134 (.261) with two homers and 22 RBIs.

At the age of 33, though, Amaro decided to retire as a player. He then moved into the Phillies' front office. Wade, who had succeeded Lee Thomas as the team's general manager in 1997, had actually first approached Amaro about his plans in spring training 1998. Wade offered a job as assistant GM right then, but Amaro wanted to see how he did during the season to come. During the summer, after discussing things with Ruben Sr. and his brother David, Amaro decided to take Wade's offer.[26]

The deal was actually announced on September 18.[27] Nine days later, in his final big-league game, Amaro drove in the go-ahead run with a single as Philadelphia beat the Florida Marlins to end the season. "It was pretty emotional for me," Amaro said. "The last three or four innings, I was fighting back the tears."[28]

"I'm actually glad that I was as bad as I was that year," Amaro later said. "It helped solidify that I absolutely made the right choice. I mean, I was done." As Wade recalled, a lot of people in the industry were surprised by his choice, and some frankly questioned it, because others had been serving their apprenticeship. Wade said that he just felt it was the right thing for the organization.[29]

Amaro worked as assistant GM for seven seasons under Wade and for three more under Pat Gillick. It bothered him at first to realize that he was no longer one of the players; his relationship with them had changed. He also still had a lot to learn on the job.[30] But he absorbed much from a Phillies institution, former GM Paul "The Pope" Owens, who was still with the franchise as a senior adviser. Amaro interviewed for the GM job after Wade was fired, but in retrospect, he realized he wasn't ready.[31]

While Amaro continued to learn, he was part of the Phillies' rise to success. Among other things, he helped obtain an important cog, Shane Victorino, and helped get Victorino into the lineup too. On November 3, 2008 – a week after the team completed its victory in the World Series – Amaro succeeded the retiring Gillick, signing a three-year contract. At the news conference, Amaro told Gillick that he was a tough act to follow.[32]

For at least the term of that contract, though, Amaro was riding high. The Phillies repeated as NL pennant-winners in 2009. They won the NL East in both 2010 and 2011 as well. Amaro enjoyed positive press and won praise for making bold deals in search of another title, such as the trades for star pitchers Cliff Lee and Roy Halladay. In March 2011, he got a four-year contract extension.

After that, however, the team's fortunes declined. They played .500 ball in 2012 but won just 73 games in both 2013 and 2014. The notoriously harsh Philly fans gave him a scathing nickname – "Ruin Tomorrow" – and the voices grew louder that he had to go. He drew fire for *everything*: letting the team get old, handing out bad contracts, making shortsighted deals, eschewing analytics, the long drought in the draft, and not acting soon enough to rebuild. Yet by 2018, the Phillies had rebounded in the standings, thanks largely to players acquired during Amaro's tenure. More time is needed for his legacy to be fully assessed.

In November 2014 Amaro got married for the second time. Jami Schnell, a children's reading specialist, had been his significant other for some time. But on the job, things got worse for the Phillies in 2015. The team won just 63 games, its worst showing since 1972. Amaro didn't last the full year – new president Andy MacPhail fired him on September 10.

After he was ousted as GM, Amaro expressed an interest in a different role: field manager. The story surfaced in the *Boston Globe* in early October that he was working with agent Bob LaMonte to remake himself, and that LaMonte was close to Tony La Russa, Walt Jocketty, and Gillick, all of whom had endorsed Amaro's new pursuit.[33]

Red Sox manager John Farrell, who had been Amaro's teammate in the Cleveland organization, saw this. Farrell asked Amaro whether he'd be interested in joining the Boston staff. Ruben thought it over and consulted with family, as well as Gillick, Wade, and Terry Francona (the Phillies' manager from 1997 through 2000). In October 2015 Amaro took the job in Boston as first base/baserunning/outfield coach.

"I guess it is unusual," he said. "But for me, I've always had kind of an itch to be back on the field … [but] had it not been the Red Sox, frankly I probably would not be doing this." He added, "I'm gonna do my best to teach what I've learned over the years. … I'm laser-focused on being the best coach I can be."[34]

After two seasons in Boston, Amaro joined Mickey Callaway's staff as the first base coach for the New York Mets in November 2017. His duties also included coaching baserunning and outfield defense. Aged just 53 as the 2018 season began, Ruben Amaro Jr. was still a baseball story in progress.

Continued thanks to Alayna Amaro.

SOURCES

In addition to the sources cited in the notes, the author relied on a number of Internet resources and purapelota.com (Venezuelan statistics).

NOTES

1. Adry Torres, "Ruben Amaro Jr. Looks to Bring Another Phillies Title to His Hometown," Fox News Latino, October 5, 2011.
2. Telephone interview, Ruben Amaro Sr. with Rory Costello, October 18, 2012.
3. As of Opening Day 2016, there have been four grandfather-father-son families in the majors: the Boones, the Bells, the Hairstons, and the Colemans. Also notable are Dick Schofield Sr. and Jr., plus Jayson Werth, nephew of Schofield Jr.
4. Mike Jensen, "Family Pick: Phillies Choose Amaro as GM," *Philadelphia Inquirer*, November 4, 2008.
5. Stan Hochman, "Phillies GM Amaro Always Will Have His Mother in His Corner," Fox Sports, December 2, 2008.
6. George Vecsey, "The Batboy Learned by Watching," *New York Times*, April 15, 1992.
7. Adam Berry, "Amaro's Grandfather Inducted Into Latino HOF," MLB.com, February 12, 2013.
8. Rob Charry, "Phillies' Amaro Has Rest of League Saying 'Roy Vey,'" Jewish Telegraphic Agency, October 5, 2010.
9. Nick DiUlio, "Ruben Amaro Jr.: Arms Dealer," *Philadelphia Magazine*, April 7, 2011.
10. Charry, "Phillies' Amaro Has Rest of League Saying 'Roy Vey.'"
11. Vecsey, "The Batboy Learned by Watching."
12. Jorge Arangure Jr., "Ruben Amaro Jr. a Confident Leader," ESPN.com, October 3, 2011.
13. "Former Stanford Great Ruben Amaro, Jr. Named Phillies GM," Stanford Athletics press release, November 4, 2008.
14. Stan Isle, "Judging Talent May Be Herzog's Greatest Gift," *The Sporting News*, August 3, 1987: 10.
15. Bob Nightengale, "Steal of the Winter," *The Sporting News*, December 23, 1991: 22.
16. Vecsey, "The Batboy Learned by Watching."
17. Gwen Knapp, "Rookie GM Amaro's Long History With Phillies," *San Francisco Chronicle*, October 25, 2009.
18. "Amaro Leads Phillies' Romp Over Cubs," *Reading Eagle*, April 9, 1992: D1.
19. Vecsey, "The Batboy Learned by Watching"
20. Frank Fitzpatrick, "Phils Deal Amaro to Cleveland in a Bullpen-Rebuilding Move", *Philadelphia Inquirer*, November 3, 1993.
21. Frank Fitzpatrick, "Amaro Shipped to Minors," *Philadelphia Inquirer*, July 25, 1992.
22. Fitzpatrick, "Phils Deal Amaro to Cleveland in a Bullpen-Rebuilding Move."
23. Ibid.
24. Bob Smizik, "Series Awards for Good, Bad," *Pittsburgh Post-Gazette*,

November 1, 1995.

25 Associated Press, "Amaro, Magee Save Phils," August 21, 1996; Arangure, "Ruben Amaro Jr. a Confident Leader."

26 Arangure, "Ruben Amaro Jr. a Confident Leader."

27 As may be seen from wire service reports of transactions.

28 "Emotional Ending for Amaro," *Reading Eagle*, September 28, 1998: D4.

29 Arangure, "Ruben Amaro Jr. a Confident Leader."

30 Tony Zonca, "New Job a Good Fit for Amaro," *Reading Eagle*, June 2, 1999: C1.

31 DiUlio, Ruben Amaro Jr.: Arms Dealer."

32 Associated Press, "Amaro Signs Three-Year Deal to Become New Phillies GM," November 4, 2008.

33 Nick Cafardo, "Apropos of Nothing," *Boston Globe*, October 4, 2015.

34 Corey Seidman, "Ruben Amaro Explains 'Unusual' Transition From GM to 1B coach," CSNPhilly.com, October 27, 2015.

PAUL ASSENMACHER

BY NICK WADDELL

Detroit native Paul Andre Assenmacher (born December 10, 1960) epitomized the somewhat obscure baseball term LOOGY (Lefty One-Out Guy) by making a "long and profitable career out of coming into a game, pitching to one or two left-handed batters, then leaving."[1]

Assenmacher, who pitched for the Aquinas College Saints (Grand Rapids) from 1981 to 1983, still held a few school records as of 2017, including most innings pitched in a season (98 in 1983), most strikeouts in a season (123 in 1981), and tied for most strikeouts in a career (246). Aquinas went 125-57 (.687) during his time there. Coming from a small school, his college stats were not enough to get him drafted, but the Atlanta Braves in 1983 signed him as an undrafted free agent. At the Braves' Gulf Coast League (Rookie) affiliate for the remainder of the season, Assenmacher teamed with future Braves Ron Gant and Mark Lemke, and future national champion football coach Urban Meyer. He pitched in 10 games, including three starts. He was 1-0, with a 2.21 ERA. Even more impressive, considering he was not a starter, was that he led the team with 44 strikeouts.

Assenmacher spent 1984 with the Durham Bulls (Class A Carolina League). He made 24 starts, going 6-11 with a 4.28 ERA, but his peripherals were good. He led all starters with a 2.83 K/BB ratio and struck out 147 batters, second highest on the team.

Assenmacher started the 1985 season back in Durham, this time pitching only out of the bullpen. This earned him a promotion to Greenville of the Double-A Southern League. As in Durham, he pitched solely out of the bullpen. He had a 6-0 record with a 2.56 ERA, and his peripheral numbers showed improvement too. He did not give up a home run in his 52⅔ innings of work. Assenmacher was viewed as one of the future arms for the Braves. His presence helped the Braves decide to not bring back veteran Phil Niekro.[2]

Assenmacher was invited to big-league spring training in 1986, and made the club. He did not disappoint, appearing in 61 games, all out of the bullpen, and ended with a 7-3 record with a 2.50 ERA. He was a bright spot for the last-place Braves, who had one of the worst pitching staffs in the National League. The strong performance garnered interest around the league, including some discussions with the Indians involving Brett Butler,[3] but the Braves elected to hang on to their young lefty.

For Assenmacher, 1987 was a rough year. While pitching on the worst staff in the National League, he had arguably his worst year as a professional. His ERA went up over 5.00. Assenmacher was still in demand; the Mets and Braves discussed a potential deal involving him and Mets outfielder Mookie Wilson, but a deal never materialized.[4]

In 1988, the lefty bounced back, with an 8-7 record and a 3.06 ERA in 64 games. His other statistics also improved. Before the 1989 season, he sought a raise to $200,000, while the Braves offered $170, 000.[5] Eventually, Assenmacher agreed to a contract for $181,000.[6] His 1989 season was even better, with an improved strikeout-to-walk ratio. On August 22 against St. Louis, Assenmacher faced five batters, striking out four. Two days later, the Braves traded him to the Chicago Cubs. The Cubs were in a race for the crown in the NL East, but Assenmacher did not provide the stability they were looking for. He had a dreadful September and October, including two appearances of a third of an inning each in Games Two and Three of the National League Championship Series against the San Francisco Giants (despite carrying a four-leaf clover in his back pocket during the playoffs[7]). His ERA was almost 6.50, and his strikeout-to-walk ratio dipped drastically in the final two months of the regular season.

The 1990 Cubs were a disappointment on the field, finishing 77-85, but Assenmacher was steady. He was the team's best pitcher out of the bullpen, going 7-2 with a 2.80 ERA. He pitched a career-high 103 innings, and made his first professional start since 1987, and the only start in his major-league career. He lasted only one inning and gave up four earned runs. Over the entire season, though, Assenmacher held left-handed batters to a .223 batting average.

Before the 1991 season, the Cubs went after Royals starter Kevin Appier with a package involving first baseman Mark Grace.[8] When that fell through, the Cubs turned to strengthening their bullpen by signing Assenmacher (who was in his walk year) to a three-year, $7 million deal (or $7.5 million, depending on the source[9]), with a club option for a fourth year.[10] Assenmacher responded by achieving career bests in games and strikeouts. His 102⅔ innings pitched were the most for NL relievers; he was second in the league in strikeouts and games pitched. The Cubs figured they would lose Assenmacher to free agency after 1992 since he had drawn so much interest during the season, and left him unprotected in the 1992 expansion draft, when Colorado and Florida joined the league. But he went unclaimed by either franchise.[11]

Assenmacher was traded to the New York Yankees in a three-team deal before the 1993 non-waivers trade deadline. The Cubs picked up minor-league power hitter Karl "Tuffy" Rhodes. Rhodes would later be known as the first player to hit a home run in his first three at-bats on Opening Day when he did it for the 1994 Cubs.

During spring training in 1994, Assenmacher was dealt to the Chicago White Sox for minor-league pitcher Brian Boehringer. The Yankees saved money but also created a roster spot for one of their prospects, Sterling Hitchcock. At the time, the Yankees had a decent bullpen; Assenmacher figured he was the one traded because "my name was pulled out of a hat."[12] The trade was important to the White Sox, considering that they were favored by many to win the AL Central crown. Over the strike-shortened season, Assenmacher held left-handers to a .196 batting average, but he was still waived at the end of the season.

Assenmacher signed as a free agent with the Cleveland Indians in April 1995 for $700,000, with another $200,000 in performance bonuses.[13] This signing was delayed because of the strike that canceled the 1994 World Series. The signing paid immediate and long-term dividends. The Indians won the AL Central five years in a row, and Assenmacher became an important part of the bullpen as a left-handed specialist.[14] He pitched in 47 games in 1995, holding lefties to a .188 batting average and .235 on-base percentage. This helped the Indians make their first postseason appearance and first World Series appearance since 1954, when they were swept in four games by the New York Giants. Assenmacher earned a hold the night the Indians clinched the division, September 8, 1995.

The Indians had the best record in baseball entering the playoffs (100-44), but never had home-field advantage. The 1995 season was the first year of the wild-card format for the playoffs. At that time, home-field advantage rotated among the division leaders. This would be the AL East and the AL West champions, Boston and Seattle respectively. Playoff rules also said that the wild-card team could not play a team in its own division in the division round, but it could not have home-field advantage either. If the Yankees had played the Indians, the Yankees would have had home-field advantage. Instead, the Yankees opposed Seattle, and the Indians faced the Red Sox.[15]

Assenmacher pitched in all three games of the sweep over the Red Sox for a total of 1⅔ innings, without giving up a run. The Indians faced the Mariners in the ALCS, and won the series, 4-2. Assenmacher pitched 1⅓ innings, without giving up a run. Perhaps his most important outing of the ALCS was Game Five. He entered the game with runners at first and third with only one out, thanks to back-to-back errors by Indians first baseman Paul Sorrento. Assenmacher got Ken Griffey Jr. to strike out swinging. Manager Mike Hargrove left Assenmacher in to face the right-handed-hitting Jay Buhner. Buhner had hit .458 against the Yankees and was hitting .389 in the ALCS up until that point. Buhner struck out on a 2-and-2 breaking ball, surprising almost everyone.

Assenmacher overall had a decent World Series, except for one pitch. Atlanta was leading the Series two games to one, heading into Game Four at Jacobs Field in Cleveland. The Braves were up 2-1 in the game, when Assenmacher entered in the top of the seventh with one out. Indians starter Ken Hill had given up a run on Luis Polonia's double. Assenmacher issued an intentional walk to his first batter, Chipper Jones, putting runners at first and second. A passed ball allowed the runners to advance, then Assenmacher struck out Braves slugger Fred McGriff. Assenmacher worked a 1-and-2 count to David Justice, and tried to get Justice to bite on a curve. Instead, the curve stayed in the middle of the plate, and Justice singled to drive in two runs.[16] One run was charged to Assenmacher, but it was unearned, as was the run charged to Hill. Atlanta won the game, 5-2, to take a three-games-to-one lead, and ultimately won the Series in six games. The Indians would have to wait another season to see if they could break the World Series drought.

Assenmacher re-signed with the Indians after the 1995 World Series. The Indians gave the lefty a two-year, $1.7 million contract.[17] He was effective in 1996 with a 3.09 ERA and he held the opposition to a .260 batting average.

The Indians finished 1996 with the best record in baseball (99-62) and faced the Baltimore Orioles in the American League Division Series. The Indians managed only one win against the Orioles, but Assenmacher picked up that Game Three victory. It was his first postseason decision.

He improved on his 1996 stats in 1997, holding batters to a .231 batting average and .289 on-base percentage. The Indians won the American League Central with only 86 wins and faced the wild-card Yankees. The Orioles had the best record in the American League, but at the time, the rule was that the wild-card team would face the best team, unless that team was in the same division. So the 96-win Yankees opened the series at home, and moved to Cleveland for the last three games. In four appearances, Assenmacher pitched 3⅓ innings and gave up two earned runs, but he played an important role in the Indians' Game Four and Game Five victories.

In Game Four, the Indians were down 2-1 going into the eighth inning. Their bullpen would have to hold the Yankees scoreless and hope that the offense would pick it up. That is exactly what happened. Assenmacher entered in the eighth and gave up a single to Paul O'Neill, but retired Bernie Williams and Tino Martinez on strikes before giving way to closer Michael Jackson. Jackson shut down the Yankees, and the Indians scored twice to win the game, 3-2. In Game Five, the Indians had a one-run lead when Assenmacher entered in the seventh. He forced O'Neill to ground into a fielder's choice, and then Bernie Williams into a double play. He faced Tino Martinez in the top of the eighth and got Martinez to pop out to the catcher. José Mesa closed out the game; the Indians won the series and faced the American League's best team, the Baltimore Orioles.

Assenmacher pitched in five of the six ALCS games and earned the win in Game Two. His stats took a hit in Game Five when he gave up two runs without recording an out, but he contributed to the Game Six win when he induced a groundout from B.J. Surhoff in the bottom of the eighth. The Indians won on a Tony Fernandez home run in the top of the 11th inning, propelling them into their second World Series in three years.

Assenmacher pitched four innings without giving up a run, but the Indians lost in the bottom of the 11th in Game Seven on Edgar Renteria's single that scored Craig Counsell. The Indians' World Series drought continued.

Lefties had more success than righties against Assenmacher in 1998. They batted .313 with a .361 on-base percentage. Conversely, right-handed batters hit .256 with a .340 on-base percentage. The Indians made the playoffs and faced the Red Sox in the American League Division Series, winning three games to one. Assenmacher appeared in three games for a total of one inning. He gave up two hits and no earned runs. The Indians played the eventual World Series champion New York Yankees in the American League Championship Series. The Indians lost, winning only two games, but Assenmacher again was steady in his role. As in the series against Boston, he did not give up a run; this time he pitched two innings.

Assenmacher appeared in 55 games for the Indians in 1999, posting a 2-1 record. But statistically speaking, it was the worst year in his career. His 8.18 ERA and 13.6 hits per 9 innings pitched were easily the worst of his career. The Indians again faced the Red Sox in the American League Division Series but lost 3 games to 2. Assenmacher pitched in just one game for a full inning, giving up five hits and three earned runs.

Assenmacher was granted free agency in November, 1999. In February 2000, Assenmacher signed a minor-league contract with the team that gave him his first shot, the Atlanta Braves.[18] He was cut at the end of spring training, having given up eight earned runs in eight innings. "My arm's just not coming around. It's for the best," he said. "Time to get on with my life. I'm 39 years old, played 14 years. It just wasn't going to happen. Nothing to be ashamed of. ... I did everything I could to keep my career going."[19]

Assenmacher retired after the season. He later said "[i]t really wore on me as a player not to see my kids enough. I just wanted to spend my retirement being at home and watching them grow up."[20]

The Cubs asked Assenmacher to come back and sing "Take Me Out to the Ball Game" in September of 2004. When he was asked if he ever thought he'd get to sing at Wrigley when he was playing with the Cubs, he replied "[n]ot really. I never thought they'd get that desperate."[21]

Assenmacher spent 10 seasons as the pitching coach at St. Pius X High School, outside of Atlanta, where he lived as of 2018 with his wife, Maggie. Together, they have five children: Jason, Candace, Lindsay, Morgan, and Clayton.

SOURCES

In addition to the sources cited in the Notes, the author also consulted the following:

Aquinas College Athletics website (aqsaints.com/d/2016-aqbaseballrecords-1.pdf).

St Pius X Athletics website (spx.org/BaseballCoaches).

NOTES

1. Murray Chass, "Left-Handed Relievers Find Long Job Security," *New York Times,* February 21, 1999: SP2
2. "Baseball," *The Sun* (Baltimore), November 21, 1985: 5C.
3. Richard Justice, "Expansion Issue Alive," *Washington Post,* December 9, 1986.
4. Tim Kurkjian, "Don't Expect Happy Ending for Yankees from Episode 5 of Martin-Steinbrenner," *The Sun,* October 25, 1987: 4B.
5. Rich Lorenz, "National League," *Chicago Tribune,* March 2, 1989: 4-5.
6. "Strawberry Bolts from Mets' Camp," *The Sun,* March 3, 1989: 4B.
7. Murray Chass, "Secret to Success: Retire Will Clark," *New York Times,* October 6, 1989: D20.
8. Murray Chass, "Joyner Signs One-Year Pact With Royals for $4.2 Million," *New York Times*, December 10, 1991: B21.
9. Ibid.
10. Andrew Bagnato, "Deal Off, Cubs Turn to Plan B," *Chicago Tribune*, December 10, 1991: 4-2.
11. Joey Reaves, "Cubs, Sox Keep Most of Their Biggest Names," *Chicago Tribune*, November 18, 1992: 4-7.
12. Jack Curry, "Yankees Trade Assenmacher (Will Hitchcock Be Moving In?)," *New York Times*, March 22, 1994: B12.
13. "Around Baseball," *Washington Post,* April 11, 1995.
14. Murray Chass, "Indians Make a Strong Pitch, Too," *New York Times,* October 16, 1995: C7.
15. Paul Hoynes, "Why Didn't the 1995 Cleveland Indians Have Home-Field Advantage in the Playoffs?" Cleveland.com, October 29, 2015. (cleveland.com/tribe/index.ssf/2015/10/heres_why_1995_cleveland_india.html accessed 6/15/2016).
16. Patrick Reusse, "Cleveland's Fortunes Take a Left Turn," *Minneapolis Star Tribune,* October 26, 1995: C1, C4.
17. "Transactions," *Washington Post*, November 3, 1995.
18. Murray Chass, "Baseball," *New York Times*, February 6, 2000: SP2.
19. Jack Wilkinson, "Braves Notebook: End of March Ends Assenmacher March," *Atlanta Journal and Constitution*, April 1, 2000.
20. "'95 Cleveland Indians – Where Are They Now?" *Cleveland Magazine,* April 2005.
21. Scott Derenger, "The Suite Life: Paul Assenmacher," *Chicago Tribune,* September 3, 2004.

CARLOS BAERGA

BY JOSEPH WANCHO

In just his third season in the major leagues, Carlos Baerga was a leader on the field. The Cleveland Indians second baseman broke into the big leagues as a third baseman in 1990. But he was moved to second, where he found a home. There was never a question about Baerga's ability to hit. He collected 205 hits in 1992, including 32 doubles and 20 home runs, and produced 105 RBIs. Those numbers added up to a .312 batting average and his first selection to the All-Star Game.

But on March 23, 1993, Baerga stepped outside the white lines to become a leader of the club off the field. The day before, the Indians were given a day off by manager Mike Hargrove. Their spring training was held in Winter Haven, Florida. The players took advantage of the free day. Some groups took their families to Disney World, others went to Universal Studios. Others stayed closer to the spring-training complex.

Tim Crews came over to the Indians via free agency from Los Angeles to Cleveland. He owned a ranch close to Winter Haven, and invited the team to his home for a picnic. Steve Olin and Bob Ojeda took Crews up on his offer. Toward the end of the day, Crews, Ojeda, and Olin climbed into Crews' 18-foot bass boat, and circled around Little Lake Nellie. Indians trainer Fernando Montes observed the trio from where the boat departed. A neighbor's dock, which extended more than 50 yards, sat on the far side of the lake. As Crews accelerated, the front of the boat rose up, blocking their vision. As soon as the boat planed out, it had run under the dock. It was too late. The accident occurred in three feet of water. "We heard this loud thump and a crash," said Montes. "And it was silence, utter silence. I knew without any hesitation that Steve Olin had passed."[1] Crews was also dead and Ojeda was badly injured.

The next day, Cleveland's vice president of public relations, Bob DiBiasio, was looking for a player who would talk to the media about the boating tragedy. "Everybody on the team was in tears," said DiBiasio. "Nobody wanted to step forward and discuss what happened."[2] Carlos Baerga stepped forward, volunteering to be the team spokesman. "I was brokenhearted," he said, "but I had a responsibility to the two good people we had lost. They were part of my life. I told God, 'Give me words, because I know it's going to be hard for me.'"[3]

Carlos Obed Baerga was born on November 4, 1968, in Santurce, Puerto Rico. He was the oldest of four children born to José and Baldry Baerga.

José worked in the credit office of Puerto Rico's largest newspaper, *El Nuevo Dia.* José managed Carlos's little league teams. At 8, Carlos was holding his own against boys 10 to 12 years old. When he reached 14, Baerga was mixing it up on the diamond with adult amateurs in their 20s and 30s in the Puerto Rican Double A League. When Baerga reached 16, he was playing in the winter leagues against major leaguers.

"I remember my father saying, 'Don't come back home if you don't have your uniform dirty,' Baerga once recalled. "Ever since, I have put it in my mind to play hard. He always pushed me. My father always watches me, he's always behind me."[4]

Longtime Indians bullpen coach Luis Isaac (1987-2008) watched Baerga grow in his native Puerto Rico. "I knew right away he'd be a big-league player," said Isaac. "Even when he was little, he was the type of kid who wanted to play two games a day. He'd be telling the other kids on the field what to do. He always played with that kind of intensity."[5]

José worked with his son on becoming a switch-hitter so that he could play every day no matter who the pitcher was. Carlos, a natural left-handed hitter, worked hard to sharpen his skill from the right side of the plate. "I've still got to practice it every day," he said in 1995. "But it has helped me. I see a guy like Randy Johnson pitching and I can't imagine having to face him left-handed. The same goes for David Cone and facing him right-handed."[6]

Word of Baerga's ability spread around the island, and soon professional scouts arrived to get a look at the 14-year-old. Luis Rosa, a scout for the San Diego Padres, got Baerga to sign for a $65,000 bonus in 1985, when he turned 17 years old. (Rosa had a keen eye for talent. At the time Baerga signed, 32 of Rosa's players had made their way to the big leagues.

Although Baerga seemed destined for big-league stardom, there was one problem. The Padres already had a second baseman in-waiting, Roberto Alomar. Baerga started his playing career at Class-A Charleston in the South Atlantic League.

"They asked me to take him with me and when (rookie level) Spokane opened up (in mid-June) he'd go there," said Charleston manager Pat Kelly.[7] Baerga, who did not speak English that well, would ask Kelly, "Coach, why me no play?" Kelly would explain to Baerga that he had to play his more experienced players. Baerga would nod, as if he understood, but he returned the next day, asking the same question. This went on for about a week. "Finally, I put him in as a pinch-hitter, and he got a hit, of course," said Kelly. "So I started him the next day, and he went like 4-for-4, and they were all (line drives). So he stayed with us the whole year."[8]

Baerga showed that he could handle the bat on the minor-league level. He was still somewhat raw, but he was still just a teenager in his first three years in the minors. Because Alomar was the second baseman of the future for the Padres, it became evident that a new position would have to be found for Baerga, even though he felt the most comfortable at second base.

When Baerga reported to Double-A Wichita in 1988, he was switched to shortstop. In 1989 he was promoted to Triple-A Las Vegas and was placed at third base. Although he made 32 errors while manning the hot corner for Las Vegas, Baerga was in the lineup to hit. He hit .275 with 28 doubles, 10 homers, and 74 RBIs. He was somewhat of a free swinger, and his strikeouts easily tripled his walks.

The Cleveland Indians were shopping outfielder Joe Carter at the 1989 winter meetings. Carter's contract was up in 1990, and the Indians knew they would not be able to re-sign him. Carter made no secret of his desire to leave the Indians, preferably to a contender, and a lucrative contract would also be nice.

The Indians found a suitor in the Padres. The teams dickered over whom the Padres would send the Indians' way for the star slugger. The Indians insisted that Baerga be included in the deal. The Padres viewed Baerga as their third baseman of the future. But the Indians' persistence won out, and they received Baerga, catcher Sandy Alomar Jr. (Roberto's brother), and outfielder Chris James for Carter. "I managed against Carlos in the Pacific

Coast League in 1989," said Mike Hargrove. "On my report at the end of the year, I recommended that we should try to acquire him. So did my coaches, Rich Dauer and Rick Adair."[9]

The Indians hired John McNamara to manage in 1990. Cleveland was putting together a solid nucleus of young talent, and it began with Baerga and Alomar. The two newcomers were blended with Albert Belle, Cory Snyder, Jerry Browne, and Brook Jacoby. Tom Candiotti, Greg Swindell, and Buddy Black anchored the starting rotation.

Alomar was a star right away. He was named the starting catcher on the 1990 AL All-Star team, won the Gold Glove, and was voted Rookie of the Year. Baerga would have to wait a bit for his time to come. Browne was entrenched at second base and Jacoby manned third. The Indians had signed Keith Hernandez to play first base. But Hernandez suffered through various injuries and played in only 42 games. His injuries offered the break that benefited Baerga; Jacoby moved to first base and Baerga became the new third baseman. "From the time he got to Cleveland, Carlos was the heart and soul of the Indians," said batting coach José Morales. "We sent him down to Triple A for two weeks in his rookie year, and team spirit just sank. When he came back, it was like a kid returning to his family. He brings an energy, a unity to the team."[10]

Baerga hit .266 his rookie season. On September 20 at Yankee Stadium, the 5-foot-11, 165-pound infielder went 4-for-5 with three doubles (a career high) and a triple with three runs scored and three RBIs. The barrage came the day after his first child, a daughter, was born. "Baerga is a hitting machine and maybe his wife should have a baby every night," said McNamara.[11] Although the Indians finished with a 77-85 record, they found themselves in fourth place in the AL East. It was something to build on for the young Tribe.

Indeed, Baerga's enthusiasm for the game was unbridled and was contagious. He was a fan favorite for his all-out hustle. But in his second season, the Indians proved unable to build on the success from 1990. McNamara was fired (Hargrove replaced him) and the team topped 100 losses.

But the pieces were beginning to come together. Charles Nagy became the leader of the pitching staff. Kenny Lofton was acquired from Houston to solidify center field and bat leadoff. Paul Sorrento was acquired from Minnesota to provide a left-handed bat and he was an above-average first baseman. The Indians worked to sign Belle, Alomar, Nagy, Belle, Lofton, and Baerga to long-term deals, selling them on the talent of the core team.

Baerga made their investment pay off. In back-to-back seasons (1992 and '93) he hit more than 20 home runs, drove in more than 100 runs, and batted over .300. He was the first second baseman to achieve these numbers in consecutive seasons since Rogers Hornsby turned the trick in 1921 and 1922.

Baerga entered the record books on April 8, 1993. He hit two home runs in the seventh inning against the New York Yankees, one from each side of the plate. He connected off Steve Howe for a two run-shot, then hit a solo home run off Steve Farr. The Indians scored nine runs in the inning on their way to a 15-5 victory. "It's exciting," said Baerga. "They told me I set a record when I got back to the dugout after the second homer, but I didn't believe them. When I got to the clubhouse after the game, Bobby DiBiasio, our public-relations man, told me I'd set a record."[12] Baerga's record night did not surprise Hargrove. "The beauty about him is that there's no way to pitch him. He hits to all fields," the manager said.[13]

Baerga made the All-Star Game for the first time in 1992 and repeated in 1993. The Indians finished with identical 76-86 records in both seasons.

In 1994 the Indians said goodbye to Cleveland Stadium and relocated to the new Jacobs Field, across downtown. The baseball-only venue was a boon for the Tribe. The Indians had brought in veteran leadership in the offseason, signing Eddie Murray and Dennis Martinez. They traded for shortstop Omar Vizquel. Manny Ramirez and Jim Thome arrived through the farm system. The results were favorable. The Indians were one game behind Chicago in the new AL Central when the season ended on August 12 because of the players strike. Although the development was a big disappointment to Tribe fans, baseball fever had indeed returned to the North Coast.

The strike wiped out the 1994 postseason and bled over into the 1995 season. Baerga finished the 1994 season with 19 home runs, 80 RBIs, and a .314 batting average.

After play resumed in late April of 1995, Cleveland broke through its 41-year stretch of not appearing in a postseason game. The Indians won 100 games and Baerga, batting third in the potent Cleveland lineup, was third on the team with 90 RBIs. He batted .314. Cleveland swept Boston in the ALDS and topped Seattle in six games in the ALCS. The Indians met the Atlanta Braves in the World Series. The old adage that good pitching will defeat good hitting proved accurate, as the Braves captured the world championship in six games.

Baerga hit .400 in the ALCS and drove in four runs in both the ALCS and the World Series. He knocked in the first two runs in the Indians' 5-2 victory in Game Two of the ALDS and three runs in their 7-6, 11-inning Game Three win in the World Series. All told, he hit .292 in the 1995 postseason.

The one constant in Baerga's career to this point was his desire to play winter ball in his native Puerto Rico. He was lauded by Puerto Rican fans for his work in the community as well as his work on the diamond. He often held clinics and his enthusiasm for the game was infectious. "They won't even let you take batting practice," Baerga said, referring to the young fans. "They come right onto the field for autographs."[14]

Baerga was also a fan favorite in Cleveland. His all-out effort between the lines and his effervescent personality off it endeared him to hard-working, blue-collar town. Thus the backlash the Indians front office received when they traded Baerga on July 29, 1996, was not unexpected. The Indians swapped Baerga and utility infielder Alvaro Espinoza to the New York Mets in a trade-deadline swap for infielders Jeff Kent and José Vizcaino. Baerga's numbers were on the downside (10 home runs, 55 RBIs, .267 batting average) through 100 games. The Indians cited Baerga's weight gain. (He was said to have been 20 to 25 pounds overweight in spring training.) His work ethic and priorities were also questioned by the Indians brass. Baerga suffered a slight fracture in his right ankle and played in only about 10 games in the winter league. He used the winter league to stay in shape, hence the weight gain. He was also battling a badly sprained left wrist and a strained groin.

"When you get close to the trading deadline, you never know what's going to happen," said New York GM Joe McIlvaine. "To be honest, when they dropped Baerga's name, I was a little surprised. I thought, 'Here's a chance to get a good, quality player.' And we did it. I don't think a year ago we could've acquired Carlos Baerga."[15]

The presence of second baseman Edgardo Alfonzo on the Mets created a question of where Baerga would be stationed. As it turned out, an abdominal strain limited Baerga to 26 Mets games, mostly at first base, and a .193 batting average.

Bobby Valentine took over for Dallas Green as the Mets manager with a month to go in the 1996 season. Over the next two seasons, Baerga recaptured his second-base spot. Alfonzo was moved to third. Manager Valentine, who at times could be as subtle as a sledgehammer, would comment about Baerga's approach to hitting as "an embarrassment."[16] Baerga felt the pressure to produce, feeling that he needed to prove his worth every day. But he did not have a strong lineup like the one in Cleveland to back him up. His batting average was .274 over the 1997 and 1998 seasons, but his power numbers were dismal. The ball was not jumping off his bat as it once had.

One longtime major-league executive explained Baerga's decline this way: "Carlos is a God-given good hitter, and sometimes a player like that takes a lot for granted, doesn't stay on top of his physical conditioning and mental preparation. And there's no doubt in my mind that is what happened to him. I mean, he's always had a thick body, but last year, well, he just got plain heavy. I think it's all related (to his weight and conditioning). I was really surprised the Mets took him. No … I was shocked."[17]

The Mets did not pick up Baerga's option year in 1999. The rest of his career was a composite of being signed, being waived, and riding the bench. St. Louis signed him for the 1999 season, but waived him at the end of spring training. Cincinnati signed Baerga, but sent him to Triple-A Indianapolis before the season, and released him after two months. In a bit of déjà vu, San Diego signed Baerga, and then traded him back to the Indians for the balance of the 1999 season.

Baerga signed on with Tampa Bay for 2000, but his contract was voided before the season began. He signed with Seattle for 2001, but was released before the start of the season. He bided his time in independent leagues and for Samsung in the Korean League. Baerga eventually made his way back to the big leagues as a role player with Boston (2002), Arizona (2003-2004), and Washington (2005). After the 2005 season Baerga retired with a lifetime batting average of .291, 1,583 hits, 134 home runs, and 774 RBIs.

Baerga worked for ESPN as a Spanish-language broadcaster for ESPN. He also helped coach the Puerto Rican National Baseball team. He also became the owner of the Bayamon Cowboys in the Puerto Rican Winter League.

Baerga married the former Miriam Cruz. They had two children, Karla and Carlos. In 2013 Baerga was inducted along with former Indians GM John Hart into the Cleveland Indians Hall of Fame. As of 2016 he was an ambassador for the Indians, making community appearances and spreading good will.

In 2016 Baerga threw out the first pitch in Game Two of the World Series at Progressive Field. He was, of course, cheered enthusiastically as he threw a perfect pitch to home plate.

NOTES

1. ESPN, Outside the Lines, "Indians Boating Tragedy," March 18, 2003. espn.com/page2/tvlistings/show155_transcript.html.
2. Frank Lidz, "Slick With the Stick," *Sports Illustrated*, April 5, 1994: 66.
3. Ibid.
4. Rick Lawes, "Baerga Has Big Talent," *USA Today Baseball Weekly*, January 13-26, 1993: 4.
5. Paul Hoynes, "Rock Solid: Carlos Baerga Is Part of the Foundation on Which the Indians Built a Winning Club," *Cleveland Plain Dealer*, July 3, 1995: 8-D.
6. Ibid.
7. Lawes.
8. Ibid.
9. Hoynes, July 3, 1995: 9-D.
10. Lidz.
11. Russell Schneider, "Tribe Rolls to Victory," *Cleveland Plain Dealer*, September 21, 1990: 1-E.
12. Paul Hoynes, "Baerga's Blasts Rip Yankees: Two-HR Inning Sets Mark," *Cleveland Plain Dealer*, April 9, 1993: 1C.
13. Ibid.
14. Lidz, 64.
15. Ray McNulty, "Net Heist Brings Baerga," *New York Post*, July 30, 1996.
16. Buster Olney, "Benching Doesn't Sit Well With Baerga," *New York Times*, April 23, 1997: B11.
17. Michael P. Geffner, "The Sound and the Fury," *The Sporting News*, May 5, 1997: 18.

DAVID BELL

BY PHILIP A. COLA

Longtime fans of the Indians know that the team did not appear in postseason play from 1954 to 1995. The 40 years in between were difficult for baseball in Cleveland. During that time, there were three waves of major-league baseball expansion into new cities with new teams finding success before the Indians returned to the postseason. The club was not the top team in Ohio during those lean years either as the Reds made it to the World Series in 1961, 1972, 1975, 1976, and 1990 while the Tribe languished as a second-tier club. However, many exciting players and traditions engaged the fans throughout these years.

For example, on April 15, 1972, David Gus Bell, better known as Buddy, made his major-league debut as a right fielder for the Indians in a 5-1 loss to the Milwaukee Brewers. He went hitless in three at-bats. The lineup for the Tribe in the losing effort included notable players such as Greg Nettles, Chris Chambliss, Ray Fosse, and Gaylord Perry. The first three went on to have careers with championship teams outside Cleveland in New York (Nettles and Chambliss) and Oakland (Fosse). Perry won the Cy Young Award that season for the Indians. The team had good players in 1972 and a rising star in Bell, but they finished in fifth place in the American League East Division, 14 games behind the Detroit Tigers.

Buddy Bell became an above-average player and a fan favorite in Cleveland. He was the Tribe's third baseman for six seasons before a trade to the Texas Rangers, for whom he earned multiple Gold Gloves for another seven seasons. He finished off the productive part of his career with three years in his adopted home town of Cincinnati. Buddy's father, David Russell "Gus" Bell, played in the major leagues from 1950 to 1964, most notably with the Cincinnati Reds from 1953 to 1961, the last of them a pennant-winning season for the club. Gus was a popular outfielder for the Reds splitting his time between center and right fields throughout his career. This introduction tells a story of a father/son combination of baseball players who both spent time in Cincinnati as major leaguers, but it is not where the family success in the major leagues, or ties to baseball in Ohio, ended.

On September 14, 1972, almost five months to the day after his major-league debut, Buddy Bell and his wife, Gloria (née Eysoldt), had a son named David. Buddy took that day off from the Indians, but he started and played center field the next day. The Indians lost to the Red Sox, 4-3, and Buddy went hitless in five at-bats from the leadoff spot in the order. However, this day became a link to a special moment in major-league history 23 years later and ironically at the start of a season in which the Indians broke their long postseason drought, and which moreover saw them win the American League pennant for the first time since 1954.

Gus Bell had moved his family to Cincinnati after a trade from the Pirates to the Reds in 1952. Cincinnati became home for the next few generations of the Bell family. Buddy had been born in Pittsburgh, but he was raised in Cincinnati and maintained his home there during his playing days in Cleveland and Texas. David was born and raised in Cincinnati.[1] He remembered being thrilled to be in and around major-league clubhouses and traveling with his father since he was 6 years old.[2] He loved the fact that his father was a major-league player, setting the stage for his future vocation.[3] David always felt that he would never be as good as his father, who he thought was a great player. His admiration for his father as a player helped mold the young David as a player and a person. The Bell family was very close and all three of Buddy's sons went on to be professional baseball players.[4]

However, before following their father's footsteps into professional baseball, David (the eldest) followed his father's lead to stardom in basketball and baseball at Cincinnati's Archbishop Moeller High School. The school often known for football success has also won seven state baseball championships, with its first in 1972, the year David was born. Seventeen years later, as a junior at Moeller, David led the team to the state title in 1989.[5] David was a three-year starter at Moeller and is the school's all-time leader in doubles.[6] Hall of Famers Barry Larkin and Ken Griffey Jr. both starred at Moeller. However, the school did not win state championships during either of their baseball careers, which preceded David's career at the school.

David had two brothers who also starred at Moeller. Michael Bell was three years younger than David and Ricky was seven years his junior. The Bell brothers starred in both baseball and basketball as did their father.[7] After David graduated from high school in 1990 (a year the Reds won the World Series), he had a baseball scholarship waiting for him to attend the University of Kentucky, which he declined when he signed with the Indians after being a seventh-round draft pick in the June amateur draft.[8]

Bell batted and threw right-handed. He stood 5-feet-10 and weighed 170 pounds during his playing career. He made his professional debut with the Gulf Coast Indians in the rookie league at age 17 in 1990. He did well, moving up to the Burlington rookie league team later that year. This began a slow but steady progression throughout the minor leagues. He spent the next two years with Columbus of the Class A Sally League and then the next season with Kinston in the Class A Carolina League. In 1993, Bell moved to Canton-Akron of the Double-A Eastern League, where his batting average for the first time rose above .260 in his minor-league career – finishing with a .292 average, 9 home runs, and 60 RBIs. His career was progressing and he seemed to be playing the game the way his father had as a good-fielding infielder, while developing in a solid, if not spectacular, fashion at the plate. In 1994, he played the entire year at Charlotte of the Triple-A International League, where he blossomed into a bona-fide major-league prospect. He hit .293 with 18 home runs and 88 RBIs. This made him a player to watch by long-suffering Indians fans, especially in a year when the major-league team was developing into a contender. However, with the Indians in contention, only one game behind the American League Central Division leading Chicago White Sox, the season abruptly ended with the players strike on August 11, 1994.

It felt unbelievable in the first year of three-division play in each league, with the Indians in the leading spot for a postseason berth as a wild-card team that the season could end in this manner. However, the future looked bright with the nucleus of star players forming what became a powerhouse of an offensive team for years to come. Additionally, there were stars in the minor leagues ready to make it to the majors and contribute to what held promise of the best baseball played in Cleveland in over four decades. Longtime fans hoped Bell would contribute to the future and follow Bell's father's example as a fan favorite in Cleveland.

Winter was somehow much longer that year; baseball had ended in August and uncertainty for the opening of the 1995 season loomed into the spring. The 1995 season opened later than usual on April 25 and with the season shortened to a 144-game schedule. As the season drew near, there was great anticipation that the Indians would reach the postseason. In addition, Bell earned the final spot on the Opening Day roster. It was a very exciting time for Indians bench coach Buddy Bell, who was able to be with his son as he made the major-league club.[9] David made his major-league debut on May 3, 1995, at the age of 22. That night the Indians trounced the Tigers, 14-7, with their high-powered offense and just enough pitching to hold them close until the offense got in gear. This was the formula for success for the Tribe, who improved to 4-2 in the young season. Bell pinch-hit for Jim Thome and replaced him at third base. Bell was hitless in his only plate appearance.

With Bell's appearance in this game, a historic achievement occurred as the Bells became only the second family ever to have three generations of major-league players. Only the Boone family had three generations of players appear at the major-league level – with Ray, Bob, Bret, and Aaron – before David helped put the Bell family in the major-league history books.

Bell's only other game for the Indians in 1995 came on May 7, when he pinch-hit for Thome in a 17-inning, 10-9 victory over the Minnesota Twins. This was Bell's only game before the home crowd in Cleveland that year. He went hitless and played third base, replacing Thome. More importantly than the Indians' victory in the Bell family that day was the sad news that Gus Bell had died at 67 in Montgomery, Ohio.

Bell did not play again that season for the Indians after a demotion to Triple-A Buffalo for more playing time. Then, on June 27, 1995, he was traded with Pepe McNeal and Rick Heiserman to the St. Louis Cardinals for starting pitcher Ken Hill. Indians fans were ecstatic to receive Hill, who had won 16 games for the first-place Montreal Expos the prior year until the strike hit. Fans were sad to see Bell go to another team without having much of a chance to prove himself in an Indians uniform. It seemed he might not assume his father's role in Cleveland as many had hoped, but the team was on its way to the pennant and he was not going to supplant Thome, Omar Vizquel, or Carlos Baerga for playing time in the Indians infield any time soon.

Bell spent the rest of the 1995 season splitting his time between Louisville of the American Association and the Cardinals. He hit .250 for the Cardinals with 2 home runs and 19 RBIs in 39 games. He played second base in 37 games and three games at third. Playing second for the Cardinals was a treat for Bell because his keystone combination partner was future Hall of Famer Ozzie Smith, whom many consider the best fielding shortstop of all time. Bell's first major-league hit came on August 19, 1995, in St. Louis. He doubled to left field on the first pitch from reliever Brad Clontz in a 5-4 win over the first-place Braves.

On August 30, 1995, Bell played his first game in his hometown of Cincinnati at Riverfront Stadium. Many friends and family attended that game to see him play (the extended Bell family is huge; Buddy was one of seven children) and he delivered his first major-league home run, a two-run shot off Mark Portugal. Bell was able to obtain the ball, which he hit over the left-center-field seats, with a little help from Reds center fielder Darren Lewis, who exchanged another ball with a fan in the outfield seats for the one that Bell hit. Bell gave that home-run ball to his mother after the game. The Cardinals finished in fourth place that year with a 62-81 record and 22½ games behind the division champion Reds. Both Ohio teams fared well that season; the Indians ran away with the American League Central Division, finishing at 100-44. Each team eventually was eliminated by the Braves. The Reds were swept in the National League Championship Series, and the Indians lost to the Braves in six games in the World Series.

Bell continued to go back and forth between the minors and majors the next two years. He spent 62 and 66 games with the Cardinals in 1996 and 1997.

He hit only .214 and .211. He was not faring much better in the minors, where his offensive struggles continued in limited playing time. In 1997 the challenges for Bell continued as he spent time back at Arkansas of the Double-A Texas League as the Indians went to another World Series. He began the 1998 season with the Cardinals and played in four games with limited productivity until he was released. The Indians claimed him off waivers on April 14, 1998. It was an exciting time to be coming back to Cleveland as a player even though his father was no longer the bench coach. The next day, April 15, 1998, Bell started at second base and hit the first inside-the-park home run ever at Jacobs Field and the first for the Indians in nine seasons. The historic hit came off future Hall of Famer Randy Johnson in the first inning with no one on base and one out giving the Tribe a 1-0 lead in an eventual 5-3 loss.

Once he rejoined the Indians, Bell was in the majors for good. He played in 107 games with the Indians, mostly as a second baseman, and began to break out as a player offensively and defensively. He hit .262 with 10 home runs and 41 RBIs. However, his big break as a major-league player came later that year when the Indians traded him to Seattle for Joey Cora on August 31, 1998. The Indians were again in the midst of a pennant race and they felt Cora brought veteran skills to the club for the playoff drive. The team won the Central Division by nine games before beating the Red Sox in the American League Division Series. They ultimately lost to the Yankees in the American League Championship Series in six games. Cora struggled in the postseason, going 1-for-17 and played in only two games against the Yankees. His playing career was over and Bell's was just beginning.

The Mariners had strong teams in the mid- to late 1990s with Randy Johnson, Ken Griffey Jr., Edgar Martinez, and Alex Rodriguez on the roster. When Bell joined the team, Johnson was gone, but the other stars remained and the future looked great. Bell hit .325 in 21 games for the Mariners to finish out the 1998 season and was primed to compete for the second-base job in 1999. He was competing with promising rookie infielder Carlos Guillen for that spot when Guillen was lost for the season with and injury. Bell became the everyday second baseman and had his true breakout year. He established career highs in home runs (21), runs (92), and RBIs (78) while batting .268. Bell led the league in putouts (313) and double plays (118) from his second-base position. The Mariners finished 79-83 and in third place in the American League Western Division, but 16 games behind division winner Texas. It was a disappointing outcome relative to the talent on the team under manager Lou Piniella. In the offseason, David married Kristi Kimener, of Cincinnati, on November 27, 1999.[10]

In 2000 Bell got his first taste of playoff baseball as the Mariners won the American League wild card with a record of 91-71 only a half-game behind the division-winning Athletics. They swept the White Sox three games to none in the Division Series before losing to the Yankees in six games in the ALCS. Bell did not repeat the success of his 1999 campaign, batting .247 with 11 home runs. Mark McLemore joined the team that season and Guillen returned from injury, forcing Bell to split playing time in the Mariners infield. This began a streak of three straight postseason appearances for Bell.

The Mariners tied the record for regular-season wins in 2001 with 116 against only 46 loses. They acquired Bret Boone (of the other three-generation family) and he exploded on the Seattle baseball scene with 37 home runs and a team-leading 141 RBIs. Guillen moved to shortstop and Bell became the starting third baseman and batted 260 with 15 home runs and 64 RBIs. Right fielder Ichiro Suzuki hit .350 and center fielder Mike Cameron had a breakout season with 25 home runs and 110 RBIs. The ever-steady Martinez hit over .300 with 23 home runs and 116 RBIs as the designated hitter. The Mariners beat the Indians, three games to two, in the Division Series before surprisingly losing to the Yankees four games to one in the ALCS. It was surprising because they had won 21 more regular-season games than the Yankees, but they were flat in four out of five games against a team that subsequently lost the World Series to the Arizona Diamondbacks. The loss to the Yankees for the second consecutive year, after the record-breaking regular season, was stunning to everyone.

Bell was solid in the ALDS against the Indians with five hits in 16 at-bats for a .313 average. He hit his first postseason home run in Game Two of the series. It was a solo drive to left field off Tribe starter Chuck Finley. However, Bell struggled, as did most of the team, in the Yankees series, hitting a paltry .188, but with four runs batted in. He became a free agent after the season, but re-signed with the Mariners in December. The Mariners traded him in January to the San Francisco Giants for Desi Relaford and cash. Bell said his time in Seattle and the lifelong friendships made there were some of the most memorable points of his career.[11]

Bell was the starting third baseman for the Giants in 2002 and played in 154 games, batting .261 with 20 home runs and 73 RBIs while playing a solid infield defense. He was a steady performer much like his father before him. He was overshadowed by monster seasons from Barry Bonds (.370, 46, 110) and Jeff Kent (.313, 37, 108), but the Giants made the playoffs, finishing 95-66-1 under the guidance of Dusty Baker. They were 2½ games behind the division-winning Diamondbacks, but they beat the Braves in the Division Series, three games to two and the Cardinals, four games to one, in the NLCS to advance to Bell's first and only World Series. He struggled in the Division Series but had an outstanding Championship Series that saw him go 7-for-17 (.412) with his second postseason home run. Bell scored the winning run in the pennant-clinching Game Five against the Cardinals. He coming home from second base on a hit by former Indians teammate Kenny Lofton.

Bell described playing in the World Series against the Angels as his career highlight. "It was that feeling" of playing in a World Series "that is the thing, I think about the most, by a long shot."[12] The Angels beat the Giants in seven games.

The Giants had all the momentum after a 16-4 bombing of the Angels in Game Five. They did not win another game. With their backs to the wall, the Angels made a historic comeback in Game Six, then bested the Giants in Game Seven for the title. Bell started all seven games at third base in the series. He won Game Four with an eighth-inning RBI single that scored J.T. Snow. He hit .304 with one home run and four RBIs, continuing his above-average postseason play. His World Series home run, in Game Two at Edison Field in Anaheim, was was a solo shot off Kevin Appier to center field in the second inning of a frustrating 11-10 loss. In the most famous play from this World Series, Bell was sprinting home with a run in the Game Five blowout after a triple by Lofton. Snow had already scored and as he crossed the plate, he grabbed Giants manager Dusty Baker's 3-year-old son, batboy Darren Baker, who was retrieving Lofton's bat, and carried him off the field, avoiding a potential serious injury. After the season, Bell won the Willie Mac Award (named after Giants Hall of Famer Willie McCovey), as voted by his teammates and the coaching staff, for team spirit and inspirational leadership.

Bell became a free agent in October 2002 and he signed a contract with the Phillies in December 2002. His first year in Philadelphia (2003) was a bust; he played in only 85 games and batted .195. He rebounded in his second year with the Phillies, hitting .291 with 18 home runs and 77 RBIs. He reunited with Jim Thome in Philadelphia in 2003 and 2004. On June 28, 2004, Bell hit for the cycle in a 14-6 Phillies rout of the Expos. He doubled in the second, homered in the fourth, and singled in the sixth. His seventh-inning triple was controversial: The ball appeared to hit of the hands of a fan in deep center field before bouncing away from the Expos' Brad Wilkerson. Expos manager Frank Robinson protested the call and the umpires met while Bell stood on third base, but the umpires ruled it a triple, much to Robinson's chagrin. Bell said he "was unaware that he hit for the cycle until third-base coach John Vukovich told him to enjoy the moment."[13] It was the first time in major-league history that a grandfather and grandson had both hit for the cycle.[14] Gus Bell had accomplished the feat on June 4, 1951, for the Pirates. Bell said he was happy to have hits in a game his team won and that he "realized that hitting for the cycle is something that doesn't happen very often."[15]

Bell's up-and-coming next two years with Phillies saw his offensive productivity in moderate decline though he remained the starting third baseman. The team was up-an- coming (once again in David's career), but it failed to make playoffs by very close margins in 2004 and 2005, finishing in second place each of those years behind the Braves. Ryan Howard had replaced Thome at first base and Chase Utley was emerging along with Howard and Jimmy Rollins as superstars in the Phillies infield. In 2006 the Phillies once again finished frustratingly second, this time to the Mets, and just three games off the wild-card pace. He spent 3½ years playing third base for the Phillies until a trade to the Brewers for Wilfrido Laureano on July 28, 2006.

Bell's career ended after he played out the 2006 season with the Brewers. He became a free agent and retired with an eye toward coaching and managing, once again following in his father's footsteps. He finished his 12-year career with a .257 batting average, 123 home runs, and 589 RBIs. In three trips to the postseason with the Mariners and Giants he batted .282 with three home runs. Bell certainly had a solid, if unspectacular, playing career in terms of productivity.

Bell managed the Double-A Carolina Mudcats, a Reds affiliate, from 2009 through 2011. He then managed the Louisville Bats of the Triple-A International League in 2012, an affiliate of the Reds He spoke hopefully about continuing to manage in the Reds' system and eventually perhaps coaching or managing with the big-league club in his hometown.[16] He spent 2013 as the third-base coach with the Chicago Cubs while his father was assistant general manager of the White Sox.[17] Bell was with the Cardinals in 2014 as an assistant hitting instructor before a promotion to bench coach for the 2015 season.[18] After spending three years as a bench coach for manager Mike Matheny's Cardinals, Bell accepted the role of vice president of player development for the San Francisco Giants after the 2017 season.[19] The position allowed Bell to be closer to his home in Scottsdale, Arizona, where he and Kristi live with their daughter, Brogan, and son, David, whom they call "Gus" just like his great grandfather.

But on October 22, 2018, Bell's career took another turn. He returned home to Cincinnati as he was named the new manager of the Reds. He succeeds interim manager Jim Riggleman, who took over for Bryan Price who was dismissed in April when the Reds broke out of the gate with a 3-15 record. Bell is the 52nd manager in Cincinnati Reds history. "It's what I always wanted and what I dreamed of," said Bell. "To have an opportunity to work with people you respect and like and truly are in it to be all together with one goal, this is what I was hoping for."[20]

The Bell family now joins another exclusive club. They are the fourth family in MLB history to have a father and son who served as managers. Buddy Bell managed in Detroit, Colorado and Kansas City. They join George and Dick Sisler, Bob and Joel Skinner, and Bob and Aaron Boone.[21]

NOTES

1. Chadwick Fischer, "Q&A with New Bats Manager David Bell," MiLB.com, January 31, 2012, milb.com/milb/news/q--a-with-new-bats-manager-david-bell/c-26525502.
2. "David Bell," Baseballlibrary.com, accessed November 25, 2014, baseballlibrary.com/ballplayers/player.php?name=David_Bell_1972.
3. "David Bell."
4. "2009 Cincinnati High School Sports Hall of Fame -- Bell, Bell, Bell, Mitts, Richter, Coaches Russo," Larosas MVP.com, accessed November 25, 2014, larosasmvp.com/fame/2009_inductees.htm.
5. Ibid.
6. Ibid.
7. Ibid.
8. Ibid. "David Bell Minor Leagues Statistics & History," Baseball Reference.com, accessed November 25, 2014, baseball-reference.com/register/player.fcgi?id=bell--004dav.
9. Derrick Goold, "Baseball Is Family Tradition for Cards' Bell," *St. Louis Post-Dispatch*, June 19, 2016, stltoday.com/sports/baseball/professional/goold-baseball-is-family-tradition-for-cards-bell/article_644365cf-04d4-5c88-b2ab-bf8d80ecfc63.html.
10. "2009 Cincinnati High School Sports Hall of Fame - Bell, Bell, Bell, Mitts, Richter, Coaches Russo."
11. Nick Piecoro, "What's Up: Ex-MLB Player David Bell," *Arizona Republic*, October 21, 2009, sec. Sports, archive.azcentral.com/arizonarepublic/sports/articles/2009/10/21/20091021spt-whatsup.html.
12. Ibid.
13. "Like His Grandfather, Bell Hits for the Cycle," *New York Times*, June 29, 2004: D6.
14.

15 "Like His Grandfather, Bell Hits for the Cycle."

16 Fischer, "Q&A with New Bats Manager David Bell."

17 Toni Ginnetti and Gordon Wittenmyer, "David Bell and Father Buddy on Opposite Sides of City Rivalry," *Chicago Sun Times*, May 27, 2013.

18 Jon Doble, "David Bell Named Bench Coach; Cardinals Roster Moves," Redbird Dugout, November 3, 2014, redbirddugout.com/david-bell-named-bench-coach-make-roster-moves/.

19 Jenifer Langosch, "Bench Coach David Bell Departs Cardinals," MLB.com, October 20, 2017, mlb.com/news/bench-coach-david-bell-departs-cardinals/c-259191112.

20 Mark Sheldon, "Reds name David Bell new manager", https://www.mlb.com/reds/news/reds-select-david-bell-as-teams-new-manager/c-299427658, October 22, 2018, accessed October 23, 2018

21 Associated Press, "New manager David Bell tasked with turning around Reds", http://www.espn.com/mlb/story/_/id/25054877/new-manager-david-bell-tasked-turning-cincinnati-reds October 22, 2018, accessed October 23, 2018

ALBERT BELLE

BY TOM WANCHO

"Joey is extremely smart. He's great with figures and crossword puzzles. He could spell backwards when he was five. Did you know my Joey was an Eagle Scout? He took French in high school, finished sixth in his class of 266. I brought him up to excel in everything. He wants to be perfect."

– Carrie Belle, Albert Belle's mother, *Sports Illustrated*, June 24, 1991.

Strike 1: It's impossible to be perfect, or bat 1.000 over the course of a 12-year major-league baseball career. Which leads to …

"Sometimes he throws coolers around. Sometimes he breaks phones in the clubhouse. There are cookies all over the place. This guy is so unbelievable, he can go three for three going into his at-bat and pop out, and he's still throwing cookies around."

– Former Indians teammate Omar Vizquel to the Associated Press, October 23, 1995.

Strike 2. In Belle's case, imperfection led to temper tantrums, shattering locker-room sinks, ripping thermostats off clubhouse walls, and firing expletives at media members. Which amped up Belle's anger inside and …

"Throughout his major league career Albert Belle has demonstrated a distinct pattern: When the surly slugger gets P.O.'d, baseballs get K.O.'d."

– Mark Bechtel, *Sports Illustrated*, July 27, 1998.

During his tumultuous career, Albert Jojuan Belle (born August 25, 1966, in Shreveport, Louisiana) almost always played pissed off. And his career statistics (a .295 batting average, a .369 on-base percentage, and averages of 32 home runs and 103 RBIs per season) second that emotion.

But when discussing Belle and/or his playing career, words speak louder than numbers. Take your pick of adjectives. Abusive and articulate. Dominant and divisive. Intimidating and intellectual. Consistent and cursing.

Belle has fond memories of growing up. "I was blessed to grow up with parents who possessed different strengths and skills," Belle wrote in an op-ed piece for the *Baltimore Sun*.[1] "Mom was and still is the 'glue' of the family, but Dad (also named Albert) was the enforcer and 'silent pillar of strength.' Mom encouraged academics and culture, and Dad always promoted athletics. Both gave me and my brother all they had." Belle's mother was a math teacher and his father, in addition to his football and baseball coaching duties at another Shreveport-area high school, was also an educator.[2]

The elder Belle pushed his twin boys hard. "To this day, I believe my late-night batting practices during my high school years were what made the difference in helping me arrive at the Major Leagues. After high school baseball practice, I would go home, eat dinner, and tackle homework. Dad would usually arrive home after a long practice with his high school team. After talking to Mom for a few minutes, he would poke his head in our room. That was our signal. My brother and I would immediately bounce up and jog out of the house up to the local junior high school, with Dad driving behind us. Dad would throw us hundreds of balls all night long."[3]

After an all-state career and National Honor Society merit at Huntington High School in Shreveport, Belle attended Louisiana State University (1985-87) in Baton Rouge, where he set school career marks for home runs (49), total bases (392) and RBIs (172).[4]

But Belle's inability to control his temper appeared on a public stage for the first time during a game at the 1987 Southeast Conference tournament. Belle attempted to run down a fan who was shouting racial slurs at him. Two of his teammates tackled him and he was suspended for the College World Series by Tigers coach Skip Bertman.

Tick, tick, tick.

It wasn't the last time Belle confronted a fan. On May 11, 1991, while with the Indians, he drilled Jeff Pillar in the chest with a fastball fired from 15 feet away after Pillar yelled, "Hey Joey, keg party at my house after the game."[5] Two years later, on September 23, 1993, Belle was with some teammates at a Cleveland nightclub when he hit William Kelly twice in the face with a ping pong paddle after Kelly chanted, "Joey, Joey"[6] (the name Belle went by before his 10-week stay at an addiction treatment center in 1990).[7]

The Indians selected Belle with their first pick in the 1987 amateur draft. Belle spent parts of five seasons in the minor leagues. Splitting time between Kinston and Waterloo during the 1988 campaign, Belle belted 17 home runs with 54 RBIs and a .293 batting average. The next year he jacked 20 home runs for Double-A Canton-Akron, earning a promotion to the major leagues. In 62 games Belle struggled with his batting average (.225) but did club seven home runs while driving in 37 runs. He was only 22 years old.

Belle's 1990 season was interrupted by his rehab stay. Re-emerging clean, Joey Belle began going by his given first name, Albert, upon leaving the facility. He made the Tribe's roster for good at the start of the 1991 season. He slammed 28 home runs in 123 games that year, driving in 95 runs while batting .282. He was just getting started.

From 1992 to 1996, there was no more dominant – or feared – batsman than Belle. His five-year averages of .303 (batting), 41 home runs, and 123 RBIs were neither equaled nor surpassed by anyone. He was named to four American League All-Star teams during that span.

Of course, Belle being Belle, there were some speed bumps along the way. In the strike-shortened 1994 season (teams refused to take the field for any of the scheduled August 12 contests and forced the cancellation of the rest of the season and the World Series) he had one of his bats confiscated by the umpiring crew during a July 15 Central Division showdown with the Chicago White Sox. Chicago manager Gene Lamont, acting on a tip, asked the umpires to check the bat for cork. A bat filled with cork can be swung faster because the cork makes it lighter and gives the baseball lift.

Following league policy, the umpires locked the bat in the umpires' room. After the incident, Cleveland pitcher Jason Grimsley, knowing that corked bats were part of Belle's arsenal, snaked his way through the maze of ductwork and ceiling tiles in the bowels of Comiskey Park II. "My heart was going 1,000 miles an hour," Grimsley said. "And in (to) the umpire's dressing room I went. I just rolled the dice. A crap-shoot."[8]

Grimsley said he quickly dropped from the top of a refrigerator to a counter and down, and immediately spotted Belle's bat in an umpire's locker. He made the exchange, as imperfect as it was: According to other members of the Indians' organization, Grimsley had to switch Belle's bat with one belonging to Paul Sorrento because every one of Belle's bats was corked.[9] As often was the endgame with Belle, he was suspended for seven games (reduced from 10).

During the strike-delayed 1995 campaign, Belle became the only major leaguer to sock 50 home runs and 50 (52) doubles in the same season, which was all of 144 games (Belle played in 143 games that year). He tied Babe Ruth's 1927 record for home runs in September with 17.[10] Like Ruth, Belle was the best player on the best team in baseball.

Despite his offensive fireworks, Belle placed second in the 1995 American League Most Valuable Player race, behind the inferior stat line of Boston first baseman Mo Vaughn. "Actually I'm surprised I got as many votes as I did," said Belle, who received 11 first-place votes to Vaughn's 12. "I'm kind of upset that they give baseball writers all this power when other media people who were former ballplayers should be involved in the voting, too. Maybe it should be 50-50 with those guys and the writers. Or maybe not let the baseball writers vote at all."[11]

The Indians ended a 41-year World Series drought when they faced the Atlanta Braves and their future Hall of Fame-loaded starting rotation of Tom Glavine, John Smoltz, and Greg Maddux. Though the Braves won in six games, Belle made headlines, although not necessarily for his offensive prowess. (Though he hit just .235, Belle had two home runs, four RBIs, four runs scored, and seven walks for an eye-popping 1.047 OPS).

During batting practice before Game Three, which for Belle was akin to a church service, he became annoyed at the number of media members in the Indians dugout. According to NBC reporter Hannah Storm, "Initially, he screamed at all the media to get out of the dugout in language that was horrible. Two or three men left. They were frightened. I was the only one who stayed, because I was waiting to do an interview with Kenny Lofton. When I stayed, he directed his tirade at me."[12]

Major League Baseball was slow to react. While it could not have approved of Belle's actions, the strong arm of the players union lurked in the background. For his part, Belle felt he should be neither fined nor suspended. "If that's what (Bud Selig) wants to do, I'll just tell him that's bull (bleep) if I have to be suspended for trying to get back some (batting) space that he as commissioner should have given us in the first place."[13]

Belle's logic was not shared by Selig. He ruled on February 29, 1996, that the outfielder had a choice: a $10,000 fine or a 10-day suspension. Belle reluctantly chose the former punishment.

Belle's agent, Arn Tellem, not surprisingly agreed with his client. "The fine is without any precedent and is totally unjustified," he said. "But we had no choice but to accept the fine given that (Selig) had no remedy to go before someone neutral to hear this matter. It would be like Marcia Clark deciding the fate of O.J. Simpson."[14]

Belle's 1995 was not over until Halloween Night, when he jumped into his truck to chase down kids from his neighborhood who had egged his house.[15] He was convicted of reckless operation of a motor vehicle and fined $1,000 for that bit of horseplay.[16]

During his 1996 free-agent walk year with the Indians, Belle continued to get the job done on the field. His 148 RBIs led the league. He clubbed 48 home runs while batting .311. Belle received his fourth straight Silver Slugger Award, finished third in the MVP voting, and won a five-year, $55 million contract with the Chicago White Sox. Just like the Babe, Belle was now baseball's highest-paid player.

For Belle, the move to a division rival represented a new beginning after 10 years and a lot of uneasiness with the same organization. His unhappiness over the Indians' 1995-1996 offseason moves was still evident one year later. "After we went to the

World Series (in '95), I told them: 'Please keep this team together. We'll win the World Series a few times, but only if it's kept together.' All they needed to do was re-sign Paul Sorrento and Kenny Hill and our offseason moves would've been over. We would've been set. We would've brought the same team back and I'm telling you we would've won more games, gone back to the Series and won it. When you go to a World Series, you can't tinker with the chemistry of a team because you fight so hard to get that kind of chemistry."[17]

At least one of Belle's ex-teammates begged to differ. "I got tired of answering questions about him," said shortstop Omar Vizquel during 1997 spring training. "He was in his own little world. He's a great player, but he didn't contribute to team chemistry. And team chemistry is important."[18]

Indians manager Mike Hargrove said, "Some of the things surrounding Albert were not good, but you take the good with the bad."[19]

The 1997 Indians did not win as many games as Belle's last Tribe team had, but still captured the AL Central by six games over his new squad. After taking care of the Yankees and Orioles in the playoffs, the Clevelanders advanced to their second World Series in three years, dropping Game Seven and the Series to the Florida Marlins.

Belle had his first of two productive seasons with Chicago. In 1997 he recorded his sixth consecutive season of hitting at least 30 home runs (30) and driving in at least 100 runs (with 116). The year after, he increased that streak to seven years with 49 homers and a career-high 152 RBIs. In two years, the White Sox slugger compiled a .301 batting average. At age 31, he was among the game's elite, and raised his salary ante to get paid like it.

Belle's original contract with the White Sox called for him to remain among baseball's top three paid players. The White Sox refused to negotiate, giving Belle and his agent a narrow window to shop his services. They found a willing suitor in the Baltimore Orioles, who showered Belle with a five-year, $65 million contract.[20]

As he had done with the White Sox, Belle played nice with the media at the start of his Orioles career, granting interviews, attending Baltimore's Fan Fest during the 1999 winter, and signing autographs during spring training. But a slow start at the plate (a .200 batting average with one RBI) led him to announce on March 14, 1999, that "I'm done with you guys." And just like that, three months of good will went right down the clubhouse drain.

He played two years in Baltimore before an arthritic right hip condition forced him to retire on March 11, 2001. He was productive up until the end, averaging 30 home runs and 110 RBIs per Oriole season.[21]

Belle considered RBIs the most important offensive statistic in the game: "Hitting for a high average is nice. So is hitting a ton of home runs. But driving in a run a game is awesome."[22]

It's too bad he did not think of media relations as highly. When his name first appeared on the Hall of Fame ballot in 2006, he received a minuscule 7.7 percent of the vote. Translated: 520 ballots were cast and Belle was recognized on just 40 of them. His second – and final – year on the ballot came in 2007 when he collected just 3.5 percent of the vote. Needing 5 percent to remain on the ballot, Belle was off his ticket to Cooperstown for good.[23]

Belle's career average 162-game season compares favorably with those of others already in the Hall, including Willie Stargell, Hack Wilson, Harmon Killebrew, Tony Perez, and Jim Rice. So why was he bounced from the ballot after just two seasons?

"His numbers were good," Paul Hoynes of the *Cleveland Plain Dealer* said. "I thought if he played one or two more years at a high level, I'd have to vote for him. But he didn't. He was a bad guy. And what goes around comes around.

"It wasn't just us. He would sit there and dare people to talk to him. He would abuse the clubhouse guy, the PR guy, everybody."[24]

According to Teddy Greenstein of the *Chicago Tribune*, who covered Belle during the 1998 season, "He was even a menace to Sox employees. He once cursed out a broadcaster for having the gall to enter the trainer's room to get an aspirin. And he belittled hitting instructor Von Joshua by forbidding him from discussing his (Belle's) swing with reporters."[25]

Belle mellowed, but only after he was retired. He visited the Indians training camps in 2012 and 2015. The father of three girls, he lives with his family near Phoenix.

In 2016, Belle was elected to the Cleveland Indians Hall of Fame. Citing family commitments, he declined to attend the ceremony.

Belle never met a fastball he couldn't crush or a writer he wouldn't berate. He played by his own rules, answering to no one. Maybe that's why one of the best players in Cleveland Indians history is not remembered fondly, but "frown-ly."

NOTES

1 *Baltimore Sun*, June 10, 2001.
2 Ibid.
3 Ibid.
4 Jim Engster, "Albert Belle, man of mystery and mastery," *Tiger Rag Magazine*, February 9, 2015.
5 *New York Post*, October 2, 1991.
6 *New York Post*, September 25, 1993.
7 *Sports Illustrated*, June 24, 1991.
8 *New York Times*, April 11, 1999.
9 albertbelle.net/timeline.php.
10 *Sports Illustrated*, October 9, 1995.
11 *Lorain* [Ohio] *Morning Journal*, January 14, 1996.
12 *USA Today*, February 6, 1996.
13 *Lorain Morning Journal*, January 14, 1996.
14 *New York Times*, March 1, 1996.
15 *Lorain Morning Journal*, January 14, 1996.
16 albertbelle.net/timeline.php.
17 *Sport Magazine*, May 1997.
18 *The Plain Dealer* (Cleveland), March 9, 1997.
19 Ibid.
20 albertbelle.net/timeline.php
21 *Sport Magazine*, May 1997.
22 Ibid.
23 Ibid.
24 *Boston Globe*, January 16, 2006.
25 Ibid.

BUD BLACK

BY NICK WADDELL

Bud Black spent 15 years as a major-league pitcher and followed that up with a long career as a manager. In 2018 he was in his 11th year as a big-league skipper.

Harry "Bud" Ralston Black was born on June 30, 1957, in San Mateo, California. He graduated from Mark Morris High School in Longview, Washington. His father, Harry Sr., was a center for the Los Angeles Monarchs of the Pacific Coast Hockey League (1945-48) and led the team in scoring in 1946.

Black pitched for Lower Columbia College (Washington) in 1976 and 1977. He was drafted twice in 1977, when the major leagues conducted two drafts a year. First, he was drafted in January by the San Francisco Giants in the third round. Then, in the June draft, the New York Mets selected him in the second round. Black declined to sign each time, deciding instead to attend San Diego State University from 1978-1979, majoring in finance. Black led the Aztecs in innings pitched and strikeouts in 1978 and 1979. Seattle drafted the left-hander in the 17th round in 1979 and Black signed with the Mariners.

Black spent the rest of 1979 in Class A, making 19 appearances with San Jose (California League) and Bellingham (Northwest League). He returned to San Jose in 1980, appearing mostly out of the bullpen. His 5-3 record and 3.45 ERA earned him a promotion to Double A to start 1981. His 2-6 record with Lynn (Eastern League) did not tell the entire story. Black led the team with a 3.74 strikeout-to-walk ratio and was third on the team in strikeouts despite making only 11 starts. He made four appearances for Triple-A Spokane before getting a September call-up with the Mariners for two games. He made his major-league debut on September 5, 1981, coming out of the bullpen against the Boston Red Sox. In the bottom of the fifth, in the midst of a six-run Red Sox rally, manager Rene Lachemann used him as a situational lefty to face one batter, Rick Miller. Black threw a wild pitch, then surrendered a single, and was replaced. He appeared in just one other game, the next day. He came on with two outs in the bottom of the sixth, and walked the batter he faced, but then picked him off first. He worked the seventh, giving up a leadoff double and walking two while getting two outs and then handing the ball over to Shane Rawley, who closed out the inning.

Seattle traded the young left-hander to Kansas City in March 1982 to complete an October 1981 deal that sent infielder Manny Castillo to the Mariners.

Black made the Royals to start 1982. Over the first month and a half, he pitched in six games, going 0-1 with a 7.98 ERA. Opponents batted .339 against him. He was sent down to Omaha, where he excelled, going 3-1 with a 2.48 ERA in four starts. Black was recalled in June 12 when David Frost was placed on the disabled list.[1] He pitched in 16 games, making 13 starts, for the rest of the season. Black finished the season 4-6 with a 4.58 ERA.

Black started 1983 with Triple-A Omaha but was recalled in May to assume a spot in the starting rotation, taking over for Vida Blue, who was sent to the pen.[2] He pitched his first career complete game as a Royal after 27 starts. The game was a 6-2 win over the Milwaukee Brewers on August 4, 1983. Black posted a solid 10-7 season for the second-place Royals. Perhaps the most memorable game of the season for Black was the "pine tar" game on July 24. George Brett hit a two-run home run in the top of the ninth to give the Royals a one-run lead. Yankees manager Billy Martin claimed that the pine tar on Brett's bat was more than the league-allowed 18 inches. The umpires agreed, calling Brett out and giving the Yankees the victory. The Royals protested the call. American League President Lee MacPhail reversed the decision of the umpires, and the game was resumed on August 18. Both the Royals and Black benefited from this reversal. Had the called stood, Black would have been the losing pitcher. Instead, Black had a no-decision.[3]

The 1984 season was Black's best as a major leaguer. He led the Royals in wins (17), starts (35), complete games (8), strikeouts (140), and ERA as a starter (3.12). He also had the distinction of giving up Reggie Jackson's 500th career home run on September 17. Black and the Royals won that game 10-1 over the California Angels.

Black made his postseason debut on October 2 in the American League Championship Series against the favored Detroit Tigers. Black had made three starts against the Tigers during the regular season, suffering one loss and two no-decisions. His ERA approached 6.00 and the Tigers hit .319 against him. This scene repeated in Game One of the ALCS. Black lasted only five innings, giving up four earned runs, as the Tigers beat the Royals 8-1.

The 1985 season was a different story. Black had a season almost statistically opposite from 1984. He led the team in losses (15), starter ERA (4.33), runs allowed (111), and earned runs (99). The Royals made the ALCS again, this time against the Toronto Blue Jays. Black started Game Two and pitched seven strong innings. Usually reliable closer Dan Quisenberry could not hold onto the lead, and the Royals fell behind in the series two games to none. Black made two more appearances in the ALCS, both relief appearances. His 3⅓-inning relief appearance in Game Six helped the Royals force a Game Seven, and they won the American League pennant. Black made two appearances in the World Series against the St. Louis Cardinals, including a five-inning loss in Game Four. The Royals won the Series in seven games, giving Black his only World Series ring. Black did not make the postseason again in his career.

The 1986 season marked a transition to the bullpen for Black. He made four starts at the beginning of the season but was moved to the bullpen in early May. Black seemed to thrive in his role. Opponents hit .198, while he carried a 2.34 ERA. The Royals finished second though, preventing a potential repeat in the postseason.

The 1987 season was the opposite of 1986; Black started in the bullpen but returned to the starting rotation in early May. His stats as a reliever again were solid (1.90 ERA, .198 batting average against) His stats as a starter were good for a back-of-the-rotation pitcher (4.01 ERA, .279 batting average against).

Black bounced back to the bullpen to start 1988 but was traded to Cleveland in early June for infielder Pat Tabler. He pitched mainly out of the bullpen for the Indians to start, but did transition back into the starting rotation late in the season.

Black was solid in the 1989 and 1990 seasons with a bottom-dwelling Indians team. He was 23-21 over that time with a 3.44 ERA. The Toronto Blue Jays needed some pitching to help them get into the playoffs, and made a mid-September trade for Black. He appeared in three games, including two starts. His last outing was one of his best for the season, eight innings of three-hit ball against Baltimore. Ultimately, though, the Blue Jays finished in second behind the Boston Red Sox.

After the 1990 season, Black signed a four-year, $10 million contract with the San Francisco Giants. Up to that point, Black was 85-83 over nine seasons, and had won only 42 games the previous five seasons combined. An anonymous National League general manager panned the signing, saying, "Maybe Bud Black will win some games for the Giants, but it looks like one of the worst signings ever."[4]

Black's first two seasons with San Francisco were mediocre. He went 22-28 but pitched almost 400 innings. The 1993 season started well, but he could not shake the injury bug. Black went on the disabled list three times during the season for elbow trouble and he did not pitch after August 3. In late September he underwent surgery to repair a tendon in his left elbow.[5] Then before the 1994 season, he had arthroscopic knee surgery.[6]

Black did not pitch until June 1994 and made 10 appearances before the season was cut short by the players strike. During the offseason, he signed a minor-league contract to go back to the Indians in 1995 but made only 11 appearances with the Indians before being released on July 14.

The Indians named Black a special assistant for baseball operations to general manager John Hart for the 1996 and 1997 seasons, before naming him the pitching coach at Triple-A Buffalo for the 1998 season. Black returned to his special assistant role for the 1999 season.

The Los Angeles Angels named Black their pitching coach in 2000, and he helmed the mound staff that helped lead the Angels to the 2002 World Series championship. His teams finished in the top five in ERA five of his seasons. He coached Bartolo Colon during Colon's 2005 Cy Young season. This success led to Black's being considered for many managerial openings. In 2002 he was a candidate for the Cleveland Indians managerial position, but later declined to continue further with the process.[7] In 2005 he declined to be interviewed for the Los Angeles Dodgers' managerial position, citing family reasons.[8] In 2006 Black was a candidate for the San Francisco Giants opening, as was then-Padres manager Bruce Bochy.[9] When the Giants signed Bochy, the Padres turned to Black. Black was named manager of the Padres on November 6, 2006.

The 2007 season was an odd one for the rookie manager. On September 23 he had a role in one of the stranger incidents in baseball. Outfielder Milton Bradley was involved in an altercation with first-base umpire Mike Winters, accusing Winters of saying that Bradley threw his bat at an umpire.[10] In an attempt to subdue Bradley, Black pulled him away. Bradley's knee buckled. That knee ultimately cost Bradley the rest of the 2007 season and may have cost the Padres a shot at the playoffs. They were 2½ games behind the first-place Arizona Diamondbacks, and had a half-game lead over the Philadelphia Phillies. The Padres and Rockies played in game 163 to decide which would be the wild-card team. The Rockies came into the game having gone 13-1 in their last 14 games. The Padres took the lead in the top of the 13th on a two-run home run by Scott Hairston, but usually steady closer Trevor Hoffman gave up three runs in the bottom half of the inning, sending the Rockies into the playoffs (and eventually the World Series). Matt Holliday scored the winning run on a sacrifice fly by Jamey Carroll, sliding head-first into home. Replays were inconclusive as to whether Holliday had actually touched home or not.

Black narrowly missed taking the Padres to the playoffs in 2010. Going into the final weekend, the Padres were three games behind the Giants for the NL West title. The Padres won the first two, but dropped the last game, giving the Giants the division. Despite not making the playoffs, Black was named 2010 National League Manager of the Year, going 90-72. This was Black's last winning season as a manager. His 2011 Padres team went 71-91, while his 2012 and 2013 teams went 76-86, and the 2014 team was 77-85. During the offseason before the 2015 season, the Padres made bold moves, including acquiring closer Craig Kimbrel, outfielders Matt Kemp and Wil Myers, and catcher Derek Norris. The Padres were 32-33 to start the season before Black was fired.

Black was not out of work for long. He was a candidate for the Washington Nationals' open managerial position and was the leading choice by all accounts.[11] Black had accepted the position, but contract negotiations broke down.[12] The Nationals eventually hired Dusty Baker, while Black returned to the Angels as a special assistant to the general manager.

Black became a leading candidate for the Colorado Rockies managerial job when Walt Weiss stepped away after the 2016 season. On November 7, 2016, the Rockies made the hiring of Black official.[13]

The Rockies got off to a hot start and were leading the West at the end of April. The Rockies, Diamondbacks, and Dodgers fought for first throughout the first half of the season, until the Dodgers pulled away from the rest of the division en route to an eventual National League pennant. Black did lead the team to an 87-75 record, and a berth in the wild-card round against the Diamondbacks. The Rockies fell behind 6-0 in that game but fought back. "Right away, all hell broke loose and from there on it was a heavyweight fight," Black said after the game. "We got close a couple times, they stretched the lead, we came back. It was a crazy game."[14] Their efforts fell short, as they lost 11-8.

In 1992, Black was inducted into San Diego State Athletics Hall of Fame.[15] He and his wife, Nanette, donated money to fund an alumni room at San Diego State's Tony Gwynn Stadium.[16]

NOTES

1. "Royals' Frost on Disabled List," *Los Angeles Times*, June 13, 1982: 3-5
2. "Royals' Blue Sent to Bullpen," *Atlanta Constitution*, May 24, 1983: 5-D
3. "Brett Not Only One Affected," *Los Angeles Times*, July 30, 1983: 3-2
4. Jerome Holtzman, "Black Deal Throws Free-Agent Curve," *Chicago Tribune*, November 15, 1990: 4-13
5. "Around the Majors," *New York Times*, September 26, 1993: 56
6. "Spring Training," *Washington Post*, February 20, 1994.
7. "Plus: Baseball," *New York Times*, October 17, 2002: D7
8. "Roundup," *New York Times*, November 24, 2005: D2
9. "Baseball," *New York Times*, October 24, 2006: D6
10. Michael S. Schmidt, "Baseball Suspends Umpire in Dispute," *New York Times*, September 27, 2007: D2
11. Chelsea Janes, "Bud Black, Washington Nationals' Choice to Be Manager, Known for his Communication," *Washington Post*, October 29, 2015.
12. James Wagner, "In End, Washington Nationals' Bet on Bud Black Goes Bust and They Land Instead on Dusty Baker," *Washington Post*, November 3, 2015.
13. Nick Kosmider, "Bud Black Reaches Agreement With Colorado Rockies to Become New Manager," *Denver Post*, November 7, 2016
14. Associated Press, "Rockies Fall Short in Wild-Card Loss to Diamondbacks," October 5, 2017.
15. Scott Miller, "Bud Black Among Inductees Into Athletics Hall of Fame," *Los Angeles Times*, November 12, 1992: C7
16. San Diego State University Baseball Media Guide, 2016.

SOURCES

In addition to the sources cited in the Notes, the author also used the following:

Baseball Reference (baseball-reference.com),

2016 Los Angeles Angels Media Guide.

JEROMY BURNITZ

BY ANNA POHLOD AND KELLY BOYER SAGERT

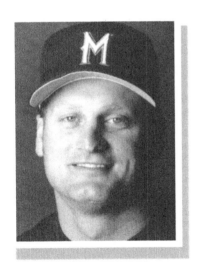

Jeromy Neal Burnitz, who was with the Indians during 1995 and most of 1996, was known for his enthusiasm (which on occasion crossed into temper), dogged persistence, and a true love for the game. During his 14-year major-league career, he also played for the New York Mets, Milwaukee Brewers, Los Angeles Dodgers, Colorado Rockies, Chicago Cubs, and Pittsburgh Pirates. He hit 315 home runs and had 981 RBIs.[1]

Burnitz was born in Westminster, California, on April 15, 1969, but spent most of his early years just outside Houston in Conroe, Texas, with his parents and three brothers.[2] After graduating from Conroe High School, he was selected by the Brewers in the 24th round of the 1987 amateur draft.[3] However, Burnitz chose to attend Oklahoma State University to raise his draft stock.

In 1990 the New York Mets made Burnitz their 17th pick in the first round. With Pittsfield of the New York-Pennsylvania League, he batted .301 in 51 games. But Burnitz truly made a name for himself in 1991 by stealing 31 bases and hitting 31 home runs for Double-A Williamsport. After one more minor-league season, with Triple-A Tidewater (International League), Burnitz was called up by the Mets.

Burnitz's power impressed the Mets, but general manager Joe McIlvaine said he was also impressed by Burnitz's psychological test, which "showed his mental toughness, desire. I believe in those things."[4] Manager Dallas Green called Burnitz "a 100 percent barrel-out guy," adding, "It's a freshness that you don't see in some guys we've been putting up with."[5]

Nevertheless, Burnitz began the 1993 season back in Triple A (Norfolk). Back with the Mets in June, he was more or less a regular. He set a Mets rookie record on August 5 with seven RBIs in a 13-inning game against the Montreal Expos. But Burnitz's freshness and enthusiasm also came with a hot temper that fueled an outburst against umpire Jim Quick during a game against the San Diego Padres. Burnitz told the *New York Times*, "If I don't do good, it ticks me off. This is it, man. This is what I do. It ticks me off when I don't do well. I'd like to play this game awhile."[6] He ended the season with 13 home runs and 38 RBIs in 86 games.

Burnitz spent much of 1994 with Norfolk, and played in only 45 games with the Mets. He encountered intense disagreement with manager Dallas Green over his refusal to play winter ball.[7] After the season, he was traded to the Indians for Paul Byrd, Jerry DiPoto, and Dave Mlicki. The Indians sent Burnitz to Triple-A Buffalo, and his only time with the Indians in 1995 was as a late-season call-up. Buffalo and the Indians both had excellent seasons, the Bisons finishing second in the American Association while the Indians won 100 games and went to the World Series. Burnitz later recalled 1995 as his favorite time in baseball.[8]

Burnitz stuck with the Indians in 1996 as a backup outfielder and pinch-hitter, but on August 31 was traded to the Milwaukee Brewers for Kevin Seitzer. For the Indians he had batted .281 with 7 home runs and 26 RBIs in 71 games. He hit two more homers for the Brewers.

While he got little time in the spotlight with the Indians, Burnitz found a home in Milwaukee.

In August 1997 he became the first Brewer to hit a home run in five consecutive games.[9] He finished the season with 27 home runs and 85 RBIs. He did even better in 1998, with 38 home runs and 125 RBIs.

The 1999 season was another big year for Burnitz with several ups and downs. Early in the year, he and his wife, Krissy, had their first child, Chloe. On July 9, he hit an estimated 500-foot, two-run home run out of Tiger Stadium.[10] Burnitz was chosen to participate in his first All-Star Game in 1999 at Fenway Park. The previous day, he finished second in the Home Run Derby. Burnitz ended the season as the Brewers' MVP. For the season he had 33 home runs, 103 RBIs, and a .270 batting average.

Burnitz, or "Burnie" to his teammates, became one of the Brewers' best players during his five-year stretch, giving the team a sorely needed strong offense. Brewers manager Phil Garner said, "Jeromy's been our offensive thrust. When he's swinging the bat and hitting home runs, we do well."[11] And while he was famous for his powerful home runs, Burnitz's performance as a runner and outfielder was also crucial to the Brewers during their late-'90s slump. At his best, he had 11 more runs than the average for right fielders in 1998, using the TotalZone scoring system.[12]

Burnitz's time with the Brewers was arguably the best period of his career. From 1997 to 2001, he never played less than 130 games per season, and he averaged 32 home runs, 103 RBIs, and a .262 batting average. Part of Burnitz's success came from learning to control his temper and being easier on himself. "I think I came to grips with the fact that I might not ever be what I thought I should be. It's tough being mad at yourself 24 hours a day. It's too hard, and with no benefit," he later said of his change in attitude.[13] In 2001 Burnitz hit 34 home runs, including three homers in a game against the Chicago Cubs.[14]

Despite early talks with the Brewers for a two-year contract, Burnitz was sent in 2002 to the New York Mets in a trade involving 11 players from the Mets, Brewers, and Rockies.[15] The Mets needed Burnitz to revamp their struggling offense: They finished the 2001 season next to last in batting average and home runs. Meanwhile, Burnitz smashed 34 home runs in 2001, approaching the 40 homers the Mets got out of all their 2001 outfielders.

The trade was a surprise to many fans, considering Burnitz's previous experience with the Mets. He told the *New York Times* that, in the mid- to late 1990s, he would never have considered playing for the Mets again.[16] His early years with the team were not his best, and his personality clash with Dallas Green still colored his opinion of the Mets organization.

But by 2002, Burnitz saw his trade back to his original team as a second chance and an opportunity to work with exceptional players like Mike Piazza and Edgardo Alfonzo. He told the *New York Times*, "If a manager hates me ever again, I don't care. I'm going to do my job the best way I can. I'm never going to have any problem with any manager ever again."[17]

However, a different scandal faced the baseball world in 2002. Fans saw a much darker side of the game after Jose Canseco and Ken Caminiti opened up about the rampant steroid use among baseball players.[18] But while Canseco estimated that around 85 percent of major-league players used steroids, Burnitz said he felt no temptation to use performance-enhancing drugs. Perhaps thinking of his younger daughter, Grace, who was born in 2002, he told the New York Daily News, "If somebody wants to do it, that's their decision. Whatever you think is fine. But when I'm 50 and I'm running around with my kids in the backyard, and you're dead, that's your deal."[19]

Baseball was not kind to Burnitz in 2002. Apart from a two-run, walk-off home run against the Cubs late in the season, it ended up being one of his worst seasons.[20] He finished with only 19 home runs, 54 RBIs, and a .215 batting average.

Though it was difficult for Burnitz to stomach, his weak season turned out to be an asset to his career. Enduring a miserable season back with his original team forced Burnitz to re-evaluate his entire approach to hitting. His new tactic was one of simplification: He eliminated all distractions and focused on identifying good pitches.

Burnitz's new attitude toward the game improved his performance dramatically. He kicked off the 2003 season with a .279 average, three home runs, seven doubles, and seven RBIs in the first three weeks.[21] Not only did his new approach improve his play, it also altered his whole attitude about the game. He told the New York Post, "I've never really liked playing too much. It's always just been work and a grind for me. Now, I like the game a lot more, and not just because I'm doing well. It's from finding an approach I'm happy with. Last year made me understand how hard it was, the game itself, and it made me appreciate what I had accomplished."[22]

Burnitz's upswing was interrupted when he broke his left hand on April 22 in a game against the Houston Astros. He returned to play on May 23 and jumped right back into his offensive stride, hitting four home runs and driving in 13 runs in his first 10 days back.[23] When Burnitz left the Mets in July, he had 18 home runs and 45 RBIs.

Despite his improved performance and attitude, the Mets traded Burnitz to the Dodgers in July 2003.[24] Though Burnitz could have blocked the trade, he was excited to play with the Dodgers as a center fielder and for the chance to play in the postseason.[25] "I played for the Brew Crew [Brewers] and the Mets when we were struggling, so to have an opportunity to go to a club that has a shot at the playoffs, it's hard for me to explain what it means," he said of the trade. More importantly, the trade brought him just two hours away from his wife and two daughters who lived in Poway, a suburb of San Diego.[26]

After injuring his hand early in the season, Burnitz tried a new approach to hitting, but his batting average fell to .239; he did, however, hit 31 home runs and finished with 77 RBIs. When he was traded, Burnitz said of the Dodgers that "the ultimate goal is for me to show up, just go crazy, hope it rubs off on everyone, and the team goes to the World Series. That's obviously what everyone wants to happen, but I'll only evaluate myself on the execution of my plan [at the plate] each day."[27] It was an appropriate decision, as even Burnitz's capable efforts that season could not push the Dodgers to the playoffs.

After the season Burnitz became a free agent and he Burnitz signed with the Colorado Rockies.[28] He started the season on a high note: His son Jake was born on March 18. Less than a month later, on April 27, he and his teammates Matt Holliday and Charles Johnson belted three home runs in a row in a game against the Miami Marlins.[29]

The 2004 season turned out to be one of Burnitz's strongest. In 150 games, he hit 37 home runs, drove in 110 runs, and batted .283. Burnitz was later chosen by the Rox Pile blog as one of the best outfielders in the Rockies' history.[30]

Burnitz declined a $3 million mutual option to stay with the Rockies after the 2004 season, instead signing a one-year deal with the Cubs.[31] He replaced star outfielder Sammy Sosa, but knew that he could not completely fill Sosa's role on the team. "All that matters is how the team does, and I'm going to go all-out with a team attitude," he said after signing. "It will all revolve around how we do as a team. I can strike out, and if we're winning, people will love me and everyone else on the squad."[32]

The 2005 season was disappointing for the Cubs, with a 79-83 record. Though the season was not a knock-out for Burnitz, either, he was one of a few consistent players who helped to keep the team afloat during the weak season. He batted .258, with 24 home runs and 87 RBIs.

After a year of active pursuit from the Pirates, Burnitz signed a one-year contract for $6.7 million. The Pirates also signed Sean Casey and Joe Randa, building a core of veteran players to add some consistency to their overwhelmingly young team.[33]

The 2006 season turned out to be disappointing for Burnitz and the Pirates alike. Burnitz batted only .230 and hit only 16 home runs with 49 RBIs. The rest of the team did not fare much better. "This is the first team I've been on in a couple years where I'm Joe High-Paid Free Agent. That, in and of itself, should tell you the big picture that the team's in. If I'm just another guy on one of those big-market, big-paying teams ... that's not the way it is here, and I understand that. I'm cool with it," Burnitz told the *Pittsburgh Post-Gazette*.[34] April 4 provided one highlight to a disappointing year. In a game against the Brewers, he hit the 300th home run of his career.

After playing major-league baseball for 14 years with seven teams, Burnitz decided to retire after the season with the Pirates. He finished with 315 home runs and 981 RBIs, and a slugging percentage of .481. After retiring from baseball and life in the public eye, he and his family settled in Agoura Hills, California.

NOTES

1. "Jeromy Burnitz Stats," ESPN. Accessed January 1, 2017. espn.com/mlb/player/stats/_/id/2903/jeromy-burnitz.
2. Tom Friend, "Steam Heat in July: It's Burnitz, Bubbling," *New York Times*, July 23, 1993.
3. "MMN Prospect Time Machine: Jeromy Burnitz." *MetsMinors.net*, September 13, 2013. metsminors.net/mmn-prospect-time-machine-jeromy-burnitz/.
4. Friend.
5. Ibid.
6. Ibid.
7. Paul Hoynes, "Looking for Opportunities: Outfielder Jeromy Burnitz Tries to Prove His Mettle to Snag Open Utility Position," *Cleveland Plain Dealer*, March 4, 1996.
8. Michael Morrissey, "Jeromy Enjoys the View," *New York Post*, August 23, 2003. nypost.com/2003/08/23/jeromy-enjoys-the-view/.
9. Paul Ladewski, "Milwaukee Brewers Defeat Struggling Chicago Cubs," *Northwest Herald* (Crystal Lake, Illinois), April 17, 2017. nwherald.com/2017/04/18/milwaukee-brewers-defeat-struggling-chicago-cubs/as4lxnb/.
10. "Burnitz, Woodard Propel Brewers Past Tigers," *Chippewa Herald* (Chippewa Falls, Wisconsin), July 10, 1999. chippewa.com/burnitz-woodard-propel-brewers-past-tigers/article_911c0c7f-7dd4-51c9-97f3-ba3229478323.html
11. ESPN, April 22, 2003.
12. Jim Breen, "Remembering Jeromy Burnitz," *Milwaukee-Wisconsin Journal Sentinel Sports Fan Blogs* (blog), December 1, 2011. jsonline.com/blogs/sports/fanblogs/134828498.html.
13. H.A. Dorfman and Karl Kuehl, *The Mental Game Of Baseball: A Guide to Peak Performance* 3rd ed. (Boulder, Colorado: Taylor Trade Publications, 2002).
14. "Burnitz's 3 HRs Lift Brewers 11-1," *USA Today*, May 11, 2001.
15. "Mets Re-Acquire OF Burnitz in Three-Team Deal," *The Daily Star*, January 22, 2002.
16. Jack Curry, "Mets' Burnitz Finds He Can Go Home Again," *New York Times*, February 22, 2002. nytimes.com/2002/02/22/sports/baseball-mets-burnitz-finds-he-can-go-home-again.html.
17. H.A. Dorfman and Karl Kuehl
18. Jason Reid, "Caminiti Admits Using Steroids," *Los Angeles Times*, May 29, 2002. articles.latimes.com/2002/may/29/sports/sp-steroids29.
19. John Harper, "No Denying Steroid Usage: Burnitz Has No Interest," *New York Daily News*, May 30, 2002.
20. Brian Lewis, "Jeromy Jolt Sends Fans Home Happy," *New York Post*, September 18, 2002. nypost.com/2002/09/18/jeromy-jolt-sends-fans-home-happy/.
21. "ESPN.Com: MLB – Burnitz out Four-to-Six Weeks with Broken Hand." Accessed January 18, 2018. a.espncdn.com/mlb/news/2003/0422/1543035.html.
22. Mark Cannizzaro, "Burnitz Made Most of Worst," *New York Post*, June 2, 2003. nypost.com/2003/06/02/burnitz-made-most-of-worst/.
23. Christian Red, "Hits Keep on Coming for Burnitz," *New York Daily News*, Accessed January 2, 2018. nydailynews.com/archives/sports/hits-coming-burnitz-article-1.658889.
24. Jason Reid, "Dodgers Add Some Offense: L.A. Acquires Burnitz from Mets, Then Signs Future Hall of Famer Henderson to Help Provide Spark to an Anemic Lineup," *Los Angeles Times*, July 15, 2003.
25. Dave Caldwell, "Rebuilding Mets Ship Burnitz to Dodgers for Prospects," *New York Times*, July 15, 2003.
26. Michael Morrissey, "The Happy Hacker: Burnitz Having Fun with New Approach," *New York Post*, May 29, 2003.
27. "Dodgers Add Some Offense."
28. Tracy Ringolsby, "Rockies Sign Burnitz, Won't Retain Payton." *Rocky Mountain News* (Denver), December 20, 2003.
29. Ben Macaluso,"The The 100 Greatest Colorado Rockies: 89 Charles Johnson." *Rox Pile* (blog), January 18, 2017. roxpile.com/2017/01/18/the-the-100-greatest-colorado-rockies-89-charles-johnson/.
30. Ibid.

31 Ken Rosenthal, "Inside Dish," *The Sporting News*, February 11, 2005.

32 Toni Ginnetti, "All Burnitz Worried About Is Helping Cubs Win," *Chicago Sun-Times*, February 3, 2005.

33 Daniel G. Habib, "Pittsburgh Pirates," *Sports Illustrated*, April 3, 2006.

34 Dejan Kovacevic, "Pirates Notebook: Burnitz Apologizes for Failing to Run Out Grounder," *Pittsburgh Post-Gazette*, May 13, 2006. post-gazette.com/sports/pirates/2006/05/13/Pirates-Notebook-Burnitz-apologizes-for-failing-to-run-out-grounder/stories/200605130175.

MARK CLARK

BY BOB LEMOINE

When Elvis Presley died, Mark Clark didn't cry. He cried when Bake McBride was traded. "Can you believe that? Elvis meant absolutely nothing to Mark?" his mother, Marjorie Clark, said. "He didn't cry for Elvis, but he cried for Bake."[1] When the king of rock 'n' roll died in August of 1977, the 9-year-old Clark exhibited no sign of distress. But earlier that summer the Clark family made one of their two-hour drives to St. Louis's Busch Stadium. Young Clark's enthusiasm for seeing the Cardinals turned to despair when he realized McBride, a Cardinals outfielder and his hero, had been traded to Philadelphia. "I cried the whole way home," Clark recalled.[2] This must truly be the only time in history Elvis and Bake McBride were ever mentioned together. But in Mark Clark's mind, McBride was king, and the Cardinals were his team. And Bake McBride had left the building.

The sobbing boy recovered, however, and one day came to wear the Cardinals uniform of his boyhood heroes. Mark Clark came from a small, cramped home with a wood stove in rural Illinois, where he loved to hunt and fish. He became a 6-foot-5, 225-pound man who pitched in big games before big crowds over a 10-year major-league career. When his career was over, he had made a lot of money and memories, and then returned home to hunt, fish, and enjoy living in the country all over again.

Mark Willard Clark was born on May 12, 1968 in Bath, Illinois,[3] to Willard and Marjorie (Lindsay) Clark, who also had four older daughters. "I'm the puppy of the family," Mark said.[4] Bath is a village in west central Illinois located between Peoria and Springfield, where baseball loyalties are split between the Cardinals and Cubs. Willard Clark, whose belly earned him the nickname "Pot," worked for the Illinois Department of Transportation, and was also a commercial fisherman. The family owned a fish market until the Illinois River became too polluted. Marjorie worked for the state Department of Public Health.[5]

Willard started teaching baseball to young Mark very early on. "He and I broke all the windows out in the back porch when he was 5 years old," Willard recalled.[6] When Marjorie and Willard watched Mark catch and pitch in Little League, they were confident he would be a major leaguer someday. "Unlike some of the other boys, his little mind was in the game, and he just knew ahead of time what plays had to be made," she said.[7] They took Mark to several Cardinals games each year, where he collected batting-practice balls to use in sandlot games on a dusty field in Bath.

Clark attended Balyki High School in Bath, which had a student body of 125. He was a standout athlete in basketball (averaging 24.2 points per game in 1985),[8] golf (he had a hole-in-one),[9] tennis,[10] and baseball. (Clark was on the all-county and all-conference baseball teams.[11]) He was dominant in baseball, but no scouts came around to see him pitch. During his high-school years Clark was a "pusher" during duck-hunting season, the "person who leads well-to-do hunters to their blinds by pushing a small boat through shallow waters with a long pole or oar." His father had done the same job for 40 years.[12]

After high school, Clark attended MacMurray College in Jacksonville, Illinois. He struggled academically, but caught the eye of his baseball coach, Randy Martz, who had pitched in 68 games in the majors with the Chicago Cubs and Chicago White Sox. Martz taught him the two-seam fastball and the pitch that would bring Clark his success, the forkball. He helped Clark through his freshman and sophomore years and saw his baseball potential. Martz encouraged Clark to transfer to Lincoln Land Community College in Springfield, Illinois, to receive more exposure. In the spring of 1988 Clark pitched 10 complete games for the Lincoln Land Loggers, winning nine, with 78 strikeouts in 82 innings pitched.[13] Scouts were now watching, and Clark was picked by the Cardinals in the ninth round of the 1988 amateur draft.

The Cardinals assigned Clark to the Hamilton (Ontario) Redbirds of the short-season New York-Pennsylvania League. On June 17 he pitched five innings of shutout ball for a win against the Saint Catherines Blue Jays, allowing three hits and one earned run,[14] then ended the season with a 6-7 record and a 3.05 earned-run average in 15 starts.

Clark spent the 1989 season with Savannah of the Class A South Atlantic League. He finished with 14 wins and a 2.44 ERA in 27 games started. On August 12 he shut out the Greensboro Hornets, 4-0, for his second straight shutout, with his forkball producing 15 groundouts. "I used the forkball for my strikeout pitch," Clark said. "By keeping the ball low, I let them make their own outs."[15] Clark flirted with a no-hitter in a seven-inning shutout against the Augusta Pirates on August 23.[16]

In 1990 Clark started 10 games and compiled a 3-2 record with a 3.05 ERA for St. Petersburg of the Class A Florida State League. Promoted in midseason to Double-A Arkansas (Texas League), Clark struggled with a 0-6 record and 5.57 ERA early on,[17] but came back to finish the season 5-11, 3.82.

Clark went to spring training with the Cardinals in 1991 but was hindered by a broken ankle suffered in an offseason automobile accident.[18] Beginning the season in Arkansas, he was 5-5 with a 4.00 ERA in 15 starts. In late July he was promoted to Triple-A Louisville (American Association), where he was 3-2 with a 2.98 ERA. On September 5 Clark was called up to the Cardinals. He entered his first major-league game on September 6 at San Diego, with the Cardinals trailing 5-0. He struck out Jim Vatcher, the first batter he faced, but gave up a solo home run to Thomas Howard.

On September 13, Clark made his first major-league start as an emergency replacement for Bryn Smith. He finished with a no-decision, giving up five hits and two earned runs in 6⅔ innings against the New York Mets. On September 30 Cardinals pitcher Jose DeLeon was hit with a line drive and had to leave the game in the first inning against the Expos. Clark provided emergency relief, pitched 5⅓ scoreless innings, and picked up his first major-league win. "It's a good feeling to get my first win, especially since we clinched second place with it," Clark said.[19]

Clark began the 1992 season back in Louisville. He lost his first four decisions, but after pitching coach Mark Riggins adjusted his leg kick, Clark threw three consecutive shutouts.[20] On June 1 he was recalled to St. Louis and remained with the club through the end of the season. He had some tough luck, starting 0-3, but "skunked" the Padres in San Diego on July 6 for his first win of the season. The game was delayed by four minutes as a skunk ran around the field. As players and umpires tried to shoo it away, it ran around the outfield and disappeared behind the wall in the Padres bullpen. "They said our bullpen stinks," San Diego reliever Larry Andersen remarked.[21]

Clark had a stretch of 17 scoreless innings in July but struggled in August and fell to 2-7 overall. He told *The Sporting News*, "Things aren't going my way right now. But they will. I'm not losing my confidence or anything. ... The record doesn't prove the way I've been pitching."[22] Clark went 0-3 in September with a 7.36 ERA and finished the season 3-10 with a 4.45 ERA. After the season he married high-school sweetheart Amy Beams, whom he had dated for nine years.[23]

Clark was considered a long shot to make the Cardinals staff in 1993.[24] Tragedy brought him new opportunity. A boating accident during spring training claimed the lives of Cleveland relief pitchers Steve Olin and Tim Crews and severely injured starting pitcher Bob Ojeda. Besides dealing with grief over the tragedy, the Indians faced a desperate need for pitching. They acquired Clark from St. Louis along with minor-league infielder Juan Andujar for outfielder Mark Whiten on March 31. "If not for the events of last week, we wouldn't have made the trade. ... But we're so thin (pitching-wise) that if we get a hang-nail we're in trouble," Cleveland general manager John Hart said.[25] "We knew we needed a starter and he's the kind of pitcher we wanted."[26]

"It's a shock," Clark said of the trade and the reality of leaving the team of his boyhood dreams. "But it benefits me. I'm going to go over there and get an opportunity to be in the big leagues."[27]

"The Indians yesterday traded a big outfielder who has trouble hitting the ball for a big pitcher who has trouble throwing the ball," wrote Paul Hoynes of the *Cleveland Plain Dealer*.[28] Clark won a shaky first start in Toronto on April 11, allowing five earned runs in six innings. "I cringed every time somebody hit a ball in the air," a bewildered Clark said.[29] After his first three starts, his ERA was 7.71, earning him a demotion to the bullpen. He struggled in relief as well, and by the end of May, his ERA was 6.42. On June 1 Clark was sent to Triple-A Charlotte (International League).

Clark pitched well in two starts in Charlotte and was recalled when the Indians released Mike Bielecki.[30] He pitched six shutout innings for a victory over Baltimore on June 19 and wore number 54 on the night the Indians wore their retro 1954 uniforms in a "turn back the clock game."[31] "When they sent me down, they told me I was going down to start. It was like a light went on. My confidence is a lot higher because I'm starting," Clark said.[32]

On July 16 Clark left the game against the Angels with a torn muscle in his right armpit and back that landed him on the disabled list for 53 days. While sidelined, Clark returned to the full hands-over-the-head delivery he had used earlier in his career until the Cardinals changed his mechanics. He returned on September 9 and looked like a brand-new pitcher. He pitched eight shutout innings in a win at Texas on September 14, took a no-hitter into the seventh inning in a win at Detroit on September 19, and pitched a complete-game victory against Milwaukee on September 25. He finished 3-0 with a 1.15 ERA in September. "Ever since I changed my windup, all my pitches seem easier to throw," Clark told *The Sporting News*.[33]

Clark signed a two-year contract with the Indians in March 1994. He won his first start, at Anaheim, and in May, he threw three complete-game victories, including a shutout over Detroit. Cleveland manager Mike Hargrove said of the sinkerball pitcher, "You can tell if he's pitching well by the number of groundballs he gets."[34] Clark's final three May starts produced 50 groundball outs to 26 fly-ball outs. He won three straight in June, and was 8-1 on June 13. Clark rose to 11-3, but his season came to a dismal end on July 20 when a line drive hit by Gary Redus of Texas broke his wrist. The players strike ended the season in August.

The historic 1995 season for the Indians was a disappointment for Clark as he never seemed to get on track. The lingering strike in early 1995 affected his rhythm and training. He gave up nine earned runs in 1⅓ innings in his first start, on April 28. In his last three starts in May, he gave up 14 earned runs in 12 innings, and was demoted to Triple-A Buffalo on the 28th. "The muscles in my hand and forearm may not be as strong as they were in the past," he said, "and that may be why my sinker is not as effective as it's been, but I can't use that as an excuse."[35]

Clark went 4-0 with a 3.57 ERA in five starts in Buffalo. When Orel Hershiser went on the disabled list, Clark was recalled on June 27.[36] He seemed rejuvenated, beating Kansas City with one earned run in eight innings. "It seemed the further I went into the game, I felt better and better," he said.[37] Clark went 3-1 with a 3.30 ERA in his first five starts after coming off the DL. Cleveland entered the playoffs for the first time since 1954, but Clark was left off the playoff roster.

After the season Clark signed a one-year contract for $900,000,[38] but on March 31, 1996, he was traded to the New York Mets for pitcher Reid Cornelius and outfielder Ryan Thompson. "There were times this spring that I felt the Indians didn't want me around," Clark complained. "Then there were times when I felt they did want me. But if they don't want me to pitch for them, I don't want to pitch for them. I'm glad I'm going someplace where I am wanted."[39]

The Mets were in desperate need of pitching, with injuries to three starting pitchers. "I'm happy about the deal," Clark said. "This is kind of a confidence builder. It's a good young team and I want to be a part of it."[40] Clark was a victim of poor run support early on but got his first Mets victory April 25 over St. Louis. "My confidence level went major high," he said after the game.[41] Clark went 4-1 with a 2.34 ERA during June and was becoming the Mets' most consistent pitcher. "I'm in a groove where I know when I throw a pitch, that it's going to go where I want it to go," Clark said.[42]

Meanwhile, Cleveland's pitching staff struggled, and Indians fans complained about the team giving up on Clark. "I'm loving it," Clark said unabashedly. "It makes me feel good. I eat it up. … The way they treated me in spring training, the way they shoved me around, I knew it was time to get out."[43] Clark won six games without a loss from June 8 to July 16. He finished the season 14-11 with a 3.43 ERA for a Mets team that finished 71-91.

Clark pitched well to start the 1997 season, and then threw back-to-back seven- and eight-inning shutout performances in May. In a June 14 win, Clark was a one-man show, holding the Red Sox hitless through seven innings and hitting a home run off knuckleballer Tim Wakefield. Clark had been hitless in 45 at-bats, which prompted his Mets teammates to place wagers on when he would finally get a hit.[44] But his ERA ballooned to 5.28 in five starts in July, and he was traded to the Chicago Cubs on August 8 with outfielder Lance Johnson and shortstop Manny Alexander for relievers Turk Wendell and Mel Rojas and outfielder Brian McRae.[45] Clark went from the Mets, a playoff contender, to the last-place Cubs. "It's nice to know that I've come to a team that wants me," he said,[46] but was snappish on another occasion, growling, "I didn't mind playing in New York, but living there was another story. There's just so much traffic. It can be a headache. And people are kind of rude out there at times."[47]

Clark pitched well for the Cubs in the final two months of the season. He had three straight victories with two complete games to start September. He was 6-1 with the Cubs with a strong 2.86 ERA, and ended up with 14 wins (14-8) for the second straight season.

Clark was rewarded with a one-year contract in 1998 for $5 million.[48] "The last couple of years I've come into my own," he commented. "I learned a lot (in Cleveland) from Dennis Martinez and Orel Hershiser – they taught me a lot of how to pitch. I had a pretty good two years in New York. I'm not going to change a thing."[49] He was a victor on opening night in Florida, striking out 11, and then threw eight innings in a victory over the Expos on April 6. But Clark then lost six of seven starts, and at the end of May was 3-6 with a 5.32 ERA. His troubles continued, and at the end of August he was 7-13 with a 5.04 ERA.

Yet Clark shined at the right moment. With the Cubs, Mets, and San Francisco Giants in a dogfight for a wild-card playoff spot, Clark won two important September starts. He struck out 10 Pirates batters in a win on September 9. His next performance bailed out the Cubs, who were reeling from five losses in six games. He defeated Houston in a must-win game on September 26, keeping the Cubs tied with the Giants and one game ahead of the Mets in the wild-card standings. "That was the biggest game of my career,"

Clark said several months later. "I knew I had to win that game. I had to give us a shot to win it. For me to go pitch the way I did, to keep us in the ballgame, it was a pretty big thrill for me. Knowing the way it all turned out, that if we hadn't won it we wouldn't have been in the playoffs, it is a good feeling."[50]

The Cubs and Giants finished tied for the wild card and had a one-game playoff in Chicago, which the Cubs won 5-3. They faced the Braves in the Division Series. Clark was the Game One starter in Atlanta against John Smoltz and allowed four runs (two earned) in six-plus innings as the Braves won, 7-1, and proceeded to sweep the Cubs. This was Clark's only postseason appearance. He finished the season 9-14 with a 4.84 ERA.

Clark became a free agent and signed a two-year deal for $9.3 million with the pitching-poor Texas Rangers, his fifth team in 10 years.[51] But his best days were behind him. His ERA at the end of April was 7.96. In four starts in June, Clark went 0-4 with an 18.24 ERA, not surviving five innings in any start. "This is by far the toughest stretch I've ever gone through," he said. "It just comes down to the simple fact that I'm not making pitches. When I need to get my sinker down, I can't, and I've never had that problem."[52] Clark was placed on the disabled list, and his 1999 season was over with a 3-7 record and 8.60 ERA.

Clark's struggles continued in 2000, and he found himself demoted to the bullpen, which his agent Barry Meister called "short-sighted and stupid."[53] Rangers owner Tom Hicks replied that Clark's signing was a "mistake."[54] Clark was not used from June 17 to 30 and on July 1, in what was his final major-league appearance, he lost to Seattle. His record fell to 3-5 with a 7.98 ERA. Clark made clear what his hopes were: "To get the hell out of here. What good is it being here? I'm not doing the club any good sitting out there in the bullpen and not pitching, and I'm not doing myself any good career-wise. Since I'm a mistake, I don't see any reason to be here. ... If that's the way they feel about me, then let me go. ... There have been nine clubs asking about me. What does that tell you?"[55]

Clark got his wish the next day, as the Rangers released him.[56] No club signed him, and Clark finished his career 74-71 with a 4.61 ERA. He ranked first three times as the best fielding pitcher of his league. However, as a hitter, his 14 hits in 242 at-bats gave him a .058 batting average, and Bill James rated him the "Worst-Hitting Pitcher" of the 1990s.[57]

Clark retired and went home to Illinois countryside, settling in the town of Kilbourne, down the road from his hometown of Bath. It was a far contrast from his baseball days, as there "is serenity as well as security, where everybody knows who he is and always has known," wrote Liz Robbins of the *Cleveland Plain Dealer*.[58] Clark followed in the footsteps of his father and grandfather in being a local hunting guide. "I grew up right on the water, and I love to hunt. ... Really nobody bothers you. ... You don't have to worry about running a stop sign in the country or four-lane highways with a ton of traffic. It's kind of like your own little place."[59]

Clark and his wife, Amy, had a son, Brandon, and a daughter, Allyson. In the September 2012 issue of *American Sports Outdoors*, Clark and Brandon were featured on the cover "getting gear lined up for early teal season. ..." An article in the issue described Clark's retirement as a busy one as "he maintains a gun club near Crane Lake Hunting Preserve called Club 54 and spends most of his time there with his cronies working and preparing it for the upcoming duck season."[60]

After the hectic pace of his baseball career, Clark said, he was more than content to be back home in Illinois. "Do I get bored?" he said. "Heck no. Never."[61]

SOURCES

In addition to the sources cited in the text, the author gathered information from Mark Clark's player file at the National Baseball Hall of Fame, Cooperstown, New York.

NOTES

1. Mike Eisenbath, "Fan-Tastic Experience for Clark. Cardinals Diehard Now on Cards Staff," *St. Louis Post-Dispatch*, September 27, 1991: 1D.
2. Ibid.
3. Population was 333 at the 2010 census. factfinder.census.gov/faces/nav/jsf/pages/community_facts.xhtml.
4. Liz Robbins, "Change of Pace: Mark Clark's Hometown Is Just What He Needs When It's Time to Get Away," *Cleveland Plain Dealer*, August 20, 1995: 1D.
5. Robbins.
6. Ibid.
7. Ibid.
8. *Rockford* (Illinois) *Register Star*, December 25, 1985: 2C.
9. *Rockford Register Star*, May 19, 1985: 2D.
10. *Rockford* (Illinois) *Register Star*, August 13, 1983: 2D.
11. Robbins.
12. Michael Bamberger, "Lucky Stiff Retired Big League Pitcher Mark Clark Was No Star, But He Got Paid Like One. And Now He's Living the Good Life – With all the Toys to Prove it," *Sports Illustrated*, May 17, 2004. Retrieved January 4, 2015. si.com/vault/2004/05/17/370175/lucky-stiff-retired-big-leagu
13. Lincoln Land Community College Loggers 2014 Media Guide. lincolnlandloggers.com/custompages/Baseball%20booklet%202014.pdf?path=baseball Accessed December 7, 2014.
14. Mark Zwolinski, "Baby Blue Jays Lose Home Opener," *Toronto Star*, June 18, 1988: B8.
15. Tom Northington, "Savannah's Mark Clark Shuts Down Greensboro," *Greensboro* (North Carolina) *News and Record*, August 13, 1989: 15.
16. Donald Heath, "Pirates' Bats Silenced Again," *Augusta* (Georgia) *Chronicle*, August 24, 1989: 2.
17. Mike Eisenbath, "Overflow San Antonio Crowd Right in the Middle of the Action," *St. Louis Post-Dispatch*, July 7, 1990: 5C.
18. Eisenbath, "Fan-Tastic Experience for Clark."
19. "Cards Rout Expos to Lock Up Second," *The Gazette* (Montreal), October 1, 1991: B7.
20. Dan O'Neil, "4-Game Winning Streak Earns Clark a Promotion," *St. Louis Post-Dispatch*, June 1, 1992: 7C.
21. Rick Hummel, "Cardinals Skunk Padres: Rookie Clark Shuts Out San Diego 4-0 in 1st Win," *St. Louis Post-Dispatch*, July 8, 1992.
22. Rick Hummel, "Clearing the Bases," *The Sporting News*, August 31, 1992: 22.
23. Robbins.
24. Dan O'Neill, "Joining Cleveland Gives Clark a Shot at Starting Rotation," *St. Louis Post-Dispatch*, April 1, 1993: 4D.
25. Dan O'Neill, "Cards Get Whiten From Cleveland: Trade Clark and Andujar for Outfielder," *St. Louis Post-Dispatch*, April 1, 1993: 1D.
26. Paul Hoynes, "Tribe Trades Whiten, Gets Cards Pitcher," *Cleveland Plain Dealer*, April 1, 1993.
27. O'Neill, "Joining Cleveland."
28. Paul Hoynes, "Tribe Trades Whiten."
29. Paul Hoynes, "Tribe Raps Jays," *Cleveland Plain Dealer*, April 12, 1993.
30. Bob Dolgan, "Tribe Releases Bielecki, Recalls Clark," *Cleveland Plain Dealer*, June 19, 1993: 5F.
31. This was for celebrating the anniversary of the last Indians team that won the American League Pennant.
32. Paul Hoynes, "Tribe Cleans Clocks," *Cleveland Plain Dealer*, June 20, 1993: 1D.
33. Mark Newman, "Insider Trading," *The Sporting News*, June 20, 1994: 20.
34. Sheldon Ocker, "Completing the Job," *The Sporting News*, May 30, 1994.
35. Burt Graeff, "Shock Wears Off for Clark," *Cleveland Plain Dealer*, May 31, 1995: 3D.
36. Paul Hoynes, "Clark Rapidly Finding Fastball: Tribe Right-Hander 3-1 Since Recall From Buffalo," *Cleveland Plain Dealer*, July 25, 1995: 1D.
37. Elton Alexander, "'General' Clark Has Command of Pitches," *Cleveland Plain Dealer*, June 28, 1995: 1D.
38. Plus an option year for $1.5 million contingent on number of innings pitched. *The Sporting News*, January 1, 1996: 46.
39. Paul Hoynes, "Indians Trade Clark: Ogea in the Rotation," *Cleveland Plain Dealer*, April 1, 1996: 1C.
40. George Willis, "Before Starting Season, Mets Trade for a Starter," *New York Times*, April 1, 1996: C3.
41. George Willis, "Mets' Victory Supplies a Variety of Hopes," *New York Times*, April 26, 1996: B11.
42. Ray McNulty, "Clark's Left Mark as Best in City," *New York Post*, June 24, 1996.
43. Jason Diamos, "Clark Wants Indians to Take Notice," *New York Times*, June 28, 1996: B11.
44. Buster Olney, "Clark Tops His Homer With 7 No-Hit Innings," *New York Times*, June 15, 1997: S7.
45. Buster Olney, "Mets Boost Bullpen in Deal With Cubs," *New York Times*, August 9, 1997: 31.
46. Paul Sullivan, "Wood Not Likely to Get Look: Pitching Prodigy May Wait for '98," *Chicago Tribune*, August 12, 1997: 8.
47. Paul Sullivan, "Cubs 4, Dodgers 2. Unlikely Heroes End a 9-Game Road Skid. Newcomer Clark, Hernandez Combine to Beat LA's Nomo," *Chicago Tribune*, August 13, 1997: 4.
48. Paul Sullivan, "Costs Mount as Cubs Re-Sign Clark, Foster," *Chicago Tribune*, January 20, 1998: 1.
49. Paul Sullivan, "Clark's Career Does 180: 'Expendable' Met a $5 Million Pitcher," *Chicago Tribune*, February 15, 1998: 3.
50. Phil Rogers, "'Clutch' Clark Finds Appreciation Elsewhere: Stretch Star Surprised Cubs Let Him Go, but Foresees Good Season With Rangers," *Chicago Tribune*, April 2, 1999: 6.
51. Phil Rogers, " 'Clutch' Clark Finds Appreciation."
52. Evan Grant, "Clark Headed to DL After Boston Pounds Him, 7-4. Righthander Knocked From Game After Just 1⅓ Innings," *Dallas Morning News*, June 20, 1999.
53. Evan Grant, "Clark's Demotion Irks Agent," *Dallas Morning News*, May 7, 2000.
54. Associated Press, "Clark Gets His Walking Papers from Texas," *The Pantagraph* (Bloomington, Illinois), July 4, 2000: 14.t.
55. T.R. Sullivan, "Peeved Clark Wants Out of Texas," *Fort Worth* (Texas) *Star-Telegram*, July 3, 2000: 4.
56. Gerry Fraley, "Rangers Let Go of 'Mistake.' Shuffle Includes Re-

lease of Clark," *Dallas Morning News*, July 4, 2000.

57 Bill James, *Bill James Historical Baseball Abstract* (New York: Simon & Shuster, 2001): 394 [Nook e-book version].

58 Robbins.

59 Ibid.

60 "Canterbury Tales," *American Sports Outdoors*, September, 2012: 1, 5. Issue retrieved from asomagazine.com/magazine/September%20 2012/001.pdf and asomagazine.com/magazine/September%20 2012/005.pdf

61 Bamberger.

DENNIS COOK

BY ALAN COHEN

"I'm just a guy who worked hard to get into this position. Nobody recruited me out of high school. The Houston kids got all the publicity. If a scout came to town, we all figured he was from the marines. I had to go to a tryout camp to get a junior college scholarship. I had to earn my way to (the University of) Texas and then into the big leagues. I was an 18th round pick. Tell you the truth, I'm glad it worked out that way. I think when the odds are against you, you work harder because there's nothing to lose. I've always been a longshot."

– Dennis Cook, March 1991[1]

Dennis Bryan Cook was born on October 4, 1962, in La Marque, Texas, in the Houston metropolitan area. His parents were William Robert and Janet Esther (Winquest) Cook. His mother and her parents had immigrated to the United States from Sweden when Janet was a child.

Dennis graduated from Dickinson High School, where he had played for coach Dale Westmoreland, in 1981, and spent two years at Angelina College in Lufkin, Texas. In January 1983, during his second year at Angelina, Cook was drafted in the sixth round by the San Diego Padres. He stayed in school and, after playing summer ball with the Alaska Goldpanners in 1983, transferred to the University of Texas for his last two years. While there, he was selected as a utility outfielder for the All-Southwest Conference Team. In each of his two years at Texas, the Longhorns lost in the final game of the College World Series.

Cook's sacrifice fly in the 10th inning of the regional final against Lamar advanced second-ranked Texas to the 1984 College World Series. That, and a three-run homer in a prior tournament win against UNLV, helped win him recognition as the Most Valuable Player in the NCAA Central Regional.[2] In the 1984 CWS, his two-out, two-run double in the eighth inning gave Texas a 6-4 win over Cal-Fullerton in the second round. In the next game, his third-inning single tied the game as the Longhorns went on to defeat Arizona State. As a senior, Cook also played in the 1985 CWS, and his five-inning scoreless relief stint against Arkansas gave Texas a place in the championship game against Miami, but the Longhorns lost to the Hurricanes, 10-6. Cook was named to the All-Tournament team as an outfielder. Indeed, he was the fifth pitcher for the pitching-rich Longhorns. Among his college teammates were pitchers Greg Swindell and Bruce Ruffin.

Cook was chosen in the 18th round of the June 1985 draft by the San Francisco Giants and signed by scout Andy Korenek. He was assigned to Clinton, Iowa, in the Class-A Midwest League. With Clinton, he was 5-4 with a 3.36 ERA in 13 games, all as a starter. The next season, at Fresno in the Class-A California League, Cook was 12-7 with a 3.97 ERA. In 1987, he got off to a great start with Shreveport in the Double-A Texas League, winning his first four decisions as his team took an early lead in the league's Eastern Division.[3] He was 9-2 with a 2.13 ERA when he was promoted to the Giants' Triple-A affiliate, Phoenix, where he was 2-5 in 12 games.

In 1988 Cook was back with Phoenix, but he was sidelined with cracked ribs and made only two appearances after July 27.[4] His record was 11-9, and he was not in the Giants' plans for the stretch drive. However, the Giants needed help when Mike Krukow was ruled out for the balance of the year, and the status of Mike LaCoss and Kelly Downs became questionable. Cook went from looking for a postseason job to figuring in the Giants plans in September.

He made his first appearance with the Giants on September 12, 1988, getting the start and keeping the opposition hitless until the fourth inning. He allowed no runs and two hits in 5⅓ innings as San Francisco defeated San Diego, 4-2. It was the first of his 64 major-league wins. After the game, he said, "I guess I was too excited to feel any pressure. I just wanted to go out, throw strikes, and let the chips fall. All my pitches were working, but my split finger and the fastball were the best."[5]

On September 25 at Candlestick Park, Cook was given the ball against the Los Angeles Dodgers. The Giants by then had been eliminated from contention and the Dodgers were on the verge of clinching the division title. Cook allowed only two hits, none after the third inning, and struck out seven as the Giants won, 2-0. In all, he appeared in four games in 1988, going 2-1 with a 2.86 ERA.

Cook started the 1989 season at Phoenix and was 7-4 when he was called up to the majors in June. After a complete-game win against Cincinnati on June 18, he was traded to the Phillies. The Phillies sent pitcher Steve Bedrosian to the Giants for Cook, Terry Mulholland, and minor-league infielder Charlie Hayes. Cook went 6-8 with Philadelphia, but finished strong, shutting out Montreal, 2-0, in his last start of the season, on September 29.

"I prided myself on being a baseball player. Not just a pitcher. Not just a hitter. But a baseball player. That's the way I played since I was eight years old, and I didn't see any reason to stop playing that way."[6]

Cook endeared himself to Philadelphia fans early on. In his third start, he was pitching against John Smoltz and the Atlanta Braves. When the Phillies came to bat in the bottom of the sixth inning, they trailed 2-1. Cook led off and dragged a bunt to the right side. Sliding head-first into first base, he was safe on the play. He was unable to advance, as he was forced at second in an inning-ending double play, but his style of play set him apart.

The hit was Cook's fourth since joining the Phillies, and after three starts, he was 4-for-9 as a hitter and 2-1 with a 1.96 ERA as a pitcher. After six starts in 1990, he was 5-0 with a 1.46 ERA. His wins included two complete games, of which one was a three-hit shutout of the Cardinals on April 20. (The shutout was the third and last of his career.) However, after his fifth win, on May 13, Cook had six starts in which he did not get a win. His record slipped to 5-2, and he was assigned to the bullpen. All but one of his remaining 29 appearances with the Phillies in 1990 were in relief, including a game at Pittsburgh on July 27 when he pitched five scoreless innings. Phillies manager Nick Leyva sent Cook into the game as a pinch-hitter in the second inning with the game tied, 2-2. He pitched innings two through six, giving up only two hits. The Phillies won, Cook's seventh win of the season.

Intensity was a big part of the Cook pedigree and on August 9, 1990, he was ejected following a brawl between the Phillies and the New York Mets. After Mets starter Dwight Gooden hit two

Philadelphia batters, the Phillies' pitcher, Pat Combs, hit Gooden on the knee, and the Mets ace charged the mound. The benches cleared and Cook, one of the first to join the fray, was thrown out of the game. During the brawl, he was thrown to the ground by umpire Joe West.[7]

With the Phillies out of contention in September, Cook was traded on September 13 to the Dodgers for catcher Darrin Fletcher. The Dodgers wanted him for the stretch run. In 42 appearances with the Phillies, he had gone 8-3 with a 3.56 ERA. On September 22 Cook made his first start and won his only game with the Dodgers, beating the Giants 6-3. It kept the Dodgers within four games of the division-leading Reds. However, Los Angeles was not able to close the gap and finished the season five games behind Cincinnati. Cook was 1-1 with a 7.53 ERA for the Dodgers.

After obtaining Cook, Dodgers general manager Fred Claire said, "We feel Dennis is an important addition to our pitching staff for the present and for the future. We've had an interest in Dennis for some time. He has advanced rapidly. The more we've seen of him, the more we like him."[8]

But the 1991 Dodgers were stocked with pitchers and there was no room for Cook. He began the season with Albuquerque in the Pacific Coast League. He went 7-3 with a 3.63 ERA in 14 games before being recalled in late June, when Jay Howell went on the DL. He pitched in 13 games with the Dodgers, all in relief, posting a 1.17 ERA in only 7⅔ innings. However, the ERA was deceiving in that he had allowed a walk or hit in all but two of his appearances. When Howell returned to the Dodgers from the DL in late July, Cook was sent to Double-A San Antonio. On August 18, he struck out 11 batters in eight innings for San Antonio, but was not involved in the decision.[9] With the Missions, his record was only 1-3, but he had a 2.49 ERA in seven appearances (all starts) and returned to the Dodgers at the beginning of September. He again was consigned to the bullpen with the Dodgers, who were eliminated from the division race on the next-to-last day of the season. On the last day, Cook had his only start of the year, pitching 5⅔ innings of shutout ball as the Dodgers defeated the Giants, 2-0. The win was Cook's only decision in the majors in 1991.

In December 1991, Cook was traded to the Cleveland Indians along with Mike Christopher for Rudy Seanez. In 1992 with the Indians, his fourth team in five major-league seasons, he went 5-7 with a 3.82 ERA in 32 games, 25 as a starter. He had begun the season as a starter, but through May 17, his record was only 1-4 with an ERA of 5.91. He then spent more than a month in the bullpen before returning to the rotation with better results. In 17 games from June 28 through October 1, he was 4-2 with an ERA of 3.20. The Indians finished the season in fourth place.

In 1993 Cook got into 25 games, six as a starter, as the Indians duplicated their 76-86 record of the prior season, finishing in sixth place. He started the season in the bullpen before starting six games between May 20 and June 17. He was ineffective during this stretch, going 1-3 with a 7.43 ERA, on a staff where there were few answers. Over the course of the season, Cleveland used 26 pitchers, 18 of them starters. Cook's season with the Indians, in which he went 5-5 with a 5.67 ERA, ended in July when he was sent to Charlotte in the International League.

The Indians let Cook go after the 1993 season and he signed with the Chicago White Sox. He pitched exclusively in relief in 1994 and had a 3-1 record with a 3.55 ERA. His season ended on August 10. At the end of the season, he was put on waivers by the White Sox and reclaimed by the Indians.

Cook's second tour with the Indians was relatively short. In mid-June of 1995, he was traded to the Texas Rangers for minor leaguer Guillermo Mercedes after having no decisions in 11 appearances with Cleveland. With the Rangers, he was 0-2 with two saves in 35 games.

In 1996 Cook went to the postseason for the first time. He was 5-2 with the Rangers and led the team with 60 appearances. In the best-of-five Division Series loss to the Yankees, Cook pitched in Games Two and Four. In the fourth game, Texas took an early 4-0 lead. New York rallied for three runs in the fourth inning. Cook came out of the bullpen with two out and runners on the corners and retired Wade Boggs to get out of the jam. He left the game at that point and looked on as the Yankees rallied to defeat Texas and move on to the League Championship Series.

Cook was once again a free agent after the 1996 season and signed with the Florida Marlins, where he was the set-up man for closer Robb Nen. Back in the National League Cook had the opportunity to show off his talents as a hitter. He had in four seasons (1988-1991) batted .250 (24-for-96) with a home run in 1990 when his overall average was .306. As a reliever, he did not have much of an opportunity to bat, but was perfect in his first four plate appearances, including his second career homer, on July 25. Against the Cardinals, he hit for himself after pitching a perfect eighth inning. He came out of the game after the homer and was credited with a hold as the Marlins won, 5-4.

On August 1 at Miami, Cook pinch-hit in the 12th inning against Atlanta. The score was tied, 2-2. There was one out and the winning run was on third base. This was his fourth at-bat and first pinch-hitting appearance of the season. His single drove in Gregg Zaun with the winning run. Over the course of the season, Cook batted .556 (5-for-9). As a pitcher, in 59 appearances, he was 1-2 with a 3.90 ERA. He struck out 63 batters in 62⅓ innings and was credited with 13 holds. His final hold, on September 23, came in a victory that secured a wild-card berth for the Marlins.

Cook starred in the Division Series against the Giants. In Game One, at Miami, he entered a 1-1 tie in the top of the eighth inning. He pitched two perfect innings, striking out three batters. In the bottom of the ninth, with two outs, Edgar Renteria singled home the winning run, and Cook had his first postseason win. In Game Three, a Marlins victory that advanced them to the National League Championship Series, he pitched a perfect eighth inning. In the NLCS he registered four outs and did not allow a hit in Florida's 5-3 Game One win over Atlanta. He got another hold in Game Three, pitching a perfect eighth inning when Florida won 5-2. The Marlins won the NLCS in six games and faced the Indians in the World Series.

Cook pitched in three games during the World Series against the Indians and was not scored upon. In Game One, he got one out in the sixth inning, pitched a scoreless seventh, and got the first out in the eighth. The Marlins won the game, 7-4 to take the lead in the series. Game Three at Cleveland was a high-scoring affair and the score was 7-7 when Cook entered the game in the bottom of the eighth inning. He allowed a leadoff single to Marquis Grissom and then retired the next three batters. With Cook the pitcher of record, the Marlins scored seven runs in the ninth inning, and Nen pitched the ninth inning. The Marlins won the game 14-11 and led the Series two games to one. Cook entered Game Seven in the seventh inning and retired the side in order. However, the Indians, his former team, had a two-run lead. The Marlins tied the game in the ninth, and when Renteria singled home Craig Counsell in the 11th inning, the Marlins had their first World Series championship and Dennis Cook had his first World Series ring.

The Marlins wasted no time in breaking up their team after the World Series. Cook was traded to the New York Mets and spent the better part of the next four seasons at Shea Stadium. Upon his arrival in New York, Buster Olney of the *New York Times* informed his readers that Cook "is all Texan from his thick prairie drawl to his pickup truck. His dog is called Stonewall Jackson, named for the Confederate general."[10] When he reported to spring training, he did it as a new father, three times over. On February 26, just before he reported, his wife, Tammy, had given birth to triplets. "It's been easy for me," he said. "My wife's doing all the work. But she's having fun. Everybody's eating. Everybody's healthy. Doesn't seem to have gotten to her yet."[11] He and Tammy, the former Tamara Paige Fitzsimmons, who studied physical therapy at the University of Texas, had been married in early 1992.

As the left-handed set-up man for closer John Franco, Cook was an iron man in the Mets bullpen. He led the team in appearances with 73 in 1998 and led the staff with a 2.38 ERA. On May 22 against the Brewers, he picked off two runners, back to back, in the eighth inning. He led all relievers in wins with eight (against four losses), and had one save. The Mets had a chance for the NL wild card but lost their last five games. After the season, the Mets signed Cook to a three-year contract worth, overall, $6.6 million.

In 1999 Cook was, outside of closer John Franco, the most reliable left arm in the Mets bullpen, and had a 10-5 record. He had four wins and a hold in his first nine April appearances, and teammates were joking about him perhaps having 20 wins in relief. Catcher Mike Piazza said, "For his sake, I do (hope so), But for our starters' sake, I don't."[12] The Mets once again were in a great position to make it to the postseason, and once again it appeared that they would fall short. On September 19, they were one game out of the division lead and had a stranglehold on the wild card. They proceeded to lose seven straight games. The last of those losses, 9-3 to Atlanta, was on September 28. Cook was the sixth of eight pitchers used by manager Bobby Valentine. He entered the game at Shea Stadium with the Mets trailing 5-1 in the eighth inning. With one out, he loaded the bases on two singles and a walk. The frustration level was high, and after the walk, Cook got into a heated exchange with home-plate umpire Alfonzo Marquez. As David Waldstein remarked in the *New York Post*, the frustration was "all right there on the face of the raging reliever, who spit fire and venom in the face of home plate umpire Alfonso Marquez, as if the man in blue were responsible for all of the Mets' losses (during the streak)."[13]

Cook was ejected from the game and later was fined $2,500 and suspended for one game by the National League. But if his implicit goal was, as Waldstein noted, "screaming at his teammates to wake up and show some fight," he succeeded.[14] The Mets got back on course, winning four of their last five games to tie Cincinnati for the wild-card slot. In a one-game playoff, they defeated the Reds, 5-0. The Mets went to the postseason as the National League wild card and faced the Diamondbacks in the National League Division Series. Cook made his presence felt in Game One. He entered the game in the sixth inning in relief of Masato Yoshii. The Mets lead in the game had been erased on a two-run homer by Luis Gonzalez. Cook registered the last two outs of the sixth inning and kept the Diamondbacks at bay in a scoreless seventh. He left the game after the seventh inning with the score tied and was a happy spectator when Edgardo Alfonzo's ninth-inning grand slam gave the Mets an 8-4 win. Cook did not appear again in the best-of-five series as the Mets won in four games to advance to the National League Championship Series against Atlanta. Cook pitched in three games in the NLCS. Although he was not charged with any runs, he did allow two inherited runners to score when Atlanta clinched the series in Game Six.

In 2000 the Mets returned to the postseason. Cook was no longer the lefty set-up man in the bullpen. That role was filled by John Franco when Armando Benitez captured the closer role. Cook was coming off an inconsistent 2000 season during which his 6-3 record was illusionary. He blew six saves and had an ERA of 5.34. He pitched in two games against the Giants in the NLDS, extending his postseason streak of scoreless appearances to 15, as the Mets won the best-of-five series in four games. In the NLCS against the Cardinals, Cook pitched only once, pitching a scoreless the eighth inning in the Mets' 8-2 loss in Game Three. The Mets won the best-of-seven series in five games and advanced to the World Series against the Yankees. Cook appeared in three games during the Series, won in five games by the Yankees. It was Cook's last appearance in the postseason. His career postseason résumé was 19 appearances, a 2-0 won-lost record, and a 0.00 ERA in 16⅓ innings.

During the offseason, the Mets were looking to unload the 38-year-old Cook, but there were no takers. On June 11, 2001, Cook was in the final season of his contract with the Mets. The team was off that day and Cook and six of his teammates had been invited to the White House to meet with President George W. Bush. During the 25-minute visit, Bush and Cook, both Texans, discussed places to fish in their home state.[15] On July 27 Cook and fellow pitcher Turk Wendell were sent to Philadelphia for Bruce Chen and Adam Walker, both of whom at the time were in the minor leagues. During his time with the Mets, Cook pitched in 255 games, won 25 games and lost 13, posted a 3.86 ERA and earned 6 saves.

When Cook returned to Philadelphia in 2001, there were no faces on the roster from the team he had left in 1990. He got into 19 games with the Phillies in the remaining months of 2001, posting no decisions. When he joined them, the Phillies were two games behind in the race for the NL wild card, but they went 29-30 in their last 59 games and did not make it to the postseason.

After the season, Cook was a free agent and signed with the Angels. He pitched in 37 games with the wild-card Angels but was not on the post-season roster. He was on the disabled list from July 6 through September 6 with a partially torn labrum.[16] After two months of rest, he made four appearances in September, but with the emergence of young reliever Francisco Rodriguez and the continued presence of Troy Percival leading the bullpen corps, Cook was left off the list.

Cook's major-league career was over after 15 seasons. He had played for nine teams (with multiple stops at Cleveland and Philadelphia). In 665 appearances, he posted a 64-46 record with a 3.91 ERA. Primarily a set-up man in the bullpen, he had saved nine games and in his early days as a starter had thrown six complete games, three of which were shutouts. His hitting prowess set him apart during his time in the National League. He batted .264 (29-for-110) with 9 RBIs.

Cook coached for the Swedish national team in the 2009 World Cup and managed them in the European Championships in 2010 (fifth place), 2012 (sixth place), and 2014 (11th place). He was a pitching consultant for the German team in the 2017 World Baseball Classic Qualifier held in Mexico City in March 2016.

As of 2018, Cook and his family lived outside of Austin, Texas. Since his retirement from big-league pitching, Cook has coached at many levels. In 2003, he coached under Tom Holliday at the University of Texas. In addition to coaching in Europe, he coached for three seasons at Lake Travis High School, near his home, when his sons were on the team. In 2018 he was named pitching coach for the Chatham Anglers in the Cape Cod League, a summer league for top college talent. One of his players was his son Asher, who after high school pitched at Navarro Junior College and moved on to Texas Christian University. Son Dawson played club baseball at the University of Mississippi.

SOURCES

In addition to the sources shown in the notes, the author used Ancestry.com, Baseball-Reference.com, and Dennis Cook's file at the National Hall of Fame and Museum Library.

NOTES

1. Mark Whicker, "Cook Known for Playing with Lot of Fire," *Orange County* (California) *Register*, March 6, 1991: D1, D8.
2. "Longhorns Prevail in 10th, Reach College World Series," *Miami Herald*, May 28, 1984: 5D.
3. Yale Youngblood, "Szeleky Kills Caps," *Times* (Shreveport, Louisiana), May 10, 1987: 3C.
4. Nick Peters, "Complicating the Plans," *The Sporting News*, September 26, 1988: 22.
5. Ibid.
6. Paul Hagen, "Cook Curious About Coaching in Retirement," MLB.com, July 19, 2017.
7. April Alfarano (United Press International), "Phils, Mets in Brawl, *Bryan* (Ohio) *Times*, August 10, 1990: 13.
8. "Will Cook Provide Missing Ingredient?" *The Sporting News*, September 24, 1990: 13.
9. Tom Griffin, "Missions Final: Angels' Ninth Buries Missions, 12-3, *San Antonio Express-News*, August 19, 1991: 1B.
10. Buster Olney, "Mets Get Cook and Still Seek Benes," *New York Times*, December 19, 1997: S4.
11. Charle Nobles, "Mets Newest Reliever Is Toughest on Lefties," *New York Times*, March 9, 1998: S3.
12. Jason Diamos, "Mets Walk on the Padres' Wild Side," *New York Times*, April 30, 1999: S1.
13. David Waldstein, "Cook Boils Over – Mets' Frustration Erupts as Reliever Goes After Umpire," *New York Post*, September 30, 1999.
14. Ibid.
15. Tyler Kepner, "Several Mets Meet Bush," *New York Times*, June 12, 2001: S6.
16. *The Sporting News*, September 23, 2002: 53.

ALAN EMBREE

BY BILL NOWLIN

Alan Embree was a left-handed reliever who pitched for 16 seasons of major-league ball and was a member of six teams that went to the postseason, going to the World Series twice – first with the 1995 Cleveland Indians and later with the triumphant 2004 Boston Red Sox.

Embree worked in 882 regular-season games, with a career earned-run average of 4.59. His won/lost record (not entirely meaningful for a specialist reliever) was 39-45. In the postseason, his ERA was a very impressive 1.66 in 31 games. Indicative of his specialist role was the fact that he worked fewer innings than games – he worked 21⅔ innings in those 31 postseason games, and 774 innings in his 882 regular-season games. His career WHIP (walks and hits per inning pitched) was 1.34.

Embree was born in The Dalles, Oregon, on January 23, 1970 and graduated from Prairie High School in Brush Prairie (Vancouver), Washington.1 He lettered in basketball, baseball, football, and volleyball. He was All-Conference in baseball. At age 19, he was selected by the Cleveland Indians in the fifth round of the 1989 amateur draft. Credit for Embree's signing goes to scout Dave Roberts and scouting director Chet Montgomery. He wasn't an easy sign, but by September came to agreement.

He was a starting pitcher during his first years in the minors. In 1990 he was 4-4 (2.64 ERA) in 15 starts in rookie ball for the Appalachian League Burlington Indians. In 1991 he pitched in Single A, for the Columbus (Georgia) Indians of the South Atlantic League. He was 10-8 (3.59), with three complete games, one of them a shutout.

In 1992 Embree pitched for two teams and was called up to Cleveland in September. He started the season with Kinston (North Carolina) in the Class A+ Carolina League (10-5, 3.30) and then was advanced to Double A, pitching for Canton-Akron in the Eastern League (7-2, 2.28). Just a couple of days after Embree was called up, manager Mike Hargrove had him start on September 15 in Toronto against the Blue Jays. Embree's teammates staked him to a 3-0 lead in the top of the first. Taking the mound, he allowed one run on no hits in the bottom of the first. (A walk, a wild pitch, and a steal of third put Robbie Alomar in position to score on a sacrifice fly.)

Later in the game Embree gave up a two-run homer to Dave Winfield, and all told allowed five runs in 4⅔ innings of work. The final score was 5-4, Jays, and Embree bore the loss.[2] He started three more games that year, two of them wins (both coming after he'd left the game). His only other decision was also a loss, in his fourth start, on October 3 in Cleveland. Baltimore beat the Tribe, 7-1. Embree had given up four runs in four innings.

The years 1993 and 1994 were both with Canton-Akron, though Embree was plagued with arm problems in 1993 and appeared in only one game all season. He started the season on the DL with an MCL injury to his left elbow; giving it time to heal did not work and he had Tommy John elbow surgery in late June. He recovered and carried a full load in 1994, starting 27 games. He wasn't as effective as he had been, with a 5.50 ERA and a 9-16 record.

The Indians decided to convert Embree into a reliever and in 1995 he began the season in Triple A with the Buffalo Bisons.

On July 13 Cleveland sent Jason Grimsley down and called up Embree, who had already appeared in 30 games with an ERA of 0.89. He relieved in 23 games for Cleveland, though his ERA was 5.11. He was credited with three wins and bore two losses. It took him only a third of an inning (and five pitches) to pick up his first big-league win. He retired the only batter he faced at Jacobs Field, getting the last out in the sixth of a scoreless game against the visiting Oakland Athletics. He was thus the pitcher of record and when the Indians scored one in the bottom of the inning, he was in position to get the win in the 1-0 game. Two days later, he pitched the 11th and 12th innings and saw the Indians beat the Athletics again. He was sent back down, but quickly recalled, was sent back down, and called up again.

Embree pitched once in the ALCS, striking out the only Mariners batter he faced, and then pitched in four games of the six-game World Series, which Cleveland lost to the Atlanta Braves. He faced 14 batters over 3⅓ innings and was tagged for two hits and one run, but it was not a decisive one. His World Series ERA was 2.70.

In 1996 Embree opened the season with the team in Cleveland, but was optioned to Buffalo in mid-April for a while. He shuttled back and forth five times during the season, and he was kept busy in both places: For Buffalo he was 4-1 in 20 games (closing in 15 of the 20), and with Cleveland he worked in 24 games, 1-1, never working more than 2⅔ innings and seven times not even a full inning (in all, he pitched 31 innings in the 24 games). His ERA for the Indians was 6.39. Cleveland made it to the postseason, but was eliminated by Baltimore in the Division Series. Embree pitched in three of the four ALDS games, for a total of one inning. He gave up one run, hitting Rafael Palmeiro, who later scored on a grand slam hit off reliever Paul Shuey.

Dissatisfied with his '96 season, Embree said in February 1997, "One month I'd be good and the next month I'd be terrible. Then things would go like that from outing to outing. ... I felt like I was a month behind all season." He kept active throwing throughout the winter months. "You can work out all you want," he said. "You can lift and run, but nothing takes the place of throwing to keep your arm strong."[3] He looked very good in spring training, said manager Mike Hargrove.

Near the end of spring training 1997, Embree was traded (with Kenny Lofton) to the Atlanta Braves for Marquis Grissom and David Justice. It was dubbed a "blockbuster" and "the biggest deal in club history" for the Braves.[4] It stunned both fan bases, and many of the players. "It was kind of like everybody's dog had been killed," said Tom Glavine.[5] Justice had hit the game-winning homer in Game Six of the 1995 World Series. Embree was described by some as a "throw-in" in the deal, to bring more balance to the deal. The deal was also one "motivated by baseball economics on both sides," according to Braves GM John Schuerholz.[6] Columnist Bob Nightengale was not kind, saying, "Embree, at best, is a mediocre pitcher. The man has a great arm, but Indians officials believe he lacks guts."[7] That Indians GM John Hart had disparaged Embree didn't sit well with him and even several years later it was reported that he had the words "No heart" and "Throw-in" written on the inside of his cap. In 2001, after Hart had announced it would be his last season with the Indians, Embree told *USA Today Baseball Weekly*, "I felt like calling him up wondering where he was going for his next job so I could stay away from him."[8]

Lofton had a very good year for the Braves, but Embree had arguably just as good a year at the tasks he was assigned. As the only left-hander in the Braves' bullpen, Embree appeared in 66 games, second only to Mark Wohler's 71, and his ERA of 2.54 was topped only by Greg Maddux (2.20) and right-handed reliever Mike Cather (2.39). He was 3-1. Getting the opportunity to work was key, in Embree's own view. "The more I'm out there, the more comfortable I feel," he said.[9]

The use of left-handed specialists had truly expanded by this time. Rangers GM Doug Melvin said, "You have to have them. You always need them. You don't necessarily need them as the closer. But you need them in the fifth and sixth or sixth and seventh for one or two batters because your starters don't go very far anymore. I think they're valuable to get one hitter out."[10] Right-handed relievers were more plentiful. Kevin Malone, Dodgers GM, said, "If you're left-handed, you've got a chance probably to pitch five years longer than one might expect."[11] Embree was what became known around this time as a LOOGY (Left-handed One Out Guy).

Embree signed a two-year deal with the Braves in January, but he traded uniforms in midseason again in 1998, traded straight up (on June 23) to the Arizona Diamondbacks for right-handed pitcher Russ Springer. It was pretty much a swap of "handedness" with the Braves needing a righty and the Diamondbacks needing a lefty (and the Braves having perhaps lost confidence in Embree). Both pitchers performed more or less the same throughout 1998, marginally better for their new club. Embree was, overall, in 55 games (35 with Arizona) with a combined 4.19 ERA. In November he was traded again, to the Giants for occasional outfielder Dante Powell. The D-Backs were looking for a center fielder.

Embree had a good 3.38 ERA in 1999 but (after signing a two-year deal in early February) slipped to 4.95 in 2000. He saw a little more postseason work in the National League Division Series with the Giants, pitching briefly in two games and retiring the five batters he faced.

In November he had minor surgery on his left elbow. After his career was over, Embree looked back on the help given him by his Tommy John surgery in 1993. "I was a power pitcher again," he said. "But I wasn't done. I took things from my rehab with me and created the maintenance program I followed throughout the rest of my career. The way I look at it is because of this maintenance program, it gave me seven to eight years onto my career."[12]

The next year, 2001, was not a good year at all. Embree appeared in 22 games for the Giants through June 26 but could never get on track. He had an 11.25 ERA for San Francisco, and it wasn't improving. Finally, they traded him, on June 29 (and had to put up some money, too), to get minor-league prospect Derek Hasselhoff from the Chicago White Sox. He pitched in 39 games for Chicago, and halved his ERA by working at a 5.03 pace. But that November, the White Sox granted him free agency. Two days after Christmas, Embree signed a one-year deal with the San Diego Padres.

It was like he'd been reborn. In 36 games for San Diego in 2002, Embree recorded an ERA of 1.26 and suddenly became a sought-after commodity. The Boston Red Sox worked a deal for him on June 23, sending the Padres two talented right-handed pitching prospects in Brad Baker and Dan Giese. He was energized, joining a team that was a possible pennant contender. He appeared in 32 games for the Red Sox with a 2.97 ERA. One outing may have exemplified his work as a lefty specialist. At Fenway Park on August 20, he was brought into a 2-1 game against the Texas Rangers in the top of the eighth. The Red Sox held the one-run lead, there were two outs, and there was a runner on third base. Embree was tasked with getting Rafael Palmeiro out. He threw one pitch. Palmeiro flied out to center. Embree's night was done. "He's throwing the ball now better than he has in his whole career," declared Red Sox manager Grady Little. "It makes you want to put him out there every single day."[13] Embree agreed he'd been going well: "This is as good as I've felt in a long time. I was scoped (elbow) the offseason before last, and that took care of the problem."[14]

In 2003 and 2004, after recovering from a shoulder injury in April 2003, Embree was a workhorse on two playoff-bound Red Sox teams, working in 65 games and then 71, with ERAs of 4.25 and 4.13. At the beginning of 2003, he was part of what the Boston media called "bullpen by committee." Red Sox GM Theo Epstein tried to be clear at the time: "That's not my choice of words." He called it "a deep, versatile, flexible bullpen with six quality options. … We believe the most critical outs in a game aren't necessarily in the ninth." They could, for instance, be in the seventh inning with the bases loaded, not in the ninth with a three-run lead."15 Actually, Embree had not reported in top condition, which he admitted, going to Florida for a while in April to get his shoulder strength back. "I didn't prepare myself. … I failed myself," he told the *Boston Globe*'s Bob Hohler.16 He'd come to love the intensity in Boston, though. "My mentality is better suited to this brand of baseball. I'm a guy that if it doesn't count, I [stink]. I've proved that. I like it when the game's on the line."17

Embree pitched in three games in the 2003 Division Series, and then in five of the seven games of the ALCS against the Yankees. In 4⅔ innings of ALCS work, he gave up three hits, but no runs. He was the winning pitcher in Game Six, securing the final two outs in the bottom of the sixth (including a one-out strikeout of Jason Giambi with men on second and third, followed by inducing a groundout), seeing the Sox score three runs to overtake the Yankees and go up 7-6 in the top of the seventh, and then not letting the ball get out of the infield in the bottom of the seventh. The score held up and he got the W.

In Game Seven, manager Grady Little left Pedro Martinez in too long and the Yankees scored three runs to tie the game, 5-5. Embree was the pitcher brought in after Pedro was taken out. He got the one batter he was asked to get. Mike Timlin closed out the inning. The Yankees' Aaron Boone homered off Tim Wakefield in the bottom of the 10th, sending the Yankees to the World Series and sending the Red Sox home.

The Red Sox got their revenge the next year, in storybook fashion. Once again they battled the Yankees in the ALCS, this time losing the first three games and getting clobbered 19-8 in Game Three. Embree gave up two runs in that game – half of the total of four he ever gave up in all his 31 postseason games. He was just one of six Red Sox pitchers to give up runs in the beatdown. Then Boston won two extra-inning games in a row, with David Ortiz knocking in the winning run both times. Embree pitched the 10th and part of the 11th in Game Four and got the last two outs in the top of the 10th in Game Five. The Red Sox took it to Game Seven, and built a very comfortable 10-3 lead over the Yankees. New York got two men on base and there were two outs. Manager Terry Francona asked Embree to relieve Mike Timlin and get the final out. That he did, getting Ruben Sierra to ground out, second to first.18 Thus, a photograph well-known in New England which shows catcher Jason Varitek leaping into Embree's arms at the end of the game. The Red Sox were bound for their first World Series since 1986.

"It was the longest ground ball of my life," Embree said of the grounder. "It was a rollover, just as I planned it, and as it passed me toward Pokey (Reese) at second, it felt like it was taking an eternity. It felt like a moment frozen in time."19

The Red Sox swept the St. Louis Cardinals in the World Series. Embree pitched in three of the four games, earning a hold in Game Four.

The very next year, he experienced something unusual – Embree started the season with the Red Sox and ended it with the Yankees. With a world championship ring to his credit, he struggled over 43 appearances and held a 7.65 ERA. The Red Sox designated him for assignment, and then simply released him on July 19. Eleven days later, he signed as a free agent with the "pitching-starved" Yankees.20 He had been in Sunriver, Oregon, fishing the Deschutes River for brown trout when he got the call. Commenting on going from the Red Sox to the Yankees, he said, "It's a beautiful ring. But that was last year. I'm trying to get one here right now."21

Embree worked in 24 games for New York, with a nearly identical 7.53 ERA. That November the Yanks released him, too.

He spent 2006 back with the Padres, and had a good year with a 3.27 ERA earned over 73 appearances. The Oakland A's worked out a two-year deal, signing Embree for 2007 and 2008. In 68 games in 2007, he worked a lot of them as the team's closer since Huston Street was injured for two months in the middle of the season. Embree filled the role well, and had a 3.97 ERA for the year.

At age 39, Embree pitched one last season in the majors, for the Colorado Rockies in 2009. He appeared in 36 games, but worked only a total of 24⅔ innings. His last decision was a win, on July 7 in a game against the Washington Nationals in Denver. The score was 4-4 after seven innings. With two outs, the Nationals got a man on first base and left-handed hitter Nyjer Morgan coming up to bat. Manager Jim Tracy called Embree in from the bullpen. Before he threw his first pitch to the batter, he picked baserunner Austin Kearns off first base, retiring the side. The Rockies scored one on a sacrifice fly in the bottom of the eighth and Tracy turned to Street, the closer, to secure the win. Embree had won the game without throwing even one pitch. Recalling the short outing after he game, he said, "I'm going, 'What just happened?' And then I came in and they went, 'You're done. Do you think you can go tomorrow?' I'm still in a daze."[22]

Three days later, Embree was hit in the leg by a line drive, fracturing his right tibia. He was out for the rest of the season.

Embree gave it one more shot in 2010 and signed a minor-league deal with the Red Sox. He appeared in eight games for the Triple-A Pawtucket Red Sox (3.68) and was called up to Boston, but wasn't used and was designated for assignment, and then released. Five days later, he signed with the White Sox again and they assigned him to play for their International League farm team, the Charlotte Knights. He was 0-1 in six games and was released on May 28. His career as a player was over.

Right near the end, the day he'd been released by the Red Sox, he expressed no anger: "I'm good with it. I've had a good career. I'm quite happy with where I am."[23]

Despite all the time he had spent in the National League, Embree's role was almost always as a lefty specialist, and so he rarely had the chance to bat. In his 882 big-league games he had only four plate appearances. He walked once, but was caught stealing. He struck out twice. His career batting average remains .000.

Embree's wife, Melanie, was a physical therapist he met during his rehab work after the Tommy John surgery. As of 2014, the Embrees lived in Bend, Oregon, where Melanie owned her own practice, Momentum Physical Therapy. Alan said, "I owe her a lot. She would probably say I didn't listen to her much, but I relied on her. I sought more advice from her than I did my trainers."[24] The Embrees have two children, Alan ("Ace") and Andie.

Embree worked as head baseball coach at Bend's Summit High School and also worked coaching the Bend Elks, an amateur team in the West Coast League, a wooden-bat collegiate baseball league in Oregon, Washington, and British Columbia.

SOURCES

In addition to the sources noted in this biography, the author also accessed Embree's player file from the National Baseball Hall of Fame, the *Encyclopedia of Minor League Baseball*, Retrosheet.org, Baseball-Reference.com, and the SABR Minor Leagues Database, accessed online at Baseball-Reference.com.

NOTES

1. Thanks to Kristin Wennerlind, librarian at Prairie High School, for explaining, "We are located in Vancouver, but many refer to the area (and location of our district) as Brush Prairie." Email to author, May 27, 2015.
2. Winfield said after the game, "The first time you face someone, you always like to leave an impression." Associated Press, "Winfield, Jays Stop Indians, 5-4," *Washington Post*, September 16, 1992: C6.
3. Sheldon Ocker, "Embree Employing Strong-Arm Tactics," *Chronicle-Telegram* (Elyria, Ohio), February 18, 1997
4. Bill Zack, "This One Really Is A BIG Deal," *Augusta* (Georgia) *Chronicle,* March 26, 1997: 6.
5. Ibid.

6. Murray Chass, "Eyes on the Bottom Line: Braves and Indians Trade," *New York Times*, March 26, 1997: B13. The deal saved the Braves a reported $7.7 million. See Associated Press, "Justice, Lofton in Monster Trade," *Oneonta Star*, March 26, 1997.

7. Bob Nightengale, Braves' Bold Move Will Haunt Them," *The Sporting News*, April 7, 1997: 24.

8. Bob Nightengale, "Chatter," *USA Today Baseball Weekly*, April 18-24, 2001: 3.

9. Bill Zack, "Embree Emerges Early as Tight Closer," *The Sporting News*, April 21, 1997: 14.

10. Murray Chass, "Left-Handed Relievers Find Long Job Security," *New York Times*, February 21, 1999: SP2.

11. Ibid.

12. Ben Montgomery, "Former Pitcher, Alan Embree, Credits Physical Therapy for Longevity," ptpubnight.com/2014/10/21/former-pitcher-alan-embree-credits-physical-therapy-longevity/

13. Bob Ryan," It's Good Work if You Can Get It," *Boston Globe,* August 2, 2002: E1.

14. Ibid.

15. Murray Chass, "Teams Are Playing Musical Chairs in Bullpens," *New York Times*, January 12, 2003: SP12.

16. Bob Hohler, "For Embree, Longer Stay Would Be Relief," *Boston Globe*, February 24, 2004.

17. Ibid.

18. Heading into the 2004 ALCS, Yankees Bernie Williams, John Olerud, and Sierra had a combined .133 batting average against Embree.

19. Ben Montgomery.

20. The phrase was used in an Associated Press article: "Embree Joins Yankees' Bullpen," *Albany Times Union*, July 1, 2005.

21. Tyler Kepner, "Boston to Oregon to Bronx, Embree Has New Uniform," *New York Times*, July 31, 2005: H5.

22. Thomas Harding, "Embree Earns 'W' Without Throwing Pitch," MLB.com, July 8, 2009.

23. Ian Browne, "Embree's Second Stint with Boston Ends," MLB.com, May 1, 2010.

24. Ben Montgomery.

ALVARO ESPINOZA

BY GREGG OMOTH

A veteran of 12 major-league seasons, Alvaro Espinoza played a variety of roles for five different teams. He went from prospect with the Minnesota Twins to starting shortstop with the New York Yankees to utility infielder with three other teams. He is best remembered by Cleveland Indians fans as a versatile backup on the 1995 American League champions. He threw out Jay Buhner of the Seattle Mariners on a grounder for the final out in the American League Championship Series, sending the Indians to their first World Series since 1954. In a career filled with unexpected success and disappointment, Espinoza found a perfect role with the Indians as the utility infielder and team prankster. He played with a passion for the game while finding ways make it fun.

Alvaro Alberto Ramirez Espinoza was born on February 19, 1962, in Valencia, Venezuela, the country's third largest city and the hub of a 3-million-strong metropolitan area. His father, Luis, a bus driver, and mother, Matilde, raised five daughters and three sons.[1] Alvaro attended the Pedro Gual School in Valencia, where he played baseball, basketball, and soccer.[2] As a youngster, baseball was his passion; after school he played in the streets with his friends and two brothers until dark. His family was not poor, but they did not have extra money for bats, balls, and gloves. He made do with no glove, a stick for a bat, and crumpled paper taped together for a ball.[3]

On October 30, 1978, Houston Astros scout Tony Pacheco signed Espinoza as an amateur free agent to $500-a-month contract with a $3,000 bonus.[4] The Astros also signed his older brother Roberto at the same time. The Astros sent them to their rookie league team in Sarasota, Florida. Roberto spent four years in the Astros system before starting a career as a coach in multiple organizations and with the Venezuelan team in the World Baseball Classic. Alvaro spent two years in the Astros organization before being released on September 30, 1980. When he was told that they were releasing him he thought he would not be allowed to play in the United States again. He returned to Valencia, where he worked selling hot dogs out of a street cart.

Espinoza continued to play in the Venezuelan winter league, where he caught the attention of Minnesota Twins scout Hank Izquierdo.[5] He wasn't sure he wanted to play again but his father persuaded him to give it another try, and the Twins signed him in 1982. They sent him to their Class-A team in Wisconsin Rapids, Wisconsin (Midwest League), where he played in 112 games, hitting .266 while splitting time between shortstop and third base.

In 1983 the Twins sent Espinoza to Visalia of the Class A California League, where he roomed with Kirby Puckett. Espinoza credited Puckett with helping him learn English by encouraging him to watch television and repeating what he heard. Hitting .319 in 130 games at Visalia while playing solid defense, he established himself as a legitimate prospect for the Twins. At the end of the season he was named to the California League All-Star team. In the winter Espinoza returned to Venezuela to play winter ball with his idol Dave Concepcion, the Cincinnati Reds shortstop and Venezuelan hero. Espinoza credited another former major leaguer, Vic Davalillo, for helping him with his hitting during this time.[6]

In 1984 Espinoza went to spring training with a chance to win a roster spot on a Twins team that did not have an established shortstop. Even with a good spring, he lost out on his bid to win the shortstop job to Lenny Faedo and was sent to the Twins' Triple-A team in Toledo. There he was installed as the starting shortstop ahead of the Twins' other shortstop prospect, Greg Gagne. In June Espinoza went on the disabled list with 21 stitches in his leg after being spiked at second base. Solid defense was the strength of his game, while his hitting was suspect at only .233 in 104 games. The Twins called him up in September and he made his major-league debut on September 14, 1984, in a game against the Texas Rangers. He entered the game as a defensive replacement in the seventh inning at shortstop, replacing Chris Speier. This was his only appearance with the Twins in 1984; he did not get a plate appearance.

In 1985 Espinoza failed to make the big-league club out of spring training and was the last infielder sent to Toledo. The Twins found their future shortstop in Gagne, making Espinoza's route to the major leagues more difficult. He had a tough year in Toledo, hitting only .229 and reinforcing the Twins opinion that he was ready to play major-league defense but not ready offensively. In August Espinoza was called up to the majors when Gagne went on the disabled list. In his first extended chance in the majors, he hit .263 in 32 games. New Twins manager Ray Miller was impressed with his defense, providing Espinoza optimism for his chances in 1986.

In 1986 Espinoza started the season in Toledo after again failing to make the Twins roster out of spring training. On July 11 he was called up to the Twins, and remained with the team for the remainder of the season. Playing in 37 games, he split time between second base and shortstop. He hit only .214.

Espinoza remained with the Twins organization in 1987 but was sent to Triple-A Portland. A knee injury in late May forced him to miss a month. Though he had a solid year, splitting time between shortstop and third base and hitting .275, he did not receive a September call-up to the Twins. On October 15 he was granted free agency and on the advice of scout Fred Ferreira, the New York Yankees signed him on November 17, as a six-year minor-league free agent.[7]

Espinoza spent most of the 1988 season with the Yankees' Triple-A affiliate in Columbus, Ohio. On August 4 he was called up to the Yankees and played in three games, going hitless in three at-bats, before being sent back to Columbus on August 12. He had a solid year at Columbus that was noticed by some of the Yankees front office people, who thought he could help the team the following year.

In the spring of 1989, Espinoza was invited to spring training with the Yankees with an opportunity to make the team as a utility infielder. When starting shortstop Rafael Santana went down with an injury in spring training, and the Yankees failed in their attempts to obtain another shortstop, manager Dallas Green named Espinoza the starter. He expected Espinoza to play solid defense but had limited expectations for his hitting. Espinoza's play turned out to be one of the biggest surprises for the Yankees in 1989; he had his best season in the major leagues, hitting .282 in 146 games. Batting second in the order, he was among the league leaders in sacrifices. He credited his improvement at the plate to his work with hitting coach Frank Howard. Manager Bucky Dent, who replaced Green in August, anticipated using Espinoza as his shortstop in 1990.[8]

Entering 1990, Espinoza was established as the shortstop and went on to play in a career-high 150 games. His offensive production was less than spectacular; he batted only .224 with 2 home runs and 20 RBIs. Espinoza did not work well with new batting coach Champ Summers, who experimented with his stance and eroded Espinoza's confidence. When Stump Merrill replaced Dent as manager and Darrell Evans became the new batting coach, Espinoza continued to struggle with the bat. He was trying too hard to drive the ball rather than making contact and moving runners along.[9] The end result was one of the worst offensive seasons for any player in major leagues in 1990.

In 1991 Espinoza was disappointed when Randy Velarde started two of the season's first three games at shortstop. This started some tension between him and manager Merrill that would carry on throughout the season. However, he quickly found himself back in the lineup as the starting shortstop, hitting .441 in the season's first 13 games. He attributed his increased production to the return of Frank Howard as the batting coach.[10] But as the season went on, his relationship with Merrill deteriorated to the point of open hostility. Late in the season, Espinoza accused Merrill of benching him so he would not meet appearance incentives in his contract.[11] He finished the season hitting .256 in 148 games, but his future with the Yankees was no longer certain.

In February of 1992 Espinoza signed a new contract with the Yankees and went to spring training competing with one of the club's free-agent acquisitions, Mike Gallego, for the starting shortstop role. After failing to trade Espinoza, the Yankees released him on March 18, in a move that saved them over $800,000. The Yankees did not believe he would be happy in a backup role after being the starter for the past three seasons. Espinoza was disappointed on being released but was also thankful for the opportunity the Yankees gave him, stating, "They gave me my chance, it was the best three years of my life. I can't say nothing bad about these guys."[12] On April 3 he signed with the Cleveland Indians and was sent to their Triple-A affiliate in Colorado Springs. He spent the season with Colorado Springs, hitting .300 in 122 games, and played in the PCL All-Star Game.

In 1993 Espinoza made the Indians' roster out of spring training as a utility infielder. He played 90 games at third base, 35 at shortstop, and two at second base. He batted .278 with 4 home runs and 27 RBIs. With his value established, he returned to the Indians for the strike-shortened 1994 season. Playing in 90 games, he split time between all infield positions, playing first base for the first time in his career.

In 1995 Espinoza's playing time was reduced because of the emergence of Jim Thome at third base and established players Omar Vizquel at shortstop and Carlos Baerga at second. His role was limited to defensive replacement and occasional pinch-hitter. With more time on the bench, he established himself as one of the team pranksters, with his favorite prank putting a bubblegum bubble on top of an unsuspecting teammate's cap and waiting for him to realize he was the victim of his prank. The Indians won the Central Division championship and faced the Boston Red Sox in the Division Series. It was Espinoza's first chance at postseason baseball. He played in Game Three as a defensive replacement for Thome at third base, getting one at-bat in the ninth inning and flying out to right field in the Indians' 8-2 win.

The Indians won the Division Series and played Seattle in the AL Championship Series. Espinoza appeared in four games, getting one hit in eight at-bats. In the World Series he played in two games, getting one hit in two at-bats. The highlight for Espinoza was a pinch-running appearance in the bottom of the 11th inning in Game Three; with no outs he scored the winning run from second base on a hit by Eddie Murray. The Indians lost the World Series to the Florida Marlins in six games.

In December Espinoza signed a new contract with the Indians and returned to his role of utility infielder for 1996. Playing at all the infield positions, he appeared in 59 games before he was traded on July 29 to the New York Mets with Baerga for Jeff Kent and Jose Vizcaino. Playing mainly at third base, he got into 48 games for the Mets, hitting .306. He filled in at all the other infield positions for the Mets. Though he was not the primary acquisition, he outperformed Baerga with the Mets after the trade. It appeared Espinoza would have a good opportunity to play for the Mets in 1997.

He went to spring training with the Mets in 1997 but was released on March 26. The Mets decided to go with younger players with better range. On April 2 Espinoza signed with the Seattle Mariners as a utility infielder. He performed well as a backup until he suffered a bruised arm and went on the disabled list on May 30. After a short rehab stint with their Triple-A team in Tacoma, he returned to the active roster on June 13. He was hitting only .181 when the Mariners released him on July 14.

In 1998 Espinoza started his coaching career as a minor-league infield coordinator with the Montreal Expos organization. In 1999 the Dodgers hired him as manager of their Florida State League team in Vero Beach. In 2000 and 2001 he was the Dodgers' roving minor-league infield coordinator. In 2002 he worked in the same capacity with the Pittsburgh Pirates organization.

In 2003 Espinoza returned to the major leagues as the infield instructor for the Pittsburgh Pirates. He continued in this role until the end of the 2005 season. In 2006 he was the club's roving minor-league infield coordinator. From 2007 to 2017 he worked as a minor-league infield instructor in the Yankees, Pirates, and San Francisco Giants organizations.

The father of seven children, Espinoza became a United States citizen in 2005. As of 2018 he lived in Florida with his wife, Corimar. In 2014 he was inducted into the Caribbean Series Hall of Fame. In a 12-year career in the Venezuelan League, he hit .368 in his three appearances in the Caribbean Series.

NOTES

1. Joe Maxse, "The Joker Utility Man Espinoza Helps Keep Teammates Smiling," *Plain Dealer* (Cleveland), September 14, 1995.
2. *1986 Minnesota Twins Media Guide*, 66.
3. Michael Martinez, "Promising Future With Yankees Doesn't Exclude Espinoza's Past," *New York Times,* September 12, 1989.
4. Charley Walters, "Smalley Sidelined by Injury to Foot," *St. Paul Pioneer Press,* March 26, 1985: 2B.
5. Tom Loomis, "Twins' Outfielder Battling Nerves: Eisenreich Promising in Exhibitions," *Toledo Blade,* March 18, 1984: D 3.
6. Ibid.
7. Bill Madden, "Espinoza Helping Yanks Forget Shortstop Problem," *The Sporting News,* May 29, 1989: 18.
8. Martinez.
9. Jack Curry, "Baseball: A Yankee and a Met Labor to Round Out Their Mastery of the Game; Espinoza Has to Be a More Selective Hitter," *New York Times*, March 19, 1991.
10. Jack Curry, "Baseball; Espinoza Goes Beyond His Fancy Glovework," *New York Times,* April 25, 1991.
11. Jack O'Connell, "New York Yankees," *The Sporting News*, September 2, 1991: 22.
12. Jack Curry, "Baseball; Double Play: Espinoza Goes and Gallego Is Given His Job," *New York Times,* March 18, 1992.

JOHN FARRELL

BY BILL NOWLIN

John Farrell began his professional baseball career as a right-handed pitcher with an 0-5 record for the 1984 Class-A Waterloo Indians in the Midwest League. He'd been drafted three times by that point, but it was certainly an inauspicious start to a career that saw him manage the 2013 Boston Red Sox to a world championship.

John Edward Farrell was born in Monmouth Beach, New Jersey, on August 4, 1962. He attended a regional high school that drew from four communities on that part of the Jersey Shore: Shore Regional High School in West Long Branch.

Farrell's father, Tom, was a left-handed pitcher, also in the Indians system, in 1953-55. He didn't advance far, but he talked baseball endlessly with John. Tom's trade was masonry, but he became a commercial fisherman and John often went out on the boat with him. "A lobster fisherman, gillnetter. That's what I thought my path was going to be."[1]

Tom Farrell was a 6-foot-3 left-hander signed by the Cleveland Indians and initially assigned to Reading in 1953. He pitched for the Sherbrooke Indians in the Provincial League in 1954, with a losing record (9-12) but a good 2.90 earned-run average. He pitched briefly in 1955 as well, 1-0 in four games, but that concluded his career. He and his wife, Suzanne, had four daughters and two sons.

John's brother played some baseball and ran track in high school, enlisted in the Air Force, and as of 2014 owned a roofing company in Dover, Delaware.

John was the ninth-round pick of Walt Jocketty and the Oakland A's in 1980, out of high school. Farrell decided to go to college instead, and went to Oklahoma State. There he was also drafted, after his junior year, a 16th-round selection by the Cleveland Indians in 1983. He elected to play one more year with the Oklahoma State Cowboys, had continued success on the mound, and was rewarded with a second-round selection (again by Cleveland) in 1984. This time he signed and was assigned to Waterloo. The Indians' signing scout was Red Gaskill, whom Farrell remembers as "a longtime scout that had an ease about him, who was willing to explain all that was involved, and what his view was and his evaluation. He almost befriended you and advised you a little bit along the way."

Tom Farrell's background had a lot to do with John's interest in baseball. "There's no doubt. In growing up south of New York City, Tom Seaver was in his prime with the Mets at the time and he was the TV prompt and teacher. My dad would break down his delivery when he was pitching on TV. That's why his picture sits right there." Farrell pointed to a framed photo of Seaver on his office wall at Fenway Park, one depicting Seaver in a Red Sox uniform. Tom Farrell died in 2003.

Playing in 1984 for the Maine Guides at Old Orchard Beach, Cleveland's Triple-A club, was John's second visit playing baseball in New England. He had spent the summer of 1982 in the Cape Cod League, playing high-level amateur ball for Hyannis. As Stan Grossfeld wrote in the summer of 2014, Farrell's stay with his host family was memorable: "Farrell spent the nights on a rollaway cot in a backyard tool-shed apartment in Osterville with skunks as neighbors."[2]

Farrell was on the varsity with Oklahoma State all four years, and the team made it to the College World Series all four years.

With the Guides, Farrell was 2-1. It was the only team he had a winning record with before he made the major leagues.

It wasn't that Farrell had superb ERA's and lacked only run support or better fielding behind him. His record was a little up-and-down:

1985 Waterbury Indians (Double-A Eastern League) 7-13 (5.19 ERA)

1986 Waterbury Indians (Double-A Eastern League) 9-10 (3.06 ERA)

1987 Buffalo Bisons (Triple-A American Association)   6-12 (5.83 ERA)

But he was learning to pitch. And in mid-August 1987, he got the opportunity every minor leaguer hopes for: He was called up to the big leagues.

Given his record at Buffalo, was Farrell a little surprised to get the call to the majors? "I got the call basically by attrition. Everybody else went down before me. I might have been the 21st pitcher that year. I was 6 and 12, I believe, before getting called up. I had been pitching well probably the four starts prior, with varying success throughout the year – mostly lack of success. But when I got to the big leagues, I felt like I was prepared, mentally as much as physically."

John Farrell's debut came on August 18, at Cleveland Stadium for manager Doc Edwards. The Indians were 45-73 at the time, in last place, 25 games behind the first-place Blue Jays, and they had indeed suffered significant staff attrition, most recently an injury to Sammy Stewart. The game with the Brewers was tied, 8-8, after 11 innings. Farrell was Cleveland's fourth pitcher of the game; he worked the top of the 12th. "I had never thrown in relief in my life," he recalled. "The first two pitches I threw were base hits. I threw two pitches and had men on first and second."

Farrell gave up back-to-back singles to Paul Molitor and Robin Yount, but then induced Glenn Braggs to ground into a double play. He walked the next batter but another grounder got him out of the inning. The Indians loaded the bases, and a two-out single by Pat Tabler gave Farrell a win. "I'm in Cleveland all of six hours, throw 13-14 pitches, and get the victory. Imagine that," he said.[3]

Farrell pitched in nine more games that year, all of them starts. His second game was a complete-game win over the Tigers. He shut out the Brewers for nine innings on three hits for his second start, but the Indians' Doug Jones coughed up a run in the 10th and lost that one. In that game, Farrell had held Molitor hitless, snapping the hitter's 39-game streak. Molitor signed a ball for him, "Wishing you a great career." By season's end, Farrell was 5-1 with a 3.39 ERA. He finally had a winning record, when it most counted. The Indians, however, finished in last place, 37 games behind.

Farrell was considered "one of the rising pitching stars of the major leagues."[4] Two more very solid seasons followed. He was 14-10 in 1988 (4.24) in 31 games, all but one a start. And, though with a losing record (9-14) in 1989, he had changed his delivery and pitched distinctly better (a 3.63 ERA), with 132 strikeouts against 71 walks. The team finished sixth both years, in the seven-team AL East. On May 4, 1989, Farrell took a no-hitter into the ninth inning against Kansas City, but an error and then a Kevin Seitzer single brought the tying run to the plate. Doug Jones came on in relief and got a double play with his first pitch, retiring the side with two more pitches. Farrell got credit for the 3-1 win.

In 1990 Farrell's elbow finally gave out on him. He'd had recurring problems with it, on the 15-day DL as early as August 1998 with "right elbow tightness,"[5] and that springtime it delayed his start a bit. He was removed during the June 24 game to have his elbow examined and he missed three months, only coming back in late September. He pitched to a 4-5 (4.28) record in 17 starts. He underwent exploratory surgery in October. He had a bone chip removed, repaired a torn ligament, and had his ulnar nerve relocated. How had Farrell kept going for the couple of years the elbow had been bothering him? "A blue-collar background," he said. "Hard work is just something I grew up with, and maybe I just expected myself to keep going. Besides, I did have periods where the elbow didn't bother me."[6]

Farrell clearly needed even more tenacity. As it turned out, he needed a second operation in September 1991 – particularly frustrating in that he had just put in 11 months of rehabilitation work. "But there was no choice. There was no option. It had to be done again. I tore the ligament completely off the bone and they reattached it rather than transplanted. So I don't think structurally the procedure would have worked, the way it unfolded. Unfortunately. Another 15-16 months of rehab and I came back and made the team with the Angels. Which I think was a little surprising to a lot of people." He missed all of the 1991 and 1992 seasons. His right arm required two elbow reconstructions. And the Indians didn't want to carry him on the roster anymore; he was released in November 1991.

The California Angels took a flyer on Farrell, signing him in early 1992, even though they knew he wouldn't be able to pitch again until 1993. The Angels' senior vice president for baseball operations, Dan O'Brien, said, "It might sound corny, but it's true. If you can bet on a man's character and ability, then you've got a good chance to succeed. He's a bulldog with enormous character. I had faith in John, and John had faith in us."[7]

When Farrell did pitch, it was a disappointment to all concerned. He started the season for the Angels, worked a stint (4-5, 3.99) for Vancouver in midseason, and then finished up with the Angels. His major-league stats were 3-12 with a 7.35 earned-run average. He pitched in three May 1994 games (1-2) but with an ERA of 9.00, the Angels had pretty much seen enough. Farrell pitched some again for Vancouver, but was released in early June. The Indians signed him again and assigned him to Charlotte. Even at Triple-A, he had a 5.61 ERA that year.

Had he tried to come back too soon? Or was it just that the elbow was unable to be reconstructed sufficiently well to pitch in top form at the major-league level? "I missed 2½ years and I lost probably 4-5 miles an hour."

A more promising 1995 and in the beginning of 1996 with Buffalo led to some interest from the Detroit Tigers and a May 14 trade for minor-leaguer Greg Granger. It was the first of only two trades in Farrell's career. The second came in October 2012, when he was manager of the Toronto Blue Jays and was traded to the Red Sox with David Carpenter for infielder Mike Aviles.

Farrell's work in the big leagues in '95 and '96 was very brief. The Indians went to the World Series in 1995, but Farrell's only big-league appearance was on September 17 at Jacobs Field. It was a battle of division leaders; the Red Sox were visiting. Dennis Martinez gave up two runs in the first inning and manager Mike Hargrove called on Farrell to pitch the second. He did, retiring the side in order. In fact, he pitched 4⅔ innings of relief but gave up four runs (only two of them earned). The Indians scored five runs in the bottom of the sixth, so Farrell was off the hook.

The Indians swept the Red Sox in the Division Series, beat Seattle in six in the ALCS, but then lost to Atlanta in six games during the World Series.

In 1996 Farrell went to spring training with the Seattle Mariners but was released in March. In April he signed with the Indians and a month later was traded to the Tigers. He pitched in two

May games for the Tigers and took a loss in both. His final major-league stats were 36-46 (4.56, with a WHIP of 1.406).

The next year, 1997, Farrell returned to Oklahoma State and worked for five years in Stillwater as assistant coach and recruiting coordinator. He had a family to support – he'd become engaged before his senior year of college and married in the winter of 1984. He and his wife, Susan, raised three sons. At the time of the August 2014 interview, all three were still in the game. Jeremy, drafted by the Pirates in 2008, was in Double A with the White Sox. Shane, drafted in 2011 by Toronto, was in the front office for the Cubs, after his own shoulder injury. The youngest, Luke, drafted by Kansas City in 2013, was in Double-A.

"I retired in '96 at the All-Star Break. I needed 22 or 24 credits to finish my degree. We were living in southern Ohio at the time and I was commuting every weekend to Oklahoma back and forth, to finish my degree that semester. During that time I had talked to Mark [Shapiro of the Indians]. I was set to graduate in December and just didn't know what my next step was going to be. He said, 'You can go back to the minor leagues and you can be a pitching coach.' I said, 'You know, I just came out of the minor leagues.' I wasn't ready to go back in. He talked about the possibility of assistant farm director. I was unsure of that. So in the last month of school, Gary Ward stepped down from Oklahoma State and I approached the assistant, who looked like he was going to be named the head coach, and said, 'If you're looking for a pitching coach, I would love to talk to you about it.' Well, that's how it unfolded. I spent five years there.

"My path has been unusual. When I look back, there's five-year cycles."

All the while, Farrell maintained contact with Mark Shapiro and when Shapiro was set to take over as Cleveland's GM from John Hart after the 2001 season, John called Mark and said he'd be interested if a position was open. He was ready to make a move. He left the Cowboys to join the Indians. Shapiro appointed him farm director (director of player development). It may have been a surprise to go outside Organized Baseball for such an important hire, but Shapiro said, "I trust John's judgment implicitly, because he doesn't do things haphazardly. He thinks them through. There's a method to everything he does."[8]

It was another five-year stint for Farrell, and many felt he was "on the GM track."[9] But he responded to a call from Boston Red Sox manager (and former Indians teammate) Terry Francona. The two had stayed in touch as well, and even had a conversation when Francona was manager of the Phillies, but that was probably for a minor-league position, and Farrell figured he'd stay put.

Now the time was right. The Red Sox hired Farrell as the major-league pitching coach, to begin with the 2007 season. Dave Wallace had been pitching coach through the 2004 World Series win and the two years that followed, but Boston elected not to renew Wallace's contract. It was the first coaching position Farrell ever had, other than at Oklahoma State in 1997.[10] "First time I was a pitching coach in pro baseball." He was someone Francona really wanted. "This isn't a thing where you start lining up friends and friendships," Francona said. "What I wanted was someone who I thought could be an outstanding pitching coach for the Boston Red Sox."[11]

One of Farrell's first challenges was dealing with newly acquired Japanese star Daisuke Matsuzaka. Farrell even devoted some time in the springtime studying Japanese with a tutor.[12] Aided as well by having superb catcher Jason Varitek behind the plate, "Dice-K" won 15 games his first year, and was 18-3 his second with a 2.90 ERA. Farrell's staff posted a league-best 3.87 ERA in 2007 and in his first year with the Red Sox they reached the heights once more, finishing first in the AL East and sweeping the Angels in the Division Series. They then had to fight all seven games to beat the Indians in the ALCS (clearly overcoming a strong Cleveland team, most of whom had been developed or acquired during Farrell's time there). The Red Sox swept the Colorado Rockies in the World Series.

"Fenway Park is an amazing place, a great place to work," he said. "The fans are so passionate. You feed off their passion."[13] Farrell served as Red Sox pitching coach in 2008, 2009, and 2010, and the Francona/Farrell working relationship seemed to be an excellent one. Their work helped produce trips to postseason play in both 2008 and 2009.

The Toronto Blue Jays made Farrell their field manager starting in 2011. He led the team for two years, and two fourth-place finishes, but the Red Sox really wanted him back after their disastrous fifth-place finish in 2012. Francona's contract had not been renewed after 2011 and Bobby Valentine had managed the Red Sox for the one season. After finishing last in the AL East, Valentine was let go. Farrell clearly wanted to come back to Boston, so Toronto chose not to stand in the way and a deal was effected, with the Blue Jays getting the very capable shortstop Mike Aviles in trade. And the 2013 Red Sox went from worst to first, winning it all. John Farrell was a world champion again, this time in his first year as field manager for the Red Sox.

It had been a lateral move, of course: major-league manager to major-league manager. Was there something about the city of Boston, or the organization, that maybe appealed to him? "All the above. All the above. Established relationships with Ben [Cherington], Mike Hazen, many others. There was a personal connection to the medical community here with our youngest son having to go through his own surgeries and radiation. There was a lot here. Plus, it always felt like a very unique place to me – whether that was coming in as a player back in the '80s and early '90s or having been here for the four years as pitching coach. It's always felt like there's been a connection here."

The 2013 Red Sox were known as the "Band of Bearded Brothers" – as the NESN retrospective DVD proclaimed. The bombing of the Boston Marathon in April had brought the team, and the city, together in a special way, but most of the team had already begun to grow beards before that, forging a certain kind of bond between the players. Since Farrell had studied Japanese with his two pitchers from Japan, why had he not grown a beard in 2013? "I've never had one, and I wasn't about to start." And there are benefits to maintaining a degree of distance between manager and players. The team could hardly have been more successful in 2013, only out of first place for two weeks in May and four days in July, winning the ALDS in four games, the ALCS over the Tigers in six, and the World Series over the St. Louis Cardinals in six games – winning a World Series in front of a Boston home crowd for the first time since 1918.

Things went south in 2014, however, and the Red Sox struggled badly, in last place at the All-Star Break – when Farrell had the honor of managing the American League team to a win. It was a worst-to-first-to-worst odyssey during the regular season with Boston back in last place again. In 2015, the Sox remained mired in last place again. Farrell had bigger problems. He was diagnosed with cancer. He had to take a leave in August to be treated for lymphoma. Torey Lovullo managed the team on August 11, and then from August 14 through the end of the season. As of August 12, the Sox were 12 ½ games out of first place in the AL East, with even fourth-place Baltimore being five games out. Farrell beat cancer and was back to lead the team in 2016. After two last-place finishes, there were many who felt that Farrell's cancer may have saved him his job. The PR nightmare of firing a manager battling cancer would have been horrific.

In 2016, the Red Sox finished first in first place. The 2016 Red Sox were, however, swept by the Cleveland Indians in the Division Series. The day after the final game of the ALDS, President of Baseball Operations Dave Dombrowski announced that John Farrell would be back in 2017.

That he was – and once more the Red Sox finished first, two games ahead of the Yankees. There was no middle ground; in the Farrell years it was either feast or famine. From 2013 through 2017, it was first-worst-worst-first-first.

The 2017 Sox lost the Division Series to the Houston Astros in four games. On October 11, despite placing first in the Al East for two years in succession, the Red Sox announced that they were replacing John Farrell as manager of the Red Sox. Alex Cora was hired as manager for 2018.

Farrell enjoyed one rare moment in 2017. On September 23, in Cincinnati, he was managing the Red Sox when Cincinnati Reds manager Bryan Price brought in John's son Luke Farrell to pitch the top of the ninth. Boston held a 5–0 lead. Luke walked two but escaped without giving up a run.

In March 2018, the Cincinnati Reds hired Farrell as an advisor and scout.[14] In the same month, he also landed a position with ESPN as a studio analyst on their *Baseball Tonight* television show.[15]

SOURCES:

In addition to the sources noted in this biography, the author also accessed Farrell's player file from the National Baseball Hall of Fame, the *Encyclopedia of Minor League Baseball*, Retrosheet.org, Baseball-Reference.com, and the SABR Minor Leagues Database, accessed online at Baseball-Reference.com.

NOTES

1. Author interview with John Farrell, August 21, 2014. Unless otherwise indicated, all quotations from John Farrell are from this interview.
2. *Boston Globe*, July 17, 2014.
3. *Cleveland Plain Dealer*, June 16, 2002.
4. *Los Angeles Times*, April 8, 1988.
5. *Cleveland Plain Dealer*, September 7, 1988
6. *Orange County Register* (Anaheim, California), February 25, 1992.
7. *Orange County Register*, April 16, 1993
8. *Cleveland Plain Dealer*, June 16, 2002.
9. *Albany Times-Union*, October 22, 2006.
10. *Cleveland Plain Dealer*, April 21, 2008.
11. *Boston Globe*, October 17, 2006.
12. "I hired a guy who went to Case Western Reserve University, a Japanese student, to get some familiarity. And then in spring training, the Red Sox had hired a language teacher. So Daisuke, Hideki Okajima, myself, and the instructor, we had three mornings a week for half an hour. The instructor would teach them English; they would teach me Japanese. It helped us kind of form a different type of relationship other than just on the field."
13. *Cleveland Plain Dealer*, April 21, 2008.
14. Anthony Castrovince, "Farrell Joins Reds As Scout," MLB.com, March 14, 2018. https://www.mlb.com/news/john-farrell-joins-cincinnati-reds-as-scout/c-268722720
15. Pete Dougherty, "ESPN Lands Former Red Sox Manager to Studio Show," *Albany Times-Union*, March 23, 2018.

BRIAN GILES

BY MARK HODERMARSKY

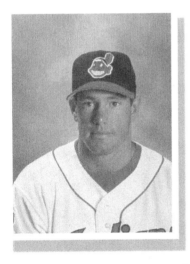

Were it not for the misfortune of attempting to break into the most talented major-league outfield of the 1990s, Brian Giles, as his post-Cleveland career confirms, might have earned a place in Heritage Park at Progressive Field as a member of the Indians Hall of Fame. In Giles' four seasons with the Tribe, 1995-1998, playing alongside stars Albert Belle, Manny Ramirez, Kenny Lofton, and David Justice limited the young slugger's plate appearances. Despite flashing admirable offensive stats and fine defensive range when inserted into the lineup, Giles was traded to the Pittsburgh Pirates after the 1998 season in exchange for reliever Ricardo Rincon in one of the worst deals in Cleveland baseball memory. Over the next 11 seasons, Giles made it impossible for Indians fans to forget the lopsided deal. For the Pirates and later the Padres, Giles proved to be one of the game's most consistent, though underappreciated, sluggers, until a chronic knee injury ended his 15-year career in 2009.

A native of El Cajon, California, in San Diego County and a 1989 graduate of Granite Hills High School, Giles was inducted into his alma mater's athletic hall of fame in 2008 for his exploits on the diamond, gridiron, and wrestling mat. He "slugged two homers in a game ... and scored four touchdowns in a game" among many other feats.[1] Granite Hills boasted one of the best high-school football backfields in the country. Running alongside Giles was Touchdown Tommy Vardell, a future star running back at Stanford, a first-round draft pick of the Cleveland Browns, and an eight-year fullback in the NFL. Giles' former baseball coach, Gordy Thompson, remembered him as "a disciplined athlete with a good sense of humor" and a "work ethic that is second to none."[2] In 1989 Giles was voted the best San Diego County Male Athlete of the Year.

Bill and Monica Giles, Brian's parents, raised four children - Brian, Marcus (seven-year big-leaguer mostly with Atlanta), Kami, and Brandi. His parents "were also crazy for baseball. Bill coached both boys in the Singing Hills Little League, and it was not unusual for the entire Giles clan to convene at a nearby ballfield for a little family BP. Dad would pitch, Brian and Marcus would hit, and Mom and the girls would play the field."[3] As is the case with most young ballplayers, Brian had a hero - Padres star and future Hall of Famer Dave Winfield. For Marcus, his hero was his big brother, Brian. Drafted by the Indians in the 17th round of the 1989 amateur free-agent draft, Giles batted .310 at Burlington (Rookie League) in 1989, .289 at Watertown (low Class

A), and .310 at Kinston (advanced Class A) in his first three years of professional ball but displayed little power, hitting only five home runs in the low minors. Promoted to Double-A Canton-Akron in the middle of 1992, the young (21) outfielder saw his career blossom. In his first full season with the Indians' Eastern League affiliate, Giles' .327/.409/.452 (BA/OBP/SLG) and his 18 steals in 30 attempts began to turn front-office heads in downtown Cleveland. As prominent was a trait that separated Giles from most other players throughout his career – plate discipline. In that season he walked 57 times while striking out only 43 times in 496 plate appearances.

Giles' physique began to swell along with his statistics. As dedicated in the weight room as he was on the field, Giles transformed his 5-foot-11, 195-pound frame into chiseled granite, and the added muscle and strength produced better power numbers as he moved up to Triple A. In Charlotte (1994) and Buffalo (1995) Giles belted 16 and 15 homers, and his slash line improved. Called up to the Indians on September 16, 1995, for an end-of-the season look-see, Giles did not disappoint, going for 5-for-9 and smashing the first of his 287 major-league home runs.

Giles' 1996 stats at Buffalo (.314/.395./.594 with 20 home runs in 83 games) made it clear to the Tribe brass that he required no additional minor-league seasoning. Called up in July, he was in the big leagues for good. In 51 games for the Indians, he hit .355 with a .612 slugging average and five home runs. Over the next two years, 1997 and 1998, Giles shared left field with David Justice and played some in center and right and at DH.

From 1996 to 1998 Giles played in three American League Division Series, two American League Championship Series, and one World Series with the powerful Indians. In the gut-wrenching seven-game 1997 Series loss to the Florida Marlins, Giles had eight plate appearances in five games and was 2-for-4 with a double.

Desperate for pitching help, the Indians traded the 27-year-old Giles for Pirates reliever Rincon on November 18, 1998, in a deal that would catapult the burgeoning slugger into National League stardom while leaving a multitude of head-scratching Tribe fans bewildered. Rincon proved to be an ordinary bullpen lefty in four years with Cleveland, posting a 3.73 ERA and crumbling in two ALDS opportunities, giving up five earned runs in 2⅔ innings.

In 1999 Giles instantly became the face of the lowly Pirates franchise by blasting 39 some runs and batting in 115 runs. His full tenure as a Pirate was equally productive. Indeed, David Golebiewski of Fangraphs makes "an argument that Giles was one of the top 10 most valuable properties in the game during his time in Pittsburgh [1999-2003]" through a sabermetric statistic, WPA/LI, that represents the sum of win expectancy per-play divided by leverage index. Golebiewski ranked Giles third in the majors in 1999 within this measurement.[4] To translate, only two players in all of baseball that year contributed more often to a win than Giles.

Another skill as a hitter that Golebiewski validated sabermetrically was Giles' plate discipline, pointing out his capacity to avoid striking out, to make contact, and to walk. As Golebiewski wrote, "If you want a player who knows the strike zone better than the man in blue behind him, then Brian Giles is your guy."[5]

For four straight seasons (1999-2002) Giles batted .300-plus with at least 35 home runs for Pittsburgh. But on August 26, 2003, before the nonwaiver trading deadline, Giles, who was enjoying another excellent year at the plate, was sent to his hometown but last-place San Diego Padres for left-handed pitcher Oliver Perez and outfielder Jason Bay.

In seven seasons with the Padres (2003-2009), Giles slammed 83 home runs despite playing at Petco Park, a very unfriendly hitters' ballpark. On April 8, 2004, in the first game at Petco Park, he got the ballpark's first hit. In 2007 he was teammates with younger brother Marcus Giles, who had a seven-year major-league career as a second baseman primarily with the Atlanta Braves.

Giles played in only 61 games in 2009 because of arthritis in his right knee. It became increasingly painful as the season wore on. He did not appear in a game after June 18. A free agent after the season, he made a comeback attempt the next year with the Los Angeles Dodgers but it lasted only briefly as the knee issues returned in a spring-training game. "Cutting in that game, I was starting to feel [knee pain]. It was getting to me, and it takes the fun out of [the game]. It's time and I'm content with it," he said at the time. "Physically, I'm not able to do what I like to do. I really have no regrets. I played the game hard, respected the game."[6]

A Padre teammate, outfielder Scott Hairston, described Giles as "one of the best I played with. He just grinded it out, each and every at-bat. … Personally, I took it as a privilege to play with a guy like that for a few years. He brought a lot of laughs to the clubhouse. He had a great career." Another teammate, closer Heath Bell, remembered Giles as "a fun guy, upbeat, even when he was hurt."[7]

Giles' focused, hardscrabble, and fearless style of play directly contrasted with his clubhouse decorum. Former Padres GM Kevin Towers said, "I'd be in (former manager Bruce) Bochy's office having a serious meeting and Brian would come in fully naked, showing his batting stance. He's normal except for the tanning booths, shaving his body and walking around with no clothes."[8]

Giles was selected for the All-Star Game twice (2000, 2001) and named Player of the Week five times. He led NL left fielders in assists (13) in 2002. Several factors have hurt Giles' legacy and fair-minded consideration as a future Hall-of-Famer.

According to Ben Jedlovec, if Giles "had been given a lineup spot rather than wallowing in Triple-A for three seasons, his career totals would have been more noteworthy. Spending six years in Petco Park probably cost him a few dozen home runs as well."[9] Playing on small-market/mostly bottom-feeding teams (Pirates and Padres) didn't work in his favor either. In addition, Giles performed during an era of record-shattering (steroid-triggered) home-run achievements, diminishing the importance of the more than respectable number he clouted. Jedlovec only 12 players have hit more home runs with a better walk-to-strikeout ratio than Giles, including Barry Bonds and Albert Pujols. "The other 10 are Hall of Famers named Williams, Musial, DiMaggio, Gehrig, Ott, Morgan, Berra, Mize, Ruth, and Hornsby. While few would group Giles with 10 inner-circle Hall of Famers, it's clear that his combination of power and patience is in elite company."[10]

A couple of events brought national attention, albeit controversial, to Giles. The first was a domestic-violence suit brought by a former girlfriend in 2008.[11] The second, and more damaging to Giles' on-the-field reputation, concerned former Pirates catcher Jason Kendall who, in a 2009 personal divorce court filing, "disclosed that Brian Giles is someone that he has known since 1997 and when asked if Giles uses Adderall [a banned MLB substance], Kendall said, 'I believe so.'"[12] Giles never admitted using a banned substance and has never been tested positive.

The Indians of 1995 will be affectionately regarded for returning the American League pennant to Cleveland for the first time in 41 years. Not to be overlooked on this powerful squad, however, should be a 24-year-old rookie, whose career achievements matched many of those posted by the more familiar names of Belle, Ramirez, Lofton, and Justice. And as the 50th anniversary of the San Diego Padres nears (2019) and Brian Giles' remarkable tenure with the Friars is re-examined, the San Diego high school legend will spark even greater regard.

NOTES

1. Leonel Sanchez, "Granite Hills Honors Alumnus Giles," *San Diego Union-Tribune,* January 24, 2008. Retrieved on November 2, 2017.
2. Ibid.
3. "Marcus Giles," jockbio.com, 2008. Retrieved November 4, 2017.
4. David Golebiewski, "Brian Giles Owns the Strike Zone," fangraphs.com, November 18, 2008. Retrieved on November 3, 2017.
5. Ibid.
6. Tom Singer and Corey Brock, "No Regrets: Giles Calls It a Career," MLB.com, March 11, 2010. Retrieved on October 24, 2017.
7. Ibid.
8. Bob Nightengale, "Welcome to the Quirky, Zany World of Brothers Giles," *USA Today,* March 17, 2007. Retrieved on October 29, 2017.
9. Ben Jedlovec, "Brian Giles, Hall of Fame Class of 2016?" *The Hardball Times,* July 22, 2014. Retrieved on November 3, 2017.
10. Jedlovec.
11. "Legal Battle Between Ex-Padres Player Brian Giles, Former Fiancé Cheri Oliver Headed Back to Court," 10news.com, June 9, 2013. Retrieved on November 6, 2017.
12. Vlad, "Jason Kendall Implicates Brian Giles, Bobby Crosby in Possible Adderall Use," bucsdugout.com, March 11, 2010. Retrieved on November 3, 2017

JASON GRIMSLEY

BY CHIP GREENE

To experience the heart-pounding thrill of espionage, the horror of a plane falling from the sky, or the dread of government agents laying siege to your home, would by itself be enough for any person's lifetime, let alone enduring all three – not to mention, all while engaged in the rigors of a major-league baseball career. Yet that's what happened to Jason Alan Grimsley. Oh, and we shouldn't overlook the World Series rings that he won.

That's quite a scrapbook for an "aw-shucks" kid from Cleveland, Texas, near Houston. Born on August 7, 1967, by all accounts Grimsley grew up, along with his brother, Joe, in a close-knit family nurtured by their parents, Johnny, a pipeline welder, and Judy. Living out in the country, the Grimsley boys undoubtedly were free to roam and play. One anecdote evokes visions of the kind of childhood they must have led, but also depicts the natural athleticism young Jason assuredly possessed. When he turned 12 years old, his parents gave him and his brother dirt bikes to ride over acres of land, owned by Mrs. Grimsley's family, that adjoined the Grimsleys' homestead. One day, while riding through his aunt's backyard, Jason caught his big toe on a tree stump. Although the toe was eventually amputated, several months later Grimsley earned a spot on his eighth-grade basketball team, and later that spring took second in the high jump at a regional competition. (Years later, after he battled throughout his professional career to conquer control problems on the mound, it would be written of Grimsley that "executives have speculated for years that his control might have been greatly improved if he had more stability on the foot he lands on in his delivery."[1])

Moving to the next scholastic athletic level, Grimsley proved even better; at Cleveland's Tarkington High School, he became a star. Besides leading the school football team as the starting quarterback, Grimsley displayed a nasty slider on the pitching mound. That drew the attention of the Philadelphia Phillies, who selected the 6-foot-3, 180-pound right-hander in the 10th round of the 1985 amateur draft.

Grimsley was as raw as a prospect could be. Beginning with the Phillies' short-season Class A Northwest League affiliate in Bend, Oregon, the 17-year-old spent the next four seasons in Utica, New York; Spartanburg, South Carolina; Clearwater, Florida; and Reading, Pennsylvania, trying to harness his often-stunning bouts of wildness and learning how to pitch. It rarely came easy, as evidenced from his body of work during that period. From his first minor-league pitch in 1985 until the evening of his major-league debut in September 1989, Grimsley pitched in 90 minor-league games (69 starts) and threw 459 innings. Over that span he averaged 6.2 walks per nine innings (down from 19.9 and 10.7 in his first 20 games), as well as 6.3 hit batsmen and 9.6 wild pitches per season (11 and 18, respectively, in his first full season). Over that same span, though, he allowed just under seven hits per nine innings and struck out almost eight, clearly a sign of his overwhelming potential.

By September 5, 1989, Grimsley finally appeared to have, if not cured, at least minimized his wildness, winning 11 games with a 2.98 ERA in 26 starts for the Double-A Reading Phillies (Eastern League); over his last five starts, his ERA had been a minuscule 1.47.[2] That day, despite having never yet pitched at Triple A, Grimsley was called to Philadelphia, where he joined the last-place Phillies in the middle of a homestand vs. the Pittsburgh Pirates.

"I thought he'd be all right to bring here [from Double A]," said Phillies general manager Lee Thomas at the time. "He's confident. He's not a shy guy. I believe if a guy can pitch at Double A, he can play here."[3]

Thus began Grimsley's often tumultuous, well-traveled 15-year major-league career.

Three days after his recall, the Phillies were in Montreal to play the Expos. With Grimsley's arrival, Phillies left-handed starter Dennis Cook had been moved to the bullpen, so that night Grimsley went to the mound as a starter in his major-league debut. Through 3½ innings the teams were scoreless. In the bottom of the fourth, the Expos nailed Grimsley for a triple and single to take a 1-0 lead. In the top of the fifth, however, the Phillies scored three times. In the top of the sixth, Grimsley was pulled for a pinch-hitter, and when Philadelphia held on for a 4-3 win, he was the winning pitcher, the first of his 42 career victories. Over the remaining three weeks of the season, Grimsley made three additional starts but struggled mightily with his control, allowing 19 walks in just 18⅓ innings. He lost each of those games.

It had been an inauspicious start for the 21-year-old, but he was solidly on the Phillies radar … for a time, at least. Grimsley opened the next season, 1990, with the Triple-A Scranton/Wilkes-Barre Red Barons. As the Phillies, showing improved play on their way to an eventual 10-win increase and fourth-place finish in the National League East, hung around the .500 mark for the first half of the season, Grimsley won eight games as a starter for Scranton and limited his walks to just over five per nine innings. Then the Phillies began to lose steam. Once again, they recalled Grimsley to Philadelphia. This time he fared much better.

Arguably, the 11 starts Grimsley made for the Phillies over the final three months of the 1990 season, during which he won three and posted a 3.30 ERA, proved the pinnacle of his career as a starter. For in the following year, after opening the season in the Phillies rotation, he endured an abysmal 1-7 record in 12 starts, and in August, following a stint on the disabled list and a rehab assignment, was optioned back to Scranton/Wilkes-Barre. It proved to be the end of his Phillies career.

(In 1999, then with the Yankees, and at the height of his career, Grimsley told a sportswriter for the *New York Daily News* about the years he had spent bouncing around the minor leagues: "Hey, I've gotten to play baseball for a living. I wouldn't have met my wife (Dana) without it, because we met when I was in spring training with the Phillies in 1991 at a Chamber of Commerce event I was obligated to go to by the club."[4] Eventually, the Grimsleys produced three children: sons Hunter and John-John, and daughter Rayne.

If Grimsley proved a frustrating prospect for Philadelphia, so too did another right-hander, Curt Schilling, prove equally frustrating for the Houston Astros. As Schilling entered the Astros' 1992 spring training "overweight, under-inspired and out of options,"[5] Grimsley, too, was out of options, meaning the Phillies had to either keep him on their 25-man roster or risk losing him to waivers. As the end of spring training neared, it was rumored that the Phillies were trying to acquire outfielder Ruben Sierra from the Texas Rangers in a trade that would include Grimsley.[6]

Whether or not that rumor was true became moot on April 2, however, when the Phillies and Astros consummated a trade of their disappointing right-handers. It was a deal that proved overwhelmingly one-sided. As Schilling blossomed, going 14-11 with a 2.35 ERA and solidified himself in the Phillies rotation, Grimsley spent the entire 1992 season at Triple-A Tucson, where he produced a hefty 5.05 ERA.

Grimsley's season was a tale of two halves. During the first half he was terrible, posting a record of 1-5 with an astronomical ERA. Over the second half, though, he finished a promising 7-2 and ended the season with 55 walks in 124⅔ innings pitched. Looking to build on that second-half success, Grimsley went after the season to Venezuela, where he pitched for Magallanes. He threw well, walking only seven batters in 30⅔ innings. There, one night, Florida Marlins scouting director Gary Hughes watched Grimsley pitch.

"The only thing that gets him in trouble," said Hughes, "is terrible control. He has real good stuff. If he's around the plate he can beat anybody, but there always seems to come a time when – boom – he loses it."[7] That night Grimsley had gone eight innings and allowed just one run, but walked five.

Later, Grimsley told the press, "Everything is upbeat. It looks like things are turning around. (Astros officials) said in the newspaper the way I threw in Venezuela, I'd put my hat in the ring for the fifth starter's spot." About his improvement in the second half of the season, Grimsley said, "I was throwing across my body. Now I have found a consistent release. All I've got to do is get consistent, throw strikes. My ball has always moved. Now I have an idea how to use that to advantage."[8] That optimism, though, proved illusory.

On March 30, 1993, Grimsley was released by the Astros. He wasn't unemployed for long. Tragically, on March 22 Cleveland Indians pitchers Steve Olin and Tim Crews had been killed in a spring-training boating accident in Florida. With starting pitcher Bob Ojeda injured in the accident, too, the Indians were desperate for pitching. On April 7 Cleveland signed Grimsley as a free agent and sent him to their Triple-A affiliate at Charlotte. Grimsley quickly set about trying to resurrect his career.

Managed by Charlie Manuel, who would later win a World Series with the Phillies, the 1993 Charlotte Knights, who finished 83-58, featured some of the players who would shortly arrive in Cleveland and take the Indians to multiple World Series, Manny Ramirez, Jim Thome, et al. Put in the starting rotation, he pitched well through mid-August, posting a 3.39 ERA and limiting his walks to 3.2 per nine innings. Then he got a call to join the Indians. On August 25 in Toronto, Grimsley made his first major-league relief appearance, surrendering three hits and two runs in 2⅓ innings. After three more relief stints, Grimsley started on September 2 at Minnesota and allowed two runs in six innings, walking five. After that game, a no-decision of Grimsley, Indians manager Mike Hargrove assessed, "I thought Jason threw very well. The only thing that bothered me is that he pitched behind in the count too much. I thought he threw enough strikes so that I didn't have to cross my fingers. I liked what I saw. He has good stuff. His ball moves all over the place."[9] Hargrove gave Grimsley five more starts before the season was ended, during which Grimsley allowed four earned runs in 19 innings over the last three games, and things looked promising for him to contend for a rotation spot in 1994. But he failed to make the squad in '94 and was sent to Charlotte.

In June the Indians, struggling to find a reliable fifth starter, recalled Grimsley. As the Indians surged to a 66-47 record and a second-place finish in the American League Central Division, Grimsley won five games and walked 3.7 batters per nine innings in the period before a strike by the players union ended the season. But it was a game in which he didn't pitch that would later garner for Grimsley the most attention.

Two noteworthy things happened during the 1994 season. One was the players strike; the other was a caper the press dubbed "Batgate."

In April 1999 Grimsley confessed to the caper, which had stumped the sport for five years. On July 15, 1994, the Indians played the White Sox in Chicago. Before the game someone tipped off White Sox manager Gene Lamont that Indians slugger Albert Belle's bat was corked. Lamont challenged the use of the bat, and umpire Dave Phillips took the bat and stored it in his locker in the umpire's room. Panic ensued among the Indians, who knew that the bat was corked. So, Grimsley volunteered to retrieve it.

"It was mission impossible," Grimsley said.[10] ... "We were sitting there in a pennant race, and for some reason I got it into my head, 'Go get the bat.' I just went over and got it."[11] Assuming that the umpires' room was on the same side of the ballpark as was the Indians' clubhouse, Grimsley climbed through the false ceiling of the clubhouse, crawled on his belly with a flashlight in his mouth, found the hatch to the umpires room, and dropped down onto a refrigerator. Once inside, Grimsley took Belle's bat from the locker and exchanged it with one that bore the signature of teammate Paul Sorrento, the evidence that ultimately led the umpires to suspect foul play. The police were called to the scene and the White Sox threatened to press charges; but in the end the Indians were told that if they supplied Belle's bat, there would be no punishment for the switch.

Throughout the caper, Grimsley later related, "My heart was going a thousand miles a second."[12] Belle received a 10-game suspension, which was later reduced to seven games. Until Grimsley's confession five years later, the culprit went unidentified.

That the stolen-bat escapade generated more excitement in baseball circles than Grimsley's pitching is indicative of his fortunes over the next four years. He labored to remain a viable major-league pitcher. As the Indians broke a 41-year drought and went to the World Series in 1995, Grimsley pitched in just 15 games for the Tribe, only two as a starter; he ended the season at Triple-A Buffalo. Then, on February 15, 1996, Cleveland shipped Grimsley and right-hander Pep Harris to the California Angels for left-hander Brian Anderson. Although Grimsley started 20 games that season for the Angels, his ERA was 6.84. In October he was released.

Over the next two seasons, Grimsley reached his nadir. Beginning in January 1997, when he signed a minor-league deal with the Detroit Tigers, he bounced among three organizations (Milwaukee, Kansas City, and Cleveland, again), without returning to the major leagues. By the end of 1998, after 52 relief appearances for Buffalo, the Indians' Triple-A affiliate, Grimsley must have questioned whether his career was over, for that fall, at age 31, he was released by Cleveland. As it turned out, though, his fortunes were soon dramatically changed.

Among pitchers, baseball history is rife with reclamation projects. That's what Grimsley was in 1999, and that season he turned his career around. As Grimsley performed well at Buffalo in 1998, the Yankees director of player personnel, Billy Connors, a former pitcher, watched him pitch and persuaded the Yankees to sign Grimsley. New York signed him to a minor-league contract with an invitation to spring training. (They also threw in a $10,000 bonus.)[13]

At spring training in Tampa, Florida, Connors persuaded Grimsley to change his repertoire, which to that point consisted of four pitches: two fastballs, a curve, and a slider; rather than mixing his pitches Grimsley would refine control of one devastating pitch, a sinking fastball. The results were immediate and impressive: Grimsley earned a spot on the Opening Day roster.

Coming out of the bullpen, he started the year strongly. Early in the season, Yankees reliever Jeff Nelson went on the disabled list, so Grimsley got lots of work. He put together a string of strong performances – so strong, in fact, that questions about the nature of those performances soon arose. It was statistically quite a stunning turnaround. Entering the season, Grimsley had compiled a major-league ERA of 5.39, allowing 450 hits in 426 innings pitched. By contrast, through the end of May 1999, he was practically unhittable: In $29\frac{1}{3}$ innings pitched he allowed only 17 hits and struck out 25 while walking only 7; with a 4-0 record, his ERA was 2.15.

Accusations arose that Grimsley was doctoring the baseball. On May 9 at Yankee Stadium, Seattle manager Lou Piniella complained to the umpire that Grimsley's pitches were "sinking and moving too much to be a product of natural forces."[14] On May 26, Boston's Jose Offerman grabbed the ball after striking out against Grimsley and checked it for cuts. No marks were found.

Whether or not Grimsley was doing something to the ball, sportswriters praised his singular "power sinker." "What Grimsley is doing could not be more simple," wrote Buster Olney in the *New York Times*. "He grips the ball with his right index and middle fingers close together, between the seams, his fingertips resting in the spot where a player might sign an autograph, and he throws as hard as he can. There is no mystery. There is no deception."[15] Yankees catcher Joe Girardi offered, "His sinker is unbelievable. The movement is so hard, and it's so late."[16]

The hitters knew Grimsley's sinker was coming; he threw it 85 percent of the time. Olney wrote, "They cannot hit it. The sinker is unusual in that it moves vertically, straight down, rather than at a downward 45-degree angle. ... The movement ... is so violent that scouts sitting behind home plate have asked each other if Grimsley is throwing a split-fingered fastball."[17]

For his part, Grimsley took all the accusations in stride, stating, "I take that more or less as a compliment. I hope everybody complains, because that will tell me my ball is moving more or less the way I want it to."[18] It was a far cry from his previous two years in baseball's wasteland.

But Grimsley's effectiveness didn't last. Over the second half of the season he began to struggle, and through one two-week stretch in September, manager Joe Torre didn't use him at all. Grimsley finished the regular season with a 3.60 ERA in 55 games.

There was one celebratory moment to come, however. Grimsley has been left off the postseason roster during the first two rounds of the playoffs (Yankees wins over Texas and Boston). For the World Series, vs. the Atlanta Braves, Torre made him eligible. In Game Three, at Yankee Stadium, Grimsley relieved starter Andy Pettitte in the top of the fourth inning with the Yankees trailing 5-1, two outs, and a man on first. Over the next 2⅓ innings, despite allowing two hits and surrendering two walks, Grimsley held the Braves scoreless, and New York eventually came back to win 6-5 in 10 innings. The next night, the Yankees won the World Series.

As 2000 arrived, Grimsley had a few productive years left – and several terrifying and frustrating episodes to experience. In January, he re-signed with the Yankees. After an inconsistent regular season (5.04 ERA in 63 games), Grimsley made what would be his final postseason appearances, facing Seattle in Games One and Five of New York's victorious ALCS. He didn't play in the World Series, and in November was released.

In January 2001, Grimsley signed with Kansas City and began what became his longest tenure with one team, pitching in 251 games over 3½ seasons for the Royals. Traded in June 2004 to the Baltimore Orioles, after the season the 36-year-old pitcher had Tommy John surgery on his pitching elbow. During his rehab period Grimsley's first terrifying episode occurred.

In 2003 the Grimsleys had bought a house in a Kansas City suburb, Overland Park, Kansas, where the family planned to settle after his career ended. On Friday morning, January 21, 2005, Grimsley left the house to drop his boys off at school and take his car to the dealer for service. Dana was home with daughter Rayne, working out in the basement. At about 9:30 a twin-engine Cessna airplane carrying five passengers heading for a golf outing in Florida took off from an airport two miles from the Grimsleys' house. A moment later the plane slammed into the house's concrete foundation and tore through the porch.

"I heard it coming down," Dana said. "I looked to my right and saw it come down. It was in a different room of the house, so I didn't see it hit. I ran upstairs from the basement with Rayne. We called 911 and ran out."[19] Neither was injured.

Grimsley's Nissan pickup was parked in front of the house. When the plane hit the house, it exploded, sending a shower of shrapnel far enough down the street to cause a police blockade two blocks long. One piece slammed into the truck, which caught fire.

When he arrived, Grimsley surveyed the damage but rejected any sense of pity for the family's loss, instead offering condolences for the passengers and admiration for the pilot. "We're going to our friends' house," he said. "And that's why we made this place our home: The people that have offered help are so gracious. But we don't need help. I'm just concerned about the family members of the gentlemen who lost their lives. They're the ones who need help."

"From what I saw, at the last second you could see the pilot did everything he could to avoid the house. ... You can see that from the angle the plane went in. His last thought was the safety of his passengers. And the fact is, he had the presence of mind and grace to do what he did."[20]

The Grimsleys eventually repaired the house and returned.

By the summer of 2005, Grimsley was finally ready to pitch again. As he prepared to return to the Orioles' active roster, Grimsley told a *Baltimore Sun* sportswriter, "I know the end is near. But this is, like, my second chance. Nobody loves going out there more than me. There's a part of you that plays this game that never grows up. Remember 'Field of Dreams'? Walking out there again between those white lines and chasing that dream – that's what I want to feel."[21]

Grimsley returned to work with the Orioles on July 15 and pitched in 22 games. After the season the Orioles released him.

In December the 38-year old Grimsley signed a one-year, $825,000 contract with the Arizona Diamondbacks. On May 31 the Diamondbacks were in New York to play the Mets. Arizona had been on a roll, winning 7 of their last 10 games. That night at Shea Stadium, the two teams went into the 13th inning tied 0-0. In the bottom of the inning, Grimsley, the sixth Arizona pitcher, came on in relief, faced three batters, and allowed the winning run. It turned out to be his last major-league appearance.

A week later, his career came to an end. On June 6 IRS and FBI agents, armed with a search warrant, raided Grimsley's home in Scottsdale, Arizona, and seized numerous items: a digital phone and answering machine; cellphone; bank and credit-card statements; checkbooks, other financial records, and other electronics. It was the culmination of an investigation that had gone on for many months. In April, investigators had traced a shipment of illegal human growth hormone (HGH) to Grimsley's home and confronted him. During interrogation, Grimsley admitted using illegal performance-enhancing drugs (PEDs) as a means to circumvent baseball's policy against illegal steroids. Grimsley also, according to later reports, named other players who were using PEDS. For that, most would never forgive him.

That night, as the Diamondbacks played the Phillies at home, Grimsley was warming up in the bullpen when he learned that his confession was soon going to be made public. The next day he asked the team to release him, confessed to his teammates, cleaned out his locker, and left the game for good. (Initially, the Diamondbacks offered to pay Grimsley the remainder of his salary, $504,000. Then they rescinded that offer. Determined to fight for his money, Grimsley eventually agreed to disburse the money among four charities.)

Had Grimsley elected to continue his career, he would have faced a mandatory 50-game suspension in 2007. Instead, he chose to retire. He was never charged with any crime. The Grimsleys returned to Overland Park determined to keep a low profile. Having made almost $10 million in his career, Grimsley was set financially. In Overland Park, he opened JOCO Baseball, an indoor batting and pitching instructional facility for youth and high school players. The academy was housed in a nondescript building that bore no marking of its owner. Additionally, Grimsley had invested with former teammate David Wells in a New York nightspot called Plum, and had also put money into a cousin's Houston-based company that managed hospital pharmacies. Grimsley was also involved in commercial properties around Kansas City; an Internet pet supply business; and a car wash.

By all accounts Grimsley still calls Overland Park his home.

SOURCES

In addition to the sources cited in the Notes, the author also consulted Baseball-Reference.com and Retrosheet.org.

NOTES

1. *New York Times* article contained in Grimsley's Hall of Fame player file.
2. *The Sporting News*, NL East Roundup, September 18, 1989: 24.
3. Ibid.
4. *New York Daily News*, May 18, 1999.
5. *USA Today Baseball Weekly*, February 23, 1993.
6. Bill Brown, NL East Roundup, *The Sporting News*, March 30, 1992: 14.
7. *USA Today Baseball Weekly*, February 23, 1993.
8. Ibid.
9. Sheldon Ocker, AL East Roundup, *The Sporting News*, September 13, 1993: 22.
10. Associated Press clipping dated April 12, 2004 In Grimsley's Hall of Fame player file.
11. *Chicago Sun-Times*, June 8, 2006.
12. *Associated Press* clipping dated April 12, 2004 in Grimsley's Hall of Fame player file.
13. Buster Olney, "Yankees Pass Pop Quiz, but Their Big Test Comes This Week," *New York Times,* May 30, 1999: SP1.
14. Buster Olney, "Piniella Accuses Grimsley," *New York Times,* May 10, 1999: D7.
15. Buster Olney, "Yankees Pass Pop Quiz, but Their Big Test Comes This Week," *New York Times,* May 30, 1999: SP1.
16. Ibid.
17. Ibid.
18. Buster Olney, "Piniella Accuses Grimsley," *New York Times,* May 10, 1999: D7.
19. *KansasCity.com*, January 22, 2005.
20. Ibid.
21. *Baltimoresun.com*, June 10, 2006.

OREL HERSHISER

BY JOSEPH WANCHO

On October 20, 1988, the Los Angeles Dodgers were on the verge of winning it all. They held a comfortable lead over the Oakland Athletics in the World Series, three games to one. LA was in a good spot for sure as its ace, Orel Hershiser, was the starting pitcher. After Kirk Gibson's dramatic pinch-hit home run in Game One delivered a victory, Hershiser blanked the A's in Game Two, 6-0. Dodgers' fans were dreaming of a world championship, and Hershiser delivered. He struck out nine on his way to a complete game, 5-2 victory. The Dodgers were world champions!

Hershiser's stat line for the Series was indeed impressive, with a 2-0 record, 17 strikeouts, two complete games, and a 1.00 ERA. "As long as we all live, none of us will ever see any pitcher accomplish what Orel has done; he'll go down in history," said Gibson.[1] Oakland manager Tony LaRussa concurred. "He's every bit as good as the season he had."[2]

What Gibson and LaRussa were referring to was the monster season Hershiser had in 1988. He led the National League in wins (23), complete games (15), and shutouts (8), and his ERA was 2.26. All of which landed him the Cy Young Award, recognition as Major League Player of the Year and NL Pitcher of the Year by *The Sporting News*, MVP of both the NLCS and World Series, a Gold Glove, and *Sports Illustrated's* pick as Sportsman of the Year. True Value should have as much hardware. Perhaps Hershiser gave the appearance of a bookkeeper or a librarian with his tall, gangly, bespectacled frame. But the right-handed hurler could throw the pill. Perhaps his biggest accomplishment was that from August 30 to September 28, he did not surrender a single run. The scoreless streak covered 59⅓ innings, breaking the record set by another Dodger 20 years earlier, Don Drysdale (58⅓ innings).

"Well, I was a little worried about Game Five," said Hershiser. "I just didn't want it to be my one bad outing, a game that would have everyone saying maybe the rest of it was lucky."[3] As it happened, that worry was totally unfounded.

Orel Leonard Hershiser IV was born on September 16, 1958, in Buffalo, New York. He was the oldest of four children born to Orel Hershiser III and Mildred Hershiser. Orel owned a business that printed newspaper advertising inserts. His business kept the family on the move, as they relocated from Buffalo to Detroit to Toronto to Cherry Hill, New Jersey, and finally back to Detroit.

After graduating from Cherry Hill East High School, Hershiser enrolled at Bowling Green State University. While living in Toronto, he had learned to play hockey and turned himself into a fairly good defenseman. Bowling Green was strong in both baseball and hockey. Hershiser leaned toward the diamond instead of the rink. He was named Outstanding Pitcher in 1979 and threw what still stands as the school's last complete no-hitter, beating Kent State 2-0 on May 4, 1979.[4] Hershiser posted a 6-2 record his junior year, and was recommended by bird dog Mike Trbovich to Los Angeles scout Boyd Bartley. The Dodgers selected Hershiser in the 17th round of the free agent draft on June 5, 1979.

Hershiser was assigned to Clinton (Iowa) of the Class A Midwest League, where he posted a fine 4-0 record. But the Dodgers viewed him as more of a relief pitcher than a starter, and for the next four seasons he toiled in the bullpen at both Double-A San Antonio (Texas League) and Triple-A Albuquerque (Pacific Coast League). While in San Antonio, he met the former Jamie Byars, whom he married in 1981 after a short courtship.

Los Angeles called Hershiser up to the big leagues and he made his debut on September 1, 1983, pitching two innings in relief of Fernando Valenzuela to earn a save. The Dodgers clinched the NL East Division with the 4-3 victory over San Francisco.

After the 1983 season, Hershiser played winter ball in the Dominican Republic. There he worked with pitching coach Dave Wallace, and together they made Hershiser a complete pitcher. "What sets him apart is his intelligence," said Wallace. "He comes out knowing what he wants to do and makes the adjustments he has to make and makes them quicker than anyone I've ever seen. He'll adjust from pitch to pitch. It takes some pitchers an inning or two to figure out what they're doing wrong. He's really broken his pitching down – his mechanics, opposing hitters. He watches and studies and just has a feeling for pitching."[5]

Hershiser made the Dodgers team in 1984, but was relegated to long relief work. Injuries to Jerry Reuss and Rick Honeycutt opened the door for him. On June 29 he defeated Rick Sutcliffe (the eventual NL Cy Young award winner) and the Chicago Cubs, 7-1. It was his first complete game in the major leagues and he struck out eight.

During the game Hershiser began a streak of $34 1/3$ scoreless innings, which ended on July 24.

As impressive as Hershiser was in his first full season, he took greater strides in 1985 when he posted a 19-3 record and a 2.03 ERA. He had a rocky beginning to the season, but righted the ship against reigning NL West Division champion San Diego, pitching a two-hitter against them on April 21, and a one-hitter on the 26th. His 19th victory came on October 2 against Atlanta. The win clinched the division title for the Dodgers. "I could watch my teammates celebrate in the dugout," said Hershiser. "It was like I was a fan, watching them."[6] After the Dodgers took a two-games-to-none lead on St. Louis in the NLCS, the Cardinals came back to take the series. Hershiser won Game Two, but was not as effective in Game Six, surrendering four earned runs in $6 1/3$ innings with one strikeout.

Over the next two years the Dodgers sank in the division standings. Hershiser pitched to a 30-30 record. Manager Tommy Lasorda gave him the nickname Bulldog, in an effort for Hershiser to have a tougher attitude on the hill. He was in the midst of five straight seasons (1985-89) with over 230 innings pitched. Hershiser picked up a great deal of his pitching acumen from Lasorda. "Tommy taught me a lot about pitching," he said. "I didn't mind if he second-guessed my pitch selection, because it was almost a Socratic method: 'Why did you throw that?' I would learn things like don't throw off-speed to a left-hander with a man on first base because he wants to hit the ball to the right side anyway."[7]

As Hershiser took the mound on September 28, 1988, in San Diego, he needed nine shutout innings to eclipse Drysdale. "It was the best I've ever seen him pitch," said the Padres' Tony Gwynn. "Oh-for-four, I grounded to second base each time, each time on a sinker, although he set me up differently each time. He sure as heck knew what he was doing out there."[8] When Hershiser tied the mark, he asked to be removed from the game, out of respect for Drysdale. But Lasorda and pitching coach Ron Perranoski persuaded him to go for the record. Hershiser pitched 10 scoreless innings in the game, which San Diego eventually won, 2-1 in 16 innings. When Drysdale was told that Hershiser wanted to be taken out of the game, he said, "I would have gone out there and kicked him in the rear."9

Hershiser displayed his leadership qualities in the 1988 NLCS against the New York Mets. He pitched in Games One and Three and got two no-decisions. But he came back in Game Four to pitch one-third of an inning of relief to earn a save. In the deciding Game Seven, Hershiser pitched a complete-game shutout, scattering five hits in the 6-0 win. "We expected to win another world championship, and didn't," said Mets skipper Davey Johnson. "I've got a bad taste in my mouth, but I don't fault the guys for anything. Orel Hershiser is unbelievable. He seemed to be in every game we played."10

In 1990 after just four starts, Hershiser felt stiffness in his right shoulder. Preliminary tests indicated that there were tears in the tissue that looked as if they had been "pounded with a hammer." His heavy workload was believed to be the cause of the discomfort. Dr. Frank Jobe performed reconstructive surgery. Although estimates of Hershiser's return were sketchy and often varied, it was not until May 29, 1991, that he made his next start.

Hershiser posted losing records in 1992 and 1993 (he led the league in losses with 15 in 1992) although he was strong as ever, topping 200 innings pitched each season. The 1994 season ended prematurely on August 12 when the players struck. The postseason was canceled. The result was 894 games being washed away. Hershiser was a free agent, and he had his choice of many suitors. "(The Dodgers) told me we're not going to re-sign you because we have other plans," Hershiser recalled. "I told them, 'Are you serious? I can still pitch.' They wanted me to retire and join the organization. I said, 'No, I can really still pitch. You guys haven't seen any offseason workouts because of (MLB's) lockout.'

"They said the only way we want you to come back is if we get a hometown discount. I think they offered me something under $1 million. Little did I know that they'd already gone out and signed Hideo Nomo from Japan and they didn't have any money to bring me back."11

Cleveland did not outbid other teams for Hershiser, but the Indians offered him the best chance at winning. He signed a two-year deal and joined a starting staff of Dennis Martinez, Charlie Nagy, and Bud Black. Cleveland pounded its opposition, clinching its first postseason since 1954, on September 8, 1995 and winning 100 games. Hershiser went 16-6 with a 3.87 ERA. From July 15 to the end of the year, he posted an 11-2 record. But he contributed more to the team than his pitching ability. "It's like he's got eyes in the back of his head," said rookie pitcher Chad Ogea. "He can be talking to you and bring up a situation in a game that just happened that you didn't even notice and he'll explain it to you. He's very knowledgeable and very easy to talk to.

"I look at the things he does, and that's who I want to model myself after, not necessarily because he's Orel Hershiser, but because of the way he pitches, his mental presence and his work ethic."12

Hershiser provided postseason experience as well, beating Boston in Game Two of the ALDS, and winning two games in the ALCS against Seattle. He surrendered just two earned runs and struck out 15 in the two wins, earning him MVP honors. "I don't throw the ball real differently from a lot of guys in the game. I just happen to be getting away with my mistakes at this time of year," Hershiser said after the Game Five win.13

The Indians advanced to the World Series after dispatching Seattle in the ALCS. Hershiser went 1-1 against Atlanta in the series, as the Braves toppled the Indians in six games.

Cleveland won the American League Central Division the next two years. Hershiser was a solid contributor to the pitching staff. He was 15-9 in 1996 and 14-6 in 1997, making him and Nagy a formidable 1-2 punch at the top of the rotation. Cleveland returned to the fall classic in 1997, against the Florida Marlins, and came up short in the seven-game series. Hershiser was knocked around by the Marlins, as he posted a 0-2 record and an 11.70 ERA.

A free agent, Hershiser returned to the senior circuit in 1998, posting an 11-10 record with the San Francisco Giants. The next year he moved on to Gotham. At age 40 (Hershiser turned 41 toward the end of the season) he was still slinging the horsehide for the New York Mets. He won

13 games in 1999 (tying Al Leiter for the team lead) and notched his 200th career win on July 22 at Montreal, a 7-4 victory. New York was the wild-card team in the 1999 playoffs. The Mets dispatched Arizona in four games in the NLDS, but lost to Atlanta in six games in the NLCS. Hershiser was relegated to bullpen duty in the postseason.

Bulldog returned to the Dodgers in 2000, signing a one-year contract. But after only six starts, he was waived on June 27, 2000. "I understand and support the club's decision of giving me my release after the way I performed," he said. "I am grateful I was given the opportunity to play for the Dodgers this season." Hershiser retired from baseball with a major-league record of 204-150, a 3.48 ERA, and 2,014 strikeouts. Hershiser shined during the postseason. He posted records of 1-0 in the LDS, 4-0 in the LCS, and 3-3 in the World Series.

Hershiser did not stray from major-league baseball, joining ESPN as an analyst in 2001. He then moved back to the field, serving as the pitching coach for the Texas Rangers from 2002 to 2005. He returned to ESPN in 2006. He was an analyst for the Little League World Series for ABC before joining the *Sunday Night Baseball* crew in 2010. As of 2017, Hershiser was in his fourth season of providing analysis for Dodger games on SportsNet LA.

Hershiser moved to Las Vegas after he and Jamie divorced in 2005. He resides in Las Vegas with his second wife, Dana. Hershiser has taken part in poker tournaments. "There's the strategy of dealing with what you have," he said of the game. "Some days you may not have your 90-mph fastball, and you have to rely on your slider and your changeup. Well, in poker, you have to play the cards you're dealt, so that means adjusting your game accordingly – and adjusting your game relative to whom you're playing against."[14]

After Hershiser's big year in 1988, he and Jamie were invited to the White House for a state dinner on November 16, 1988, honoring British Prime Minister Margaret Thatcher. Among the other guests were Henry Kissinger, Tom Selleck, and Mikhail Baryshnikov. "It's around midnight and we're walking down the long hall in the White House that goes from the ballroom to the front door," said Hershiser. "While we're walking, I'm telling Tom Selleck and his mother that we feel like Cinderella at the ball, and that if we don't hurry up, our limousine is going to turn into a pumpkin. When our car pulls up, a marine opens one door for Jamie, and I help her with her dress, and then I walk to the other side of the car where another marine is holding the door for me.

"Now this marine is just like me, about my age. But he's standing there, staunch and upright, his chin out, like I am some head of state. So I decided to make a little joke and, and I put my hand in my pocket, pull it out, and say 'I'm sorry, but I don't have any singles.'

"The guy never cracks a smile. He just says, 'That'll be all, Cy Young.' "[15]

Hershiser may not have been a head of state in 1988, but for certain he was baseball royalty.

NOTES

1   Dave Nightingale, *The Sporting News*, October 31, 1988: 10.
2   Ibid.
3   Ibid.
4   Bowling Green State University *2016 Baseball Media Guide*, 51.
5   Gordon Edes, *Los Angeles Times Magazine*, April 9, 1989: 39-40.
6   Gordon Verrell, *Sporting News*, October 14, 1985: 15.
7   Steve Wulf, *Sports Illustrated*, December 19, 1988: 69.
8   Wulf: 63.
9   Ibid.
10 Joseph Durso, *New York Times*, October 13, 1988: D26.
11 Paul Hoynes, Cleveland.com, accessed October 14, 2015.
12 Tim Warsinskey, *Cleveland Plain Dealer*, July 30, 1995: 10D.
13 Bonnie DiSimone, *Cleveland Plain Dealer*, October 16, 1995: 4S.
14 Bill Ordine, Baltimoresun.com, February 23, 2008.
15 Wulf, 62.

KEN HILL

BY GREGORY H. WOLF

Right-hander Kenny Hill flashed the kind of stuff that made batters think twice before they came to the plate. He had a wicked split-finger fastball which made his low-to-mid-90s heater look even faster, and his hard slider was generally regarded as one of the best in baseball. Three times he won a career-best 16 games, including in the strike-shortened 1994 campaign when he tied Greg Maddux for the NL lead. But had Hill had a little luck and a healthy elbow, he might be remembered as one of the best pitchers of the 1990s instead of a coveted journeyman hurler who posted a 117-109 record in a 14-year career (1988-2001) with seven teams, most notably the Montreal Expos, Cleveland Indians, and Texas Rangers.

On December 14, 1965, Willie and Rosemary Hill welcomed their seventh of eighth children to the world, Kenneth Wade Hill. The Hill children were born in Lynn, an old industrial city of about 100,000 residents located 10 miles northeast of Boston. The elder Hill, known as "Sonny Boy," was a well-known and respected African-American baseball coach in local youth leagues, and raised his six boys with the same passion for the sport that he had. "We were just an athletic family," recalled Ken. "We all pitched and played different positions."[1] Tall and agile, Ken excelled in basketball and soccer at Lynn Classical High School, but baseball was his calling. He played second base and pitched, posting a 6-2 record as a senior and leading the team to the playoffs.

After graduating in 1984 Ken attended North Adams State College (now called Massachusetts College of the Liberal Arts), a small Division III school situated in the Berkshire Hills of Western Massachusetts. Packing only about 145 pounds on his 6-foot-4 frame, Hill was initially slotted for the infield on the Trailblazers, but coach Joe Zavattaro quickly recognized the power of Hill's right arm. "He had great velocity," said Zavattaro while seeing Hill compete in a fall league.[2] Nicknamed "Thrill" by his teammates, Hill helped guide the club to a then team-record 25 victories (10 losses) and to the Massachusetts State College Association title and a berth in the NCAA tournament. "When I'm out on the mound, it's all business," said Hill of his moniker. "But I guess it's also a show."[3] Far removed from the rounds of big-league scouts, Hill relied on some assistance to attract their attention. Tipped off by Dick Champa, Hill's American Legion coach, Joe "Skippy" Lewis, baseball lifer and scout for the Detroit Tigers, signed the skinny undrafted teenager as an amateur free agent in 1985.

Hill began his professional baseball career with the Gastonia (North Carolina) Jets in the Class-A South Atlantic League in 1985, but lasted only a year and a half in the Tigers organization before he was sent along with first baseman Mike Laga to the St. Louis Cardinals for catcher Mike Heath. In his first full season on the Cardinals farm (1987), Hill split his time between Single- and Double-A ball, struggled as a middle reliever and spot starter (4.75 ERA in 94⅔ innings). With an unimpressive 17-22 record in three seasons in the minors, Hill surprised the Redbirds in the Florida Instructional League in 1987. "He opened every scout's eyes in Florida," said Lee Thomas, the Cardinals' director of player personnel. "If he keeps throwing the way he's thrown, he's a year away from the big leagues."[4] Those words were prescient.

Added to the Cardinals' 40-man roster, Hill participated in his first big-league spring training in 1988. With his dream in hand's reach, Hill suffered his first injury in a career defined by them. Bothered by a pulled muscle in his rib cage, Hill was ultimately assigned to the Arkansas Travelers in the Double-A Texas League, and started the season on the DL. He overcame a 0-6 start to finish 9-9 despite an unsightly 4.92 ERA in 115⅓ innings. After whiffing 21 batters in 13 innings in his last two starts, Hill was promoted to the big leagues.[5] He debuted in a blowout to Houston in the Astrodome on September 3, yielding two runs and six hits in three innings.

Hill began the 1989 season with the Louisville Redbirds in the American Association, but his first experience in Triple A was brief. The Cardinals staff was decimated by the end of spring training; starters Danny Cox and Greg Mathews suffered season-ending injuries; and southpaw Joe Magrane, who had led the NL with a 2.18 ERA in 1988, was suffering from Crohn's disease. Recalled in mid-April, Hill was thrust into the starting rotation, and became an immediate, albeit short-lived sensation. In his first appearance, he held Montreal to five hits and two runs over seven innings, and knocked in a run, to notch his first big-league victory on April 20. As part of a career-best stretch of 24⅔ scoreless innings, Hill fired a three-hit shutout and struck out nine against Los Angeles on May 4. "He looks like one of the hardest throwers in the National League," said Dodgers skipper Tommy Lasorda.[6] Primarily a fastball pitcher, Hill attributed his success to two pitches and keeping hitters off balance. Said Hill, "I used to be a thrower and not a pitcher. Now I'm out there mixing my pitches well." He began throwing a split-finger fastball that he learned the previous season from former big-league reliever and then Cardinals minor-league pitching instructor Darold Knowles, and a hard slider. "I couldn't throw the slider last year," revealed Hill. "It was all over the place. Suddenly I found the release point."[7] While St. Louis battled Chicago and Montreal in a tight race in the NL East, Hill hit a brick wall the last nine weeks of the season, losing nine of 10 decisions. His 33 starts were the most for a Cardinals rookie since Reggie Cleveland's 34 in 1971. He tied for the NL lead in losses (15) and paced the circuit in walks (99) while posting a 3.80 ERA in 196⅔ innings.

Hill's relationship with the Cardinals and manager Whitey Herzog soured in 1990. Slated for long relief to start the season in light of the club's offseason acquisition of southpaw John Tudor and right-hander Bryn Smith, Hill was demoted to Louisville after just three ineffective appearances. "I thought I deserved a better opportunity," said Hill angrily.[8] The Cardinals GM, Dal Maxvill, was unapologetically blunt in his decision. "He was brought in because he had a good arm and all the people we had go down," said the former Cardinals infielder. "He still needs a lot of work."[9] The demotion, though painful, proved productive. Working closely with Cardinals minor-league pitching coach Bruce Sutter to hone his split-finger fastball, Hill was "nearly unstoppable" with Louisville, posting a 6-1 record and 1.79 ERA in 85⅓ innings.[10] He was recalled in late July when pitcher Rick Horton was released, and finished the season with a 5-6 record and a 5.49 ERA in 78⅔ innings.

While skipper Joe Torre guided the Cardinals from the cellar to a second-place finish in the NL East in his first full season with the club in 1991, Hill returned to the rotation only to battle the elbow pain that accompanied him for the remainder of his career. After a three-week stint on the DL in

August, Hill fashioned an excellent September, including a steak of 24 scoreless innings, to finish with an 11-10 record and a 3.57 ERA in 181⅓ innings; he was also the third-hardest pitcher to hit in the league (7.3 hits/9 innings). With his future seemingly firmly secure in the Gateway City, Hill was unexpectedly sent to Montreal in exchange for slugger Andres Galarraga on November 25 in a trade that was panned by the press. St. Louis sportswriter Bernie Miklasz wondered why the team would exchange a "live arm" for a "dead bat" (Galarraga had batted just .219 with nine home runs).[11]

Hill's three-year stint in Montreal was the most productive period in his career. Described as an "emerging talent" by Expos GM Dan Duquette, Hill tossed a four-hit shutout against the Mets at Shea Stadium in his first appearance in the red, white, and blue Expos uniform.[12] In his next meeting with the Mets, at Olympic Stadium in Montreal on June 8, the big 26-year-old fired a one-hit shutout. Duquette's acquisition of Hill seemed like a stroke of good fortune. While Galarraga struggled in St. Louis (10 homers and .243 batting average), a healthy Hill finally realized the success so many had predicted. He won a career-best seven consecutive decisions (in eight starts) in midsummer, including a personal-best 10-strikeout outing against San Francisco on July 10, en route to tying veteran Dennis Martinez with a club-high 16 victories, and posting a career-low 2.68 ERA in 218 innings. "[Hill's] always had quality stuff," said pitching coach Joe Kerrigan, unsurprised at the hurler's success. "It was just a matter of throwing first-pitch strikes."[13] Several factors contributed to Hill's season-long consistency: he was freed from the expectations in St. Louis; he established better control of his pitches, lowering his walk total to 3.1 per nine innings; and he connected with Kerrigan, whose counsel he sought well after leaving Montreal. "I see a man who is maturing," said Expos skipper Felipe Alou, who took over for Tom Runnells in mid-May. "He's always had the physical part, but now he's growing mentally."[14]

Hill thrived in the closely-knit Expos clubhouse, and talked shop with other pitchers, especially graybeard Martinez, 12 years his senior. In 1993 Hill got off to a blistering start, winning his first six decisions, including consecutive four-hitters. But his 6-0 record and 2.42 ERA at the end of May masked a strained right groin that had bothered him since spring training. In late June he landed on the DL and missed three weeks. Lacking the early-season power and control upon his return, Hill finished with a 9-7 slate and 3.23 ERA in 183⅔ innings.

Hill revealed a different side of himself in 1993. Typically described as stoic, quiet, private, and observant (qualities he said he learned from his father),[15] a more mature and confident Hill became assertive as his stature with the club grew. Though the Expos were widely considered front-runners to win the NL East, the club's offense sputtered for much of the season. On June 25, the Expos trailed Philadelphia by 13 games. Montreal sportswriter Jeff Blair reported that Hill was among the most vocal players who criticized the small-budget Expos' failure to land a much-needed offensive threat, such as highly prized slugger Gary Sheffield whom San Diego ultimately traded to the Florida Marlins.[16] Hill's laid-back demeanor off the field often clouded his intense personality, will to win, and team-oriented attitude. Liz Robbins of the *Cleveland Plain Dealer* characterized Hill as a "fortress, insulated with confidence and solitary purpose."[17]

Hill's vocal leadership was evident at the beginning of the 1994 season as the Expos, once again expected to compete for the NL East crown, got off to a horrible start (4-9). "Teams just don't respect us anymore because we're too laid back," said Hill, upset with his teammates, but also with management, which had traded away budding star and leadoff hitter Delino DeShields. "[T]he intensity is just not there."[18] Unlike his team, Hill was firing on all cylinders, and won eight of his first 10 decisions. In his last start before the All-Star break, Hill tossed a sparkling five-hit shutout against San Diego for his major-league-leading 13th victory (tied with the Yankees' Jimmy Key) against just three losses, pulling the Expos to within a game of the division-leading Braves. Pitching coach Kerrigan cited Hill's "maturity, experience and understating [of his] delivery," as the reasons for his emergence as the league's best pitcher not named Greg Maddux. "[Hill] self-correct[s] himself with two or three pitches. In the last two years, it was taking six, seven or eight"[19] In his first and only All-Star berth, Hill tossed two scoreless innings, issuing just a walk, in the NL's 8-7 dramatic victory on teammate Moises Alou's walk-off double in the 10th inning. With the threat of the players strike looming, Montreal went on a tear, winning 20 of its last 23 games from July 18 to August 11 to sit atop the division, a comfortable six games in front of the Braves. The strike interrupted play the next day, and eventually lasted 232 days, wiping out the entire postseason and the World Series.

The Expos and Hill were left to wonder "What if?" Hill finished with 16 victories, tied with Maddux for the NL lead, and finished a distant second in Cy Young Award voting behind Maddux, who garnered all 28 first-place votes to win his third of four straight awards. In a poll conducted that season by *The Sporting News*, peers ranked Hill's slider as the best among NL starters (tied with Atlanta's John Smoltz and Montreal's Jeff Fassero); only relievers Bryan Harvey and Hill's teammate Mel Rojas received more votes in the NL.[20] The Expos had the best record in baseball (74-40), yet were robbed of one of the best chances to their first pennant.

The strike cast a dark shadow over baseball for almost eight months. It also confused and confounded players and owners, especially regarding the status of free agents. In light of the owners' vote in December to implement a salary cap, Hill was expected to become a restricted free agent. Highly coveted by several clubs, he signed an offer sheet from the Florida Marlins widely reported as a four-year deal worth $20 million. In ongoing negations between the Major League Players Association and owners, the salary cap was deemed unfair by the National Relations Labor Board, and the rules governing free agents were altered yet again, thereby invalidating Hill's offer sheet with the Marlins.[21] Hill was eligible for salary arbitration, but not yet free agency. Unable to afford the increased salaries that were sure to come from salary arbitration, Montreal moved quickly to discard players. Over a two-day period in early April the Expos traded Hill to St. Louis for three unheralded prospects, shipped closer John Wetteland to the New York Yankees, and sent All-Star center fielder Marquis Grissom to Atlanta; two days later they lost All-Star right fielder Larry Walker to Colorado in free agency. The loss of four major contributors decimated the Expos, who fell to fifth place in 1995. Never again did Montreal challenge for the NL East crown. With dwindling attendance and absentee ownership, the franchise relocated to Washington for the 2005 season.

"[It] took a lot out of me," Hill admitted about his odyssey in 1995 which took him from Montreal to Florida, back to Montreal, to St. Louis, then to Cleveland, and finally to free agency and a multiyear contract with the Texas Rangers.[22] "I had 20 million dollars on the table and that got swiped away from under my feet," he recalled. "And then I got traded to St. Louis. ... [T]he atmosphere wasn't good."[23]

Rick Hummel, a sportswriter with the *St. Louis Post-Dispatch*, described Hill's short-lived reunion with the Cardinals as an "uneasy marriage" and Hill's performance a "bust."[24] Hill, whose one-year contract worth approximately $4.5 million made him the highest-paid pitcher in Cardinals history, sparred in the press with GM Walt Jockety, who refused to entertain contract talks.[25] "I can't say I'm excited," said Hill when asked about his return to St. Louis, a bad club mired in the cellar in the NL Central. By midseason the only question about Hill was to which team the Cardinals would send the disgruntled hurler before they lost him in free agency. Complicating matters was Hill's poor pitching. "I'm having a tough time," said the dejected hurler.[26] Hill was also concerned about the grave health of his mother. After skipping a start to be with her when she had a tumor removed, Hill joined the club in Philadelphia where he was pummeled for eight runs in just 2⅓ innings on July 23.[27] Four days later he was shipped to the Cleveland Indians for three prospects.

Hill joined the first-place Indians en route to their first pennant since 1954 and shored up a staff led by former Expos teammate Dennis Martinez (12-5), Charles Nagy (16-6), and Orel

Hershiser (16-6). After his disastrous stint with the Cardinals (5.06 ERA), Hill was steady, though far from spectacular, winning four of five decisions and posting a 3.98 ERA in 74⅔ innings. "I didn't pitch well with St. Louis," said Hill. "I gave it up. I just wanted to go somewhere where I could get into the postseason and show what I could do."[28] The Indians finished with the best record in baseball (100-44), led the majors in runs scored (840), home runs (207), and batting average (.291), and paced the AL in team ERA (3.83). The importance of Hill's acquisition was revealed in the playoffs. In his first postseason appearance, he tossed 1⅓ scoreless innings in the first game of Cleveland's three-game sweep of Boston in the ALDS. He picked up the win when Tony Pena clouted a walk-off home run in the bottom of the 13th. With Cleveland trailing two games to one in the ALCS, Hill held the Mariners to five hits over seven scoreless innings to win Game Four. "Hill pulled a poor man's Bob Gibson," mused Cleveland sportswriter Terry Pluto.[29] "I went out there and pitched the way I know I'm capable of," said Hill, who threw 121 pitches.[30] In Game Four of the World Series, Hill held Atlanta scoreless for 5⅓ innings before yielding a solo home run to Ryan Klesko. He was knocked out the next frame, charged with six hits and four walks in 6⅓ innings in the Indians' 5-2 loss at Jacobs Field. Atlanta clinched the title in Game Six, 1-0, behind Tom Glavine's sparkling one-hitter over eight innings. Hill faced just one batter in relief, yielding a leadoff single to former teammate Marquis Grissom in the seventh.

Finally granted free agency in the offseason, Hill was spurned by Cleveland which signed right-hander and former Cy Young Award winner Jack McDowell, and instead inked a two-year deal with Texas, which had lost its top hurler, Kenny Rogers, to the New York Yankees. Hill emerged as the ace of an unheralded staff which boasted five starters with at least 10 victories (Hill 16, Bobby Witt 16, Roger Pavlik 15, Darren Oliver 14, Kevin Gross 11) as Texas finished in first place for the first time in franchise history (dating back to its expansion in 1961 as the Washington Senators). Consistent and healthy all season, Hill recorded career bests in many categories, including wins (16 for the third time), innings (250⅔, third-most in the AL), and strikeouts (170); he also finished sixth in the Cy Young voting. On May 3 he tossed his second and last career-one hitter to defeat Detroit, 11-0, at Tiger Stadium. The next day Pavlik tossed a one-hitter (allowing only a solo home run) to beat Detroit, marking just the eighth time in big-league history that teammates tossed consecutive one-hitters. In the Rangers' four-game loss to New York in the best-of five ALDS, Hill surrendered three hits in six innings in a loss in Game Two at Yankee Stadium.

Seemingly at the top of his game, Hill's final five years in the big leagues (1997-2001) were characterized by chronic injuries and pain, stints on the disabled list, and trades and unconditional releases. Bothered by a strained right shoulder for much of 1997 and shelved for three weeks in May, Hill (5-8, 5.19 ERA) was sent to the Anaheim Angels on July 29 for catcher Jim Leyritz in a salary dump for the underachieving Rangers. Angels beat reporter Mike DiGiovanna opined that the 31-year-old Hill "appeared to be a bust," posting a 6.82 ERA in his first six starts before making a stunning turnaround and emerging "as the staff ace."[31] While the Angels battled the Mariners for the AL West crown (ultimately finishing in second place), Hill made a "strong statement" with a 1.37 ERA in 46 innings in his final six starts, which included a two-hit victory over Texas, while holding opponents to a .128 batting average.[32] According to pitching coach Rene Lachemann, Hill's reversal was just a matter of correcting mechanics. Hill had flattened the arm angle in his delivery because of shoulder pain, leading to an inconsistent release point and poor control. (Hill led the AL with 95 walks.)[33] After the change, he was one of the hottest pitchers in the majors.

Granted free agency in November, Hill re-signed with the Angels, who committed an estimated $16 million for a three-year deal. It looked like money well spent when Hill won seven of his first ten starts through just 44 games of the 1998 season. Three weeks later, Hill was on the DL with elbow pain. He career was in jeopardy when he underwent an operation by team physician Lewis Yocum in mid-June to remove bone spurs and bone chips.[34] According to sportswriter DiGiovanna, the Angels knew about Hill's problems even before they signed him, but had hoped that Hill could undergo the procedure after the 1998 season.[35] Hill hurled six innings to defeat Boston on August 28 in his first appearance since surgery, but it proved to be his final win of the season.

As bad as 1998 was for Hill, 1999 might have been worse. He was placed on the DL twice, struggled as a starter, and ultimately was relegated to the bullpen in the final month of the season with a 4-11 record and an ERA approaching 5.00. The demotion set off an "ugly and controversial" reaction by Hill, who claimed that race played a role.[36]

The injury-prone Hill returned to the Angels to finish out his contract in 2000. In constant pain, he tinkered with his windup and delivery to relieve stress and discomfort on his arm. Sidelined for almost seven weeks for what *The Sporting News* called "severely torn rib-cage muscles," Hill made only 16 ineffective starts (6.52 ERA) and was given his unconditional release on August 7. He signed with the Chicago White Sox 11 days later, but made just two appearances, yielding eight earned runs in three innings, before he was released by the end of the month.

In 2001 Hill was signed and released by three different teams, Tampa Bay (for whom he made his final five appearances), Cincinnati, and Boston. After 14 seasons in the big leagues, Hill hung up his spikes. He posted a 117-109 record and 4.06 ERA in 1,973 innings. His adjusted ERA, which measures his ERA in relation to the pitcher's ballpark and the league's ERA, was 106 (above 100 is better than average). Hill was especially tough on Terry Pendleton (2-for-26), Luis Gonzalez (4-for-40), and Ken Griffey (3-for-22; but was hit hard by Jose Valentin (11-for-21), Tim Raines (11-for-20), and Mo Vaughn (13-for-25).

After his playing days, Hill settled with his wife, Lorrie, and their two children Ken Jr. and Marcus, in Southlake, a suburb of Dallas, where he resided as of 2016. He was involved in coaching his sons in youth baseball, and managing their amateur athletic profiles. A highly recruited high-school football player, Ken Jr., made national headlines on August 28, 2014, when he passed for 511 yards in his first start as quarterback for Texas A&M to break former Heisman Trophy winner Johnny Manziel's school record in a victory over the University of South Carolina.

SOURCES

In addition to the sources noted in this biography, the author also accessed Hill's player file and player questionnaire from the National Baseball Hall of Fame, the Encyclopedia of Minor League Baseball, Retrosheet.org, Baseball-Reference.com, the SABR Minor Leagues Database, accessed online at Baseball-Reference.com, and *The Sporting News* archive via Paper of Record. Special thanks to Bill Mortell for his assistance with genealogical research.

NOTES

1 Liz Robbins, "Getting a New Start," *Cleveland Plain Dealer*, August 6, 1995.

2 Ibid.

3 Ibid.

4 *The Sporting News*, November 16, 1987: 54.

5 *The Sporting News*, August 1, 1988: 36; and September 12, 1988: 25.

6 *The Sporting News*, May 22, 1989: 16.

7 Ibid.

8 "Ken Hill Sent Down After Bad Outing," *St. Louis Post-Dispatch*, April 29, 1990: F3.

9 Rick Hummel, "Demoted Hill Thinks Cardinals Slighted Him," *St. Louis Post-Dispatch*, April 29, 1990: F1.

10 *The Sporting News*, June 18, 1990: 31.

11 Bernie Miklasz, "A Live Arm for Dead Bat? Wait and See," *St. Louis Post-Dispatch*, November 26, 1991: 1C.

12 *Oneonta Star*, November 26, 1991.

13 Joe Donnelly, "Hill's Mission: Control," *New York Newsday*, April 11, 1992.

14 Ibid.

15 Robbins.

16 *The Sporting News*. July 5, 1993: 18.

17 Robbins.

18 *The Sporting News*, April 25, 1994: 17.

19 *The Sporting News*, August 1, 1994: 19.

20 *The Sporting News*, July 11, 1994: 17.

21 AP, "Salary Cap's Demise Brings Confusion, Hope for Accord," *St. Louis Post-Dispatch*, February 4, 1995: C3.

22 Paul White, "This Ranger Is Now King of the Hill," *USA Today Baseball Weekly*, March 25, 1997.

23 Robbins.

24 Rick Hummel, "Hill Takes His Leave of Birds," *St. Louis Post-Dispatch*, July 28, 1995: D1; *The Sporting News*, October 16, 1995: 24.

25 *The Sporting News*, June 19, 1995: 24.

26 *The Sporting News*, July 3, 1995: 21.

27 Rick Hummel, "Phillies All Got Dumber in Slump," *St. Louis Post-Dispatch*, July 22, 1995: 27.

28 Associated Press, "Indians Finally Get to See the Real Hill," *The Tennessean* (Nashville, Tennessee), October 15, 1995: 58.

29 Terry Pluto, "Belle's Injury Tempers Indians Celebration," *Akron Beacon Journal*, October 15, 1995: C 5.

30 "Indians Finally Get to See the Real Hill."

31 *The Sporting News*, October 6, 1997: 57.

32 *The Sporting News*, September 22, 1997: 52.

33 *The Sporting News*, April 20, 1998: 20.

34 "Angels Hurler Hill Has Surgery on Elbow," *Courier-Journal* (Louisville, Kentucky), June 16, 1998: D4.

35 *The Sporting News*, June 22, 1998: 50.

36 *The Sporting News*, January 10, 2000: 62.

WAYNE KIRBY

BY ED GRUVER

Most major-league players dream of doing something good on Opening Day.

On April 4, 1994, Wayne Kirby did something that was not just good. It was historic.

Teeing off on a 3-and-1 fastball from Seattle reliever Kevin King, Kirby christened the Cleveland Indians' sparkling new ballpark, Jacobs Field, in style. Stroking a game-winning single to left, the opposite field, in the 11th inning, Kirby capped a 4-3 comeback win.[1]

For Kirby, the dramatic moment remained a favored memory of his eight-year major-league career. It proved to be a prologue for the Indians' historic 1995 season, when they won their first American League Central Division title and reached the World Series for the first time in 41 seasons. Cleveland's come-from-behind win on that sun-soaked, chilly Monday afternoon at Jacobs Field proved pivotal in the Tribe's history since it came in a game dominated over the first seven innings by Mariners ace and future Hall of Famer Randy Johnson.

Locked in a mound duel with Indians ace Dennis Martinez, Johnson hurled seven hitless innings and owned a 2-0 lead before the Indians tied it in the eighth when Manny Ramirez pulled a two-run double to deep left.

That set the stage for Kirby, who had entered the game in the bottom of the 10th inning to run for Ramirez. Kirby took third on Jim Thome's double off King and scored on Omar Vizquel's groundout to tie the score at 3-3. In the decisive 11th inning, King surrendered a one-out double to Eddie Murray. Murray headed to third on Paul Sorrento's fly to center and King walked Sandy Alomar Jr. intentionally to get to Kirby.[2]

Kirby's dramatic walk-off single to score Murray stole the spotlight from President Bill Clinton, who had provided the pageantry by throwing out the ceremonial first pitch. It also proved a portent of things to come. Before opening Jacobs Field the Indians had called aging Municipal Stadium home. The Tribe and their fans had endured plenty of mistakes by the lake, but in 1995 fans at Jacobs saw the Tribe rally to win 51 times, 28 of those in their final at-bat. They swept 15 series, went 54-18 at home, won 100 games in a shortened season, boasted six .300 hitters in the starting lineup. and posted the lowest earned-run average (3.83) in the league.

Going to The Jake on game days, Kirby told Cleveland sportswriter Steve Eby, was awesome. Kirby would go on the field early and watch the seats fill up. He knew fans believed they were going to see a good team take the field, and they did. The '95 Indians did all the things necessary to win. For the Tribe, it was all about winning.[3]

Batting left-handed and throwing right-handed, the 5-11, 185-pound Kirby started 36 games in 1995 and appeared in 101 of the 144 regular-season games, the season starting later than usual because the players strike that canceled the end of the 1994 campaign also delayed the start of the 1995 campaign. Because of his speed and defensive skills, Kirby was used primarily as a pinch-runner or late-inning defensive replacement. He played solid defense when presented the opportunity, spending 236 innings in center field to spell Kenny Lofton, 141 2/3 innings in right field and 2 innings in left field. He ranked fourth on the team in stolen bases with 10 in 13 attempts.[4]

Kirby had his shining moments at the plate and could deliver the big hit when called upon. On May 10 his pinch-hit single off Kansas City Royals closer Jeff Montgomery tied the score in the ninth inning in a game the Indians won; on June 30 he homered in the seventh to help beat Minnesota; and on August 20 against Milwaukee, Kirby drove in the go-ahead run with an eighth-inning single off Cincinnati Reds reliever Rob Dibble. In all, Kirby contributed six multihit games in his 36 starts. He added a couple of hits in the postseason as well, appearing in 11 games in October and starting Game 4 of the American League Championship Series against Seattle in place of the injured Albert Belle.

Kirby said during the 1995 season that the Indians believed they were never out of a game, that they could always come back to win. "We came back a lot," he told Eby. "It was a team effort. It was 25 men working together. We stuck together and it was a unity. We hit a ton of home runs, we played great defense and it was just fun. There was no score that we couldn't come back from."[5]

Comebacks, in baseball and in life, were something Kirby was familiar with.

Born on January 22, 1964, in Williamsburg, Virginia, Wayne Leonard Kirby attended Tabb High School in Tabb, Virginia. His brother Terry, younger by six years, played 10 seasons (1993-2002) in the National Football League as a running back for the San Francisco 49ers, Oakland Raiders, Miami Dolphins, and Cleveland Browns.[6]

Ever the teacher, Wayne helped prepare Terry for his football career. Wayne and his friends played a lot of sandlot football, baseball, and basketball when they were growing up, and even though Terry was big at age 5, older kids warned him he would get hurt if he played ball with them. When Terry replied that he didn't care if he got hurt, Wayne didn't take it easy on his brother. Wayne would go on to rush for more than 3,500 yards as a high-school running back, but his prowess on the field did not prevent young Terry from coming back for more on the sandlots.

Wayne and Terry played several sports and Wayne credited his parents with keeping them busy. Good grades in school allowed the brothers to participate in sports and they chose to play multiple sports to learn which one they excelled in. Gifted athletes, they excelled in all sports and eventually had to make a choice. Wayne chose baseball; Terry football, and Wayne helped coach his younger brother into becoming a record-setting running back in high school.[7]

Wayne was still teaching two decades later when he found himself the fourth outfielder on the 1995 Indians team that had young stars in Ramirez, Belle, and Lofton. All three were named to the American League All-Star team in 1995 and all owned strong personalities. His young protégés looked up to the 31-year-old Kirby because he was a seasoned veteran who had spent 12 seasons in professional baseball, most of them in the Los Angeles Dodgers organization.

Belle, Lofton and Ramirez would ask him questions: What are we supposed to do on this play? What do we do on that play? Kirby understood their line of questions because he knew that when players came out of the minor leagues early there was still a lot of baseball to understand.[8]

Because Kirby had spent so much time in the minors, he knew how to play the game. Graduating from Tabb High School, he entered the Newport News (Virginia) Apprentice School. He planned to become a mechanic if he did not succeed in baseball. But he was determined to not have his dreams die because he was outworked.[9]

As a minor leaguer in the Los Angeles organization, Kirby was a most artful Dodger. He was selected by the Dodgers in the 13th round of the January 1983 draft. Kirby played in 60 games in 1983 with the Gulf Coast League Dodgers, batting .292 with 13 RBIs and 23 stolen bases. The next season he spent time with three Dodgers farm teams, the Great Falls (Rookie League), Vero Beach, and Bakersfield (Class A). He hit a combined .281 in 119 games with one home run, 42 RBIs and 38 steals. He played the entire 1985 season with Vero Beach and batted .261 with 28 RBIs and 31 steals in 122 games.

Kirby was back with Vero Beach in 1986 and he hit two homers, drove in 31 runs and stole 28 bases in 114 games. In 1987 Kirby split time between Bakersfield and the San Antonio Dodgers, playing the bulk of his season (105 of his 129 games) for Bakersfield. He batted a combined .264 with one homer, 43 RBIs, and 62 stolen bases.

In 1988 Kirby again split time between Bakersfield and San Antonio, but this time most of his games (100 of 112) were with the latter. His numbers dropped to a batting average of .244 with 25 RBI and 35 steals. Kirby rebounded in 1989 by batting combined .302, driving in 37 runs, and stealing 40 bases in 122 games with San Antonio and the Triple-A Albuquerque Dukes. He stayed with Albuquerque in 1990 and hit .278 with 30 RBIs and 29 steals.

Kirby became a free agent after the 1990 season and signed with Cleveland. Playing for the Indians' Triple-A affiliate, the Colorado Springs Sky Sox, in 1991, Kirby hit .294 with one home run, 39 RBIs, and 29 steals in 118 games. He was called up in September and made his major-league debut on September 12, replacing Albert Belle in left field in the eighth inning. He got his first major-league hit on September 17 when he stroked an RBI double off Detroit's Walt Terrell at Municipal Stadium.

Kirby spent his second season in the Indians' organization with Colorado Springs, posting a .345 batting average with 11 homers, 74 RBIs, 51 steals, and 162 hits in 123 games. His totals were the best of his minor-league career. In September he got 21 plate appearances with the Indians. His three hits included his first major-league home run, a pinch-hit drive off Duane Ward at the SkyDome in Toronto on September 15.

Kirby made it to Cleveland just in time to be a part of the Indians' breakout success in the mid-1990s. He became an everyday outfielder in 1993. Kirby played in 131 games and led the American League in outfield assists with 19. He batted .269 with 60 RBIs and 17 stolen bases, and placed fourth in the American League Rookie of the Year voting. Still, he was placed in a reserve role for the 1994 season behind Ramirez, the young phenom who took over in right.[10]

After six seasons (1991-96) with Cleveland, Kirby's playing career came full circle when he returned to his Dodgers roots and was claimed off waivers by Los Angeles on June 24, 1996. He hit .245 in 111 games through 1997, signed a free-agent deal with the St. Louis Cardinals and was then traded to the New York Mets. Kirby closed his pro playing career after the Mets released him in mid-September of 1998.

Even while he was a player, Kirby was becoming a coach as well. His coaching career officially began in 2002 when became the hitting coach for the Burlington Indians of the Rookie Appalachian League. The following season he was the hitting coach of the low Class-A Lake County Captains in the South Atlantic League. In 2004 Kirby moved to the Kinston Indians of the high-A Carolina League as hitting coach, and in 2005 he moved up to Double A ball as hitting coach of the Akron Aeros of the Eastern League.[11]

From 2006 to 2010 Kirby was the minor league outfield and baserunning coordinator for the Texas Rangers and in 2011 joined the Baltimore Orioles as first-base coach, a position he still held as of 2018.

A student of baserunning and outfield play, Kirby was considered by the Orioles a jack-of-all-trades coach. Manager Buck Showalter called him a "blueprint for what a coach is supposed to be."

Kirby learned the finer points of basestealing and bunting from Maury Wills; was taught the mechanics of the swing by hitting guru Charlie Manuel; and learned how to better drive the ball from Von Joshua.[12]

Kirby and his wife, Cara, settled in Las Vegas. They have two daughters, Caylee and Cabria, and a son, Cayden. They teach them about life, about what it takes to be successful.[13]

Kirby gets credit for helping kick-start the greatness of the 1995 Cleveland Indians. "I knew we had a great group of guys, hungry guys," Kirby told Eby. "We knew we could hit. (General manager) John Hart ended up getting the right pitchers for this team and we had the young guys coming. We knew it was special."[14]

NOTES

1 Steve Eby, "Did the Tribe Win Last Night?" *Countdown to Indians Opening Day 73: Catching Up With Wayne Kirby*, January 22, 2016. didthetribewinlastnight.com/blog/2016/01/22/catching-up-with-wayne-kirby/. Accessed September 27, 2018.

2 Ibid.

3 Ibid.

4 Jason Lukehart, "Wayne Kirby Provided Speed and Defense Off the Bench," SB Nation. letsgotribe.com/2015/4/17/8442201/1995-cleveland-indians-wayne-kirby-news. Accessed September 27, 2018.

5 Eby.

6 Terry Kirby Stats, Pro Football-Reference.com.

7 Lukehart.

8 Eby.

9 Norm Wood, "Top Teacher," *Newport News* (Virginia) *Daily Press*, July 30, 2011: C1.

10 Ibid.

11 Wayne Kirby, Baltimore Orioles official website, m.mlb.com/bal/roster/coach/117114/wayne-kirby. Accessed September 27, 2018.

12 Wood: C5.

13 Rich Dubroff, "Everybody Loves Kirby," pressboxonline.com, May 15, 2017, forum.orioleshangout.com/forums/index.php?/topic/28761-cover-story-on-wayne-kirby/. Accessed September 27, 2018.

14 Eby.

JESSE LEVIS

BY CHIP GREENE

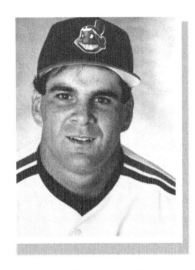

In the American criminal justice system, and under the United Nations Declaration of Human Rights, a person accused of a crime is considered innocent until proved guilty. But often the mere fact that he is accused can deprive him of his chosen profession and forever alter his life. So it was with Jesse Levis.

A Philadelphia native, born on April 14, 1968, Levis (pronounced LEV-is) was one of those baseball commodities managers often covet – a left-handed-hitting catcher. Levis's childhood revolved around two primary pursuits: baseball and religion. Raised in a Conservative Jewish household, the future major leaguer attended Hebrew school; baseball games and practices were scheduled around his religious activities. "I got it done," Levis said in 1996. "I had a bar mitzvah and I respected all the holidays. I had plenty of time for school, baseball, and friends."[1]

After learning the game in Little League, Levis became a star at Philadelphia's Northeast High School, where he had, in the words of his coach, Ben Rosner, "a terrific high-school career,"[2] winning All-Public League honors three consecutive seasons. During those years his school competed against Phoenixville High School, 30 miles northwest of Philadelphia. The Phantoms were led by All-County first baseman Mike Piazza, who in 2004 said of his relationship with Levis, "We reminisce about high school all the time and have fun with it."[3] Levis always kept newspaper clippings of their rivalry.

In 1986, the 18-year-old Levis graduated from Northeast High School. He had a choice to make. The Phillies selected Levis in the 36th round of the June amateur draft. He was also highly recruited by several major colleges. Levis declined the Phillies' offer and enrolled at the University of North Carolina.

The Phillies "offered me maybe $15,000 out of high school," Levis recalled in 2002. "I weighed that versus a college education and getting better in college at a top-flight Division 1 college." It was "tough not to sign. If I had known I was going to (Veterans Stadium), I'd have signed. But I was going to Oshkosh, Wisconsin, or somewhere. ... The hometown side came into effect with me. That was my team growing up, watching Bob Boone and Mike Schmidt and Pete Rose. I've tried to get back there the last few years. Seems like when you turn them down, they don't make another offer."[4] (In 2002 Levis did sign with the Phillies, but by then his best days were behind him.)

At UNC, Levis, a communications major, validated his decision to spurn the Phillies offer and fully realized his potential. Over the next three years, in the highly competitive Atlantic Coast Conference, he played well enough to earn, by his junior season, first team All-ACC and third team All-American honors. His maturation had undoubtedly been enhanced the previous summer when Levis joined the Orleans Pelicans in the Cape Cod League, where he competed against some of the finest collegiate players in the country. After an outstanding sophomore season (.317, with 10 home runs and 37 RBIs), the UNC coach, Mike Roberts, had suggested that Levis play in the Cape Cod League, and Levis had been up to the challenge, batting .295 with 3 homers and 17 RBIs. Most importantly, while with the Pelicans, Levis focused on his defense. "My main concern is keeping the runners from stealing bases," he said. "I try to keep them close as much as possible. In addition to that, I want to keep my passed balls down to a minimum."[5] Presciently, Levis understood that his defense would be scrutinized at the next level, a fact he soon became acutely aware of.

On June 5, 1989, when the Cleveland Indians selected Levis in the fourth round of the draft, Levis joined the professional ranks. Thus began a seven-year uninterrupted run through the Cleveland organization, during which he played in 72 major-league games. From the beginning, Levis proved he could hit. Through stops at Burlington, North Carolina (Rookie League); Kinston, North Carolina (Class A); Canton-Akron, Ohio (Double A); and Colorado Springs, Colorado (Triple A), his least impressive offensive showing produced a slash line of .264/.333/.372, at Double A, in 1991; while the next season, at Triple A, he delivered a robust .364/.444/.522 in 87 games. Meanwhile, Levis also continued to work diligently to improve his defensive deficiencies, which were marked primarily by a relatively weak arm.

By 1992, the Indians considered Levis ready to help them at the major-league level, where a glaring problem at catcher almost assured he'd get a chance to play. That problem was the fragile health of the starter, Sandy Alomar Jr. In the winter of 1989, Cleveland had made a blockbuster trade with the San Diego Padres in which they'd sent perennial Joe Carter to San Diego for three players, including Alomar, a highly gifted catching prospect. In his first season with Cleveland, Alomar lived up to his hype, making the All-Star team, winning a Gold Glove and being named the American League Rookie of the Year. But then he got hurt. In 1991, battling shoulder and hip injuries, Alomar played in only 51 games; in 1992, plagued by injuries to his knee and hand, he played in only 89 games. That opened the door for Levis.

As Junior Ortiz, whom Cleveland had signed as a free agent in December 1991 for just this situation, assumed the starting role during Alomar's frequent absences, Levis, who had begun the year at Triple-A Colorado Springs, was recalled by the Indians in early April to back up Ortiz. In that supporting role, Levis made his major-league debut, grounding out as a pinch hitter on April 24 vs. the Milwaukee Brewers. On May 4, at home versus Kansas City, Levis pinch-hit again and this time, against right-hander Mike Boddicker, singled to right field, for the first of his 167 career hits. On May 10, Levis made his first start, went 2-for-3, and by May 17 was 4-for-11 in nine games. That day Alomar returned from the disabled list, and Levis was sent back to Colorado Springs.

In late August, with Alomar again hampered by injuries, Levis was again recalled by the Indians. Over the remainder of the season he played in 19 more games, eight as a starter. On September 26 in Detroit, Levis hit the first of his three major-league home runs, a solo blast off the Tigers' Kurt Knudsen. In all, Levis hit .279 in 43 at-bats in 1992. Behind the plate, though, he threw out just two of nine attempted base stealers, so the jury was out as to whether or not he had the makings of a big-league catcher. Despite four years in the minor leagues, as he returned for the winter to Philadelphia, Levis still had much to prove.

As 1993 spring training approached, the Indians had four catchers under contract for what would likely be two roster spots. In March 1989, as a backup to Andy Allanson, Cleveland had obtained Joel Skinner in a trade from the Yankees. As

Alomar established himself that season, Skinner proved a capable backup, and in 1990 signed a three-year contract. Over the next two seasons, though, as injuries limited Alomar's playing time, Skinner's playing time increased, and in 1991 he led the club in starts at catcher. But that season Skinner experienced pain in his throwing shoulder and in November underwent surgery, which necessitated the signing for 1992 of Junior Ortiz. Frustratingly for the Indians, as Skinner's shoulder failed to heal, he remained disabled for the entire 1992 season.

The Indians hoped Skinner would return in 1993 to once again back up Alomar, who they hoped was over his own injuries. Guarding against the unavailability of either, though, over the winter Cleveland had re-signed Ortiz. And Levis would be back, of course.

It soon became apparent that Skinner would not be ready for spring training, so the battle to be Alomar's backup would again be between Ortiz and Levis. At a Cleveland luncheon in February, manager Mike Hargrove was asked whether the club would consider keeping three catchers on their roster.

"We would consider anything," Hargrove answered, "but the probability of us carrying three catchers is very slim."[6]

The previous fall, asked to assess Ortiz and Levis, Hargrove had said, "Jesse moves better behind the plate, but Junior throws better. Jesse is the better hitter, but he runs like me."[7] ... "I think Jesse really needs to work on his throwing. Jesse doesn't have the strongest arm in the world, but he's very accurate with it. He just needs to make up for that lack of arm strength by getting rid of the ball quicker."[8]

Cleveland had no doubts about Levis's bat. The Indians "don't want to spoil his line-drive, spray-to-all-fields style by turning him into a big swinger."[9] That warning came after a Levis at-bat early in spring training when he hit a home run off the roof of the building that housed the team's batting cages. Sounding like a man who knew what was expected of him, and fearful of hurting his chances, the next day Levis explained,

"I wasn't trying to hit a home run yesterday, believe me. I never try to hit home runs. Not even in batting practice. I take BP seriously. I want to work on my game, which is hitting line drives to all fields."[10]

Asked to assess his chances that spring, Levis said, "I've got to catch and throw consistently. They haven't told me anything, but it seems they have confidence in my hitting."[11] He would do his best to influence the club's decision.

In the end, Levis's best wasn't good enough. That season, as Ortiz again backed up Alomar, Levis once again began the year in Triple A. (Cleveland had changed affiliates, from Colorado Springs to Charlotte in the International League.) On May 3 the Indians again placed Alomar on the disabled list and recalled Levis. He remained with the Indians until the first week of August. Between May 3 and August 5, Levis made 16 starts, but when Alomar was reactivated on August 8, Levis was returned to Charlotte, where he played for the rest of the year. In 1994, the year of the players strike, the Indians signed veteran catcher Tony Peña to back up Alomar, and Levis, except for one game (in which he pinch-hit but didn't catch), spent the entire season at Charlotte. Clearly, it seemed, Levis no longer fit into the Indians' long-range plans.

If Levis had any doubts heading into the 1995 season regarding his future with the Indians, all his questions were soon to be emphatically answered. For a brief moment, though, it appeared Levis might finally have found his place. With spring training delayed after the strike ended, Alomar and Peña entered camp in late April as locks to be Cleveland's catchers. Ortiz had departed the organization and Skinner's career appeared over, so Levis was once again the team's third catcher, which meant he was likely once more bound for Triple A. However, in the last week of April, for the fifth consecutive year, Alomar went on the disabled list. For the first time, Levis broke camp with the Indians. With Alomar due to return early in May, Hargrove said, "We're as covered at catcher as we can be. Tony Peña was a starter up until last season. Obviously, we want Sandy to be our everyday catcher, but we feel we'll be

OK with Tony and Jesse."[12] As to Levis's playing time, Hargrove said, "I wouldn't be afraid to start Jesse, but Tony will start most of the games."[13]

As indeed Peña did. Between Opening Day and his last appearance before being sent to Triple A on May 15, Levis played in just seven games (three starts). On May 13 he started a game in Baltimore; then two days later received what must have been quite a jolt when the Indians announced they had traded left-handed pitcher Matt Williams to the Houston Astros in exchange for 29-year-old catcher, Eddie "Scooter" Tucker, who boasted a .157 career batting average and just 91 plate appearances in 34 major-league games.

"He's an upgrade on Jesse, as far as defense is concerned," explained Hargrove,[14] and certainly Levis must have gotten the message. Although he later made several late-season appearances for Cleveland after returning to the club, the acquisition of Tucker signaled the end of Levis's days as an Indians prospect. (Over the remainder of the 1995 season, Tucker made 27 plate appearances and was 0-for-20. He never played in the major leagues again and finished his career with 103 at-bats and a lifetime batting average of .126.)

Despite an inglorious end to his regular season, 1995 nonetheless ended joyously for Levis, in more ways than one. First, the Indians went to the World Series against the Atlanta Braves. While he wasn't on the postseason roster, Levis, the team's emergency catcher, traveled with the team, warmed up pitchers in the bullpen and earned an American League championship ring. Greater still, however, he got married.

About that day, there's an interesting anecdote. Levis's fiancée was Joan Greenspan. At the outset of the World Series, she told a writer from the *Philadelphia Inquirer* the couple's potential nuptial dilemma. The wedding, to be held in Cherry Hills, New Jersey, was scheduled for Sunday night, October 29, 1995, one year to the day from when Levis had proposed to Joan. The food was ordered, the guests invited and all was made ready – but there was one small problem: October 29 was also the scheduled date for Game Seven of the World Series. At the time the couple set the date, they thought the Series was scheduled to end on October 28, not 29. By the time they discovered their mistake, it was May. They had two choices: either move the wedding back a day, or move it to an earlier time on the 29th, to 11:00 A.M. They chose the latter to, as Joan put it, "stick with Sunday and pray."[15]

"I reserved him a flight from Atlanta [both Games Six and Seven were to be played at the Braves home field] that leaves at 7 in the morning [on the 29th]," Joan said. "Then we'd get married from 11 to 3. Then I'd get him on a plane back to Atlanta, and he could be there by game time. But I don't know if he'd be too nervous if he comes back and gets married in between games."[16]

For his part, Levis admitted, "You try all your life to get to this point, to be on a team that plays in the World Series. And you never know if you'll get there again. But at the same time, you want to be able to go to your own wedding. So at this point, we're just taking it day by day."[17]

"Hopefully," he concluded, "we'll win this in five games – and none of this will be a problem."[18]

Perhaps the couple had mixed emotions when the Indians lost Game Six, and the Series, on Saturday night.

As spring training opened in 1996, Levis was out of minor-league options. In order to return him to Triple A (now the Buffalo Bisons in the American Association), the Indians first had to expose him to waivers. On April 1 Cleveland designated Levis for assignment. Three days later, having passed through waivers, he was traded to the Milwaukee Brewers for left-handed pitcher Scott Nate and a player to be named (later, right-handed pitcher Jared Camp). Over each of the next two seasons, Levis finally spent the entire season in the major leagues.

As a Jewish player, Levis was one of a select few in professional baseball. In 1996, wrote reporter Michael Gelbwasser of *Jewish Weekly* magazine, only four other players in addition to Levis were reputed to be Jewish (pitchers Mike Milchin, of the Twins, and Jose Bautista, of the Giants; Padres catcher Brad Ausmus; and Toronto outfielder Shawn Green). In August of that year the magazine published Gelbwasser's interview with Levis, under the title, "The catcher wore a kippah: Jesse Levis of the Brewers." (A kippah is the yarmulke, or skullcap, worn by pious Jews.)

With regard to Yom Kippur, the holiest day on the Hebrew calendar, Gelbwasser reported that if Levis anticipated playing the next day, he fasted on the Thursday night before the high holy day. Also, Levis attended minyan (prayer services) when possible and, although he didn't keep kosher, asked for kosher restaurants when on the road. (In another article, published in 2012, Levis recalled playing on Yom Kippur in 1996, explaining that because he wasn't a superstar, he didn't feel he had a choice, although he did fast that day. "I'm not Sandy Koufax," Levis said. "I'm a major-league player trying to make a living."[19])

When asked by Gelbwasser about anti-Semitism in the majors, Levis admitted he'd heard "jokes and stuff about being cheap," but nothing malicious. "There's not a whole lot of anti-Semitism," Levis said. "But some people may talk behind your back."

Finally, wrote Gelbwasser, Joan Levis, too, came from an Orthodox household, and her family, said Levis, had been "really supportive" of his career, even though he couldn't practice Judaism as much as he'd like.[20]

Now a Brewer, in 1996 and 1997 Levis split catching duties with right-handed-batting Mike Matheny. Over that period, Levis played 203 games, half of them (102) as a starter, and posted slash lines of .236/.348/.283 and .285/.361/.335. Also, however, his caught-stealing percentages versus the league average in each year were less than perhaps the Brewers desired, 27 percent versus 30 percent, and 26 percent versus 33 percent. He appeared to be the catcher the Indians knew they had in their system all along.

On April 14, 1998, Levis turned 30 years old. Little could he have imagined that his playing career would soon be effectively over. After a hot start during which he collected five hits in six at-bats in early April during one two-game stretch, on May 8, as the Brewers started a three-game homestand versus the Houston Astros, Levis was batting .351. That night, however, after starting and batting twice, Levis left the game after the fifth inning when he felt his shoulder pop on a throw to second base. X-rays failed to reveal any damage, but when the pain in his shoulder increased, Levis was placed on the disabled list. Shortly thereafter he had rotator-cuff surgery and was subsequently shelved for the rest of the season. It was the end of his Brewers career. At season's end, Milwaukee released him.

For the next six years, Levis just tried to hang on. In December 1998, he signed a minor-league contract with the Tampa Bay Devil Rays. Included in his deal was a clause that allowed him to become a free agent if not back in the majors by July 15, 2000. When he was not, Levis exercised his option and returned to Cleveland, signing a contract for the remainder of the season. He played in 10 games. From 2001 to 2004, he signed with the Braves, by whom he was released without playing in the majors; re-signed with the Brewers, for whom he played his last major-league game, on October 7, 2001; and then played in the minor-league systems of the Reds, the Phillies, and the Mets. After 10 games in Norfolk for the Mets, in 2004, Levis's playing days came to an end.

His nightmarish period, however, was soon to begin. In 2005, Levis managed in the Mets system, piloting their Rookie League club in Kingsport, Tennessee, to a 28-40 record. Then he became a scout. After a stint with the Mets, Levis took the same job with the Boston Red Sox. It was in that capacity that his world was turned upside-down. On March 2, 2008, Levis was staying in Room 215 of the Springhill Suites hotel, in Port St. Lucie, Florida. In the outdoor pool below, teenage girls were swimming. Shortly, Levis was arrested and charged with two felony counts of committing lewd and lascivious acts in the presence of children: a hotel manager told police that Levis had allegedly been seen masturbating in front of his window, in full view of the children. Moreover, stated the manager, Levis may have been involved in a similar incident the previous year.

In short order, the manager retracted his story about the previous incident, and Levis passed a lie-detector test. Levis's lawyer, Jayne Weintraub, was prepared to introduce evidence that proved

Levis was on his computer during the time he was allegedly exposing himself and had then gone to dinner at the Ruby Tuesday restaurant, next door to the hotel. There were pictures showing a large palm tree between the pool area and the window, which could have obscured the view of any potential witnesses. Yet, Levis later recalled, the police "didn't listen to anything I said. They didn't care about my lie-detector test. They didn't want to listen to my attorney or anything. It was just, 'You're guilty.' And the internet just ran with it."[21]

Levis's defense suggested monetary reasons for the charges. When the young women complained to the hotel manager, they were accompanied by an adult male. "It was a baseball hotel," Levis said. "Players stay there, scouts stay there, reporters. If somebody thinks they can get something from somebody by saying something … I don't know. They thought they had a big-shot ballplayer doing something or they can pretend or make up a story."

Commented Weintraub, "I honestly believe what motivated them was a lawsuit or quick settlement with the Mets, or the Red Sox, thinking he was connected with one or the other team."

Eventually, the charges were dropped from felonies to misdemeanors, and for quite some time the prosecution tried to build their case. During that period, Levis and the Red Sox parted ways. The case "was a mess," said Levis. "It sat in limbo for almost two years. A lot happened in the middle of that as far as losing my job. The Red Sox held on to me as long as they could. They put me back to work and I worked that whole 2008 season. They didn't renew my contract because [the case] was still pending."

Ultimately, said Weintraub, "The reality is that we finally said, 'Enough is enough.' We filed a demand for a speedy trial. No witnesses came forward and the case was dismissed. The state could have appealed it. They appeal these things all the time if they want to go forward. The state didn't want to go forward because I'm sure they have no evidence."

"This was handled in a very horrific way. The prosecutors were just lazy, looking to make a name for themselves. They turned it over. There were four different prosecutors who handled the case. Nobody had the guts to try it, because there was no evidence. They didn't want an acquittal in front of a jury. And nobody had the guts to dismiss it because they didn't want egg on their face."

On January 27, 2010, the charges were dropped altogether. Explained Judge Philip Yacucci, who signed the discharge order, "The state was faced with evidentiary proof problems. And that, combined with an unfavorable ruling as far as a speedy trial, dictated they ask that the charges be dropped."

"He got a break. He got off on a technicality. We had witnesses prepared to testify. We believe we could have proven our case beyond a reasonable doubt," said Assistant State Attorney Gayle D. Braun, the final prosecutor who handled the complaint.

With the ordeal behind him, Levis has focused on family. As of 2015, he and Joan lived in Fort Washington, Pennsylvania. Joan returned to work as a physical therapist, while Levis has remained home with their children. "I try to look at the bright side," he said. "It's over with. It's behind me. My name is cleared. I've gotten to spend a ton of time with my family, my wife and my children. I've been their T-ball coach. I've gone back to school and I'm getting close to my degree. I want to be a teacher, I think, if baseball doesn't work out.

Levis continues to try to get back into the game. He has called all 30 major-league general managers, offering his services as a scout, coach, or in player development.

"Hopefully, my reputation will be rebuilt and I'll be able to prove again that I can really help an organization," he said wistfully. "That's the bottom line. I think I have a lot to offer an organization as far as my knowledge and experience. So, hopefully, somebody will give me a chance."[22]

NOTES

1. jweekly.com/article/full/3846/the-catcher-wore-a-kippah-jesse-levis-of-the-brewers/.
2. articles.philly.com/1988-08-18/news/26254833_1_summer-baseball-league-public-league-cape-cod.
3. nytimes.com/2004/03/12/sports/baseball-goal-for-mets-levis-is-to-beat-the-bushes.html.
4. reds.enquirer.com/2002/03/17/red_q_a_with_reds.html.
5. articles.philly.com/1988-08-18/news/26254833_1_summer-baseball-league-public-league-cape-cod.
6. *Sandusky* (Ohio)*Register*, February 7, 1993.
7. *The Sporting News,* September 7, 1992.
8. *Sandusky Register,* February 7, 1993.
9. *Elyria* (Ohio) *Chronicle Telegram,* March 8, 1993.
10. Ibid.
11. Ibid.
12. *Elyria Chronicle Telegram,* April 25, 1995.
13. *Sandusky Register,* April 26, 1995.
14. *Elyria Chronicle Telegram,* May 16, 1995.
15. *Philadelphia Inquirer*, October 23, 1995.
16. Ibid.
17. Ibid.
18. Ibid.
19. jewishbaseballnews.com/tag/jesse-levis/.
20. All quotations from the Gelbwasser article are from jweekly.com/article/full/3846/the-catcher-wore-a-kippah-jesse-levis-of-the-brewers/.
21. articles.philly.com/2010-06-22/sports/24966563_1_hotel-manager-springhill-suites-hotel-legal-system.
22. All quotations are from the Philly.com article. The author left a voicemail at the Levis home requesting an interview, but the call was never returned.

KENNY LOFTON

BY RICHARD BOGOVICH

"In a way, Kenny Lofton is the real instrument of terror for the Indians," *Los Angeles Times* sports columnist Jim Murray wrote during the 1995 World Series. "He is kind of like the scout for the cavalry. He forages ahead of the main force, scans the terrain, probes for weak spots, sets the tone for the attack. Custer would have died in bed if he had one."[1]

Though 13 different Indians were named American League All-Stars from 1995 to 1999, Lofton stood out to teammates like Jim Thome, who called him "the most talented player in baseball."[2] Opponents also deeply admired him. "Kenny Lofton is such a great offensive weapon," said Alex Rodriguez in 1998, in the wake of a confrontation that saw Seattle teammate Randy Johnson and Lofton ejected from an April game.[3] Toward the end of his career, fans were often calling Lofton the "Mayor of Cleveland."[4]

As intense as Lofton could be during a game, in the spring of 1995 a *Sports Illustrated* profile noted that "when the season's over, Lofton avoids the spotlight."[5] That largely remained true during the rest of his major-league career. "The Kenny Lofton that [he] shows the public is not the same Kenny Lofton those closest to him know," wrote *Plain Dealer* reporter Jodie Valade when Lofton's career was winding down in 2007. "He likes it that way, keeping the world at a distance from his private life."[6] Still, details have trickled out here and there, and Sam Smith of the *Chicago Tribune*, for one, believed that some of those facts served to shed light on Lofton's personality off the baseball field. "Lofton's longtime personal reserve grew from the spartan upbringing" he experienced growing up in East Chicago, Indiana, in a home that "had concrete floors and broken windows," Smith wrote. "Food was made to last and extravagances were unknown."[7]

Kenneth Lofton was born prematurely to Annie Mae Person on May 31, 1967. Mentions of his birth weight have ranged from 2½ to 4½ pounds but sources tend to say he weighed about 3 pounds.[8] Annie was just 14 years old when Kenny was born. She wanted to focus on completing school so she asked her widowed mother, Rosie, to raise Kenny. Annie eventually moved away. "Kenny never knew his daddy," Rosie said in 1995. "We don't know if he's dead or alive. It was one of those one-night stands."[9]

One of the first descriptions in a prominent media outlet of Lofton's modest upbringing came when he was a prominent college athlete. Two

Chicago Tribune columnists wrote about Rosie's role in his life, noting that Kenny was just one of eight grandchildren whom she raised or helped to raise. She did that despite having been blind for a number of years. "She used to come to all the games when I was in high school," Lofton said, "and the people next to her would tell her what I was doing."[10]

Even before Rosie lost her sight, the glaucoma that eventually claimed it kept her from being employed, but she did not go on welfare and accepted only Social Security benefits. She enrolled Kenny in the local Head Start program and he would overcome a speech impediment. She also fostered a love of baseball in Kenny. She was a diehard Chicago Cubs fan and often listened to games on the radio. As a result, when Kenny was a toddler he would watch neighborhood games played in the street and occasionally scamper after a stray ball. Soon enough, he was the proud owner of a Wiffle ball and bat. Though he would grow up playing basketball often, baseball reportedly came first.[11]

It was Rosie who taught Kenny how to throw his first baseball. However, by the time he was 9 years old he would find himself providing additional play-by-play descriptions to his grandmother by watching their television. Kenny started attending East Chicago's Washington High School in the fall of 1981 and toward the end of that school year he made the baseball team. The lefty was a starter all four years, and did well as a pitcher and outfielder.[12]

Nevertheless, it was as a basketball player there that Lofton's name would regularly get into newspapers across Indiana. After spending his first season on the freshman squad, he leapfrogged the junior varsity and started playing for the varsity team in 1982-83 as a 5-foot-11 sophomore. The team improved from 3-18 that season to 11-9 in Lofton's junior year, and when he was a senior in 1984-85 the squad went 24-2 and went to the semifinals of the state championship.

Lofton received a scholarship to the University of Arizona to play basketball. He started as a guard during his sophomore year to replace injured teammate Steve Kerr, later an NBA star. In his third season he played a crucial sixth-man role as Arizona reached the Final Four of the 1988 NCAA tournament. Lofton's high school, which had closed the year after he graduated, had the unusual distinction of producing the only two athletes to play in both a Final Four and a World Series, the earlier graduate being pitcher Tim Stoddard.

Lofton started playing for Arizona's baseball team on a limited basis as a junior, and at mid-year he was signed by the Houston Astros as a 17th-round pick in the 1988 amateur draft. That summer he played 48 games for the Auburn Astros of the New York-Penn League. Though he struggled at bat, hitting .214, he stole 26 bases in 30 attempts. Success on the basepaths would become one of his defining attributes. Lofton declined an assignment to play in the Instructional League into October because he wanted to honor his commitment to his grandmother, Rosie, to earn a college degree. Thus, as a senior he was the starting point guard as Arizona reached the Sweet 16 of the 1989 NCAA tournament. Lofton "might be the quickest player in America," wrote one sportswriter.[13]

Lofton was awarded a degree in studio production, which he would put to good use years later, but it was back to minor-league baseball for the summer of 1989. He returned to Auburn and improved his batting average to .264, then was promoted to the Asheville Tourists in the South Atlantic League for 22 games, in which he hit .329. Rarely did Lofton hit below .300 for any team over the next decade. He next spent the 1990 season with the Osceola Astros of the Florida State League, where he hit .331. In 1991 he played at the Triple-A level with the Tucson Toros in the Pacific Coast League, where he hit .308. He was named to that circuit's all-star team and the Toros won the championship. Lofton earned a final-month call-up by Houston, and made his major-league debut on September 14, 1991, in a game against the Cincinnati Reds. Lofton impressed that day. In four at-bats he had three hits, one of them a double, and he added a walk while scoring three runs. But over his 20-game audition he hit only .203.

The Astros were committed to Steve Finley as their center fielder, so during the offseason Lofton and infielder Dave Rohde were traded to Cleveland for backup catcher Eddie Taubensee and pitcher Willie Blair. "There was nary a scout who didn't think the Houston Astros erred big-time in giving up speedy center-field prospect Kenny Lofton," said a Knight-Ridder news service report on the winter meetings.[14] By mid-March, Associated Press baseball writer Jim Donaghy was proclaiming, "The closest thing to a favorite for the AL Rookie of the Year has to be Cleveland center fielder Kenny Lofton." He added that the trade "could be the steal of the year."[15]

Lofton, who wore uniform number 7, did not disappoint. He hit .285, and his 66 steals set a record for American League rookies. He led the AL in steals for the next four years as well. How fast was he? Sportswriter Wayne Stewart reported that Lofton could "rocket from home plate to first base in a blistering 3.1 seconds."[16] Lofton finished second in AL Rookie of the Year voting to Pat Listach of the Milwaukee Brewers. After the 1992 season he signed a contract totaling $6.3 million over four years. In 1993 his .325 batting average was fourth highest in the AL, his on-base percentage was .408, he scored 116 runs, and he received the first of four consecutive Gold Glove Awards.

The strike-shortened season of 1994 was a special one for Lofton in several regards. On May 2, an open date before a series in Chicago, he went home to see Rosie, and the syndicated TV show *This Week in Baseball* recorded their visit for a segment about Mother's Day. That summer he was named an All-Star for the first of six seasons in a row. In the top of the seventh inning he rapped a two-run single. (The AL lost the game in the 10th.) "The funniest moment of the night was when Bob Costas suggested that All-Star Kenny Lofton did his communications thesis on [Bob] Uecker's *Mr. Belvedere*" TV series, asserted one reporter.[17] Lofton concluded the season leading the AL in hits on his way to a .349 average, and finished second with 105 runs scored in his 112 games. His on-base percentage was .412. Most impressively, he finished fourth in Most Valuable

Player voting, behind winner Frank Thomas, Ken Griffey Jr., and teammate Albert Belle.

The 1995 season was another solid one for Lofton. He hit .310 and led the AL in triples with 13. He had three multi-triple games, the first player to accomplish that obscure feat since the American League's expansion in 1961. In the American League Championship Series against the Mariners, he batted .458 in six games, and saved the best for last: "The biggest moment in a season full of them was Kenny Lofton's dash home from second base on a passed ball in the final game of the ALCS in Seattle," declared Bob Dyer in *The Top 20 Moments in Cleveland Sports,* ranking the feat number 9 in his list.[18] In the World Series loss to the Braves, Lofton hit only .200, though in the third game, won by the Indians in extra innings, he was 3-for-3 plus three walks, a stolen base, and three runs scored.

The 1996 season was another productive one for Lofton. He batted .317 with 210 hits and 132 runs scored. However, in March of 1997 he and pitcher Alan Embree were traded to the Braves for outfielders David Justice and Marquis Grissom. Lofton hit .333 for Atlanta in '97 but went on the disabled list twice with groin injuries and stole only 27 bases while leading the National League in times caught stealing.

A free agent after the 1997 season, Lofton returned to Cleveland for the next four seasons. In three of those his average was below .300. He did score more than 100 runs in the first three of those years, and on September 3, 2000, he tied an American League record by scoring in an 18th straight game, matching Red Rolfe's achievement in 1939 for the Yankees. His salary peaked in 2001 at $8 million. That year, as part of the franchise's centennial celebration, a group of experts named Lofton one of the Top 100 Greatest Indians.

In February 2002 Lofton returned home by signing as a free agent with the Chicago White Sox. He donated $125,000 to create new ball fields in East Chicago, and the venue was christened the Kenny Lofton Little League Complex. In June, less than two weeks after his 35th birthday and on the day after he stole the 500th base of his major-league career, Lofton spoke to local youngsters at the site. "I started here just like you, and look where I am now," he said. "All your dreams can come true if you work hard enough. Maybe one day I'll be out in the audience clapping for one of you guys about what you've done for the city of East Chicago."[19] That same year, Rosie's role in Kenny's life would be one of the stories told in a documentary called *Apple Pie: Raising Champions*.

At the July waiver deadline, Lofton was traded to the contending San Francisco Giants and reached the World Series for the second time in his career. He was 9-for-31 as the Giants lost to the Angels in seven games. From 1995 through 2007 Lofton reached the postseason each year except for 2000 and 2005.

From 2002 through 2007 Lofton played with a different team – or two – in each season. He split 2003 between the Pittsburgh Pirates and the Chicago Cubs, toiled with the New York Yankees in 2004, played for the Philadelphia Phillies in 2005, and spent 2006 with the Los Angeles Dodgers. He started 2007, his final season, with the Texas Rangers but fittingly finished with Cleveland. Personal highlights were sprinkled throughout his travels. For example, from April 29 to May 30, 2003, he had a 26-game hitting streak for the Pirates.

Also, in 2005 Lofton's batting average was .335 in 110 games, and at age 39 the next year he had the second-most triples of his career, 12. In 2006 he stole 32 bases in 37 attempts. In 2007 he scored the 1,500th run of his career, and at the time that put him at number 54 on the all-time list, just behind Frankie Frisch. In the subsequent playoffs with the Indians he stole two bases to end his career with 34 in the postseason, breaking Rickey Henderson's record. Lofton's 622 regular-season stolen bases put him at number 15 on the all-time list, and he retired with a career batting average of .299.

Lofton and David Wells share the record for playing for the most different teams in the postseason, six. Lofton wore the uniforms of 11 teams overall, only one fewer than the record of 12 held by Mike Morgan. Toward the end of his career Lofton's many relocations were made light of in a TV commercial aired by the DHL Express delivery service.

In early 2004 Lofton co-founded a television production company, FilmPool Inc., and as of 2015 was still its CEO. He has co-produced two TV shows, *The Audition* and *Burnin'*. He kept a foot in the baseball world as a pregame and postgame analyst for Fox Sports West/Prime Ticket broadcasts of Dodgers games.

In August of 2010 Lofton was inducted into the Cleveland Indians Hall of Fame. In 2011 the Indians hired him for spring training to coach baserunning and outfield defense, and in 2012 he was brought back for a weekend as a guest instructor. Lofton's relationship with his main team turned a bit sour in January of 2014. He appeared at the second annual TribeFest at Progressive Field (formerly Jacobs Field) and expressed his disapproval of considering the Indians' wild-card loss to have been a playoff appearance, ending their postseason drought since Lofton's final year. "People look at it as a playoff game, it wasn't a playoff game," he said. "A playoff is a series, not one game. It's not the Super Bowl."[20]

It wasn't widespread news until mid-March that Nick Swisher took such exception to Lofton's dismissive commentary that Swisher debated heatedly with him.[21] Lofton then reportedly received numerous cold shoulders when he appeared at the Indians' spring training site. (His mood may have been decidedly negative around then for a very different reason: His beloved grandmother was very ill. Rosie Person passed away on February 25, 2014.)

Lofton became eligible for the National Baseball Hall of Fame in 2013. Leading up to the vote, Ted

Keith of *Sports Illustrated* provided a long analysis of his Hall-worthiness. "Despite his excellence, Lofton was somewhat underrated in his day, and he scores surprisingly well by some measures when it comes to the Hall of Fame – better than some of the more heralded centerfielders on this year's ballot, at the very least," Keith wrote. "He's in danger of getting lost among the flashier candidates on the ballot, so it's important to give his case its due."[22]

Lofton received votes from only 3.2 of the voters and therefore didn't qualify to remain on the ballot. Matt Snyder, writing for CBSsports.com, flagged him as one of the three biggest names to have fallen out of consideration, characterizing Lofton's result as "amazingly low considering his body of work and how few voters appear to have voted for their maximum of 10 players."[23] These form just the tip of the iceberg of what an Internet search about his candidacy will generate. Granted, there has been plenty of opining online that Kenny Lofton isn't a Hall of Famer, but for someone with so few votes the debate about his merits sure has been robust.

NOTES

1. Jim Murray, "Indians Missing a Spark," *Los Angeles Times*, October 26, 1995.
2. Dave McKibben, "Teammates Think Highly of Lofton, Even If He Doesn't," *Los Angeles Times*, August 15, 1996.
3. Ken Berger (Associated Press), "In Lather over Shave," *Pittsburgh Post-Gazette*, April 17, 1998: C-5.
4. Kim Schneider, "Turn Back the Clock," *Cleveland Magazine*, August 2010.
5. Michael Silver, "Close to the Heart," *Sports Illustrated*, May 1, 1995: 97.
6. Jodie Valade, "Cleveland Indians' Kenny Lofton Wants His World Serious," *Plain Dealer* (Cleveland), October 15, 2007.
7. Sam Smith, "Lofton Ready to Run Again," *Chicago Tribune*, March 17, 2002. Several of the following details about Lofton's humble early years are also from Smith's account.
8. His weight was reported as 2½ pounds by Bruce Jenkins in "Lofton Is Starring in Leading-Man Role," *San Francisco Chronicle*, October 10, 2002, quoting from the *Dayton Daily News* in 1995. Lofton's weight was given as 4½ pounds in the 2002 documentary *Apple Pie: Raising Champions*. See applepiemovie.com/html/kennyandrosie.html. Additional information about Lofton's youth has been taken from the latter.
9. Bruce Jenkins, "Lofton's Grandmother Was Listening." *San Francisco Chronicle*, October 25, 1995. This is also the source of subsequent details about Lofton's youth.
10. Linda Kay and Mike Conklin, "Odds & Ins," *Chicago Tribune*, December 25, 1987.
11. Bonnie DeSimone, "A Leader of the Pack," *Chicago Tribune*, October 1, 1996.
12. Mark Stewart, *Kenny Lofton: Man of Steal* (Chicago: Children's Press, 1998), 15.
13. Steve Bisheff, "Wildcats Looks Similar to Bruins of Old," *Orange County Register* (Anaheim, California), March 13, 1989: C8.
14. For example, see "Many Free-Agent Players Didn't Strike It Rich," *The Telegraph* (Alton, Illinois), December 22, 1991: C-4.
15. For example, see Jim Donaghy, "Solid Rookie Class for Baseball Season," *Aiken* (South Carolina) *Standard,* March 19, 1992: 7A.
16. Wayne Stewart, "Baseball's Greyhounds," *Boy's Life*, May 1994: 10.
17. Jeff Hasen, "Uecker Underutilized During All-Star Game," *Deseret News* (Salt Lake City), July 15, 1994: D3.
18. Bob Dyer, *The Top 20 Moments in Cleveland Sports: Tremendous Tales of Heroes and Heartbreaks* (Cleveland: Gray & Company, 2003), 260.
19. Jim Masters, "Lofton hits a home run in E.C.," *The Times* (Munster, Indiana), June 9, 2002.
20. Stephanie Storm, "Indians Notebook: Former Ace Pitcher Charlie Nagy Glad to Be Back in Organization," *Akron* (Ohio) *Beacon Journal*, January 25, 2014.
21. For example, see Jonathan Lehman, "Why Nick Swisher Is Beefing with Kenny Lofton," *New York Post*, March 18, 2014.
22. Ted Keith, "JAWS and the 2013 Hall of Fame Ballot: Kenny Lofton," SI.com, December 17, 2012.
23. Matt Snyder, "Murphy, Lofton, Williams headline those falling off Hall of Fame ballot ," CBSsports.com, January 8, 2013.

ALBIE LOPEZ

BY HARRY SCHOGER

Albert Anthony "Albie" Lopez, of Mexican heritage, was born in Mesa, Arizona, on August 18, 1971, the oldest child of Albert and Gloria Lopez. The elder Albert owned a construction business. Although Albie learned the basic skills of his father's trade, he showed little interest in pursuing it. His love and focus was always baseball. When he was inducted into the Mesa Public Schools Hall of Fame in 2013, he told the Mesa Community College student newsletter, the *Mesa Legend*, "My entire life has been about baseball. My parents tell me I picked up a baseball at the age of 3, and I haven't put it down yet."[1] By the age of 6 he was playing organized Little League.

Albie had a brother, David, and a sister, Amanda. In spite of a six-year difference in ages the boys formed a tight bond growing up. Although they played baseball together as youths, the boys followed two distinctively different paths in life.

Albie started his primary education in parochial school, while most of his friends attended public school. At age 10 he asked his parents to let him go to public school to be with his friends. His folks assented.[2] He attended Westwood High School in Mesa, where he was a right-handed pitcher for the Warriors. In 1989, his senior year, he played for the US Junior Olympic team, which won Gold and Bronze Medals.[3] He was also drafted in the 46th round of the 1993 amateur draft by the San Francisco Giants but declined to sign. His father was adamant that Albie was too young at only age 17.[4]

Lopez's baseball talents earned him a full scholarship to Mesa Community College. He led his team to the 1990 Junior College World Series and earned First Team All American honors.[5] The Seattle Mariners drafted him in the 19th round of the 1990 amateur draft. He declined for a second time. "The Mariners offered me $50,000, but they kept telling me I couldn't make it," Lopez said. "I knew I could play so I didn't like their attitude. My dad didn't either. He told them I wasn't interested."[6]

His parents, especially his mother, opposed Lopez's goal of playing professional baseball. She felt he could never make the kind of money he could in private business. In 1991 he was drafted by the Cleveland Indians in the 20th round. By this time he had apparently exhausted his parents with his dream of playing professional baseball, left his scholarship on the table and joined the Cleveland organization. Even though the Indians' offer was less than half that of the Mariners,

Cleveland persuasively pitched the impression that it wanted him.[7]

For the 1991 season Lopez, a slender 6-foot-2 185-pounder, was assigned to the Burlington Royals of the Rookie Appalachian League, where he started 13 games and posted a record of 4-5. In 1992 he advanced to Columbus (Georgia) of the Class A Sally League, where he went 7-2 with a 2.88 ERA and was promoted to Kinston of the High A Carolina League and posted a record of 5-2 with a 3.52 ERA. In 1993 he was assigned to Canton-Akron Indians of the Double-A Eastern League. He was 9-4 record with a 3.11 ERA, third best in the league, and was an Eastern League All-Star.

Because of injuries, the 1993 Indians were in dire need of healthy starters, and called Lopez up for a one-game stint in Oakland on July 6. His parents had driven 2,100 miles from Mesa to Canton to watch him pitch for the Double-A Indians. They arrived just a few hours before Albie had to catch his plane to Oakland. Not all was lost, though. Al and Gloria had planned a month's vacation in the Canton-Akron-Cleveland area. They were able to watch him several times.

Lopez had a promising start against Oakland's Bob Welch, leaving in the seventh inning with a 6-2 lead but got a no-decision when the A's tied the game, 8-8, in the eighth inning. The Indians won the sloppily played contest, 11-8, on a three-run homer by Carlos Martinez. The next day Lopez was optioned to Canton-Akron.

On July 18 the Indians brought him back for another start, and he pitched 7⅓ scoreless innings while earning his first major-league win, 2-1 over the California Angels, 2-1, beating All-Star pitcher Mark Langston. Inserted into the starting rotation, on the 23rd he won again as the Indians beat the Seattle Mariners, 9-4.[8]

Manager Mike Hargrove knew his freshman pitcher would someday have a bad outing.[9] On July 28 his premonition was rewarded. Lopez didn't finish the second inning before giving up five hits, five walks, and nine runs. One of those hits was a grand slam by Robin Ventura as the White Sox coasted to a 9-4 win. Lopez bounced back in his next start, leading the Indians to a 9-4 win over Detroit in a rain-shortened seven-inning game.

Lopez made four more starts in August with no decisions. After showing promise in five starts, he regressed to the point where it was evident he was not ready for prime time. Pitching coach Rick Adair thought he should use his changeup more. Lopez used it less. Accordingly, he was demoted to Charlotte of the Triple-A International League for the balance of the season.

Lopez spent most of the 1994 season at Charlotte, where he pitched well, chalking up a 13-3 record and 3.94 ERA. He was called up twice by the Indians for a total of 19 days in July and August. He started four games, pitched 17 innings, and went 1-2 with an ERA of 4.24. His pitching coach at Charlotte told Albie he needed to develop more mental toughness if he wanted to stay in "The Show." As it was, Lopez still got a paycheck from Charlotte while the Indians players got none when the players went on strike.

The 1995 season was more of the same for Lopez. He spent most of his playing time with the Buffalo Bisons of the Triple-A American Association. The Indians brought him up again. He started two of the six games in which he played and had no decisions. Although it was an AL pennant-winning year for the Indians, Lopez was not on the postseason roster. The next season, 1996, was a step up for Lopez as he split his time between Cleveland and Buffalo. With the Indians he pitched 62 innings in 13 games, 10 of which he started, compiling a 5-4 record with a bloated ERA of 6.39. As usual he had a much better year statistically with the minor-league Bisons, going 10-2 with a 3.87 ERA. Again he failed to make the Indians postseason roster.

Lopez spent all of 1997 as a major leaguer, except for 12 innings with Buffalo. However, his role began to change. He started only 6 of the 37 games in which he was used. In the other 31 games he was a middle/long reliever. He finished the season 3-7 with a 6.93 ERA. His third and last win was a relief stint in St. Louis on June 14 in Cleveland's first-ever interleague game.

Again the Indians were in the playoffs and Lopez was not on the roster. He took a comment from manager Hargrove the wrong way (according to Hargrove), believing it indicated he was on the roster. After telling Lopez of his omission, Mike asked him to stay in shape and accompany the team to New York for the Division Series vs. the Yankees in case he was needed to replace an injured player. Lopez became incensed, refused to board the bus to the airport, and drove home. In response to Lopez's behavior, Hargrove decided that Lopez had pitched his way off the roster. It is most likely that the incident played a part in his future with the Tribe.[10]

An expansion draft was scheduled for November 18. Two new franchises were to be formed: The Tampa Bay Devil Rays would join the AL and the Arizona Diamondbacks the NL. The local newspapers in the Cleveland area began taking polls to determine whom the fans would most prefer to protect from the draft. Lopez made embarrassingly negative headlines as the one player the fans would least want protected.[11] He was put into the draft pool and taken by Tampa Bay.

Lopez's somewhat checkered career with the Indians was over. He had shown signs of genius interspersed with periods of mediocrity. After five years in the Indians organization he had pitched 228 innings in 69 games with the parent club. He started 31 games, completing only one. His record was 12-14 with an ERA of 5.99. Not only was his hurling inconsistent but his demeanor toward Tribe management was critical, sometimes publicly. Considering that he had been optioned 18 times in a 3½-year period, there was certainly some degree of merit to his criticism.

Lopez reported to the Rays spring training for a fresh start on a new team. By this time he weighed 240 pounds. He made the Opening Day roster and was a fixture on the Tampa Bay team for most of four seasons. His hope of making the starting rotation would not materialize his first two seasons. He was used as a set-up man. However, the work was steady. He played in only six minor-league games while a Devil Ray. In 1998 he worked 79⅔ innings, went 7-4 and enjoyed his career-best ERA at 2.60. In the same role in 1999 he worked 64 innings, earned a 3-2 record and watched his ERA move up to 4.64.

An event in February of 1998 involving his brother David was painful for Albie and the entire family. David was charged with attempted murder. The man he allegedly shot was paralyzed from the neck down. The police said that David was the perpetrator and there was "bad blood" between him and his victim. Bond was set at $2.5 million, and David sat in jail for 18 months before his trial. Albie insisted David was innocent. In spite of his belief, the trial determined otherwise. David served 8½ years. He did not get out until 2006.[12]

The 2000 season was perhaps Lopez's banner year. He was moved into the starting rotation during the course of the season. Of the 45 games in which he played he started 24, throwing four complete games, including a shutout. He compiled an 11-13 record and had a 4.13 ERA. He was named AL player of the week for August 13.

The next season, 2001, was notable for multiple reasons. First of all, Lopez got the nod to start the home opener at Tropicana Field against Toronto. He pitched eight strong innings, allowing only one run and seven scattered hits. The Rays' offense backed him up with 15 hits on the way to an 8-1 victory, the first-ever franchise home-opening win.

When the glow of the Opening Day win faded, reality set in. Lopez had pitched in 20 games, winning 5 and losing 12. His ERA was up to 5.34. The Arizona Diamondbacks, who were in the thick of a battle for their division championship, needed a seasoned starter. On July 25 they made a deal that included Lopez, who was excited to be close to home, where he could be near his family and visit imprisoned David on a regular basis. In addition, he would team up with two of the best pitchers in professional baseball, Curt Schilling and Randy Johnson.

Lopez made his first start on July 28 against the San Francisco Giants with 144 members of his fan club in the upper deck. They had little to cheer about as he gave up 10 hits and 7 runs in an 11-4 drubbing by the visitors. His second outing was another loss, but he got no help from a dormant offense in a 1-0 game. The third start was a repeat of the first one when he again allowed 10 runs while extending his record to 0-3. He won his next three starts in a row. Inconsistency set in again, as he ran his record to 3-7 before winning a crucial game down the stretch to avoid losing his 20th game of the season. As it was, his 19 losses led the majors.

At last Lopez made a postseason roster. He lost an NLDS start against St. Louis and had no decision in the NLCS against Atlanta. He was relieved after three innings. He pitched once in the World Series against the Yankees. It was a relief appearance in Game Five. Chuck Knoblauch singled and moved to second base on a sacrifice bunt by Scott Brosius. Albie then gave up a walk-off single to rookie Alfonso Soriano down the right field line on which Knoblauch managed to reach home before Reggie Sanders's throw arrived. Soriano's hit marked the end of Lopez's one and only World Series appearance and the last game of his career as a Diamondback. Lopez went 0-2 in the postseason. He was granted free agency on November 6 after the Diamondbacks had gone on to win the Series in seven games.

Lopez signed with the Atlanta Braves as a free agent on December 20. He worked mostly in middle relief for the 2002 Braves, for a 1-4 record and 4.37 ERA. The Braves gave him free agency on December 28.

In 2003 Lopez hooked a ride with Kansas City, where he worked 22 innings, enjoyed a winning 4-2 record but compiled a whopping 12.71 ERA. He worked his last game for the Royals and the last game of his major-league career at home against the Twins on June 19. By the time he was called in to relieve starter Kyle Snyder the score was already 7-0 for the visitors. Lopez worked two-thirds of an inning, faced 10 batters, and gave up six hits (including a home run), seven runs, and two walks. The devastation at the end of day was 16-2, Twins. It was a no-decision for Lopez but the end of his major-league career. He was released that same day. On that sour note he took a break from baseball for 2004.

On March 23, 2004, his wife Crystal's birthday, Lopez was "out of baseball, out of shape, and out of sorts." He was up to 260 pounds. He had been casually relaxing, watching baseball games and helping Crystal with their three children.[13] He committed himself to getting back into playing shape and did so with unwavering commitment. He met his goal but not the end result he was hoping to achieve, a return to the majors.

Lopez did sign with the Pittsburgh Pirates in January of 2005 but was released on March 23 before the season began. In April he signed with the Mariners but was released on May 19 without having any playing time. He caught on for a short stint with the Tacoma Rainiers of the Pacific Coast League, pitching three relief stints, losing one game, and suffering a 12.60 ERA.

Lopez stayed out of pro ball until 2010 when he joined the Tucson Toros of the independent Golden Baseball League. He signed on as a starting pitcher and started 15 of the 16 games in which he played. His record was 7-5 and an ERA of 3.93. Jay Zucker, owner of the Toros, announced the team would take 2011 off.[14] Lopez then jumped to the newly formed North American League to play for the former Golden Baseball League Edmonton Capitals. He played in six games, all of which he started, going 3-0. The team folded at the end of the season, but not before winning the league championship series vs. Rio Grande Valley.

Lopez, at best a journeyman pitcher, never racked up any stats in his 11-year major-league career that approached All-Star caliber by any measure. He never reached the potential many baseball experts had predicted for him. He had a good arm, was a hard thrower, a power pitcher. Inconsistency was his nemesis. In reality, he had a sparkling minor-league career but one that was unspectacular at the major-league level. He was known for always smiling but on a few occasions off the field created tension with management, especially in Cleveland. These incidents went public, diminishing his image with the fans. Coupled with erratic pitching performances, these events managed to alienate the fan base of at least three of the big-league teams he served.

To be fair, he was bounced between the parent Cleveland Indians and the minors like a yo-yo. For 54 percent of his major-league career (per innings pitched), he toiled for Tampa Bay, a perennial last-place team. The problems of his brother David likely added mental distraction to his performance on the mound. He spent a total of 16 seasons, including minor-league service, plying his trade. In 11 major-league seasons he pitched 841⅓ innings (92 starts) and recorded a 47-58 won-lost record with a 4.94 ERA, yielding 112 homers.

In spite of his parents' misgivings, Albie did make a financial success of baseball.

As of 2018 Lopez lived in Gilbert, Arizona. He develops young professional aspirants by coaching and teaching in the instructional camps and clinics he advances, works and/or runs in the Mesa area.

SOURCES

In addition to the sources cited in the Notes, the author also consulted Baseball-Reference.com, the Baseball Cube, MLB.com. and Fox Sports.

NOTES

1. Mesa Community College Alumni Association website: mesacc.edu/alumni-association/hall-fame/albie-lopez
2. Richard Obert, "Return Home Doesn't Ease All of Lopez's Pain," *Arizona Republic* (Phoenix), August 17, 2001.
3. Mesa Community College Alumni Association website.
4. Sheldon Ocker, "Albie's Mom and Pop Operation," *Akron Beacon Journal*," July, 30, 1993.
5. Mesa Community College Alumni Association website.
6. "Albie's Mom and Pop Operation."
7. Ibid.
8. Lopez gave up a history-making homer to Ken Griffey Jr., the fourth in a string of eight consecutive games with a home run, tying a record held by Dale Long (1956) and Don Mattingly (1987).
9. Sheldon Ocker, "Indians Clobber Mariners' Johnson 9-4. Rookie Pitcher Has Strong Outing, Gets Second Big-League Win," *Akron Beacon Journal,* July 24, 1993.
10. Sheldon Ocker, "Irritated Lopez Refuses to Make Trip," *Akron Beacon Journal*, September 30, 1997.
11. Michael Weiner, "What, No Albie Lopez?" *Akron Beacon Journal,* November 16, 1997.
12. "Return Home Doesn't Ease All Lopez's Pain," *Arizona Republic,* August 17, 2001.
13. Peter Diana, "Lopez's Comeback Taking Shape," *Pittsburgh Post-Gazette,* February 21, 2005; "TB Stat Sheet," *Tampa Tribune,* March 30, 1998. Lopez had two children from his first marriage: Kelli Ryan and Albie Jr. At the time of this article they were in California.
14. "Toros on Hiatus; Triple A Beavers Plan to Play at TEP," *Arizona Daily Star* (Tucson), October 26, 2010.

DENNIS MARTINEZ

BY RORY COSTELLO

In 1976, Dennis Martínez became the first Nicaraguan to play in the big leagues – and he remains by far the most successful. Indeed, his 245 major-league wins are the most by any Latino pitcher, two ahead of Juan Marichal. Martínez got more than half of those wins after overcoming an alcohol problem that nearly derailed his career. His single most outstanding performance came on July 28, 1991, when he became the 13th pitcher to throw a perfect game.

El Presidente – as Martínez is often known in the U.S. – was a nickname he first received in 1979 from Orioles teammate Ken Singleton.[1] In later years, Martínez's name was bandied about as a candidate for president of Nicaragua, but only by a fringe party. The U.S. press ran with the idea, and it went mainstream in the States. His countrymen refer to Martínez as *El Chirizo*, which refers to his shock of mestizo hair. Without dispute, though, he has long been an enormous hero at home. In 1998, Nicaragua renamed its national stadium in his honor.

Denis José Martínez Ortiz was born on May 14, 1955 – or maybe 1954. Journalist Tito Rondón, who grew up in Nicaragua and is an authority on baseball there, noted that the daily *La Prensa*'s listing of the Nicaraguan team competing in the 1972 Amateur World Series showed 1954. Various other local press sources also show the earlier date of birth, but pending official confirmation, this biography will use 1955, in accord with Martínez's own belief.

Rondón added, "When he signed with the Orioles, he chose the name José Dennis Martínez. As mother's maiden name he wrote 'Emilia,' his mom's first name – Emilia Ortiz de Martínez was her complete name. The Major League name became official when Dennis became an American citizen [in 1993]. When the stadium in Managua was named after him and they put up his name in lights, he insisted (and it was done) that they add the second 'n'."[2]

Martínez comes from Granada, a small city on the western shore of Lake Nicaragua and not far from the Pacific Ocean. Doña Emilia was in her forties when she gave birth to Dennis, her seventh child. He followed three brothers (Enrique, Guillermo, and Carlos) and three sisters (Lilliam, Aminta, and Adilia).[3] He came ten years after his previous sibling, and this meant that he grew up a lonely child, as he told Bruce Newman of *Sports Illustrated* in 1991.[4]

What's more, Dennis's father, Edmundo Martínez, became estranged from Emilia while she was expecting Dennis. He too had a drinking problem. Edmundo had inherited land from his father, and Emilia ran a stall in which she sold the products that came from the farm.[5] "My dad was...the quietest, most lovely drunk I ever saw," Martínez told Newman. "He was very gentle...But when he was drinking, he would sell our pigs to get money for liquor."[6]

"Emilia was a wonderful, honest, hard-working woman," said Tito Rondón. "When Dennis reached the majors, he asked her to retire, and he kept asking her, but she never did. She always went to the market to put up her stall and sell fruit, cheeses, beef and other staples."

In 2012, Martínez also recalled his childhood in a chat with *La Prensa*. "I was a rascal when I was a kid [the word he used was *pícaro*, the root of picaresque]. I grew up in the streets. They called me a bum, but I was a baseball bum." He recalled using balls made of socks and that he was 13 years old when he held a real baseball for the first time.[7] In sandlot ball, however, he was a third baseman.[8]

According to Tito Rondón, "Dennis started to play in an organized way as an infielder in a youth league in the area between Granada, Masaya, and Jinotepe in 1971." He also did some pitching and first attracted national attention that year when he led his team, Prego Junior, to the juvenile championship of Nicaragua. He threw a 1-0 shutout, allowing just a single infield hit and driving in the game's only run with a homer.

Nicaragua's first winter professional baseball league had folded in 1967, but an amateur summer league was established there in 1970. Founder Carlos García called it the First Division, and indeed it featured the nation's best players. In 1972, Martínez stepped up to that level. The skinny 17-year-old pitched for his hometown team, the Granada Tiburones (Sharks). Tito Rondón recalled, "Before the season he tried out for San Fernando from Masaya. Their old catcher 'Guaracha' Castellón would say tongue in cheek, years later, 'My claim to fame is that I fired Dennis Martínez from San Fernando.'

"Dennis then decided to try out for the Tiburones, and manager Heberto Portobanco also told him that he could not make the team. But he liked his strong arm, so he asked his brother, coach Joaquín 'Chapuliche' Portobanco, to take the youngster to the bullpen and teach him how to throw so they could evaluate him as a pitcher. He made the Granada team and the national squad."

Most of the other Nicaraguan big-leaguers (12 altogether as of early 2013) also started in this league. Number two was pitcher Tony Chévez of León, whom the Orioles signed along with Martínez. Chévez was the bigger star at home, and expectations were higher for him.[9] Yet after a fine early minor-league career, he pitched just four games with the 1977 Orioles. He hurt his shoulder in the fourth outing and was never the same.

That year, the Nicaraguan playoffs featured star performances from Martínez and Chévez. It was a four-team round robin that came down to a best-of-three tiebreaker between León and Granada. After Martínez won Game One on June 21, the series finished with a doubleheader on June 22 at the National Stadium in the capital city, Managua. In the opener, Chévez won 5-0 – but in the nightcap, Granada beat León with five innings from Martínez in relief.[10] "You just took the ball," said Chévez in 2009. "Everybody was watching."[11]

In August 1972, the Torneo de la Amistad (Friendship Tournament) was held in Santo Domingo, Dominican Republic. Rookie Martínez got a surprise start against Cuba in a game that Nicaragua won, 5-4 – its first victory over the regional powerhouse in 20 years.[12] Later that year, the 20th Amateur World Series was held in Managua from November 15 through December 3. The hosts, Nicaragua, won the bronze medal with a 13-2 record. Martínez pitched in five games, starting two; he was 1-1, 1.86.

Less than three weeks later, on December 23, 1972, Managua suffered its devastating earthquake. That New Year's Eve, as Roberto Clemente left for Nicaragua on his mercy mission, his plane went down off Puerto Rico, killing all on board. Martínez had come to know Clemente because

Roberto had managed the Puerto Rican team in the Amateur World Series. More than 40 years later, Martínez said, "I had two idols – one as a pitcher, Juan Marichal, and the other, Clemente, as a human being. I took him as an example. He got me to think more about helping your neighbor, helping children, which was his goal and now mine too."[13]

In 1973, there was a split in Nicaragua's top amateur ranks that would last through 1977. Two leagues evolved under rival federations: the Roberto Clemente League and the Hope and Reconstruction League, or ESPERE. Martínez played for the Granada entry in ESPERE in 1973.

When he was nearly 18, on April 29, 1973, Martínez married Luz Marina García, a fellow student from Granada. "She was 15," said Tito Rondón. "Dennis signed several months later, and left Nicaragua in March 1974. Friends told her to leave him, that in the U.S. he would forget her. But he had told her to wait for him, and she had faith in him. And in 1977, when he returned to the U.S., to the Orioles, she was with him." They had four children: Dennis Jr., Erica, Gilberto, and Ricardo. Martínez has often credited the support of his wife in helping his life get back on track and remain there.

Owing to a conflict between international baseball organizations FIBA and FEMBA, two Amateur World Series were held in parallel in 1973. The FEMBA event took place (without Cuba) in Managua from November 22 through December 5. Following the quake, the National Stadium was in ruins and the Nicaraguan economy was still suffering. Yet the hosts still spent a precious $500,000 to stage the tourney.[14]

Nicaragua faced the U.S. in the gold medal game, held in León; 9,000 fans thronged the 6,000-seat stadium. The Nicaraguans had to settle for silver, though, as Martínez lost a 1-0, 10-inning duel to Rich Wortham, who pitched in four seasons in the majors (1978-80; 1983). "I heard Dennis plead with his teammates, 'Please get me just one run, one is all I need,'" recalled Tito Rondón, who got to sit in the dugout for the first six innings. "But Wortham was much superior to the Nica hitters. Dennis had tougher foes and he tired in the 10th."

Manager Tony Castaño told Chévez – and Martínez too, one may infer – "You gotta go north. There's nothing for you here."[15] He tipped off his fellow Cuban, Julio Blanco Herrera, a bird dog for Baltimore.[16] Regional scouting supervisor Ray Poitevint then entered the picture. He later said, "Dennis looked like a pencil. But he had natural talent, as much as anyone. And he was hungry. He wanted to be something."[17] When he was signed, Martínez weighed a mere 135 pounds.[18] As a scout, though, Poitevint projected how his prospect would look when mature. Martínez filled out to 160 pounds by the time he reached Baltimore, eventually weighing 185 as a veteran. He stood 6-feet-1.

Tito Rondón and a colleague named Hans Bendixen were actually in Poitevint's hotel room, having an engrossing conversation about scouting with Ray and Julio Blanco Herrera, when Doña Emilia arrived with Dennis. "The signing was cloak and dagger stuff," said Rondón. "Ray and Julio asked us a favor; not to publish or talk about it." Accounts vary as to the bonus Baltimore paid, but whether it was $10,000 or as little as $3,000, Poitevint later called it "the best money I ever spent."[19]

According to Tito Rondón, keeping the signing quiet enabled Martínez to play for Granada at the beginning of the 1974 Nicaraguan season. At that time, he was also an engineering student at La Universidad Nacional Autónoma – he had a good mind for mathematics. He went there for just the first year, though, before going to the United States – Doña Emilia was not best pleased that he quit school.[20]

In March 1974, Dennis and Tony started their pro careers with Miami in the Florida State League (Class A). They had traveled the world before with the national team and had pitched in big stadiums, so they were not overwhelmed. Martínez ascended rapidly through the Baltimore system. In his first year with Miami, he was 15-6 with a 2.06 ERA. He struck out 162 men and allowed just four homers in 179 innings. He started the 1975 season with Miami again, but after going

12-4, 2.61, he was promoted to Double-A Asheville. He finished the season with two games at Triple-A Rochester.

Martínez pitched strongly again at Rochester in 1976 (14-8, 2.50). There were warning signs – "Unnamed teammates stated that the pitcher had developed 'bad night-time habits,' and enjoyed the party life." Even so, he was the International League's Pitcher of the Year, winning the Triple Crown of pitching. It was only the second time it had been done in the league's history.[21]

Thus, in September the big club rewarded him with his first call to the majors. Rochester manager Joe Altobelli thought that Martínez would be a better big-league pitcher than Mark Fidrych, who was then enjoying his marvelous rookie year for the Detroit Tigers. Baltimore superscout Jim Russo agreed, saying, "We haven't rushed Dennis, and our patience should pay off." (Of course, the Orioles had that luxury back then, since their pitching was so deep.) Russo added, "Martínez and Fidrych have similar styles. They keep the ball down and have exceptional sinking stuff."[22]

Martínez later described his repertoire to Orioles historian John Eisenberg. "My stuff was decent. I had a good curveball. My fastball was decent. My curveball made my fastball better. Everyone was aware of my curveball, so my fastball went right by them. But mostly, I had a big heart. . . .It isn't the stuff you have, it's how you execute it. With desire, determination, that's how I did it."[23] Looking back in 2011, he added, "As soon as I got a changeup, I blossomed."[24]

Martínez's debut came in long relief against the Tigers at Memorial Stadium on September 14, Ross Grimsley and Dave Pagan gave up seven runs between them in the first four innings. The rookie entered and struck out the first three batters he faced. He didn't allow a run the rest of the way either, and he got the win because the Orioles scored four in the bottom of the seventh. After that he started three times, losing two of them, including a 1-0 decision to Boston at Fenway Park in the second-last game of the season.

As part of his development, that winter Martínez went to play in Puerto Rico with the Caguas Criollos. Thomas Van Hyning, who has chronicled Puerto Rico's winter league in two books, wrote, "Martínez was part of the Baltimore-Caguas axis between 1976-77 and 1980-81. During this period he helped Caguas win three titles." Van Hyning added, "Puerto Rico was a second home to Martínez. . .the quality of play appealed to [him], and he gave it his all, including the 1978-79 championship game when he bested Mayagüez's Jack Morris."[25]

Wayne Garland, who won 20 games for Baltimore in 1976, signed as a free agent with the Cleveland Indians. Martínez therefore had a good chance to crack the starting rotation in 1977. Instead, he wound up as a swingman, starting 13 games in 42 appearances. He was 14-7, though his ERA was 4.10. In those days, four-man rotations were still the norm; Jim Palmer, Rudy May, Grimsley, and Mike Flanagan – who won the #4 starter job – started 143 games among them that year, completing 59. Manager Earl Weaver "was inclined to go with Martínez and Scott McGregor when he had to make a call on the bullpen. . .mainly because both rookies have displayed an ability to get the ball over the plate."[26]

Martínez entered Baltimore's rotation in 1978, along with McGregor. In December 1977, May had been traded to the Montreal Expos, and later the same month, Grimsley signed with the same club as a free agent. Martínez was 16-11, 3.52 in 40 games (38 starts). He had a poor first half, but at the All-Star break, pitching coach Ray Miller asked Dennis's wife what Martínez was doing differently that he hadn't done in the minors. Luz Marina replied that he was dipping his shoulder.[27] He also addressed how he was tipping his pitches with facial expressions by sticking a big chaw of tobacco and bubblegum in his cheek – it became his visual trademark.[28] In the second half, Martínez was 9-4, 2.30. He threw complete games in 11 of his last 14 starts, and in two of the other three games, he went 11 and 8 innings.

When Baltimore won the AL pennant in 1979, Martínez led the league in starts (39), complete games (18), and innings pitched (292 1/3). His results were so-so, though – 15-16, 3.66. After losing two of his first three starts, Martínez reeled off 10 straight wins in 14 outings from April 22 through June 20. He didn't pitch that badly the rest of the way, but had little to show for it – he didn't really pitch well enough to win much of the time either.

Some Orioles insiders, according to New York sportswriter Dick Young, cited Martínez's insistence that Dave Skaggs catch him rather than Rick Dempsey.[29] Skaggs joked, "When I die, they're going to bury me 60 feet, six inches away from Dennis Martínez."[30] Martínez told John Eisenberg, "I had a lot of disagreements with Dempsey. Whatever I was doing, it wasn't good enough or I wasn't doing things the right way."[31] Dempsey too acknowledged the battle and the two-way frustrations, but he said, "Earl made sure I knew what he wanted us to do with each hitter. I know Dennis didn't like it, but we won that way."[32]

At least at some level, worries about his family back in Nicaragua may have been a factor too. The Sandinista revolution was in full swing, and amid the civil war, Martínez could not reach Doña Emilia by telephone. Dictator Anastasio Somoza Debayle resigned on July 17. It was soon thereafter that Ken Singleton said, "You're going to be *El Presidente*," and the name stuck.

In the postseason, Martínez started Game Three of the AL Championship Series versus the California Angels. At Anaheim Stadium, he took a 3-2 lead into the ninth inning, but after Rod Carew's one-out double, Weaver called for Don Stanhouse, who couldn't hold the lead.

Martínez appeared twice in the World Series against the Pittsburgh Pirates. He started Game Four at Three Rivers Stadium, got knocked out of the box in the second inning – but the Orioles' six-run rally in the eighth inning got him off the hook. In Game Seven, he was the fifth pitcher that Weaver used in the ninth inning, when the Pirates scored two crucial insurance runs. Dennis came on with the bases loaded and hit Bill Robinson with a pitch, but then got Willie Stargell to hit into a double play.

The 1980 season was a setback for Martínez. A sore shoulder kept him out of action for most of two months from mid-May through mid-July. He was able to pitch only 99 2/3 innings, with 12 starts in 25 appearances. Bullpen coach Elrod Hendricks made an interesting observation – Martínez had not played winter ball in the 1979-80 season. "A lot of Latin pitchers cannot go without pitching in the winter," Ellie said. "They simply develop their arms a different way."[33]

Trade rumors circulated around Martínez after that off year, but his market value was low, and it turned out to be better for them that he stayed. *El Presidente* bounced back nicely in the strike season of 1981 – his 14 wins led the AL, and he lost just five while posting a 3.32 ERA. He came in fifth in the voting for the Cy Young Award. General Manager Hank Peters said that June, "We didn't want to break up our pitching staff and we've always felt Dennis had the arm and the ability. It was just a matter of him putting it all together."[34]

Martínez signed a five-year contract with Baltimore after the '81 season. He was a workhorse again in 1982, starting 39 games and going 16-12. However, his ERA was on the high side at 4.21. That September, he had to return to Nicaragua for the funeral of his father.[35] "He was walking and a truck hit him and killed him in Granada," Martínez recalled in 1985, suspecting that alcohol was likely a factor.[36] Despite Edmundo's grave alcoholism, Dennis still loved his father greatly – though he later regretted drinking together with him when he went back home.[37]

The year 1983 was when Martínez's personal problems came to a head. It was reflected in his performance on the mound – 7-16, with a career-high ERA of 5.53. The Orioles did not use him in either the AL Championship Series against the Chicago White Sox or the World Series against the Philadelphia Phillies. Nonetheless, Martínez is still proud of his championship ring from '83, even though he thought the '79 squad was more talented. "This was the year I got help for my alcohol problem," he said in 2002. "It was a bad year, but I got a new start."[38]

After Martínez was arrested for drunk driving in December 1983, the Orioles staged an intervention. He entered rehab in Baltimore's Sheppard Pratt Hospital. He told UPI sportswriter Milton

Richman that he was still in denial at first, but then his counselor encouraged Martínez to find strength in prayer. "That," he told Richman, "was the turning point of my life."[39] He stayed in control with the ongoing help of Alcoholics Anonymous meetings.[40]

It took more than three years for Martínez to re-emerge as an effective pitcher, though. He was 6-9, 5.02 in 1984. "I was happy to see the improvement in my mental problem," he told Richman. "That was my prime concern. Baseball was second."[41]

As part of his effort to rebound on the field, Dennis returned to Puerto Rico near the end of the 1984-85 winter season, joining the Santurce Cangrejeros.[42] Martínez got another chance to be a rotation regular for Baltimore in 1985 after Mike Flanagan ruptured an Achilles tendon. He did post a 13-11 record, but his ERA remained lofty at 5.15. "Physically, he is back," said Ray Miller that June. "Mentally, he is in the upward direction."[43]

Martínez's stock fell in 1986. He pitched just four games for Baltimore in April and then – bothered again by a sore shoulder – suffered a demotion to Rochester. In mid-June, the Orioles traded him to Montreal with a player to be named later, receiving a player to be named later in return. During the second half of the season, he started 15 games and relieved in four for the Expos, with no particular success (3-6, 4.59). He considered quitting.

After the '86 season, Montreal refused to offer more than $250,000 to Martínez, who had been making $500,000 in the last year of his Baltimore pact.[44] He became a free agent, but there were no takers, and he was barred from re-signing with the Expos until May 1, 1987. He went back to the minors again to get in shape, pitching for the independent Miami Marlins (Class A). He then re-signed with Montreal for the minimum salary. He was just 3-2, 4.46 for the Expos' Triple-A club in Indianapolis, but when Montreal farmed out Jay Tibbs in June, Martínez got another chance.

From then on, it all came together. During six and a half seasons with the Expos, Martínez was consistently among the best pitchers in the National League. His winning percentage was good (97-66, .595), but that wasn't all. His ERA was 2.96, including a major-league-best 2.39 in 1991. He was an NL All-Star in 1990, becoming the oldest player to make his All-Star debut, and repeated that honor in '91 and '92. He again received Cy Young consideration in 1991.

Along with attaining inner peace, Martínez had become a master craftsman on the mound. In 1988, he told Montreal sportswriter Ian MacDonald, "Before, when I was drinking, I used to think I was good. I didn't think about pitching. . .I used to just try to throw the ball past the hitter. Now I think. I don't say it makes it easy, but it makes it easier." He moved the ball around, changed speeds, focused on the weaknesses of the hitters, and made constant adjustments, setting up batters based on their reactions from pitch to pitch.[45] He also hid the ball well with his motion and threw from varied arm angles.

Many insights also come from James Buckley's book *Perfect: The Inside Story of Baseball's Twenty Perfect Games*. Ron Hassey, the catcher for Martínez's flawless gem, said, "He had to hit his spots; he had to have his command to get guys out. But Dennis had outstanding control, and he knew how to pitch." Center fielder Marquis Grissom said, "It was like an artist making a painting." Opposing catcher Mike Scioscia also noted how fine Martínez's command was, saying, "We might have played 20 innings against him and never gotten a hit." Tito Rondón, then with *La Prensa*, said, "Dennis Martínez was already the most popular man in [Nicaragua] before he pitched a perfect game. Now he's just more popular."[46]

In December 1993, the 38-year-old veteran signed as a free agent with the Cleveland Indians. General manager John Hart viewed his club as a contender, and owner Richard Jacobs was willing to open up his wallet. Montreal had been paying Martínez around $3 million a year from 1991 on, but Cleveland gave him a two-year contract for $9 million. This was vast wealth by the standards of Nicaragua, where his needy countrymen already counted heavily on him.

Martínez continued to pitch well for the Indians – 32-17 (.653) with a 3.58 ERA in his three seasons there. He was particularly effective in 1995, when he made the AL All-Star team and helped Cleveland to win the pennant. In his first return to the postseason since 1979, he started once against Boston in the Division Series, getting a no-decision. He was 1-1 in the ALCS against Seattle, including seven scoreless innings in the decisive Game Six against fearsome Randy Johnson, even though his whole body hurt.[47] He was 0-1 in two starts against Atlanta in the World Series.

Martínez pitched only once in 1996 after the end of July, though – elbow problems disabled him. He became a free agent again that November, and it took him until late the following February before he landed with a new team, because his elbow was perceived as too risky. The Seattle Mariners finally took a chance, and as he approached his 42rd birthday, Martínez won a spot on the roster.

He was a good influence in the clubhouse and showed initial signs that he was not done yet, but Martínez made only nine ineffective starts for the Mariners. Although his elbow held up, a surprising 29 walks in 49 innings led to a 1-5 record and 7.71 ERA. Seattle released him in May 1997. The following month, he decided to retire, citing the lack of an opportunity to keep pitching.[48] He established the Dennis Martínez Foundation in 1997, with the goal of helping children, primarily in Nicaragua but also elsewhere in Latin America.

In the winter of 1997-98, however, Martínez decided to go back to Puerto Rico once more to play winter ball. As he had the previous year, he was again hoping to catch on with the Florida Marlins, since he had made his home in Miami for many years and the Nicaraguan population in south Florida was sizable. Various teams watched Martínez in his playoff showcase with the Mayagüez Indios, but Atlanta was the only one to show serious interest.[49]

During his 23rd and final season in the majors, Martínez was mainly a reliever, making five starts in 53 appearances. He was 4-6, 4.45 in 91 innings pitched. On June 2, he finally tied his old idol Juan Marichal for most wins in the majors by a Latino pitcher. It came with a complete-game 12-hit shutout at Milwaukee. He went ahead with a victory in relief over the Giants in San Francisco on August 9. His last win, #245, came in middle relief at Atlanta's Turner Field on September 25. He retired all four New York Mets he faced.

Martínez got into four NLCS games for Atlanta in 1998, getting one of the Braves' two wins against the San Diego Padres. In February 1999, he announced his final retirement, saying, "There is nothing more to do."[50]

A couple of months later, the Nicaraguan Baseball Federation named Martínez coordinator of the national team for the Pan American Games, to be held in Winnipeg that July. He said that he might even join the team if it needed pitching.[51] When July rolled around, he was still planning to work an inning or two in exhibition games, with an eye toward appearing against Cuba or the U.S. if Nicaragua made it as far as the semifinals. He was motivated because the Pan Am Games were an Olympic qualifying event.[52] It only got as far as an exhibition appearance in Panama, though.[53] A bad knee was one reason, but Mexico knocked out Nicaragua in the quarterfinals.

After retiring, Martínez worked for the Nicaraguan Visitors and Travel Bureau. He also helped coach at Westminster Christian High School in Miami. His youngest son, Ricky, was a player there. In the spring of 2005, with all his children out of school except for Ricky, he returned to the Orioles organization as a pitching instructor in camp. Old teammate Mike Flanagan, who was in the Baltimore front office, had kept in touch with him over the years about a possible return.[54]

Martínez spent six years (2007-12) as a minor-league pitching coach in the St. Louis Cardinals organization. He enjoyed helping many young prospects develop; among them was his son Ricky, who signed with the Cardinals as a non-drafted free agent in 2010. However, Dennis was hoping to get a shot at the big-league level.[55] In November 2012, he got that chance when the Houston Astros named him as their bullpen coach.

Martínez also remained involved with the Nicaraguan baseball scene. He managed the national team in the 2011 Baseball World Cup, as well as the 2013 World Baseball Classic qualifying tournaments, held in September and November 2012. Son Ricky was part of the squad for the WBC qualifiers.

In 2004, Martínez became eligible for the Baseball Hall of Fame in Cooperstown. He received 16 votes from the Baseball Writers Association of America. That level of support meant he was "one and done" – off the ballot in 2005. Five years later, baseball author Joe Posnanski wrote, "When you add it all up he has a very similar case to Jack Morris, who is gaining Hall of Fame momentum."[56] It remains to be seen if the Veterans Committee may eventually consider Martínez. In 2011, however, he became a member of the Latino Baseball Hall of Fame in La Romana, Dominican Republic.

One may conjecture that without the lost years in the middle of his career, Dennis Martínez might be an even stronger candidate for Cooperstown. But the flip side of that argument is that his career only became what it did because of the resurrection. "I never did," he said when asked in 2002 if he thought he would pitch for 23 years. "I think after recovery I had more of an effort to live life. And the competitor in me wanted to keep going. I did everything that God allowed me to do.

"I think the key to my longevity was staying in shape and changing my life after my addiction. Before that, I did not take good care of myself. . .But I had my family and I had a lot to play for."[57]

NOTES

1 "Former Oriole Dennis Martinez ponders political pitch," *Baltimore Sun*, January 7, 1994.

2 E-mail from Tito Rondón to Rory Costello, March 6, 2013 (based on Rondón's personal knowledge of the situation).

3 "Pésame a Denis Martínez por la pérdida de su madre," *La Prensa* (Managua, Nicaragua), May 4, 2001.

4 Bruce Newman, "Return of the Native," *Sports Illustrated*, December 30, 1991.

5 Bob Finnigan, "13 Years Of Sobriety, Dennis Martinez Has Been A Responsible Family Man, A National Hero In His Native Nicaragua And One Of Baseball's Best Pitchers," *Seattle Times*, April 25, 1997.

6 Newman, "Return of the Native"

7 Amalia del Cid, "Denis Martínez," *La Prensa*, October 14, 2012.

8 Newman, "Return of the Native"; Finnigan, "13 Years Of Sobriety"

9 Hernández, Gerald. "Everth Cabrera es el décimo nicaragüense en Grandes Ligas, quiere triunfar en San Diego". Puro Béisbol website (http://purobeisbol.com.mx/content/view/1255/1/). See also George Vecsey, "Nicaragua's Best Pitcher," *New York Times*, September 27, 1981: S3.

10 Ruiz Borge, Martín. "Asoma el tercer duelo," *El Nuevo Día* (Managua, Nicaragua), March 16, 2003.

11 Rory Costello, "Tony Chévez," SABR BioProject (http://sabr.org/bioproj/person/94643812)

12 Edgard Tijerino, "Denis, prepárate," *El Nuevo Diario*, September 18, 2011.

13 Antolín Maldonado Ríos, "Dennis Martínez fue influenciado por Clemente," *El Nuevo Día*, January 4, 2013.

14 Jordan, Pat. "Dubious Triumph In Florida," *Sports Illustrated*, December 9, 1974.

15 "Tony Chévez"

16 Edgard Tijerino, "¡Qué difícil fue!" *La Prensa*, January 13, 2003.

17 John Eisenberg, *From 33rd Street to Camden Yards* (New York, New York: Contemporary Books, 2001), 282.

18 Steve Henson, "The Frontiersman: Poitevint Blazes Trail for Angels as Global Scout," *Los Angeles Times*, September 17, 1993.

19 Finnigan, "13 Years Of Sobriety." The Orioles made Julio Blanco Herrera a full scout as a result of the Martínez/Chévez signing.

20 Vecsey, "Nicaragua's Best Pitcher"

21 Brian Bennett, On *a Silver Diamond: The Story of Rochester Community Baseball from 1956-1996* (Scottsville, New York: Triphammer Publishing, 1997), chapter 4.

22 "A Better Bird," *The Sporting News*, September 18, 1976, 32.

23 Eisenberg, *From 33rd Street to Camden Yards*, 283.

24 Derrick Goold, "Dennis Martinez makes his mark as pitching instructor," *St. Louis Post-Dispatch*, August 14, 2011.

25 Thomas Van Hyning, *Puerto Rico's Winter League* (Jefferson, North Carolina: McFarland & Co., 1995), 160.

26 Jim Henneman, "Orioles Toss Burning Problem to Fireman Drago," *The Sporting News*, July 2, 1977, 18.

27 Peter May, "If Birds Ever Need a Pitching Coach…," United Press International, September 13, 1978.

28 Newman, "Return of the Native"

29 Dick Young, Young Ideas," *The Sporting News*, October 20, 1979, 20.

30 Phil Pepe, "Phil Pepe's Patter," *The Sporting News*, November 3, 1979, 16.

31 Eisenberg, *From 33rd Street to Camden Yards*, 305.

32 Newman, "Return of the Native"

33 Peter Gammons, "Don't Expect Many of Those Deadline Deals," *The Sporting News*, June 21, 1980.

34 Ken Nigro, "Dennis Martinez Is O's New Ace," *The Sporting News*, June 27, 1981, 15.

35 Tom Flaherty, "Orioles Serve Weaver One Last Hot Roll," *The Sporting News*, October 4, 1982, 12.

36 Milton Richman, "Orioles' Dennis Martinez Has a New Goal: Staying Sober," United Press International, March 10, 1985.

37 Edgard Tijerino, "Era mi padre, lo quería," *El Nuevo Diario*, August

28, 2011. Finnigan, "13 Years Of Sobriety"

38. Gary Washburn, "Where have you gone, Dennis Martinez?" MLB.com, September 12, 2002 (http://baltimore.orioles.mlb.com/news/article.jsp?ymd=20020912&content_id=126757&vkey=news_bal&fext=.jsp&c_id=bal)

39. Richman, "Orioles' Dennis Martinez Has a New Goal: Staying Sober"

40. By most accounts, he stayed consistently sober, but according to one story, he had a few relapses. Ian MacDonald, "The only Montreal Expo to ever pitch a perfect game is now teaching a new generation," Canwest News Service, March 15, 2008.

41. Richman, "Orioles' Dennis Martinez Has a New Goal: Staying Sober"

42. Van Hyning, *Puerto Rico's Winter League*, 160.

43. Jim Henneman, "Martinez's Pitching Quiets Trade Talks," *The Sporting News*, June 17, 1985, 20.

44. *The Sporting News*, December 22, 1986, 48.

45. Ian MacDonald, "Heeding Expos' Call for Arms," *The Sporting News*, September 12, 1988, 15.

46. James Buckley Jr., *Perfect: The Inside Story of Baseball's Twenty Perfect Games* (Chicago, Illinois: Triumph Books LLC, 2012), 166, 167, 169.

47. Terry Pluto, *Our Tribe* (New York, NY: Simon & Schuster, 1999), 237.

48. "Dennis Martinez Retires From Baseball," *Seattle Times*, June 18, 1997.

49. Mike Berardino, "Martinez Making A Brave Comeback Try," *Palm Beach Sun-Sentinel*, March 8, 1998.

50. "Dennis Martinez retires," Associated Press, February 7, 1999.

51. "Still pitching?" *Seattle Times*, April 19, 1999.

52. Stephen Canella and Jeff Pearlman, "Dennis Martinez's Plans – One More Time: Pan Am Games," *Sports Illustrated*, July 19, 1999. This article also confirmed that Martínez showed his year of birth as 1954 in documentation he presented for the event.

53. Dick Heller, "Coach Martinez makes pitch for himself in Pan Am Games," *Washington Times*, July 12, 1999.

54. Gary Washburn, "'El Presidente' happy in new job," MLB.com, February 20, 2005 (http://mlb.mlb.com/news/article.jsp?ymd=20050220&content_id=946722)

55. Goold, "Dennis Martinez makes his mark as pitching instructor"

56. Joe Posnanski, "Taking a look at the Hall of Fame ballot's one-and-done club," SI.com, December 2, 2009 (http://sportsillustrated.cnn.com/2009/writers/joe_posnanski/12/01/hall.of.fame/index.html)

57. Washburn, "Where have you gone, Dennis Martinez?"

JOSÉ MESA

BY JOSEPH WANCHO

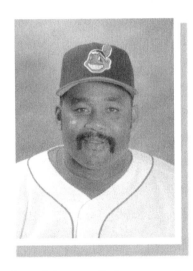

"What have you done for me lately?" is a common refrain heard among fans of all sports. Die-hard and casual fans are known to be a fickle bunch. Any time a player has an outstanding performance in one game, he or she is the toast of the town. The next day they falter and they are a bum. It is unfortunate that in many instances the boos are louder and last longer than the cheers. Except for the elite athlete, no player is exempt from getting "the business" or the "Bronx cheer" from the public.

On October 15, 1997, the Cleveland Indians were at Camden Yards to face the Baltimore Orioles in Game Six of the American League Championship Series. A pitcher's duel between the Indians' Charles Nagy and the Orioles' Mike Mussina was a delight. Both pitchers went deep into the game (Nagy 7⅓ innings and Mussina eight) without surrendering a run. The bullpens were equally stingy until the top of the 11th inning, when the Tribe's Tony Fernandez walloped a two-out home run to give Cleveland the slimmest of margins, 1-0.

Indians manager Mike Hargrove called on José Mesa to close out the O's and send Cleveland to its second World Series in three years. Mesa allowed a two-out single to Brady Anderson, and then struck out Roberto Alomar for the third out. It was the second save of the series for Mesa, who had lost his role as closer to Mike Jackson during the season.

Eleven days later, on October 26, Mesa was called on again by Hargrove in Game Seven of the World Series to close out the Florida Marlins in the ninth inning. If he was successful, it would be Cleveland's first World Series championship since 1948.

The Indians led 2-1 as Mesa trudged to the mound. But Moises Alou led off with a single to center field. Mesa struck out Bobby Bonilla, but Charles Johnson followed with a single to right field. Craig Counsell's sacrifice fly scored Alou to pull the Marlins even with Cleveland. The Marlins eventually won the game, 3-2 in 11 innings, and their first World Series championship.

Just as a team that wins has many contributors, the same is true when it loses. However, in the competitive world of professional sports, where winning is the only thing that matters, fingers seemingly must be pointed at the reason for a team falling short of the ultimate goal. Unfortunately, those fingers pointed at Mesa then, and to this day. For a closer the pendulum has big swings: lights out today, bum tomorrow.

But Mesa rose above that, became a successful closer for Philadelphia and enjoyed a 19-year major-league career. He reinvented his game to become one of the greatest relief pitchers of his time. As of 2018 Mesa ranked in the top 20 in career saves with 321.

Jose Ramon Mesa was born on May 22, 1966, in Pueblo Viejo, Azua, in the Dominican Republic. He was the 12th of 15 children born to Narciso and Maria Mesa. The Mesa family resided on a farm where they grew potatoes, green peppers, watermelons, and a surplus of coconut and banana trees. All of the Mesa children put in time working on the farm. Narciso left and started another family that produced nine more children. Narciso died suddenly in 1976 of a stroke.

At age 15, Mesa went to a tryout given by the Toronto Blue Jays. His main position was outfielder; he had never tried pitching. "I was a center fielder, with a little pop in my bat," said Mesa. "(Blue Jays scout Epy Guerrero) timed me in 7.4 seconds in the 60-yard dash, which meant I was probably too slow to play the outfield. But he still had me throw from the outfield."[1]

Mesa showed off his greatest asset for Guerrero, his powerful right arm. Even though Mesa had never pitched, Guerrero had him throw off a mound. After a few hours, Guerrero signed the teenager to a contract for $3,000. "I was the man of the family, and I had to get a job to help support my mother," said Mesa. "When I signed and went over to the States to play, I'd send money back to her every two weeks."[2] When Mesa left home, he had completed only the seventh grade in school.

Mesa reported to Rookie League ball in the Gulf Coast League in 1982. He pitched well, posting a 6-4 record with a 2.70 ERA. He led the league in shutouts with three.

However, Mesa never pitched higher than Double A for Toronto. On September 4, 1987, he was the "player-to-be-named-later" to complete a deal in which Baltimore sent pitcher Mike Flanagan to Toronto for pitcher Oswaldo Peraza and, subsequently, Mesa.

In spite of his relative inexperience pitching at higher levels, the Orioles activated Mesa immediately and he made his major-league debut on September 10, 1987, at Boston. Mesa gave a decent accounting of himself; he went six innings and surrendered three earned runs while striking out four batters. He won his first major-league game on September 30 at Detroit. The win dampened the Tigers' efforts to catch Toronto for the AL East crown. "I was just going after them," said Mesa. "I didn't care who they were."[3] Mesa, who worked 8⅔ innings, threw 150 pitches and struck out four.

Baltimore returned Mesa to the minors for more seasoning. Unfortunately for Mesa, both the 1988 and 1989 seasons were cut short due to surgery on his right elbow both years. He pitched in only 21 games over those two seasons between Double-A Hagerstown and Triple-A Rochester. Mesa returned to Baltimore late in the 1990 season. He won three games in a row to post a 3-2 record with a 3.86 ERA.

Mesa received his first extended playing time in the big leagues with the Orioles in 1991. The Orioles as a franchise were in a bit of a free-fall from the winning teams that they usually fielded. From 1986 to 1991 their average record was 71-91. Mesa posted a 6-11 record in 1991 with a 5.97 ERA. He totaled 64 strikeouts against 62 walks in 123⅔ innings pitched. Incredibly, Mesa was tied for third on the staff with the six wins, as Bob Milacki led the way with 10 victories.

Although he did not give up a run in spring training in 1992, his performance did not transfer over to the regular season. In 12 starts he was 3-8 with a 5.19 ERA. He whiffed 22 batters, but he also issued 27 free passes. That was the book on Mesa. He could throw 95 mph, but he lacked control. Baltimore traded Mesa to Cleveland on July 14, 1992, for minor-league outfielder Kyle Washington. "He pitched well against us last year," said Hargrove. "He throws hard and he's had control problems. But when he's thrown strikes, he's been effective."[4]

Mesa became the answer to a trivia question on September 9, 1992, when he gave up Robin Yount's 3,000th career hit at County Stadium.

Yount had also gotten his 1,000th and 2,000th career hits off Cleveland pitching. "I saw that and said, 'Well, maybe the guy's going to get No. 3,000 off Cleveland too,'" said Mesa. "And he did."[5]

The 1993 season was shrouded in black. It was bound to be an emotional season for many as the Indians were playing their last season at Cleveland Stadium. Although a brand new, open-air, baseball-only ballpark awaited them in 1994, there were many who had wonderful memories of the lakefront stadium.

But that all took a backseat on March 22, 1993, when Steve Olin, Tim Crews, and Bob Ojeda were involved in a boating accident on Little Lake Nellie near the team's spring training facility in Winter Haven, Florida. The trio ran head-first into an extended dock. Olin died instantly and Crews the next day. Ojeda recovered to pitch later that year.

The impact of that accident shadowed the team all season. Mesa, however, had a breakout year of sorts. Although his record was 10-12, he led the club in wins, complete games (3) and strikeouts (118). He was learning to pitch and not just throw hard. His strikeouts to walks (118/62) indicated he was making great progress. After one of those complete games, a 6-2 victory over Kansas City on May 12, Cleveland pitching coach Rick Adair gave a hint to Mesa's success. "When (Mesa) is pitching well, he is not overthrowing the ball, which he started to do at the end," said Adair. "I just told him to stay within himself, to not overthrow the ball. When he's throwing the ball right, he's got three good pitches which he did tonight."[6]

The 1994 season breathed fresh air into the Indians franchise. The Tribe was in their new digs at Jacobs Field and they were suddenly the hottest ticket in town. Dennis Martinez, Tony Peña, and Eddie Murray signed as free agents in the off-season and Jack Morris came aboard just before the season started. Omar Vizquel came over in a trade with Seattle. These five players provided instant credibility and veteran leadership to an otherwise young team that already had talented players Jim Thome, Albert Belle, Manny Ramirez, Carlos Baerga, Kenny Lofton, Charlie Nagy, and Sandy Alomar Jr.

The Indians' new pitching coach in 1994, Phil Regan, talked to Mesa about moving to the bullpen. He had one of the key attributes to being a successful closer, a fastball that had been clocked at 98 mph. "I told him I didn't know that I could do the job," said Mesa.[7]

The coaches brought him along slowly, using him initially as a middle reliever, then a set-up man, and then a closer. At the last step, closer, he had problems. Mesa failed to protect four of six closer opportunities. "I wasn't prepared," said Mesa. "I didn't understand the job."[8]

However, Mesa finished the season with a 7-6 record, a 3.82 ERA, and two saves. He continued to master control of the strike zone, posting 63 strikeouts against 26 walks.

The 1994 season had brought a new alignment of the divisions in the major leagues. The Indians were now in the AL Central, and finished the season one game behind the White Sox. The season ended prematurely due to a players strike on August 12. The work stoppage canceled the entire postseason and delayed the start of the 1995 season until April 25, 1995.

Mesa's finest year in the big leagues was in 1995. He was successful in 46 of 48 save opportunities as he blew batters away with his blazing fastball. His 46 saves are a franchise record. "I love to watch those batters swing and miss against Jose," said catcher Peña. "Some of them say, 'Oh, my God.' I just tell them 'You better start your swing early.'"[9]

At one point in the season, Mesa converted 38 save opportunities in a row. He was selected to his first All-Star Game, pitching a scoreless inning at the Ballpark at Arlington. "He's been our MVP," said Paul Sorrento. "What he's done is unbelievable – 38 in a row and 44 out of 46. When he comes in, you know the game is over."[10] Mesa was the AL Rolaids Relief Man of the Year and was named AL Fireman of the Year by *The Sporting News.*

Cleveland won the Central Division in 1995 by 30 games over Kansas City, The Indians returned to the postseason for the first time since 1954. Mesa recorded a save in both the ALCS and the World Series, although the Indians fell to the Atlanta Braves in six games.

It would seem near-impossible to duplicate such a great season, but Mesa came close in 1996. He converted 39 of 44 opportunities for Cleveland. The Indians returned to the postseason, but were bounced by Baltimore in the ALDS. In Game Four, Mesa gave up a run to the Orioles that knotted the score at 3-3. He gave up the winning run. Mesa had pitched 3⅔ innings, the most he had pitched in two seasons. "It was very obvious how much the situation had to do with us sending Jose back out there," said Hargrove. "We haven't done that in two years. But he was very strong the inning before. We went to him and asked him if he could still pitch and he said 'yes.'"[11]

Jose Mesa had a tumultuous year in 1997 on and off the baseball field. It actually began on December 22, 1996, when he was arrested for gross sexual imposition in a suburban motel just west of Cleveland. A charge of concealing a loaded handgun was added later when the weapon was found in the console of Mesa's vehicle at the time of his arrest.

Mesa was free on $10,000 bond and reported to spring training in Winter Haven with the rest of the Indians. However, the whole ordeal was on his mind, and his ERA in spring training was 6.93. He still had the power in his right arm, but the old bugaboo of location crept up again.

A court date was set for March 31, just two days before the start of the 1997 season. Defense attorney Gerald Messerman did not even put on a defense. The jury deliberated for eight hours before coming back with a verdict of acquittal. The credibility of Mesa's accusers was called into question. "Regardless of whether a crime occurred or not, the bottom line was that there wasn't enough evidence to convict beyond a reasonable doubt," said juror Bruce Pixler.[12]

After the verdict came down, a tearful and grateful Mesa said, "It's been tough. I was nervous, but I knew God was with me. And with God I can do the next thing: to win the World Series."[13]

The concealed-gun charge, which was tried separately, was also dismissed. The judge ruled that the police officers had seized it unlawfully.

Mesa lost his closer's role to Mike Jackson, and he was constantly taunted in his own ballpark with shouts of "Rapist!" He was a free man in the eyes of the legal system, but not in the court of public opinion. In his first 19 appearances, his record was 0-3 with a 7.45 ERA. "José had to handle a crisis in his life a lot bigger than baseball," said Hargrove. "An experience like that shakes you right to your core, and when he returned, he didn't have the same confident attitude."[14]

Mesa eventually regained his status as closer and saved 16 of 21 games in 1997. But it is the Game Seven loss in the World Series that proved to be his legacy in Cleveland. "I just didn't do my job," said Mesa. "It hurts a lot to think we were just two outs away."[15]

Mesa never recovered from his 1997 season. After he went 3-4 with a 5.17 ERA in 1998, he was included in a five-player deal that sent him to San Francisco on July 23, 1998.

Mesa signed in the offseason with Seattle. He converted 33 of 38 saves for Seattle in 1999. But his control problems were once again an issue, as he walked 40 batters while striking out 42. He was moved out of the Seattle closer role in 2000 in favor of Kazuchiro Sasaki. He appeared in 66 games as the Mariners finished second to Oakland by a half-game in the AL West. Seattle swept Chicago in the ALDS, and Mesa was credited with the win in Game One. But the Mariners were eliminated in six games by the Yankees in the ALCS.

After the season Mesa opted for free agency and signed with Philadelphia, a reported two-year deal for $6.8 million. He showed he was worth the money, saving 87 games over two seasons. In 2001 the Phillies finished two games behind Atlanta in the NL East. Philadelphia sprinted out to a 34-18 record in April and May and enjoyed an eight-game lead over Atlanta. But the Phillies couldn't hold the lead, playing under .500 the rest of the season. The one bright spot was Mesa, who converted 42 of 46 save opportunities. "When we signed him there were a lot of snickers in baseball – 'How can you give this guy this kind of money?,'" said Phillies manager Larry Bowa. "But he's definitely been tremendous. I have no idea where we'd be without this guy. People will say all this stuff about his character. But all I can say is that in two years, he's a solid citizen."[16]

Mesa showed 2001 was no fluke by racking up 45 saves in 2002, fourth in the NL. However, he tied for the league lead in blown saves with nine. Nonetheless, the 45 saves were the most by a Phillies reliever since Mitch Williams saved 43 games in 1993. In 2003 Mesa converted 24 of 28 save opportunities. He left the Phillies after the 2003 season, ranking number one in franchise history with 112 saves. He was eventually surpassed by Jonathan Papelbon, in 2015.

In April 2002 Mesa's former teammate Omar Vizquel published an autobiography, *Omar!: My Life On and Off the Field*. Chapter One focused on Game Seven of the 1997 World Series. It said, "The eyes of the world were focused on every move we made. Unfortunately, José's own eyes were vacant. Nobody home. You could almost see right through him. Not long after I looked into his vacant eyes, he blew the save and the Marlins tied the game."[17]

"If I face him, I'll hit him," said Mesa. "I won't try to hit him in the head, but I'll hit him. And if he charges me I'll kill him."[18] Mesa responded by hitting Vizquel with a pitch on June 12, 2002, at Cleveland. He beaned Vizquel three times after the book was published. The last occurrence came on April 22. 2006. Mesa was pitching for Colorado and Vizquel was with the Giants. Mesa drew a four-game suspension for his actions.

Mesa moved on to Pittsburgh in 2004, and pitched for the Pirates in 2004 and 2005. He showed that he could still hum the old pea across the plate, saving 70 games for the Pirates. He later pitched for Colorado (2006), Detroit, and Philadelphia (2007). On July 26, 2007, Mesa pitched in his 1,000th game. He became only the 11th major-league pitcher to reach that plateau.

José Mesa retired after the 2007 season. In 19 seasons his career record was 80-109 with a 4.36 ERA. He struck out 1,038 batters and walked 651. He totaled 321 saves.

Mesa and his wife, Mirla, settled in the Atlanta area. They have five children and grandchildren. Mesa helps coach their little-league teams. He keeps a close eye on José Jr., a pitcher in the New York Yankees farm system, who was named the Pinstripes Prospect Comeback Player of the Year in 2017.

On June 19, 2016, the Cleveland Cavaliers defeated the Golden State Warriors for the franchise's first world championship. It also ended the 52-year drought since the last time a professional Cleveland team won a world title. Shortly after the game ended, Jose Mesa Jr, tweeted "There you go Cleveland now leave the past in the past and build on this!"[19] It was his way of saying, get off his dad's back and stop blaming him for the city's failure to win.

NOTES

1 Paul Hoynes, "Rise and Sign," *Cleveland Plain Dealer*, July 16, 1995: 1-D.

2 Hoynes, "Rise and Sign": 16-D.

3 Tim Kurkjian, "Mesa Defies Logic and Tigers, Gives Orioles 7-3 Win," *Baltimore Sun*, October 1, 1987: F-1.

4 Paul Hoynes, "Indians Reneging on Changes," *Cleveland Plain Dealer*, July 17, 1992: 1-E.

5 Rick Braun, "Mesa Enjoys Making History," *Milwaukee Sentinel*, September 10, 1992: 1B.

6 Russell Schneider, "Mesa Perfect Cure for What Ails Tribe," *Cleveland Plain Dealer*, May 13, 1993: 4F.

7 Jerome Holtzman, "There's No Mess When Cleveland Calls In Mesa," *Chicago Tribune*, September 21, 1995: 4-10.

8 Ibid.

9 Hoynes, "Rise and Sign": 16-D.

10 Holtzman, "There's No Mess When Cleveland Calls in Mesa."

11 Paul Hoynes, "A Dream Slips Away; Indians Eliminated by Orioles," *Cleveland Plain Dealer*, October 6, 1996: 1-D.

12 James F. McCarty and James Ewinger, "Mesa Found Not Guilty: Indians Star Says Justice System, God On His Side," *Cleveland Plain Dealer*, April 11, 1997: 1-A.

13 Ibid.

14 Tim Crothers, "Trial and Errors," *Sports Illustrated*, January 18, 1998: 57.

15 Ibid.

16 Claire Smith, "Veteran Mesa Has Steadied the Phillies," *Philadelphia Inquirer*, July 23, 2001: E5.

17 Omar Vizquel with Bob Dyer, *Omar!: My Life On and Off the Field* (Cleveland: Gray and Company Publishing, 2002), 1.

18 "Mesa Being Investigated by Commissioner's Office," ESPN.com, March 12, 2003, Player's File, Baseball Hall of Fame.

19 Jose Mesa Jr., Twitter.com, June 19, 2016, accessed online at https://twitter.com/JoeTable/status/744728829000884225, July 19, 2016

EDDIE MURRAY

BY ALAN COHEN

"That night might have been the best thing anyone has done in baseball in the last 10 years."

– Mike Downey, August 28, 1985

In 1985 Eddie Murray drove in a career-high 124 runs, had a career-high 37 doubles (a total he matched in 1992), and reached the 30-home-run mark (31) for the fourth time. He was elected to the All-Star team as a starter for the first time and finished fifth in the MVP balloting. It was a season that would very much define Murray. In December 1984, his mother had died and in February 1985 his sister Tanya was hospitalized with a kidney ailment that caused Murray to miss some of spring training. In April his sister Lucilla died from a heart ailment and Murray missed five games for the funeral. They were the only games he missed since the beginning of the 1984 season. Indeed, he had played every inning of every game except for the time spent mourning his sister – until August 26, 1985.

On that night, Eddie Murray homered in three of his first four at-bats against the Angels in Anaheim. It was the third and last of Murray's three-homer games (the homers came in the first five innings), and his father, Charles, was among the spectators who rose and cheered as Eddie was taken out of the game for a pinch-runner after walking in the ninth inning. Reggie Jackson (who had a famous three-homer night in the 1977 World Series), then with the Angels, called it "the best performance anyone's seen in baseball in the last 10 years." Earlier that month, Murray had made a generous donation to establish a park in Baltimore in memory of his mother, Carrie. Wrote Mike Downey of the *Los Angeles Times, that* was the best thing anyone had done in baseball in 10 years.[1]

"It always seemed I was able to hit. I remember when I was 8 or 9 years old and I was trying out for the Little league team. The coach would throw the ball in hard and you had to run (laps) if you didn't hit it. I always did (hit it)."

Murray in spring training before his rookie year on March 6, 1977.[2]

"Most of the time the other pitchers try to walk him. He's the best all-round player we've had – can play any position. Eddie has a good bat, most of the scouts are interested in his hitting. He's strong and rangy, has good wrist action,

and is a power hitter. He's got all the equipment to make it in the big leagues and a real good attitude as well. He hits the long ball, doesn't strike out much, and would probably hit for a much higher average if we didn't have him pitching too."

– High school coach Art Webb talking about Prep Athlete of the Month Eddie Murray on May 2, 1973[3]

"His game never has been one of knock-'em-dead showmanship, but of delicious subtlety and nuance. And an unwavering focus on singular goals – a strict attention to, and the repetition of, the smallest of details, executed game after game, year after year, with a wonderous mechanical efficiency. It is a game so blatantly understated, so incredibly unpretentious, that it has made Eddie Murray the most underrated and misunderstood player of his generation." [4]

"Few great hitters have ever stepped up under pressure with such a sense of flexibility and enjoyment. Murray mixes the intuitive and the analytic in a purely personal way. Nobody talks or thinks hitting like Murray."

– Michael P. Geffner, July 3, 1995, shortly after Murray's 3,000th career hit on June 30.[5]

"Few great hitters have ever stepped up under pressure with such a sense of flexibility and enjoyment. Murray mixes the intuitive and the analytic in a purely personal way. Nobody talks or thinks hitting like Murray."

–Thomas Boswell, September 23, 1982, during a typical Murray stretch run.[6]

Eddie Clarence Murray was born in Los Angeles on February 24, 1956, the eighth of 12 children (five boys and seven girls) His parents, Charles and Carrie Bell Fairchild Murray, had moved the family from Cary, Mississippi, to East Los Angeles in 1946, and Charles spent most of his years there as a forklift operator for the Ludlow Rug Company, retiring after 30 years. All five of the boys played professionally. Eddie's oldest brother, Charles, played six seasons in the Houston organization, making it as far as Double A. In 1964, his third year of pro ball, Charles slammed 37 homers and had 119 RBIs for Modesto in the Class A California League, second only to Ollie "Downtown" Brown. Brothers Leon and Venice were in the Giants organization. Leon played one season of rookie ball in 1970, and an injured arm kept him from continuing. Venice played a season Cedar Rapids (Class A) in 1978 and tore up his knee.

Eddie played baseball only during his senior year at Alain Leroy Locke High School in Los Angeles, where he was a star pitcher and was named Prep Player of the Month for April 1973 by the *Los Angeles Sentinel*. The newspaper also made mention of the team shortstop, Osborn Smith, who was hitting .304 after being named the Marine League co-player of the year in basketball.[7] Thirty years later, in 2003, Murray and Ozzie Smith were reunited on the podium at Cooperstown for Murray's Hall of Fame induction. (Smith was inducted the year before.)

Locke High School was in a troubled area of Los Angeles and the sound of gunfire was not uncommon. Murray's parents made sure that he and his siblings distanced themselves from the gang violence that gripped the Watts neighborhood. When he wasn't pitching for Locke, Murray played first base and left field. In his senior year, his 6-1 record and .500 batting average led his team to the Marine League championship. His younger brother, Rich Murray, was his catcher that year and was named second-team all-league.[8]

Murray was picked in the third round of the June 1973 draft by the Orioles and was signed by Ray Poitevint. Younger brother Rich was drafted by the Giants in the sixth round two years later. Rich played parts of two seasons with San Francisco.

Eddie started his professional career with Bluefield in the Appalachian League. In 50 games, he batted .287, hit 11 homers, had 32 RBIs, and was voted the league's Most Valuable Player. His next stop, in 1974, was at Miami in the Class A Florida State League, where he was once again named to his league's All-Star team at first base and batted .289. His 48 extra-base hits led his team, and his 29 doubles led the league. At the end of the season, Murray played briefly at Double-A Asheville (Southern League), and he spent the entire 1975 season at Asheville, batting .264. Four months into the season, he was slumping, and manager Jimmie Schaffer encouraged Murray to switch-hit. The experiment was met by skepticism in the Orioles organization, but Murray was determined to succeed.[9] He began the 1976 season with Charlotte as the Orioles shifted their Southern League team from Asheville. After 88 games (enough to be named to the postseason All-Star team), he was promoted to Triple-A Rochester (International League). Between Double A and Triple A, he hit 23 home runs and had 86 RBIs.

Although initially slated to return to Rochester in 1977, Murray made it to the majors with the Orioles at the start of the 1977 season. However, he was a man without a position. First base was occupied by veteran Lee May, and Murray wound up primarily in the DH role (110 starts). He got into 42 games at first base and 6 as an outfielder. He was named the American League Rookie of the Year after batting .283 with 29 doubles, 27 homers, and 88 RBIs.

Murray followed up with two similar successful seasons. Playing regularly at first base (May was by now the regular DH), "Steady Eddie" as he came to be known, batted .285 with 27 homers and 95 RBIs in 1978 and was named to his first All-Star team. (He did not play in the game.) In 1979 Murray he batted .295 with 25 homers and 99 RBIs as the Orioles won the AL East and advanced to the postseason.

> *"I stepped off the rubber. All the guy at first base (Doug DeCinces) wanted to do was get my attention. By the time I realized what was happening, it was too late."*

- Chicago White Sox pitcher Guy Hoffman, August 15, 1979.[10]

On August 15 Murray displayed a side of his game not generally noteworthy. The Orioles were playing the White Sox and the game was still tied in the bottom of the 12th inning. With two outs, Murray was on third and Doug DeCinces was on first. The count was 1-and-2 to Baltimore's Benny Ayala when manager Earl Weaver resorted to his bag of tricks.[11] As the pitcher went into the stretch, DeCinces intentionally stumbled off first base and Murray made a mad dash for home. Pitcher Hoffman, distracted by DeCinces, was not able to prevent Murray from stealing home. Two weeks later, Murray arrived home in a more customary fashion and did it three times. His three homers against the Twins at Minneapolis in the second game of a doubleheader on August 29 led the Orioles to a 7-4 win. It was the first of three times during his career that Murray would homer three times in one game.

Baltimore won the best-of-five ALCS against the California Angels in four games as Murray batted .417 (5-for-12) with a homer and five RBIs. In Baltimore's 9-8 win in Game Two, he singled in a run in the first inning and slammed a three-run-homer in the second inning that extended the Orioles' lead to 8-1. (The Angels mounted a comeback that fell one run short.) In the clincher, won by the Orioles, 8-0, Murray drove in a run.

Murray hit a home run in Game Two of the World Series, against the Pirates, but his performance was otherwise subpar (4-for-26) as the Pittsburgh won in seven games.

Murray had his best season to date in 1980, but it almost ended prematurely. On July 13 the Orioles were playing Kansas City. Murray had not missed a game all season. In the top of the eighth inning, with one out and runners on first and second for the Royals, George Brett hit a hard groundball in Murray's direction that took a bad hop and struck Murray above his right eye. The ball bounded off Murray into center field for a run-scoring double. Murray left the game. He was stitched up and missed four games. Although his vision was slightly impaired, he was able to adapt and went on to complete the season with a flair.[12] In his last 76 games, he batted .316 with 18 homers and 59 RBIs. He finished the season batting .300 and exceeding 30 homers (32) and 100 RBIs (116) for the first time. He finished sixth in the MVP balloting.

In 1981, a not-so-funny thing happened on the way to Murray's most productive season yet. The ballplayers went out on strike and 57 games were cut from the schedule. Playing in 99 games, he led the American League with 22 homers and 78 RBIs while batting .294. For the second time, he was named to the All-Star team. He went 0-for-2 after entering in the game in the sixth inning. Again he finished in the top 10 of the MVP balloting – this time fifth.

In 1982 Murray had another excellent season – it was getting habitual at this point. His batting average increased to .316 and his 32 homers and 110 RBIs reverted to pre-strike norms. He secured his first Gold Glove for his work at first base. He placed second in the MVP balloting, losing out to Robin Yount of the American League champion Brewers.

> *"That is the only time I actually got to win [the World Series]. ... [I]t's awesome when you win. ... There were times when guys would play 25 years and never got to win the World Series. It lets you know how special that is because that was the only one I got."*
>
> – Eddie Murray, March 17, 2003, speaking about 1983 during a Hall of Fame visit.[13]

The Orioles had finished second to the Brewers in the American League East in 1982, and the race had been tight with Baltimore just one game behind Milwaukee, unofficially known that year as Harvey's Wallbangers in honor of manager Harvey Kuenn. The Orioles emerged victorious in 1983. They had a season-long duel with the Detroit Tigers before pulling away in September to win the division by six games. Murray batted .306 with 33 homers, a career high, and 111 RBIs. He was named to his third consecutive All-Star Game, finished second again in the MVP balloting (this time to teammate Cal Ripken Jr.), won another Gold Glove at first base, and collected his first Silver Slugger Award.

In the ALCS, Baltimore, after losing the first game to the White Sox, came back to win three games and advance to the World Series. In Game Three of the ALCS, Murray hit a three-run homer in the Orioles' 11-1 win. The finale was scoreless through nine innings. In the top of the 10th, Murray's single was a key element as the Orioles won, 3-0, and moved on to face the Phillies in the World Series.

The Orioles dropped the first game in the World Series, then came back to win four straight. Murray's bat was quiet for most of the Series, but in Game Four he singled during a two-run fourth inning, and in Game Five he had the game of his life on the biggest of stages. He led off the second inning with a homer off Charles Hudson to give Scott McGregor a 1-0 lead. Rick Dempsey homered in the third inning to put Baltimore ahead 2-0. In the fourth, with Ripken on base, Murray hit another homer for a 4-0 lead. Baltimore added another run and McGregor pitched a five-hit shutout, securing the Orioles' first World Series win since 1970.

Over the next several seasons, Murray was a picture of consistency. In 1984 Murray, who had already played in at least 150 games in each of his first six full seasons, played in all of his team's 162 games. His .410 on-base percentage led the American League and he was again named to the All-Star team. His sixth-inning double was his first hit in All-Star competition. He won his third Gold Glove and his second Silver Slugger Award. Once again, he finished in the top five in MVP balloting.

Toward the end of his memorable 1985 season, in which Murray overcame family tragedy to bat .297, slug 31 homers, drive in 124 runs, and finish in the top five of the MVP balloting for the fifth consecutive year, Murray was rewarded with a five-year contract extension worth $13 million, making him at the time baseball's highest paid player.[14]

In 1986 Murray batted .305 and was elected to the All-Star team for the seventh and last time as an Oriole. However, he did not play in the midsummer classic. He had injured a hamstring on July 3 running out a groundball in the first inning and left the game in the eighth inning. It was the first inning he had missed because of injury since 1983.[15] He remained in the lineup as a DH through July 6, when he aggravated the injury and left the game. After pinch-hitting appearances on July 8 and 9, he went on the disabled list on the 10th and was idled until August 7. Toward the end of the 1986 season, a rift began to grow between Orioles owner Edward Bennett Williams and Murray. Williams publicly questioned whether Murray was giving the team his best effort. Murray, on the other hand, felt that Williams was not building the team as it went downhill after the World Series win in 1983. In 1986 the team had dropped to last place in the division. Things would only get worse.

The rift continued through the 1988 season. Murray had long since stopped talking to the media, which portrayed him as sullen. His lower productivity coupled with the continuing plunge of the Orioles (they went 54-107 in 1988) resulted in loud and numerous insults showering Murray at Memorial Stadium. Although he hit 58 homers in 1987 and 1988 and became the first switch-hitter ever to homer from both sides of the plate in consecutive games (May 8-9, 1987), he failed to drive in 100 runs in either season and his batting averages were .277 and .284 respectively. After the 1988 season, Murray was traded to the Los Angeles Dodgers for Juan Bell, Brian Holton, and Ken Howell.

> *"I think I'm going to have fun again. The key thing is having fun when playing this game. It's going to be a learning experience (playing in the National League for the first time), but I've never been one to shy away from a challenge."*
>
> – Eddie Murray in 1989 spring training.[16]

When Murray returned to his home in Los Angeles, there had been changes in the household of his youth. His mother had died in December 1984 and his sister Lucilla died from a heart ailment in April 1985. His youngest sister, Tanya, who had been hospitalized for kidney troubles shortly after her mother died, was still experiencing problems in a fight that would go on until 2003.

Nevertheless, there was optimism that with a new team, life would be better on the field. Despite a new lease on life, Murray's first year with the Dodgers, 1989, was a disappointment. He batted only .247 with 20 homers and 88 RBIs. Los Angeles finished fourth in the NL West with a 77-83 record. But the following season was a rebirth for Murray as his batting average soared to a career-high .330, he clubbed 26 home runs, and he drove in 95 runs, his most RBIs since 1985.

He was awarded the Silver Slugger Award for the third and final time while finishing fifth in the MVP balloting. The Dodgers finished in second place, five games behind the Reds. On June 23, 1991, Murray was honored as Baseball's Man of the Year in Los Angeles at a banquet sponsored by the Board of Governors of Cedars-Sinai Medical Center.[17] He was previously honored as Sportsperson of the Year at the first Los Angeles Black Sports Hall of Fame ceremony on January 12, 1991.[18]

In 1991 Murray's numbers slipped slightly. After getting off to a good start and batting .300 for the first two months of the season, he went into a three-month slump and saw his average drop to .247 by the end of August. Nevertheless, in July the 35-year-old first baseman was named to the National League All-Star team. It was his last All-Star appearance.

If Reggie Jackson is Mr. October, then Eddie Murray is Mr. September.[19]

Writer Tom Boswell said this in 1982 when Murray kept the Orioles in the hunt by hitting 11 homers with 38 RBIs in 31 games from August 17 through September 16. In those days, Murray always seemed to save his best for the stretch run. Could he do it again at age 35?

Murray's performance in September kept the Dodgers in the race for the division title. He had hit safely in his last five games in August and the streak continued through his first three games in September. In those three games, he went 6-for-11 with a pair of home runs. The Dodgers were tied for first place with the Braves as they took the field on September 4. Murray was given the night off (only the ninth time he hadn't started in 1991), as he had a sprained ankle and was nursing a sore back. Los Angeles was hosting St. Louis and the Cardinals took a 3-0 lead into the bottom of the seventh inning. With two outs, the Dodgers mounted a rally as Mike Sharperson and Alfredo Griffin singled.

> *"I figured if I ever needed a home run, it was right now. I had Murray for one shot. I figured*

that we may not get this chance again. I had to go for it."

– Tommy Lasorda, September 4, 1991.[20]

Manager Tommy Lasorda dispatched coach Bill Russell to the training room and Murray limped to the plate to hit for pitcher Tim Belcher. Mitch Webster, who was ready to pinch-hit and was standing at the plate, was called back to the dugout. Steady Eddie, in a scene eerily reminiscent of Kirk Gibson's appearance in the 1988 World Series, limped to the plate. The count went to 2-and-2. Rheal Cormier's next pitch was just off the plate and called ball three by umpire Doug Harvey. Murray fouled off the sixth pitch of the at-bat and then launched a fly ball just beyond the reach of left fielder Milt Thompson's extended glove. The ball sailed into the stands above the 370-foot sign. The game was tied, and the crowd chanted, "Eddie, Eddie!" The Dodgers scored five runs in the next inning to win the game, 8-3.

The homer was Murray's fourth in five days and the second pinch-hit homer of his career. It was a magnificent September for Murray, who batted .351 for the month. On September 30 he singled in the third inning off Dennis Rasmussen of the Padres in a 7-2 Dodgers win. The hit was the 2,500th of Murray's major-league career. The win kept the Dodgers one game ahead of the Braves as the season entered its final week. The Dodgers lost three straight games and were eliminated on the final Saturday of the season. They finished one game behind the first-place Braves.

In the offseason, Murray became a free agent, but the Dodgers were not willing to offer him more than a one-year contract. On November 27, 1991, Murray signed a two-year deal with the Mets estimated at $7.5 million. In his two years with New York, they were not in contention. In 1992 he batted .261 with 16 homers and a team-leading 93 RBIs in a forgettable season – except for one game. On May 3 against the Atlanta Braves in Atlanta, in a one-sided game, the Mets took a 6-0 lead into the top of the eighth inning. Murray's fifth-inning double had keyed a five-run uprising that gave David Cone all the runs he would need. Marvin Freeman came on to pitch for the Braves and Murray greeted him with the 400th home run of his career. In 1993 he batted .285 with 27 homers and a team-high 100 RBIs in 154 games. It was Murray's last season with 100 or more RBIs. But the Mets hit rock-bottom, finishing in seventh place in the NL East, 38 games behind the division champion Phillies.

On November 1, 1993, Murray became a free agent, and in December he signed with the Cleveland Indians. In his first year with Cleveland, he played in 108 games and had a .254 batting average with 76 RBIs and 17 home runs before the season was cut short by the players strike in August.

In 1995, with the 3,000-hit mark within his sights, Murray began the year hitting in 16 of his first 17 games. He returned to iron man status, playing in each of Cleveland's first 60 games. Game 58 was played on June 30 at Minneapolis and not only was Murray chasing hit 3,000 but the Indians were chasing a trip to the World Series for the first time in more than 40 years. He was batting .309 with 2,999 career hits as the Indians took the field with a 40-17 record. Murray, the DH, was hitless in his first two plate appearances. The score was tied, 1-1, as the game entered the sixth inning. Murray, the second batter, stepped to the plate with Albert Belle, who had led off with a double, at second base. "Steady Eddie," batting left-handed, pulled a Mike Trombley offering, and the groundball found its way into right field, giving Murray his 3,000th hit.

Two days later, he was injured in the final game of the series with the Twins and missed 25 games. He returned to action on August 1 and, playing in 113 of his team's 144 games (the schedule was abbreviated to allow for a brief spring-training period after the strike ended), batted .323 for the season, his best average since 1990. His 21 doubles marked his 19th consecutive season (each of his major-league seasons) with 20 or more doubles. He had 21 homers and 82 RBIs as the Indians won the AL Central Division by 30 games and advanced to the postseason for the first time since 1954. In the Division Series' three-game sweep of the Red Sox, Murray was 5-for-13 with an RBI single in Game One and a two-run homer in Game Two. In the Championship Series against

Seattle, the Indians were down two games to one before winning the next three games to advance to the World Series. Murray played a pivotal role in two of those wins. In Game Four, his two-run homer in the first inning propelled the Indians to a 7-0 victory. In Game Five, he drove in the first Cleveland run with a single and after doubling in the sixth inning, he scored ahead of Jim Thome when Thome's homer put the Indians ahead to stay as they won 3-2.

In the World Series, the Indians lost to the Braves in six games. Murray's second-inning homer in Game Two gave the Indians a 2-0 lead, but they lost the game and were down, 2-0. In Game Three, the Indians pulled the game out in the bottom of the 11th inning when Murray's single off Alejandro Pena scored Alvaro Espinoza with the winning run. It was the Indians' first World Series game win since they defeated the Boston Braves in the 1948 World Series. But in 1995 Atlanta won two of the remaining three games and the Series.

In 1996 Murray was on the precipice of reaching a plateau reached only by Willie Mays and Henry Aaron. At the end of the 1995 season, he had 479 homers and 3,071 hits. He was 21 homers away from becoming the third player with 500 homers and 3,000 hits. After 97 Indians games (he played in 88 of them), he was batting .262 with 12 homers. On July 21 he was traded from Cleveland to Baltimore for pitcher Kent Mercker. The trade was made pursuant to the request of Orioles owner Peter Angelos, who wanted to see Murray get his 500th homer in an Orioles uniform. Murray was very much in favor of the trade.[21]

On September 6, 1996, the Orioles were playing the Tigers. Baltimore was in second place in the AL East and contending to advance to postseason play for the first time since 1983. The Orioles were trailing the Tigers, 3-2, in the bottom of the seventh inning when Murray strode to the plate. Facing pitcher Felipe Lira, Murray homered to tie the score. It was the 500th homer of his career, and his ninth since the trade; he finished the season with 501 career homers. Although Baltimore did not win on September 6, they gained a wild-card berth in the 1996 postseason.

In the American League Division Series, the Orioles faced the Indians, with whom Murray had begun the season and for whom he had hit 12 homers in 1996. The Orioles won the best-of-five series in four games. Murray had one RBI, his double driving home Bobby Bonilla in a Game Two victory. The Orioles faced the Yankees in the ALCS. The Yankees won the best-of-seven series in five games. In Game Five, a 6-4 Orioles loss, Murray, batting right-handed against Andy Pettitte, homered in the eighth inning. It was Murray's last postseason at-bat. In 44 postseason games, he hit nine homers, drove in 25 runs, batted .258 (41-for-159) and, in 1983, as an Oriole, won his only World Series ring.

There was still more baseball to be played by Murray, but it would not be with the Orioles. As 1996 had been a homecoming to the city of Murray's greatest baseball achievements, 1997 would be a homecoming to the city of his youth, Los Angeles. A free agent after the 1996 season, he signed with the Angels during the offseason. He was with the Angels through August 14, appearing mostly as a designated hitter. He hit the last of his 504 homers on May 30 off Bob Tewksbury of the Minnesota Twins. Six days after being released by the Angels, for whom he batted .219, he signed with the Dodgers. He made nine pinch-hitting appearances, going 2-for-7 with a pair of walks. The last of his 3,255 career hits, on September 6 off former Cleveland teammate Dennis Cook, produced the last of his 1,917 RBIs. Only 12 men have had more hits, and 10 more have had more RBIs. He is the all-time leader in RBIs by a switch-hitter.

"His best year was every year. He never won an MVP Award – but he was an MVP candidate every year."

– Bill James[22]

When he left the field for the last time as a player, Eddie Murray did so with an expansive list of achievements, not the least of them being his six finishes in the top five in MVP balloting.

His career batting average of .287 included a 1990 season in which his .330 average was the best in the majors. (Willie McGee clinched the NL title that year before completing the season in the AL.) He had 1,333 walks and, in 1984 his league-leading 107 bases on balls along with a .306 batting average produced a league leading .410 on-base percentage. In six seasons, Murray played 160 or more games, and his 3,026 games played is tied with Stan Musial for sixth most in the history of the game. He was an RBI machine and was particularly dangerous with the bases loaded. His 19 grand slams put him fourth on the all-time list and he batted .399 with the bases jammed. On three occasions, he homered three times in a game, and as of 2018 he held the career record for sacrifice flies (128).

Defensively, Murray's numbers were not only far above those of his contemporaries but ranked him with the all-time greats. He played more games at first base (2,413) than anyone else, and his 1,865 assists are the major-league record. He led his league in fielding percentage three times, and he corralled three Gold Glove Awards.

Murray's number 33 has not been worn by an Orioles since he arrived in Baltimore in 1977. It was not worn between 1988 and 1996, when he playted elsewhere. The number was retired in 1989, but Murray, then with the Dodgers, was not inclined to accept the recognition at that point in his life. A formal ceremony, at which Murray appeared, was held in 1998.

After playing 21 major-league seasons. Murray became a coach, first with the Orioles, serving as bench coach in 1998 and 1999 and as first-base coach in 2000-2001. He then moved on to the Indians, for whom he was the hitting instructor from 2002 through June 2005. He was released by Cleveland in 2005. He accepted a similar position with the Los Angeles Dodgers in 2006 but was released in June of the following year.

The first time Murray's name appeared on the Hall of Fame ballot, he was named by 85 percent of the electors and entered the Hall of Fame in 2003. On January 2, shortly before the announcement of his election, Murray's youngest sister, Tanya died at the age of 38 from kidney disease. The day of the announcement, January 7, was also the day of Tanya's funeral. The press conference for the inductees, Murray and Gary Carter, was moved to January 16 to allow Murray sufficient time between the funeral and the meeting with the press.

You are the Voice of Heaven.

It was Jack O'Connell's task to notify Murray of his selection to the Hall of Fame. It was Phil Niekro who had labeled O'Connell the "Voice of Heaven" in 1997. But 2003 was a bit different. It was by O'Connell's admission one of his more challenging assignments.[23] Murray's relationship with the print media was not good. He had ceased speaking with reporters after an unflattering article appeared on the eve of the 1979 World Series. O'Connell was trying to reach Murray by phone while the family was heading to the funeral in Los Angeles. O'Connell finally got through to Murray's wife's cell phone. Understandably, Eddie was quite distraught. He got on the phone, was given the news, and said, "Thank you." But the news had not really registered, and he didn't tell the family. On the way home, the family's limousine stopped at a Costco so they could pick up items for the reception back at the house. Upon seeing Murray, the cashier, who recognized him and had learned the news when it was made public, said "Congratulations." Eddie Murray was a Hall of Famer.[24]

At the induction ceremony, Murray was joined in Cooperstown by his four brothers and five surviving sisters. With him also was his wife, Janice, and his daughters, Jordan and Jessica. Janice and Eddie subsequently divorced. It was a time to reflect and remember those who had help him along the way from his family to his Little League coach Clifford Prelow to his teammates and managers at the major-league level.

> *"I'd like to be able to touch someone's heart the way that camp (which he attended at age 13) touched mine."*
>
> – Eddie Murray, 1985.[25]

After his playing days Murray continued his philanthropic efforts and was nominated for the Roberto Clemente Award on multiple occasions.

In Baltimore he contributed generously (a sum estimated at $500,000) to the Carrie Murray Outdoor Recreational Campus in Leakin Park. The program, which was announced in August 1985 and honored his mother, who had died the prior winter, stressed personal challenge, self-control, intergroup relations, and outdoor camping experience.[26] During his time in Baltimore, and Los Angeles, he was involved with the Sickle Cell Disease Foundation, the American Red Cross, the United Way, and United Cerebral Palsy.[27]

And in New York, Claire Smith of the *New York Times*, while alluding to the various visions that fans, the press, and teammates had of him, called Murray "a quiet supporter of children and their support organizations, an ambassador for his team who rarely says no."[28]

There would be more honors for Murray. In 2012 he and five other Orioles Hall of Famers were honored with bronze statues at Orioles Park at Camden Yards. Murray was also, along with Cal Ripken Jr., inducted into the Hall of Legends at Camden Yards. The Sports Legends Museum, administered by the Babe Ruth Birthplace Foundation, is reserved for the elite of Maryland's sports culture.

SOURCES

In addition to Baseball Reference.com, Eddie Murray's file at the National Baseball Hall of Fame, and the sources shown in the notes, the author used:

Edes, Gordon. "Baseball '89 A Preview: He's Back Where He Belongs," *Los Angeles Times*, April 2, 1989: S-1.

Faulkner, David. "Murray's Quiet Inner Drive," *New York Times*, June 2, 1986: C5.

Geffner, Michael P. "Great Big Stick," *The Sporting News*, July 3, 1995: 10.

Wulf, Steve. "Eddie Is a Handy Dandy," *Sports Illustrated*, June 21, 1982: 34.

O'Connell, Jack. "Murray's Family Paved Way," *Hartford Courant*, January 17, 2003: C-6.

NOTES

1. Mike Downey, "Good Man Has a Night of Greatness," *Los Angeles Times*, August 28, 1985: C1.
2. Ken Nigro, "Murray Wears Birds' Spring 'Can't Miss' Label," *Baltimore Sun*, March 7, 1977: C5.
3. Brad Pye Jr., "Prep Athlete," *Los Angeles Sentinel*, May 3, 1973: B3.
4. Michael P. Geffner, "Great Big Stick," *The Sporting News*, July 3, 1995: 10.
5. Thomas Boswell, "Eddie Murray Hits Stride in September: Mr. September Is in Full Swing Again," *Washington Post*, September 23, 1982: E-1.
6. Ibid.
7. Pye.
8. "Johnson, Murray Win Honors in City Baseball," *Los Angeles Times*, June 14, 1973: F6.
9. Joe Christensen, "Switch-Hitting Experiment Paid Off," *Baltimore Sun*, January 8, 2003.
10. Richard Dozier, "O's Steal One from Sox," *Chicago Tribune*, August 16, 1979: C-2.
11. Ibid.
12. Paul Hoynes, "Murray Is Supervisor with Super Vision," *Cleveland Plain Dealer*, March 9, 2003: C1, C8.
13. Dean Russin, "Murray Does It His Way," *Daily Star* (Oneonta, New York), March 18, 2003: 11.
14. A.S. Doc Young, "Eddie Murray Signs $13 Million Contract," *Los Angeles Sentinel*, August 15, 1985: B-1.
15. Richard Justice, "Once More, Orioles Are Losers, 11-7: Murray Injures Hamstring," *Washington Post*, July 4, 1986: D3.
16. Gordon Edes, "Eddie Is Ready," *Los Angeles Times*, February 23, 1989: 3-1.
17. Allan Malamud, "Notes on a Scorecard," *Los Angeles Times*, May 1, 1991: C-3.
18. "L.A. Black Hall of Fame Awards Set for January 12," *Los Angeles Times*, December 7, 1990: 15.
19. Boswell.
20. Bill Plaschke, "Murray's Dramatic Timing Gives Dodgers Big Lift, 8-3," *Los Angeles Times*, September 5, 1991: C-1.
21. Tim Kurkjian, "Coming Home," *Sports Illustrated*, July 29, 1996.
22. Bill James, *The New Bill James Historical Baseball Abstract* (New York: Free Press, 2001), 434.
23. Jack O'Connell, "The Hall's Messenger: Cheers and Tears on the Other Side of the Line," *Hartford Courant*, January 27, 2003: C-6.
24. Jack O'Connell, "Sounds from Down Around the Hall," *Hartford Courant*, July 27, 2003: C-6.
25. Justice, "10 Who Made a Difference," *Baltimore Sun*, December 15, 1985: 10.
26. Eunetta Boone, "Murray Makes His Biggest Hit," *Evening Sun* (Baltimore), August 16, 1985: C-4.
27. "Eddie Murray: Baseball Man of the Year!" *Los Angeles Sentinel*, May 9, 1991: B1.
28. Claire Smith, "The Game Face of Eddie Murray: A Quiet Superstar Takes Stock," *New York Times*, February 12, 1993: B-13.

CHARLES NAGY

BY STEVE WEST

He was an everyman, a solid but not spectacular New Englander who went out and did his job every time. Never a dominant pitcher, he was once called the "master of the 11-hitter."[1] He never liked attention; all he wanted to do was take his place in the rotation. Even when his arm gave out, he hung on for years, just hoping that somehow it would all come back and he could go to the mound again.

Charles Harrison Nagy was born on May 5, 1967, in Bridgeport, Connecticut, to Richard Nagy and the former Beverly Harrison. His father was of Hungarian ancestry, the name Nagy meaning great or big in Hungarian. As a child Charles lived in St. Petersburg, Florida, for six years, where he played Little League baseball, and lived in the same condo development as Tom Seaver.[2] Returning to live in Fairfield, Connecticut, he spent much time with his brothers (Richard Jr., two years older, and David, two years younger), playing baseball and football, being coached by their father.

He played baseball, football, and basketball at Roger Ludlowe High School in Fairfield, Connecticut, and was a standout in all three sports. Despite being recruited for baseball, Nagy chose to go to Cornell to play football, but after one semester he transferred to the University of Connecticut, where he joined the baseball team and his career took off. Playing two seasons with the Huskies, Nagy was named Big East Pitcher of the Year in 1987 and 1988, dominating with big strikeout numbers, including a conference-record 17-strikeout game in 1988. Despite this, his most memorable moment was a bad one, at the Big East Tournament in 1987, when future major leaguer Mo Vaughn hit one of his pitches out of the ballpark.

In the summer of 1987 Nagy pitched in the Cape Cod League, and in 1988 he was invited to try out for the US Olympic team, making the team prior to the Seoul Olympics that year. Pitching from the bullpen throughout the summer, he made 19 appearances, going 3-1 with a team-leading 1.05 ERA and six saves. Alongside future major leaguers like Jim Abbott, Ben McDonald, and Andy Benes, Nagy helped the US team win Olympic gold. His efforts were acknowledged in 1999 when he was named to the 15-man all-time USA Baseball team.

During the summer Nagy became the first UConn player to be drafted in the first round, taken 17th overall by the Cleveland Indians. He quickly signed with the team for a bonus of $126,000,³ and in 1989 he started his professional career with Kinston in the High-A Carolina League. After dominating there (8-4, 1.51 ERA), he was quickly moved up to the Double-A Canton-Akron Indians (Eastern League). Results weren't as spectacular (4-5, 3.35), but Nagy still performed well enough to be noticed.

Before the 1990 season, Nagy married his high-school sweetheart, Jacquelyn Schuh. He returned to Double A, but only for a short time; he performed well enough to get the call to the big leagues in June. On June 29, 1990, he made his major-league debut in Cleveland against the California Angels, pitching against his former Olympic teammate Jim Abbott. Nagy struggled in his debut, losing and giving up four runs in 4⅓ innings on seven hits and four walks. "I was pretty nervous. ... I'm pretty happy that my first start is over with," he said.⁴ His next game he was a little better, three runs in seven innings against Seattle, but still took the loss. In his next start he was terrible, six runs in 1⅓ innings, and he was sent back to the minors with an 0-3 record and a 9.24 ERA.

It didn't take long for Nagy to return. Brought back at the end of August for a longer look, he got in another six games, five of them starts, and toward the end was starting to look much better. He got his first win on September 18 against Milwaukee ("I'm just real excited right now," he said),⁵ and by the end of the season had brought his record to 2-4, 5.91. Not a great start, but Nagy certainly showed the promise the team was looking for.

In 1991 Nagy looked good in spring training, appearing to have become more composed, and began the season in the Cleveland rotation. His first start was a complete game. He gave up just one run in eight innings against Kansas City, but the Indians couldn't score, and Nagy took the 1-0 loss. Pitching against the Royals again on April 22, he was perfect through six innings, creating some excitement before giving up a leadoff double in the seventh. On July 4 he threw his first career shutout, against Milwaukee, a six-hitter. He was inconsistent all season long, having streaks of a few really good games followed by a few really bad games. The result: Nagy ended the 1991 season with a 10-15 record despite a 4.13 ERA.

The Indians began improving with a core of home-grown players, with the likes of Albert Belle, Sandy Alomar Jr., and Carlos Baerga joining Nagy in the big leagues. Most of the prospects coming up were hitters, and the team was trading its veteran pitchers away, leaving Nagy as the default number-one starter in 1992. On Opening Day he was the starting pitcher in the new Orioles ballpark, Camden Yards. Despite being named the number one, Nagy didn't get too excited: "If I start getting too happy, balls start flying around all over the place."⁶

Nagy stepped up to the task of staff ace, going 17-10 on a team that finished 10 games below .500. No other starter won more than six games, and Nagy established himself as the Indians' star. He was pitching so well that he was selected to the All-Star Game in San Diego, and pitched a 1-2-3 seventh inning. With the AL running out of players, manager Tom Kelly left Nagy in to bat in the top of the eighth (he had to borrow a helmet), and he led off the inning with an infield single – the first AL pitcher to get a hit in the All-Star game since Ken McBride in 1963. "I didn't know what was going on. I just closed my eyes and ran," he said.⁷ He also came around to score a run as the AL dominated the NL, 13-6.

On August 8 Nagy had perhaps his best game in the major leagues, throwing a one-hitter with two walks in Baltimore. The only hit was in the seventh inning, a groundball by Glenn Davis deep in the hole to shortstop, and the next batter grounded into a double play. Typically self-effacing, Nagy said, "The result was one of my best, but it wasn't a thing of beauty."⁸

Again the ace in 1993, Nagy started the season slowly. On May 15 he faced just six batters before leaving the game in the first inning with a sore shoulder. A few days later he had surgery for a torn labrum and was expected to miss a couple of months. He came back late in the season, starting the final game in the old Cleveland Stadium on October 3. His final record of 1993 was 2-6 with a 6.29 ERA, a disappointment in an injury-ravaged season.

Now that they had a core of young hitting, the Indians were in need of pitching, and they signed veteran free agents Dennis Martinez and Jack Morris for 1994, taking the pressure off Nagy as he came back from his injury. "I don't know if our pitching staff will ever gain a lot of respect," Nagy said. "We do get overshadowed by our hitting."[9] In 1995 the team replaced Morris with Orel Hershiser, and they took off. Dominating throughout the season, they ended up winning their division by 30 games, with Nagy and Hershiser having identical 16-6 records. Nagy was amazed at how the team had grown around him. "You couldn't even imagine a couple of years ago that we'd be here today."[10]

The Indians swept the Boston Red Sox in the American League Division Series, got by the Seattle Mariners in six games in the Championship Series, but then lost the World Series to the Atlanta Braves in six games. Nagy faced John Smoltz in Game Three and cruised through the early innings. He gave up solo home runs in the sixth and seventh innings to make the score 4-3 Indians. In the eighth he gave up a single and a double to the first two batters before being pulled, with manager Mike Hargrove being criticized for leaving Nagy in too long. The Indians blew the lead, but rallied to win the game in the 11th inning. Nagy would not pitch again though, being scheduled for Game Seven before the Indians lost in six.

Nagy started 1996 with a new contract, a two-year, $6.75 million deal. He celebrated by having his best year in the major leagues, going 17-5 with a 3.41 ERA. Back in the All-Star Game, he was selected by his manager, Mike Hargrove, to start for the American League – facing John Smoltz, whom he'd pitched against in the World Series the previous fall. This time his All-Star performance was not successful; he gave up three runs in two innings and took the loss. He started Game One of the ALDS against the Orioles and struggled, taking the loss with seven runs in 5⅓ innings. Brought back in Game Four, he did better, allowing two runs in six innings, and was in line for the win until Jose Mesa blew the save in the ninth and the Indians lost in the 12th, ending their season. Nagy finished fourth in the Cy Young Award voting.

In 1997 the Indians were back in the playoffs, and in ALCS Game Two Nagy struggled, leaving in the sixth inning down 4-2 to the Orioles, but the team rallied to get him off the hook. He was back in Game Six, facing Mike Mussina and the pair settled in for a pitching duel. Mussina was excellent, eight innings of one-hit ball, but Nagy matched the score with 7⅓ innings of nine-hit ball. Again the game went to extra innings, and this time a home run by Tony Fernandez in the 11th won the game and the series. Back in the World Series for the second time in three years, the Indians had high hopes against the Florida Marlins. With the series tied, Nagy got the start in Game Three, but struggled, giving up three home runs and a bases-loaded walk. He left having given up five runs in six innings, but had a 7-5 lead that the bullpen again could not hold, and the Marlins eventually won the game, 14-11, on the back of a seven-run ninth.

The Indians fought back to take the series to a Game Seven. After agonizing over his decision, manager Mike Hargrove decided to start Jaret Wright instead of Nagy, saying that Nagy looked tired and Wright had the hot hand. Wright vindicated the decision by giving up one run in 6⅓ innings, but Jose Mesa blew it with two out in the ninth, giving up the tying run on a sacrifice fly. In the bottom of the 10th Hargrove turned to Nagy – who had warmed up four times already – with two on and two out, and he got Moises Alou to fly out and end the inning. Then came perhaps the defining moment of Nagy's career. In the bottom of the 11th, with the bases loaded and two out, Edgar Renteria lined a single that tipped off Nagy's outstretched glove and fell in center field for the game-winning hit. All Nagy could do was walk off the field as Marlins leapt and celebrated around him.

Nagy didn't pitch well in 1998, his 15-10 record hiding a 5.22 ERA. The Indians made it back to the postseason, and he beat Boston in the ALDS. He pitched well in Game Two of the ALCS against New York, but received a no-decision in the Indians' 4-1 win. In Game Six, Nagy gave up six runs (three earned) in three innings on the way to the season-ending loss. The Indians still had faith though, and signed the 31-year-old to a four-year contract that would pay him $6 million per season through 2002. Nagy celebrated by donating $100,000 to UConn to establish a baseball scholarship.

In 1999 Nagy improved a little, and was back in the All-Star Game for the third time. The Indians reached the playoffs once again. In the ALDS he won Game Two, putting the Indians up 2-0, but the Red Sox won three in a row, including Game Five, in which Nagy got a no-decision despite giving up seven runs (including Troy O'Leary's grand slam) in three innings, and somehow leaving with an 8-7 lead after three.

Everything changed in 2000. Nagy started the season poorly, and with a 7.19 ERA he was placed on the disabled list in May, and had surgery to remove bone chips from his elbow. With the injury he broke his personal streak of 192 consecutive starts over eight seasons. He managed to return for three outings in September, but he wasn't any better, giving up 15 runs in 10⅔ innings and taking three losses. Despite hope for recovery in the offseason, Nagy started 2001 on the DL again, trying to build up arm strength in the minor leagues. Returning to Cleveland in June, he lasted through August but pitched poorly. Another offseason of rest helped get him going again, and in 2002 the team decided he would be better coming out of the bullpen for a while. After a couple of months this wasn't working, and when Nagy gave up nine runs in two innings to Minnesota on June 4, he was put back on the DL. Coming back to the rotation in July he got five more starts, and then was put back in the bullpen to finish the season.

With his contract over at the end of 2002, and the team seeing little hope that he would be effective again, Nagy became a free agent. Despite the desire early in his career to be a one-team man, he signed a minor-league deal with the San Diego Padres for $500,000 in December. He started 2003 at Triple-A Portland, and was brought up on May 16 for a spot in the bullpen. After just five appearances, he was sent back down on June 2, and was released on June 6.

Nagy returned to the Indians a few weeks later as a special assistant to GM Mark Shapiro, working in the front office and on the field. He was hired by the Angels to be pitching coach for the Triple-A Salt Lake Bees in 2006, but after two seasons there he decided to spend some time at his home in San Diego. Nagy always kept his personal life private, talking little about his family and his life growing up. He preferred to let his work on the field tell his story. He and his wife, Jacquelyn, had two daughters, Makeala and Lily. "My kids are at a certain age and I was missing a lot," he said.[11] After a couple of years of being home with his family, they could tell he still had baseball in him, and urged him to return to the game in some capacity.

In 2007 Nagy was inducted into the Indians Hall of Fame, and in 2009 he returned to the team, this time as pitching coach at Triple-A Columbus. He spent one year there, then took another year off, but he was back in the major leagues in 2011, this time hired by the Arizona Diamondbacks as pitching coach, in part due to his relationship with GM Kevin Towers, who had been GM in San Diego when Nagy was there.

The Diamondbacks pitchers had been struggling for a while, but in Nagy's first year as pitching coach they improved their team ERA by a full run. Nagy tried, as always, to deflect any credit to others, saying, "I really didn't bring much to the table. ... I just tried to communicate as much as possible."[12] Nagy's players disagreed, calling him optimistic, calming and reassuring as a pitching coach. However, the Diamondbacks showed no further improvement over the following two years, and at the end of 2013 Nagy was fired. He quickly returned to his roots in Cleveland again, this time as a roving pitching instructor in the Indians minor-league system.

Nagy returned to the Diamondbacks as their pitching coach in 2016. However, it turned out to be only for a year. As of 2018, Nagy will be in his second season as the pitching coach for the Los Angeles Angels.

Charles Nagy was driven out of the big leagues by his injuries, spending much of his last four seasons on the disabled list. His New England drive kept making him try again and again, but led to some regrets and some might-have-beens.

NOTES

1. Tom Boswell, "Indians Could Rock or Get Rolled by M's," *Spokane Spokesman-Review*, October 13, 1995.
2. Tom Yantz, "A reluctant No. 1," *Hartford Courant*, April 28, 1992.
3. Tracy Ringolsby, "Frey Takes Charge, Shakes Up Cubs Scouting Staff," *Traverse City* (Michigan) *Record-Eagle*, November 5, 1988: 19.
4. "Baseball," *The Sporting News*, July 16, 1990: 13.
5. "Segui's Home Run Sparks Orioles to Win Over Bosox," *Daily Gazette*, September 19, 1990: C2.
6. Sheldon Ocker, "Expect No Miracles, G.M. Hart Warns," *The Sporting News*, April 6, 1992: 25.
7. Dave Ruden, "Fairfield's Nagy Living His Baseball Dream," *The Advocate* (Stamford, Connectivut), November 28, 1992: B4.
8. Sheldon Ocker, "Dugout Chatter," *The Sporting News*, August 17, 1992: 36.
9. "Pitching Is the Key to Indians' Success," *Roswell* (New Mexico) *Daily Record*, October 8, 1995: 15.
10. Paul Sullivan, "Here's the Pitch: Don't Overlook Cleveland's starters," *Chicago Tribune*, October 19, 1995.
11. Nick Piecoro, "Arizona Diamondbacks Pitching Coach Charles Nagy Quietly Effective," *Arizona Republic* (Phoenix), March 17, 2011.
12. Chris Elsberry, "Nagy's Calm Reassurance a Plus for D'Backs," *Connecticut Post* (Bridgeport), May 13, 2012.

CHAD OGEA

BY DAVID E. SKELTON

On June 7, 1994, the nation was glued to the live broadcast of police chasing a white Ford Bronco on Los Angeles' Interstate 405. In the home clubhouse 2,300 miles away, the Cleveland Indians were no less riveted as they prepared for a match against the Boston Red Sox. Never confused for an intellectual titan, slugger Manny Ramirez sat before the clubhouse television wondering why the police were chasing his teammate Chad Ogea (pronounced OH-jay).

Three years later such bewilderment with O.J. Simpson, the driver of the Bronco, ceased to exist as Ogea carved his own reputation in the nationwide headlines. The right-handed hurler's postseason success appeared destined for the 1997 World Series Most Valuable Player Award until the Florida Marlins' Game Seven ninth-inning rally and 11th-inning bases-loaded single snatched the world championship from the Indians' grasp. Despite this disappointment, a bright future loomed for the 26-year-old hurler until a series of injuries ultimately waylaid his career.

Chad Wayne Ogea was born on November 9, 1970, the second of three children of Arthur Ray and Laura Jeanette (Eagle) Ogea, in Lake Charles, Louisiana. Ogea attended St. Louis Catholic High School, where he led the Saints to two state titles. He was named Louisiana's 1988 High School Baseball Player of the Year and through 2015 remained the only Saint to advance to the major leagues. Drafted by the New York Yankees in the 41st round of the June 1988 amateur draft, Ogea instead chose to trek 130 miles east to Baton Rouge where he became "one of the most productive pitchers in [the long] history" of Louisiana State University's successful baseball program.[1]

LSU appeared in the College World Series in each of the three years Ogea pitched for the Tigers (1989-1991). In 1991 the second team All-American led the Tigers to a university-record-tying 55 wins. They were the first team in nine years to go undefeated through both the NCAA Regional Tournament and the College World Series. Ogea won two games in the Series including the June 8, 1991, clincher over Wichita State that delivered the university's first national championship. The success of the Series sweep stirred Louisiana Congressman Richard H. Baker to rise before his Washington colleagues to read a congratulatory notice into the *Congressional Record*.

On the advice of scout Buddy Mercado, the Indians selected Ogea in the third round of the 1991 draft just days after his championship win (Mercado's influence was evidenced in the next round when Cleveland selected Ogea's college roommate, Paul Byrd, who went on to carve out a 14-year major-league career). Ogea wasted little time acclimating himself in the Indians' system. In 1992 he was named Cleveland's Minor League Player of the Year after leading the Class-A Carolina League Kinston Indians in wins (13), ERA (3.49), strikeouts (123), complete games (5), and shutouts (2). His campaign earned him a late-season promotion to Double-A Canton-Akron (Eastern League), where a 2.20 ERA produced six wins in his seven starts. The 19 combined wins garnered national attention: "Cleveland has been nurturing several top young players. ... Pitcher Chad Ogea and outfielder Manny Ramirez are prime Class-A prospects."[2]

Ogea earned an invitation to the Indians' 1993 spring-training camp as a nonroster player. Initially ticketed for assignment to the Triple-A International League, Ogea outpaced expectations with a strong Grapefruit League campaign. A March 22 boating accident that claimed the lives of two Cleveland hurlers and severely injured a third suddenly thrust Ogea into competition to be the team's fifth starter. But as intended the Indians assigned the youngster to the Charlotte Knights for more minor-league seasoning. Ogea placed among the league leaders in wins (13), starts (29), innings pitched (181⅔), strikeouts (135), and (more disturbingly) homers yielded (26) as he paced the Knights to a pennant in their inaugural season in the International League. (It was also Charlotte's first season as a Cleveland affiliate.) In the offseason Ogea's name surfaced among the many Indians prospects sought by the New York Mets when Cleveland attempted to secure two-time Cy Young Award winner Bret Saberhagen via trade.

Ogea earned another nonroster invitation to spring training in 1994. This time he found the competition much steeper. One third-place finish had proved Cleveland's high-water mark in the preceding 34 years, a signature futility that included a franchise-worst 105 losses three years earlier. Through free agency and trades – including the acquisition of veteran hurlers Dennis Martinez and Jack Morris – general manager John Hart sought to reverse this long collapse. The varied moves left Ogea little room to compete as he bounced between Charlotte and Cleveland. On May 3, 1994, Ogea made his major-league debut in mop-up duty against the Chicago White Sox. Entering the sixth inning with an 8-0 deficit, the righty induced a groundout of Julio Franco and a strikeout of Robin Ventura to get out of the frame. Ogea survived the seventh unscathed but walks proved his undoing the next inning as the White Sox touched him for three runs. Ogea made three additional appearances in the strike-shortened season, including his first major-league start on August 7 against the Boston Red Sox (filling in for injured righty Mark Clark). Ogea was dominant his first time through the lineup – one hit and five strikeouts versus the first 10 batters. But the second time through proved less successful. Ogea pitched into the seventh inning and sustained a 4-1 loss in his first big-league decision.

Most of Ogea's 1994 season was spent in Charlotte, where he attained mixed success. A brilliant start – 6-3, 2.83 to place among the league leaders – crumbled to a second-half record of 3-7, 4.98. This decline was likely the result of a left knee injury that prevented Ogea from solidly planting his foot in his follow-through. (The knee would hamper him throughout his career.) After the season he underwent arthroscopic surgery that delayed by two months his participation in the Venezuelan Winter League.

Meanwhile the Indians' general manager remained active both before and during the 1995 campaign. Free-agent signings (including veteran hurlers Orel Hershiser and Bud Black) followed later by the acquisition of righty Ken Hill made for a very crowded field. (In July Cleveland failed in a bid for Toronto All-Star righty David Cone in which Ogea was vigorously pursued by the Blue Jays.) Ogea began the season in Buffalo but an injury to reliever Paul Shuey made for a quick recall. A strong relief performance against Minnesota on May 6 was rewarded with a return to the American Association. But this second stay in Buffalo would also prove short.

On May 9 the Indians captured a first-place stake in the American League's Central Division. They never relinquished that hold. The most powerful offense in the major leagues masked the difficulties sustained by the back end of the rotation as veterans Clark and Black both struggled. A brief dalliance with Jason Grimsley ended June 4 when the righty surrendered seven first-inning runs against the Blue Jays. (The only out secured was on a sacrifice bunt.) Manager Mike Hargrove turned to Ogea in relief. The Louisiana native held Toronto to one run over 6⅔ innings that allowed the Indians' juggernaut offense to mount a comeback. A ninth-inning walk-off homer by Paul Sorrento earned Cleveland a 9-8 win. Though Ogea was not credited with the win, the impressive outing earned the righty his second major-league start. Five days later he captured his first big-league win with a 7-4 triumph over the Milwaukee Brewers. Ogea won four of his next five starts including an 8-1 complete-game victory over the Seattle Mariners on July 6 (a Tino Martinez home run the only barrier between Ogea and his first major-league shutout).

Not all went swimmingly for the youngster. A record of 0-2, 8.00 in Ogea's next four starts – including two consecutive outings in which he did not survive the third inning – produced concerns that his days in the rotation were numbered. Ogea explained, "It's a matter of not going after the hitters. "I need to quit trying to think too much. I have to go on my natural instincts."[3] Those natural instincts resurfaced when Ogea finished the season with a record of 3-0, 1.80 in his last seven appearances (four starts). He concluded his rookie campaign with a respectable 8-3, 3.05 in 106⅓ innings. Ogea was relegated to the bullpen when Hargrove selected his playoff rotation. The righty made just one appearance: a mop-up role in Game Four of the American League Championship Series against the Mariners.

With Boston and California in the vanguard, Ogea attracted great trade interest in the offseason. Cleveland made clear that because of his versatility as a starter and reliever, Ogea was unavailable. But Ogea's chances of moving into the rotation were diminished with the December 14 free-agent signing of former Cy Young Award winner Jack McDowell. A strained elbow muscle in March 1996 only served to set Ogea back further. When the regular season began, four of Ogea's first five appearances were in relief. Despite two wins – continued testament to Cleveland's explosive offense – Ogea had a 10.12 ERA in 13⅓ innings. A second injury – tendinitis in his right shoulder – shelved the hurler for over a month.

Ogea returned to the mound on June 9 and picked up his third victory of the season in the second of two successful relief appearances. Following a few middling starts in June, Hargrove moved Ogea into the rotation in July after Dennis Martinez began suffering elbow problems. Ogea's July 7 win over Chicago avoided a four-game sweep and allowed the Indians to put some space between themselves and the hard-charging White Sox. A month later he yielded just a disputed infield hit over eight innings to beat the Mariners, 2-1. (Hargrove drew criticism for lifting Ogea before the ninth.) A record of 3-1, 3.52 in September – including Ogea's only career shutout, a four-hit, 7-0 win over Milwaukee on September 4 – assisted Cleveland to a .731 winning percentage in September and ensured another postseason for the Indians. Relegated again to the bullpen, Ogea faced just two Baltimore batters in the Division Series (in the ninth inning of the Game Four clincher) as the Indians fell to the Orioles, three games to one.

Spurned in the offseason by free-agent pitchers Roger Clemens, John Smoltz, and Alex Fernandez and outfielder Moises Alou (the latter two would play significant roles for Cleveland's 1997 World Series competitors), the Indians entered spring camp with Ogea as their number-four starter. A more relaxed Ogea confided that "in the past I couldn't help but worry if I was going to have a job at the big-league level. I was always fighting that."[4] In March his 18-9 mark over the preceding two years was rewarded with a three-year, $3.35 million contract. Ogea opened the 1997 season with two wins over the Anaheim Angels followed by two miserable starts against Boston.[5] He continued this seesaw approach – three straight wins in May, five consecutive losses in June – until a strained elbow resulted in a June 24 disabled-list assignment. A long recovery ensued as Ogea also suffered a recurrence of the knee injury that originally hampered him in 1994. Meanwhile reports surfaced that the Indians were "not happy with his professionalism and work ethic."[6] But when Ogea rejoined the team on September 1 after a brief rehab stint in Buffalo, his return was welcome relief. The team was racked with injuries to the staff, with Hargrove at one point complaining, "We have guys lined up and waiting to go on the disabled list."[7] Ogea's record of 3-1, 3.21 in his final five appearances helped lift the Indians to their third consecutive division flag.

Ogea's first appearance in the 1997 playoffs was of the dubious sort. Trailing the Yankees 2-1 in the fourth inning of Game Three of the Division Series, he entered a bases-loaded situation and yielded a grand slam to outfielder Paul O'Neill.[8] Ogea settled down to retire the next 13 batters in a 6-1 loss. He did not appear again until two starts in the Championship Series against the Orioles. Though he pitched well Ogea absorbed both losses in Cleveland's four-games-to-two Series win. But he drew further (and much unwanted) attention after Orioles manager Davey Johnson accused Hershiser of doctoring the ball. Ogea fueled these suspicions when he claimed that the veteran hurler "cheats, and everybody else does. … [Hershiser] showed me how to cheat."[9] The brouhaha disappeared after Hershiser claimed Ogea was simply teasing with the reporters.

Ogea drew the Game Two World Series assignment against Marlins All-Star hurler Kevin Brown. Both teams scratched out first inning runs until the Indians broke through with three runs in the fifth (aided by a sacrifice bunt from Ogea). Frequently the Marlins succeeded in getting runners into scoring position but Ogea wriggled out unscathed. Lifted in the seventh inning, Ogea was credited with a 6-1 win to knot the Series at one win apiece. Praise came from all quarters, including Marlins manager Jim Leyland: "[Y]ou have to credit Chad Ogea, he changed speeds and mixed pitches. He pitched outstanding."[10]

With the Indians facing elimination in Game Six, Ogea again took the mound against Brown. In a second-inning bases-loaded situation Ogea came to the plate with Hershiser's bat.[11] With just two major league at-bats under his belt (no hits) he delivered a line-drive single to right field to score two runs. Three innings later Ogea came around to score the Indians' third run after stroking a leadoff double (becoming the first pitcher since Mickey Lolich in 1968 to get two hits and two RBIs in a World Series game, and the first Indians hurler to drive in a Series run since 1920). Meanwhile Ogea's fastball (thrown at two speeds), slider, and changeup held the Marlins to a single hit through four innings. A leadoff walk in the sixth caused an anxious Hargrove to turn to the bullpen but Ogea came away with his second win of the Series.

"In my wildest dreams, I didn't think I'd be in this situation," Ogea said afterward. "I worked hard on the DL, came back healthy, rearranged my routine and got with it. And I started throwing the ball really well in September and it just carried over into the postseason."[12] Despite his fine mound work, the primary focus turned to his hitting. "I think the last time I had (a hit) was in high school," Ogea said. "I was just trying to go up there and make contact. It was fun."[13] Teammate Brian Anderson joked, "I think Chad is available to pinch-hit in Game 7."[14]

An Indians win in Game Seven seemingly ensured a Series MVP award for the pitching-and-hitting hero. But that win was not forthcoming. With Florida trailing 2-1 in the ninth, Marlins outfielder Moises Alou (whom Cleveland had sought in free agency) scored the tying run to send the game into extra innings. An 11th-inning tally secured Florida's world championship, with two-game winner Livan Hernandez awarded MVP honors.

Despite the Series disappointment, Ogea's stock had risen considerably. In January 1998 the Minnesota Twins were reportedly prepared to trade two-time Silver Slugger winner Chuck Knoblauch to the Indians in a package deal that included the righty hurler. The next month Ogea reported to spring camp as Cleveland's projected number-three starter. Instead injury spelled much of his 1998 season. He arrived in Florida wearing a knee brace. It was revealed that Ogea had no cartilage in his left knee and he began taking a gelatin-like injection to lubricate the knee. He began the season on the disabled list. A strain of the right pectoral muscle in May, followed by a diagnosis of tendinitis in his right middle finger in August, resulted in the combined loss of nearly three months. Ogea recovered in time to make the Indians' postseason roster with just 69 innings in the regular season (5-4, 5.61 in 19 appearances, nine starts).

Sophomore hurler Jaret Wright, who had moved into the rotation in Ogea's absence, got the Game One start against the Yankees in the ALCS. He did not survive the first inning. Brought in in relief, Ogea surrendered a run-scoring single before holding the Yankees into the sixth. On the strength of this performance Hargrove selected Ogea as the Game Five starter. If the manager hoped to resurrect Ogea's postseason success of the preceding year, he had cause to worry when the first batter was hit by a pitch. It went downhill from there as the Yankees scored three times on two hits, two walks, and another hit batter. A strikeout of third baseman Scott Brosius with the bases loaded spared further disaster. But Ogea surrendered another run in the second and was replaced by Wright. The Indians went on to a 5–3 defeat. They were eliminated in the Series two days later.

Ogea's name surfaced on the trade block shortly thereafter. Rumored to be headed to Atlanta in a three-way trade with Milwaukee, he was instead traded to Philadelphia on November 13 for reliever Jerry Spradlin. Cleveland's hesitation in making the swap was evident when general manager Hart stated, "We may regret trading Chad Ogea to the Phillies when he wins 20."[15] Meanwhile Philadelphia was ecstatic. Anticipating the loss of righty Mark Portugal to free agency, they projected Ogea as the club's number-two starter behind ace Curt Schilling.

Except for a difficult start in Atlanta on April 6, Ogea appeared poised to meet the Phillies' lofty expectations. He did not surrender an earned run over his next 19⅔ innings, capturing two wins in three appearances. But a 7.46 ERA over five starts resulted in two additional losses, drawing a sharp appraisal from the Philadelphia press: "[Ogea] is meticulous about his mechanics to the point it can affect his mental approach."[16] He was replaced in the number-two role by his former college roommate Paul Byrd (who had been acquired by the Phillies in August 1998).

After Ogea worked closely with pitching coach Galen Cisco, glimpses were seen of his successful past. A changed delivery produced a 3.12 ERA and two wins over four starts into August. "Ogea has lessened the leg kick in his windup – he felt it was "too violent" – and has started to work faster on the mound. … The result has been a more crisp breaking ball and improved velocity and location on his fastball."[17] But a record of 0-3, 8.04 in Ogea's ensuing five starts – including a league-leading 32nd home run surrendered on August 18 – relegated the righty to the bullpen. He made eight additional appearances (mostly in mop-up duty) and finished the season at 6-12, 5.63. Ogea was granted free agency three days after the season ended. In November the Detroit Tigers signed him to a minor-league contract. A month later the Tampa Bay Devil Rays selected Ogea in the Rule 5 draft. They projected him as a fourth or fifth starter for the then two-year-old franchise, but continued injury prevented Ogea from progressing beyond the early spring camp. He retired and went home to Louisiana.

Ogea returned to Louisiana State University to secure a degree in landscape architecture. "This is a very wide-ranging field," he told *Cleveland Magazine* in a 2005 "Where Are They Now?" piece. "It involves design, site analysis, drainage. It goes all the way from city development down to small-scale stuff like people's back yards. It's fascinating. … I've always liked the design part of it, the artistic part. … I like the outdoors, so that really kind of sparked my interest in this program."[18] (The article also noted Ogea's wife, Anne, and two daughters, Madelyn and Hannah.) Ogea ventured into lawn care and landscaping enterprises, including one with former LSU pitching coach Dan Canevari aptly called Diamond Cutters.

A strong religious faith was a stable throughout Ogea's life thanks to the mentoring and fostering of a Class-A coach years earlier. But the constant throughout Ogea's life remained baseball. He enjoyed working with children and developed a baseball training camp in which he successfully tied his faith to his instruction. Ogea proudly proclaimed, "God has given me a platform, through baseball, to reach children."[19] He also spent time with the nonprofit fundraising 2 Seam Dream Foundation, a group of former professional baseball players dedicated to the eradication of cancer. In 2008 Ogea was inducted into the Kinston (North Carolina) Professional Baseball Hall of Fame. Seven years later he returned to Cleveland to participate in the 20th-anniversary celebrations of the Indians' 100-win campaign.

In 1997 an injury-racked rotation caused Indians' manager Mike Hargrove to turn to Ogea as a primary starter in the postseason. The ensuing results nearly captured a World Series MVP award for the 26-year-old righty. But it was injuries that also waylaid Ogea's once-promising career. His six major-league seasons produced a record of 37-35, 4.88 in 128 appearances (including the postseason). With a rapid advance through the minors, plus considerable interest shown by numerous competitors, a far more brilliant career seemingly loomed for the former collegiate star.

The author wishes to thank Rod Nelson, chair of the SABR Scouts Committee, and Karl Green, chair of the Collegiate Research Committee for their valuable input. Further thanks are extended to Bill Nowlin and Len Levin for review and edit of the narrative.

SOURCES

Baseball-reference.com.

Ancestry.com.

nesn.com/2014/06/relive-the-o-j-simpson-ford-bronco-chase-on-events-20th-anniversary/.

indiansprospectinsider.com/blog/chad-ogea-inducted-into-kinston-hof-8613.

14-0productions.com/Louisiana_Baseball.html.

books.google.com/books?id=EU4FWOay3tgC&pg=PA14634&lpg=-PA14634&dq=chad+ogea+lsu&source=bl&ots=g5Bj7V7KBB&sig=-NynIbJgK7G5qHZ98twOtz9-XHY&hl=en&sa=X&ved=0CDYQ6AEwBDgeahUKEwjFiuSK7ofHAhWBhQoKHd6mAPE#v=onepage&q=chad%20ogea%20lsu&f=false.

rayscoloredglasses.com/2014/12/11/tampa-bay-rays-rule-5-draft-history-selections/.

businessreport.com/article/entrepreneur-dan-canevari-and-chad-ogea.

thegoal.com/players/baseball/ogea_chad/ogea_chad.html.

2seamdreamfoundation.com/index-2.html.

wmanfm.com/articles/wman-local-news-122687/cleveland-indians-celebrate-the-20th-anniversary-13693134/.

NOTES

1 Bryan Wideman, "After LSU: Life in the Pros for Former Tigers," LSUreveille.com (February 20, 2002). (lsureveille.com/after-lsu-life-int-he-pros-for-former-tigers/article_3f6c9f1f-cb1a-50fd-9a5c-5436b78b617c.html).

2 "Minors: Cleveland Indians," *The Sporting News*, October 12, 1992: 33.

3 "A.L. Central: Cleveland Indians," *The Sporting News*, August 14, 1995: 31.

4 "A.L.: Cleveland Indians," *The Sporting News*, March 10, 1997: 37.

5 Extending into 1998, Ogea became the second pitcher in history to surrender six earned runs to the Red Sox in four consecutive appearances.

6 "The book on … CHAD OGEA," *The Sporting News*, November 3, 1997: 40.

7 "Rotation Is Rocked as Injuries Roll," *The Sporting News*, July 21, 1997: 27.

8 The Yankees first playoff grand slam in 33 years.

9 "Davey Johnson Accuses Hershiser of Cheating," *Los Angeles Times*, October 13, 1997.

10 Steve Eby, "Eighteen Crazy Nights – Looking Back at the 1997 Cleveland Indians," Did The Tribe Win Last Night? (didthetribewinlastnight.com/blog/2014/10/19/eighteen-crazy-nights-looking-back-at-the-1997-cleveland-indians-17/).

11 Hershiser was the last pitcher to get three hits in a World Series game.

12 "In Defense of the Defense," *The Sporting News*, November 3, 1997: 41.

13 Eby.

14 Ibid.

15 "Caught on the Fly," *The Sporting News*, January 24, 2000: 8.

16 "Schilling Evolves, but Battles with G.M. Linger," *The Sporting News*, May 31, 1999: 33.

17 "Surprise Team of N.L. Must Now Face Injuries," *The Sporting News*, July 5, 1999: 29.

18 Jeannie Roberts, "'95 Cleveland Indians – Where Are They Now?" Cleveland Magazine.com (clevelandmagazine.com/ME2/dirmod.asp?sid=E73ABD6180B44874871A91F6BA5C249C&nm=Arts+%26+Entertainemnt&type=Publishing&mod=Publications%3A%3AArticle&mid=1578600D80804596A222593669321019&tier=4&id=B36B8A00D4D448F79AEFC9EB084DA9B4).

19 Lawrence Conneff, "Former Major Leaguer Ogea Leads Week Of Champions Clinic," Bluffton Today (blufftontoday.com/bluffton-sports/2013-06-23/former-major-leaguer-ogea-leads-week-champions-clinic#.VcqFVzZRHIV).

GREGG OLSON

BY WYNN MONTGOMERY

Gregg Olson, the only son of a highly successful high-school baseball coach, distinguished himself on the diamond at Omaha's Northwest High School and went on to "pioneer the position of late inning [college] closer at a time when no one put their most talented pitcher in the bullpen."[1] That talent made him a first-round draft pick and an almost immediate major-league star. His mound dominance lasted for five years until he was sidelined by a serious arm injury. After trying for four frustrating years to recover his mastery, he finally found new life with an expansion team and added four years to his résumé.

Greggory William Olson was born on October 11, 1966, in Scribner, Nebraska. His parents were Bill and Sandra "Sandy" (née Cassell) Olson. In 1971 the family, which by then included younger sister Tammi, moved to Omaha when Gregg's father became the first baseball coach at Northwest High. Gregg grew up there, playing youth football, basketball, and baseball throughout his childhood.[2]

Olson credited his father with shaping him "into a major leaguer."[3] A significant component of that process was teaching the youngster at age 13 to throw the curveball that would become his trademark "Uncle Charlie," but for a year limiting him to one per game.[4]

In 1982 Gregg joined his father's baseball squad at Northwest High, and over the next four years, the Huskies won four Class-A state championships as Gregg compiled a 27-0 record and a microscopic 0.76 ERA while fanning 276 opposing batters.[5] After the third of those championships, the father and son were featured in *Sports Illustrated*'s "Faces in the Crowd," which noted Gregg's performance in the championship game when he "struck out 10, hit two homers, and drove in [all] four Husky runs."[6]

That article also cited Northwest's 40-game winning streak, which had begun in 1983. The streak ended at 53 games in 1985, Gregg's senior year, but the Huskies won their fourth consecutive title, and Gregg capped his high-school career by hitting .857 (18-for-21) in the state tournament and throwing a no-hitter (the fourth of his career) in the championship game.[7]

Gregg's high-school teams were ranked among the top three nationally by *Collegiate Baseball* magazine for three consecutive years (1983-85).[8] In 1984 he was a member of the USA Junior Olympic Team that won a Silver Medal,[9] and he was named a High School All-American in 1985.[10] With that track record, college baseball was the logical next step, so Gregg passed up a football scholarship from the University of Nebraska.[11] From some 30 Division I baseball offers, he chose a "full ride" from Auburn University because he would be able to "play right away" for Hal Baird, whom he considered "an exceptional pitching coach."[12]

In his first collegiate year, Gregg made 14 starts, completing one, and relieved in five other games. He compiled a 7-3 record with a 5.72 ERA and 62 strikeouts (0.79 per inning).[13] The next year, Coach Baird "changed the college game forever"[14] by giving the big (6-foot-4, 210-pound) right-hander what was at the time a new role. He became the Tigers' closer, appearing in 78 games over the next two years, compiling an 18-4 record with 20 saves and fanning 209 batters (1.4 per inning).

After leading the NCAA with a 1.26 ERA in 1987, Olson was named an All-American by *Baseball America*. He then played on the USA National Team that handed Cuba two home losses in July. That team went 8-0 in the Pan American Games in Indianapolis before losing the championship game to those same Cubans. Olson was a vital part of Team USA's success, appearing in 21 of its 56 games, amassing a 3.53 ERA, and leading the team with 69 strikeouts.[15]

In 1988 Olson's 2.00 ERA led the Southeastern Conference, and he became Auburn's first two-time baseball All-American.[16] Following that successful junior year, the Baltimore Orioles made him the fourth overall pick in the 1988 amateur draft – the highest pick ever for a college relief pitcher[17] -- and offered him a contract that stipulated that he would be in the majors by September 1.[18] He had also been selected to play for Team USA in the 1988 Olympics, but contracted mononucleosis and was unable "to finish the Olympic experience."[19]

On June 28, 1988, Olson signed with the Orioles for a reported bonus of $200,000[20] and was assigned to Hagerstown in the Class-A Carolina League to begin his professional career. After closing eight games and earning one win and four saves for the Suns, Olson was promoted to Double-A Charlotte. He pitched in only eight games there before he and teammate Curt Schilling were summoned to join the Orioles in Seattle.[21] During that brief stint in Charlotte, Olson acquired the nickname ("Otter") that Schilling brought to the majors with them and that followed Olson throughout his career.[22]

Olson made his major-league debut in Seattle on September 2, 1988, entering the game in the bottom of the eighth inning with nobody out and a runner on first and the O's trailing, 3-1. He fanned Steve Balboni on a called third strike. The next hitter singled but was out at second trying for a double. After issuing a walk, Olson retired the side with another strikeout. In the ninth, after the Orioles scored three times, Tom Niedenfuer held the Mariners scoreless, and Olson had his first major-league victory. He pitched 10 more innings that year and was charged with one loss and no saves.

Olson staked his claim to the Baltimore closer's job early in 1989. He earned his first save on April 15 in Boston in his fifth appearance. He followed that performance with two middle-relief stints and a three-inning closing effort against the Twins that earned him a win. On April 26 Olson earned what he later called "my first real save"[23] when he entered a game in Oakland in the bottom of the eighth with the Orioles leading 2-1. After retiring the side in order, he returned in the ninth and struck out Dave Parker, Dave Henderson, and Mark McGwire to preserve the win. It was the second save of his career, and he was now the Orioles' closer. He converted his first 15 save opportunities, went through a brief slump in July, and finished the season with 27 saves in 33 opportunities.

Late in the season, manager Frank Robinson said of Olson, "I don't know where we'd be without him" but added, "He always makes it interesting."[24] It seems that 1-2-3 innings were not Olson's usual approach. One Baltimore sportswriter described his season this way: "Close game. He pitches into trouble. He pitches out of trouble. Orioles win."[25] Unfortunately for the Orioles, he didn't always pitch out of trouble. In his last appearance of the season, he had a rare blown save when his wild pitch allowed the Toronto Blue Jays to tie and eventually win a game that gave them a two-game lead over the Orioles with only two games left to play. Another loss the following day ended the Orioles' hopes of a pennant.

It had, however, been a turnaround year for the Orioles – climbing from the AL East cellar in 1988 to a second-place finish. Olson's role in that transformation was rewarded when he was named AL Rookie of the Year, the first relief pitcher to be so honored. On December 16, 1989, he made the year even more memorable by marrying Jill Johnson, whom he had met on a blind date during his junior year at Auburn.[26]

Olson followed his outstanding rookie season with another stellar year, being named to his only All-Star team by Oakland Athletics manager Tony La Russa and finishing the season with 37 saves, his career high and an Orioles' record until it was eclipsed in 1997 by Randy Myers' 45 saves. That was the first of three consecutive 30-plus-save seasons during which Olson became (at age 25) the youngest player at the time to record 100 saves. Perhaps the most unusual and historic of those saves occurred at Oakland-Alameda County Coliseum on July 13, 1991. Olson came into the game to start the bottom of the ninth inning with the Orioles leading the Athletics, 2-0. He was the O's fourth pitcher of the game, after Bob Milacki (6 innings pitched), Mike Flanagan (1 IP), and Mark Williamson (1 IP), and he was trying to preserve their combined no-hitter. He needed only 12 pitches to do just that, getting Dave Henderson to ground out and fanning Jose Canseco and Harold Baines.

When the 1993 season started, Olson had established himself as one of the premier closers in the league, and he was headed for yet another 30-plus saves until disaster struck on July 31. He entered a game in the ninth inning to protect a 4-0 lead over the Red Sox (a non-save situation). He did his job, striking out the side. He later called that game's final strike, which fanned Mo Vaughan, his "best curveball EVER,"[27] but it also was his worst curveball ever because it resulted in a torn ligament. That injury did not receive immediate attention as he pitched in four games over the next eight days. He earned saves in the first three of these appearances to bring his season total to 29 and lowered his ERA to a career-best 1.60, but on August 8 he allowed an inherited Cleveland runner to score a tying ninth-inning run. The Orioles eventually won that game in extra innings, but Olson's career in Baltimore was over. He faced (and walked) only one more batter that season (on September 22).

In August, the orthopedic surgeon Frank Jobe had recommended Tommy John surgery to repair the damaged elbow, but Olson wanted to avoid the knife.[28] He talked with Nolan Ryan, who had rehabbed through a similar injury, and decided to try Ryan's approach. In January 1994, Dr. James Andrews found that the ligament had fully healed although such tears rarely mend on their own. But Olson had not paid enough attention to his mechanics,[29] and he was no longer the pitcher he had been.

In his five full seasons with the Orioles. Olson had become a fan favorite, relying on his knee-buckling curveball and a "90-plus-mph fastball"[30] to earn 160 saves, a team record that has stood for more than years. He also set the franchise record of 41 consecutive scoreless innings (in 29 appearances between August 4, 1989, and May 4, 1990). When asked about that streak, Olson said, "I don't think of it as a streak. Cal Ripken has the Streak. This [was] just a little run."[31]

Considering what he accomplished in Baltimore, it is not surprising that Olson was hurt when, in his words, "Baltimore ditched"[32] him after the 1993 season, opting not to risk arbitration with an injured pitcher. The Orioles tried unsuccessfully to develop a mutually acceptable "incentive-laden"[33] contract, and so many other teams showed interest that during January 1994 every issue of The Sporting News included articles related to some aspect of the "Olson Derby."[34]

Although it didn't take him long to find a new team, Olson was about to begin what he later called "a run of total, frustrating hell."[35] Despite the disappointments and frequent uniform changes, he never considered quitting. He no longer felt "invincible," but he got close enough often enough to being what he had been[36] that he was sure there was light at the end of the tunnel.

Eventually, he was correct, but the tunnel was longer and bumpier than he expected.

Olson signed in February 1994 with Atlanta. His one-year contract was for less than he had made in Baltimore, but included a potential bonus if he was healthy enough to pitch in 60 games.[37] In one of life's (or at least baseball's) little ironies, pitcher Greggory William (Gregg) Olson signed with the Braves just two months after Atlanta released catcher Gregory William (Greg) Olson. The two "namesakes" had met only once – in 1990 when they were on opposing sides in the All-Star Game, staying in the same Chicago hotel, and dealing often with the confusion of receiving each other's phone calls, messages, and laundry.[38]

Olson's Atlanta bonus money was in doubt from the outset; he went on the disabled list during spring training, rehabbed in Richmond, and then struggled through the season, appearing in only 16 games and compiling a record of 0-2 with a single save and a 9.20 ERA. The Braves released him at the end of the season, and Olson spent the next three years (1995-97) trying to resurrect his career.

That quest took him to seven major-league teams and three minor-league affiliates. His journey began when he signed with Cleveland after being released by the Braves. He also considered returning to Baltimore, but decided that Cleveland's need for a relief pitcher was greater.[39] He started the 1995 season with Triple-A Buffalo and then joined the Indians, where he compiled an ERA of 13.50 in three games. In mid-July, his wife was at home expecting their first child, and the Indians were scheduled for a 10-day road trip after the All-Star break. The team denied Gregg's request to be released but allowed him to miss the road trip so he could be at home for the birth.[40] Shortly afterward, Kansas City purchased his contract. His numbers with the Royals were much more respectable – three saves, a 3-3 record, and a 3.26 ERA in 20 appearances, but in November he again became a free agent when Kansas City's best offer for the next year was a minor-league contract.[41]

The Olson merry-go-round moved even faster in 1996; he became the property of four major-league teams, but played for only two. The St. Louis Cardinals signed him in January, but released him after he was injured during spring training.[42] The Cards having traded for Dennis Eckersley shortly after acquiring Olson probably made him more expendable.[43] Cincinnati signed Olson immediately; assigned him to Triple-A Indianapolis, where he earned four saves in seven appearances; and traded him to Detroit in late April for infielder Yuri Sanchez, who would spend 14 years in the minors without ever making it to "The Show."

Olson appeared in 43 games (43 innings) for the Tigers, earning eight saves and compiling a 3-0 record and a 5.02 ERA, before being traded in late August to Houston, where he appeared in nine games and earned another win. When the Astros released Olson in October, he was once again a free agent, but while with Detroit he had added a pitch to his repertoire that he later credited with helping him in his comeback efforts. Olson said that Tigers pitching coach Jon Matlack taught him to throw a changeup, giving him "a pitch nobody expected."[44]

Olson's road back had a few more stops. He signed with Minnesota in December 1996, and opened the 1997 season with the Twins. In 11 games, his ERA was an astronomical 18.36, and he was released in the middle of May. The Royals signed him again a week later and returned him to his hometown Omaha Royals, where for the first time in years he was used as a starter as well as reliever. He pitched in nine games, starting five and closing two others, compiling a 3-1 record and a 3.31 ERA, and was promoted to Kansas City in July. In 34 games (41⅔ IP), mostly as a middle reliever, his ERA (3.02) was the lowest since his final year in Baltimore, perhaps because his strikeout-to-walk ratio (1.65) was also his best since that same year. Olson later credited Royals coach Bruce Kison with helping him regain his earlier form. He said, "With the Royals I started feeling like my old self. It began coming naturally again."[45] Even so, he was released in October.

In the spring of 1998, Olson appeared in the training camp of the brand-new Arizona Diamondbacks, one of the National League's two expansion teams. He made the team and was expected to be the setup man with Felix Rodriguez as the closer.[46] That was his role on April 20, when he entered a duel of the expansion teams at Bank One Ballpark in Phoenix with Arizona leading Miami 7-4. The Diamondbacks continued to add runs, and Olson stayed in the game for 2⅔ innings. As a result, he found himself in an unfamiliar spot – the batter's box. He had batted twice before in the majors – once in Baltimore, once in Atlanta – and had struck out both times. He batted twice in this game, striking out again in his first appearance. In his second at-bat, he smashed a two-run homer off right-hander Oscar Henriquez. He would walk in his only other major-league plate appearance, so upon retirement he became the 12th member of an elite club[47] -- players whose only major-league hit was a home run.

In May, with Rodriguez' ERA hovering around 7.00, about twice as high as Olson's, their roles were reversed. On May 1, Gregg closed his first game as a Diamondback, pitching the last two innings of a loss to the Expos. Three days later, he pitched the 10th and 11th innings against the Mets and earned his first win. After two more middle-relief appearances, Olson garnered his first save on May 14 with a perfect ninth inning against the Brewers to preserve a 4-1 victory. At that time, the Diamondbacks owned an 8-31 (.205) record. From that point forward, with Olson closing another 46 games, earning 29 more saves, and lowering his ERA from 4.08 to 3.01, Arizona's record was 57-66 (.463).

Among those 29 saves was perhaps the oddest of Olson's career. On May 28 he entered a game in the bottom of the eighth with Arizona clinging to a 7-5 lead over San Francisco. The Giants had already scored twice in the inning and had a runner on first with two outs and Barry Bonds at the plate. Gregg walked Bonds and then threw a wild pitch that put the tying runs in scoring position. He issued another walk to load the bases before fanning Rey Sanchez to end the inning. The Diamondbacks scored once in the ninth to gain a three-run cushion, and Olson stayed in the game. After fanning the leadoff batter, he issued two more walks, a double, a run-scoring groundout, and yet another walk, bringing Bonds back to the plate with the bases loaded and Arizona's lead reduced to two runs. Following manager Buck Showalter's orders, Olson intentionally walked Bonds to force in another run. That rare[48] strategy "worked," but it took a while. Brent Mayne fouled off five full-count pitches before drilling a line drive that the right fielder lost in the lights before making a "dramatic, game-ending catch."[49] Arizona prevailed, 8-7, and Olson earned a save while giving up two runs on one hit and six walks (only one of which was intentional). He had thrown 56 pitches to record four outs.

At the end of the season, another Greg (Padres' outfielder Greg Vaughn) was named NL Comeback Player of the Year by *The Sporting News* and by the Players Choice Awards program. Vaughn had an All-Star season (.272/50 home runs/119 RBIs), which was vastly better than his previous year (.216/18 homers/57 RBIs), but did his bouncing back from one bad year outweigh what Olson accomplished for the Diamondbacks after four years as a baseball vagabond? Perhaps the voters found it easier to recognize a rapid rebound from a single bad season than to recall how good Olson had been five years earlier and how long and often discouraging his comeback road had been. Olson's performance did receive some recognition; Arizona's baseball writers named him the Diamondbacks' Most Valuable Pitcher.[50]

In 1999, for the first time in five years, Olson did not have to look for a new ballclub; Arizona was happy to have him back. Even with a 30 percent raise (to $850,000), he was a bargain. His numbers declined a bit as he returned to a set-up role after blowing several saves early in the season[51] and spending time on the disabled list because of back spasms,[52] but he appeared in 61 games, earning 14 saves to go with a 9-4 record (his career high in wins) and a 3.71 ERA. When the Diamondbacks won the NL West, Olson got his only (and very limited) postseason experience, facing two batters in two games, and being charged with the game-tying run (unearned) in the deciding game of the Division Series won by the Mets.

After that season, Olson again tested the free-agent market. Now, however, he had two successful seasons on which to base negotiations, and he landed a guaranteed two-year $3 million contract with the Los Angeles Dodgers. However, he went on the disabled list early (on April 11) – with a strained right forearm. He then tore a tendon in the same arm while on the mound in a rehab assignment in Class-A San Bernardino.[53] He appeared in only 13 games (17⅔ IP) in 2000, acquiring one loss and no saves. The following year, his performance deteriorated even further. On June 22, 2001, he entered a game in the top of the ninth with one out and two runners aboard. The visiting Padres had already scored twice to take a 6-4 lead. Olson gave up a walk, a sacrifice fly, and a hit. When he finally retired the side, both inherited runners had scored, he had been charged with a run, and the Padres had a 9-4 lead.

That was Gregg Olson's last game in the major leagues. After 28 games, he had an 8.03 ERA, a record of 0-1, and no saves. In his last four games, he had been charged with 10 runs (all earned) in 3⅓ innings (a 27.00 ERA) – an inauspicious end to an amazing comeback. Olson himself said that "it wasn't a total surprise"[54] when the Dodgers announced his release.

Olson, his wife, Jill, and their four children (Brett, Brooke, Ashley, and Ryan) remained in Newport Beach, California, where they had moved in 2000. Brett, a right-handed hitter and pitcher[55] like his father, joined the Auburn baseball team as an infielder in 2015. Gregg served for four years as an advance scout for the San Diego Padres and became part-owner and president of Toolshed Sports International, a manufacturer of high-performance athletic undergear.

Olson was inducted into the Nebraska High School Sports Hall of Fame (along with his father) in 1999. That same year, *Sports Illustrated* named him one of Nebraska's "Fifty Greatest Sports Figures of the Century."[56] In 2001, his plaque was placed on "Tiger Trail" in downtown Auburn, Alabama, which honors former Auburn University athletes. In 2008 he was inducted into the Baltimore Orioles Hall of Fame, and two years later, he was one of the first four players (along with Frank Thomas, Bo Jackson, and Tim Hudson) to be enshrined on the Wall of Fame at Plainsman Park, Auburn's baseball stadium.

In 2013 Olson became associated with yet another honor when he agreed that his name could be attached to a new annual award that would recognize college baseball's "Breakout Player of the Year." This award, sponsored by Toolshed Sports International, recognizes a player who receives no preseason All-American mention but "elevates his game to an elite level"[57] during the season. The winner of the inaugural 2013 Gregg Olson Award was Ball State pitcher Scott Baker.

Olson also co-edited and contributed several stories to *We Got to Play Baseball: 60 Stories from Men Who Played the Game.* In his "Dedication" to that volume, he wrote: "Baseball is a great life, but not an easy one." His own career certainly supports that belief.

SOURCES

Books

Olson, Gregg, and Ocean Palmer, ed. *We Got to Play Baseball: 60 Stories from Men Who Played the Game* (Houston: Strategic Book Publishing and Rights Company, 2012).

Newspapers

Baltimore Sun.

Los Angeles Times.

Sports Illustrated.

The Sporting News.

Washington Post.

Online Resources

Auburn Tigers Baseball (auburntigers.com).

Baseball Almanac (baseball-almanac.com).

Baseball Cube (thebaseballcube.com).

Baseball Library (baseballlibrary.com).

Baseball-Reference.com (baseball-reference.com).

City of Auburn, Alabama (auburnalabama.org).

Gregg Olson Award (olsonaward.com).

MLBlogsNetwork (mlb.com).

Nebraska High School Sports Hall of Fame Foundation (nebhalloffame.org).

Retrosheet (retrosheet.org).

SB Nation: The Good Phite (thegoodphite.com).

The Sports Illustrated Vault (si.com/VAULT).

Personal Correspondence

For six weeks, starting in mid-December 2014, the author and Gregg Olson exchanged voicemails. Between January 9 and 11, Olson reviewed a first draft of the biography and provided feedback and answers to questions raised by the author. In a January 26, 2015, telephone discussion, after reading a revised draft, Olson answered additional questions, discussed his career, and approved the biography.

The author is also indebted to Richard French, his former neighbor in Atlanta and Gregg Olson's college roommate, for making the introduction that facilitated this effort.

NOTES

1 Hal Baird, head baseball coach at Auburn University (1985-2000), quoted on olsonaward.com.
2 Gregg Olson, email, January 11, 2015.
3 Gregg Olson, "Introduction" to *We Got to Play Baseball* (Houston: Strategic Book Publishing, 2012), xii.
4 Jonathan Hacohen, "Gregg Olson Interview: Talking Ball with One of the Greatest Closers in MLB History," MLBreports.com, April 6, 2012.
5 nebhalloffame.org.
6 *Sports Illustrated*, July 16, 1984.
7 nebhalloffame.org.
8 Gregg Olson, email, January 11, 2015.
9 Gregg Olson, "Jim Abbott: Troublemaker in Cuba," *We Got to Play Baseball* (Houston: Strategic Book Publishing, 2012), 26.
10 nebhalloffame.org.
11 Ibid.
12 Gregg Olson, email, January 11, 2015.
13 The Baseball Cube (thebaseballcube.com).
14 olsonaward.com.
15 Ibid.
16 auburntigers.com.
17 olsonaward.com.
18 Hacohen.
19 Gregg Olson, "Jim Abbott: Troublemaker in Cuba," *We Got to Play Baseball* (Houston: Strategic Book Publishing, 2012), 26.
20 baseballlibrary.com.
21 Hacohen.
22 Gregg Olson, email, January 11, 2015.
23 Amanda Comack, "Closer Olson Enters O's Hall of Fame," Mlb.com, August 9, 2008.
24 John Eisenberg, "As Olson Goes, So Go the Orioles," *Baltimore Sun*, September 10, 1989.
25 Ibid.
26 Gregg Olson, email, January 11, 2015.
27 Hacohen.
28 Tom Boswell, "Arms Control Tough Task," *Washington Post*, September 29, 1993.
29 Gregg Olson, email, January 11, 2015.
30 Comack.
31 Tim Kurkjian, "Between the Lines: What Streak?" *Sports Illustrated*, May 14, 1990.
32 Hacohen.
33 Peter Schmuck, *The Sporting News*, January 3, 1994: 27.
34 Peter Pascarelli, "Baseball Report," *The Sporting News*, January 24: 31.
35 Jeff Pearlman, "Inside Baseball: Gregg Olson Redux: Diamondback's Comeback," *Sports Illustrated*, August 24, 1998.
36 Gregg Olson, telephone conversation, January 26, 2015.
37 *Los Angeles Times,* "Gregg Olson, Braves Agree on One-Year Deal," February 9, 1994 (from Associated Press).
38 Gregg Olson, telephone conversation, January 26, 2015.
39 Gregg Olson email, January 11, 2015.
40 Ibid.
41 Gregg Olson, telephone conversation, January 26, 2015.
42 Ibid.
43 Gregg Olson, telephone conversation, January 26, 2015.
44 Pearlman.
45 Ibid.
46 Ibid.
47 David S. Cohen, "For Tommy Medica – One Hit, One Home Run Careers,"(thegoodphight.com), September 12, 2013. Note: At least five more members joined the club after Olson's retirement.
48 baseball-almanac.com reports six bases-loaded intentional walks. The first was issued in 1881, the most recent in 2008.
49 Gregg Olson, "A Very Intentional Walk," *We Got to Play Baseball*

(Houston: Strategic Book Publishing, 2012), 107-110.

50 Pedro Gomez, "Arizona: White Named Team MVP," *The Sporting News*, October 12, 1998: 70.

51 Jason Reid, "Olson Suffers a Setback," *Los Angeles Times*, May 13, 2000.

52 *Los Angeles Times*, "Around the Majors," July 4, 1999 (from the Associated Press).

53 Reid.

54 Chris Foster, "Olson Not Surprised at Being Cut Loose," *Los Angeles Times*, June 24, 2001.

55 auburnbaseball.com

56 "The Master List of the 50 Greatest Sports Figures of the Century from Each of the 50 States," *Sports Illustrated*, December 27, 1999.

57 olsonaward.com.

TONY PEÑA

BY BLAKE W. SHERRY

In Tribe folklore, Tony Peña will always bring back moments of elation and unbound hope for a world championship after he crushed an early-morning pitch toward left field for a walk-off homer in the 13th inning of Game One of the 1995 American League Division Series. For the Indians, it was their first postseason since 1954, and left Indian fans dreaming, "Would this be the Indians' year?"

Antonio Francisco (Padilla) Peña was born on June 4, 1957, in Monte Cristi, Dominican Republic. He was born into a family of hard-working parents. His father, Octaviano, was a farmer, and his mother, Rosalia, a teacher for more than 30 years. Tony was raised with three brothers and a sister. While his father worked long hours, it was his mother who took it upon herself to teach Tony the finer points of baseball. Tony once said it was his mother who was the star of the family. "She was a real all-star," he said his rookie year. "She played softball and she pitched and hit better than most men."[1] Rosalia was strict with the family getting their education, insisting that Tony and his brothers keep up with their studies and not just play baseball. If he or any of his siblings had an exam the next day, studying had to come first.

Tony Peña was signed as an amateur free agent in July of 1975 by the Pittsburgh Pirates. Originally signed as an outfielder, he switched to catcher in his second year in the minors. He made his way through the Pirates farm system with stops with their Gulf Coast Rookie League team, Salem (Class A), Charleston (Class A), Shreveport (Double-A), Buffalo (Double-A), and Portland (Triple-A) before getting a call-up to the Pirates when rosters expanded on September 1, 1980. In eight games he hit a robust .429 (9-for-21).

Peña made the Pirates roster in 1981 but was initially stuck behind the strong backstop platoon of Steve Nicosia and Ed Ott. That had taken the Bucs to the 1979 world championship. However, it was not long before Peña became the starting catcher. His strong end-of-season showing in 1980 allowed the Pirates to trade Ott to the California Angels in April of 1981. At that point manager Chuck Tanner insisted that he now had two starting catchers in Peña and Nicosia.

After seeing action in just 66 games in that strike-shortened season of 1981, Peña emerged as the starting catcher toward the end of the season. One of the attributes of his game that fans noticed early in his career was his love for the game, not unlike the joy of one of his Pirates predecessors, the perpetually smiling Manny

Sanguillen. Said Peña, "I would love this game even if I wasn't getting paid to play."[2] Tanner saw even bigger things coming, stating, "It's just a matter of time before Peña is recognized as one of the outstanding catchers."[3] Tanner was not alone in his observations; Atlanta manager Bobby Cox said that Peña "looks like an excellent prospect."[4] Peña's .300 batting average and excellent defense garnered him a sixth-place finish in the Rookie of the Year voting. He was named Topps Rookie All-Star catcher and was selected to the UPI Rookie All-Star Team. Peña's hard work and desire to get better would serve him well. At year end, he said, "I will be better next year because of the experience I got this year," adding, "I made some mistakes. Chuck talked to me about them."[5]

As the Pirates' starting catcher in 1982, Peña began to hit his stride. In July he was named to the NL All-Star team. He batted .296 and hit 11 home runs in his first full year as a starter. He would subsequently be named to four more All-Star teams in his career. He had arrived.

In 1983 Peña established himself as one of the stars of the game. He was awarded his first Gold Glove while hitting a full-season career high .301. He added some power to go with the high average with a career-high 15 home runs and 70 runs batted in. Over the next three years, Peña was a fixture for the Bucs, becoming known for his low crouch behind the plate with one leg fully extended. Pittsburgh fans also loved his exuberance for the game, and he was a crowd favorite during his stay.

The 1983 season was a good one for the Pirates as well. They were tied for first place as late as September 17 with the Phillies. But the Bucs faded the last two weeks of that season, and then entered a down phase for the franchise that lasted nearly through the end of the decade. A miserable team in 1985 went 57-104 and failed to draw even 750,000 fans for the season. During that period it took a major push lead by Mayor Richard Caliguiri to put together a consortium of local businesses just to keep the Pirates in town.[6]

As the Pirates struggled in the mid-'80s to field a competitive team and to stay in Pittsburgh, Peña's ability to maintain his zest for the game was challenged. With three consecutive last-place finishes, the game was not as much fun. The 1985 season was the low point of his career. "It was no fun – no fun at all," he said. "There were the drug trials, the club was up for sale and we were losing, losing, losing. I am not a loser."[7] A number of major leaguers, including several Pirates, but not Peña, were called before a Pittsburgh grand jury investigating cocaine use. As someone who had not taken drugs, Peña resented the guilt by association that all the Pirates endured. "The world thought that Pittsburgh was on trial," he said. "Everywhere anyone went, they heard about ball players and drugs, and heard about Pittsburgh. It was unfair. It was not right. Pittsburgh is a good town."[8] It wasn't until 1988 that the Pirates started to win back their fans.

In 1986, Peña's last with the Pirates, he hit a respectable .288 and made the All-Star team for the third consecutive year, but the team lost 98 games. Offensively, Peña's Pirates years were among the most productive of his career. His consistency on defense supported by his three Gold Gloves, four All-Star Game appearances, and a .286 composite batting average during his seven seasons in Pittsburgh garnered him consideration for the All-Time Pirate lineup. The baseball.about.com website ranked Peña in the top four Pirate catchers of all time by MLB expert Scott Kendrick.[9]

On April 1, 1987, Peña was part of a blockbuster trade that brought the Pirates two key players for their string of NL East crowns in the early '90s, and led Peña to his first World Series appearance. He was traded to the St. Louis Cardinals for pitcher Mike Dunne, catcher Mike LaValliere, and future All-Star and Gold Glove outfielder Andy Van Slyke. Given Peña's popularity, it was a surprise to Pirate fans, but gave reason for excitement to the Cardinals and their fans. Said Cardinals general manager Dal Maxvill, "We are getting one of the premier players of the game, as evidenced by what we had to give up to acquire him."[10]

Pena, however, was emotionally hurt by the trade. "I cried for a week,' Pena said. " The trade hurt me psychologically. I lost my stroke."[11]

Peña spent the next three years with the Cardinals, and ended up being one of the key ingredients for their run at a championship in 1987. Getting his first taste of postseason baseball that season, he hit .381 in the NLCS as the Cardinals topped the San Francisco Giants in seven games and then hit a strong .409 in a losing cause in the World Series, won by the Minnesota Twins in seven games.

A year after the trade, on April 21, 1988, Peña got some personal satisfaction during an early-season return to Pittsburgh. He went 3-for-4, with two home runs and three runs scored in a 9-3 Cardinals victory over the Bucs. "It was nice to be back in my old ballpark," said Peña. "I've tried to put the trade behind me, and I just want to forget about that and do my job."[12] He played two more years in St. Louis and made another All-Star Game appearance in 1989.

Peña left St. Louis as a free agent after the 1989 season and signed with the Boston Red Sox. He spent the 1990 through 1993 seasons with the Red Sox. His leadership abilities again emerged in the Red Sox clubhouse, all while adapting to the American League. Similar to his stays in Pittsburgh and St. Louis, Peña displayed excellent defense and pitching staff management, which was exactly what Red Sox general manager Lou Gorman was expecting. Peña said Gorman told him, "I want you to catch, call the game and throw people out. That's what I need."[13] Peña made good on those expectations, winning a fourth Gold Glove in 1991. (He became only the second catcher to win a Gold Glove in each league; Bob Boone was the first.)

Red Sox pitching coach Bill Fischer went even farther with his praise, ranking him above Hall of Famer Johnny Bench, whom he watched for five years in Cincinnati as a coach. "I think Pena's the best catcher I've ever seen," Fischer said. "Bench made a lot more noise with his bat, but as far as catching goes I think Pena's better. He's so important to the pitching staff because of the way he handles a game and the way he keeps them loose."[14]

Yet, a humble Pena shies away from such praise. "I don't think I can take much credit," he said,

They (the pitchers) threw the ball and made the pitches. They had the success. My job is to help the pitcher as much as I can. If something goes wrong, my job is to fix it. I keep full concentration on the game."[15]

Peña paid special attention to Latin players on the Red Sox, like Carlos Quintana and Ivan Calderon, to encourage them to assimilate into the team. In addition, he assisted the Latin community. (As an example, he took part in an event in the heavily Latino city of Lawrence to raise money to help immigrant Hispanic families.[16])

On February 7, 1994, the 37-year-old Peña signed a free-agent contract with the Cleveland Indians as a backup to Sandy Alomar Jr. It was the first time Pena signed as a non-starter. Worried about the Indians backup, General Manager John Hart approached Pena while in the Dominican Republic that winter. He gave a Tribe hat to Pena and asked him to think about being the backup catcher in Cleveland. A few days later, Pena called Hart and told him, "I'm wearing my Indians hat,"[17] and that's how Hart knew he had him in the fold. In a part-time role, he provided both spark and veteran leadership to help manage the pitching staff for the Indians. Peña spent the next three seasons as part of the Tribe.

The 1995 season started with Alomar on the disabled list, so Peña found himself back in the starting lineup. The Indians got off to the best start in baseball, going 41-17. With Peña catching, the pitching staff had the lowest ERA in the league through July 1. Peña played the whole first half of the season and ended up playing more than half the games that season as the Indians won their Central Division going away, winning 100 of their 144 games in a strike-shortened season. They won the division by a whopping 30 games.

Pena was one of the key ingredients to the success. Peña hit .262. As a catcher he was noted for his quick, productive mound visits with pitchers when he felt they weren't focused enough. "Tony has a master's degree in the game'" said Indians pitching coach Jeff Newman. "He gets the performance he should out of a pitcher. If a pitcher doesn't anything on a certain day, there is nothing a catcher can do. But if the pitcher has good stuff, a good catcher can make him put it in certain spots by calling the right pitch at the right time. Not every catcher can do that, but we have two who can."[18] Returning from the disabled list, Alomar was back behind the plate for the playoffs.

It was vindication for Pena. "I know there was a lot of doubt about me," Pena said. "They didn't know if I could catch every day. But I caught every day in winter ball in the Dominican to get ready for the season. I've done it every year I've played in the big leagues." He added that he feels 'the human body is like a car. If you drive your car every day for six months, and then shut it down for six months, it will break down when you start it up again. That's why I never take time off.[19]

With Alomar back, Peña played little in the postseason. But on October 3, he made it count. Peña's bottom-of-the-13th inning walk-off homer in Game One of the American League Division Series against the Red Sox gave early momentum to the Indians. The home run came off Boston's reliever Zane Smith some six hours after the game was supposed to start. It was the Indians' first postseason victory since their championship in 1948, a drought of 47 years. Of his blast, Peña said, "I wasn't sure if I was supposed to take or not. But when he [Red Sox pitcher Zane Smith] threw the pitch, it was too good to let go by."[20]

The Indians went on to beat Boston in the ALDS, and then Seattle in the AL Championship Series, before succumbing to the Atlanta Braves in six games in the World Series. Peña played in four games in the ALCS but in only two games of the World Series. Despite the Indians' loss of the World Series, Peña's ALDS home run continues to be cited as one of the most memorable moments in Indians history. The website didthetribewinlastnight.com described the home run as "the biggest moment in the biggest year in franchise history."[21]

Peña played in 67 games with the Indians in 1996. A free agent after the season, he signed with the Chicago White Sox in January 1997. He played in just 31 games with White Sox before being traded to the Houston Astros on August 15. He played in nine games with the Astros and, now 40 years old, was released after the season.

Pena spent that winter as a player/manager for the Aguilas Cibaenas in the Dominican League. As the season wore on, he played himself less and less despite getting some key hits early on. He retired as a player at the end of that season and began focusing on managing and coaching.

Pena spent the next several years as a minor-league manager before positioning himself as a major-league coach and ultimately a major-league manager. He managed the White Sox' Arizona Fall League team in 1998. He then took over as the manager of the New Orleans Zephyrs in the Pacific Coast League for the Houston Astros organization. There he won a PCL East title in 2001, before becoming a bench coach for the Astros in 2002.

Early in the 2002 season, on May 15, Peña was hired to manage the Kansas City Royals after the dismissal of Tony Muser. He became only the third Dominican to manage a major-league team. On June 25, as he and manager Luis Pujols of the Detroit Tigers exchanged lineup cards, they became the first Dominicans to do so in the major leagues. As fate had it, Felipe Alou, the first Dominican manager, was also there. He was a bench coach for the Tigers. Dominican Republic President Hipolito Mejia was also present for a special presentation from Commissioner Bud Selig. It was not the first time Peña and Pujols, also a former catcher, had been managerial opponents; they previously managed against each other in the Dominican Winter League.

In 2003, Peña's first full major-league season as a manager, he experienced initial success for the Royals as they finished above .500 for the first time since the strike-shortened season of 1994. He had restored enthusiasm and accountability to the budget-constrained team. He was an easy choice for American League Manager of the Year by *The Sporting News* and the Baseball Writers Association of America, getting 24 of the 28 first-place votes and becoming only the fifth manager to win the award in his first full season.

The Royals could not capture the magic again in 2004 and lost 104 games. After another slow start to the 2005 season (8-25), Peña resigned on May 10. After the final 3-1 loss to the Blue

Jays, he said, "I can't take it anymore. We are not playing well. It's tough going to the ballpark and lose game after game. I haven't been eating. I haven't been sleeping."[22]

In November of 2005, Peña was hired by the New York Yankees as a first-base coach, a position he held until he became the bench coach in 2009. He also served as the team's catching instructor. In 2015 Peña returned to the role of first-base coach and was still currently in that role during there during the 2017 post-season run for the Yankees.

On February 11, 2012, in a ceremony in La Romana, Dominican Republic, in La Romana, Dominican Republic. Peña was inducted into the Latino Baseball Hall of Fame.

In March of 2013, Peña managed the championship Dominican Republic team in the World Baseball Classic. The team went an unprecedented 8-0, winning the final game 3-0 over Puerto Rico. The team was led offensively by the tournament's MVP, Robinson Cano. Pitcher Fernando Rodney had seven saves for the Dominicans. He managed the defending Champions again in 2017, but was eliminated in the second round of pool play winning one and losing two games.

Peña has a number of notable accomplishments as a player. As of the start of the 2015 season, he was sixth among major-league catchers with 1,950 games behind the plate, eighth in career putouts (11,212), and sixth in career double plays turned by a catcher (156). He had numerous seasons ranking in the Top 10 for Defensive WAR (wins above replacement).

Peña married the girl down the street, Amaris, who lived just three houses down from his. They had three children together: sons Tony Jr. and Francisco Antonio, and a daughter, Jennifer Amaris. Tony Jr. was signed as an amateur free agent shortstop by the Atlanta Braves in 1999. He made his major-league debut in 2006 and had a four-year major-league career. Francisco Antonio, has been in the minor leagues since 2007, and as of 2015 was playing in the Royals' farm system. Peña daughter, Jennifer Amaris, won the Miss Dominican Republic-USA beauty pageant in 2007.

One of Tony's younger brothers, Ramon, also played major-league baseball. He appeared in eight games as a relief pitcher for the Detroit Tigers in 1989. He registered no decisions and had a 6.00 ERA in 18 innings pitched.

NOTES

1 Charley Feeney, "Tanner Rates Pena All-Star of the Future," *The Sporting News*, October 17, 1981: 31.

2 Charley Feeney, "Bucs Given Strong Charge By 'Dominican Connection'," *The Sporting News*, June 20, 1981: 31.

3 Feeney, "Tanner Rates Pena All-Star of the Future."

4 Feeney, "Bucs Given Strong Charge By 'Dominican Connection'."

5 Feeney, "Tanner Rates Pena All-Star of the Future."

6 Ron Cook, "A Terrible Time of Trial and Error," *Pittsburgh Post-Gazette*, September 29, 2000: CC-3.

7 Charley Feeney, "Pena Wiser After Nightmare of '85," *The Sporting News*, March 10, 1986: 39.

8 Ibid.

9 Scott Kendrick, "Pittsburgh Pirates All Time Lineup," About.baseball.com, March 27, 2017, Retrieved December 5, 2017.

10 "Pirates Deal Pena to Cardinals," *New York Post*, April 4, 1987. Player's file, National Baseball Hall of Fame.

11 Paul Hoynes, "What a Catch," *Plain Dealer* (Cleveland), July 2, 1995.

12 "Pena Finally Gets Back at Pirates," *Los Angeles Times,* April 22, 1988: Part 3-7.

13 Robyn Norwood, "This Free Agent Was A Catch for the Red Sox," *Los Angeles Times*, August 9, 1990: C6.

14 Joe Giuliotti, "Red Sox catch Pena Fever," *Boston Herald,* April 11, 1991: R27.

15 Sean McAdam, "A Good Guy to Have," *Providence Journal*, May 15, 1991.

16 Paul Lafond, "Sox' Tony Pena: I really like to help kids who are needy'," *Lawrence Eagle-Tribune,* June 29, 1990: 25-27.

17 Hoynes: 11-D.

18 Ibid.

19 Ibid.

20 Jim Ingraham, "Picture-Perfect Play," *The Morning Journal,* March 4, 1996: B1.

21 Steve Eby, "The Greatest Summer Ever: Tony Pena," Didthetribewinlastnight.com, June 20, 2015. Retrieved December 5, 2017.

22 Bob Dutton, "Royals Manager Tony Pena Resigns," KansasCity.com, May 11, 2005. Retrieved December 5, 2017.

HERB PERRY

BY JAY HURD

If hard work and commitment are needed for a successful baseball career, Herb Perry learned those lessons early. He grew up on a farm where chores and responsibility were the norm.

Herbert Edward Perry Jr. was born on September 15, 1969, to Herbert Edward and JoAnn Perry of Mayo, east of Tallahassee in rural northern Florida. The Perrys owned a dairy farm in Mayo. Herb was born in nearby Live Oak. Young Herb's days were filled with farm chores, school, and sports, among other things. He learned through his father about athletics, competition, and baseball; Herbert Sr. had coached Little League baseball for 32 years and was an associate baseball coach in high school for 14 years.[1] From his parents Herb learned the importance of commitment to family, church, and community. His younger brother Chan learned the same lessons, and had a brief major-league career with Cleveland and Kansas City.

Although he did his chores, he did seek other activities. He said, "There's nothing else to do. You played sports, and I loved to play."[2] He would rush home from school, run to his grandmother's house, fashion a piece of wood into a bat and hit rocks in his makeshift baseball diamond. "I'd throw up a rock and hit it. I had a fence made up of weeds and stuff. If I hit it over this weed, it was a home run. If it landed on this side, I had to hit it again. I just played hours and hours by myself, just sitting there making up scenarios. At that time I was a Dodger – it was all Yankees and Dodgers in those days – and I'd be facing Goose Gossage or somebody like that.[3]

A natural athlete, familiar with hard work, Herb became a significant contributor to team sports in Mayo and at Lafayette High School. A three-sport athlete, he earned MVPs in football, basketball, and baseball. As starting quarterback for the Lafayette High Hornets, Herb followed a path opened by his friend and fellow quarterback, Kerwin Bell, who graduated from Lafayette in 1985. During his senior year, 1987, Perry passed for 834 yards and nine touchdowns.[4] He excelled at baseball, pitching a perfect game and three no-hitters; he set a state record with 210 strikeouts in one season,[5] hit .565 his senior year,[6] and had a 37-game hit streak and an eight-game home run streak.[7]

Perry attracted the attention of the Toronto Blue Jays and the University of Florida football program. The Blue Jays hoped to sign him to a major-league contract while the Gators offered a scholarship to play Division I football. He opted for the university offer, as had Kerwin Bell two years earlier.

Perry's athletic prowess reflected only a part of his ambition. In addition to being elected high-school Student Council president, he was a member of the Future Farmers of America. His 1986 FFA forestry team finished first in the state competition and earned a ticket to the National FFA Convention in Kansas City. He recalled that "FFA was one of the most enjoyable things I had going through school. I played sports, but I always looked forward to having the forestry contests, land judging and livestock judging. I was on all those teams, plus all the other stuff – parliamentary procedure and public speaking.[8]

At the University of Florida, under coach Galen Hall, Perry was the third-string quarterback behind Kerwin Bell and Pepe Lescano. As the coach sought to identify a starting quarterback, Perry had his practice and game opportunities. However, in 1988, after a game in which he was sacked seven times by the Vanderbilt University Commodores and he "definitely got hit harder than usual,"[9] he reflected on whether he ought to pursue football or baseball. His fine performance on the baseball team that spring – he had opted to play baseball rather than participate in spring football – helped him decide. "I wasn't cut out to be a quarterback," he said later. "I don't have the mental makeup to be a quarterback. I understood that, and I didn't stick around and fight myself about that."[10] Although he also played as the team's punter, the connection to football weakened as he played more baseball.

Initially, Florida baseball coach Joe Arnold doubted that a young man coming from a small high-school program (there were only 400 students at Lafayette High) could play ball at the Division 1 level. Having played football as much as he did, he needed time to improve his batting and his throws from third base to first. Still, Perry had an impressive baseball career at Florida. His father was not surprised: "I have put pressure on these boys [Herbert and Chan]. I expected them to give everything they had. To be your best, you have to give everything."[11]

By his senior year at Florida, Perry felt that he had a better chance to play professional baseball than professional football. He played on two Florida teams that went to the College World Series, in 1988 and 1991. Perry's numbers as of 2015 still ranked him in the top 10 in nine individual season categories at Florida, including fourth in home runs with 25 and second in runs scored with 142. In 1989 he had 90 hits, 59 RBIs, and a team-leading batting average of .370. In 1991 he hit 15 home runs.[12]

In 1991 Perry earned a degree in agricultural operations, and was selected by the Cleveland Indians in the second round of the amateur draft. Perry began his professional baseball career, at the age of 21 with the Watertown (New York) Indians, a Class A short-season club in the New York-Pennsylvania League. This began an annual pattern of progression up the minor-league ladder. In Watertown, he played in 14 games and batted .212 (11-for-52).

The following year, 1992, Perry moved up to the high Class A Kinston (North Carolina) Indians. Here he improved each aspect of his game, appearing in 121 games with 53 games in the field alternating between first base, third base, and the outfield. He had 19 home runs and 77 RBIs. In 1993, he moved to the Double-A Canton-Akron Indians (Eastern League), where he had a .269 batting average and a .422 slugging percentage.

At age 24, in 1994, Perry played with the Charlotte (North Carolina) Knights in the Triple-A International League. In 102 games and 426 plate appearances he achieved a .327 batting average and a .505 slugging percentage. His progress and his play in Triple A prepared him for a call-up to the Indians team in May. He debuted with Cleveland on May 3 and played four games, two at first base, and two at third base. He had one hit in nine at-bats, for a .111 average.

The players' strike ended the 1994 season in early August. The Indians finished second, behind the Chicago White Sox, in the American League Central Division. Perry's season was replete with "what ifs."

The strike ended in 1995, but the season did not open until April 25. Perry started the year with the Triple-A Buffalo Bisons. He was hitting .317 and fielding well, and on June 13, 1995, when Dave Winfield went on the disabled list with a strained shoulder, Perry was called up to Cleveland.

On June 17, in his second game back, Perry hit his first major-league home run, off the Yankees' Andy Pettitte, in the fourth inning of a game at Jacobs Field. In the sixth he hit his second home run. He finished the day with a single. When Winfield came off the DL, Perry's batting had not cooled – his .315 batting average, 3 home runs, and 23 RBIs had earned him a spot on the team for the remainder of the season, and into the postseason and the World Series.

Perry did not hit well in the postseason, going 0-for-8 in the American League Championship Series vs. the Seattle Mariners. He played in three games for the Indians in the World Series against the Atlanta Braves and went 0-for-5 at the plate. However, he made a stellar fielding play that preserved the Indians' victory in Game Three. In the top of the ninth inning, Perry replaced Paul Sorrento at first base. A sportswriter described the play and its consequences: "With two outs and runners at first and second, Chipper Jones pulled a ball down the first base line, and Perry fielded a strange hop and stepped on first. 'It definitely saved the game,' Hargrove said."[13] Perry told the University of Florida campus newspaper he was grateful for playing well in the majors, and playing in a World Series, saying, "There's always that chance I'll never be here again. … To be involved in the championship of the world is incredible."[14]

Perry injured his knee and had surgery in 1996. He played in only seven games, then sat out the entire 1997 season. After the season the Indians placed him on the unprotected list for that fall's expansion draft, and he was chosen by the Tampa Bay Devil Rays.

Around this time a mutual friend fixed Perry up with Sheila Glover, the daughter of an Anniston, Alabama, preacher. Sheila had been in an unsuccessful marriage and had divorced her first husband. Sheila was hesitant to meet Herb, as she had heard about ballplayers – she often sang the National Anthem at spring-training games in Lakeland, Florida, and had experience around ballplayers. Rather than follow through with a first date, she "stood him up," Sheila admitted.[15] But when she did meet him, and recognized his qualities – polite, firm values – she wrote to him while he tended to his injuries in Cleveland. The two were married on November 1, 1997. Sheila had one son from her first marriage, 7-year-old Ethan, whom Herb adopted. Their family would grow in time: son Drew, born in 1999; daughter Gabrielle, born in 2000; and a daughter, Olivia, adopted from Ukraine in 2009.

Perry spent all of 1998 in the minors, playing for the St. Petersburg Devil Rays of the Florida State League, the Gulf Coast League Devil Rays, and the Triple-A Durham Bulls of the International League. He was hit by a pitch early in the season, broke his hand and saw limited playing time. He began the 1999 season with Durham and was called up to the Devil Rays on May 6, remaining with the team the rest of the season. In April 2000 the Devil Rays put Perry on waivers and the Chicago White Sox claimed him. By this time, having had surgeries on both knees and a series of nagging injuries, he thought about leaving baseball and returning to the dairy farm. But he put off retiring, and played two seasons with the White Sox. In 2000 he batted .308 as the White Sox went to the postseason. (They lost to Seattle in the American League Division Series.) "Being able to play every day here is awesome," he said. "This is the best time I have had in baseball, by far. This is a great bunch of guys. [Manager] Jerry [Manuel] is a great person. The whole coaching staff has made it easy for me."[16] In Chicago a new nickname, the Milkman, took hold. When he hit the ball well, broadcasters would proclaim, "The Milkman delivers."[17]

Perry could not stay healthy for the 2001 season. A strained Achilles tendon limited his playing time. In November the White Sox traded him to the Texas Rangers for pitcher Corey Lee. His time with the Rangers included a career season in 2002 – he played in 132 games and hit 22 home runs.

Injuries continued to plague Perry into the 2003 season. Once again he spent time in the minor leagues, playing with the Frisco Rough Riders of the Double-A Texas League. He was called up to the Rangers on May 10 and played through May 28 until a shoulder injury ended his season. He finished his career in 2004 with the Texas Rangers playing in 49 games, with a stint in late July with Frisco.

Perry played all or part of nine seasons in the major leagues with four teams. His highest salary, $1,700,000, came in his last season, 2004 with the Rangers. He played in two postseasons. Injuries restricted his time on the field, but he remained consistent with attitude and persistence. GM John Hart of the Cleveland Indians perhaps summed up Perry's career by saying: "Herbert was a good player for us, when he played. The promise was there. But we just couldn't keep him healthy."[18]

On December 18, 2004, Herbert Edward Perry Sr. died unexpectedly. The following March, the Mayo community sports complex was renamed the Edward Perry Sports Complex.

After leaving baseball, Herb devoted his time to operating the family dairy farm. His brother Chan – who had a brief career in the major leagues – and other family members also were involved. Perry also remained active in the Alton Church of God, and supported its sports ministry in Cuba.[19]

NOTES

1. Obituary of Herbert Edward Perry Sr., *Suwannee Democrat*, posted December 21, 2005, accessed March 7, 2015, suwanneedemocrat.com/obituaries/article_716213c5-8258-5a79-8f7f-ca4869f77ea2.html?TNNoMobile.
2. Erich Gaukel, Internet Archive, "Chicago White Sox Slugger Talks Baseball and the FFA," *The Magazine of the National FFA Organization*, May/June/July 2001, accessed March 7, 2015, archive.org/stream/ffanewhorizons4952001unse/ffanewhorizons4952001unse_djvu.txt
3. Gaukel.
4. Tim Povtak, "Duo Thrown Into Gators' Qb Race," *Orlando Sentinel*, December 22, 1987, accessed March 7, 2015, articles.orlandosentinel.com/1987-12-22/sports/0170070288_1_perry-passed-perry-mind-kerwin.
5. Gaukel.
6. Povtak.
7. *Player Profiles Page*, "Perry, Herbert," accessed March 7, 2015, baseball.playerprofiles.com/sampleplayerprofile.asp?playerID=1872.
8. Gaukel.
9. Jeff Brown, "Gator Quarterback Making His Mark in Baseball," *Sun Sentinel*, accessed March 6, 2015, articles.sun-sentinel.com/1989-04-22/sports/8901210130_1_herbert-perry-perry-s-baseball-field.
10. Liz Robbins, "Quiet Success Herbert Perry Often Underestimates His Ability but His Rookie Performance Speaks for Itself," *Cleveland Plain Dealer*, September 28, 1995.
11. Rogers.
12. University of Florida, *Gator Baseball History and Links*, accessed March 7, 2015, gatorzone.com/baseball/history.php?his=1999/season1999.html.
13. Buster Olney, *Baltimore Sun*, October 25, 1995, articles.baltimoresun.com/1995-10-25/sports/1995298051_1_cleveland-carlos-baerga-world-series.
14. Jacob Luft, "Perry Enjoying Indian Summer," *University of Florida Alligator*, October 24, 1995.
15. *Player Profiles Page*, accessed March 7, 2015.
16. Phil Rogers, "Holy Cow: A Season Worth Milking," *Chicago Tribune*, October 1, 2000, accessed March 7, 2015, articles.chicagotribune.com/2000-10-01/sports/0010010421_1_dairy-farmer-herbert-perry-father Holy Cow.
17. Rogers.
18. Rogers.
19. Alton Church of God, Mayo, Florida, *Honoring the Father, Athletes Testimonies*, Herbert Perry – Baseball: Cleveland Indians, Chicago White Sox, Texas Rangers, honoringthefather.com/multipage.php?id=3484.

ERIC PLUNK

BY TED LEAVENGOOD

The very best parts of a game always were at the end for Eric Plunk. He was a starting pitcher early in his career, but like many hard throwers, he had problems with his command, especially with his secondary offerings, and he found his highest and best use in major-league bullpens for 14 seasons. Plunk's best moment on the mound came on September 17, 1996, when he pitched the last three innings against the White Sox to save the game in the Indians' 9-4 win that clinched their second consecutive Central Division title and marked a return to the postseason for a team bursting with talent.

Eric Vaughn Plunk was born on September 3, 1963, in Wilmington, California, to Melva and Kenneth Plunk. Kenneth worked as a foreman in the farm-machinery business. Eric grew up in the Los Angeles suburbs along with a brother, Gerald. He graduated from Bellflower High School in 1981, and was selected in the fourth round of that June's draft by the New York Yankees. A right-handed pitcher, he stood 6-feet-5, and weighed 210 pounds as a mature ballplayer, and had a perfect build for a pitcher. Early scouting reports acknowledged Plunk's above-average fastball along with a strong curve, but also noted his lack of command and a fastball that tended to be straight up in the zone.[1] In the summer of 1981 he began his minor-league career in the Gulf Coast League with the Yankees' rookie affiliate and progressed to the Fort Lauderdale of the Florida State League in 1983, where his record as a starter was 8-10 with an ERA of 2.74. The Yankees continued to stretch Plunk out as a starter in 1984, and at Fort Lauderdale he won 12 games against 12 losses with a 2.86 ERA.

After the season Plunk began what would be a staple of his career when he was traded by the Yankees to the Oakland Athletics in a deal that was notable for bringing Rickey Henderson to New York. Plunk went to Oakland along with Stan Javier, Jose Rijo, Tim Birtsas, and Jay Howell. In return Oakland sent Henderson and Bert Bradley to the Yankees.

In the Oakland organization, Plunk continued his steady progress, beginning with the 1985 season with Huntsville, Alabama, in the Southern Association and ending that year with the Tacoma Rainiers of the Pacific Coast League. Between the two teams, Plunk posted an 8-7 record and a 4.42 ERA. He returned to Tacoma in 1986, but received his first call-up to the major leagues, making his debut against Toronto on May 12, giving up four runs in 5⅓ innings of relief. Plunk finished the season with the Athletics, logging 120⅓ innings as the Athletics finished third out of seven teams in the American League's West Division.

Plunk started 15 of the 26 games he pitched in for the Athletics in 1986, but by the end of the 1987 season he had shifted to the bullpen exclusively and over the course of his 14 seasons in the major leagues, he was used almost without exception as a reliever. He established himself as a quality set-up man in 1988 for Oakland in a bullpen led by future Hall of Fame closer Dennis Eckersley. Plunk threw 78 innings that season as a reliever and pitched to an ERA of 3.00 and a record of 7-2.

Plunk came of age as a major leaguer with an exceptional group of talented Oakland players. The 1988 Athletics won 104 games under manager Tony La Russa and finished in first place in the American League West. They were led by two players who achieved notoriety during the era of performance-enhancing drugs, Mark McGwire and Jose Canseco. The pitching staff was led by Dave Stewart and Bob Welch and the combination of solid pitching, a quality bullpen, and unmatched power led the team to the World Series, where they were beaten by the Los Angeles Dodgers in five games. In the 1988 postseason, Plunk pitched in three games, two of them in the World Series. He was unscored upon in a total of two innings of work. He began the 1989 season with Oakland, but in June the Yankees completed a trade that sent Rickey Henderson back to the Athletics with the Yankees receiving Plunk, Greg Cadaret, and Luis Polonia.

Plunk spent three seasons in New York and in his last year there, 1991, the Yankees once again employed him as a starter. He threw 111 2/3 innings that season and saw his ERA soar to 4.76, the highest it had been since 1987. Those disappointing numbers led the Yankees to part company with Plunk, who signed with the Cleveland Indians as a free agent before the 1992 season.

Used exclusively out of the bullpen again, Plunk saw his numbers improve and once again he was part of a talented young team that would achieve great success. In spring training before the 1993 season, Indians closer Steve Olin was killed in a tragic accident and Plunk was forced into the closer role, which he shared with Derek Lilliquist and Jerry Dipoto. Plunk earned 15 saves that season, the most on the team, and had a 2.79 ERA in 71 2/3 innings. It may have been his best season, but Cleveland managed only a sixth-place finish in the American League East despite the presence of Kenny Lofton leading off and Albert Belle hitting in the middle of the order.

In 1994 the Indians' bullpen situation remained uncertain and Plunk was the best late-inning relief that manager Mike Hargrove could call upon. He threw 70 innings and posted a 7-2 record to go with a team-leading 2.54 ERA and three saves. As with Oakland, the Indians were building a team of strong young talent that would coalesce in 1995 and fuel a run of playoff excellence. Plunk was a favorite of Mike Hargrove, if not always of Cleveland fans who were often frustrated by stretches of wildness that plagued Plunk even in his best years.[2]

The biggest change that season for Plunk was the emergence of Jose Mesa as the Indians' closer. Mesa had 46 saves and a 1.12 ERA and Plunk and Julian Tavarez were the primary set-up pitchers in the late innings. The Indians bullpen was crucial to the success of the team in 1995, because veteran pitchers like Dennis Martinez and Orel Hershiser had limit their innings to remain effective. Paul Assenmacher and Jim Poole were part of a capable cadre of relievers who limited the stress on the starting rotation to the point that no 1995 starter pitched more than 187 innings.

The team won the American League pennant by beating Boston and Seattle in the playoffs. Plunk made only one appearance in the Division Series against the Red Sox, an inning and a third of scoreless relief. Against the Mariners in the League Championship Series, he was used more often. In Game Three, in Cleveland, Plunk came on in the 11th inning with the score tied, 2-2, a runner on base, and one out. Plunk retired the Mariners' Edgar Martinez on a foul pop. With two out, manager Hargrove ordered Plunk to intentionally walk Tino Martinez to face Jay Buhner. Buhner hit a long home run to right field that "may still be orbiting to this day."[3] The mortal blow in the Mariners' 5-2 victory was struck off Plunk, but Julian Tavarez was the losing pitcher.

In Game Five, Plunk came on in the eighth inning and was able to escape a jam of his own making after he walked two batters. Luis Sojo of the Mariners scorched a line drive that shortstop Omar Vizquel was able to turn into an unassisted double play to end the inning. Plunk did not pitch in the World Series against the Atlanta Braves, who beat the Indians in six games.

In 1996 Plunk was again an integral component in the excellence of the Indians pitching staff. He threw 77⅔ innings of relief and had a 2.43 ERA with two saves. At 32, Plunk had what may have been his best campaign in the majors, logging more innings than he had previously and striking out more than a batter per inning with 85 K's by season's end. However, in the American League Division Series against the Baltimore Orioles, Plunk again had problems with the long ball. In Game Two, he relieved Orel Hershiser and threw two scoreless innings. But manager Mike Hargrove pushed his luck and sent Plunk back out in the bottom of the eighth inning against the heart of the Orioles batting order. He walked Bobby Bonilla and allowed a ground-rule double to Cal Ripken to put runners at second and third. He intentionally walked Eddie Murray to load the bases. Paul Assenmacher and Julian Tavarez relieved Plunk and allowed three runs to score, all of which were charged to Plunk, who took the loss. In the decisive Game Four of the series, Plunk pitched a hitless eighth inning with two strikeouts. Jose Mesa blew the save in the ninth inning and the Indians lost the game in extra innings and the series to Baltimore, three games to one.

In the following year, 1997, the wear and tear began to show on Plunk. He allowed an uncharacteristic 12 home runs in 65⅔ innings and had a 4.66 ERA. The Indians were in the playoffs once again and went to the World Series, where they lost to the Florida Marlins. Plunk pitched in Game One of the Division Series against the Yankees and gave up four runs in an inning and a third. Again, it was the long ball that proved his undoing. In the bottom of the sixth inning, he gave up back-to-back home runs to Tim Raines and Derek Jeter as the Yankees won, 8-6.

In the ALCS, Plunk threw a scoreless two-thirds of an inning as Cleveland beat the Orioles to advance to the '97 World Series. However, against the Marlins, he was ineffective again. He pitched two scoreless innings in Game One after Orel Hershiser surrendered seven runs in the first five innings. In Game Three, a slugfest won by the Marlins, 14-11, Plunk took the loss after giving up two singles, two walks, and three earned runs. In his last postseason appearance, Plunk threw a scoreless third of an inning in Game Five, a loss to the Marlins. Although he was often effective, Plunk had an unsightly ERA of 7.53 in 14⅓ innings of relief in his postseason career. His record as a reliever in the month of October is defined by several innings of less than desirable result.

Plunk pitched in both 1998 and 1999, for Cleveland and Milwaukee, but his best years were behind him. He retired after the 1999 season with a career mark of 72-58, 35 saves, and an ERA of 3.82. His endurance and longevity – 14 seasons in the majors – were the true tale of his abilities.

After his playing career, Plunk devoted himself to his family and teaching baseball. He and his wife, Billie, had two sons, Eric Jr. and Alden, and two daughters, Abigail and Allison, who died in infancy. The family lives in Corona, California. Plunk has been a pitching instructor with both Power Alley Sports and as of 2018, with the Hitting Pro in Corona.

SOURCES

In addition to the sources cited in the notes, the author also consulted genealogical information supplied by Bill Mortell, Baseball-almanac.com, Baseball Reference.com, and *The Sporting News*.

NOTES

1. Steve Vrablik, Scouting Report, Diamond Mines, Baseball Hall of Fame Research Library.
2. Steve Eby, Didthetribewinlastnight.com, "The Best Summer Ever: Eric Plunk," June 23, 2015.
3. Ibid.

JIM POOLE

BY CHIP GREENE

It was October 28, 1995. In Atlanta's Fulton County Stadium, the Cleveland Indians and Atlanta Braves squared off in Game Six of the World Series, with the Braves leading, three games to two.

Through 5½ innings the teams were scoreless. As the contest entered the bottom of the sixth inning, 29-year-old left-handed pitcher Jim Poole took the mound for Cleveland and prepared to face the Braves' fifth, sixth, and seventh hitters. That Poole was in the game in the sixth was due to a move for which Indians manager Mike Hargrove would afterward receive a barrage of criticism. With two outs in the bottom of the previous inning, Cleveland starter Dennis Martinez allowed a walk and a single; so with left-handed slugger Fred McGriff due up for Atlanta, Hargrove replaced Martinez with Poole, his situational lefty. As he had done so often against left-handed hitters during the regular season, Poole fanned McGriff, on three pitches, and preserved the scoreless game.

With no Cleveland runs on the board, perhaps that should have been it for Poole. So impressed had Hargrove been with the relative ease with which Poole had dispatched McGriff, however, and with another left-handed hitter due to lead off the bottom of the sixth for Atlanta, instead of making another pitching change Hargrove left Poole in the lineup, batting ninth. (In that spot, he he would bat second for Cleveland in the top of the sixth inning. If Poole came to the plate, it would be his first major-league at-bat.) Hargrove would take his chances with Poole at bat if it meant having his clutch southpaw on the mound in a pressure situation.

If dreaming of playing in a World Series is a part of many boys' childhoods, it surely must have seemed a remote one for young James Richard Poole. Born April 28, 1966, in Rochester, New York, young Poole moved with his parents, Rick and Judy, from Rochester to the Philadelphia area. At LaSalle College High School (Class of 1984), in Wyndmoor, 15 miles north of the city, Poole by all appearances Poole was an undistinguished kid playing on mediocre-to-poor teams.

As Poole recalled of those years, "Most of my coaches didn't let me pitch."[1] His high-school record was just 2-16, "and," he added, "I had to go 10 innings for one of those wins."[2] Such futility couldn't have given Poole much expectation for a career in the sport; and indeed, many years later, having accomplished an 11-year major-league career, he said, "I have gone far beyond any expectations I set when I was a kid."[3]

Poole's fortunes changed dramatically when he attended college. Apparently intent on earning an electrical-engineering degree, he enrolled at Georgia Tech University. At the same time, though, he appears to have wanted to extend his baseball career, for, as he later explained, "I recruited myself by writing the [baseball] coach letters. They kept me on the team so I could help the freshman grade-point average."[4] Soon he had excelled far beyond that rather humble status.

By the end of his senior year, Poole was one of the best college relievers in the country. From 1985 to 1988, he played on four straight Atlantic Coast Conference championship teams, and was a pivotal contributor throughout, primarily in his final two seasons, during which he saved 19 games and was each year named to the All-ACC team. When Poole retired from the major leagues in 2000, he stood first in Georgia Tech history, with 22 career saves.

By his junior season, 1987, Poole had drawn the attention of major-league scouts. In June he was selected by the Los Angeles Dodgers in the 34th round of the amateur draft. Wanting to complete his electrical-engineering degree, Poole declined the chance to turn pro, and instead returned to school. The following season the Dodgers again drafted him, this time in the ninth round. So, armed with his degree, Poole began his professional baseball career.

Speaking years later about his mindset on the mound in tough situations, Poole recalled one particular collegiate day in 1985, his freshman season. "It was a game that changed my course in baseball. What happened that day was bad, but it actually turned everything around for me. Tech had qualified for the NCAA Regionals and we had a three-game series with Mississippi State as kind of a warm-up. Coach (Jim) Morris decided to use me to determine if I was ready to help the team in the regionals.

"I went out there scared to death and fell to pieces against a team that had four future major leaguers (Will Clark, Bobby Thigpen, Rafael Palmeiro, and Jeff Brantley). I walked two batters and never got anyone out. Needless to say, I didn't make the squad for the regionals.

"After that game I made a vow that win or lose, from then on I would give the best I had. I made up my mind to relish a situation such as that rather than let the pressure overcome me. Actually, I used that game as motivation throughout my career at Tech and in the majors."[5]

It didn't take long for Poole to establish himself as a prospect. Over his first two minor-league seasons, at Vero Beach, in the Class-A Florida State League (with one game also at Bakersfield in the Class-A California League in 1989), he proved he was already a polished reliever. In 1989, he pitched in a league-leading 60 games and was dominant, leading the club in wins (11) and strikeouts (93 in 78⅓ innings), posting a 1.61 ERA, and finishing second in the league with 19 saves. That performance earned Poole a promotion to San Antonio of the Double-A Texas League, where he was again effective, saving 16 games with 77 strikeouts in 63⅔ innings. Midway through that 1990 season, the Dodgers called.

On June 14, 1990, with the San Diego Padres visiting Los Angeles the next day to begin a three-game series, the Dodgers' two left-handed relievers were both on the disabled list, leaving the team without a left-hander in their bullpen. That day, Poole was told by his San Antonio manager that he was to immediately join the Dodgers in LA.

"I thought I'd been traded," Poole stated at the time. "It was the last thing I expected. It felt great. It's every young boy's dream. But it took me completely by surprise."[6]

"I guess they need someone to come in for one batter and get a left-hander out now. I was just lucky enough to get the break."[7] That was undoubtedly so; although if he could have known who his first batter was to be, maybe Poole's outlook would have been different.

The Padres and Dodgers went to the 11th inning with the scored tied, 1-1. To begin the 11th, manager Tommy Lasorda sent Poole to the mound. For San Diego, future Hall of Famer Tony Gwynn led off. If Poole was nervous, he never confessed as much. In short order, Gwynn was called out on strikes, and Lasorda immediately removed Poole from the game.

Six years later Poole recalled of his debut, "That was unbelievable. As a kid, you dream of striking out a batting king in your first big-league game. I couldn't believe it. I could barely sit down afterward in the clubhouse."[8]

It was to be the highlight of Poole's first major-league season. Poole made six more appearances before he was returned to San Antonio on July 1. When the rosters expanded on September 1, he was back with the Dodgers and pitched nine more times, including a game at Houston, on September 26, when he allowed his first major-league home run, to Franklin Stubbs, in a 10-1 loss. In all, Poole worked 10⅔ innings in 16 games, registering neither a decision nor save. In December the Dodgers designated Poole for assignment, and on December 30 traded him to the Texas Rangers for two minor leaguers. It wouldn't be the last time in his career that Poole changed teams.

The year 1991 began for Poole a somewhat nomadic existence. Over the next 10 years, he wore seven different major-league uniforms. After attending major-league camp with Texas, Poole began the season with Triple-A Oklahoma City, in the American Association. There, he registered three saves and averaged over a strikeout per inning. When the Rangers placed pitcher Brad Arnsberg on the disabled list on May 7, Poole was recalled. It was to be a brief engagement, however. After just five appearances, including his first major-league save, registered at home on May 18 versus Roger Clemens and the Red Sox, on May 25 the Rangers placed Poole on waivers, and he was quickly claimed by the pitching-challenged Baltimore Orioles. Poole remained with Baltimore for four seasons, and pitched in 123 games, his second-most with a single organization.

At Rochester, the Orioles' Triple-A affiliate in the International League, Poole again drew notice, saving nine games with 29 strikeouts in 29 innings. By July 31, 1991, the 40-60 Orioles made wholesale pitching changes, demoting three to Rochester and recalling three, including their top prospect, Mike Mussina, as well as Poole. Over the remainder of the 1991 season, Poole proved a valuable asset in Baltimore's bullpen, as he tossed 36 innings in 24 games and posted three wins, an ERA of 2.00, and 34 strikeouts. For a while, at least, Poole seemed to have found a home.

The following season, 1992, Poole experienced his first bout with an injury, which severely limited his major-league activity. Bothered at the beginning of the season by left shoulder tendinitis, Poole began the year on a rehab assignment with the Hagerstown (Maryland) Suns in the Double-A Eastern League. Wanting to improve the strength in Poole's arm, the Suns gave him the first three starts of his professional career. Soon he went to Rochester, and, still bothered by his injury, for the first time struggled on the mound; his final numbers were 1-6 and a 5.31 ERA in 42⅓ innings, although he did save 10 games. Despite that performance, though, when the rosters expanded on September 1 and Poole was recalled to Baltimore, he pitched in only six games, for a total of 3⅓ innings. He went home hopeful that the injury was behind him.

Much to the Orioles' relief, the next year proved that Poole's injury was, in fact, healed. The 1993 season was arguably his best in the majors. That "was a breakthrough year for me," Poole said. "I got off to a good start with 12 straight scoreless outings. That gave me confidence, and also gave the team confidence in me."[9] Indeed, only twice in his career did Poole make more appearances than his 55 that season, and never did he exceed the 50⅓ innings worked (although he twice later tied that mark). As Baltimore, playing its second season in Camden Yards, improved to third place under manager Johnny Oates, Poole came in time and again to face the opposition's toughest left-handed hitters, and invariably got the best of the battle. With a 2.15 ERA, Poole's batting average versus right-handed hitters was just .174, and against left-handers, .177. Poole also got two of his four major-league saves in 1993.

That was Poole's final quality season for the Orioles. The next year, 1994, as Baltimore finished second in a strike-shortened campaign, Poole's performance significantly deteriorated: In 38 games, covering just 20⅓ innings, he allowed 32 hits and his ERA ballooned to 6.64. On December 23 Poole became a free agent, and he ended 1994 unemployed. He wouldn't remain that way for long, though; and the following season Poole found himself on baseball's biggest stage.

On March 18, 1995, Poole signed a minor-league contract with the Cleveland Indians. With the players strike winding down, he began the season with the Triple-A Buffalo Bisons. When the strike ended, Poole joined the Indians at spring training. Given his poor 1994 performance in Baltimore, he had much to prove. Displaying a quality curveball, which had eluded him the previous year, Poole pitched his way onto the team and opened the season in the bullpen. In his first appearance, on April 28 at Texas, he entered a 9–9 tie game in the bottom of the sixth inning and gave up a solo home run to Mickey Tettleton in the eighth. Poole took the loss. But on May 7, at home versus the Minnesota Twins, in a 17-inning Cleveland victory, Poole threw the final four innings of another 10–9 slugfest, allowing just one hit while striking out three, to earn his first Cleveland win. That performance established his place on the staff and Poole recorded a solid season, finishing 3–3 with a 3.75 ERA in 50⅓ innings. Most impressive were his .217 batting average against and .156 average against with runners in scoring position. Clearly, Poole had righted his ship.

For the Indians, 1995 was their first World Series since 1954. For Poole, it was his first postseason. He saw action in every series. As the Indians swept the Red Sox in the American League Division Series, Poole appeared in Game One, at Cleveland's Jacobs Field. Beginning the 11th inning of a 3–3 tie, he allowed a home run to Boston's Tim Naehring to fall behind, 4–3, but Tony Peña's home run in the bottom of the 13th won the game for Cleveland. Against the Seattle Mariners in Game Four of the Championship Series, Poole entered in the top of the eighth inning at home with the Indians ahead 7–0 and retired all three men he faced, striking out two.

Then came the World Series.

After Atlanta won Game One, the second game took place on October 22, in Atlanta. Entering the sixth inning, the game was tied 2–2. However, after Cleveland was held scoreless in the top of the sixth, Indians starter Dennis Martinez allowed a two-run homer in the bottom of the inning to give Atlanta the lead. In the top of the seventh, the Indians got one run back, and in the bottom of the inning Poole came on to start the inning against the heart of the Braves' order. In succession, he retired sluggers Chipper Jones, Fred McGriff, and David Justice to keep the score at 4–3, but Cleveland couldn't score, and that's where the game ended.

Poole remained in the bullpen as the Indians took two of the next three games in Cleveland, and as the Series returned to Atlanta, the Braves held their 3-games-to-2 lead. For Poole, Game Six would be one of those games that will forever live in infamy.

Having struck out Fred McGriff swinging to end the bottom of the fifth inning, Poole was the second batter scheduled in the top of the sixth. Entering the inning, Braves starter Tom Glavine had tossed a no-hitter. That lasted one batter. Hitting eighth and leading off the inning, Indians catcher Tony Peña singled for what would be the only hit allowed by Glavine that night. That brought Poole to the plate.

Allowing Poole to hit was, of course, a questionable move in a tie contest, one for which Hargrove was afterward lambasted by the press. In compiling his Series roster, Hargrove had elected to keep on his bench two utilitymen perfectly suited for such a situation, Alvaro Espinoza and Ruben Amaro, both excellent bunters. (Amaro had been added to the roster at the expense of future Hall of Famer Dave Winfield.) Moreover, in the bullpen Hargrove had two left-handed pitchers remaining, Alan Embree and Paul Assenmacher, either of whom could be used to face the Braves' left-handed hitters. In any event, though, Hargrove elected to send Poole to the plate with instructions to bunt. Poole failed on three tries, the last one a foul popup to the first baseman.

After Poole's failed bunt, Glavine retired the next two batters, on a fielder's choice and, after a stolen base, a foul popup. So Poole went to the mound to face the Braves in the bottom of the sixth.

Leading off for Atlanta was left-handed-hitting David Justice, whom Poole had retired in Game

Two on a long fly ball to right field. Now, Poole threw two pitches outside to Justice, a ball and a strike. On the third pitch, Poole attempted to go low and outside again with a fastball, and the ball tailed inside. Turning on it, Justice drove the ball over the right-field wall to stake the Braves to a 1-0 lead. It was only the third home run Poole allowed all season to a left-hander – he had earlier allowed home runs to Baltimore's Harold Baines and California's J.T. Snow – and it was a back-breaker.

Poole retired the side, but the damage was done. In the bottom of the seventh, Ken Hill relieved Poole, and four pitchers followed, including the two left-handers. Atlanta never scored again but neither did Cleveland, and Justice's home run stood as the only run of the game. Atlanta won the Series in six games.

Having failed both at the plate and on the mound, Poole could have avoided sportswriters after the game by escaping to the sanctity of the trainer's room. Instead, he stood at his locker, fielded every question, and accepted blame for the defeat, reasoning, "It isn't a pleasant part of the job, but you are paid to perform and paid to talk about your performance."[10]

Regarding his bunt attempts, Poole said, "It should not be that big a deal to lay down a four-seam fastball. That was my job."[11]

And as to whether his at-bat impacted his pitching: "I went up there fully confident that I could sacrifice Tony Pena to second. I promise you I didn't take my failure to do that out to the mound with me, even though Justice was the first man I faced."[12]

Finally, Poole also proved that he hadn't lost his sense of humor when he quipped, "Justice had no business looking inside after everything I threw was away."[13]

He had kept it all in perspective.

The following spring, columnist Bill Livingston of the *Cleveland Plain Dealer* had nothing but praise for Poole's attitude with the press that night. Although Justice's home run was "the most deflating home run yielded by an Indians pitcher since Bob Lemon's to Dusty Rhodes in the 10th inning of the 1954 World Series. ... the test of the inner person in any sport comes away from the champagne and celebrations. Poole came up big in that measure of a man. He would not let himself be diminished by defeat." Besides, Livingston continued, "Poole made one bad pitch. But when any pitching staff gives up only one run, it has done its job. The Tribe's silent bats were the reason the World Series ended that night."[14]

It was a sentiment Poole had undoubtedly considered.

As the 1996 season approached, Poole, who that night had assured the press that "I won't dwell on it. I will try to use this on days during the winter in which I don't want to work out, to push myself. And it will remind me that you have to make every pitch better because one pitch can make a season,"[15] likewise assured them, "I know that we will have plenty of motivation this season, after we had to watch the Braves celebrate."[16]

"The World Series "was all a fantasy," he continued, "until the last pitch. I suppose I'll hear about it out of frustration if I get off to a bad start."[17] As it turned out, he had only half a season to find out.

By July 9, Poole had appeared in 32 games for Cleveland and fared very well, amassing a 4-0 record and 3.04 ERA in 26⅔ innings. That day, though, Poole was traded to the San Francisco Giants for outfielder-first baseman Mark Carreon. With starting first baseman Julio Franco nursing a strained hamstring, and backup Herbert Perry undergoing knee surgery, Cleveland sought a right-handed hitter to fill in at first and come off the bench. Carreon filled that need.

"Mark gives us greater flexibility," manager Hargrove said. "We are not excited to lose a pitcher like Jim Poole, but you can't have your cake and eat it too."[18]

For the remainder of that season, Poole served as the Giants' primary left-handed specialist (35 games) and finished the season strongly, 2-1 with a 2.66 ERA in 23⅔ innings pitched. (He did not play in the Giants' Division Series loss to Florida.) But it was to be his last impressive showing. In 1997 Poole spent the entire year with San Francisco but endured a ghastly 7.11 ERA in a career high 63 games, caused primarily by 13 earned runs allowed in his final five appearances. By July 1998, Poole's 5.29 ERA had convinced the Giants that the left-hander was no longer effective, and on July 15, he was released.

Poole had one more moment in the spotlight, however. Perhaps feeling they could rekindle his prior success, the following week the Indians signed him to a minor-league contract and sent him to Buffalo, where he was lights-out for 10⅓ innings (16 strikeouts and a 0.87 ERA). Assured by their first-place standing of another postseason appearance, Cleveland promoted Poole to their roster in time for him to be postseason-eligible, and that fall he pitched twice in the Tribe's Division Series win over Boston and four times in the Championship Series loss to the Yankees.

In December 1998, Poole returned to Philadelphia, signing a one-year, $500,000 contract with the Phillies. Having watched Poole twice retire tough left-handed Yankee Paul O'Neill during the 1998 ALCS, Phillies manager Terry Francona was convinced Poole could fill the specialist role in his bullpen. For his part, Poole said, "The Phillies were always my first love. My parents are just as excited about this as me."[19] After 51 appearances, though, Poole was released in August, and once again signed by the Indians, where he once again made the playoff roster, but this time did not participate during the Division Sereies loss to Boston.

The 2000 season was Poole's last, and was not without controversy. On December 20, 1999, he agreed to a minor-league contract with the Detroit Tigers and in the spring made the club. On April 22 in Chicago, the Tigers and White Sox played a scrappy 14-6 contest, won by the White Sox, which featured a brawl that resulted in 16 members of the two teams being suspended for a total of 82 games. Although Poole, who worked two-thirds of an inning, didn't participate in the on-field fighting, he did return to the field after leaving the game, for which he was fined $500. On May 17, saddled with a 7.27 ERA, Poole was released by Detroit, and subsequently signed by the Montreal Expos to shore up their injury-depleted bullpen. In two innings Poole allowed eight hits and six runs before the Expos released him and on June 9, perhaps fittingly, he was signed a final time by the Indians and sent to Buffalo, where he pitched the final 10 games of his career.

Over his career, Poole earned over $4 million. While a student at Georgia Tech he had met Kimberly, his future wife. In 1996, Poole told a reporter: "We bought a house in Georgia, just outside of Atlanta [in Alpharetta, where the couple still lived in 2015]. We decided it was time to put down some roots, especially for our two boys. We had lived for the past four years near Baltimore. My wife has put her career on hold for me. She has a bachelor's degree in industrial engineering, and a master's degree in finance. Now, it will be her chance. I'll follow her."[20]

For the young man who won two high-school games, it had been quite a ride. In 11 years he pitched in 431 games for eight teams and won 22 games. Yet he'd always be remembered for one inside fastball on a sultry night in Atlanta.

SOURCES

Jim Poole player file from National Baseball Hall of Fame, Cooperstown, New York.

Baseball-reference.com.

Retrosheet.org.

Ramblinwreck.com/sport.

NewsPaperArchive.com.

NOTES

1. *Sports Collectors Digest*, June 21, 1996.
2. Jim Salisbury, "New southpaw, dogged, lucky", *Philadelphia Inquirer*, February 22, 1999: D-1.
3. *Sports Collectors Digest*, June 21, 1996.
4. Salisbury.
5. ramblinwreck.com/sports/m-basebl/spec-rel/100401aaa.html.
6. *National Sports Daily*, June 15, 1990.

7   Ibid.
8   *Sports Collectors Digest,* June 21, 1996.
9   Ibid. It was actually 12⅔ scoreless innings pitched by Poole.
10 Bill Livingston, "Poole's One Pitch Didn't Lose Series", *Cleveland Plain Dealer,* March 13, 1996: 1D.
11 *New York Post,* October 30, 1995.
12 Livingston.
13 Ibid.
14 Ibid.
15 *New York Post,* October 30, 1995.
16 Livingston.
17 Ibid.
18 *USA Today,* July 10, 1996.
19 Salisbury: D-6.
20 *Sports Collectors Digest,* June 21, 1996.

MANNY RAMIREZ

BY BILL NOWLIN

"Manny being Manny" – the simple phrase seemed to instinctively capture the essence of his baseball persona. He was one of the greatest right-handed hitters of the past 50 years. As of 2015, he ranked ninth all-time in career slugging percentage (.5854), has 555 major-league home runs (placing him number 14 – and he's got another 29 postseason home runs – more than any other player), and is number 32 in career on-base percentage (.4106). He won the American League batting crown in 2002 and was World Series MVP for the Boston Red Sox in 2004. He's a 12-time All-Star, with nine Silver Slugger awards, and he's third all-time in grand slams.

And yet his judgment was questionable. He was suspended for 50 games for testing positive for banned substances in 2009, and when he tested positive again in 2011, he retired rather than take the prescribed 100-game suspension.[1]

He's been called a hitting savant. And with his "fielding miscues, baggy uniforms, flowing dreadlocks, big hits, and tired anecdotes, the public is left with caricatures of Manny as a carefree goofball and spoiled superstar."[2] He earned over $200 million as a major leaguer. Yet biographers Rhodes and Boburg also write that, however inscrutable he may be, he "defines himself by what he is least known as – a dedicated athlete, a well-regarded teammate, and a beloved father, husband, and son."[3]

Ramirez was also beloved by fans entranced by his hitting and his charisma at the three main stops on his career route – Cleveland, Boston, and Los Angeles. Each time, he burned bridges behind him, leaving fans disappointed, or worse, though one wouldn't know that from the statistical record alone.

Named after his father (and a statesman of ancient Athens) as Manuel Aristides Ramirez, he was born on May 30, 1972, in Santo Domingo. His high school, though, was George Washington High School in New York City. An outfielder throughout his career, he was a first-round pick of the Cleveland Indians (the 13th pick overall) in the 1991 draft.

Manny moved to New York when he was 13. His mother, Onelcida, had worked a desk job at a dermatological institute in the Dominican Republic but in New York had to take a job as a seamstress in a sewing factory. Father Aristides had worked as an ambulance driver and then, after marriage, driving tank trucks. In New York he was a factory worker and sometimes in and out of work. Manny was the only son in what seemed a matriarchal family, with his mother and his grandmother Pura; he had three older sisters. They moved into an apartment building in a Washington Heights neighborhood that was heavy with drug dealers and murders.[4] But Manny himself had started playing baseball at age 5, playing with the proverbial stick and bottlecap in the DR – and even announcing at 7 his ambition to play professionally. In New York he found Highbridge Park near the apartment and signed up for Little League under coach Carlos "Macaco" Ferreira. Bizarrely, Manny kept baseball separate from family and not even his sisters or mother knew he was ultimately named New York City Public High School Player of the Year, his sister Evelyn admitting, "When we found out that Manny was drafted, we had no idea. I mean, nobody knew about it. Somebody called us and told us to turn on the television ... the six o'clock news. We knew he loved to play baseball, but we had no idea."[5]

Manny was active in Brooklyn's Youth Service League ball from the age of 14, and played here and there in the various boroughs, not always letting school get in the way of baseball. He was often the first on the field and the last to leave. It is likely that school attendance being a prerequisite for sticking on the high-school team helped get him through school. He may also have been cut a little slack; "maybe that was when he began to realize that for a gifted athlete like him, the rules did not apply."[6]

Manny's lack of English-language skills left him unsure of himself in situations where conversation was called for, but his work ethic showed from an early age in punishing workouts, waking as early at 5 A.M. on a regular basis to get in his running – and quite often running up hills in the city, tugging a 20-pound tire behind him secured by a rope around his waist. Even years later, teammates on, say, the Boston Red Sox, mentioned that no one worked harder in the weight room and with training than Manny Ramirez. Under the baggy uniforms was a sculpted body that might have been featured in a fitness magazine; as a major leaguer, he was listed as an even 6 feet tall and 225 pounds.

Once on the Washington High team under coach Steve Mandl, Manny truly excelled. As early as age 17, he made the first of two trips to New Mexico with the Youth Service League to play in the Connie Mack World Series.[7] He hit for a .630 batting average in his junior year and was named to the All-City team. In his senior year, he surpassed that, batting .650. He was named New York City Player of the Year.

Needless to say, scouts began to pay attention – even if it meant making the trip into neighborhoods one could understatedly deem dodgy. Cleveland Indians scout Joe DeLucca followed Ramirez carefully, but also at a bit of a distance so the other scouts wouldn't see how interested he was. He wanted to make Manny a first-round pick, but there were 12 other teams picking first. Indians scout George Lauzerique told DeLucca, "No Latin-American immigrant kid has even been drafted in the first round," but that didn't faze DeLucca, who stuck to his guns.[8] The Indians selected Ramirez in the June 1991 draft, and signed him with a $250,000 bonus.

The Indians had Ramirez attend a two-week minicamp and then go to Burlington, North Carolina, for rookie ball in the Appalachian League. He did well – hitting .326 with 19 homers and more than one RBI a game – 63 RBIs in 59 games.

Ramirez's 1992 season was a tougher one. The Indians asked him to play winter ball in the Dominican Republic, but he quit after 15 days and returned to New York. Playing for the Kinston Indians, in the high Class-A Carolina League, he got off to a very slow start, but he started to hit in June and the beginning of July – when he broke the hamate bone in his left hand, costing him the rest of the season. He hit just .278 in 81 games.

In 1993 Ramirez was assigned to the Canton-Akron Indians (Double-A Eastern League), got into 89 games (.340, 17 HR, 79 RBIs) and got himself called up to Triple-A, to the Charlotte Knights (International League). He played in another 40 games and drove in 36 runs, with a .317 average – and also got himself called up to the major leagues, to Cleveland. He was later named *Baseball America*'s Minor League Player of the Year.

When he got the call, Ramirez asked Charlotte manager Charlie Manuel, "Can you come with me?"⁹ The sentiment was emblematic of his attachment to certain mentors along the way. Needless to say, Manuel couldn't drop everything – he had the Knights on the way to the league pennant. Ramirez joined the Indians in Minneapolis on September 2 and was 0-for-4, though three of the balls were well-hit fly balls. The very next day, they played at Yankee Stadium, with lots of Manny's family and friends at the game. He hit a ground-rule double to left field his first time up, flied out in the fourth, hit a two-run homer to left in the sixth off Melido Perez, and then hit another one – also to left – off Paul Gibson. Two homers, three RBIs, and a 7-3 Cleveland victory.

It was quite a splash but Ramirez struggled from that point on, getting only six more hits in 45 at-bats, with two more runs batted in and no more extra-base hits of any kind. With one exception, he DH'd, and pinch-hit in four games – and, perhaps a little oddly, pinch-ran in five. He ended the season, after appearing in 22 games, batting .170.

The Indians, once again, asked Ramirez to play winter ball. It was another fiasco; he even took one of the team buses and drove off, AWOL for the day. He wasn't welcomed back.¹⁰

The 1994 season ended with a players' strike. The Indians played 113 games, and Ramirez appeared in 91 of them. It was his official rookie year, and he came in second in Rookie of the Year voting, though compared to the rest of his stats, it was one of his least productive years. He did drive in 60 runs.

The Indians opened the 1995 season in Texas. The team went on to Detroit, and after they left, there was a typical Manny moment – he'd left his paycheck in a boot underneath his locker. It had to be shipped onward to him. Ramirez himself hit 11 homers in just the month of May. (He was named AL Player of the Month.) He made the All-Star team for the first time, drove in 107 runs (helped by 31 homers), and helped the Indians reach the World Series. He hit only .222 in the Series itself (with a .364 on-base percentage), with one homer, but there was only one Indian who hit higher – Albert Belle with .235. The Cleveland offense was clearly lacking – 19 runs in six games, losing to the Atlanta Braves.

Ramirez's early career was replete with a number of fielding and baserunning lapses. He was cut slack, of course, given his hitting – in 1996 he drove in 112 runs, with 33 homers. He hit for a higher average in 1997 (.328) but his RBIs declined to 88. Matt Williams, Jim Thome, and David Justice each drove in just over 100. The Indians made the postseason again, and went all the way to the World Series once more, playing the Florida Marlins. At one point or another, the Indians held a lead in each of the seven games, but in the end they lost four. Ramirez contributed some key hits in the first couple of rounds, but was 4-for-26 (.154) in the World Series. Average alone was deceptive; he drove in six runs in the seven games.

Occasional lapses aside, Ramirez had a strong and accurate arm. Twice he led the AL in assists from his position: 1996 as a right-fielder, with 19, and in 2005 as a left-fielder, with 17.

There was a time when Manny paid an unannounced visit to his old high school, and wandered into the gym where coach Steve Mandl was talking to the baseball team. Asked if he wanted to say anything to the team about hitting, Manny said, as simply as possible, "See the ball. Hit the ball."¹¹

With 45 homers and 145 RBIs in 1998, Ramirez had an exceptionally productive season, despite a batting average six points under .300. At one point in September, he homered in four at-bats in a row and eight times in a five-game stretch. It was the second year he made the All-Star team, and the first year in what became a string of

11 consecutive annual All-Star selections. The Indians beat Boston in the ALDS but lost to the Yankees in the ALCS. Ramirez hit two homers in each round, batting .357 and .333 respectively.

There were thoughts, though, that Ramirez's fielding may have cost the Indians the chance to get to another World Series. It was Game Six, at Yankee Stadium, and the Indians had just scored five runs in the top of the fifth to pull to within a run of New York. (Thome hit a grand slam, but Ramirez had struck out with the bases loaded.) In the bottom of the sixth, Derek Jeter tripled to right field to drive in two big insurance runs – but the ball was a catchable one. A *New York Times* article was headlined: "Ramirez: Big Bat, Blunders." Ramirez had leapt to catch the ball, only to have it land at his feet. He wasn't charged with an error, but he had clearly erred in anticipating the ball's trajectory.

Ramirez drove in 20 more runs (to a total of 165, tied for 14th all-time for single-season RBIs) in 1999. He hit .333 (with a .442 on-base percentage) and scored 131 runs. He homered 44 times. For the fifth year in a row, the Indians made the postseason, but this time lost to the Red Sox in the Division Series. Ramirez got just one base hit in 18 at-bats (.056), but he did draw four bases on balls and scored all five times he got on base. Ramirez placed third in the MVP voting, the highest he ever ranked. (It was a ranking he tied in 2004.)

The year 2000 was Manny's contract year in Cleveland and he got off to a great start, but he was on the disabled list with a serious hamstring injury from May 29 to July 13, missing 39 games. Despite missing a quarter of the season, he still had 122 RBIs and 38 homers. He hit .351 and led the league in slugging (.697) and OPS (1.154). There was no doubt Ramirez was due for a big contract.

Red Sox GM Dan Duquette won the bidding war. Ramirez was a huge fan favorite in Cleveland and the Indians kept upping their offer, but he signed with the Red Sox for a reported $160 million/eight-year deal.[12] Manny had one final condition before signing: that the Red Sox hire Cleveland clubhouse man Frank Mancini, to accompany him to Boston.[13] It was reminiscent of him wanting Charlie Manuel to come with him from Charlotte. It also didn't happen.

Some wondered if Ramirez could handle the intensity of the Boston market. Rhodes and Boburg quoted Macaco as saying that "Manny's lack of anonymity at shopping malls was one of his primary dissatisfactions with life in Boston." Bizarre as that may seem, "Manny always wants to go to shopping malls. Sometimes we'll go two or three times a day." And it wasn't necessarily to buy anything.[14] He just liked going to malls, but quite naturally didn't want to be relentlessly fawned over and followed by fans.

Ramirez was the Red Sox DH into June, when he began to play left field. In late August he reverted to DH. (He was DH for 87 games and left fielder for 55.) He had a career high in strikeouts, with 147, but still achieved a .405 on-base percentage (hitting .306), and drove in 125 runs, 37 more than anyone else on the Red Sox. He had 41 homers, 14 more than Trot Nixon's second-place 27.

Ramirez lost more than a full month in 2002 due to a broken left index finger, fractured on a head-first slide into home plate on May 11 (he was out), and not returning until June 25. In 120 games, he drove in 107 runs, with 33 homers. His .349 average (.450 OBP) won the American League batting title.

It was back to the playoffs in 2003, the first full year under new ownership. Ramirez played in a career-high 154 games, and led the league in on-base percentage (.427). He hit .325, just one point behind the AL batting champion, teammate Bill Mueller. He hit 37 homers, drove in 104 runs (one behind teammate Nomar Garciaparra), and scored 117 runs. Too often, there seemed to be a discordant note. In late August the Yankees came to Boston for what was really a key series. Manny was excused from the game due to throat inflammation – but was discovered in the Ritz-Carlton bar with Enrique Wilson of the Yankees, which didn't go over well with the Red Sox fan base. Neither Ramirez nor David Ortiz hit that well in the Division Series, but the team pulled through and Manny's three-run homer in Game Five made all the difference in the 4-3 win.

Ramirez homered twice and drove in four runs in the ALCS against the Yankees, a series that went to seven games and seemed to be in Boston's hands until manager Grady Little (who'd been the bench coach on the Indians in Manny's last years there) put Pedro Martinez back into the game when he seemed so obviously out of gas. The Yankees rallied and tied the game, then won it on Aaron Boone's home run leading off the bottom of the 11th. Little was fired, and Terry Francona hired as manager for 2004.

Ramirez had more than once expressed a wish to get out of Boston. At the end of October the Red Sox placed him on waivers – they could have called him back if any team had claimed him, but none did. There was, after all, close to $100 million remaining on his contract. Perhaps the Red Sox did it just to make a point with Manny about what a good deal he had – so good no other team was willing to pay the freight to get him.

There was also discussion about trading Ramirez, as part of two trades that would have brought Alex Rodriguez from the Rangers for Manny and Jon Lester, and sent Garciaparra to the White Sox for Magglio Ordonez. A-Rod wanted to come to Boston and was willing to take a $25 million pay cut to do so, but the Players Association refused to sign off on such a hefty cut.

Early in 2004 Ramirez became an American citizen and, when he took his position before the game on May 11, he ran out to left field carrying a miniature American flag. He then handed it off to a spectator. He later joked, "Now they can't kick me out of the country." Before his first at-bat, the team played the song "Proud to Be an American" on the sound system.[15]

Manny Ramirez was World Series MVP in 2004, the Red Sox this time rolling over Anaheim in the Division Series (he had seven RBIs in three games) and then losing the first three games of the ALCS to the Yankees, only to come back and win an unprecedented final four in a row. Oddly, Ramirez didn't have even one RBI in the ALCS, though he hit .300 and scored three times.

Facing the St. Louis Cardinals in the World Series, Ramirez looked like a stumblebum in left field, committing two errors in Game One. He overran a ball in the top of the eighth, allowing one run to score, and then made an awkward slide to try to catch a ball on the very next play, letting it get past him as another run – the tying run – scored, costing the Red Sox the lead. He was 3-for-5 in the game with two RBIs.

In Game Three, he homered in the first inning and drove in another run later in the game, a 4-1 Red Sox win. Derek Lowe shut out St. Louis in Game Four and the Red Sox swept the Series. It was their first World Series win in 86 years. Any number of Red Sox players might have been voted MVP, but Ramirez (1-for-4 in Game Four, without either an RBI or run scored) got the nod, perhaps in recognition of his having had at least one base hit in every one of the 14 playoff games in which the Red Sox had played.

The Ramirez work ethic was noted earlier. Billy Broadbent, the Red Sox video coordinator, said Manny put in as much time with video as any other player or more, and he added a few twists to his study. Preparing for whomever he might face, if it was a pitcher against whom he'd not previously batted, he'd call up at at-bats of another right-handed slugger, like Miguel Tejada, and look to see how the pitcher had worked Tejada. "It's something he came up with all on his own," said Broadbent. "It's nothing we suggested. He came up to these determinations on his own. He was one of the hardest workers that you'd ever want to see."[16]

Ramirez may have seemed oblivious at times, or just downright goofy, but there were perhaps two unexpected aspects to the approach he took to hitting. First of all, the way he slipped into a kind of zen mode helped to create an almost preternatural focus, slowing down time and allowing all that he had learned to be brought to the fore. He could tune out distractions. Simply put, in the words of Jim Thome, "He's good at not letting things get to him."[17] He was perhaps like the "absent-minded professor, whose mind is so specialized and consumed by his craft that he is as helpless as a lamb outside the lab."[18] There was also craftiness in the way he would try to set up pitchers. Allard Baird reportedly told columnist Joe Posnanski that he believed "Manny will swing and miss at a pitch in April so that the pitcher will throw him the same pitch in September."[19] Alex Rodriguez told the *New York Times*, "When it comes to his craft, his art, his skill, he's as smart as anyone in the American League. And he takes it as seriously as anyone in the game."[20] If he was a savant, he was a studious savant. That doesn't mean he wasn't also a little flaky and a little naïve.

Ramirez never once hit over .300 in 2005, and was as low as .224 more than a quarter of the way through the season (on May 27, after game number 47). One month later, on June 26, he was leading the American League in RBIs (with 66) and he finished the season with career highs in homers (45, matching his 1998 season in Cleveland) and drove in 144 runs, just four behind the league leader, David Ortiz. This was the season when Manny stepped inside the Green Monster during a conference on the mound and didn't come out until after the first pitch after play resumed. He was also marching to his own drummer, when he insisted on taking a scheduled day off despite teammate Trot Nixon having suffered an oblique strain in late July. There was tension in the Red Sox clubhouse, which had a player apparently unwilling to set his personal wishes aside to help out his team in a pennant race. There was a stronger sense of him quitting on the team in 2006, when he reported himself unable to play because of patellar tendinitis and he missed 22 games from late August into September. He still drove in 102 runs but the Red Sox failed to make the postseason (they'd gotten into the ALDS in 2005, but were swept in three games, Ramirez hitting .300).

In 2007 the Red Sox won the World Series again. Ramirez started slow, got hot for a stretch, and then suffered his own oblique strain. His power numbers were down on the year, with only 20 homers and 88 RBIs (the first time he'd been below 100 in a decade, since 1997), but come the playoffs, he contributed. In Game Two of the Division Series, when Angels manager Mike Scioscia had Ortiz walked to get to Ramirez with two outs in the bottom of the ninth, it may have triggered something in Ramirez – he hit a walkoff three-run homer. His fourth-inning homer in Game Three was literally the game-winner, giving Boston a 2-1 edge in a game they won, 9-1.

In the 2007 ALCS, Ramirez was facing his former team, the Indians. He drove in 10 runs, with two more homers and a .409 average. The Red Sox swept the Rockies in the World Series; he hit .250 and drove in two runs, but all in all, he was .348 with 16 RBIs in the 14 postseason games.

The last guaranteed year of Ramirez's Red Sox contract was 2008. It was the year he joined the 500-HR club, homering off Chad Bradford in Baltimore on May 31. June was a tough month for Manny's reputation in Boston. First he got into a fight with Kevin Youkilis in the Red Sox dugout during a game. Then, on June 28, he got in an argument over complimentary tickets with traveling secretary Jack McCormick and shoved the 64-year-old man to the ground.[21] There were a couple of game-play situations where Ramirez seemed not to be giving his all. There were thoughts he was provoking the team into trading him. On July 31, at the trading deadline, two deals were done: Ramirez's contract was transferred to the Los Angeles Dodgers, who agreed to pick up the money remaining on his contract (the Red Sox freed him from the two option years), and Boston acquired left fielder Jason Bay from Pittsburgh to take his place.

If he'd been dogging it, it wasn't entirely self-evident; Ramirez had hit .347 during July. But he'd worn out his welcome in Boston. Once he hit Los Angeles, he became an instant sensation and he reveled in the "Mannywood" moniker given him. In 53 games, he drove in 53 runs, and he hit for a .396 average. The Dodgers won the NLDS (Manny hit .500 with two homers), but lost the NLCS in five games (Manny hit two more homers and drove in seven runs, batting .533).

Come 2009, however, Manny's hitting came back to earth – he was 37 years old, and hit .290 in 104 games, with 63 RBIs. He likely would have played more games, but he tested positive for a banned substance and was suspended for 50 games during the season, from May 7 through July 2.[22]

In 2010 Ramirez got off to a good start with the Dodgers, and was batting .322 through the end of June. But he played in only two games in July and, after a month, returned to play in five late-August games. The Dodgers placed him on waivers and he was selected by the Chicago White Sox on August 30. For the White Sox, he played in 24 September games but hit for only a .261 average, with just one home run and only two RBIs in 24 games. The White Sox chose not to try to re-sign him. At the end of January the Tampa Bay Rays signed Ramirez on perhaps something of a flyer but he again tested positive for a performance-enhancing drug and thus faced a 100-game suspension. He played in five games (batting .059) but then announced his retirement.[23]

After the 2011 season was over, however, Ramirez struck a deal under which he would accept a 50-game suspension and be permitted to return. He signed with the Oakland Athletics for 2012. He played in 17 games, batting .302 without a home run, for Oakland's Triple-A club in Sacramento, but never played for Oakland itself. The Athletics released him in June.

Ramirez played in Taiwan for the EDA Rhinos, but left at the midpoint of the season. His agent, Barry Praver, said, "The reason he decided not to return for the second half was to free himself to be available to play in the United States. This whole thing with Manny in Taiwan was a phenomenon. He invigorated the league. Attendance went through the roof. It was a very positive experience for both sides."[24]

The Texas Rangers signed Ramirez to a minor-league deal in July 2013, but six weeks later, after he hit .259 for Triple-A Round Rock in 30 games, they released him.

Near the end of May 2014, Ramirez signed with the Chicago Cubs and he was again asked to play in Triple-A, this time for the Iowa Cubs as a player/coach. He claimed he was a new man, that he and his wife, Juliana, had been in church for almost four years. "Now, I realize that I behaved bad in Boston," he said. The *Boston Globe*'s Christopher L. Gasper wrote, "Manny being Manny means something entirely different now if you are to believe Ramirez, who will turn 42 on Friday. Chastened by time, the diminishing of his skills, and his newfound faith, he has finally found a manager he likes – God."[25] Of course, time will tell. The Cubs' president of baseball operations, Theo Epstein, hoped he would become a mentor for Cubs prospects. He played in 24 games and hit .222 with three home runs.

NOTES

1 The 2009 drug was human chorionic gonadotropin, a fertility drug for women. See *New York Times*, May 10, 2009.

2 The best source for much more information about Manny Ramirez and the primary source for this biography is Jean Rhodes and Shawn Boburg, *Becoming Manny: Inside the Life of Baseball's Most Enigmatic Slugger* (New York: Scribner, 2009). The quotation noted here is from page 3.

3 Rhodes and Boburg, 5.

4 The "Ramirez family settled in one of New York City's most dangerous and drug-infested neighborhoods (between 1987 and 1991 there were 462 homicides, 58 percent of them drug-related, in Washington Heights' police precinct)." Rhodes and Boburg, 49.

5 Rhodes and Boburg, 9, 10.

6 Sara Rimer, *New York Times*, April 26, 2011. Rimer's lengthy profile of Ramirez, someone she had met and observed since his high school years is recommended to readers.

7 Rhodes and Boburg, 84, 85, 96.

8 Rhodes and Boburg, 111, 118.

9 Rhodes and Boburg, 147.

10 Rhodes and Boburg, 152, 153.

11 Rimer, *New York Times*.

12 *New York Times*, December 12, 2000.

13 Rhodes and Boburg, 193.

14 Rhodes and Boburg, 128, 143.

15 *Boston Globe*, May 12, 2004.

16 Author interview with Billy Broadbent on June 28, 2013.

17 *New York Times*, July 22, 1999.

18 Rhodes and Boburg, 290.

19 Rhodes and Boburg, 292.

20 *New York Times*, April 17, 2008.

21 It wasn't the first time Ramirez had struck a team employee. In 1998 he slapped Cleveland clubhouse assistant Tom Foster. See *New York Times*, March 30, 1998.

22 For a full report on the suspension, see the May 8, 2009, *New York Times*.

23 *New York Times*, April 9, 2011.

24 espn.go.com/mlb/story/_/id/9403816/manny-ramirez-parts-ways-eda-rhinos-taiwan-league. Posted June 20, 2013.

25 *Boston Globe*, May 29, 2014.

BILLY RIPKEN

BY JIMMY KEENAN

Infielder Billy Ripken attacked the game of baseball with reckless abandon and paid the price, sustaining an inordinate number of injuries during his career. He never changed his all-out, hustling style of play, earning the reputation of a player who left it all on the field.

The Ripkens were a baseball family. Bill's father, Cal Ripken Sr., was a solid minor-league player and one of the most valued and respected managers/coaching instructors in the Baltimore Orioles organization. Two of Billy's uncles were also outstanding ball players in the semiprofessional Susquehanna League. One of these uncles, Bill's namesake, had a successful yet brief career in the Brooklyn Dodgers minor-league chain.

Bill's older brother Cal Jr. was a Hall of Fame shortstop and is now known as the most durable player in the history of major-league baseball. The younger Ripken would turn out to be one of the best defensive second baseman that ever donned an Oriole uniform.

Unlike his brother, who was ensconced in the starting lineup, Billy had to compete for a roster spot for most of his 12-year major-league career. When asked about fighting for a job each season Billy said, "There were times I went to spring training as a non-roster player and I was the 28th or 29th on the depth chart. But I felt strongly that if I went there and showed what I could do, I'd come out on the top 25 and the roster."[1]

When asked to compare the two brothers, baseball executive John Hart, who managed the younger Ripken in the minors, told sports writer Jim Henneman in an August 31,1995, interview with the Baltimore Sun, "Bill and Cal are similar in that they are both extremely intelligent players, but you really can't compare them. Cal is like the strong power forward and Billy is like a scrappy point guard. As for Bill's injuries, some of it is just bad luck. The rest of it is the way he plays--diving all over the place."[2]

In a subsequent interview with ESPN.com, Hart offered the following opinion on the younger Ripken: "He was a big-time gamer who played the game the right way. Cal Sr. is as proud of Billy as he is of Cal Jr. Billy was just like him." Hart went on to say, "Bill was vastly underrated for his versatility, defensive skills and knowledge of the game."[3]

William Oliver Ripken was born in Havre de Grace, Maryland, on December 16, 1964. He was the youngest of four children born to the former Violet Gross and Calvin Ripken Sr.

Billy played baseball at Aberdeen High School and was an 11th-round pick of the Baltimore Orioles in the 1982 amateur draft. He started his professional career at shortstop with Bluefield in the Appalachian League. During his first few years in the minors he showed his versatility by playing every position in the infield except first base. Unfortunately, Billy was plagued by a myriad of nagging injuries and couldn't stay healthy long enough to make an impression on the Baltimore front office.

That all changed when he switched over to second base at the beginning of the 1986 season. Playing with Double-A Charlotte, Billy had his best offensive year as a pro up to that point, hitting .268 with five home runs and 62 RBIs. At second base, he led the loop in five defensive categories and was named to the Southern League All-Star team. These accomplishments earned him an invitation to the Orioles major-league camp in 1987.

At the start of spring training Cal Ripken Sr., who was now managing the Orioles, commented, "I never got to see him play much. He's shown me some things this spring that made me say darn I did not know he could do that. He's shown me that he is a very sound basic fundamental player."[4]

On March 23, 1987, after playing extremely well in camp, Bill was optioned to the Triple-A Rochester Red Wings when the Orioles made their first cuts. When asked about being sent back to the minors, Billy told a reporter, "Sure it's a disappointment when you get sent down from a major league club. But you realize that it's best that you go out and play…. put on a uniform and go to work."[5]

Billy meant what he said and after reporting to the Rochester team continued to play well. On July 11, 1987, the Orioles released veteran infielder Rick Burleson and called up Billy up to the major league club. Ripken was hitting .286 at the time, which included a recent 11-for-12 tear at the plate. He also connected for eight consecutive hits before his promotion.

When asked by Gordon Beard of the *Associated Press* what it would be like to be the first big league manager to have two of his sons on the same team, Cal Sr. replied, "I don't think about that… I think about the ballplayers. I'm happy for any young kid going to the big leagues. I spent a lot of time down there, [13 years as minor-league manager] and I was just as thrilled to send them as they were to go."[6]

With the addition of the younger Ripken, Baltimore proceeded to win 11 of their next 12 games. Billy was full of enthusiasm, and his youthful exuberance put some life into the low-key Baltimore clubhouse. Orioles coach Elrod Hendricks simply said, "To us, he was a breath of fresh air."[7]

When Bill and Cal teamed up in the middle of the Oriole infield, they became the fourth set of brothers to form a double play combination in the major leagues.[8]

Billy's first major-league hit was a double off the left-field wall against Kansas City's Charlie Leibrandt on July 16. Three days later, he belted his first major-league home run, off the Royals' Bud Black. Billy's season ended on September 15 when he took a misstep over an Astroturf seam while fielding a groundball at Toronto's Exhibition Stadium and tore the lateral ligament in his right ankle.

Bill played 58 games for Baltimore that year, finishing the season with a .308 batting average. Defensively, he made only three errors at second base in 298 chances. Ripken didn't make his first error until his 26th game, the same night he handled 14 other chances flawlessly.

When he reported to the Orioles in the spring of 1988, Billy told Marty Klinkenberg of the *Miami News*, "I'm not trying to fill the shoes of my brother. He's an established major league star. I just want to be an established major league player, period. This year my goals are to the make the major league team and play every day."[9]

The Orioles started off the 1988 campaign with six straight losses, and Cal Ripken Sr. was let go as manager. Both Ripken siblings were taken aback by the abrupt firing of their father but continued to go about their business on and off the field as professionals.

Cal Sr. wore number 7 and after the firing, Billy changed his number from three to seven in honor of his Dad's service to the team. When asked about the change, Bill replied, "Obviously, I was hurt by the whole thing. I just looked at Dad as being No. 7, and I really didn't want anything going on during the course of the year and it just occurred to me that someone else could be given No. 7, and I just didn't like the thought very much. I just couldn't bear to think about it at the time."[10]

On the day that the Orioles won their first game of the season after starting out 0-for-21, Billy was severely beaned by Chicago White Sox pitcher John Davis. With none out and a man on first, Ripken squared around to bunt and Davis' pitch sailed in and hit him in the temple. He lay there motionless for a few moments and was eventually taken off the field on a stretcher. Never one to be sidelined long, Ripken returned to the Baltimore lineup three days later. Bill didn't hit as well as he did in his first season, but defensively, he was solid, handling 761 chances while making only 12 errors and turning 110 double plays.

In spring training of the following year, Billy suffered a broken left hand after he was struck by a pitched ball. The injury caused him to miss the first two weeks of the 1989 campaign. A few months later, on August 23, Bill was put on the disabled list with a strained right shoulder, and veteran infielder Tim Hulett was called up to replace him. Ripken returned to the Baltimore lineup on September 7. Bill hit .239 that season, and his .985 fielding percentage was the third highest of American League second basemen.

That same year, Ripken's 1989 Fleer baseball card was issued, and inscribed on the bottom of the knob of the bat he was holding was a glaring two-word expletive. Ripken explained in subsequent interviews with the media that he had written on one of his practice bats to distinguish it from his game bats. While hastily preparing to have his photograph taken for his Fleer baseball card, Billy grabbed the wrong bat by mistake. Fleer eventually performed damage control by reissuing a number of different variations of the card with the white-out version being the most sought-after by collectors.

Bill played in 129 games for the Orioles in 1990 but missed most of August with a stress fracture in his right foot. The injury occurred when he had to retreat back to second base on a failed sacrifice bunt attempt by Brady Anderson. He rejoined the team on August 21. Infielder Jeff McKnight was sent down to triple A Rochester to make room for Ripken on the Orioles roster. On September 15, Billy and brother Cal hit home runs off Toronto pitcher David Wells in the same inning. The two would accomplish this same feat six years later on May 28,1996, against the Seattle Mariners' Scott Davison in the ninth inning of an Orioles win. Cal hit three that day and drove in eight runs; Bill hit a solo shot. Davison played his last game two days later.

Billy led the Orioles with a .291 batting average in 1990 while tying his brother Cal for the most doubles (28) on the ballclub. An outstanding bunter and unselfish player, Bill led the American League with 17 sacrifices.

The Ripken brothers made a formidable double-play combination for the Birds, executing 296 twin killings from 1987 through 1992. Bill also led all American League second basemen in fielding percentage in 1992.

In December of 1992, the Orioles released Ripken when they acquired free-agent second baseman Harold Reynolds. Asked about the move Baltimore general manager Roland Hemond replied, "We felt it would be difficult for Billy to be confronted with the signing of Harold Reynolds. Ripken has difficulty at not playing. It really eats at him. He's become accustomed to playing every day."[11]

Ripken found out about the release from his agent, Ron Shapiro. In an interview with WMAR-TV in Baltimore, Billy said he was more shocked than bitter about his release.

"I've been hearing things for a long time now that we needed another second baseman and I guess it finally caught up. Who knows? I might get bitter later. It's just one of those things. You realize that baseball is just a business. I really realize that at this point in time."[12]

In late January of 1993, Texas Rangers starting second baseman Jeff Frye injured his right knee while jogging. A short time later, Texas general manager Tom Grieve contacted Billy about joining the team. Ripken eventually signed a minor-league contract with the club, which included an invitation to attend the Rangers' major-league camp for spring training.

Billy made the Rangers team out of spring training but injures plagued him for most of the season. He appeared in only 50 games while spending 87 days on the disabled list. Although he did not hit much (.189) his versatility allowed Rangers manager Kevin Kennedy the luxury of having a reliable utility man who could play every infield position.

The injury bug continued to haunt Bill in 1994, but he performed well when he was in the Rangers lineup, hitting .309 in 32 games. At the end of the season, Texas designated Ripken and catcher Junior Ortiz for assignment to the minor leagues. Both players declined the offer, choosing to test the free agent market instead.

In March 1995, Bill signed a contract to play shortstop for the Cleveland Indians' Triple-A affiliate in Buffalo. The Indians management made it clear that they were happy with Omar Vizquel at shortstop and Carlos Baerga at second base in addition to having Alvaro Espinoza as their utility man. There would be no chance of making the big-league roster; Ripken was strictly covering them in case one of their infielders was injured.

Major-league baseball was also in the midst of a strike at this time, and there was talk of starting the season with replacement players. Billy was absolutely not interested in that scenario. When asked by a reporter for the Associated Press about the possibility of crossing the picket line, Billy replied, "It's a straight Triple A deal with no implications about being a replacement player. That's the way I wanted it. I don't feel guilty as far as playing in the minor leagues, nor do I think people look at me in a different way for doing it."[13]

Billy went on to have an outstanding year for Buffalo, playing 126 games at shortstop and four others at second base while hitting .292 with 34 doubles. His all-around fine play earned him a selection to the Triple-A All-Star team, which featured the best players from the highest level of the minor leagues.

The major-league strike was eventually settled, and in September 1995 Bill was called up to the majors. He ended up playing in eight games for the Indians, raking the ball for a lofty .412 batting average.

That same month Billy attended Camden Yards in Baltimore when his older brother Cal broke Lou Gehrig's consecutive games record.

In December 1995, the Baltimore front office, which was disappointed in the play of second baseman Bret Barberie, signed Billy to a one-year minor-league deal.

Billy ended up making the major-league club, earning his spot on the roster as the team's utility man. In the middle of May, starting third baseman B.J. Surhoff went on the disabled list with a sprained ankle. At first, manager Davey Johnson considered moving Cal Ripken from shortstop over to third base. Johnson, choosing not to tamper with the infield continuity, decided to go with Billy Ripken at third instead. The younger Ripken was no stranger to the position, having played there during his first stint with Baltimore and more recently with Texas. Billy wound up playing 25 games at the hot corner for the Orioles, handling 41 chances without an error.

Baltimore chose not to resign Billy after the 1996 season, and on December 10 he joined back up with the Texas Rangers. Initially, Benji Gil won the shortstop job for the Rangers but by early June, Ripken had taken over the position.

Unfortunately, Billy suffered a herniated disc in his back while running the bases against Colorado and had to go on the disabled list. Texas called up infielder Hanley Frias from Triple-A Oklahoma to take his place on the roster. Ripken played in 71 games for the Rangers in 1997, appearing at every infield position and hitting .276.

On December 16, Billy, who was now a free agent, signed a minor-league deal with the Detroit Tigers and was invited to spring training as a non-roster player.

The following February, Tigers starting shortstop Deivi Cruz broke his ankle playing winter ball. At that time, Detroit manager Buddy Bell informed the press that Billy would take over at shortstop until Cruz was ready to return to the lineup. Unfortunately, Billy injured his knee in late April and had to be placed on the disabled list. After a brief rehab with Toledo, the Tigers released him on July 20. By this time, Cruz had returned to the Detroit lineup, and the team had a number of other players who could play the infield if necessary.

Bill Ripken hung up his spikes for good at this time, finishing his big-league career with a .247 batting average. Defensively, his .987 lifetime fielding percentage at second base places him 20th on the all-time list.

The following spring, Cal Ripken Sr. died of lung cancer. Bill and Cal, along with other family members, started the philanthropic Cal Ripken Sr. Foundation in honor of their family's beloved patriarch.

In 2002, Billy Ripken was elected into the Maryland Sports Hall of Fame.

In February of 2005, Bill and his brother Cal signed on with XM satellite radio to host a weekly baseball show. Billy later became a studio analyst for the MLB network.

When brother Cal was inducted into the Hall of Fame in 2007, Billy spoke proudly of his former double play partner: "He did things at shortstop that would wow me every week. I don't think people give him enough credit. He was big and he was long, but he did have range. To lead the league in total putouts and total chances, you can't be a desert cactus."[14]

As of 2016, Billy currently remains heavily involved with the Ripken baseball camps and clinics. The brothers have also co-written two well-received instructional books on baseball. Among Bill's many duties, he is the co-owner and executive vice-president of Ripken Baseball, which was founded in 1998. This sales and marketing company oversees all of the baseball activities of the family business, which include the Youth League tournaments that are held at the Ripken Stadium complex as well as their interests in the Aberdeen Iron Birds and the Augusta Green Jackets

In addition to his many commitments to Ripken Amateur Baseball, Ripken Management and Design, Ironclad Authentics and the Cal Ripken Sr. Foundation, Bill is now working as an analyst for Fox Baseball. On February 3, 1989, he married the former Candace Cauffmen. The Ripkens currently reside in Harford County, Maryland, and they have four children, Miranda, Anna, Reese, and Jack.

SOURCES

In addition to the sources cited in the Notes, the author consulted Baseball-Reference.com, *Lewiston Journal, Pittsburgh Press, Seattle Times, Toledo Blade,* and *The Dispatch (Richmond, Virginia.)*

Acocella, Nick. "Tip Your Cap to Baseball's Newest Iron Man," ESPN Classic, November 19, 2003.

Ripkenbaseball.com, "Growing the game of baseball the Ripken way."

A special thanks to Bill Haelig for his much-appreciated assistance with this biography.

NOTES

1. Jeff Seidel, *Baltimore Orioles: Where Have You Gone?* (Champaign, Illinois: Sports Publishing LLC, 2006), 8.
2. Jim Henneman, "Billy Ripken: Finally His Own Man," *Baseball Digest,* July 1991.
3. Jerry Crasnick, "It Wasn't Always Easy Being the Little Brother," ESPN MLB.com, July 27, 2007. Accessed September 29, 2018.
4. Ron Cook, "Then There Were 3: Two Cals, Billy the Kid," Northwest Herald (Woodstock, Illinois), April 2, 1987: 23.
5. Ken Rosenthal, "Ripkens' Reunion Comes to an End," *Baltimore Evening Sun,* March 24, 1987: B7.
6. Marty Klinkenberg, "Billy Ripken Seeks Identity," *Miami News,* March 10, 1988: 4B.
7. Patti Singer, "Hart's Number Finally Comes Up with Orioles," *Democrat and Chronicle* (Rochester, New York), November 18, 1987: 7D.
8. Granny and Garvin Hamner, with the Philadelphia Phillies in 1945, twins Johnny and Eddie O'Brien, with the Pittsburgh Pirates from 1953 through 1958, along with Frank and Milt Bolling, with the Detroit Tigers in 1958, were the only other sibling double-play combinations in major-league history.
9. Klinkenberg.
10. Seidel, 7.
11. Associated Press, "O's Ink Reynolds to One-year Deal," *Daily Times* (Salisbury, Maryland), December 12, 1992: 17.
12. Peter Schmuck, "Reynolds Comes, B. Ripken Goes," *Baltimore Sun,* December 12, 1992: 2C.
13. Sheldon Ocker, "Not Lost in the Shuffle," *Akron Beacon Journal,* March 23, 1995: C7.
14. Seidel, 8.

JOE ROA

BY CLAYTON TRUTOR

Joseph Rodger Roa pitched in 120 major-league games over six seasons between 1995 and 2004. The 6-foot-1 right-hander played 16 seasons of professional baseball between 1989 and 2005. Nicknamed "The Roa Constrictor," he moved frequently from one franchise to another. Roa was traded on five occasions during his career and played for 12 organizations. He spent his six major-league seasons with the Cleveland Indians (1995-1996), San Francisco Giants (1997), Philadelphia Phillies (2002-2003), Colorado Rockies (2003), San Diego Padres (2003), and Minnesota Twins (2004).

Roa was born on October 11, 1971, in Southfield, Michigan, a Detroit suburb. His parents were Ralph and Patricia Roa. Roa graduated from nearby Hazel Park (Michigan) High School, in 1989. He excelled on the Hazel Park Vikings' baseball team, a perennial Michigan powerhouse which a decade earlier produced future Cy Young Award winner Bob Welch. In June 1989 the Atlanta Braves drafted the 17-year-old Roa in the 18th round of the amateur draft. The Braves sent Roa to their Gulf Coast League affiliate for first-year players.

Working primarily as a reliever, Roa excelled in his first year of professional baseball, posted a 2.89 ERA with a 2-2 record in 13 appearances. Building on his success in 1989, the Braves elevated Roa in 1990 to the Pulaski Braves of the Appalachian League, another Rookie instructional league. Roa started in 11 of his 14 appearances in Pulaski, compiling a 4-2 record with a 2.97 ERA.

The Braves moved the 19 year-old Roa up to Macon of the Class A Sally League in 1991. He began the season as a middle reliever before being turned into a starting pitcher in late May. Roa asserted himself as the ace of the staff, amassing a staff-best 13-3 record and a 2.17 ERA, the best among the team's starting pitchers. *The Sporting News* took notice of Roa's Sally League success in August 1991 in a brief item entitled "Red Hot Roa," noting his 6-1 record since becoming a starting pitcher.[1]

On August 29, 1991, Roa was traded; the Braves sent hot prospect Roa and left-handed reliever Tony Castillo to the New York Mets for journeyman right-hander Alejandro Pena. Roa spent 1992 with the St. Lucie Mets of the Class A Florida State League. He finished second on the club with nine wins while compiling a 3.63 ERA. Roa advanced to Binghamton of the Double-A Eastern League in 1993, where he posted a 12-7 record with a 3.87 ERA. He split 1994 between Binghamton and Triple-A Norfolk, where he compiled a combined 10-9 record with a 3.31 ERA.

After the 1994 season, Roa was traded for the second time. He and right fielder Jeromy Burnitz, a highly regarded prospect who had been butting heads with Mets management, were traded to the Cleveland Indians for three right-handed pitchers, Paul Byrd, Jerry Dipoto, and Dave Mlicki, as well as a player to be named later who became minor-league utility infielder Jesus Azuaje. New York apparently made the move in an effort to bolster its aging pitching staff.[2]

The Indians assigned Roa to the Buffalo Bisons of the Triple-A American Association for the 1995 season. Roa had a breakout year in 1995, leading the league in wins with a 17-3 record. He had a 3.50 ERA. He made his first major-league appearance late in the season as a September call-up for the American League champion Indians. Roa started on September 20 at Comiskey Park against Jason Bere and the Chicago White Sox. (That was 12 days after the Indians clinched the AL Central, securing the Tribe's first playoff appearance in 41 years.) Roa pitched six innings in a losing effort, surrendering four earned runs on nine hits, including a two-run home run by Chris Snopek. The Indians lost 4-3 in Roa's only major-league appearance of the season.

The 24-year-old Roa, already a veteran of seven seasons of professional baseball, returned to Buffalo in 1996. Bob Nightengale of *The Sporting News* made note of the depth of the Indians' pitching at the Triple-A level entering 1996, describing Roa as one of several pitchers in Buffalo who were "legitimate major league starters."[3] Roa had another strong season in Buffalo in 1996, going 11-8 with an improved 3.27 ERA. He received another brief September call-up with the Indians, pitching 1⅔ innings in relief and allowing two earned runs to Texas in his only major-league appearance of the season.

After the 1996 season, Roa was traded again, this time to the San Francisco Giants. He was the player to be named later in a blockbuster deal that sent Giants slugger Matt Williams to Cleveland in exchange for three future major league stalwarts, future All-Star second baseman Jeff Kent, journeyman reliever Julian Tavarez, and longtime utility infielder Jose Vizcaino. Roa joined Kent, Tavarez, and Vizcaino on the Giants as a hot young pitching prospect who figured to be a part of the parent club in San Francisco in 1997.[4] The Matt Williams trade was extremely popular in Cleveland, where fans regarded it as providing the Indians with the final piece they needed to win the World Series after the postseason disappointments of 1995 and 1996. In San Francisco, the trade "elicited vulgar phone mail" from hundreds of angry fans and served as fodder for a winter's worth of vitriolic local newspaper columns and sports talk radio harangues.[5] Giants management had the last laugh on the trade, though. The 1997 Giants won the NL West in part because of Jeff Kent's breakout 29 home-run, 121-RBI season, Julian Tavarez's steady bullpen work, and Jose Vizcaino's solid hitting and fielding.

Roa earned a spot on the Giants' 1997 Opening Day roster, beating out right-hander Dan Carlson for the final position in San Francisco's bullpen.[6] Roa started the season strong, posting a 2.08 ERA in seven April appearances before having his ERA balloon to nearly 6.00 by the middle of May. The Giants considered demoting him to Triple-A Phoenix, but he was able stay in San Francisco by reducing his ERA to as low as 3.56 through a series of strong late May and June performances.[7] Roa's ERA began to rise again in late June and July, exceeding 5.00 as the trade deadline approached. In an effort to bolster their pitching staff as a whole for the pennant race, the Giants acquired veteran starters Wilson Alvarez and Danny Darwin as well as reliever Roberto Hernandez from the Chicago White Sox in exchange for six minor-league pitchers. As a result of the acquisition of the three new pitchers, Roa was demoted to Phoenix for the remainder of the season.[8] In his 28 major-league appearances in 1997, he compiled a 2-5 record with an ERA of 5.21.

Twenty-seven-year-old Joe Roa spent the 1998 season with Triple-A Fresno, the Giants' new Pacific Coast League affiliate. He posted a 12-9 record in 27 starts, but his ERA was an unimpressive 5.17. After the season, the Giants released Roa, but he quickly signed with the Kansas City Royals. Troubled by a nagging elbow injury, Roa failed to impress the Royals in spring training and they released him in late March. Roa spent 1999 out of Organized Baseball and underwent elbow ligament replacement surgery.[9] He signed a minor-league deal with the Cleveland Indians in March 2000. Roa made 19 appearances, primarily as a starter, during the 2000 season with the Double-A Akron Aeros, still recovering from the previous year's elbow surgery. He was 6-5 with a 3.41 ERA. The Indians released Roa after the season, but he was soon signed by the Florida Marlins. Roa split the 2001 season between Double-A Portland (Maine) and Triple-A Calgary, posting a combined 6-8 record with a 3.71 ERA. Florida released Roa on March 19, 2002, and three days later, on the 22nd, he signed with the Pittsburgh Pirates. Six days after that, the Pirates traded Roa to the Phillies to complete a previous minor-league transaction.

At the age of 30, Roa had his finest season as a professional in 2002, both at the minor-league and major-league levels. Working with a reconstructed elbow, he changed his approach as a pitcher, relying on craftiness, an arsenal of off-speed pitches, and control, while leaving behind the power pitching of his 20s. Roa dominated the International League in 2002 with the Scranton/Wilkes-Barre Red Barons, going 14-0 with a 1.86 ERA. The Phillies called him up in July, and he spent the remainder of the season as a starter.[10] For the Phillies he was 4-4 with a 4.04 ERA in 71⅓ innings of work.

Roa opened the 2003 season on the Phillies roster as the number-five man in the rotation. He struggled in his early starts and was sent to the bullpen in late April. In early June the Phillies released Roa. He then signed with the Milwaukee Brewers, who assigned him to Triple-A Indianapolis. After he made four shaky starts for Indianapolis, Roa was released on June 3. He signed the next day with the Colorado Rockies. Roa made four appearances for the Rockies in July before being placed on waivers. He signed with San Diego in late July, and remained with the Padres for the rest of the season. Roa made 18 appearances for the Padres, posting a 1-1 record with a 6.75 ERA. His major-league log for 2003 was 1-3 in 28 appearances with a 6.14 ERA. After the season the Padres released the 32 year-old pitcher.

"Baseball's charm, the strange allure of this peculiar summer game, extends well beyond a soaring home run by Barry Bonds or a Red Sox-Yankees series in Boston. It can also be found on the back of journeyman Joe Roa's baseball card," Dan Campbell wrote of Roa in a profile of his frequent moves published in June 2004 on ESPN.com.[11] By the time the profile appeared, Roa had signed a one-year, $320,000 contract with the Minnesota Twins. The "Roa Constrictor," as sports talk radio hosts in the Twin Cities called him, was a relief pitcher for the Minnesota Twins.[12] Roa made a career-high 48 appearances for the Twins in 2004, serving primarily as a middle reliever. He pitched well early in the season, managing a 2.17 ERA as late as June 3. His ERA increased significantly over the second half of the season, leaving him with a 4.50 ERA for the season with a 2-3 record.

The 2004 season was Roa's last in the major leagues. After the season the Twins released the soon-to-be 33-year-old pitcher. The Pittsburgh Pirates signed Roa off waivers in November and assigned him to Indianapolis. Roa pitched in six games for Indianapolis in 2005 before retiring in May. As of 2015 he resided with his wife and family in Chesterfield, Michigan, a Detroit suburb.

NOTES

1   Mike Eisenbath, "Minor League Report," *The Sporting News*, August 19, 1991: 37.

2   "The New York Mets," *The Sporting News*, November 28, 1994: 36; "Cleveland Indians," *The Sporting News*, December 5, 1994: 49-50.

3   Bob Nightengale, "There Is Clearly No Die in This Dynasty," *The Sporting News*, April 8, 1996: 24.

4   "San Francisco Giants," *The Sporting News*, February 17, 1997: 22.

5   Joan Ryan, "What a Turnaround," *The Sporting News*, June 23, 1997: 8.

6   "San Francisco Giants," *The Sporting News*, April 28, 1997: 28.

7   "The Fabulous Baker Boys," *The Sporting News*, June 9, 1997: 35; "San Francisco Giants," *The Sporting News*, June 9, 1997: 43.

8   "San Francisco Giants," *The Sporting News*, August 11, 1997: 26.

9   "Philadelphia Phillies," *The Sporting News*, August 26, 2002: 30.

10 "Philadelphia Phillies," *The Sporting News*, July 15, 2002: 25; "Philadelphia Phillies," *The Sporting News*, August 26, 2002: 30.

11 Dan Campbell, "Long Baseball Journey Brings Roa to Twins' Bullpen," ESPN.com, June 9, 2004. Accessed on November 11, 2014: sports.espn.go.com/espn/wire?section=mlb&id=1818796.

12 Ryan Hoffman, "Forgettable Twins #80: Joe Roa," *81 Forgettable Minnesota Twins*, April 7, 2009. Accessed on November 11, 2014: forgettabletwins.blogspot.com/2009/04/80-joe-roa.html.

PAUL SHUEY

BY CHARLES F. FABER

The flame-throwing right-hander Paul Shuey was selected by the Indians in the first round (second overall pick) of the 1992 amateur baseball draft, ahead of such future luminaries as Derek Jeter and Todd Helton. With good reason the Indians expected Shuey to become their star closer. However, a series of injuries prevented him from attaining the stature that had been predicted for him. Nevertheless, he fought back from injury after injury to carve out an 11-year career as a big-league middle reliever and set-up man.

Paul Kenneth Shuey was born on September 16, 1970, in Lima, Ohio, the son of Teresa Bernice (Mason) and Kenneth Claude Shuey. During his childhood, the family moved to Raleigh, North Carolina. His father, an electrical engineer, taught him how to pitch, and he played American Legion and Babe Ruth League baseball as well as high-school ball. He became an outstanding baseball player at Raleigh's Millbrook High School, where he was a starting pitcher and right fielder. In high school he pitched a no-hitter and was named to the All-State team. He said, "I loved to hit and high school was the last place where I was able to play baseball the way I wanted to play, where I could hit and pitch. I had some at-bats in college and in the big leagues, but it wasn't the same as high school."[1]

At the University of North Carolina at Chapel Hill, Shuey wasted no time in becoming a star. In his first year (1990), he made the freshman All-America team, based on an 8-1 won-lost record and eight saves as he led the Tar Heels to the Atlantic Coast Conference championship. In 1991 he suffered a patella tendon rupture, the first of many injuries that were to plague him throughout his career. In limited action, Shuey led the Tar Heels with a 1.70 earned-run average. During the summer he pitched for the US national baseball team in the Pan American Games. He came back strong in 1992, earning his place in the first round of the June baseball draft. In his collegiate career Shuey was 18-4 with a 2.67 ERA and 16 saves. He struck out 87 batters in 69 innings.

Shuey signed with the Indians, eschewing his senior year of college. His father, a certified public accountant, and his mother negotiated their son's contract. At age 21, Shuey stood 6-feet-3 and weighed 215 pounds. In addition to his blazing fastball, he was equipped with a splitter and a sharp-breaking curveball. His fastball topped out at 98 mph and the split-finger pitch could reach 90 mph. The Indians told Shuey to abandon his high leg kick, which slowed his delivery and made it easy for baserunners to steal against him. It didn't work, so he was told to throw the way he wanted. "I tried it in one outing for the first three batters," Shuey said, "but I bagged it for the fourth hitter, because a guy stole second even when I used the low kick."[2] The Indians sent Shuey to the Columbus Red Stixx of the Class-A South Atlantic League in 1992, where he started 14 games and went 5-5. In 1993 he was assigned to Kinston of the high Class-A Carolina League, where he won his only decision before being promoted to Canton-Akron of the Double-A Eastern League. A losing record (4-8) caused Shuey's demotion to Class-A Kinston to start the 1994 season.

Shuey quickly earned one win and eight saves for Kinston. Desperate for relief pitching, the Indians called him up. It is rare for a player to leap from Class A to the major leagues, but Shuey's case was not unprecedented. From the moment the Indians drafted him they had regarded him as their closer of the future. Shuey made his major-league debut at Baltimore on May 8, 1994, in relief of Jose Mesa, with the Indians trailing, 8-6. He retired the first batter he faced, Mark McLemore, and finished the inning, giving up one hit and striking out one. On May 14 he made the highlight reels by striking out four batters in one inning. However, he could not quite master the closer's role. Although he saved five games, he had a horrific ERA (8.49) and was sent down to Triple-A Charlotte, where he won two of three decisions, saved 10 games, and compiled a 1.93 ERA.

Shuey started the 1995 season with Buffalo, the Indians affiliate in the Triple-A American Association. He pitched reasonably well for Buffalo until he was sidelined with an injured hamstring. The Indians brought him back up briefly, but he had two losses with no saves or wins. He was not on the postseason roster for Cleveland's run to the 1995 World Series. During the next several seasons, Shuey shuffled back and forth between Cleveland and the minors and spent an amazing amount of time on disabled lists. He was on the DL three times in 1997. In 1999 he injured his right hip. Shuey explained this injury: "I have what you'd call a violent pitching motion, with a lot of torque involved. I was pitching on a wet mound in Cleveland, and I started slipping. Then I felt something funny." Over the next several seasons he underwent multiple surgeries on his hip. In 2001 Shuey was placed on the DL with a strained ligament in his elbow. In his nine years in Cleveland, Shuey was 34-21 with a 3.60 ERA. He struck out 450 batters in 404⅔ innings while walking 202.

On July 22, 2002, Shuey was traded to the Los Angeles Dodgers for pitcher Terry Mulholland and minor leaguers Francisco Cruceta and Ricardo Rodriguez. As a middle reliever for the Dodgers in 2002 and 2003, he enjoyed some success, compiling an 11-6 record with one save. He had surgery on his hip in October 2003. By spring his pitches had not recovered their effectiveness, so the Dodgers planned to put him on the DL. The injury bugaboo struck again during spring training in 2004. He tore a ligament in his thumb and reinjured his hip while undergoing rehabilitation, causing him to get a hip replacement and miss the entire season. The Dodgers paid Shuey his full salary ($3.25 million) even though he did not pitch a major-league inning in 2004, expecting to recover the expense from the insurance company (Hartford). However, the policy had expired the day before the tendon tear. The club claimed his disability was caused by the hip problems and should be covered. Hartford argued that Shuey's disability was caused by the thumb injury and thus was not covered. The Dodgers sued, and the case dragged on for years. In December 2011 the club and the insurance company agreed to accept an arbitration procedure.[3]

During the offseason Los Angeles let Shuey go, and he signed to rejoin Cleveland, but he never pitched a game for the Indians. He announced his retirement, but in February 2007 Baltimore signed him, and he attempted a comeback. He had very little success, losing his only decision and collecting only one save.

In his next-to-last major-league appearance, on August 22, 2002, Shuey gained considerable notoriety by allowing the last nine runs as the Texas

Rangers defeated Baltimore, 30-3, an American League record for the most runs scored by a team in a game. Shuey made his final appearance in the big leagues four days later. After 11 injury-plagued seasons and at least 13 trips to the DL, he had accumulated 45 major-league wins, 28 losses, 23 saves, and an ERA of 3.87.

The Orioles released Shuey on September 5, 2007. In January 2008 the Indians signed him to a minor-league contract. They assigned him to their Akron farm club, but Shuey had to give it up; the pain was too much. "It's a sad day," he said in announcing his retirement. "It's pretty much the end of the baseball career, and that's always tough to think about it actually being over, especially when I know I'm leaving and still can probably get some guys out with my 84 to 86-mph pitches. I can still throw the split and the curves, but … I had the pain that I had in 2003 in the back of the hip. … As soon as you are sitting there with your hip throbbing again and limping around, you realize this is not what we had hoped. … The writing was pretty much there for me as soon as I had pain."[4]

In retirement Shuey settled in Wake Forest, North Carolina, with his wife, Julie, and their three daughters: Morgan (born 1997), Casey (1998), and Kate (2006). He signed on as an assistant coach of the Barton College women's soccer team, but his chief avocation was bass fishing. From 2009 through 2013, the ex-pitcher competed in the Walmart Fishing League. Since 2012 he has competed in the Fishing League Worldwide tour. Shuey has participated in 21 tournaments, in which he has caught 89 bass, weighing a total of 210 pounds, and earned $1,787 in prize money.[5]

NOTES

1. "Millbrook High School Hall of Fame," wcpss.net/athletics/hallfame, December 22, 2013.
2. Sheldon Ocker, "Cleveland Indians Team Notes," *The Sporting News*, September 12, 1994: 50.
3. Bill Shaikin, "Dodgers Still Fighting Over Paul Shuey's Salary," *Los Angeles Times*, December 16, 2011: 38.
4. indians.scout.com. April 27, 2005, Accessed August 14, 2014.
5. flwoutdoors.com. Accessed August 14, 2014.

SOURCES

In addition to those cited in the notes, the principal sources consulted were baseball-reference.com. and beenverified.com.

PAUL SORRENTO

BY ALAN COHEN

Paul Sorrento was with the Cleveland Indians for four seasons, during which they rose from fourth place (76-86) in 1992 at dingy old Cleveland Stadium (nicknamed "the Mistake by the Lake") to first place (100-44) in 1995 at their new ballpark, Jacobs Field.

Paul Anthony Sorrento was born on November 17, 1965, in Somerville, Massachusetts, the youngest of three children and the only son.[1] His mother, Margaret Helen (Reuter) Sorrento, saw him play at Fenway Park for the Twins and Indians, but died of cancer on May 9, 1994, two months shy of her 58th birthday, the season before Paul made it to the World Series. She had battled cancer for four years. Not long after her death he said, "It would be nice just to be able to talk to her after you have a good game. Not to talk about the game, but you know."[2]

The family lived in Peabody, Massachusetts, when Paul was growing up, and his father, Tony, followed his progress through high school, where Paul starred on the gridiron as well as the diamond. Speaking about Paul's football prowess, Paul said that when the opposition tried to get around his defensive position, "you could hear the sound of the hits in the stands." In his senior year at St. John's Prep, Sorrento was named to the 1982 *Boston Globe* All-Scholastic Football team. Switching to baseball the following spring, he was his team's MVP, batting .442 with five homers in 17 games, and was named to the *Globe*'s All-Scholastic baseball squad.

During the summer months, he honed his baseball skills at a camp in New Hampshire run by former Red Sox players Jerry Moses and Mike Andrews. They wrote to colleges and helped Sorrento get into Florida State University, where he hit 17 home runs as a freshman. But his coaches felt he was a one-dimension player. In the words of Coach Mike Martin, he "hit our fall conditioning program hard. He lost weight, got stronger, and picked up some quickness. By his junior year, he was the straw that stirred our drink."[3]

As a junior, Sorrento led number-one ranked FSU with 22 home runs and 86 RBIs. In the Metro Conference championship game, against South Carolina, his homer and single propelled his team to a win that gave them a berth in the 1986 NCAA Regionals.[4] They swept through the regionals to advance to the College World Series for the first time in six years, and lost to Arizona in the title match. Sorrento had a grand slam in an earlier loss to Arizona, but provided a single and a double as his squad came back to defeat Oklahoma State 6-5 in an elimination game that kept them alive in the tournament.

After his junior year, Sorrento was selected by the California Angels in the fourth round of the 1986 amateur draft and was signed by scout Al Goldis.

His first stop was at Quad Cities in the Class A Midwest League, where he batted .356 in 53 games but did not have enough plate appearances to qualify for the batting crown. He was moved to Palm Springs in the California League before the end of the season and stayed with the team through the 1988 season. He had a weak 1987 season, and got off to a slow start in 1988, batting .257 with 5 homers and 40 RBIs at the All-Star break.[5] However, he went on a second-half surge and lifted his season's batting average to .286 with 14 home runs and 99 RBIs.

After the season Sorrento was traded with minor-league pitcher Rob Wassenaar and little-used relief pitcher Mike Cook to the Minnesota Twins in a deal that brought Bert Blyleven and minor-league pitcher Kevin Trudeau to the Angels. After spending spring training with the Twins in 1989, he was assigned to Orlando of the Double-A Southern League and led the league with 35 doubles and 112 RBIs. He hit 27 home runs and earned a spot on the circuit's All-Star team.

A late-season call-up, Sorrento made his major-league debut on September 8, 1988, walking as a pinch-hitter against Kansas City. On September 12 against Toronto, he had his first major-league hits, both off Todd Stottlemyre, going 2-for-4.

Sorrento split the next two summers between Minnesota and the Triple-A Portland Beavers. With Portland he batted .302 and .308 and mustered 32 home runs over the two seasons, but with the Twins, his numbers were not stellar. In 1990, after starting the season with Portland, he was recalled on June 22, and hit his first major-league homer on June 24 off Storm Davis of Kansas City. After batting .200 in 23 games, he was sent back to Portland on July 19. He was recalled at the end of August and finished 1990 batting .207 with 5 homers and 13 RBIs for the Twins. One of the home runs was the Twins' first pinch-hit home run of the season. The game-winning 10th-inning two-run blast came in a 3-1 win at Oakland on September 13. Sorrento said, "I was just basically trying to get a hit, not a home run. I was just trying to keep the rally going, honestly."[6]

In 1991 Sorrento was once again optioned to Portland at the beginning of the season and recalled on July 1. On July 11, he had another pinch-homer, this time against the Red Sox, to cement a 7-3 win. Two days later, he was sent back to Portland, and returned to the Twins in September. In September he batted .294 in 20 games with 3 homers and 9 RBIs as the Twins concluded their worst-to-first run and won the AL West by eight games. In his only at-bat in the LCS, he stuck out as a pinch-hitter in Game Three. The Twins advanced to the World Series and Sorrento went 0-for-2 with a walk in three pinch-hitting appearances as the Twins beat the Atlanta Braves in seven games. With Kent Hrbek holding down first base for the Twins, Sorrento did not fit into their plans and before the 1992 season he was dealt to the Cleveland Indians for Curt Leskanic and Oscar Munoz.

Sorrento spent four years with the Indians. He was the regular first baseman in 1992, and on Opening Day got the first hit at the new Orioles Park at Camden Yards, a single off Rick Sutcliffe. On May 17 he had his first career multi-homer game, blasting two off former teammate Kevin Tapani. Over the course of his career, Sorrento homered twice in a game 10 times. He ended the season with a .269 average and 18 home runs. In 1993 he again had 18 homers along with 65 RBIs and a .257 batting average. That season he slugged the first of his nine career grand slams, on June 25 off Tom Gordon of Kansas City.

In 1994 Sorrento rocketed two homers in a 6-5, 10-inning win over the Angels on April 13, and batted .286 with 3 homers and 18 RBIs in April as the Indians, in their new ballpark, won 13 of their first 22 games and were tied for the lead in the Central Division of the American League. In May he missed five games after his mother died, and his average sank to .237 on May 17. But he was encouraged when his leadoff ninth-inning homer on May 27 was the difference in a win over Oakland. "That's probably the first one I've hit like that in the ninth. I hope there's many more to come."[7] He caught fire in July and hit five homers in as many games between July 19 and 23, bringing his total to the season to 12 and lifting his batting average from .261 to .275. On the 19th he slugged two homers and had five RBIs. Through August 10, Sorrento had 14 homers and 62 RBIs, and was on a pace to set career highs in both figures. His .280 batting average was his highest to date. And the Indians were on the way, possibly, to a postseason berth for the first time in 40 years when the players strike ended the season.

Just before the strike Sorrento found himself in the middle of controversy. Teammate Albert Belle had been suspected of corking his bat. Umpire Dave Phillips had confiscated Belle's bat. Before he could send it to league headquarters to be examined, it disappeared and was replaced by one of Sorrento's bats. Belle claimed that there was no switch and that he had been using Sorrento's bat. His argument did not convince league officials and he was suspended.[8] Sorrento, unwittingly in the middle of the mess, commented, "I was sure he was using my bat, but they've changed bats so many times since then, I don't know now. Maybe we should call in Judge Wapner."[9]

During his early years with the Indians, Sorrento met Melissa Thacker while the team was on the road in Kansas City. They were married on October 29, 1994, and settled in Largo, Florida.

In 1995, when Cleveland completed its evolution into a winning team, Sorrento was part of a first-base platoon, sharing playing time with Dave Winfield, Eddie Murray, and newcomer Herbert Perry. The left-handed-hitting Sorrento got into 104 games, slugged 25 homers and batted in 79 runs with only 76 hits. Of his team, he said, "It's like night and day. We were a bad team and now we're winning. It's a lot of fun to be part of it."[10]

The evening of June 4 was a major turning point, and Sorrento was a major factor. The first-place Indians were hosting Toronto and the Blue Jays jumped off to a 7-0 lead in the first inning. With David Cone pitching for Toronto, the Indians began to cut into the lead. A run in the third, two runs in the fourth, two runs in the fifth, and a run in the sixth made the score 8-6 Toronto. In the bottom of the ninth, the Indians had a run to make the score 8-7. Sorrento came to the plate. Looking back on the moment, he said, "You could have bet the mortgage that we wouldn't have come back, but even the fans seemed to sense something. They stayed around and started getting louder and louder in the eighth and ninth inning. You just sit back and say to yourself, 'This kind of thing (the comeback) will end one day,' but it hasn't."[11] Sorrento swung and ended the game with a two-run homer to right field off Darren Hall. The 9-8 win kept Cleveland's division lead at five games.

But it was frustrating not to be playing every day. "I've accepted it for the team," he said. "I'm not happy with it. But I'm accepting it for the team."[12] Although he hit with power, he batted only .235 as the Indians won the AL Central Division race and advanced to the postseason for the first time since 1954.

Sorrento batted .300 in the Divisional Series as the Indians swept the Red Sox. In Game One he singled off Rick Aguilera. In Game Two, he walked in the fifth inning and scored the only run the Indians would need as Orel Hershiser pitched a 4-0 shutout. In the next game, Sorrento's single in the sixth inning plated the first of five sixth-inning runs as Cleveland broke things open, winning 8-2 to advance to the League Championship Series.

Sorrento, despite hitting only .154 in the LCS and staying on the bench when lefty Randy Johnson pitched for the Seattle Mariners, was a factor in his team's win over Seattle. In Game Two he scored two runs as Cleveland won and evened the series at 1-1. The Indians won the series in six games and faced Atlanta in the World Series. In the Indians' seven-game loss, Sorrento batted .182. When his pinch-hit fly ball fell into the waiting glove of Braves center fielder Marquis Grissom for the second out of the ninth inning in Game Seven, he had taken his last swing as a member of the Cleveland Indians.

The Indians chose not to pick up Sorrento's option after the season, electing to go with veteran

Eddie Murray at first base. Sorrento signed with He replaced Tino Martinez, who had been traded to the New York Yankees.

Sorrento was looking forward to playing regularly. In his last two years with Cleveland, he had played in only 199 of his team's 257 games. Before the season he said, "I'm looking forward to the challenge of getting 500-600 at-bats. That's something I've never done in my career. I was a role player in Minnesota. I never got too many at-bats there. I got more in Cleveland, but it was about the same. I'm coming over to a good club that has some great players. I'm looking forward to helping this team win."[13]

In 1996 Sorrento got off to a slow start. Although he had a two-homer game on April 6, his average was only .229 at the end of April. He turned things around in May, batting .361 with five homers, but the Mariners had yet to catch fire, and on May 14 were victimized by Dwight Gooden's no-hitter. Sorrento reached base in the second inning on one of six walks issued by Gooden. In the top of the ninth inning, Seattle put runners on second and third and Sorrento came to the plate as the lead run. When his popup fell into the waiting glove of Derek Jeter, the Yankees had a 2-0 win and Seattle was in second place, 5½ games out of first in the AL West.

They were still in second place, three games over .500, when May came to a close, but Sorrento was about to really catch fire. His average for the season went over .300 when he hit in 11 consecutive games (21-for-44) in June, and as late as August 20, he was batting .300 with 20 homers and 72 RBIs. But on that date, the Mariners were essentially a .500 ballclub, trailing the division-leading Texas Rangers by seven games.

The deficit grew to nine games on September 11 but the Mariners were not about to give up. They won 10 in a row, including a four-game sweep of first-place Texas to pull within one game of the division lead. In the 10th win, on September 21, the Mariners went on a homer barrage in the third inning that prompted Tom Verducci of *Sports Illustrated* to write, "Pitching to the Seattle Mariners is like ordering coffee with extra sugar at one of Seattle's ubiquitous coffee shops. You take your lumps and end up feeling buzzed."[14] In the space of four pitches, Oakland's Dave Telgheder gave up home runs to Alex Rodriguez, Ken Griffey Jr., and Edgar Martinez and took a 6-0 lead. Martinez's blast tied the team record for extra-base hits in a season (580), set by the Yankees in 1936. After Jay Buhner struck out, Sorrento came to the plate against Telgheder and hit a homer that gave the Mariners the extra-base-hit record.[15] They finished the season with 607 extra-base hits.

During the 10-game winning streak, Sorrento hit in seven consecutive games. But the team could not keep up the momentum and lost six of its last eight games to finish in second place, 4½ games behind the Rangers. For the season, Sorrento batted a career-high .289 with 23 homers and a career-high 93 RBIs. He played in 143 games and had a career-high 471 at-bats.

In 1997 the story had a happier ending. Sorrento made it to the postseason for the third time in seven years when the Mariners won the AL West. Although his average slipped to .269, he contributed 31 home runs (with 80 RBIs), and was one of six Mariners to hit at least 20 home runs as Seattle hit a record 264 homers. During the season, Sorrento became a father for the first time when his son, Ashton, was born on July 19. Not only was Sorrento hitting for power, but he was fielding his position well. He made only four errors all season and was second in the league in fielding percentage (.996).

In the Divisional Series against Baltimore, Sorrento was 3-for-10 with his only postseason home run. The Mariners lost the best-of-five series in four games

In two years with the Mariners, Sorrento enjoyed playing in the Kingdome and hit 54 home runs, 31 of them at home. "It's a real good hitter's park, one of the better ones in the league, so that's obviously helping, and batting on turf helps out as well, so there are a lot of advantages to hitting in the Kingdome," Sorrento said in 1996.[16]

After the season Sorrento became a free agent and signed with the expansion Tampa Bay Devil Rays. After signing, he said, "It feels good to be wanted. With the players they've signed, it shows that management is as serious about winning as the players."[17]

He became the Devil Rays' first designated hitter on Opening Day 1998 and hit the team's first grand slam on May 3, part of a 4-for-5 game in which he had six RBIs, a team record that stood until 2007.[18] Most of his appearances were as a DH and he batted .225 with 17 homers and 57 RBIs. Despite a lineup that included names like Wade Boggs and Fred McGriff, the team finished last in the AL East, 36 games below .500.

In his second season with Tampa Bay, Sorrento batted .235 with 11 homers and 42 RBIs in 1999. His 491-foot homer on May 19 against the Rangers at the Ballpark in Arlington was the longest home run ever hit at the ballpark. Paul and Melissa welcomed their second child, Arabella, in August. That season he played in 99 games, but was the designated hitter in only seven of them, otherwise playing left field and first base. The 33-year-old Sorrento batted .235 with 11 homers, and the Devil Rays did not pick up his option after the season.

In 2000 Sorrento went to spring training with the Kansas City Royals but was released at the end of spring training as the Royals found his defensive skills subpar. He signed with the Sacramento River Cats, the Oakland A's affiliate in the Pacific Coast League, and batted .273 with 6 homers and 32 RBIs in 40 games. He retired at the end of the season.

For his major-league career, Sorrento batted .257 with 166 home runs and 565 RBIs.

In 2012, after a dozen years away from baseball, Sorrento became the hitting coach of the Inland Empire 66'ers, an Angels farm team in the California League. The next season he was the roving hitting instructor for the Angels. He was slated to be in that role again in 2014, until major-league hitting coach Don Baylor broke his femur in a freak injury while squatting to catch the ceremonial first pitch from Vladimir Guerrero on Opening Day, March 31, putting him on the shelf for 12 weeks. Assistant hitting coach Dave Hansen took over for Baylor, and Sorrento was added to the coaching staff to assist him.[19] Once Baylor rejoined the Angels in June, Sorrento resumed his duties as a rover, continuing in that role through the 2015 season. When Hansen was named hitting coach for the Angels for the 2016 season, succeeding Baylor, who had been fired, Sorrento was named assistant hitting coach.[20]

During Sorrento's time with the Mariners, his family relocated to Washington State. As of 2015 they were living in Issaquah, a suburb of Seattle.

SOURCES

In addition to the sources cited in the Notes, the author also relied on Ancestry.com, Baseball-Reference.com, Sorrento's file at the National Baseball Hall of Fame Library, and these articles:

Newnham, Blaine. "Sorrento Wants a Chance: M's Will Oblige," *Walla Walla* (Washington) *Union Bulletin*, March 5, 1996: 13-14.

Morgan, David Lee Jr. "Even Better at 31: Former Indian Sorrento Continues to Improve as Mariners' First Baseman," *Akron* (Ohio) *Beacon Journal*, July 24, 1997: B1.

NOTES

1   Tony Massarotti, "Sorrento's Fan Club a Family Affair," *Boston Herald*, April 16, 1993.

2   Terry Pluto, "Sorrento Plays Through Pain of Loss," *Akron Beacon Journal*, August 6, 1994.

3   Paul Hoynes, "Platoon Leader: Indians Sorrento Still Sits Against Lefties, but Other Things Are Going Right," *Cleveland Plain Dealer*, June 25, 1995: 1D.

4   *Index-Journal* (Greenwood, South Carolina), May 12, 1986: 12.

5   *San Bernardino* (California) *County Sun*, August 13, 1988: C5.

6   *Santa Cruz* (California) *Sentinel*, September 14, 1990: B1.

7   *Post-Standard* (Syracuse, New York), May 28, 1994: C4.

8   Hoynes, "Ump Says Bat He Took From Belle Was Swiped," *Cleveland Plain Dealer*, July 17, 1994: 1A.

9   Thomas Stinson, "Belle's Cork Chicanery Does Baseball's Underbelly Proud," *Atlanta Journal Constitution*, July 23, 1994: D2.

10 Hoynes, "Platoon Leader."

11 Ibid.

12 Ibid.

13 Larry Whiteside, "It's a Fresh Start in New Home as Sorrento Hits Kingdome," *Boston Globe*, March 25, 1996.

14 Tom Verducci, "What a Week! Seven Days in September Were Filled With Feats on the Field and Pennant Fever from Coast to Coast, Just Like in the Old Days," *Sports illustrated*, September 26, 1996.

15 Bob Sherwin,"10 in a Row, M's Show Might but Gain No Ground," *Seattle Times*, September 22, 1996: D1.

16 Jim Greenidge, "A Hot Time for Sorrento," *Boston Globe*, May 23, 1996.

17 Fred Goodall, Associated Press, December 9, 1997.

18 Marc Lancaster, "Rays Go Batty on Baltimore," *McClatchy-Tribune Business News* (Washington, D.C.), September 6, 2007.

19 Greg Beecham, Associated Press, April 2, 2014.

20 *Los Angeles Times*, November 4, 2015: D7.

JULIÁN TAVÁREZ

BY PAUL HOFMANN

Controversial, flamboyant, excitable, volatile, hot-headed, crazy, wild, and emotional are among the many adjectives used to describe Julián Tavárez during his 17-year major-league career spent with 11 teams. Over the course of his career, Tavárez developed a reputation as an unpredictable pitcher who was not afraid to pitch inside. The 6-foot-2, 165-pound right-handed hurler hit 96 batters, which ties him for 102nd on baseball's all-time list as of 2017.[1] He was a starting pitcher, closer, long man, and setup specialist (at different times during his career) who played a brash brand of baseball that led to multiple bench-clearing brawls.

Julián Tavárez Cameron was born on May 22, 1973, in Santiago de los Caballeros, Dominican Republic. He was one of eight children and the youngest of seven boys, born to Francisco Tavárez and Maria Carmen.[2] Francisco worked off and on in the construction industry and was often absent from the home. Maria rolled cigarettes and cigars. Julián grew under challenging circumstances. The combined earnings of his parents were barely enough to keep food on the table. The small family home had a dirt floor, tree leaves for a roof, and a sewage-filled river running behind.[3] Tavárez said, "Most of the money my father made went for rice and beans."[4]

There are conflicting reports as to how much formal education Julián received. Some accounts state he had a sixth-grade education.[5] Others say he never attended school.[6] Regardless of the amount of time he spent in a classroom, it is clear he received little education. Later in life, Tavárez revealed that he was illiterate.[7]

At the age of 15, Julián left home to find work. The teenager, who had become tired of living in poverty, sold pineapples and newspapers on street corners, tried his hand at construction, cleaned shoes, and did other odd jobs to make money. As he did whatever he needed to do to subsist, the one constant in his life was his passion to play baseball. From an early age Julián knew he wanted to be a baseball player.

Tavárez was a lanky, top-rated shortstop prospect who weighed only 135 pounds when he was first spotted by major-league scouts. When he signed as a free agent for $1,200 with the Cleveland Indians in March 1990, the Tribe had other plans for the 16-year-old.[8] Tavárez began his transformation from infielder to pitcher in the Dominican Summer League in 1990 and 1991.

The Indians originally projected Tavárez as a starter. Unable to speak English, he first came to the United States in 1992. He was assigned to the Burlington (North Carolina) Indians of the Appalachian League and inserted into the team's starting rotation. He made 14 starts at the rookie-league level and went 6-3 with a 2.68 ERA.

Tavárez started the 1993 season with the Kinston (North Carolina) Indians of the Class-A Carolina League. After going 11-5 with a 2.42 ERA, he was promoted to the Canton-Akron Indians of the Double-A Eastern League. In his three appearances with Canton-Akron, he went 2-1 with a 0.95 ERA and one shutout. He was called up to the Indians in early August and made his major-league debut on August 7, 1993, against the Baltimore Orioles at Camden Yards. Opposing the Orioles' Fernando Valenzuela, Tavárez pitched two scoreless innings before being roughed up the second time through the order. The big blow was a three-run homer by Cal Ripken. In three innings, he gave up five runs (all earned) on six hits while walking three and striking out one. Seven days later, he earned his first major-league victory when the Indians beat the Texas Rangers, 8-5, at Cleveland's Municipal Stadium.

Tavárez went 2-2 with a 6.57 ERA in eight appearances with the Indians that year. While he had only two quality starts among the seven he made, he had established himself as one of the Indians' top prospects. However, it was clear he needed additional seasoning. Late in the year, he was joined on the Indians by fellow Dominican Manny Ramirez, who was coming up in the Indians organization at the same time. The two remained best friends.

Tavárez spent most of the 1994 season with the Charlotte Knights of the International League. He did get called up early in the year to make a spot start against the Boston Red Sox at Fenway Park on May 26. Despite being staked to a two-run first-inning lead, Tavárez yielded eight runs (four earned) on six hits in 1⅔ innings and absorbed the loss. He was optioned back to Charlotte, where he finished the year with a 15-6 record and a 3.48 ERA.

Since Tavárez had limited success as a starter during his first two cups of coffee with the Indians, the team decided to use him as a reliever to start the 1995 season. He was particularly effective during the first half of the season. At the All-Star break Tavárez was 5-0 with a 1.18 ERA and 9 holds. Middle relievers were rarely given consideration as All-Stars then, and Tavárez was left off the squad.9 After the break, Tavárez went 5-2 and posted a 3.89 ERA. He finished the season 10-2 with a 2.44 ERA. His 57 appearances were second on the team to closer Jose Mesa (62). He finished tied for sixth in the American League Rookie of the Year voting and was named to the Baseball Digest Rookie All-Star Team. The Indians went 100-44 and won the American League Central Division by a whopping 30 games.

Tavárez had his first taste of postseason baseball in Game One of the 1995 American League Division Series against the Boston Red Sox. The gangly rookie was called on by manager Mike Hargrove in the top of the seventh inning to relieve Dennis Martinez and protect the Indians' 3-2 lead. He retired the Red Sox in order in the seventh before giving up a game-tying home run to second baseman Luis Alicea to start the eighth. After he surrendered a single to John Valentin, his night was over. The game went late into the night and was decided when the Indians' Tony Peña hit a two-out, walk-off home run in the bottom of the 13th inning. Tavárez appeared in two more games during the series. He came on in relief of Orel Hershiser in the top of the eighth of Game Two and retired Valentin, the only batter he faced, on a popup to second. He also pitched the eighth inning of series-clinching Game Three, giving up one run on three hits.

Tavárez made four appearances in the American League Championship Series against the Seattle Mariners and was a tough-luck loser in Game Three. After pitching a scoreless 10th, he gave up a leadoff single to Joey Cora, the only batter he faced in the 11th inning. Cora later scored the winning run when Mariners slugger Jay Buhner hit a three-run homer off right-hander Eric Plunk. Tavárez was used frequently in the World Series, against the Atlanta Braves. He pitched in five games and tossed a combined 4⅓ innings of scoreless ball. The Indians lost the Series in six games. The image of a distraught, bawling Tavárez in the Indians dugout as the Braves celebrated is one of the most lasting from the 1995 World Series.

It would be quite some time before Tavárez enjoyed another season like 1995. He failed to regain the form that made him one of the premier set-up men in baseball and struggled throughout the 1996 season. He finished 4-7 with an inflated ERA of 5.36 (more than double his ERA from his outstanding rookie year). On May 31 he threw a fastball behind the Brewers' Mike Matheny, sparking a bench-clearing brawl. During the melee, Tavárez flipped umpire Joe Brinkman onto his back. He was suspended for five games, later reduced to three, for his role in the fracas.10 This was the first of many on-field incidents Tavárez would be involved in during his career.

In 1996 the Indians went 99-62 and again won the AL Central Division title. Tavárez made mop-up appearances in the first two games of the 1996 ALDS against the Baltimore Orioles, a series the Indians lost three games to one. During the offseason, Tavárez was traded with Jeff Kent, Jose Vizcaino, and a player to be named later (Joe Roa) to the San Francisco Giants for right-handed slugger Matt Williams and a player to be named later (Trenidad Hubbard).

Tavárez had an up-and-down season in 1997. He pitched in a league-leading 89 games and finished with a 6-4 record with a 3.87 ERA. His season was defined by three distinct periods. In his first 12 appearances of the season Tavárez recorded six holds and had an ERA of 2.45. Then he experienced a deep slump. In his next 17 appearances he went 1-2 with only three holds with a gaudy 10.67 ERA. As the season progressed, Tavárez rebounded and went 5-2 with 17 holds and a 2.57 ERA in his final 60 appearances of the year. The Giants won the NL West by two games over the Los Angeles Dodgers and, for the third year in a row, Tavárez found himself headed to the postseason.

Tavárez pitched in all three games of the 1997 NLDS against the Florida Marlins. In Game One he came on in relief in the eighth inning of a 1-1 tie. After throwing a scoreless eighth, Tavárez gave up a leadoff single to Jeff Conine and then hit Charles Johnson to begin the ninth. Roberto Hernandez came on in relief of Tavárez and two outs later gave up a game-winning single to Edgar Renteria. Tavárez took the loss. He pitched the sixth and seventh innings of Game Two and gave up a solo home run to Gary Sheffield in the Giants' 7-6 loss. He also pitched a scoreless seventh in the Giants' 6-2 Game Three loss. Seven long years passed before Tavárez appeared in another postseason game.

The 1998 season was another roller-coaster year for Tavárez. The first half was one of his better stretches in the majors. He was 3-3 with a 2.71 ERA before he landed on the disabled list in July. After his return, he went 2-0 with a 6.85 ERA. On September 9, an on-field confrontation with umpire Sam Holbrook earned Tavárez a three-game suspension.

Tavárez struggled during the 1999 season from beginning to end. He pitched in only 47 games, the fewest in his five full seasons in the majors to that point and finished with a 2-0 record and a 5.93 ERA. After the season he was claimed off waivers by the Colorado Rockies. This ushered in the true journeyman era of his major-league career.

Tavárez started the 2000 season in the Rockies' bullpen but moved into the starting rotation by the end of July. He made 12 late-season starts and went 6-3 with a 3.75 ERA over that stretch. On September 5 he tossed his first complete game when he beat the Chicago Cubs, 10-2, at Coors Field. He finished the season with a record of 11-5 and a 4.43 ERA. After the season, Tavárez opted for free agency and signed with the Chicago Cubs. The Cubs thought Tavárez's repertoire would be a good fit for Wrigley Field. He was a fastball-slider-sinker pitcher who kept the ball down, a tremendous asset when the wind starts to blow out of the Friendly Confines.[11]

The 2001 season got off to an eventful start for Tavárez. During a spring-training game against the Giants on March 26, he was involved in another incident. Tavárez appeared to gloat after striking out Giants third baseman Russ Davis to end the inning. The right-handed-hitting Davis took exception and met Tavárez near the first-base line where a scuffle ensued after Tavárez attempted a karate-style dropkick directed toward Davis.[12] Major League Baseball fined Tavárez and suspended him for five games for "fighting, kicking, and provoking a bench-clearing incident."[13] He was also ordered to take sensitivity classes.[14]

The fight led to another incident on April 28 when Tavárez returned to San Francisco, where he was booed by Giants fans who were unhappy with his role in the fight with Davis. After the Cubs' 5-0 loss to the Giants, a reporter inquired about the fans' reaction toward the former Giant. Having learned nothing from John Rocker's outburst and resulting condemnation in 1999, Tavárez spewed the following: "Why should I care about the fans? They're a bunch of assholes and faggots here."[15] The comments set off a firestorm of criticism around the league and among LGBT groups around the country. Amazingly, after issuing a scripted apology, Tavárez was spared the same heavy-handed response from MLB that Rocker received. *Chicago Sun-Times* columnist Jay Mariotti opined in *The Sporting News* that Commissioner Bud Selig "went mushy on Tavárez. He didn't issue a suspension and deferred to the Cubs, who criticized Tavárez, slapped him with a fine and pointed him toward the mound, where he kept his place in the rotation."[16] Again, Tavárez was ordered to take sensitivity classes.[17]

Tavárez was unable to keep his spot in the Cubs' rotation for the entire year. After his start on August 14, he stood at 8-8 with a 3.77 ERA, but after three subpar outings he was relegated to the bullpen for the remainder of the season. In his final 10 appearances of the year, he had an ERA of 9.00. Tavárez finished the season with a 10-9 record and a 4.52 ERA. His late-season struggles, anti-LGBT comments (the Cubs have one of longest track records of any major-league franchise of embracing their LGBT fan base), and dissatisfaction with being demoted to the bullpen all contributed to Tavárez being traded before the 2002 season.[18]

Tavárez had entered spring training with the hope of returning to the Cubs rotation. However, when the Cubs floated the idea of moving him back to the bullpen Tavárez balked at the idea. On March 27 the Cubs traded Tavárez with minor-league pitcher Jose Cueto, catcher Ryan Jorgensen, and left-handed pitcher Dontrelle Willis to the Florida Marlins for right-handed closer Antonio Alfonseca and right-handed starter Matt Clement. Tavárez, who was set to make $2,750,000, reacted to the trade by saying, "They had two choices, let me start or trade me.[19] I waited until the end of the month ... and I felt like it was for sure I was going to be the number-five starter. I guess I was wrong about that."[20]

Tavárez took Clements' spot in the Marlins rotation as the number-five starter and struggled from the beginning of the season. He made 27 starts for the Marlins and finished with a record of 10-12, a 5.39 ERA, and a 1.705 WHIP. Now 29 years old, Tavárez found himself at a crossroads in his career.

On January 28, 2003, Tavárez signed a one-year, $750,000 contract to join the Pittsburgh Pirates. He proved to be a solid addition to the Pirates bullpen, despite the volatile unpredictability he brought to the club. He was suspended once again for coming out of the bullpen and throwing punches during a brawl in the Pirates' 12-9 victory over the Tampa Bay Devil Rays on June 14. Tavárez claimed he was acting in self-defense. Tampa Bay manager Lou Piniella said the fight was subsiding until "Tavárez came out of the bullpen and started throwing right hands."[21]

Tavárez assumed the closer role after the Bucs traded Mike Williams to the Philadelphia Phillies. He finished the year with a 3-3 record, 11 saves, and a 3.66 ERA, a good comeback year that positioned himself to once again test the free-agency market during the offseason.

On January 9, 2004, Tavárez signed a free-agent contract the St. Louis Cardinals, his sixth team in six years. The Cardinals were rewarded with one of Tavárez's best seasons. He pitched in 77 games (all in relief) for St. Louis and finished with a record of 7-4, four saves, and a career-best 2.38 ERA. The Cardinals won the NL Central Division title with a 105-57 record, in part because Tavárez had regained his form to once again become one of the best set-up pitchers in the game.

However, the season was not without incident. On August 20, 2004, Tavárez lasted just one out in a 5-4 victory over the Pittsburgh Pirates in the opener of a day-night doubleheader. Umpire crew chief Joe West conducted a lengthy inspection of Tavárez's cap before tossing Tavárez, who made a flamboyant exit. First, Tavárez put his arm around home-plate umpire Ron Kulpa and suggested the two get a beer after the game and then flipped his cap to a fan in the stands behind the dugout on his way off the field.[22] After the game, Tavárez explained to reporters the exchange that proceeded this ejection. "He (West) asked me if it was pine tar and it was like 'No, it's just a dirty hat,'" Tavárez said. "Every pitch I throw I touch my hat, just like a lot of guys. I asked him if I could wear another hat and he said, 'No, you're out of the game.'"[23] Tavárez was suspended for 10 games.

Tavárez's erratic behavior was not limited to exhibition or regular-season games. It also carried over into Game Four of the 2004 NLCS vs. Houston. Tavárez gave up a go-ahead solo home run to Carlos Beltran in the bottom of the seventh. Frustrated that he had given up the lead, Tavárez sailed a pitch over the head of Astros first baseman Jeff Bagwell. The pitch almost brought the two to blows and resulted in the pitcher being fined $10,000.[24] After the inning, Tavárez returned to the dugout and attacked a water cooler and punched a phone during a nationally televised meltdown that resulted in two broken fingers on his left hand.[25]

Tavárez made two appearances in the World Series against the Boston Red Sox. He entered Game One to start the bottom of the eighth with the score tied, 9-9. With one out, Jason Varitek reached on an error. Red Sox second baseman Mark Bellhorn followed with a two-run, go-ahead home run to put the Red Sox up 11-9. Tavárez was tagged with the loss. He also pitched a scoreless ninth in the Cardinals' 4-1 Game Three loss. The Red Sox went on to sweep the Series in four games, denying Tavárez a World Series ring for the second time.

Tavárez returned as the Cardinals set-up man for the 2005 season. He pitched in 74 games and finished with a 2-3 record, a 3.43 ERA, and four saves. The Cardinals posted their second consecutive 100-win season and captured the NL Central title by 11 games.

Tavárez made two appearances in the Cardinals' three-game sweep of the San Diego Padres in the 2005 NLDS. He came on in relief of left-hander Mark Mulder in Game Two with two on and two outs in the top of the seventh inning to retire Ryan Klesko on an inning-ending fly ball. He loaded the bases with two outs in the eighth before hitting Xavier Nady to force in a run and forcing manager Tony La Russa to call on Randy Flores to get out of the inning. Tavárez was again called upon in the bottom of the eighth of Game Three. The first batter he faced, Ramon Hernandez, hit Tavárez's first offering into the left-center-field bleachers for a solo home run. Tavárez retired the next hitter before giving up a single and giving way to Cardinals closer Jason Isringhausen.

Tavárez made three appearances in the Cardinals' six-game upset loss to the Astros in the NLCS. In Game Two he came on in relief in the top of the eighth with the Astros leading 2-1. Houston touched Tavárez for a pair of runs and went on to even the series at one game each. He pitched a scoreless eighth inning in Game Three, a 4-3 Astros victory. He made the final postseason appearance of his career in Game Six. With a runner on second and two down, Tavárez was summoned from the bullpen to keep the Cardinals deficit at 4-1. Morgan Ensberg greeted Tavarez with an RBI single to center to increase the Astros lead to 5-1. Tavarez finished the seventh and pitched a scoreless eight to finish his postseason career.

On January 18, 2006, Tavárez agreed to a two-year, $6.7 million contract with the Red Sox, a hefty contract for a set-up man at that time. One Cardinals fan summarized his feelings about the pitcher's departure from the Cardinals in a blog post on *Deadspin*:

As Cardinals fans, the level of enjoyment we derived from having Julian Tavárez on our team the last few years is exceeded only by the relief we felt when he left. Tavárez was an excellent setup man, but every relief appearance was fraught with peril: Is this the time he's going to snap? Every time Tavárez took the mound, you crossed your fingers: Blue wire, or red wire? Fingers crossed … *whew*. Our favorite moment was the NLCS two years ago, when, a day after breaking his finger by punching a wall, he took a line drive back up the middle, right off that finger, and still got out of the inning. Exciting, effective, crazy … but a little *much* sometimes.[26]

Tavárez's tenure with the Red Sox got off to a Tavárez-like start. On March 27, only six days after appearing in his first game in a Red Sox uniform and a week before the start of the regular season, Tavárez was involved in another fight.[27] The fight erupted when the Tampa Bay Devil Rays' Joey Gathright spiked the hot-tempered Tavárez when he slid into home in the eighth inning. Tavárez stepped on the outfielder's right arm while Gathright was still on the ground. As Gathright tried to extricate himself and get to his feet, he was met with a stiff right hand to the jaw, a punch Devil Rays outfielder Carl Crawford referred to as a sucker punch.[28]

When asked if he regretted hitting Gathright, Tavárez quizzically replied, "What do you mean, 'regret'? I wish I don't have to [throw a punch], because I'm not here to fight, you know. Little things happen in baseball, you know. No big deal."[29] When probed as to whether he thought he would be suspended, he said, "I don't know what is going to happen. But Major League Baseball, they make a decision and there is nothing you can do about it."[30] Tavárez was given a 10-day suspension for his role in the bout.

Tavárez did not appeal the suspension and did not make his regular-season debut with the Red Sox until April 13. He made 52 relief appearances (2-4, 4.71 ERA) before moving into the rotation for the final month of the season. On September 22 he scattered seven hits in a 7-1 victory over the Toronto Blue Jays, the second complete game of his career. He finished the year with a 5-4 mark and 4.47 ERA while the Red Sox finished 86-76, a distant third behind the New York Yankees.

The 2007 season brought renewed hope that the Red Sox would be able to return to championship form. Tavárez started the season as the team's fifth starter, but relinquished his spot in the rotation in late July when his ERA still hovered about 5.00. Among his few highlights that season was a play on May 27 when he retired the Rangers' Frank Catalanotto on a comebacker to the mound by rolling the ball to first base. He finished the year with a record of 7-11 and an ERA of 5.15. While the Red Sox won the AL East title and went on to win the World Series, Tavárez was left off the postseason roster. He was awarded a World Series ring for being on the roster during the regular season.

After the 2007 season, the Red Sox exercised a $3.85 million club option on Tavárez. He started the season in the Sox bullpen but was designated for assignment on May 11 after nine appearances that included three highly ineffective outings. He was 0-1 with a 6.39 ERA at the time of his designation. Unhappy about the demotion, Tavárez left his $20,000 World Series ring from the year before in his locker.[31] The Red Sox released him on May 22. Five days later he signed with the Milwaukee Brewers. He made only seven appearances with the Brewers, going 0-1 with an 8.59 ERA before being released on June 25. On July 8 he signed with the Atlanta Braves. In 36 games with the Braves, Tavárez went 1-3 with a respectable 3.89 ERA, demonstrating to potential suitors that he still had some baseball left in him.

There was little interest in Tavárez during the offseason. On March 12, 2009, he signed a minor-league contract with the Washington Nationals and was invited to spring training. The Nats were coming off a 59-102 record in 2008 and were in desperate need of pitching help. Addressing a group of reporters after signing, Tavárez provided an analogous explanation as to why he opted to sign with the team. "When you go to a club at 4 in the morning, and you're just waiting, waiting, a 600-pounder looks like J. Lo. And to me this is Jennifer Lopez right here. It's 4 in the morning. Too much to drink. So, Nationals: Jennifer Lopez to me," said Tavárez.[32] This was the 35-year-old, 16-year veteran's roundabout way of saying he had no other offers.

Tavárez earned a spot in the Nationals' bullpen coming out of spring training. He made 42 appearances and had a 3-7 record with a 4.89 ERA before being released on July 29. With no offers from other teams, Tavárez retired. While his career never reached the heights projected when he originally came up with the Indians, it was nonetheless a memorable one. He finished with a record of 88-82, a 4.46 ERA, and 23 saves.

As of 2017 Tavárez split time between his home in Broadview Heights, Ohio, and his native Dominican Republic. He worked as a youth baseball coach in both the Dominican Republic and United States. In 2017 he worked for Elite Squad Baseball as a 9U coach alongside former major-league outfielder Todd Hollandsworth. He has a son, Trent Siebert.

SOURCES

In addition to the sources cited in the Notes, the author also relied on Baseball-reference.com and Retrosheet.org.

NOTES

1. Steve Eby, "The Greatest Summer Ever: Julian Tavarez," August 8, 2015. didthetribewinlastnight.com/blog/2015/08/08/the-greatest-summer-ever-julian-tavarez/.
2. Roger Rubin, "No Relief in Sight for Tavarez," *New York Daily News*, May 22, 2007. nydailynews.com/sports/baseball/yankees/no-relief-sight-tavarez-article-1.253769.
3. Teddy Greenstein, "Not in His Vocabulary: Profane Outburst Unusual for Tavarez, Say Friend, Teammates," *Chicago Tribune*, May 10, 2001. articles.chicagotribune.com/2001-05-10/sports/0105100206_1_dominican-republic-insult-julian-tavarez.
4. Mike Kils, "Cartoons a Kick for Tavarez," *Denver Post*, July 21, 2000. extras.denverpost.com/rock/rox0721.htm.
5. Greenstein, "Not in His Vocabulary."
6. "No Relief in Sight for Tavarez."
7. Rick McNair, "Red Sox: Julian Tavarez Welcomes the Rays to Spring Training," bosoxinjection.com/2017/02/21/red-sox-julian-tavarez-rays-spring-training/.
8. Greenstein, "Not in His Vocabulary."
9. Jason Lukehart, "Julian Tavarez Became One of the Best Setup Men in Baseball in 1995," July 24, 2015. letsgotribe.com/2015/7/24/9022213/1995-cleveland-indians-bullpen-julian-tavarez-news.
10. "A.L. Reduces Suspensions Handed to Belle, Tavarez," *Spokane Spokesman-Review*, June 19, 1996, spokesman.com/stories/1996/jun/19/al-reduces-suspensions-handed-to-belle-tavarez/.
11. "Chicago Cubs," *The Sporting News*, August 6, 2001: 41.
12. Teddy Greenstein, "Penalty Surprises Tavarez: Pitcher Is Fined, Suspended for Brawl With Giants," *Chicago Tribune*, March 30, 2001. articles.chicagotribune.com/2001-03-30/sports/0103300260_1_cubs-manager-don-baylor-davis-teammate-julian-tavarez.
13. Ibid.
14. Gordon Edes, "Tavarez' Tantrums," *Boston Globe*, March 28, 2006. archive.boston.com/sports/baseball/redsox/articles/2006/03/28/tavarez_tantrums/.
15. Jim Buzinski, "They're a Bunch of … Faggots," *Outsports*, May 2, 2003. outsports.com/2013/2/26/4033778/theyre-a-bunch-of-faggots.
16. Jay Mariotti, "Hearing an Ugly Side to Athletes," *The Sporting News*, May 14, 2001: 7.
17. "Tavarez' Tantrums."
18. Jim Buzinski, "Baseball and Gay Fans Come Together," *Outsports*, August 3, 2004. outsports.com/2013/2/26/4034138/baseball-and-gay-fans-come-together.
19. "Cubs Get Closer Alfonseca In 6-Player Deal," ESPN, March 28, 2002. static.espn.go.com/mlb/news/2002/0327/1359044.html.
20. Ibid.
21. "Tavarez' Tantrums."
22. "Reliever Ejected for Dirty Cap," ESPN, August 23, 2004. espn.com/espn/wire/_/section/mlb/id/1864051.
23. Ibid.
24. Chris Kolb, "Boston Red Sox: The 5 Most Embarrassing Players/Coaches in Franchise History," November 14, 2012. bleacherreport.com/articles/1408311-the-top-5-most-embarrassing-red-sox-players-coaches-in-franchise-history. See also "Tavarez' Tantrums."
25. Ben Bolch, "Tavarez's Tantrum Causes Broken Bones," *Los Angeles Times*, October 19, 2004. articles.latimes.com/2004/oct/19/sports/sp-nlrep19.
26. "Julian Tavarez Is Crazy, Man, Crazy." *Deadspin*, March 28, 2006. deadspin.com/163355/julian-tavarez-is-crazy-man-crazy.
27. "Tavarez-Gathright Ejected in BoSox-Rays Brawl," ESPN, March 27, 2006. espn.com/mlb/news/story?id=2386484.
28. Gordon Edes, "Tavarez: One Strike, One Brawl," *Boston Globe*, March 28, 2006. archive.boston.com/sports/baseball/redsox/articles/2006/03/28/tavarez_one_strike_one_brawl/.
29. Ibid.
30. Ibid.
31. Dan Lamothe, "Julian Tavarez Loses World Series Ring," May 29, 2008. blog.masslive.com/redsoxmonster/2008/05/julian_tavarez_loses_world_ser.html.
32. Chico Harlan, "The Nats Love Don't Cost a Thing," *Washington Post*, March 15, 2009. voices.washingtonpost.com/nationalsjournal/2009/03/the_nats_love_dont_cost_a_thin.html#more.

JIM THOME

BY JOSEPH WANCHO

All right up there, drop down the ladder from your clubhouse. A new member is joining you. Henry, show him the secret handshake. Willie, educate him on the secret password. Babe, don't hog all those s'mores. Junior, slide over a bit. Gentlemen, please welcome Jim Thome to the 600 Home Run Club.

It may seem a bit of tomfoolery to think of an actual tree house hosting some of the greats of the game of baseball. But on August 15, 2011, that is exactly the scene one might envision. Minnesota Twins slugger Jim Thome joined that elite group when he hit home runs 599 and 600 against the Detroit Tigers at Comerica Park. He became the eighth player to achieve the monumental feat, and he became the first to hit numbers 599 and 600 in the same game.

Thome stepped to the plate in the in the top of the sixth inning, with Jason Kubel on first base and no one out, and homered to break a 3-3 tie. In the seventh inning, he connected for a three-run homer off pitcher Dan Schlereth. The ball sailed over the left-field wall for number 600. Detroit left fielder Delmon Young, who had been traded to the Tigers from Minnesota earlier that day, leapt in vain to catch the baseball. "If Delmon would have caught that, I might have went out there and kicked his butt," said Twins manager Rod Gardenhire.[1]

As Thome rounded third base and headed to home, his teammates were there to greet him. Detroit baseball fans, a knowledgeable bunch, recognized a historic moment when it presented itself, stood, and showered Thome with thunderous applause. "I wasn't really aware of it. I knew he was close to 600, but I didn't know if that was going to be the one," said Schlereth. "I'm not exactly happy about it, but he's a great player, and I'm a huge fan of his. He did a great thing tonight, and … I felt kind of awkward, I didn't know whether to clap or what."[2]

Said Thome, "It's an unbelievable night. You dream about it, but when it happens it's kind of surreal. You envision, is it ever going to happen? You don't know. At 40 years old, approaching 41, you don't know. I never tried to take it for granted."[3] It was fitting that Thome hit the historic blast against the Tigers, as he had hit more home runs against Detroit (66) than any other club in his 22-year career.

Thome reached the 600-home-run plateau in 8,167 at-bats. Only the Babe was faster; it took the Bambino 6,821 at-bats. "It's an honor and a privilege to welcome another member to the 600-home-run club, especially someone like Jim Thome, who is not just a great baseball player, but a great person as well," said Ken Griffey Jr. "I offer Jim my heartfelt congratulations."[4]

James Howard Thome was born on August 27, 1970, in Peoria, Illinois, one of Chuck and Joyce Thome's five children. Chuck Thome worked as a foreman at Caterpillar Industries Inc. There was baseball lineage in the Thome family. Chuck played fast-pitch softball on teams sponsored by Caterpillar. His sister Carolyn played fast-pitch as well and was inducted into the National Softball Hall of Fame in 1966. Jim's grandfather, Chuck Sr., played baseball in the minor leagues. Thome paid tribute to his grandfather by wearing his socks pulled all the way up. He noted, "My dad told me that my grandfather hit a home run off Bob Feller when Feller was barnstorming through the Midwest one year."[5]

The story that is often told of Thome as a young boy is how he idolized Chicago Cubs slugger Dave Kingman. On one visit to Wrigley Field with his father, young Jim sought out Kingman for an autograph. But his attempts were unsuccessful. Not to be deterred, he bounded into the Cubs dugout. Thome was returned to Chuck Thome via a delivery from Cubs catcher Barry Foote.

Thome was a two-sport star at Limestone High School in Bartonville, a Peoria suburb, garnering All-State recognition in both basketball and baseball. After high school Thome enrolled at Illinois Central College, where he excelled in both sports. The Junior Athletic Association named him an All-American in baseball. Cleveland scout Tom Couston remembered Thome hitting ropes all over the field. "There were a bunch of scouts there, but they'd all come to see another player," Couston said. "Thome was playing shortstop, and he went 1-for-4 or maybe it was 0-for-4. But every ball he hit was a rocket. His swing was so quick and powerful that I was surprised he didn't kill somebody. "[6]

Couston asked the coach for permission to speak to Thome. "First of all, he sent over the wrong kid," said Couston. "I told him I don't want you, I want the shortstop. When Thome came over, I didn't want any of the other scouts to see me talking to him. So we're standing back-to-back. Jimmy kept calling me sir and turning around to talk to me and I kept saying 'Don't look at me, keep looking into the distance.' He probably thought I was a wacko. I asked him, 'If we draft you, will you sign?'"[7] Thome said he would.

Cleveland selected Thome in the 13th round of the June 1989 free-agent draft. He was assigned to the Indians rookie-level Gulf Coast League team, where he struggled, with little power. The following year Thome established a relationship that would serve him through his career and beyond. At the end of spring training, he was not assigned to a minor-league team, and stayed in extended spring training waiting for one of the Class A short-season teams to begin its schedule. Charlie Manuel, Cleveland's big-league hitting coach, was named manager of the Indians' Triple-A affiliate in Colorado Springs for 1990. Manuel took note of how hard Thome hit the baseball, and worked with him on his swing. A relationship was formed and then strengthened from 1991 to 1993, when Thome spent parts of all three years playing for teams Manuel managed.

From 1991 through 1993, Thome spent the beginning of each season at the minor-league level, but he made his way to the big-league club during each year. He made his major-league debut on September 4, 1991, at the Hubert H. Humphrey Metrodome in Minneapolis. Thome played third base and went 2-for-4 at the plate, with an RBI and a run scored.

Thome demonstrated a high aptitude for hitting. Except for his initial year in 1989, he hit well over .300 in each year in the minors. In Charlotte in 1993, under Manuel's tutelage, Thome smacked 25 home runs and drove in 102 runs while batting .332. Thome, like Manuel, was a left-handed hitter. Manuel noted that Thome was unable to pull the ball to right field. One day in the clubhouse, some players were watching the movie *The Natural*. "In the movie, Robert Redford would point the bat out in front of him and then bring it back," said Manuel. "I thought that might work for Thome. He was so tense at the plate that he'd bow his back. This way, he could point the bat out in front of him, take a deep breath and bring it back."⁸ Manuel also had Thome open up his stance so he could pull the ball more to right field.

When the 1994 season began, Cleveland was in a new ballpark, Jacobs Field. Thome started at third base, but mostly only against right-handed starters. The players strike halted the season on August 12, with Cleveland one game behind Chicago in the American League Central Division. Expectations were high in 1995. Thome had hit .304, with 18 homers and 43 RBIs against right-handed pitching in 1994. Overall, he batted .268 with 20 homers and 52 RBIs.

The 1995 season offered little resistance for Cleveland. With a lineup including Albert Belle, Manny Ramirez, Kenny Lofton, Paul Sorrento, Eddie Murray, and Thome, the Indians decimated their opponents. They led the league in batting (.291) and ERA (3.83). They clinched their division on September 8, 1995. Thome caught the final out to send the Indians to the postseason for the first time since 1954.

Cleveland swept through Boston in the Division Series and toppled Seattle in the ALCS in six games. But in the World Series the Indians lost to Atlanta in six games. Thome had four homers and 10 RBIs in the postseason.

The Indians won the division title again in 1996 with little trouble. Thome's 38 homers and 116 RBIs were second on the team to Belle's 48 and 148. Thome walked 123 times, and had an on-base percentage of .450. He was named the third baseman on *The Sporting News* AL All-Star Team in both 1995 and 1996. "He's a natural-born hitter," said Sandy Alomar. "He's gotten better since he's been in the big leagues, and I think he can continue to improve."⁹ In 1996 the Indians were eliminated in four games by Baltimore in the ALDS.

First baseman Paul Sorrento left Cleveland after the 1995 season. The Indians signed Julio Franco to replace him. As it turned out, eight different players started at first base in 1996. It was a situation that general manager John Hart addressed in the offseason, acquiring third baseman Matt Williams from San Francisco, and moving Thome across the diamond to first base for 1997. "When you get a Matt Williams, that's two pretty good corner guys who can hit the ball," said Thome.¹⁰

Other changes were made. Belle left the club through free agency, and Lofton was traded to Atlanta for David Justice and Marquis Grissom. The 1997 Indians were a much different club than in 1995, but they won their second pennant in three years and reached the World Series. Thome was selected to his first All-Star Game, the first of three straight. He led the team in home runs with 40 and finished second to Williams in RBIs with 102. Thome led the league in walks with 120. But the Tribe fell short, losing to the Florida Marlins in seven games in the Fall Classic.

Over the next few years the Indians returned to the playoffs, but were not able to get back to the Series as they were defeated in the ALDS (1999 and 2001) and the ALCS (1998). Meanwhile Thome became the face of the franchise. He was a dependable, hard-working, blue-collar type of ballplayer whom fans cheered for, referring to him as a "throwback." In 1998 Thome hit 30 homers and drove in 85 runs. Pretty good numbers considering he missed five weeks of play after breaking a bone in his left hand at Tampa on August 7. After the 1998 season, Thome tied the knot with Andrea Pacione on November 7 in Chicago. Pacione was a newscaster at a local TV station. They had two children, Landon and Lila.

Over the next four seasons (1999-2002), Thome averaged 42 home runs and 114 RBIs each year. He hit the longest home run in Indians history on July 3, 1999. He hammered a 3-and-1 fastball from Kansas City Royals pitcher Don Wengert an estimated 511 feet. The ball hit a pillar to the right of the bleachers in center field and ricocheted through an iron fence and on to Eagle Avenue behind the park. "I don't think I've ever seen a ball hit that far," said manager Mike Hargrove.¹¹

Thome broke the single-season home-run mark of 50 set by Belle in 1995 when he smacked 52 in 2002. From June 25 through July 3, Thome hit a home run in seven straight games. He missed tying the major-league record of eight games, shared by Dale Long, Don Mattingly, and Ken Griffey Jr.

"It was a nice run," said Thome. "Streaks always come to an end. They're fun while they last."[12]

But perhaps the most important achievement for Thome in 2002 was receiving the Roberto Clemente Award. The award is given to the major-league who "best exemplifies the game of baseball, sportsmanship, community involvement, and the individual's contribution to his team." Thome was the second Cleveland Indian (Andre Thornton was honored in 1979) to be so honored. "My father and brother told me when I was young what kind of player Roberto Clemente was," said Thome. "They told me he was the best player who ever lived. But I really didn't know what kind of man he was."[13] Thome helped raise more than $200,000 for the Children's Hospital in Peoria, and another $200,000 with the United Way.

Thome was at the apex of his career. A 32-year-old free agent after the 2002 season, he was looking for long-term security for himself and his family. That offer came from the Philadelphia Phillies, who signed the left-handed slugger to a six-year deal worth $85 million. Thome may have inked a big contract, but it did not change his personality one iota. He made an immediate impression on Phillies manager Larry Bowa in spring training. "Jim Thome hasn't missed a road trip," said Bowa. "I've given him the option. He says: 'I like to ride the bus. I get to bond with my players.' I've never heard that in my life."[14]

Bowa had to like what he saw of his new first baseman on the diamond. Thome clubbed 47 home runs to lead the senior circuit in 2003 and his 131 RBIs were third in the league. He provided dependable glove work, fielding at a .997 clip, his highest fielding percentage in the majors. His home-run total came up one short of the franchise record. (Mike Schmidt cracked 48 homers in 1980). But the Phillies could not catch the Braves.

Thome's mother, Joyce Thome, died of lung cancer on January 5, 2005. "In a lot of different ways, she was my best friend," said Thome. "My mom was the really go-to lady in our family. She was the rock. She was the foundation. We all kind of fed off what she did."[15]

On the baseball front, Bowa was replaced by Charlie Manuel. But the Thome-Manuel reunion was short-lived. Thome suffered through elbow and back injuries, limiting him to 59 games in 2005. With the emergence of Ryan Howard, who won Rookie of the Year honors that season, the Phillies traded Thome and cash to the Chicago White Sox for outfielder Aaron Rowand and pitcher Gio Gonzalez.

The White Sox were world champions in 2005, and both Jim and Andrea though it was divine intervention on his mother's behalf that brought him back home. Chicago had a team with good power, including Paul Konerko, Jermaine Dye, and Joe Crede. Now they were adding Thome to the lineup as their designated hitter. "The DH role should help him stay healthy," said White Sox manager Ozzie Guillen. "We want to save him from the wear and tear on the field. We feel confident he can be the hitter he's always been."[16]

In essence, Thome was replacing Frank Thomas, the White Sox' all-time home run leader. The Big Hurt was a free agent and like Thome had battled injuries in 2005. Thomas signed a deal with Oakland over the winter. "I knew (general manager Kenny Williams) was going to go out and get us a bat," said first baseman Konerko. "I had no idea it'd be someone the caliber of Jim Thome. That clinched it. It showed me that not only were we trying to stay on top, but we were also trying to get better. From what I've seen so far this spring he's going to hit 30, 35 home runs by accident."[17]

Maybe Konerko should have given up his day job to become a full-time prophet, and then some. Thome clubbed 42 home runs, drove in 109 runs, totaled 107 walks and batted .288 in 2006. It was the ninth time in a run of 11 seasons that Thome posted at least 30 homers, 100 RBIs, and 100 walks. The two seasons in which he did not exceed these numbers were cut short by injury. He was named Comeback Player of the Year by *The Sporting News* and Major League Baseball.

On September 16, 2007, Chicago was hosting the Anaheim Angels. The score was tied, 7-7, in the bottom of the ninth inning. The White Sox' Darin Erstad led off the inning with a single to right field against his former team. Thome stepped to the plate and hit a home run to left-center field off Angels reliever Dustin Moseley. Not only did the blast give the White Sox a win, but it was the 500th career home run for Thome, in his 2,000th big-league game. He became the 23rd player to reach the 500-HR plateau, and the first to do it in walk-off fashion. "Just can't believe it, I really can't," said Thome. "I never would have imagined doing that as a walk-off. It's hard to explain what's going through me right now. What a great day. It's hard to hit home runs when people want you to."[18]

Three days later Thome and his father made the 14-hour drive from Peoria to Cooperstown to deliver the home-run ball to the National Baseball Hall of Fame. For Thome, it was the first time he would see the entire shrine, as his only visit up to that day had been for exhibition games.

After falling shy of making the postseason, the White Sox returned in 2008, winning the AL Central Division by one game over Minnesota. But they were eliminated in the Division Series, losing in four games to Tampa Bay. On August 31, 2009, Thome was dealt to the Los Angeles Dodgers. Back in the NL, with no DH, Thome was employed solely as a pinch-hitter.

A free agent after the 2009 season, Thome signed with the Minnesota Twins on January 26, 2010. He was used as a designated hitter and pinch-hitter for Ron Gardenhire's club. Even in limited duty, Thome hit 25 home runs, drove in 59 runs, and batted .283. The Twins won the AL Central, but were swept in the Division Series by the New York Yankees. Thome was traded back to Cleveland on August 25, 2011, for a player to be named later. The move was in part symbolic, as Thome had just hit his 600th home run 10 days earlier. But the Tribe's DH, Travis Hafner, was out for the season and Thome filled the void. In the last home game of the season on September 25, 2011, the Indians inserted Thome at third base for one play, as he bade farewell to the fans upon his exit.

Thome signed with Philadelphia in 2012, reuniting him again with Manuel. He was used mostly as a pinch-hitter and as a designated hitter in interleague games. On June 17, 2012, at the Rogers Centre in Toronto, Thome hit his fourth home run of the season. With that blast, Thome became only the fourth major leaguer to hit 100 home runs with three different clubs. (Alex Rodriguez, Reggie Jackson, and Darrell Evans preceded him) Thome hit 337 homers for the Indians, 134 for the White Sox, and 101 for the Phillies.

Not long after that, Thome was on the move again, traded to the Baltimore Orioles on June 30 for two minor leaguers. The Orioles won the wild card game over Texas, but lost in the ALDS to the Yankees in five games.

Even though he would not officially retire for two more seasons, Thome's playing days had come to an end. In a career that spanned 22 years, he hit 612 home runs and had 1,699 RBIs, 451 doubles, 1,747 walks, a batting average of .276, and a slugging percentage of .554. As of January 2016, Thome ranked seventh all-time in both home runs and walks.

On August 2, 2014, the Cleveland Indians dedicated a statue to their all-time home-run hitter. The pose is of Thome with his bat extended out in front, just as Charlie Manuel made him bat over 20 years before. "How do you ever imagine, when you play this game, getting an opportunity to have an organization put a statue up for you?" Thome said. "I'm a little lost for words. It's much bigger than all of us. What's going to be cool is that it will stay. I mean like now, in the snow. I always look up at Bob Feller's statue and No. 1 you appreciate the player, but the fact that it's up all year and people can come see it. If you were their favorite player, maybe they pass on a memory to a kid, it's humbling."[19] Before the unveiling ceremony, Thome signed a one-day contract with Cleveland, so that he could retire as an Indian.

As of 2016 Thome was a special assistant to Chicago White Sox general manager Rick Hahn. Someday he would like to manage on the big-league level. In 2017, Thome joined the MLB Network as a studio analyst, in addition to his duties with the White Sox. Jim Thome was elevated to the Baseball Hall of Fame in 2018, becoming only the second player in Indians history, after Bob Feller, to be elected in his first year of eligibility. On August 18, 2018, Thome's uniform number 25 was retired by the Indians. He joins Earl Averill, Lou Boudreau, Larry Doby, Mel Harder, Bob Feller, Frank Robinson and Bob Lemon as the only other players to be so honored.

In 2012 Steve Aschburner wrote a biography of Harmon Killebrew, for which Thome wrote the foreword. Thome wrote of his career parallels with Killebrew: their pursuit of 500 home runs, the need to practice hitting home runs in batting practice. Thome ended the foreword by detailing the "living legends" he encountered on his journey in the major leagues. "All those guys, they came back and gave their time to the game. It's important that guys today appreciate that. You're talking about the living legends."[20]

Include yourself in the mix, Jim. Indeed, you are a living legend.

NOTES

1. Brian Murphy, *St. Paul Pioneer Press*, August 16, 2011.
2. Noah Trister, SF Gate.com, August 16, 2011.
3. Murphy.
4. Murphy.
5. Paul Hoynes, "Playing the Family Game, Baseball Scouts Didn't Notice Jim Thome's Potential Until After High School", *Cleveland Plain Dealer*, August 27, 1995: 12-D.
6. Hoynes.
7. Hoynes.
8. Hoynes.
9. Linda Feagler, "Who's on First?", *Cleveland Magazine*, April, 1998: 33.
10. Steve Herrick, "Thome Willing to Move for Team", *Elyria* (Ohio) *Chronicle-Telegram*, November 15, 1996.
11. Burt Graeff, "Thome Hammers Out Place in Tribe History", *Cleveland Plain Dealer*, July 4, 1999: 5C
12. Murray Chass, *"My-Make That Thome's-Historic Bid"*, *New York Times*, July 5, 2002. D3
13. Paul Hoynes, "Thome Wins Clemente Award". *Cleveland Plain Dealer*, October 23, 2002: 04
14. Murray Chass, "Like 2002, Mets, Phillies Add Veterans", *New York Times*, March 19, 2003 D4
15. Todd Zolecki, *Philadelphia Inquirer*, April 4, 2005.
16. Peter King, "The Defending Champs Add Some Big Hurt to Their Lineup", *Sports Illustrated*, April 2, 2006.
17. Ibid.
18. ESPN.com, September 16, 2007.
19. Paul Hoynes, "Indians Will Unveil Thome Statue on Aug. 2", *Cleveland Plain Dealer*, January 26, 2014: B10
20. Steve Aschburner, *Harmon Killebrew: Ultimate Slugger* (Chicago: Triumph Books, 2011), X.

EDDIE "SCOOTER" TUCKER

BY RICHARD CUICCHI

Scooter Tucker was not unlike millions of boys who have aspired to play in the big leagues. It was a dream of his from an early age to play professional baseball. His influential mentors as a youth taught him how to play the game. His sports role models were former major leaguers from his hometown. His college coach was a former major-league player and coach. All of them helped shape his passion for the game.

Tucker achieved success at all levels of baseball as he pursued his goal. Indeed, he reached the major leagues, able to share his debut game milestone with his ill father. However, several events kept him from keeping a steady job in the majors. He came close to reaching the pinnacle of baseball in 1995 – playing on a World Series team, but that didn't work out either. Yet Tucker always felt fortunate to have had the opportunity to compete at the highest level of baseball. His career found its way back into professional baseball as a coach and manager, almost 15 years after his playing career ended.

Eddie Jack Tucker was born on November 18, 1966, in Greenville, Mississippi, to Nolan and Jacqueline (Pope) Tucker, Mississippi natives. Although that area of the Mississippi Delta was largely known for its farmlands, Tucker's parents held jobs outside of the agricultural industries. Nolan worked as a terminal manager for Chevron and later for U.S. Gypsum, while Jacqueline was a bookkeeper for a local Otasco retail store. Tucker has a younger sister, Stephanie.

Eddie's grandfather gave him the nickname Scooter at an early age. "I'm not sure why he did," Tucker said in a telephone interview. "He must have thought I was going to be faster than I am. I was in the second grade before I knew my name was Eddie."[1] The nickname stuck with him.

Nolan Tucker was an avid baseball fan and encouraged his son to play. Eddie began playing as a 6-year-old. As he grew up, he competed in all the age groups of the youth leagues in town. By the time he was 10 years old, he was regularly playing the catcher position, and continued throughout his high school, college, and professional careers.

Tucker attributed his initial passion for baseball to two local residents who provided influences throughout his teen years. One, Tommy McGehee, was his coach for two years on the Greenville Phillies in a local summer league. Tucker recalled that McGehee was a gritty, hard-nosed person who taught him mental toughness and helping form his initial passion for catching. The other,

George Hood, was a local baseball enthusiast who nurtured Tucker's baseball interests and later helped him evaluate college baseball and football scholarship offers.

Tucker had two other sports role models, both former major-league players from Greenville, on whom he could draw encouragement. His father had grown up with Bobby Etheridge, who played parts of two seasons with the San Francisco Giants in the late 1960s. And Tucker played baseball with the son of George Scott, who had a 14-year major-league career, most notably with the Boston Red Sox, during the 1960s and 1970s.

Tucker attended the private Washington School in Greenville, where he was a standout in baseball and football. As an offensive and defensive end, he lettered three years in football and won All-Conference selection for two seasons and All-State honors as a senior. He was a letterman in baseball all four years of high school, recognized as an All-Conference player three times and All-State in his senior year. His baseball team was a conference champion and state playoff semi-finalist in his sophomore season, and Tucker's passion for baseball was fueled by his success in high school. (The school has retired his baseball jersey number.[2])

Tucker graduated from high school in 1985 and with the advice of George Hood, he chose to attend Delta State University in Cleveland, Mississippi, which offered him a full scholarship to play baseball. Other offers included only partial scholarships, while several four-year colleges and junior colleges offered football scholarships.

At Delta State, an NCAA Division II school, he started at catcher in his freshman season in 1986 and was named Freshman of the Year, based on a batting average of .344, 5 home runs, and 27 RBIs. His sophomore season was similar, with an average of .381, 8 home runs, and 35 RBIs. As a junior, Tucker's numbers included a .356 batting average, 7 home runs, and 51 RBIs, as Delta State won the Gulf South Conference Championship and went to the NCAA Division II Regional tournament.[3] Tucker was named to the All-Gulf South Conference team in each of his three seasons (1986, 1987, and 1988) with Delta State, and was selected for the All-American team in 1988.

Tucker attributed his development at Delta State to the coaching of Dave "Boo" Ferriss, the longtime baseball coach who had pitched for the Boston Red Sox in the 1940s and was the team's pitching coach for several years in the 1950s.

On the field, Ferriss leveraged his own big-league experience to tutor Tucker as a catcher – taught him how to call a game, watch tendencies of hitters, and pay close attention to game details. Ferriss stressed to Tucker that catchers should be leaders. Off the field, Ferriss often gave fatherly advice to Tucker and took a personal interest in his schoolwork. Ferriss arranged for Tucker to play in college summer leagues, where he got exposure to other styles of baseball and a higher level of competition.

The San Francisco Giants selecting Tucker in the fifth round of the 1988 June Amateur Draft. He didn't return to Delta State for his senior year, instead deciding to sign with the Giants. (It is noteworthy that tiny Delta State has sent two other catchers to the major leagues, Barry Lyons and Eli Whiteside.)

At 6-feet-2 and 205 pounds, Tucker was assigned to Everett of the Class A Northwest League in 1988. He was named to the league's postseason all-star team.[4] The next season he was moved up to Clinton of the Midwest League. On July 6, 1989, Tucker played in a 25-inning contest against Waterloo, the longest game in Midwest League history. The game was suspended by curfew after the 19th inning and 5 hours and 46 minutes of play, and resumed on August 17. Waterloo won, 4-3, after 7 hours and 37 minutes of total play. Tucker batted 11 times in that elongated game.[5] He recalled that he didn't get a hit in the game, with his at-bats including hitting into a double play and a bloop fly out to the outfield that started a triple play. He remembered coming back to the dugout after one of his frustrating at-bats late in the game, demonstrating one of the few tantrums of his career. Tucker said Clinton manager Keith Bodie shouted to him, "At least you made only one out in that at-bat!"

At Class A San Jose in 1990 Tucker threw out 50.4 percent of potential base-stealers (59 of 117 attempts). He played in the California League All-Star Game that year.[6] He was promoted to Double-A Shreveport for the 1991 season, and again excelled defensively, leading the league's catchers with a .995 fielding average and 70 assists. From April 25 to July 18, he had a stretch of 67 consecutive errorless games. In 110 games, he batted .284, with 4 home runs and 49 RBIs, and was selected to play in the Texas League All-Star Game.[7]

Shreveport won the Texas League championship in 1991. Tucker was placed on the Giants' 40-man roster, and thought his future looked bright. But while taking part in a postseason camp for promising young Giants farmhands, he was put on waivers. The Giants told him the team needed to make room for more pitching help after a number of hurlers were sidelined by injuries during the season.

The Houston Astros claimed Tucker off waivers. The Astros figured that if he showed he was ready for a big-league roster spot, he could become part of a plan to allow incumbent catcher Craig Biggio to shift to second base and focus more on the offensive part of his game. The Astros were thinking Tucker and Scott Servais would share the catching duties in the new lineup.[8]

The Astros sent Tucker to play winter ball in Venezuela, but he had to come back after being felled by a stomach virus.[9] Tucker thought he had a good chance to make the Astros out of spring training in 1992. However, the team had also acquired catcher Ed Taubensee in a trade with Cleveland, and Tucker was sent to Triple-A Tucson instead.

A right-handed hitter, Tucker was batting .329 at Tucson through June 12, when he was called up by the Astros. He made his major-league debut on June 14. Recalling recalled his feelings about his first game, Tucker said, "I was grateful for getting the chance. There was a lot of emotion surrounding the event since my father had been ill, and I had been dealing with that. My father was able to attend the game, but died three weeks later. I was blessed to have him witness the realization of our shared dream."

In his debut game, Tucker drew a walk from the Giants' Dave Righetti, but then was picked off at first base after getting a steal signal. Tucker remembered Giants first baseman Will Clark consoling him by indicating the Giants had stolen the Astros' signal. Two days later against San Diego, Tucker got his first major-league hit, a single to right field off Rich Rodriguez, his first of three hits in the game, and had three RBIs in an Astros blowout. The next day, despite not being known for the speed that his nickname would imply, he again got the steal signal and this time successfully swiped second base. Tucker said he never got another steal signal in the majors.

Astros manager Art Howe liked what he saw from Tucker in his first games. "He's a take-charge guy and that's what you want to see in your catcher," Howe said. "Once he gets used to the pitchers, I think he's going to do a good job calling games."[10]

Tucker started 13 games in 17 appearances during his first call-up with the Astros, but was returned to Tucson on July 21, when he failed to routinely get on base. He hit .302 with Tucson for the season, but his power numbers were low, including only one home run and 29 RBIs in 83 games. Recalled by the Astros in September, he played in only three more games.

Servais and Taubensee remained as the Astros' primary catchers in 1992, and Tucker played most of the 1993 season with Tucson, where he helped the Toros win the Pacific Coast League championship over Portland. He was the Most Valuable Player in the championship series, hitting .391 with one home run and five RBIs.[11] He got a September call-up to the Astros, starting seven of the Astros' final 18 games.

Tucker had decided to change his hitting approach a few years earlier. More of a contact hitter than a power hitter, mainly hitting between the left-field and right-field gaps and not striking out much, he came to realize he would have to add more power to better his chances of reaching the big leagues. In 1990 he had gone to San Diego in the offseason to work with former major leaguer Deron Johnson on his new hitting approach. Tucker recalled, "I put myself in a sink-or-swim situation with this change." By the end of the 1993 season, his confidence in his hitting had improved, and he was starting to realize the benefits of the change.

Tucker was one of four catchers competing for the Astros' catcher job in 1994. Tony Eusebio came onto the scene in spring training, making for a difficult decision by Astros manager Terry Collins.[12] Since Tucker did not have a guaranteed contract, he was sent back to Tucson. With the help of hitting coach Dave Engle, Tucker had a breakout year with Tucson, accomplishing career highs in batting average (.321), home runs (14), and RBIs (80). He finished second in the Astros minor-league system for RBIs, and was the best defensive catcher in the Pacific Coast League with a .993 fielding average.[13] However, in August Tucker was hit in the face by a pitched ball. "I never felt like I fully recovered from that injury," he recalled. "I lost my comfort factor in the batter's box. In a way, it turned out to be the beginning of the end of my career."

Meanwhile, major-league players went on strike on August 12. In September the remainder of the regular season and the postseason were officially canceled.[14] A court ruling brought an end to the strike on March 31, 1995. The start of the 1995 season was delayed until April 25 to allow for an abbreviated spring-training extension.[15] Tucker recalled, "It was hectic because of the late start. There was a hurry to get things going, getting pitchers up to speed in order to be ready for the regular season. However, it was exciting when I made the major-league roster out of spring training."

Tucker hit his only major-league home run on May 6, off St. Louis Cardinals pitcher Ken Hill. (He recalled that when an Astros coach attempted to retrieve the home-run ball from the stands, he asked the fan who caught the ball, "What would it take to get the ball?" The fan responded, "A new ball," obviously having little regard for catching the first home-run ball of a little-known rookie like Tucker.)

Tucker played in five games for the Astros before being traded on May 15 to the Cleveland Indians for pitcher Matt Williams. The Indians' regular catcher, Sandy Alomar Jr., had been on the disabled list since the beginning of the season, leaving veteran Tony Peña to perform most of the everyday catching duties. Tucker was acquired to serve as a backup for the 38-year-old Peña.

The Indians were loaded with big-name players that season. In addition to Peña and Alomar, veterans Dave Winfield and Eddie Murray, who later became Baseball Hall of Fame inductees, were the designated hitters. Omar Vizquel, Jim Thome, Manny Ramirez, Albert Belle, Carlos Baerga, and Kenny Lofton were regular position players. Orel Hershiser, Dennis Martinez, Charles Nagy, and Jose Mesa highlighted the pitching staff. "I couldn't believe all the talent on this team," Tucker said. "It was a unique, awesome experience being around the caliber of those players. What really impressed me were the leadership, work ethic, and attention to details many of them brought to the team."

With the Indians on their way to winning 100 games in the strike-shortened season, the recently opened Jacobs Field was selling out many games. Tucker observed, "There was a fan resurgence going in Cleveland. They were really paying attention to the details of the games. For example, I was once congratulated by a fan after a game for laying down a sacrifice bunt, because it had been instrumental in winning a game."

Tucker played in 17 games for the Indians, primarily as a late-inning replacement for Peña. He aggravated a rib-cage muscle on his left side, but nursed himself through the injury rather than go on the disabled list. He wanted to remain active so that he could stay around for what he saw as a potentially pennant-winning team. However, Tucker became expendable when Alomar returned from the disabled list in late June. He figured he would be sent to Triple-A Buffalo after clearing waivers and then rejoin the team in September to continue being part of a championship club. Furthermore, Tucker was optimistic that he and Alomar would be the catching tandem in 1996.

But the Atlanta Braves altered Tucker's hopeful course when they claimed him off waivers. He didn't get his shot at experiencing the Indians' American League pennant-winning team and their first World Series appearance since 1954. Tucker finished the season with the Braves' Triple-A club in Richmond.

Disappointed with the outcome of the 1995 season and unable to regain his hitting edge after being hit in the face a year earlier, Tucker decided to retire. However, Kansas City's manager, Bob Boone, persuaded him to come to spring training with the Royals in 1996. Tucker signed with the Royals in December 1995. He spent part of the 1996 season with Triple-A Omaha and then retired from playing baseball, his dream ending at age 29.

Tucker's major-league career included 51 games played, a .126 batting average, one home run, and seven RBIs in 103 at-bats. His minor-league stats included 744 games, a .276 average, 32 home runs, and 342 RBIs during parts of nine seasons.

Tucker worked for a home manufacturing and development company from 1996 until 2004. He also worked with a recreation ministry in Pensacola, Florida, for five years and conducted sports clinics in Korea and Russia.

In 2007, at the age of 40, Tucker started tinkering with baseball again, when a friend of his got a job with an independent minor-league team in Pensacola. Tucker offered to pitch batting practice and, as he put it, "an itch became a rash" to return to baseball in some capacity. It also rekindled his thoughts when he retired that he might want to coach one day.

After some part-time scouting for the New York Mets in 2010 and 2011, Tucker got back into baseball full time with the Cleveland Indians organization in 2012 as a hitting coach for the Class A Carolina Mudcats. He felt that he was a great fit in the Indians organization and managed the Class A Lake County Captains in 2013. He returned to the Mudcats in 2014 as manager and in 1915 was promoted to minor-league catching instructor.

Tucker married Teresa Coghlan, whom he met while attending Delta State, on November 9, 1991. They have four daughters, Courtney, Torey, Hailey, and Anna Grace. Tucker was named to Washington School's Sports Hall of Fame in 1990 and the Delta State University Hall of Fame in 2002.[16]

SOURCES

In addition to the sources cited in the Notes, the author also consulted:

Delta State University Baseball 1987.

Gillette, Gary, and Pete Palmer, eds. *The ESPN Baseball Encyclopedia, Fifth Edition* (New York: Sterling, 2008).

Johnson, Lloyd, and Miles Wolff, eds. *Encyclopedia of Minor League Baseball, Third Edition* (Durham: Baseball America, 2007).

Simpson, Allan, ed. *Baseball America 1996 Almanac* (Durham: Baseball America Inc., 1995).

Scooter Tucker telephone interviews with author, November 12, 2014, and December 8, 2014. Except where cited, the information for this biography was obtained in these interviews.

NOTES

1 *The Sporting News*, April 6, 1992: S-22.
2 *Cleveland Indians Information & Record Book 2012*, 255.
3 *San Francisco Giants Information Guide 1991*, 120.
4 Ibid.
5 bghotrodsblog.mlblogs.com/2013/08/31/scooter-tucker-one-of-the-mwls-marathon-men/.
6 *San Francisco Giants Information Guide 1991*, 120.
7 *Houston Astros Media Guide 1995*, 101.
8 *The Sporting News*, October 28, 1991: 23.
9 *The Sporting News*, December 16, 1991: 35.
10 *The Sporting News*, June 29, 1992: 20.
11 *Houston Astros Media Guide 1995*: 101.
12 *The Sporting News*, March 28, 1994: 22.
13 *Houston Astros Media Guide 1995*: 101.
14 Alan Schwarz, "Damaging Labor Impasse Casts Black Cloud Over Baseball," *Baseball America 1996 Almanac*, 5-9.
15 Ibid.
16 *Cleveland Indians Information & Record Book 2012*: 255.

OMAR VIZQUEL

BY AUGUSTO CÁRDENAS

Venezuela has been a cradle of shortstops since 1950, when Alfonso "Chico" Carrasquel made his debut in the majors with the Chicago White Sox.

In his steps followed Luis Aparicio, the only Venezuelan in the Hall of Fame in Cooperstown, David Concepción, Ozzie Guillén, and then another shortstop who played more games at that position than at any other in the majors: Omar Enrique (González) Vizquel.

Vizquel was born in Caracas on April 24, 1967, to Omar Santos Vizquel and Eucaris González, the eldest of three children. He has a younger brother, Carlos Alberto (born 1970), and Gabriela (1980).

"My dad was an electrician in Caracas. My mother was a woman of the household, enterprising, with a very strong character," Vizquel remembered. "We are a very close family, very quiet."[1]

"I grew up in a neighborhood called Bloques de Santa Eduvigis. That is the height of Palos Grandes, in Caracas. There I attended the Santa Gema School for two years, and then we moved to a neighborhood called El Cafetal, where I attended the Josefa Irausquín López School. There I spent most of my school until I graduated and went to Antonio López Méndez School," he recalled. "I ended up graduating in Francisco Espejo College, in El Cafetal. That was the year I received an offer to sign a professional baseball contract. ... so I did not attend my graduation party but traveled directly to the United States, after I finished the school year, in 1984."

His love for baseball was instilled by his father, who passed away in 2016.

"My dad played on an amateur team and took me to the games on weekends. That began to motivate me, and I grew to love the game. I was given a Venezuelan brand Tamanaco baseball glove, blue, that was one of my favorites, and with that I started playing baseball to follow the footsteps of my father."

He played baseball in his spare time. "All my friends always invited me to play and I was very happy at Santa Eduvigis blocks with all those friends playing with balls that we (made) with adhesive tape and guava sticks that we used as a bat."

When he was 8, Omar's father took him to the Lyceum Gustavo Herrera to join a children's team, Gran Mariscal, of the Leoncio Martinez League, an affiliate of the Criollitos of Venezuela Corporation, a youth movement similar to the Little League organization.

"The coach put me to play shortstop and I was on that team until I was 16 years old."

With Gran Mariscal Vizquel developed his skills and managed to represent Miranda state in several national and international tournaments, along with another future big leaguer, Carlos Hernández, who caught for the Los Angeles Dodgers.

In 1977, in a Little League Baseball World Series, contested by 12 countries at Universitario Stadium in Caracas, Vizquel's glove work began winning him fans and was instrumental in Venezuela's winning the title. He was only 10 years old.

"At that age you do not feel that you are famous or anything. You are simply playing sports, and not looking to see if you are in newspapers or anything like that," he said. "But the organizers noticed, and when you went to a national or other World Series, your name would stand out. Two years after that World Series, I went to a national tournament, where I won the award for the best infielder. Every two years I was going to a National and I represented Miranda state a couple of times, and I won the best infielder award, and I was invited to numerous competitions."

These tournaments were played in one of the stadiums of the Venezuelan professional baseball league before winter league games, so Vizquel had the opportunity to meet some of his predecessors, Chico Carrasquel, Aparicio, and Concepcion, his main idol and the starting shortstop for the Cincinnati Reds, who also played in Venezuela with Tigres de Aragua.

"We did not go often to the stadium to watch the winter ballgames, just when Dave Concepción was going to play with Tigres de Aragua. My dad, who was a big fan of Dave Concepción, took me to see him play and we sat in the third-base stands to see him play ball," he recalled. "I really liked his style and I followed in his career when he was with the Cincinnati Reds. That's why I wore the famous number 13 in my career, in honor of Dave Concepción."

The shortstop of the Big Red Machine was a big influence and motivation to Vizquel when he decided to pursue the dream of becoming a professional baseball player.

"When I was 14, I knew I had skills to play the sport, and this was actually when I started to get serious with baseball. Back then I worshipped Dave Concepción. I followed his games, was more aware of the details of how he made a double play, how he fielded a grounder, to get the right position when fielding, all these little things that could help me to develop my own game. I also went to a clinic that Alfonso Carrasquel gave and I began attending activities that had to do with baseball to learn a little bit more about it."

One of his teammates on the Gran Mariscal team was Luis Morales, son of Pablo Morales Chirinos, one of the owners of Leones del Caracas, the Venezuelan Winter League team to which he was invited to attend practices at age 16.

"When I went to train with Leones del Caracas, I met Marty Martínez that afternoon, a scout for the Seattle Mariners. In two days I had signed a contract. I was very lucky, because there were players who were training three to four months and had not been offered a contract. But with me it was different. I had just two days' training and Marty had offered me a contract to go play with the Mariners. I was very lucky."

Vizquel signed as a free agent with a nonguaranteed bonus of $4,500, in 1984. He received $2,500 up-front with the rest to come in installments of $500 at each step up the ladder.

He immediately went to America and played Rookie League ball with the Butte Copper Kings; he hit for a .311 average in 15 games.

"The minor-league process was normal. Every year I had the opportunity to move to a different league. I started in rookie league, because I was 16, and then I was promoted to Class-A short-season ball (1985 Bellingham Mariners), then to Class A (1986, Wausau Timbers), and then switched to Class A Advanced (1987, Salinas Spurs). At each level, I was able to develop further."

His participation in winter ball with Leones del Caracas also helped him mature as a player and to better develop his skills.

"When I was in Class A I was added to the roster of Leones del Caracas, playing as a 19-year-old with players from Double A and Triple A. When I got to Double A, I got the chance to play as a starting shortstop in Venezuela and I think that made me a much faster player, because I was already playing with major-league players. I remember that Andrés Galarraga was the first baseman, Baudilio "Bo" Díaz was catching, Antonio "Tony" Armas was one of the outfielders, along with Lloyd McClendon and Donell Nixon; Jesús Alfaro was at third base and Edgar Cáceres at second. I was the youngest guy and I had the nickname 'Chamo Menudo,' because the youth music group Menudo was the band of the moment."

That experience helped Vizquel on his journey through Double A (Vermont Mariners) and Triple A (Calgary Cannons), in 1988, when he became a switch-hitter on the recommendation of Mariners hitting instructor Bobby Tolan.

"In 1988 they took me to the Instructional League to learn to bat left-handed, because they saw that my right-side numbers were a little weak. They thought that batting lefty I could exploit a little more speed and batting skills; it was a change that benefited me a lot and maybe was the key to success for me in the big leagues."

During 1989 spring training the Mariners had Rey Quiñones as first-string shortstop, but he reported late because of a contract dispute, which began to open the doors of the majors to the young Venezuelan shortstop.

"Supposedly that year I had to go to Triple A, but with Quiñones out, Mario Díaz had to play," Vizquel recalled. "He was the shortstop in Triple A and had good numbers, but was injured during spring training and there was nobody else to play shortstop so they threw me into the ring to see what I could do and I surprised the manager, Jim Lefebvre."

Díaz injured his right elbow and Vizquel had the opportunity to display his defensive talents, and he impressed Lefebvre, despite his weaknesses as a batter.

"He liked the way I played, how I defended, and he knew I was learning to bat from the left side that year, but I knew it was going to get difficult to stay in the big leagues, but they made the decision, traded Rey Quiñones to the Pirates, and left Mario Díaz as the utility player, because he continued to suffer arm problems. That left me as the shortstop."

At just 21 years old, a few days shy of 22, Vizquel received the news on the last day of spring training.

"I had to ask one of the coaches, 'What do I do with my bags? Am I going to Triple A? Am I going to be in the big leagues? I need to know, because people are packing,'" he recalled. "I was not told I was going to be the team's shortstop until the last day of spring training. After the final out, they gave me the news. It was a total surprise because the last thing I thought was that I was staying in the majors that year."

Vizquel's debut came on Opening Day, April 3, 1989, at the Oakland Coliseum, facing the reigning American League champions, the Oakland Athletics. Vizquel was not the only rookie debuting in Lefebvre's lineup. So was Ken Griffey Jr., from the start a media sensation.

Vizquel did not make the best of impressions in his debut, with a fielding error on Carney Lansford's roller in the third inning, followed by a Mark McGwire home run, which made all the difference in the A's 3-2 win over the Mariners.

"I felt bad for the error, but I never felt that I was going to be affected by it in the future. They had already given me the confidence to go out and play my game. The manager told me, 'We know you're not ready for this kind of work, but we like the way you play and you will be our regular shortstop.'"

Vizquel's first campaign was not his most productive. He finished with a .220 batting average, the lowest of his career, but he learned how to handle the pressure of playing as a shortstop in major-league baseball.

"I had many things against me. First, I was learning to bat from the left side; it was not going to be easy to learn to bat left-handed against big-league pitchers. The Mariners knew that I wasn't really ready to play in the majors, but I got the job and they gave me the opportunity. By asking questions, and working all day every day with the guys who were there, like Alvin Davis, Harold Reynolds, who were regulars in the organization, learning the little things they were always telling me – how to bat from the left side, it all helped me gradually to become a better player."

Vizquel began the 1990 season on the disabled list after suffering a sprained MCL in the left knee; he played in only 81 games, batting .247 and making seven errors. He played 142 games in 1992; his batting average slipped to .230. Nevertheless, Seattle remained confident in his abilities.

"Obviously the bat was not the reason that I was in the majors. That's for sure. It was the way I played and my glove," he said. "The glove was my best asset, and I could steal some bases, could play the ball, could do hit-and-run. Those are the things that you try to instill in young boys today who expect to reach the majors just hitting all the time. There are other things you have in your repertoire that you can develop, and you can stay in the majors doing small things. That was my case."

By 1992 Vizquel was considered one of the best defensive shortstops in the American League. That season he made only seven errors for a .989 fielding percentage, the best in the majors. For the first time he was a candidate for the Gold Glove Award, though Cal Ripken Jr. got the nod.

"I was very pleased with the work I had done, so was the organization, and that was all that interested me," said Vizquel, who hit a strong .294 that season. "I was improving my game in both batting and fielding."

His reward came the following year, when he turned 108 double plays, tied for the league lead. His fielding percentage of .980 and the growing appreciation of his talent combined to win him his first Gold Glove. One standout moment occurred on April 22, when he preserved Chris Bosio's no-hitter against the Red Sox by making a barehanded grab of an Ernest Riles chopper and firing to first for the last out of the game.

Vizquel felt settled in Seattle, where he took up residence and married his first wife, Nicole Tonkin, but his plans changed when he was surprised with the news that he had been sent to the Cleveland Indians on December 20, 1993, in a trade for Félix Fermín, Reggie Jefferson, and cash. The Mariners were making room for a talented youngster named Alex Rodríguez.

"When I got the news that they traded me to Cleveland I felt pretty bad. I was down. I wanted to be on a team for 20 years. I did not want to move anywhere else," he said. "I felt good with the Mariners. I had married that year, had bought my house. It was like they gave me a slap in the face, and I had to move to another organization where I knew no one.

"The first time you are traded you think about a lot of things. The first is that the team does not like you, that they trade you because they don't like what you're doing. But I took it otherwise. I took it the positive side. When I got to spring training and met the players and the kind of talent that the team had, I felt much better and I clicked very well on that team. With all the Latin players there, I had a very good time that year with the Cleveland Indians."

Vizquel joined a group of Latinos who helped the Indians change their image from that of a perennial loser, which was satirized in the 1989 movie *Major League*. The Indians had put together a very competitive club in 1994 with Manny Ramírez, Carlos Baerga, Sandy Alomar Jr., Tony Peña, Dennis Martínez, José Mesa, Julián Tavárez, Álvaro Espinoza, Rubén Amaro Jr., and Candy Maldonado.

That group, together with Kenny Lofton, Albert Belle, Jim Thome, Eddie Murray, Charles Nagy, and Jack Morris, helped the Indians to a 66-47 mark, just a game behind the Chicago White Sox for the American League Central lead when the season was suspended because of the players strike.

"You could tell that team was coming together well," said Vizquel. "We had good chemistry and everyone was filled with confidence. The team chemistry was growing and we thought we had a chance to be champions that year; however the strike prevented us finishing the season."

Vizquel, who on April 7 that year got the first stolen base in the history of Jacobs Field, the Indians' new home ballpark, won the second of nine consecutive Gold Gloves in the American League.

There was no strike to stop the 1995 Indians, who were reinforced by veterans like Orel Hershiser and Dave Winfield, and reached their first World Series since 1954.

"In 1995 we felt like we were indestructible," Vizquel said. "We felt that no one could beat us. We had offense, pitching, we ran bases. We had a great team. I was very happy that we finally got to where any player wants to go: the World Series."

The Tribe swept the Red Sox in three games in the Division Series and dispatched the Seattle Mariners in six games in the American League Championship Series, after having 100 victories in a regular season limited to 144 games by the delayed start of the season.

"With this record we looked unbeatable. I never thought we were going to lose, even with the pitching of the Atlanta Braves, but certainly we lacked experience," he said. "I think that was the only thing we lacked; the Braves had a team with more postseason experience."

The Braves, with the future Hall of Famer Bobby Cox as manager, had reached the fall classic in 1991 and 1992, but in 1995 their pitching looked even better with future immortals Greg Maddux, Tom Glavine, and John Smoltz.

"We were like wild horses. What we did was just play ball, score runs, stole bases, and they played a different style of baseball, pitching around," said the Venezuelan, who in his first postseason hit just .138. "They could score two runs and win a game with their relievers. That was what happened. We couldn't hit. Their pitching was dominant. With these three future Hall of Famers (Maddux, Glavine, and Smoltz) it was difficult for us to see the light and we lost that World Series."

In 1997 Vizquel returned to the fall classic with the Indians after playing a key role in eliminating the defending champion New York Yankees in five games in the ALDS.

With the Yankees ahead in the series, two games to one, Vizquel forced a fifth and deciding game at Jacobs Field, hitting a single that drove in Marquis Grissom from second base in a 3-2 walk-off victory. The Tribe won the next day, 4-3. Vizquel ended the series with a .500 (9-for-18) batting average and four stolen bases.

In the ALCS the Indians had their revenge on the Baltimore Orioles, who had eliminated them in 1996, and beat them in six games to advance to the World Series against the Florida Marlins.

"We thought we had more experience than the Marlins. It was a fairly new team, which came almost all from different teams, and we thought we could win."

Vizquel was never closer to winning a World Series ring than that year and again was a key to forcing a decisive contest, Game Six of the Series.

The Marlins led the Series three games to two. In Game Six at Miami's Pro Player Stadium, Cleveland had a 4-1 lead after five innings, due in large part to Vizquel's glove. In the sixth inning, with men on second and third and two outs, the Marlins' Charles Johnson hit a grounder in the hole and Vizquel made a spectacular diving catch to throw him out at first and prevent two runs from scoring.

"Everyone in Cleveland will remember that play, because of the magnitude of the moment. World Series plays are special moments," he said. "It was the biggest play of my career. Logically the moment marked that play. When I talk about the Seattle Mariners, people always remember the play in Chris Bosio's no-hitter. If I had to pick one play, it would be the World Series one, but if you talk about Omar Vizquel the infielder, people always remember the barehanded plays because I made it very often and it's like a brand, the dude grasping a ball without a glove. I'm also recognized by that."

In the deciding Game Seven, with Cleveland two outs away from winning the ultimate prize, the Marlins tied the game in the ninth inning and then won it, 3-2, in 11 innings on Edgar Renteria's walk-off hit.

"We went to Game Seven and couldn't achieve the ultimate victory. It was a game that went to extra innings and in extra innings anything can happen," Vizquel said. "I think that the beauty of this Series was going to Game Seven. It's like a dream that everybody has: Play the seventh game of the World Series. There is no further, everyone is watching the game, and everything is magnified three times. The challenge to be there playing and trying to do your best for your team was one of the things that has filled me as a player. Knowing that I could handle that moment, because not everyone can handle that kind of pressure, made me feel very good about myself."

In 2001, Vizquel won his ninth Gold Glove, matching the American League record held by Hall of Famer Luis Aparicio. He also played in his last postseason.

The golden years of the Tribe were over. Only Vizquel and Jim Thome remained from the winning core that had been formed in the mid-'90s.

Thome left as a free agent after the 2002 season, in which Vizquel set career highs in home runs (14) and RBIs (72), and took part in his third and final All-Star Game, being the sole representative of the Tribe.

The Indians were rebuilding in 2003 and Vizquel, with an injured right knee, played in just 64 games. In 2004, at the age of 37, he returned with a solid .291 average, but the Indians had other plans for 2005 and gave the position to rookie Jhonny Peralta.

"Everybody had already left the team. I was the last that remained of that generation that made the playoffs, the World Series," Vizquel noted. "That's why the people of Cleveland showed me so much affection. But this is a business. I was fortunate that I lasted 11 years in the organization. They treated me great, and I will always take pride in those years."

On November 16, 2004, Vizquel signed a three-year, $12.25 million deal with the San Francisco Giants, moving his magic glove and experience to the National League.

"I knew I still had a lot of baseball ahead. (The Indians) believed that I was going downhill. The knee operation affected me and I think that influenced their decision to let me go. When San Francisco signed me, thank God I made it to a number-one organization, one where I felt good, was offered all possible respect, and could even trust myself. That helped me win two more Gold Gloves at the age of 38 and 39 years."

In 2005 Vizquel had a brilliant debut in the Bay Area, winning his 10th Gold Glove to surpass Luis Aparicio's record for the most Gold Gloves won by a Venezuelan. The following year he repeated the honor and became the oldest shortstop to obtain the distinction.

On May 13, 2007, Vizquel broke the record for most career double plays turned by a shortstop after reaching 1,591, surpassing the 1,590 of Ozzie Smith. His years as a regular shortstop ended the following season, but not until after he established a major-league record for most games for a shortstop with 2,584, surpassing another mark held by Luis Aparicio. When he retired, Vizquel's career total at shortstop was 2,709.

He maintained his physical condition at the highest level, despite his 41 years, but clubs were not very interested in giving him a starting spot. He was seen as a utility player and mentor of young figures, like fellow Venezuelan Elvis Andrus when Vizquel went to the Texas Rangers in 2009.

"I think he was very helpful for me," Andrus said of Vizquel. "And I imagine, putting myself in his shoes, it's hard to play your whole career as a starter and have to change to the role he had here, as a substitute, or as my mentor, actually. He helped me a lot and I feel super blessed. Having him in my first year in the big leagues was like having a bible of how to do things, how to play baseball, how to prepare to play. Mentally I think Omar is one of the best shortstops in the whole story and I think that he helped me very much since day one. He always gave me advice and helped me, especially during the bad times I had that year to keep focused on the positive things and never let the negative consume me. These were tips that I continue to use to this day."[2]

"It was strange to play after turning 40 and hear the comments of people saying I couldn't keep playing baseball. They were wondering if I could be a shortstop, because a 40-year-old shortstop is not the same as a 24-year-old kid in an organization. That boy is going to be as versatile as you, but they never took into account the experience, or anything like that," he said. "It was a stage, in which the mind began to change, to see the game different, with another vision, and I had to make changes, adjustments in every sense of the word, and thank God they were noticing some of the records I was setting and they offered me the opportunity to reach these personal records."[3]

In his one year with Texas he played only 62 games and made no errors, having his only perfect defensive year. On June 25, in Arizona, he surpassed Aparicio as the Venezuelan with the most major-league base hits, with 2,678.

In 2010 Aparicio graciously allowed Vizquel to wear his retired No. 11 jersey with the Chicago White Sox, after the newly-acquired utilityman failed to secure his usual number 13 – that was worn by his new manager Ozzie Guillen, who was also a Dave Concepcion fan.

"That was a truly enjoyable time, because at the time I signed with the White Sox, I was giving a baseball clinic with Luis Aparicio in Venezuela, and the question came up whether I could wear #11 in tribute to him. It was a nice gesture from him to call the owners of the White Sox and let me wear the number not only in his name but on behalf of Venezuela as well."[4]

In 2012 he signed a minor-league contract with the Toronto Blue Jays and managed to make the team in spring training. This time he wore number 17, in honor of Chico Carrasquel, because Brett Lawrie had number 13. He participated in 60 games, his last game at shortstop coming on October 3 in Toronto. In his final game, he went 1-for-3 against the Minnesota Twins, getting his 2,877th hit and passing Mel Ott on the career hits list. (Two weeks earlier, on September 19, he had collected hit number 2,874, passing Babe Ruth.) He finished his career as the only player with 24 straight seasons at shortstop and, at age 45, the oldest player to play that position.

Just other five major-league shortstops have more career hits than Vizquel: Derek Jeter, Honus Wagner, Cal Ripken Jr., Robin Yount, and Alex Rodríguez, all with over 3,000.

"I think the hits record makes me proud the most,". People believe that is the Gold Gloves one, a record hard to achieve as well. Winning 11 Gold Gloves is not easy at the highest level of baseball, but to connect for 2,800 hits, nearly 3,000, is something especially since I had never been considered a hitter."

Vizquel finished with a career line of .272/.336/.352, with 456 doubles, 77 triples, 80 home runs, 1,445 runs, 951 RBIs, and 404 steals, and he is one of just 11 players to accomplish 2.800 hits and 400 stolen bases. But his trademark was his fielding excellence.

The Venezuelan finished his career with a .9847 fielding percentage, the best in MLB history, just above Troy Tulowitzki (.9846) as of 2018. He the leader in games (2,709) and double plays (1,734) as a shortstop, and ranks third in assists (7,676). His 11 Gold Gloves ranke him second as a shortstop, just behind the 13 that the first-ballot Hall of Famer Ozzie Smith won, another glove wizard with whom he was often compared.

After 24 seasons playing in the majors, Vizquel decided to start a coaching career after spending his last four years mostly on the bench, as a utility player, passing his knowledge to young players while accumulating personal records when he got the chance to go to the field.

"I felt very happy that in each of those organizations in which I played I could break records that meant something beautiful for me on a personal level. I did not play because I wanted to break those records, I just felt really good about myself and my knees were responding fully. I was a gym freak and able to maintain my body in good shape. Even after I retired with the Blue Jays, when I was in Anaheim, I had some regret that I'd retired because I felt I could continue playing, but I was ready to be a coach."

On January 30, 2013, Vizquel was hired as a roving infield coach by the Los Angeles Angels. The next year he returned to the majors with the Detroit Tigers, who made him their first-base coach and infield and baserunning instructor. That association ended after the 2017 season.

"That's something I had to do because I want to be a manager and that was one way of preparation, hearing all the comments from the coaches. Right now I love my job. The fact that I can help a boy to develop his game pleased me very much."

Vizquel, who was a candidate to manage the Tigers in 2018 (Ron Gardenhire was hired), got his first managerial experience with Venezuela in the 2017 World Baseball Classic, but his team couldn't pass the second round.

"The WBC was spectacular. Although we didn't reach the final goal, which was to reach the last playoff, we were able to sneak into the second round. It was a shame we did not score the necessary runs and that the pitching dropped a little bit, because in a short competition anything can happen," Vizquel said. "As a first experience as a manager, I had a great time."

Vizquel came back to the White Sox organization in 2018 as the manager of their Class-A affiliate at Winston-Salem. He still resided in Seattle as of 2018, along with Blanca Garcia, his wife since 2014. They live near his two children, Nicholas, born in 1995, and Kaylee, who was adopted in 2007.

Vizquel was inducted into the Cleveland Indians Hall of Fame on June 21, 2014, and was chosen by the fans as one of the Tribe's Franchise Four in 2015, alongside Bob Feller, Tris Speaker and Thome.

Vizquel had his first shot at election to the Hall of Fame in 2018, when Chipper Jones, Vladimir Guerrero, Jim Thome, and Trevor Hoffman got the call, but he fell short with 37 percent of the votes.

"I'm very happy," he said. "When you are first eligible for the Hall of Fame you do not know what kind of support you will receive from the voters. As time goes by you can increase or you can stay in the same position. I believe that it will continue to increase, although in the sabermetrics there are numbers that do not benefit me, but who saw me playing ball knows the game, knows what I did, knows my skills, what I was able to do and that (is) not numbers. You work for that on the field and the rest is on the part of the voters to discuss it."

Nevertheless, his debut on the ballot was better than that of Aparicio, who finished with 27.8 percent in his first chance and finally made in his sixth opportunity.

"I hope he gets into the Hall of Fame, because he deserves it, but I think the change of position (from shortstop) is going to hurt him," said Aparicio. "It also depends on who else is on the ballots, but I think he's going to make it. I think about the shortstops that I saw and there is none like that little fellow, because he fields grounders like nobody else."[5]

"You flip back and see how time flew," Vizquel said. "Playing 24 seasons in the majors and having all those memories, records, and stats make me feel very humble. I never thought I could go up to the heights of a player like Luis Aparicio and get to have so many good numbers."

SOURCES

baseball-reference.com/.

baseballhall.org/hof/2018-bbwaa-ballot.

cbssports.com/mlb/news/2018-baseball-hall-of-fame-ballot-the-cases-for-and-against-omar-vizquel/.

cleveland.com/tribe/index.ssf/2018/01/path_to_cooperstown_will_not_b.html.

espn.co.uk/mlb/news/story?id=3419650.

mlb.com/es/news/tiene-autenticos-argumentos-omar-vizquel-para-el-salon-de-la-fama/c-262497102.

Vizquel, Omar, and Bob Dyer. *Omar! My Life on and Off the Field* (Cleveland: Gray & Company, Publishers, 2002).

Cárdenas Lares, Carlos Daniel. *Venezolanos en las Grandes Ligas* (Fundación Cárdenas Lares, 1994).

Various Authors. *Todo lo que usted debe saber sobre Omar Vizquel* (Grupo Editorial Macpecri, 2012).

NOTES

1 Author interview with Omar Vizquel on January, 7, 2015. Unless otherwise noted, all comments by Vizquel are from this interview.

2 Author interview with Elvis Andrus on March, 10, 2018. Unless otherwise noted, all comments by Andrus are from this interview.

3 Luis Aparicio and Augusto Cárdenas, "Mi Historia: Luis Aparicio," 2011.

DAVE WINFIELD

BY DOUG SKIPPER

It is fitting that Dave Winfield's bust at Cooperstown wears a San Diego Padres cap. Winfield was the franchise's first superstar and represented the team in the first Major League Baseball All-Star game to be hosted the by city. Long after eight magnificent and contentious seasons in San Diego, his charity work continued to impact "America's Finest City," even as he sustained his assault on pitchers in other venues. After he concluded one of the baseball's most glorious and eventful careers, the team retired the number 31 he sported on his navy blue and sand brown uniform on his sleek, powerful frame and he was named to the club's Hall of Fame.

Imposing, confident, complex, charismatic, and controversial, Winfield ranks as the greatest multi-sport athlete to emerge from the State of Minnesota. Drafted by five different teams in five leagues in three major sports, Winfield chose baseball and compiled a first-ballot Hall of Fame career.

At 6-foot-6 and 220 pounds, the powerfully-built right-hander wielded a menacing black bat. His long, sweeping swing started with a distinctive hitch. Then, with sudden ferocity, he uncoiled and laced line drives to all parts of the park; sometimes clearing fences and walls, more often slamming into them. He ran the bases aggressively and with purpose. He was a good base stealer, but a great base runner. He played defense with equal enthusiasm. Athletic and graceful, he gobbled up ground with long strides, sported a steady glove and boasted one of the most lethal throwing arms in the history of the game. Though blessed with tremendous physical ability, it was Winfield's preparation and determination, along with his ability to make adjustments at the plate and in the field that made him a player greater than his tremendous physical talent.

Winfield grew up in St. Paul and excelled in baseball and basketball at St. Paul Central High School and then at the University of Minnesota. "Winnie" averaged 10.3 points and 6.7 rebounds in 40 Gopher basketball games and posted a 19-4 record for the baseball squad. While at Minnesota, Winfield was a First Team All-America in 1973 and a two-time All-Big Ten selection in 1971 and 1973. He was 9-1 in his senior season with a 2.74 earned run average and 109 strikeouts in 82 innings of work. He batted .385 with 33 runs batted in in 130 at bats that season.

Winfield jumped straight from college to the major leagues, and compiled 3,110 hits, 465 home runs and a .283 batting average in 22 seasons with the San Diego Padres, New York Yankees, California Angels, Toronto Blue Jays, Minnesota Twins and Cleveland Indians. He played in 2,973 games, batted 11,003 times, collected 1093 extra base hits, stole 223 bases, made 5,012 putouts and 168 assists, and appeared in 12 All-Star games and two World Series. He was just the fifth player in the history of baseball to compile 3,000 hits and 450 home runs.

But there is so much more to the man than the numbers.

There is Winfield's charity. He was the first active athlete to establish a charitable foundation. For 22 years, The David M. Winfield Foundation provided health care, holiday meals, game tickets, educational scholarships, and hope to underprivileged families. Under Winfield's leadership, the foundation developed "Turn It On," an international community action campaign to prevent substance abuse. For his charitable work, Winfield has earned the YMCA Brian Piccolo Award for Humanitarian Service, baseball's first-ever Branch Rickey Community Service Award, the American League's Joe Cronin Award, the Josh Gibson Leadership Award, and Major League Baseball's Roberto Clemente Award. He was also awarded an honorary Doctorate of Laws from Syracuse University[1] and recognition by Derek Jeter's Turn2 Foundation. Jeter is one of a number of players who credit Winfield's philanthropic efforts for the inspiration for their own charitable organizations.[2]

There is Winfield's business acumen. In addition to serving as president of the Winfield Foundation for years, the big slugger from St. Paul – who once played for Padres owner and McDonald's founder Ray Kroc – possessed a string of Burger Kings, art galleries, a lighting design and contracting company, and a diverse and powerful stock portfolio. He has served on the board of directors for President Bill Clinton's National Service Program, the Morehouse School of Medicine and the Century Council and on the advisory boards for the Peace Corps and MLB's Baseball Players Trust.[3] Since December 2013, he has served as the special assistant to the executive director of the Major League Baseball Players Association (MLBPA), Tony Clark.

There is Winfield's literacy and culture. He is a prolific reader of fiction and non-fiction, collaborated on his best-selling 1988 autobiography, and outlined his plan of action to revitalize baseball in 2007 in *Dropping the Ball*. He penned *Turn It Around, There's No Place Here for Drugs*, authored *The Complete Baseball Player*, and collaborated on Frank White's *They Played for the Love of the Game: Untold Stories of Black Baseball in Minnesota*. A music lover, he served as host and narrator for the Baseball Music Project, a series of concerts that featured songs about the national pastime.[4]

There is Winfield's race relations leadership. As an African American youngster in St. Paul, and later as a major-league baseball player, Winfield encountered racism and battled it with dignity and determination. Granted a public forum by virtue of his occupation, Winfield has spoken and written about race relations, providing a powerful voice in the community. He helped develop the idea of the honoring former Negro League's stars at MLB's 2008 draft.[5]

Winfield's guidance is not restricted to race relations. A highly respected motivational speaker with a smooth, silky voice, Winfield has addressed clubs, schools, and business about sports, education, health, fitness, teamwork, substance abuse prevention, and youth issues.

There is also Winfield's ego. "Much of America's current self-esteem crisis could be overcome just with Winfield's excess," *Sports Illustrated* observed in 1992. "Nobody knows better than Winfield that he is handsome, buffed, richly appointed with all the options, well read, well-spoken and well paid."[6]

And then there is Winfield's pride. After eight successful seasons in San Diego, Winfield signed a contract with New York Yankees owner George Steinbrenner that made him the most highly paid player in baseball. But Steinbrenner quickly developed buyer's remorse, the two squabbled, "The Boss" publicly declared that Winfield was not worth the money, disparaged him, and tried to trade him. "Steinbrenner, who did so much to make Winfield's life miserable in the eight-plus years he played for the Yankees, never appreciated the type of player he had," the *New York Times* observed. "All he did was look at Winfield's hitting statistics. When they lacked lusty numbers, he criticized Winfield. Unlike players and managers from other teams, Steinbrenner never understood the contributions Winfield made with his outfield defense and his base running."[7]

Eventually Steinbrenner even went so far as to pay a known gambler to discredit his star slugger. "Winfield would become the target of owner Steinbrenner's downright vicious crusade to force him out," the *New York Times* observed later. "No doubt he is having the last laugh, but there are times when Winfield sounds like someone who succeeded in spite of his father, and sometimes feels the hurt an abused child must feel all his life." [8] Stung by Steinbrenner's criticism that he was great in the regular season and awful in his first postseason, Winfield cast off the "Mr. May" label with a strong 1992 World Series performance. He earned the Babe Ruth Award as the player with the best performance in the Fall Classic, and placed his decade of discontent with the Yankees behind him. After Winfield revived his career in California, won a World Series in Toronto, collected his 3,000th career hit in Minnesota, and closed out his playing days in Cleveland, he and the Boss made a form of peace.[9]

In recent years, Winfield also made peace in his complicated personal life. Devoted to the mother who raised him, he reconnected with his father after her 1988 death. That same year he married, and formed a relationship with a child from a previous relationship. Later, he fathered two more children with his wife Tonya. As a special assistant to the executive director of the Major League Baseball Players Association., he travels the world as an ambassador for baseball, delivers motivational speeches, continues his charitable work, and spends time with his family.[10]

David Mark Winfield was born in St. Paul on October 3, 1951 – the day that Bobby Thomson hit "The Shot Heard Round the World," the pennant-winning home run for the New York Giants. David was the second son for Frank Charles Winfield, a World War II veteran and a Pullman porter on the Great Northern Railroad's flagship train, the *Empire Builder*, and Arline Vivian (Allison) Winfield, a St. Paul native. Frank, who lived in Duluth before he entered military service, met Arline through her brother. The couple divorced by the time David turned 3, and Frank eventually moved to Seattle, remarried and became a skycap for Western Airlines. Though they saw one another on occasion, David and his father remained estranged for much of their lives.[11]

Arline, who never remarried, raised David and his older brother Stephen in their home in a row house on Carroll Avenue, west of the state capital and just south of the swath that Interstate 94 now cuts through St. Paul. Arline earned a modest living at her job in the St. Paul School District's audio-visual department, and raised her sons with the assistance of her mother, Jessie Hunt Allison, who lived a block away, and an extended family of aunts, uncles and cousins. Arline stressed the value of education to her sons, showed them educational films she borrowed from the school district, and taught them a new word every night. The family lived in a primarily African American neighborhood and worshipped at the African Methodist Episcopal St. James Church on Central Avenue, a couple blocks north of their home.[12] "More than anything Ma and I *did*, I learned from the example she set, learned the value of education, family, work and a positive attitude,"[13]

As youngsters, Dave and Steve played baseball and hockey in St. Paul, and followed the Minnesota Twins when they moved to the Upper Midwest in 1961. Bill Petersen, a former University of Minnesota catcher, coached the pair at the Oxford Playgrounds, and the Winfield boys later led his Attucks-Brooks Post 606 baseball team to two American Legion state championships.[14]

The brothers also excelled at St. Paul Central High School, at the corner of Marshall and Lexington. Steve lettered in baseball three times, captained the team his senior season, 1968, and was named to the school's Athletic Hall of Fame in September 2007. Younger brother Dave earned All-St. Paul and All-Minnesota honors in both baseball and basketball for the Minutemen, and was named to the Central's Athletic Hall of Fame in 1995.

At the end of his senior year, Dave stood 6-foot-6 when on June 5, 1969, the Baltimore Orioles selected the younger Winfield in the 40th round of baseball's amateur draft. He passed up that opportunity, and accepted a baseball scholarship from the University of Minnesota, where older brother Steve was already enrolled.

The scholarship covered only tuition, and as a freshman, Winfield commuted 12 miles by public bus each day to attend class, to play forward for the freshman basketball team and pitch for the freshman baseball squad. He went 4-0 for the Gopher frosh in the spring of 1970, then 8-0 in the Metropolitan (St. Paul) Collegiate League that summer, before he and a friend were caught snatching a pair of snow blowers from a local business. Winfield pled guilty to a charge of felony theft and was sentenced to three years in the St. Cloud Penitentiary, a sentence that was suspended, and years later, based on his public service and good works, expunged.[15]

Winfield made a repentant return to campus and embraced his second chance. He and Steve led a team dubbed "The Soulful Strutters" to the campus intramural basketball championship, and were invited to scrimmage regularly against the Gopher junior varsity.[16] After he posted an 8-3 record and a Big Ten-best 1.48 earned run average for Dick Siebert's Minnesota varsity baseball team, Winfield pitched and played outfield for the Fairbanks Goldpanners of the Alaska Summer League, coached by college baseball legend Jim Dietz.[17]

Back on campus for his third year in the fall of 1971, Winfield worked out with the junior varsity basketball team, where he caught the eye of Gopher assistant coach Jimmy Williams. Williams invited him to try out for new head coach Bill Musselman, and Winfield earned a spot on a veteran squad that included Jim Brewer, Ron Behagen, Clyde Turner, Keith Young, Bob Murphy, Bob Nix, and Corky Taylor. The veterans were slow to accept Winfield, but he won them over with his hard work, hustle and powerful elbows.[18] "He was the best rebounder I ever saw," Musselman, who would go on to coach in the American and National Basketball Associations, later said.[19]

"Making the team, I give up my half baseball scholarship for a full basketball scholarship," Winfield's autobiography stated. "Anyway, for the first time I can go to classes, go to practices, live away from home, and not have to worry whether I'll be able to afford my meals, my books, or transportation."[20]

If life was more settled off the court, it was frantic on the hardwood, where Musselman coached his players to be aggressive and physical, a style Winfield embraced. "From Musselman I learned to get on that man, to get inside his jersey, his shorts, his jock. I learned first and foremost to *be* there. To get up in his face when he tried to dribble, and to stay there when he tried to shoot."[21]

On January 25, 1972, "Musselman's Musclemen" became too aggressive. Trailing late in a Big 10 showdown with Ohio State before a frenzied Williams Arena crowd, Taylor committed a hard foul on Ohio State center Luke Witte. The Gophers had been unhappy with the way Witte was throwing elbows during the game. When Taylor helped Witte up off the floor, he kneed him in the groin. Behagen who had fouled out earlier, jumped in off the bench, and stomped on Witte's head and neck. Quickly, the floor was a sea of players, fans, coaches and officials. Winfield, who had been sitting on the sidelines, entered the fray, running across the floor to throw punches ''like I was spring-loaded.'' Winfield later told *Sports Illustrated*, ''Hey, I'm not denying I was involved. There was a fight with my team. I was swinging.''[22] Though he was later blistered by media members, he escaped the punishment assessed Behagen and Taylor, season-ending suspensions. Instead, he stepped into Behagen's spot in the starting lineup. As one of the Gophers "Iron Five," Winfield led Minnesota to its first conference championship in 35 years and an appearance in the NCAA Tournament.

The baseball season went less well. In an early season game against Michigan, Winfield damaged tendons around his right elbow and missed the remainder of the season. Despite the injury, Dietz asked him back for the summer, and Winfield hit .315 with 15 home runs for the Goldpanners as an outfielder, and struck out 36 batters as a relief pitcher. He was named team MVP after he led Fairbanks to the ASL title.[23]

Winfield returned to campus and guided Minnesota's basketball team to a second-place Big Ten finish and a berth in the National Invitational Tournament in New York. When the Gophers were knocked out, he joined Siebert's baseball team in Texas, where he lost his season debut. After that, Winfield was magnificent. He won 13 straight, posted a 2.74 ERA, and hit .385 with 33 runs batted in to earn first-team All-America honors. Appointed team captain, Winfield led Minnesota to the Big 10 title and to the College World Series in Omaha. Along the way, he pitched a nine-inning 1-0 shutout with 14 strikeouts against Oklahoma. On the tournament's final day, the Gophers lost to Arizona State, then met Southern Cal. Thorough eight innings, Winfield limited a Trojan team that included Roy Smalley and Fred Lynn to just one hit, and struck out 15. Leading 7-0, but after nearly 140 pitches, Winfield ran out of gas and surrendered a pair of runs in the ninth. With one out, he left the mound and moved to left field. USC rallied and won 8-7. Despite a third-place finish for the Gophers, Winfield was named CWS MVP.

After the season, four different teams in four different leagues in three different sports drafted Winfield. San Diego made him the fourth pick of the major-league baseball draft on June 5. The Atlanta Hawks picked him in the fifth round of the National Basketball Association draft, the Utah Stars drafted him in the fourth round of the American Basketball Association draft, and – even though he never played high school or college football – the Minnesota Vikings selected Winfield in the 17th round of the National Football League draft. Winfield, Texas Christian's Mickey McCarty, and Colorado's Dave Logan are the only players ever drafted by professional baseball, football, and basketball teams.

Winfield signed with San Diego for $15,000 and jumped straight to the major leagues at the age of 21. He commenced his assault on big-league pitchers with a single and a stolen base in four at-bats against the Houston Astros on June 19, 1973, then collected hits in each of his next five games. Used most often in left field and against lefthanders by manager Don Zimmer, the St. Paul slugger collected 39 hits, with four doubles, a triple, and three home runs, batted .277 and drove in 12 runs in his 56-game rookie campaign. He also began to buy blocks of tickets to Padres games for families who otherwise could not afford to attend.[24]

Over the next three seasons, the youngster continued to provide tickets to poor families and power and speed to the Padre lineup. Between 1974 and 1976, he slugged 64 doubles, 10 triples, and 38 homers, despite playing his home games in cavernous Jack Murphy Stadium. He also stole 64 bases, with a career-high 26 in the bicentennial year. John McNamara, who replaced Zimmer at the start of the 1974 season, used Winfield in left and center, but most often penciled in the youngster into right field. Winfield remembered, "After the All Star Break, McNamara said to me, 'Kid, I'm going to give you a chance to play every day. Play well and the job is yours.'"[25] He did, and for his efforts, the young slugger, who created a scholarship fund for minority student athletes from St. Paul that still exists, saw his pay rise to around $40,000 in 1975 to $57,000 in 1976.[26]

Winfield was unhappy with the contract the Padres offered in 1977, and elected to play out his option at a 10 percent pay cut.[27] The contract squabble pitted him against Padres General Manager Buzzie Bavasi, and when it looked like Winfield might be dealt, signs appeared in the ballpark that urged, "Keep Dave, Trade Buzzie."[28] In early July, with the two sides $100,000 apart, Winfield's friend and representative, Al Frohman, came up with an ingenious solution. Under Frohman's plan, The David M. Winfield Foundation for Underprivileged Youth, an official 501 (c)(3) organization, was established. The team paid the Foundation the $100,000 difference between what Winfield wanted and the Padres were willing to pay, the Foundation handed it right back to the club in exchange for 100,000 game tickets at a dollar apiece, and the Foundation distributed the tickets to underprivileged families.[29] Everybody won.

Winfield got the four-year, $1.4 million contract he wanted, the Padres sold an extra 100,000 tickets, thousands of kids got to sit in the Dave Winfield Pavilion at San Diego's Jack Murphy Stadium – and Frohman picked up a sizeable commission.[30]

Winfield signed the contract in early July, in the midst of his breakout season. Just 25, he batted .275 with 25 home runs and 92 runs batted in, clubbed 29 doubles, seven triples, and was named to the National League All Star team. Winfield made the first of his 12 consecutive appearances in the Mid-Summer Classic, smacked a double and drove in the winning runs with a single off Sparky Lyle in the NL's 7-5 victory.

The Dave Winfield Foundation drew support from a number of corporations, formed a relationship with the Scripps Foundation to provide free medical checkups to needy families, and delivered an anti-drug message and provided holiday dinners and scholarships to those who otherwise could not get them.[31]

In 1978, he was named the first team captain in Padres history, was the NL Player of the Month for June, hit .300 for the first time, slugged 24 homers, 30 doubles, and five triples, drove in 97 runs and scored 104, and stole 21 bases. When San Diego hosted the All-Star Game, the Winfield Foundation bought its usual allotment of pavilion tickets. On local radio, the slugger from St. Paul, scheduled to play in his second All-Star Game, urged "all the kids of San Diego" to attend. When they responded by showing up in droves, major-league baseball opened practice sessions for the first time, starting a tradition that continues to the present day.[32] It was a highlight in a special season for San Diego. Under new manager Roger Craig, with a roster that included Winfield, Rollie Fingers, Gaylord Perry, and rookie shortstop Ozzie Smith, the Padres posted a winning record for the first time, though they finished fourth in the NL's Western Division.

A year later, San Diego slid back to 25 games under .500, though Winfield enjoyed what may have been his finest season. The 27-year old batted .308 again, with 34 home runs, 27 doubles, 10 triples, and 15 stolen bases. Winfield

drove in a career-best and NL high 118 runs, scored 97, won his first Gold Glove, and finished third in the league's Most Valuable Player Award voting behind Keith Hernandez and Willie Stargell. He drew a career-high 85 walks, and led the league in intentional passes with 25. "I became a lot more patient," Winfield said later. "I learned the strike zone a lot better and I realized that sometimes it's better to take a walk than to make an out on a bad pitch."[33]

Winfield grew less patient with the Padres, and there were suggestions that he was not a team player. "If the Padres go places, I will be a main reason," he said. "But it they falter, I'll still shine."[34] With his contract set to expire at the end of the 1980 season and no extension in sight, Winfield played in all 162 games for Jerry Coleman, his sixth manager in eight years, and won another Gold Glove, but slipped to 20 home runs, 87 RBIs, 23 steals, and a .276 batting average. When the season ended, so did his tenure as a Padre. Not everyone was sad to see him go. "Dave Winfield thinks he is holier than thou," Smith said later. "He always acted as if it were his God-given right to tell other people how to do things."[35]

On December 15, 1980, New York Yankees owner George Steinbrenner signed Winfield to a 10-year, $23.3 million contract. Slugger Dave Winfield was leaving San Diego to play at Yankee Stadium and to become baseball's highest paid player.

It seemed like a match made in heaven; it would begin a decade of pure hell between the two men. From the start, there were problems. Steinbrenner, who took great pride in his negotiation skills, didn't understand or didn't fully read the cost of living escalator clause that Frohman, a man *Sports Illustrated's* Rick Reilly described as "a rumpled and retired New York caterer, a two-pack-a-day, fast-talking, 5 ft., 4 in., 220-pound chunk of walking cholesterol – with no experience as a sports agent," had negotiated for Winfield.[36] That clause made the contract worth seven million dollars more than the $16 million that Steinbrenner thought it was worth, and when alerted by a media member, the Boss was livid.[37] It was made worse when Frohman, who collected a 15%, $3.5 million commission on the deal, reportedly told the *New York Daily News*, "If he ever touches a hair of my boy's head . . . I'll blow the lid. I've got stuff on George that if it ever came out, he would be in big trouble. It's very easy to be friends with George if you have blackmail on him."[38]

After heated exchanges, Winfield and Steinbrenner reached a compromise – an addendum to the contract that adjusted the cost of living increase, reportedly for $3 to $4 million less over the life of the contract. Winfield also reached an agreement with the Padres, mediated by Baseball Commissioner Bowie Kuhn, which called for the Dave Winfield Foundation to meet a $35,000 contractual obligation to continue to buy tickets for underprivileged children to attend Padres home games. Winfield had already arranged for $3 million ($300,000 per year for 10 years) of his salary to be donated to the Foundation, which funded the Dave Winfield nutrition center at Hackensack University Medical Center and collaborated with Merck Pharmaceuticals to create a bilingual substance abuse prevention program called "Turn it Around."[39]

In his first season in pinstripes, Winfield hit .294 with 13 homers and 68 RBIs in 105 games in the strike-shortened 1981 season. He batted .350 with two doubles and a triple to lead the first-half champion Yankees over the second-half champion Milwaukee Brewers in the AL Divisional playoffs. The Bronx Bombers went on to beat Oakland in the AL Championship Series, but with Reggie Jackson and Graig Nettles injured, and Winfield collecting only one hit in 22 at bats, dropped a 4-2 decision to the Los Angeles Dodgers in the World Series, a loss that stuck firmly in Steinbrenner's craw. After his lone hit, a single, Winfield, perhaps in jest, asked for the ball, which made the Boss even madder.[40]

The Yankees never returned to the postseason with Winfield in the lineup, though he was one of the top players in baseball over the next seven years. He was selected to play in the All-Star Game each year, won five Gold Gloves, and drove in 744 runs. In 1982, the 30-year-old slugger clubbed 37 home runs and drove in 106 runs, batted .280, and slugged a career best .560 for musical chairs managers Bob Lemon, Dick Howser, and Clyde King. A year later, Winfield batted .283 with 32 homers and 116 RBIs for Billy Martin, but the most notable day of his season came on August 4, 1983. Warming up in the outfield before the bottom of the fifth inning, Winfield hit and killed a seagull with a throw at Toronto's Exhibition Stadium. When he tipped his cap in a mock salute to the bird, the hometown crowd reacted by hurling obscenities and objects at him. When the game ended, Winfield was escorted to the Ontario Provincial Police station, booked on charges of cruelty to animals and forced to post a $500 bond before he was released, Martin joked, "It's the first time he's hit the cutoff man."[41] After the charges were dropped the next day, Winfield remarked to the media. "I am truly sorry that a fowl of Canada is no longer with us."[42] Although Winfield attempted to placate them,[43] Blue Jays fans booed Winfield every time he appeared in Toronto until he joined the Jays in 1992.[44]

In 1984, Winfield and Yankee teammate Don Mattingly waged a dramatic and wrenching race for the AL batting title. Winfield homered 19 times, drove in 100 runs, and batted .340, but Mattingly collected four hits – and a standing ovation each time he batted – against Detroit on the season's final day to finish at .343. The two walked off the field together with clasped hands after the finale, but Winfield was clearly hurt that many of his teammates – and the Yankee ownership – had openly rooted for Mattingly, who was white, over Winfield, a black man. "Most of their teammates were clearly pulling for Mattingly, raising questions about the possibility of race as a factor," the *New York Times* later observed.[45] "I've experienced racism in my life," Winfield told sportscaster and writer Art Rust, Jr. "It was all around me when I was on the Yankees and competing with Don Mattingly for the batting title. Here we both were, two guys on the same team, fighting one another for the same thing against a background of manipulative media and the perceptions of hundreds of thousands of fans that were created by that media. There was a vast difference in the amount of encouragement each of us got from the press and the public."[46] Winfield cleaned out his locker and left without speaking to the media after the final game, and some suggested he was resentful of Mattingly. ''There was nothing between Donnie and I,'' Winfield later said. "We lived different lives. He was a young player who had a lot of support. I just know what I experienced the entire year. It was much different than my teammate did at the same time.'' [47]

Already strained by the Boss's buyer's remorse and his attempt to deal his big slugger to Texas in 1984, the relationship between Steinbrenner and Winfield worsened in 1985, though New York's best all-around player drove in 114 runs, batted .275, scored 105 times and clubbed 26 home runs for Yogi Berra and Martin. Late in the season, with the Yankees out of the postseason for a fourth straight year, the Boss said bitterly, "I got rid of Mr. October (Reggie Jackson) and got Mr. May (Winfield)."[48] Winfield later told the *New York Times*, "It was irreverent, it was off-color, it was improper, it doesn't fit. I always rejected it. It doesn't apply. It was an inappropriate remark at the time. I didn't appreciate it then.'' [49]

Nor did he appreciate Steinbrenner's attempts – public or private – to ruin his reputation, even as he smacked 76 homers and drove in 308 runs between 1986 and 1988 for Lou Piniella and again under Martin. In 1986, Steinbrenner ordered Piniella to platoon Winfield; when he refused, the owner was livid.[50] In 1987, the Boss began to withhold payments he owed to his star slugger to be donated to the Winfield Foundation, despite three court orders to make the payments. Winfield and his new agent, Jeffrey Klein, endured lengthy, heated meetings with Steinbrenner's acerbic attorney, Roy Cohn, often on game days.[51] When Winfield sued, the Boss countersued to have Winfield removed from leadership from the foundation, suggesting that Winfield was running the foundation for personal gain and that his star slugger could not be trusted. A report in *Newsday* suggested that the foundation spent $6 for every $1 it gave away; Steinbrenner's lawyers provided the numbers. ''There is no way to fathom what was being done to me,'' Winfield told Reilly. ''It was immoral, improper and reprehensible. It was a battle for everything, your performance, your credibility. Do you know what it's like to have people fooling with your career?'' [52]

Steinbrenner continued to make his managers bench or move Winfield down in the batting order, tried to trade him to the Detroit Tigers for Kirk Gibson in 1987, and stepped up the efforts just before Winfield's 1988 autobiography, *Winfield, A Player's Life*, was published.[53] But with 10 seasons in the majors and five for the same team, Winfield could not be traded without his consent. At times, Winfield was able to joke about the situation. "These days baseball is different. You come to spring training; you get your legs ready, your arms loose, your agents ready, your lawyer lined up."[54] After setting an AL record with 29 RBIs in April 1988, he quipped, "We go on to May, and you know about me and May."[55] Whatever levity he might have felt faded away in the Fall of 1988. His mother Arline died of breast cancer in October; he suffered a herniated disk and endured offseason back surgery. He was forced to miss the entire 1989 season, which ended his string of 12 straight All Star Game appearances. And when it looked like things between he and Steinbrenner could not get worse, they did.

Back in 1981, Frohman had introduced Winfield to Howard "Howie" Spira, a gambler with alleged mafia connections, and arranged for Winfield to make a $15,000 payment owed to Frohman instead to Spira. Five years later, Spira approached Winfield and asked for money in exchange for information that "would ruin Steinbrenner." After Winfield refused, Spira visited Steinbrenner, who was desperate for any information that would make his highly paid player look bad, and the Boss made a secret, illicit deal with the mercenary gambler. Eventually, Spira publicly accused Winfield of betting on baseball, and in the shadow of the Pete Rose investigation, the commissioner's office launched another inquisition. The investigation uncovered no evidence that Winfield had bet on baseball, but revealed that Steinbrenner had paid Spira $40,000 for his dubious information. The investigation also discovered that Steinbrenner had suggested turning over "potentially damaging" information about the Winfield Foundation to the Internal Revenue Service.[56] On June 30, 1990, Baseball Commissioner Fay Vincent ordered Steinbrenner to resign as the club's general partner and banned him from day-to-day operation of the team for life, a sanction that was lifted two and a half years later.[57] Spira was later found guilty of trying to extort an additional $70,000 from Steinbrenner, and sentenced to 30 months in prison for his role in the sordid affair.[58]

In the shadow of the inquiry, Winfield began the 1990 season in pinstripes. Angry that the Yankees left him off the All-Star ballot, he batted just .213 over 20 games with a pair of home runs and 19 runs batted in before the club traded him to the California Angels on May 11, 1990 for pitcher Mike Witt. Winfield argued that his contract did not allow him to be traded without his consent, but accepted a negotiated deal on May 16.[59] "It's been an ordeal to a large degree," Winfield said. "Maybe things didn't work out (in New York), but I know they are going to work out in California."[60]

Although he had moved to the opposite side of the country, Winfield continued to stick in Steinbrenner's craw. On July 6, Baseball Commissioner Fay Vincent ordered the Yankees to pay the Angels $200,000 – in addition to a $25,000 fine – for tampering with Winfield after he was traded to California.[61]

For the Angels, Winfield was brilliant. He batted .275 with 19 home runs and 72 runs batted in 112 games to earn The Sporting News AL Comeback Player of the Year honors. A year later, Winfield smacked 28 more home runs, 27 doubles, and drove in 86 runs for the Angels. He homered three times on April 13 at Minnesota and on June 24, he went 5-for-5 and hit for the cycle for the first time in his career, the oldest major-league player ever to do so, at 39. On August 14, 1991, Winfield became the 23rd player to hit 400 career home runs when he connected at his hometown ballpark, the Metrodome in Minneapolis. "Three-ninety-nine sounds like something you'd purchase at a discount store. Four hundred sounds so much better."[62] At the end of the year, he again became a free agent.

On December 19, 1991, Winfield embarked on the most successful year of his career when he signed a one-year contract with Toronto. For the 1992 AL East champs, Winfield batted .290, smacked 33 doubles and 26 homers, scored 92 runs, and drove in 108, the first 40-year old ever to drive in 100. His numbers as a designated hitter and right fielder were impressive, but it was his hard work and hustle that made him a fan favorite and earned him absolution for the seagull incident. Winfield, the Blue Jays' cleanup hitter, implored fans to be supportive of the team, and the phrase "Winfield Wants Noise" quickly appeared on t-shirts, signs and the Sky Dome scoreboard. "He is asked about his longevity," *Sports Illustrated* reported, "and he says, 'For the last few years people have seen me and acted surprised that I'm still playing. Still playing? I'm kicking butt.'"[63]

Winfield smacked a pair homers and a double in Toronto's four-games-two victory over Oakland in the AL Championship Series, then drove in three runs against Atlanta in the World Series. Two came home when he smashed a double down the third-base line in the 11th inning of the Game Six to give Toronto a 4-3 lead. When the game and the Series ended on Otis Nixon's unsuccessful bunt in the bottom half of the inning, Winfield went from "Mr. May" to "Mr. Jay." He was presented the Babe Ruth Award as the player with the best performance in the World Series. After the season, he also received the Branch Rickey Award, presented for exceptional community service.

"I've been thinking about this," Winfield told *Sports Illustrated*. "If my career had ended (before Toronto), I would not have been really happy with what baseball dealt me. I would have had no fulfillment, no sense of equity, no fairness. I feel a whole lot better now about the way things have turned out."[64]

With a World Series win under his belt, Winfield set out to accomplish another calling, playing for his hometown team. On December 17, 1992, the St. Paul native signed a free agent contract with the Minnesota Twins. In 143 games, most as Minnesota's designated hitter, he batted .271 with 21 home runs and drove in 76. On September 16, 1993, he collected his 3,000th hit, a ninth-inning single off Oakland reliever Dennis Eckersley that plated Kirby Puckett.

In 1994, at age 42, he hit 10 more home runs, but the Twins fell out of contention, and on July 31, Minnesota dealt him for to Cleveland for a player to be named later. Two weeks later, on August 12, before Winfield ever appeared as an Indian, major-league baseball players went on strike, and after a short impasse, owners cancelled the rest of the season. Winfield became a free agent in October, and Cleveland never sent a player to the Twins in the deal, but when executives of the two teams went to a dinner after the season, the Indians reportedly picked up the tab to settle the score.[65] After the season, Winfield received the Roberto Clemente Award, which annually recognizes the player who best exemplifies sportsmanship, community involvement and contribution to his team."[66]

On April 5, 1995, as baseball resumed, Winfield signed on with Cleveland. At 43, major-league baseball's oldest active player spent part of the season on the disabled list with a rotator cuff injury, appeared in 46 games, hit the 464th and 465th home runs of his career and batted .191 for the Indians, who won their first pennant in 41 years. On September 28, he rifled a pinch-hit single to center field at the Metrodome. Two days later, he collected the 3,110th and final hit of his career, at Jacobs Field, and on October 1, 1995 at Cleveland, he made his final appearance in the major leagues, a pinch-hit ground out. Cleveland won the AL title, but Winfield did not appear in the postseason. After the Indians lost a heart-wrenching World Series, the St. Paul slugger retired.

Winfield served as a Fox television baseball broadcaster, starting in 1996, hosted a Los Angeles morning drive time radio show, *On the Ball*, served as a spokesperson for the United Negro College Fund, the Drug Enforcement Administration, the Minnesota Board of Education, and the Discovery Channel. He also appeared in the film *The Last Home Run*, hosted the syndicate television show "*Greatest Sports Legends*," and appeared on *Married with Children*, the *Drew Carey Show*, and *Arli$$*.

In 1999, *The Sporting News* ranked Winfield 94th on its list of Baseball's Greatest Players, and he was nominated for MLB's All-Century Team. In 2000, he was inducted into the San Diego Padres Hall of Fame and his number 31 was retired. Winfield had one year earlier been named to the Breitbard Hall of Fame, honoring San Diego's greatest athletes, and enshrined in the San Diego Hall of Champions

Early in 2001, Winfield and Puckett each were elected to Baseball's Hall of Fame in their first year of eligibility. Steinbrenner issued a statement that said he was delighted by Winfield's election and that he was "probably one of the greatest athletes I have ever known."[67]

Steinbrenner and Winfield had started to patch up their complicated relationship a few years earlier. "All of that never should have happened," the Boss said in early 1998. "Dave Winfield was one of the greatest athletes I've ever known. What part of it is me, I'll take the blame."[68] Just before the HOF election, the *New York Times* reported that, "Steinbrenner also acknowledged the problems the two men encountered, though he didn't say he instigated them, and said that 'today we are good friends.'"[69]

Winfield didn't go that far, but said more than once that Steinbrenner had "apologized for what he's said and what he's done."[70] The reconciliation survived yet another dust up when Steinbrenner publicly stated that Winfield's HOF bust should wear a Yankees cap, and the Boss reportedly was irked when Winfield chose to be the first player represented with a San Diego Padres cap.[71]

On August 5, 2001, Winfield and Puckett became the seventh pair of teammates to be inducted into the Hall in the same year. Puckett recalled the time during his rookie year when Winfield had invited him to dinner, and imparted lessons about baseball and life. "From that point on, Dave Winfield was a friend of mine," Puckett said. "He's a great friend of mine. Any time I can spend in his company is special, not just when we're going into the Hall of Fame."[72]

In his induction speech, Winfield was conciliatory towards Steinbrenner.[73] The two had talked earlier, and "There were a lot of things we got out in the open," Winfield said. "He said things that made me believe he regretted what had happened."[74]

Things between the two had improved enough that on August 18, 2001, the St. Paul slugger was honored with Dave Winfield Day at Yankee Stadium. "Here's a day we thought we might not see, but it's here and it's beautiful," Winfield said.[75] The Yankees unveiled his old number 31 (though they didn't retire it), painted along the first- and third-base stands, and he was presented with keys for a sports car by his old teammate, Don Mattingly. Although Steinbrenner didn't attend, he did call Winfield, who thanked the Boss for inviting him back. "I'm not the one that's been behind trying to make a Dave Winfield Day at Yankee Stadium," Winfield told the *New York Times*. "It's been his doing. Things are certainly good now."[76]

The relationship continued to thaw. In 2008, Winfield played in the final Old Timer's Day Game at Yankee Stadium in August, and took part in the Final Game Ceremony at the Stadium in September. Earlier that summer, Winfield told *Newsday* that Steinbrenner "definitely has to be considered" for the Hall of Fame. "I might not have thought this years ago," Winfield said, "but he's had a lot to do with resurrecting the Yankees franchise and their brand and they've done really, really well during his tenure."[77] However, the Boss was not elected before he died in 2010.

Meanwhile, Winfield, who had joined the front office of the San Diego Padres as an executive vice president and senior advisor in 2001, appeared as an analyst on ESPN's *Baseball Tonight* from 2009 to 2012, and become the assistant to the Executive director of the MLBPA in 2013, continued to collect honors and accomplishments.

In 2004, ESPN named him the third best all-around athlete in the history of sport, behind only Jim Brown and Jim Thorpe.[78] He was one of the inaugural class of five players named to the College Baseball Hall of Fame in 2006, and inducted on July 4, 2007. One year later, he was selected to the California Athletic Hall of Fame. In 2010, Winfield was named the All-Time Left Fielder the National Sports Review Poll, and named as one of 28 member of the NCAA Men's College World Series Legends Team.[79]

On July 14, 2014, Winfield was one of four St. Paul natives to throw out the first pitch for the 2014 Home Run Derby, along with Joe Mauer, Paul Molitor, and Jack Morris.

He journeyed to Cuba in March 2016 as a representative of Major League Baseball when President Barack Obama visited the island nation, participated in a press conference in Havana with Joe Torre, Derek Jeter, and Luis Tiant and attended an exhibition baseball game between the Tampa Bay Rays and the Cuba National Team.[80]

In July, the 2016 Major League Baseball All-Star Game at Petco Park was dedicated to Winfield, who had represented the Padres at the San Diego's first All-Star Game at Jack Murphy Stadium in 1977.

Away from baseball, as he did with his dealings with Steinbrenner, Winfield set some of the relationships in his equally complicated personal life in order.

In 1988, he married Tonya Turner in New Orleans, seven years after they had met. Arline, battling cancer, sat in the front row. Shortly before she died in October, Winfield established contact with his daughter Lauren Shanel Winfield, who he fathered with Sandra Renfro, a Houston flight attendant in 1982.[81] Renfro, who never lived with Winfield, filed a common-law marriage suit against the ballplayer in 1985, after he had supported her for several years. Renfro won a $1.6 million judgement against Winfield in 1989.[82] It was overturned in 1991, and the two reached a legal agreement in 1995 that decreed that no marriage ever existed between them. Winfield agreed to continue $3,500 monthly child support payments,[83] and continued to be involved in Shanel's life. Winfield also reconnected with his father. Frank attended Arline's funeral, and with the encouragement of Tonya's mother, the two began to communicate more frequently.[84]

Dave and Tonya welcomed twins Arielle and David Jr in 1995. Both enrolled at the University of Pennsylvania in 2013, where Arielle played women's volleyball and David Jr played men's basketball.

Winfield followed his children's athletic careers, and remembered his own. ''I miss going first to third in somebody's face,'' he told the *New York Times* just before he was inducted into the Baseball Hall of Fame in 2001. "I miss throwing someone out from the outfield. Going from first to third, scoring from first on a double, for a big guy, those are things I really enjoyed. You can hit a ground ball right at an outfielder and if you're busting your backside from home plate, you have a chance for a double. Those are things I enjoyed. Playing defense is something you have to work on and something you have to love. When I first started, I wasn't a good defensive outfielder. I focused on it, enjoyed it, worked on things like charging the baseball. Little things that you do consistently become big things. Defense was a big part of my game.''[85]

SOURCES

In addition to the sources cited in the Notes, the author also consulted:

Books

James, Bill. *The Bill James Historical Baseball Abstract,* (New York: Villard, 1985).

Madden, Bill and Kerin McCue. *Steinbrenner: The Last Lion of Baseball,* (New York: Harper, 2010).

White, Frank and Dave Winfield. *They Played for the Love of the Game: Untold Stories of Black Baseball in Minnesota,* (St. Paul: Minnesota Historical Society Press, 2016).

Winfield, David with Michael Levin. *Dropping the Ball, Baseball's Troubles and How We Can and Must Solve Them* (New York: Scribner, 1987).

WEBSITES

www.aparchive.com, web.baseballhalloffame.org, www.baseball-almanac.com, www.baseball-reference.com, www.central.spps.org, www.davewinfield.com, www.davewinfieldhof.com, www.gophersports.com, www.mlb.com, www.retrosheet.org, www.spn.com, www.si.com/vault, www.sabr.org, www.sicnn.com, www.thebaseballpage.com, and www.upi.com/archives.

NOTES

1. http://davewinfieldhof.com
2. Ryan Mink, "Turn2 Foundation Celebrates 10th Anniversary; Jeter's Youth Outreach Organization Helps Kids," mlb.com, June 29, 2008.
3. http://davewinfieldhof.com
4. Ibid.
5. Tim Kurkjian, "Negro League Players Will Be Recognized at Draft," ESPN.com, June 4, 2008. A group that included Winfield, then Commissioner Bud Selig and MLB executive Vice President for Baseball Operations Jimmie Solomon provided the idea and the inspiration for the June 5, 2008 special draft of former Negro League players. Each of the 30 major league teams drafted one surviving Negro League player, representing all of those who were excluded from the major leagues.
6. Rick Reilly, "I Feel a Whole Lot Better Now; Dave Winfield's 20-Year Baseball Career, Often Touched by Trouble and Trauma, Has Taken A Happy Turn in Toronto," *Sports Illustrated*, June 29, 1992. Reilly's incisive interview with Winfield at a time he was a member of the Toronto Blue Jays provides a rich look into Winfield's personality, his background and his motivations.
7. Murray Chass, "Some Slights Endure for Winfield," *New York Times*, January 18, 2001: D4.
8. Harvey Araton, "Sports of the Times; One Went; One Stayed; Both Yearn," *New York Times*, September 22, 1993: B13.
9. "Winfield Honored by Yankees," *New York Times*, August 19, 2001: D4.
10. http://davewinfieldhof.com
11. Dave Winfield with Tom Parker, *"Winfield; A Player's Life* (New York: W.W. Norton and Company, 1988, 39-40.
12. Winfield with Parker, 40-41 and Gene Schoor, *Dave Winfield, The 23 Million Dollar Man* (New York: Stein and Day, 1982), 9-16 both provide details about Winfield's formative years, his mother Arline, and his close relationship with his brother Steve.

13 Winfield with Parker, 43.

14 Ibid., 35-39.

15 Ibid,. 62-66.

16 Ibid., 73-75.

17 Ibid., 68-72.

18 Ibid., 77.

19 Ibid., 77.

20 Ibid., 78.

21 Ibid., 76.

22 Winfield described the incident to Reilly in the 1992 profile for *Sports Illustrated.*

23 Winfield with Parker, 83-86.

24 http://davewinfieldhof.com

25 Winfield with Parker, 111.

26 Schoor, 61.

27 According to Baseball-Reference.com, *The Sporting News* Salary Survey, published April 23, 1977, listed Winfield's salary at $90,000.

28 Winfield with Parker, 128-131

29 Ibid., 130-131

30 Reilly. Years later, according to http://davewinfieldhof.com Winfield learned that Toronto Blue Jays teammate David Wells had been one of the "Winfield Kids" who sat in the Winfield Pavilion.

31 Winfield's exceptional philanthropy is well known. Schoor, 57-58, 89-91, 160, and 161 provides details, as does the http://davewinfieldhof.com/winfield-foundation/ website.

32 http://davewinfieldhof.com

33 Phil Collier, "Hot-Hitting Winfield Shuns HR Swing," *The Sporting News,* May 5, 1979: 27.

34 Schoor.

35 Reilly.

36 Ibid.

37 The media member was the *New York Times* writer Murray Chass.

38 Reilly.

39 http://davewinfieldhof.com

40 Thomas Boswell, "Winfield's Single Merely a Souvenir," *Washington Post*, October 26, 1981.

41 Bill Pennington, *Billy Martin: Baseball's Flawed Genius* (Wilmington, Massachusetts: Mariner Books, 2016), 393.

42 UPI writer David Tucker reported Winfield's comment in "New York Yankees' slugger Dave Winfield Was Arrested Thursday" https://www.upi.com/Archives/1983/08/05/New-York-Yankees-slugger-Dave-Winfield-was-arrested-Thursday/8533428904000/. The story ran in a number of newspapers.

43 Winfield with Parker, 201-203. Winfield told Parker that he donated two pieces of art to Easter Seals charity auctions he attended in Toronto the next two off seasons, worth $70,000. Despite the charity, he was heckled by arm-flapping fans on each return to Toronto prior to 1993.

44 Herschel Nissenson, "Winfield Arrested for Killing Seagull," *Daily News*, August 5, 1983: 25. See also Jane Gross, "Winfield Charges Will be Dropped," *New York Times,* August 5, 1983: 29. Pennington, 393, provided comments from Martin. [Is this the *New York Daily News*?]

45 Murray Chass, "Some Slights Endure for Winfield," *New York Times*, January 18, 2001: D4.

46 Art Rust, Jr. *Get That Nigger off the Field, The Oral History of the Negro Leagues* (Los Angeles: Shadow Lawn Press, 1992), 190.

47 Chass, "Some Slights Endure for Winfield."

48 Murray Chass, "Murray Chass on Baseball; Familiar Problem for Piniella, *New York Times*, December 15, 1985: S7, and "Murray Chass, "On Baseball: Sorry, Harvey," www.murraychass.com, 14.

49 Chass, "Some Slights Endure for Winfield."

50 Bill Madden and Moss Klein, *Damned Yankees: Chaos, Confusion, and Craziness in the Steinbrenner Era,* Chicago, Triumph Books, 2012 (reprint). Steinbrenner denied he ordered Piniella to platoon Winfield, but that he might do so. Ross Newhan, "Baseball: Drug Death's Don't Change the Real Issue," *Los Angeles Times*, July 13, 1986.

51 Reilly.

52 Reilly.

53 E.M. Swift, "Yanked About by the Boss; Bringing Their Feud to a Head, George Steinbrenner Sought to Discredit, to Humiliate and Unload Dave Winfield," *Sports Illustrated*, April 11, 1988, and Michael Martinez, "Baseball; Dark Cloud Obscures Winfield," *New York Times*, May 1, 1988: S1.

54 Murray Chass, "Winfield is Hoping Yanks Will Focus on Play, Not Feuds," *New York Times*, February 27, 1983: S3.

55 Michael Martinez, "Baseball; Winfield Ties R.B.I. Mark as Yankees Roll," *New York Times*, May 1, 1988: S2. Winfield broke the AL record and tied the major-league record held by Ron Cey of the Dodgers and Dale Murphy of the Braves. Martinez wrote that Winfield reportedly be a part of a three-way trade between the Yankees, Toronto, and Houston later that week.

56 David E. Pitt, "Baseball; Steinbrenner Had Ex-I.R.S. Man Check Winfield," *Publication*, August 26, 1990: 2.

57 Kevin McCoy and Richard T. Pienciak, "Gone! The Boss Gets the Thumb: Loses Control of Yankees, *New York Daily News,* July 31, 1990: 1, 4-5. Vincent lifted the ban on March 1, 1993. "A History of Steinbrenner's Career with the Yankees," *Newsday*, July 13, 2010.

58 Bill Brubaker, "Steinbrenner, Winfield and Friend A Tangled Web," *Washington Post*, March 30, 1990: S1; David E. Pitt, "Baseball; Steinbrenner Had Ex-I.R.S. Man Check Winfield."

59 Robert McG. Thomas, Jr. "Winfield Approves Trade to the Angels," *New York Times*, May 17, 1990: B13.

60 Helene Elliott, "Winfield Reaches Settlement, Ready to Join the Angels: Baseball: He Gets Contract Extension for One Year, Plus Two Option Years. Package is Worth as Much as $9.1 Million," *Los Angeles Times*, May 17, 1990.

61 "Yanks Must Pay $225,000 for Winfield Tampering," *New York Times*, July 6, 1990: A17. *The Times* reported that "Winfield challenged the trade and threatened to take the case to arbitration. Steinbrenner met with Winfield on May 14 and said the outfielder would still have a place on the Yankees if he won in arbitration. Winfield then agreed to go to the Angels and accepted a three-year, $9 million contract extension." Baseball Commissioner Fay Vincent explained: "'Mr. Steinbrenner's statement that Mr. Winfield would be welcomed back to the Yankees if he won the arbitration and should play on a full time basis was clearly improper," Vincent said in a statement yesterday. "It follows therefore, that Mr. Steinbrenner's improper statements harmed the Angels' bargaining position.'"

62 Robyn Norwood, "No Place Like This for Winfield's 400th: Angels; He Becomes 23rd Player to Reach Home Run Milestone, Doing It in the Area Where He Grew Up," *Los Angeles Times*, August 15, 1991.

63 Reilly.

64 Ibid.

65 The Associated Press story that appeared in the *New York Times* on September 1, 1994, under the headline: "Baseball; It's a Deal: Indians Grab Winfield" said that the Indians had obtained Winfield for a player to be named later. According to Tom Keegan, "Owners Try on Global Thinking Cap, *Baltimore Sun*, September 11, 1994, that if the season did not resume, Indians General Manager John Hart had agreed to pay the Twins $100 and take Minnesota's Andy MacPhail out to dinner. MacPhail had already left the Twins to join the Chicago Cubs at that point. Several sources claim that Indians team personnel treated Twins team personnel to dinner after the season to settle the score.

66 https://www.mlb.com/search?page=1&q=roberto%20clemente%20award&type=all

67 Chass, "Some Slights Endure for Winfield."

68 Murray Chass, "Baseball; Mr. Break-It and Mr. Fix-It," *New York Times*, January 4, 1998: 1.

69 Chass, "Some Slights Endure for Winfield."

70 Tyler Kepner, "Winfield Recalls Reconciliation with Steinbrenner," *New York Times*, July 13, 2010.

71 Murray Chass, "Winfield Chooses Padres Over Yanks," *New York Times*, April 14, 2001: D1 and Harvey Araton, "Sports of the Times: Winfield and Steinbrenner and Reconciling the Past," *New York Times*, July 18, 2008: S1.

72 Puckett's comments were included in an Associated Press story that appeared in several newspapers, including the *Arizona Daily Sun*, which titled it "Hall Open Doors to Puckett, Winfield," on January 16, 2001.

73 Jason Stark, "Détente? Winfield Gives Thanks to the Boss," ESPN.com, Monday, August 6, 2001.

74 Araton, "Sports of the Times: Winfield and Steinbrenner and Reconciling the Past."

75 "Winfield Honored by Yankees," *New York Times*, August 19, 2001.

76 Ibid.

77 Jim Baumbach, "Even Winfield Believes in Boss," *Newsday*, July 26, 2008.

78 Jeff Merron, "The Best All-Around Athletes," ESPN.com, April 26, 2004.

79 https://amp.ncaa.com/amp/news/baseball/article/2010-05-06/ncaa-and-cws-inc-announce-college-world-series-legends-team.

80 "MLB goes to Cuba," *Newsday*, March 22, 2016; "Why Derek Jeter Agreed to Accept Spotlight of Cuba Trip," *New York Post*, March 22, 2016; Rays Beat Cuban National Team 4-1 in Havana," *Orlando Sentinel*, March 22, 2016.

81 Reilly.

82 "Winfield Loses Palimony Suit," *Los Angeles Times*, March 22, 1990.

83 "Winfield Ends 10-Year Legal Battle," UPI Archives, November 7, 1995.

84 Reilly.

85 Murray Chass, "Some Slights Endure for Winfield."

THE COACHING STAFF

MIKE HARGROVE

BY GREGORY H. WOLF

His nickname says it all: The Human Rain Delay. In the years before seemingly every big-league ballplayer stepped out of the box after every pitch to go through a routine of incessant equipment adjusting, Mike Hargrove was an anomaly and drove pitchers, managers, fans, and even broadcasters mad. "With machine-like precision," wrote Bob Sudyk, "Hargrove approaches the plate, calls time, grabs some dirt, taps at his pants, sleeves, hitches up his waistband, adjusts his hair, taps down his helmet, squeezes his hand deeper into his batting glove, drains all the moisture from his mouth and steps in after raking some dirt in the batter's box with his cleats."[1] The origins of Hargrove's routine are innocent. After damaging a nerve at the base of his left thumb as a minor leaguer, in 1973, he devised a sponge doughnut ring to minimize the pain. "It was hard to break in," Hargrove once explained, "and if I didn't screw it down my thumb, it would fly off."[2] He claimed his preparation helped him concentrate, but he also admitted candidly, "I wouldn't like to pitch to myself. ... If it also bothers the pitcher, well and good. Maybe he'll hang a curve."[3]

Hargrove hit his fair share of hanging curves. Two years after playing semipro ball, he made an improbable jump to the big leagues and was named AL Rookie of the Year with the Texas Rangers, batting .323 in 1974. The line-drive-hitting first baseman antagonized pitchers, hitting a robust .290 over 12 seasons, the final seven with the Cleveland Indians. Regularly among the league leaders in walks, he finished with a .396 on-base percentage. After his active playing career, he made a seamless transition into coaching. He was a big-league manager for 16 years; the first nine of those were with the Indians, whom he led to five consecutive AL Central crowns and two pennants (1995 and 1997).

Dudley Michael Hargrove was born on October 26, 1949, in Perryton, Texas to Dudley and Rita Ann (Hurter) Hargrove. Like many of the roughly 8,000 residents of the town, located in the northeastern corner of the Texas Panhandle, the elder Hargrove worked in the oil industry, as a pumper; his wife was a nursing-home administrator. The Hargroves provided a sturdy middle-class lifestyle for the four children (Mike, followed by Dennis, Cynthia, and Paula) and instilled in them a relentless work ethic. His father had tryout offers from the Dodgers and Giants in the mid-1940s but couldn't make either one because of his duties on his family's farm. Mike played Little League and Babe Ruth baseball and was later coached by his father in American Legion and YMCA ball, but did not take baseball too seriously. A natural athlete, Mike's passion was football, the king of sports in the state. At Perryton High School he was a defensive back and punter, an accomplished golfer, and an all-conference basketball player, but his school did not field a baseball team. Upon graduation in 1968, Hargrove accepted a basketball scholarship to Northwestern State College (now known as Northwestern Oklahoma State University), in Alva, about 150 miles from Perryton.

At the insistence of his father, Hargrove tried out for the college baseball team. "The first thing I noticed about Michael was how quick his hands were, the way he picked up the ball and threw it," said coach Cecil Perkins of his initial reaction to the walk-on.[4] Hargrove played football and basketball for two years, but his interest gradually shifted to baseball. The stocky 6-foot, 195-pound left-hander was a consistent hitter in college and a capable defensive first baseman but possessed neither the power nor the speed to be considered a hot prospect. He gained additional experience playing semipro ball during the summers. After graduating with a degree in education in 1972, Hargrove moved to Liberal, Kansas, less than 50 miles north of Perryton, where he worked in a meat-packing plant and played semipro ball for the Bee Jays. "I planned to become a high-school coach," he once said, but those plans were derailed when the Texas Rangers selected him in the 25th round of the draft that June.[5]

Hargrove's rise from semipro ball to AL Rookie of the Year in just over two years is as unlikely as it is surprising. After batting just .267 and slugging .350 in his first year of professional baseball, with the Geneva (New York) Senators in the short-season Class A New York-Pennsylvania League in 1972, Hargrove was assigned to the Single-A Gastonia (North Carolina) Rangers in the Western Carolinas League. Among the oldest players on the squad, Hargrove enjoyed a season-long surge and was named league MVP by pacing the circuit in hitting (.351), hits (160), doubles (35), and slugging (.542).

Hargrove's numbers naturally caught the attention of the Rangers' brass, who sent him to the Florida Instructional League in the fall of 1973. While there, he was heavily scouted by Billy Martin, who had taken over as the Rangers' pilot in the last month of the season. Martin liked Hargrove's compact body and natural swing, was impressed by his hustle, and ultimately invited the prospect to spring training in 1974.

The Rangers were coming off a horrible season in 1973 (57-105) in which they had ranked dead last in runs scored. Martin was in the process of rebuilding the team in his likeness – hardworking, scrappy ballplayers whose commitment to win and playing hard trumped any personal gains. That description fit Hargrove perfectly. Beat writer Merle Heryford reported that Hargrove was widely expected to be sent to Triple-A at best.[6] "I'll never forget how shocked he was when I told him he made the team," said Martin. "I think he made me repeat it several times."[7] The 24-year-old rookie, described as having the "rugged good looks of a West Texas Brahma bull rider," made an immediate impact and established himself as the club's most consistent hitter.[8] He saw most of his action against right-handed pitchers. Platooning with Jim Spencer at first base and serving as a designated hitter, Hargrove got off to a fast start, going 13-for-32 (.406) in his first three weeks in the big leagues as the Rangers unexpectedly held down first place at the end of April. "You watch him hit, then you talk to him, and you forget he's a rookie," said Martin of his prized Texan. "He's mature and he's got all the tools, including the right kind of head."[9] While the Rangers were the surprise of baseball, finishing in second place (84-76), Hargrove collected 134 hits, good for a .323 average (which would have ranked second had he had enough at-bats to qualify for the title). "I don't consider myself a power hitter or pronounced pull hitter," said Hargrove, who tallied just 4 homers and 18 doubles. "My best hitting is in right center, but I try to go with the pitch."[10]

Hargrove began his sophomore season platooning again with Spencer at first base. Recognizing that he needed his most consistent hitter in the lineup every day, Martin switched Hargrove in mid-May to left field, a position he had never played save for a few games the previous year. Hargrove understandably struggled and never felt at home. "I'll admit I never counted on being an outfielder," he said.[11] A streaky hitter, Hargrove batted .432 (51-for-118) over a 34-game stretch from May 10 to June 20 to raise his average to .365 while the Rangers fought to play .500 ball. Named to his first and only All-Star Game, Hargrove pinch-hit and popped out in his only appearance in the AL's 6-3 loss. [The AP reported that residents of Perryton cast 96,000 votes in an effort to get their hometown hero selected to the game.[12]] With the Rangers failing to live up to expectations, Martin was replaced by Frank Lucchesi on July 21. The former Philadelphia Phillies skipper righted the ship, leading the club to a 35-32 record, but Hargrove entered a prolonged slump, batting just .229 from July 28 through September 18, and saw his average dip under .300 before a late-season surge pushed his average to .303, easily the best mark on the club. He pounded righties for a .329 clip but struggled against lefties (.212).

In 1976 Lucchesi moved Hargrove back to first base, where he was once again the Rangers most consistent hitter, leading the fourth-place club in average (.287), runs (80), and hits (155). He led the AL with 97 walks and finished second with a .397 on-base percentage. In the field, however, the laid-back Texan had a season evoking memories of Dick "Dr. Strangeglove" Stuart. Hargrove committed 21 errors, the most by an AL first baseman since Stuart's 24 in 1964. "I get sick every time I think about it," a disappointed Hargrove said after the season.[13]

"We almost have to be better," Hargrove told Rangers beat writer Randy Galloway as he headed to spring training in 1977. "Our consolation is that we can't be any worse than we were in July and August last season (20-41)."[14] The season reached its nadir after an ugly incident on May 28. Disgruntled second baseman Lenny Randle, who had lost his job to Bump Wills, attacked Lucchesi, knocking him out. The brouhaha resulted from Lucchesi's incendiary comments just days earlier, "I'm tired of these punks saying play me or trade me. Anyone who makes $80,000 a year and gripes and moans all spring is not going to get a tear out of me."[15] The fight led to Randle's suspension for 30 days (and ultimate trade) and to Lucchesi's dismissal. With the team floundering (34-35) in fifth place, but only 5½ games off the lead, Billy Hunter took over as the skipper. After hitting primarily third in 1976, Hargrove batted in every position in the chaotic campaign before Hunter made an unusual decision. "Let's just say that I'm not a classic example of what most people expect out of the guy who bats first in the order," said the slow-footed Hargrove.[16] Almost exclusively leading off for the rest of the season, Hargrove batted .308 with a .440 on-base percentage in the final 74 games. Even more surprising was his sudden power surge; he belted 16 home runs in just 260 at-bats. Hargrove's also improved his glove work dramatically, finishing fifth among first sackers in fielding percentage and becoming a Gold Glove candidate. Texas responded to Hunter, winning 60 of 93 games to finish in second place with a franchise-record 94 wins. "Grover," as Hargrove's teammates called him, led the club in hitting (.305), runs (98), hits (160), and on-base percentage (.420).

On paper the 1978 Rangers seemed like one of the best teams in baseball. They had acquired two All-Stars, left fielder Al Oliver and DH Richie Zisk, in the offseason, and Bobby Bonds in a mid-May trade; they had arguably the best defensive catcher in the league (Jim Sundberg), one of the best third basemen (All-Star Toby Harrah), and Hargrove. Widely expected to capture its first division crown, Texas unexpectedly struggled to score runs and was under .500 as late as mid-September before a season-ending surge (15-2) provided window dressing to what beat writer Randy Galloway called a "bad season."[17] Hargrove was mired in a season-long slump, batting just .251, though he led the AL with 107 free passes. A disappointing season was made worse when he injured his left ankle jumping back to first base to avoid a pickoff throw by Oakland's Matt Keough on September 16. He was carried off the field and missed the final two weeks save for one pinch-hitting appearance.

Even before the season ended, trade rumors swirled around Hargrove, whom *The Sporting News* called "one of the most popular players ever to wear a Rangers uniform."[18] On October 25, 1978, the financially strapped Rangers sent Hargrove to the San Diego Padres in a multiplayer and cash deal. Hargrove reacted bitterly to the trade: "There are some real (bleeps) on this team. Not a lot of them, but three of four of those 'hooray for me, the heck with you guys [types].'"[19] Al Oliver saw Hargrove as the glue that kept the team together. "This team is going to miss [him] next season. Mike has the same qualities of a Bob Moose and Roberto Clemente," he said, comparing Hargrove to his Pirates teammates, both of whom died tragically.[20]

The contact-hitting Hargrove seemed ideally suited for the expanse of San Diego Stadium, but he hit rock bottom in his move to the NL. He batted a hard-to-fathom .192 and lost his starting job. "I didn't go to San Diego with the best attitude in the world," said Hargrove. "I went there with a lot of misgiving."[21]

In what proved to be one of the more lopsided trades in baseball history, the Padres sent Hargrove to the Cleveland Indians on June 14, 1979, for utilityman Paul Dade. While Dade made only 375 more at-bats and was released after the 1980 season, Hargrove resurrected his career and remained with the organization for the next 20 years as a player, coach, and manager.

The Indians' acquisition of Hargrove initially seemed like a bad move. With first base occupied by slugger Andre Thornton, Hargrove was moved to left field, where the transplanted Texan continued his batting woes (9-for-52, .173). He turned to coaches Dave Duncan and Joe Nossek for help. "They noted I wasn't setting up the same way as (1976 and 1977)," said Hargrove. "[So] I lowered my bat and opened my stance slightly and I could wait longer on the pitch." With his new stance and primarily leading off, "Grover" hit at a .353 clip with a .463 on-base percentage from July 6 through the end of the season for the sixth-place club (81-80). "A good hitter has to be tough mentally, and Mike is a tough, tough kid," said skipper Dave Garcia, who took over on July 23 and led the Indians to a 38-28 record.

"He fights the pitchers. He battles to win. You never hear him complain."[22]

Described by Cleveland sportswriter Bob Sudyk as "the possessor of one of the sweetest swings in the game," Hargrove put together a career-best 23-game hitting streak (32-for-84, .381, .500 OBP) early in the 1980 season. Since the offensive explosion throughout baseball beginning in 1977, teams had increasingly relied on the long ball for success; however, the Indians seemed out of place, ranking last in the AL in home runs (89). Hargrove's 11 round-trippers tied for second on the club, trailing only rookie Joe Charboneau's 23. Remarkably, the club finished with a 79-81 record despite the worst pitching staff in baseball (4.68 ERA). Dubbed "The Incredible Twitching Machine," the 30-year-old Hargrove batted .304, set a new team record with 111 walks, and drove in a career-high 85 runs.[23]

Hargrove was an "old school" player before there was an old school. He wasn't flashy, lacked power and the physical attributes of first basemen like Eddie Murray or Cecil Cooper, avoided the spotlight, and rarely criticized publicly his teammates or coaching staff. "The paycheck is anything but Mike's first consideration," Nossek once said of the Indians' acknowledged team leader. "He's gonna play the game no matter what kind of money he makes. I think he's one of the big reasons why this club has grown over the years. Not so much because of what he says but by the example he sets."[24] In a poll of players and media, *The Sporting News* named Hargrove to the All-Hustle team in 1980, and the Cleveland chapter of the Baseball Writers Association of America selected him as Man of the Year in 1980 and 1981.

In the strike-shortened season of 1981, Hargrove was one of the few bright spots for the Indians, who finished in sixth place for the fourth of five consecutive seasons. A paragon of consistency, Hargrove batted a team-high .317 and led the AL with a .424 OBP. In interviews after his playing career, he often mentioned playing in right-hander Len Barker's perfect game against the Toronto Blue Jays on May 15 as "probably the highlight of my career."[25]

A remarkably healthy player during his big-league career, Hargrove matched his career high by playing in 160 games in 1982. His batting average fell to .271, though the left-hander drew 101 walks for the sixth-place Indians. His final three years with Cleveland (1983-1985) marked one of the low points in the franchise's history, as the club finished last in attendance each season while fielding horrible teams. Hargrove, entering his mid-30s, saw his playing time gradually reduced, and was platooned in '84 and '85 as Cleveland went to a pronounced youth movement.

Granted free agency after the 1985 season, Hargrove wanted to continue playing but went unsigned. "I talked to some ballclubs and there was some interest and all of a sudden there was no interest at all," he said. "Since then, with the collusion being proved, I think that was just as much as anything."[26] After batting just a combined .275 and slugging .343 in the previous two seasons, he had a brief tryout with the Oakland A's as a non-roster invitee during spring training in 1986. His release signaled the end of a 12-year playing career. The classic contact hitter collected 1,614 hits in 1,666 games, belted 80 home runs, and drove in 686 runs. His on-base percentage (.396) was higher than his slugging percentage (.391), an oddity for first basemen in the post-Deadball Era. He wore out Gaylord Perry (18-for-35, .514), Dick Tidrow (12-for-24, .500), and Wilbur Wood (9-for-18, .500) and had troubles with Dave Righetti (1-for-18, .056), Dick Bosman (1-for-15, .067), and Mike Flanagan (3-for-38, .079).

Given his attention to detail, his cerebral and selfless approach to the game, and his leadership skills, Hargrove seemed destined to become a coach. His 21-year career in coaching began in 1986 when Cleveland named him hitting instructor for the Batavia Trojans of the Class A (short season) New York-Pennsylvania League. A rising star in the organization, Hargrove quickly moved up the ladder. He piloted three different teams in as many years from 1987 to 1989 and was twice named manager of the year (with the Kinston Indians of the High-A Carolinas League and with the Triple-A Colorado Sky Sox of the Pacific Coast League). "As a coach and manager you've got 23 or 24 guys all wanting your time," said Hargrove about his learning curve. "So your time is a lot less yours than as a player. That took a lot of adjusting to."[27]

Hargrove was back in a big-league uniform in 1990 when he joined the Indians staff as first-base coach. The following season he replaced skipper John McNamara after a dreadful start (25-52), thus inaugurating his nine-year tenure as the Tribe's manager. The easy-going Hargrove had an ideal temperament for a manager. In an interview with Bonnie DeSimone of the *Cleveland Plain Dealer* he explained that he learned one of his guiding principles from his college basketball coach, Roy Pennington, who "almost never chewed a player right after a mistake but waited until the emotion of the moment had passed and quietly made a correction."[28]

"I've tried to take a little bit from every manager that I've been around and seen what I've thought he's done well and what I've thought he didn't do well and try to incorporate that into the way I treat my players and the way I run my ballclub," said Hargrove.[29] He cited Billy Martin as a great tactician and Dave Garcia as the best people-person. Players respected Hargrove for his candor, compassion, and patience. "They know they'll get a truthful answer even if it is not the one they want," said Indians coach Jeff Newman."[30]

Hargrove's first three full seasons (1992-1994) as Indians manager were marked by frustration, tragedy, and an eye toward a promising future. After two consecutive 76-86 records, the Indians were enjoying their best season in four decades since the days of Bob Lemon, Early Wynn, Mike Garcia, and Herb Score. In second place (66-47) but just one game behind the Chicago White Sox, the Indians saw dreams of their first postseason berth since 1954 dashed by the baseball strike which began on August 12, 1994, and ultimately forced the cancellation of the playoffs. A year earlier, Hargrove consoled his players after pitchers Steve Olin and Tim Crews were killed in a boating accident during spring training.

Hargrove guided the Indians to five consecutive AL Central crowns from 1995 to 1999, thus ending the club's 41-year playoff drought. Favored to win the World Series in 1995 after barreling through the shortened regular season (100-44), the Indians lost the fall classic in six games to the Atlanta Braves. Two years later, the Indians were two outs away from their first title since 1948 when the Florida Marlins broke the hearts of Cleveland fans by tying Game Seven in the ninth inning, 2-2, and then winning in the 11th. Hargrove was never known as a tactician and was often criticized for his handling of relievers and the way some players seemed ill-prepared or even lackadaisical on the field. Blessed with sluggers, speedsters, and superstars, Hargrove got the most of his players while dealing with a cast of diverse characters, from the surly Albert Belle, whose contempt for the media and even fans was well documented; Manny Ramirez, whose sometimes bizarre on-the-field indifference helped engender his moniker, "Manny Being Manny"; to switch-hitter Eddie Murray, whom the *Chicago Tribune* called "the most churlish player ever."[31] The Indians' success corresponded to their departure from cavernous Cleveland Municipal Stadium, which seated approximately 78,000 for baseball games, and move into fan-friendly Jacobs Field (later renamed Progressive Field) in 1994. The Tribe set a big-league record by selling out 455 consecutive games, from June 12, 1995, to April 4, 2001. Hargrove was fired in 1999 after the Indians squandered a two-games-to-none lead against the wild-card Boston Red Sox in the Division Series.

Hargrove's experiences as a winner in a talent-laden Cleveland organization sharply contrasted with his four-year stint with the Baltimore Orioles (2000 to 2003). He guided the weak-hitting, pitching-challenged club to four consecutive losing seasons and four fourth-place finishes in the competitive AL East.

Hargrove took over the Seattle Mariners in 2005 and guided them to consecutive fourth-place finishes. With the club in second place, riding an eight-game winning streak, and playing their best baseball in four years, Hargrove unexpectedly resigned on July 1, 2007. "It was not a knee-jerk reaction," he said. "It was something I turned over 15,000 ways."[32] Almost immediately speculation arose that he was forced out because of his increasingly toxic relationship with the team's star, Ichiro Suzuki. "[Hargrove] never truly explained himself – to his bosses, players, fans or himself," wrote the *Seattle Times*.[33]

Hargrove never donned a big-league uniform again as manager or coach. In 16 seasons as skipper, he amassed a record of 1,188-1,173 (.503).

In an interview with Linda Feagler of *Cleveland Magazine.com*, Hargrove said that he had lived in at least 23 cities in 13 states and had moved at least 100 times throughout his 35 years in professional baseball. The one constant, however, was his wife, Sharon. "No matter what we did or where we went, we did it together," said Hargrove. "Sharon and I emphasized that our home was a safe haven and that family mattered above anything else."[34] High-school sweethearts, Mike and Sharon married at ages 20 and 19 respectively, in 1970, and raised five children, Kim, Missy, Shelly, Pam, and Andy. A big, 250-pound first baseman, Andy was drafted by the Seattle Mariners in the 47th round of the 2005 draft and spent three years in the Mariners organization.

Hargrove never forgot his roots, never let success go to his head, or let the millions of dollars he earned in baseball change him. "[He's] a home-town boy," said his father.[35] After resigning from the Mariners, Hargrove's path came full circle when he returned to Liberal, Kansas, to manage the semipro Bee Jays in the summers of 2008 and 2009. He also remained close to his alma mater. In 1992 Northwestern Oklahoma State University inducted him into its Hall of Fame, and in 2007 the school honored him on Mike Hargrove Day by retiring his number 30. He was inducted into the National Association of Intercollegiate Sports (NAIA) Hall of Fame in 1999.

Hargrove's ties to the Indians also remained strong. His success as a player and especially as manager of the Tribe received more critical acclaim after he retired. The club inducted him into its Hall of Fame in 2008; five years later he was inducted into the Cleveland Sports Hall of Fame. He returned to the Indians in 2011 as a special adviser and was a regular presence at spring training through 2014, and also occasionally broadcast games.

As of 2018 the Hargroves reside in the Cleveland area.

NOTES

1. Bob Sudyk, "Pokey Hargrove Streaks to Hot Start For Tribe", *The Sporting News*, May 31, 1980: 33.
2. Gary Herron, "'The Human Rain Delay.' Former first sacker Mike Hargrove interviewed," *Sports Collectors Digest*, June 22, 1990: 130.
3. Hal Lebovitz, "Can the Tribe keep Hargrove," *Cleveland Plain Dealer*, August 26, 1979: III, 2.
4. Bob Colon, "Time's Up! Hargrove Is the First," Newsok.com, July 9, 1991. newsok.com/times-up-hargrove-is-the-first/article/2362281.
5. Dan Coughlin, "The Hargrove Mystery," *Cleveland Plain Dealer*. [1979; undated article in player's Hall of Fame file]
6. Merle Heryford, "Sizzling Hargrove Confirms Billy's Early Sizeup", *The Sporting News*, July 20, 1974: 18.
7. Associated Press, "Mike Hargrove: Ranger rookie just a natural," *The Morning Herald* (Hagerstown, Maryland), June 28, 1974: 19.
8. Ibid.
9. Randy Galloway, "Huge Leap by Top Rookie Hargrove", *The Sporting News*, November 16, 1974: 46.
10. Heryford, *The Sporting News*, July 20, 1974: 18.
11. Merle Heryford, "Soph Jinx Merely Myth to Hot-Hitting Hargrove", *The Sporting News*, October 18, 1975: 33.
12. Associated Press, "8,000 Residents of Home Town Cast 96,000 Votes for Ranger Hargrove," *Gettysburg* (Pennsylvania) *Times*, July 3, 1975: 17.
13. Randy Galloway, "Hargrove Looks For Different Year", *The Sporting News*, February 12, 1977: 38.
14. Randy Galloway, "Hargrove Looks For Different Year", *The Sporting News*, February 12, 1977: 39.
15. Jeff Merron, "Put up your dukes," ESPN.com. espn.go.com/page2/s/list/basebrawl.html.
16. Randy Galloway, "Sizzling Sundberg, Hargrove Fuel Ranger Surge", *The Sporting News*, September 3, 1977: 5.
17. Randy Galloway, "A Bad Season Already Over For Hargrove", *The Sporting News*, October 7, 1978: 28.
18. Randy Galloway, "Rangers, Short of Funds, Decide to Gamble", *The Sporting News*, November 11, 1978: 47.
19. Ibid.
20. Randy Galloway, "Ranger Revolving-Door Policy Ticks Off Oliver", *The Sporting News*, December 2, 1978: 51.
21. Merron.
22. Lebovitz.
23. Merron.
24. Milton Richman (United Press International), "Neither side wants strike," *Ukiah* (California) *Daily Journal*, May 26, 1981: 4.
25. Merron.
26. Merron.
27. Merron.
28. Bonnie DeSimone, "Affair of the heart," *Cleveland Plain Dealer*, October 1, 1995: 20-D.
29. Merron.
30. DeSimone, 21-D.
31. Dan McGrath, "Stuff The Ballot Box," *Chicago Tribune*, January 3, 1999.
32. Larry Stone, "Mariners manager Hargrove resigns," *Seattle Times*, July 1, 2007.
33. Art Thiel, "Resignation is inexplicable, even for Hargrove," *Seattle Times*, July 1, 2007.
34. Linda Feagler, "A New Ballgame," *Cleveland Magazine.com*: clevelandmagazine.com/ME2/dirmod.asp?sid=E73ABD6180B44874871A91F6BA5C249C&nm=&type=Publishing&mod=Publications%3A%3AArticle&mid=1578600D80804596A222593669321019&tier=4&id=09B4813C341044E991A7C06DFD943494.
35. Joe Christiansen, "Old Indian guide hasn't lost his way," *Baltimore Sun*, March 19, 2002.

BUDDY BELL

BY JOSEPH WANCHO

The Boston Red Sox were clinging to the slimmest of leads in the American League Central Division. They had just lost two of three games to the Milwaukee Brewers at County Stadium. A quick look at the standings on July 4, 1975, showed that the Red Sox were in a virtual tie with the Brew Crew, ahead by a couple of percentage points. Boston traveled to Cleveland next, to tangle with the Tribe in a four-game set that kicked off the July Fourth holiday weekend. As for Cleveland, they were eight games off the pace.

The Indians won the opener, 3-2. The second game was not nearly as close, as Buddy Bell's grand slam in the second inning off Boston starter Steve Barr staked the Indians to a 6-0 lead. He added a solo home run in the fourth frame and a run-scoring double in the eighth. Bell was 3-for-5 with three runs scored and six RBIs, a career high. Indians starter Roric Harrison went the distance as the Indians coasted to a 12-2 victory.

Bell had been the whipping boy in Cleveland, batting .232 to that point in the season. "Sure I heard them but I'm a professional and I try not to let it bother me, but it did," Bell said of the booing fans.[1] Bell was simplistic in describing his grand slam. "I never try for homers. All I wanted to do was get a hit. The bases were loaded and a single would have put us up by three. The pitch came down the middle and I just ripped, that's all."[2] Bell continued his fine hitting for the balance of the season, batting .271 for the year. "It's a great feeling to come back like that after the start I've had this season," said Buddy of his big day.[3]

After the Indians split a Bat Day Doubleheader with the Bosox the following day, Cleveland had won 13 of its last 17 to pull within six games of the division-leading Red Sox. But Boston got the last laugh, winning the American League pennant in 1975.

The Indians third baseman made headlines off the field a few days after the Boston series. The All-Star Game was to be played in Milwaukee on July 15. Bell finished second in the fan voting to the Yankees' Graig Nettles. AL skipper Alvin Dark picked Bell as the backup to Nettles. However, Bell rejected the appointment. "I did it because in my heart, I know I don't deserve it as much as some of the other guys who are playing better than me right now," he explained.[4]

"Now that it's final—I talked to (AL President) Lee MacPhail and Mr. Dark yesterday—I feel like a burden has been lifted off my shoulders. For two weeks, ever since the balloting was printed in the newspapers, and I was leading the third basemen. It has been eating up my insides, because I knew I didn't deserve it."[5]

"Now I feel better, so relieved, because I know I'm doing the right thing. There are other guys who deserve it more, and I know how I'd feel if I were in their shoes."[6]

"I wanted Buddy because I think he could help us win the game, "said Dark. "There's no doubt but that Buddy is one of the stars of baseball and belongs in the All-Star Game. I'd be honored to have him on the team. But I couldn't convince him.

"Once he made his decision, and I knew it was irrevocable, I told Buddy I admire his attitude and his courage for doing what he thinks is right, no matter the consequences. And now I have even more respect for Buddy Bell."[7]

David Gus Bell was born on August 27, 1951, in Pittsburgh. He was one of seven children born to Gus and Joyce Bell. At the time, Gus Bell was in his second year as an outfielder for the Pittsburgh Pirates. His 15-year career was played entirely in the National League with Pittsburgh, Cincinnati, the New York Mets, and Milwaukee. He was a four-time All-Star, all while he was a member of the Reds. Gus started in right field for the Mets in their inaugural game, on April 11 1962, at St. Louis's Busch Stadium. His single to center field in the second inning was the first hit in Mets history.

Gus gave Buddy his nickname to differentiate him from another family member also named David. Although David was born in Pittsburgh, it was Cincinnati where he spent his formative years. Bell was a two-sport star at Archbishop Moeller High School, excelling in basketball and of course baseball. In his three seasons on the varsity, Bell compiled a .410 batting average. He was the first real "star" to walk the halls at Moeller. Ken Griffey Jr., Barry Larkin, Adam Hyzdu, and Buddy's sons David and Mike would all wear the Crusader blue and gold.

The assumption by many was that Buddy, being the son of a major-league star, was the beneficiary of Gus's instruction on the finer points of playing baseball. But the opposite was true. "Most people say to me, 'I guess you were able to help him quite a bit,' but the fact is that I did help a little at the beginning, but not much after that," said Gus.

"I don't think you can push a kid. You can try to lead them but I feel that whatever they try to do, just encourage them. Tim Rose [Moeller coach] taught Buddy a lot of the fundamental things, like base running, how to play the position, and that sort. I don't claim very much of the credit."[8]

After graduation, Bell was selected in the 16th round of the June free-agent draft by the Cleveland Indians on June 5, 1969. Cleveland general manager Gabe Paul and assistant general manager Phil Seghi were both in the Cincinnati front office when Gus Bell was a member of the Reds. They had both known Buddy since he was a toddler. Bell spent three years in the Indians farm system, culminating in 1971 at Wichita of the American Association. In 129 games there, Bell hit .289, with 11 homers and 59 RBIs to go with 136 hits. He was named the league's Rookie of the Year, as well as MVP of the Aeros.

Bell also wed the former Gloria Eysoldt in 1971. They had five children: David, Michael, Ricky, Kristi, and Traci. David and Michael both played in the major leagues, making the Bell family one of only four three-generation families in major-league history. (See also the families of Sammy Hairston, Ray Boone, and Joe Coleman)

At 1972 spring training prior it looked as if Bell might be ticketed to the minors again. But given the opportunity, he was able to show the Indians brass that he was needed on their big-league team. "I hadn't played in any of the Indians exhibition games and there were only two weeks of camp left. The team had left for Yuma and the rest of us were left at Tucson. They needed an outfielder for the "B" game that morning so I was sent out there.

"I had a good day at the plate, going 3-for-4. Then the office got a phone call from Yuma, saying that they needed a replacement that afternoon for outfielder John Lowenstein, who had been hurt, and I was sent over there for the afternoon game.

I played right field and went 4-for-5, had three RBIs and drove in the winning run. The next day they used me in the outfield again at Phoenix and I had two RBI singles and a three-run homer to win the game. From then on I was in the regular lineup and was signed to a Cleveland contract."[9]

During his minor-league years Bell was primarily situated at third base, although he also saw time at second base. But the path to third base was blocked by Graig Nettles. However, Bell's talent was evident, and on April 15, 1972, he was the starting right fielder for Cleveland on Opening Day.

Joining Bell in Cleveland was Ken Aspromonte, his manager at Wichita, who was also promoted to the big leagues. Bell split his time between right and center fields, batting .255. The Indians hit .234 as a team and were inept offensively. Nettles, who often clashed with Aspromonte, led the team in homers (17) and RBIs (70). But in the offseason, Nettles was traded to the New York Yankees in a six-player swap. The deal proved to be disastrous for Cleveland. Gabe Paul left the Indians shortly after the deal was announced. His departure raised more than a few eyebrows when it was learned that he had joined the ownership group that purchased the Yankees. (Paul returned to Cleveland in 1978 and subsequently made a similar deal, sending star pitcher Dennis Eckersley to Boston. Bell said at the time, "Maybe Gabe's going to Boston in a couple of years.")[10]

Bell was back in familiar territory in 1973 making a smooth transition back to third base. "The important thing to me was playing in the big leagues," he said. "Sure, I had some qualms about moving to the outfield, and I did again when I moved back to third base. Both required adjustments, but I think I made those adjustments satisfactorily."[11] Bell's bat heated up in May and June, as he batted .320 and .350 in those months. He was selected to his first All-Star Game on July 13 at Kansas City. In his lone appearance at the plate, he smashed a pinch-hit triple off Claude Osteen.

Over the next several years, Bell was a model of consistency both in the field and at the plate. He missed some time in 1974 due to a right knee strain. But from 1975 to '78, Bell hit between six and 11 homers, drove in between 59 and 64 runs, and got between 39 and 51 walks. His batting average fluctuated between .271 and .292. In the field he led the league in putouts in 1975 (146) and in assists in 1978 (355). He was considered one of the top third basemen in the American League.

But what was also consistent was the losing ways of the Cleveland Indians. By the end of the 1974 season, Aspromonte was a lame-duck manager, and was replaced by Frank Robinson. Robby knew it would be a tough road with the Tribe. He encouraged the front office to promote promising minor leaguers to the big-league team. Duane Kuiper, Rick Manning, Dennis Eckersley, and Jim Kern were added to the mix of veterans on the club. Bell was upbeat about the opportunity to play for Robinson, a teammate of his father's in Cincinnati. "Frank is going to be a big inspiration to us by the way he plays the game," said Bell. "He's always aggressive, and I know that's how he'll want us to be. I remember when I first played against him and I thought he was slowing up. But this one time he slid into third base and nearly took my hand off."[12]

But the losing continued and on June 15, 1977, Bell walked out on the Indians. The reason for his AWOL status was termed "personal," but it was uncharacteristic of Bell to up and leave. "I've got a personal problem. I really don't want to discuss it," he said."[13] He missed one game, and one exhibition game in Toledo. Three days later, Robinson was fired and replaced by Jeff Torborg.

Bell met the same fate as Eckersley at the conclusion of the 1978 season. On December 8 he was sent to Texas in a straight-up deal for Toby Harrah. Harrah provided a bit more power and run-producing ability. Bell was bringing his defense to the Rangers. "Buddy has hurt us in the past few years because he moved the ball around so well," said Texas manager Pat Corrales. "We weren't able to defend against him. I was impressed. I think he'll make a good second hitter."[14]

The Rangers had tied California for second place in the American League's West Division in 1978, five games behind Kansas City. Bell was inserted to a 1979 lineup that included Richie Zisk, Al

Oliver, Bump Wills, and Pat Putnam. Bell played in all 162 games, leading the league with 670 at-bats. He hit 18 home runs, and he drove in a career-high 101 runs. Bell also established career bests in doubles (42) and runs (89). He batted .299. While his offensive numbers were indeed impressive, it was his defense that was getting rave reviews. He was honored with the first of six straight (1979-1984) Gold Glove Awards as a third baseman. It is the second longest streak for an American League third baseman, behind Brooks Robinson. Bell's streak was later equaled by Eric Chavez of Oakland (2001-2006).

"I take a lot of pride in my defense," said Bell. "I've always had pretty good hands but I've also worked very hard at defense. But to win a Gold Glove puts you in the class of a Nettles or a Brooks Robinson. For a third baseman, that's a big thrill for me."[15]

Others began taking notice of Bell and his mastery of the hot corner. "Nobody can play third better than Buddy Bell," said California manager Gene Mauch. "Nettles is a great one, too, but Bell amazes me. One thing about Nettles is how deep he plays at third. That makes the big play easier. What he's doing is telling the pitcher to field the soft stuff and the bunts and he'll take care of the hot stuff."[16]

Speaking of Bell's former Indians teammate, it was often Nettles who Bell went to for input on playing third. "I go to him for advice," said Bell. "I ask him about different hitters and how he plays them. For a long time I never played as far off the line as I do now, but Graig told me to move over more, and I did. His explanation was that there were more balls hit in the hole than down the line. And he was right."[17]

In 1980, Bell batted .329, hitting 17 home runs and driving in 83 runs. He was selected to the All-Star Game, the first of four All-Star games over the next six seasons. Bell became a star in Texas. But while his abilities were appreciated, the Rangers could not make any headway in the West Division. While the talent seemed to be there, Texas could not rise to the top. California, Chicago, Kansas City, and Oakland all took turns winning division titles during Bell's stay with the Rangers.

After he hit .315 in 1984, Bell's batting average plummeted to .235 at the All-Star break in 1985. He had also committed 16 errors to that point in the season, and the Rangers were mired in last place. On July 19, 1985, Bell was dealt to his hometown team, the Cincinnati Reds, for outfielder Duane Walker and pitcher Jeff Russell. Cincinnati had been using a platoon system at third base, employing Nick Esasky and Wayne Krenchicki. "Esasky and Krenchicki were doing a fine job for us," said Reds skipper Pete Rose. "But this makes us better overall and when you have a chance to get a guy like Buddy Bell, you do it. I hope the ballclub plays the way Buddy Bell plays. He is consistent, year in and year out, and that's what we're looking for."[18]

Player Dave Parker had a slightly different take on the trade: "Bell is a hometown boy who can help us on and off the field. He'll certainly help at the gate and I am sure that was taken into consideration. By getting him, it shows everybody that the front office wants to win."[19] The Reds were in third place at the time, trailing the division-leading Dodgers by five games.

Bell stepped right in, with the red numeral 25 on the back of his white Reds uniform, the same number Gus had worn three decades earlier. But Bell did not fare well, batting .219 in 67 games. His fielding was also subpar; he made nine errors and fielded at a .946 clip. Although the Reds won 15 of 21 to close out their schedule, they could not catch the Dodgers.

Bell bounced back the following two years. He posted career highs in home runs (20) and walks (73) in 1986 while collecting 75 RBIs and batting .278. In 1987 he hit 17 homers, drove in 70 runs, and hit .284. His .979 fielding percentage was tops among third basemen in the National League. Cincinnati finished second in both years.

Bell lost his starting position to rookie Chris Sabo in 1988. He was traded to Houston on June 19 for a player to be named later. Cincinnati also made the move to clear a roster spot for outfielder Eddie Milner. Bell's time with the Astros was short and he was released on December 21, 1988. Bell signed a one-year deal with the Rangers. But he was released after just 34 games, and retired on June 24, 1989. He announced his retirement without fanfare, no bells or whistles. "My career was pretty much a secret to begin with, I might as well keep it that way," said Bell.[20]

Buddy Bell retired from baseball with a batting average of .279, 201 home runs, 1,106 RBIs, and 2,514 hits over 18 seasons. He played in 2,405 major-league games. As of 2018 he ranked fourth all time in games played without appearing in the postseason, behind Ernie Banks, Luke Appling, and Mickey Vernon.

Bell did not stray too far from the game he loved. In 1990 he joined the Cleveland organization as a roving minor-league hitting instructor. Next he moved to Chicago, where he was the director of minor-league instruction for the White Sox from 1991 through 1993.

In 1994 Bell joined Cleveland manager Mike Hargrove's staff as an infield coach. He stayed with the Indians for two seasons. Times had changed for the Indians, and Buddy was able to witness the rebirth of the Indians, who made it to the World Series for the first time since 1954. It was doubly nice for the Bell clan as son David was an Indians utility player for part of the 1995 season. However, it was not all good news, as Gus Bell passed away on May 7, 1995, just as the season was getting under way.

Bell managed the Detroit Tigers from 1996 to August 31, 1998. He finished second in the Manager of the Year voting in 1997, after guiding the Tigers to a 26-game improvement over the 1996 team. He managed the Colorado Rockies from 2000 to April 25, 2002. Bell returned to Cleveland and served on manager Eric Wedge's staff as the bench coach from 2003 through May 30, 2005. He left the Indians when he was named to replace Tony Pena as manager of Kansas City, a position he held through the 2007 season. His won-lost record as a manager was 514-715 (.418).

In 1999 Bell was at the helm of the US Baseball Team in the Pan American games in Winnipeg, Canada. They won four games to advance to the medal round, eventually losing to Cuba in the championship game. Their performance enabled the United States to qualify for the 2000 Olympics in Sydney, Australia.

In 2005 Bell co-wrote, with author Neal Vahle, *Smart Baseball: How Professionals Play the Mental Game*. In the book, Bell examines the mental makeup of players, past and present, and how they prepare themselves. If it is believed that ballplayers are in top physical condition when they take the field, often it is their mental approach to the game that will determine if they succeed or fail, he maintained.

In 2005 Bell suffered a personal loss. His nephew Lance Cpl Timothy Bell was killed with 13 other Marines when their amphibious assault vehicle was blown up during combat operations in Iraq. He was the 165th Marine interred at Arlington National Cemetery as a result of Operation Iraq.

In 2006 Bell took a leave of absence from the Royals at the end of the season. It was discovered that he had throat cancer. He made a full recovery, returning to the Royals in 2007, and he managed the entire year.

In 2017 Bell was in his 10th season working in the front office of the Chicago White Sox. He was the vice president/assistant to general manager Rick Hahn and director of player development. In 2015 he received the Sheldon "Chief" Bender Award, given annually to someone who has been instrumental in player development. "I am incredibly humbled by this award as I had the distinct honor of working alongside Chief in the Reds organization in 1999," Bell said. "I learned something new every day. The knowledge I gleaned has been invaluable to me ever since, and I am thrilled to be joining the impressive list of recipients who have received this award before me."[21]

After the 2017 season, Bell returned to his hometown of Cincinnati. He was named the Reds' senior advisor to General Manager and president of baseball operations, Dick Williams.

Buddy was joined in Cincinnati be his son David, who was named the 52nd manager in Reds history on October 21, 2018. The Bell family now joins another exclusive club. They are the fourth family in MLB history to have a father and son who served as managers. Buddy Bell managed in Detroit, Colorado and Kansas City. They join George and Dick Sisler, Bob and Joel Skinner, and Bob and Aaron Boone.[22]

NOTES

1. Joe Giuliotti, "Bell Didn't Try for HRs," *Boston Herald*, July 6, 1975: 35.
2. Ibid.
3. Chuck Heaton, "Bell's Two HRs Nail 4th in a Row," *Cleveland Plain Dealer*, July 6, 1975: 3-2.
4. Russell Schneider, "Bell Rejects All-Star Bid," *Cleveland Plain Dealer*, July 11, 1975: 1-C.
5. Ibid.
6. Ibid.
7. Ibid.
8. Joe Quinn, "Buddy Bell: From Moeller to the Majors," *Greater Cincinnati Sports*, September 1978 (In Bell's Hall of Fame File).
9. Quinn.
10. Dan Coughlin, "Indians' Bell Waiting for Other Shoe to Fall," *Cleveland Plain Dealer*, March 31, 1978: 38.
11. Russell Schneider, "Bell's Hot Stick Sounding Alarm to A.L Hurlers," *The Sporting News*, June 16, 1973: 28.
12. Associated Press, March 4, 1975 (In Bell's Hall of Fame file.)
13. Chuck Heaton, "Buddy Takes Night Off," *Cleveland Plain Dealer*, June 16, 1977: 1-E.
14. Randy Galloway, "Bell Says Difference Is Talent," *Dallas Morning News*, December 9, 1978: 2B.
15. Randy Galloway, "Bell, Sundberg Voted Gold Glove Awards," *Dallas Morning News*, November 22, 1979: 2B.
16. Randy Galloway, "Nettles the Greatest? Someone Forgot Bell," *Dallas Morning News*, October 25, 1981.
17. Ibid.
18. Hal McCoy, "Deposed Reds Voice Gripes," *The Sporting News*, August 5, 1985: 16.
19. Ibid.
20. T.R. Sullivan, "Bye-bye Buddy," *Fort Worth Star-Telegram*, June 25, 1989: 2.
21. Rhett Bollinger and Joey Nowak, "Bell Honored with 'Chief' Bender Award," milb.com, accessed November 29, 2015.
22. Associated Press, "New manager David Bell tasked with turning around Reds", http://www.espn.com/mlb/story/_/id/25054877/new-manager-david-bell-tasked-turning-cincinnati-reds October 22, 2018, accessed October 23, 2018

LUIS ISAAC

BY RICHARD BOGOVICH

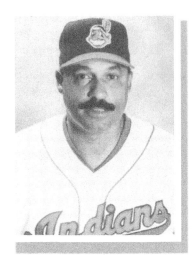

"Bullpen coaches are probably the most underappreciated of any uniformed member of a Major League staff," MLB.com reporter Evan Drellich once wrote, "just because they're well out of the public eye."[1] If that's a credible rule, then Luis Isaac must have been an exception when he held that job for the Cleveland Indians, because local members of the Baseball Writers Association of America (BBWAA) twice named him winner of the Frank Gibbons/Steve Olin Good Guy Award, 10 years apart. From 1968 through 2017, only four other men won it twice.

Luis Isaac was born on June 19, 1946, in Río Piedras, a municipality near San Juan that was annexed by the Puerto Rican capital city in 1951. He played PONY League and Babe Ruth League baseball in his youth. He added track and field when he attended high school in neighboring Carolina.[2]

Luis, who played 99 percent of his minor-league games as a catcher, signed his first professional contract with the Pittsburgh Pirates. In 1962 he made his debut with Kingsport in the Class-D Appalachian League. He played in just seven games and had one hit, one RBI, and one run in 18 at-bats. The only member of the Kingsport Pirates that year who played in the major leagues was fellow catcher Carl Taylor, who played in 40 of the team's 69 games.

Luis was still only 16 in April 1963, and thus at least two years younger than his teammates on the Pittsburgh affiliate in Gastonia, North Carolina. He had reached his maximum height by then, 5-feet-11, but reportedly weighed only 150 pounds.[3] Luis played only one game for Gastonia, though it was a good one for him, 2-for-5 with a walk. He played in 31 more games that year for two other Pittsburgh farm teams at the A level, eight games for Batavia, New York, and 23 with Reno.[4] Isaac didn't play pro ball at all in 1964 but that was the year he graduated from high school in Carolina.[5] By late October he was listed on the roster of Puerto Rico's Arecibo Wolves, without a professional affiliation. He was to be managed by Tony Castaño and projected to catch the likes of Mike Cuellar of St. Louis and Jim Roland of Minnesota, while trying to catch basestealers with throws to Sandy Alomar of Milwaukee or Cookie Rojas of Philadelphia.[6]

In 1965 Isaac returned to pro ball with the Waterloo Hawks of the Class-A Midwest League, an affiliate of the Boston Red Sox. He made at least one trip to the disabled list[7] and played in just 21 games; after that season he almost always played in at least 50 games yearly. In the November 1965 minor-league draft, Isaac was drafted by AA teams. Several of the AA selections, including Isaac, cost $8,000, while the others cost $4,000. At the time he was the property of Winston-Salem, another of Boston's Class-A farm teams, and he was chosen by Reading, then of the Double-A Eastern League.[8] Reading ended up without a club in 1966. Instead, Isaac played in Pawtucket, Rhode Island. In 56 games, he homered (and tripled) for the first time. Both of his home runs that season came in the same game, a few days after his 20th birthday, in what was probably one of his top career highlights. Pawtucket was trailing York by one in the eighth inning but exploded for six runs, four thanks to a grand slam by Isaac.[9] Isaac and two other catchers each played about the same number of games for Pawtucket. One of the other two was Fran Healy, who was three years away from the start of a nine-year major-league career.

Though Isaac's batting average was only .184, for 1967 he was promoted to Cleveland's Triple-A team in Portland, Oregon. That was the first of six straight seasons at Triple A, either at Portland or Wichita. In 1967 Isaac played in 94 Triple-A games, a season high for him. He batted little better in 1967 than he did at Double A in 1966. In his third season at Portland, 1969, Isaac reached his career-best Triple-A batting average, .266 in 93 games. In his second season with Wichita, 1971, he came close to that by hitting .261 in 93 games. In 1969 and 1970 Isaac shared time with another young catcher who'd already played a few seasons in the majors, Ken Suarez. It's possible that 1970 was the first time Isaac appeared on a baseball card, a McDonald's set of 18 Wichita Aeros that was listed in at least one catalog at $350.[10]

Isaac was invited at least once to spring training with the Indians. In March of 1971 he was a nonroster invitee in Tucson, but was returned to Wichita toward the end of the month.[11]

From 1973 through 1977 Isaac was a player-coach for Cleveland farm teams at different levels, beginning with Class-A Reno.[12] In 1974, with Double-A San Antonio, he played in a personal high 115 games. Isaac returned to Triple-A Oklahoma City for part of 1975 and Toledo for all of 1977. During winters he continued to play with Arecibo,[13] and by the 1975-76 season he was their player-manager, known for having "a keen mind for baseball strategy."[14]

In 1978, he began the season as a coach at Triple-A Portland,[15] and a second cousin of his, longtime minor-league infielder Juan López, was on Spokane in the same league.[16] That assignment didn't last long, because by the end of June Isaac started his lone year as a manager in the minors, for short-season Batavia, which had been one of his first assignments 15 years earlier. He led the team for its entire season, and it finished with a record of 34-38. One player eventually made it to the majors: Ramon Romero, who pitched briefly for Cleveland in 1984 and 1985.

In 1979 Isaac played one final season, for Double-A Chattanooga at the age of 33, and thus logged 16 years in the minors without making it to the majors. In eight years at Triple A he caught in 480 games and made 35 errors, for a fielding percentage of .989.

By the late 1970s, Isaac had switched to Santurce in Puerto Rico's winter league. Santurce at the time was led by former Indians manager and future Hall of Famer Frank Robinson (who put himself into a few lineups as designated hitter during 1978-79.[17] In 1980, Isaac became a scout for Cleveland and continued in that role through mid-1987, while also coaching rookie league teams.[18] His 1981 baseball card as a Batavia Trojan identified him as the pitching coach (and in contrast to common photos of him years later, he was clean-shaven). He was identified as the hitting coach on the 1992 baseball card that he shared with fellow coach Dyar Miller.

One of the first players he recruited as a scout made it to the majors: Bernardo Brito was signed out of the Dominican Republic in 1980 and played in 40 games for the Minnesota Twins from 1992 through 1995.[19] In 1981 he signed another Dominican, shortstop Wilson Uribe, who played eight seasons of minor-league ball, was a major-league bullpen catcher from 1989 through 1995, and for the 2011 and 2012 seasons was a coach for the Arizona Diamondbacks.[20]

One prospect with whom Isaac had a very long acquaintance was Sandy Alomar Jr. In 1990 Alomar was named an All-Star for the first of six times in his major-league career, and that season Isaac reminisced about interacting with him around 1970, then reconnecting in 1983. "I remember Sandy when he was 4 or 5 years old," Isaac told one reporter early in 1990. "I played winter ball with his father at Santurce, and Sandy was always around the clubhouse." The two would play catch. "He would squat down like a catcher and give me the sign. I would tell him, 'I'm going to make you a catcher.' Of course, I didn't know it was going to come true, although that's what he always said."[21]

About two months later, after Alomar was named an All-Star, Isaac was a little more candid about that early contact. "I used to put catcher's equipment on him and throw hard to him, tried to hurt him," Isaac recalled. "I'd come to the ballpark and try to make him cry. I never thought he would be the type of catcher he is now."[22] Another reporter might have provided an explanation for Isaac's purported animosity, and the source appeared to be Sandy's Hall of Fame brother, Robby, who said back then that "Sandy was always doing the crazy, dangerous things," including sneaking away with Isaac's mitt.[23] By 1983, Isaac's feigned animosity changed to admiration when Sandy Alomar was suddenly a 17-year-old Caribbean phenom. "I told [Cleveland] about Alomar, but we never did talk money," Isaac said. "There were about 15 scouts around and his price was up around $100,000. I didn't think we would be in the running."[24] Alomar signed with the San Diego Padres but after only eight games with them the Tribe acquired him in December of 1989, along with Carlos Baerga and Chris James, in a trade for Joe Carter.

In the mid-1980s Luis Isaac experienced two changes in his personal life. On Valentine's Day in 1984 he married the former Marilu Morales, and on September 15, 1985, they welcomed their son, Luis Isaac III, into the world. Luis already had three daughters: Veronica, Monica, and Jennifer. On the job front, less than two years later Pat Corrales was fired as manager of the Indians and replaced with Doc Edwards, and on July 16, 1987, Isaac was named the bullpen coach. He returned to coaching in the minors in 1992, was rehired as bullpen coach on November 9, 1989,[25] and continued in the role through 1991.

The last day of Isaac's first half-season in the majors proved memorable for a surprising reason. The Indians finished the season against the Angels on Sunday, October 4, and at 4:00 that morning there was an earthquake in the Los Angeles area, and at least a few Indians panicked in their Anaheim hotel. For example, "Dave Clark and Junior Noboa abandoned their rooms and slept in a van in the parking lot," according to an Ohio newspaper. "Coach Luis Isaac was seen running down the 11th-floor hallway pulling his trousers on over his underwear," the newspaper's account said. "Isaac ended up sleeping in the lobby."[26]

In 1992 Isaac returned to coaching in the minors with the Colorado Springs Sky Sox. In 1993 he switched to coaching for Charlie Manuel's Charlotte Knights, and Manny Ramirez recalled Isaac being something of a joke-teller after a few beers, as well as a coach whom he felt comfortable sassing playfully.[27] Years later, Isaac and Cleveland pitcher Jake Westbrook received attention for their humor in a *Sports Illustrated* feature: "The Best Jokes We Can Tell in *Sports Illustrated*." Isaac's joke was: "An ant and an elephant marry. The first night of their honeymoon, the two make love, but the elephant has a heart attack and dies. The ant is devastated and says, 'Five minutes of passion, and now I have to spend the rest of my life digging a grave.'"[28]

Isaac returned to the major-league club as the Indians' bullpen coach in 1994. The strike by players in August, which ended up canceling the World Series, motivated most Puerto Rican major leaguers to play in their native island's winter-league season. As a result, San Juan Senadores manager Luis "Torito" Melendez had a difficult time choosing among many worthy candidates to represent Puerto Rico on its 1995 Caribbean Series team. Isaac was one of four coaches who helped Melendez make those impossible choices. The resulting "Dream Team," which won the Series, included Roberto Alomar, Edgar Martinez, Juan Gonzalez, Bernie Williams, Ruben Sierra, Carlos Baerga, and Carmelo Martinez.[29]

On their way to playing in the 1995 World Series, the Indians clinched the AL Central crown on September 8. Paul Hoynes of Cleveland's *Plain Dealer* wrote that "No one connected with the Indians today could be happier than bullpen coach Luis Isaac. Because no one among the Indians' current players, coaches and managers has worn a Cleveland uniform longer than him," Hoynes wrote. "Mel Harder is the only person to wear a Tribe uniform longer. Isaac has been in uniform 30 years; Harder wore his for 36 years as a pitcher and coach."[30]

A month into the 1996 season the Indians suffered through another unusual early-morning incident at a hotel, this time in Toronto. At 2:00 A.M. on a Sunday in early May, guests staying at the Westin Harbour Castle were awakened by a fire alarm that sounded at length. A voice over the public-address system stated that the cause was under investigation but seemed to say that vacating the building was optional. "At first I wasn't going to go," said Indians manager Mike Hargrove. "Then I said: 'If there is a fire, I'm going to look pretty stupid.'" Hargrove walked down 33 flights of stairs and found various guests already in the lobby but only three of his – coaches Dave Nelson, Mark Wiley, and Luis Isaac – plus a lone player, Eric Plunk. "I guess that means there's only five intelligent people on this club," Hargrove concluded.[31] When Hargrove managed the AL All-Stars in 1998, for the second time, he took four of his own coaches with him and that quartet included Wiley and Isaac,[32] two of his "intelligent" employees. It was a few months later, in November of 1998, that Isaac was rewarded in a different way, when the Baseball Writers Association of American chapter named him the newest embodiment of Frank Gibbons and Steve Olin.

Isaac remained bullpen coach into the new century, but his continuation was jeopardized by a health scare during spring training in 2002. He was hospitalized for eight days at the beginning of March after surgery to remove 14 inches of his small intestine. One aftereffect was a brief attack of gout, which he had been controlling the previous two years with medication, but very soon he was back with the team.[33]

Isaac was fired abruptly at the end of the 2008 season. He was 62 years old and had been with the Cleveland organization since age 19. "Luis was as loyal as the day is long," said manager Eric Wedge. "Ultimately, I felt we needed a different dynamic in the bullpen for that role. It's been something I've been thinking about for a while." Wedge added that Isaac would not be reassigned within the organization.[34] Asked by a sportswriter if he was angry, he replied, "How am I going to be angry when I've been 44 years with the Indians? How am I going to do that? When you're running a team and you think the best thing is to do this or that, how am I going to be angry when they are the ones that run the team? You can't be upset."[35]

Isaac also disputed Wedge's implication that he hadn't been offered a different position in the organization. Luis said general manager Mark Shapiro did offer him something else but Isaac declined and said he'd search for a coaching job on his own. He added that if he didn't succeed in that hunt, he might rethink Shapiro's offer. "Or I'll stay in Puerto Rico playing golf," he said.[36] That very day he said he shot an 83 at Cocoa Beach, the golf course that hosted the Puerto Rico Open.

Isaac could afford to do that because he reported having earned more than $1 million over the years, and was fully vested in Major League Baseball's pension plan. He summed up his reaction by saying," I hope that Mr. Shapiro and Mr. Eric Wedge go to the World Series and win. I'll be happy because I think they're my Indians. For 44 years, I loved the Indians, and the Indians are my team."[37]

Despite Isaac's classy reaction, outrage on his behalf was expressed swiftly by Bill Livingston, a sports columnist for the *Plain Dealer* since 1984. "The fall guy for Indians General Manager Mark Shapiro and his bullpen of walking gas cans is apparently coach Luis Isaac," Livingston wrote. "Isaac was one of the guys fans don't know much about, but he deserved better. It was a small, mean way to dismiss a man who had been part of the Indians' organization for 44 years in the big leagues and the bushes.

"Isaac didn't just have longevity. He had baseball knowledge," Livingston wrote. "Brian Anderson was the winning pitcher in relief the day Charlie Nagy got out of trouble in every inning and the Indians won their last pennant in 1997." Anderson credited Isaac with developing his changeup. Isaac told him to drag his back foot to slow down his arm motion. "Yet third-base coach Joel Skinner, he of the 'Merkle moment' in the playoffs, is still here. Remember Game 7 against the Red Sox, and how the words 'Swing, and a single to left, and here comes Lofton to tie the game' weren't spoken?" Livingston asked, as he concluded. "How was Skinner absolved of holding Kenny Lofton at third? How does Isaac alone take the fall for the season?"[38]

Whether equally angry or simply saddened, the next month the BBWAA chapter paid its respects, so to speak, by naming Luis Isaac winner of the Frank Gibbons/Steve Olin Good Guy Award for a second time.

NOTES

1. Evan Drellich, "With Tuck retired, Lavarnway turns to Epperson," mlb.com/redsox/news/c-41333894/print, February 1, 2013.
2. *1991 Cleveland Indians Media Guide*, 14.
3. Neale Patrick, "Pat's Peckings," *Gastonia* (North Carolina) *Gazette*, April 26, 1963: 2-B. Patrick had bad notes about Luis, calling him a "Negro from the Dominican Republic," but correctly stated that he had appeared in seven games for Kingsport the previous summer. The *1991 Cleveland Indians Media Guide* reported Isaac's weight as 195 pounds.
4. "Two New Players Assigned Pirates," *Gastonia Gazette*, June 29, 1963: 6.
5. *1991 Cleveland Indians Media Guide*, 14.
6. "Puerto Rico Player Rosters," *The Sporting News*, October 31, 1964: 27.
7. "Hawks Use Disabled List to Reach Limit," *Waterloo* (Iowa) *Daily Courier*, June 9, 1965: 24. Team statistics on that page show that Isaac was hitting .250 in 16 at-bats at the time.
8. "Red Wings Get Pair in Annual Minor Draft," *Rochester* (New York) *Democrat and Chronicle*, November 30, 1965: 2D.
9. "Mets Drop Elmira 6-4 after Coming from 3-0 Deficit," *The Express* (Lock Haven, Pennsylvania), June 24, 1966: 13.
10. See mention of 2002 catalogue at worthpoint.com/worthopedia/1970-mcdonalds-wichita-aeros-luis-isaac-minor.
11. "Sports Highlights," *Circleville* (Ohio) *Herald*, March 25, 1971: 13.
12. *1991 Cleveland Indians Media Guide*, 14.
13. He appeared regularly on Arecibo rosters printed in *The Sporting News*, e.g., November 2, 1968: 47; November 29, 1969: 47 (though listed as an infielder); November 28, 1970: 55; November 13, 1971: 55; and November 4, 1972: 26.
14. Thomas E. Van Hyning, *The Santurce Crabbers: Sixty Seasons of Puerto Rican Winter League Baseball* (Jefferson, North Carolina: McFarland & Company, Inc., 1999), 130.
15. *1991 Cleveland Indians Media Guide*, 14.
16. Juan López was born in Río Piedras in 1952 and played in the minor leagues from 1971 to 1984. He coached at various levels and peaked as batting-practice coach and advance scout coordinator for the New York Mets in 2002 and 2003, and as their bullpen coach in 2008. See *2006 New York Mets Media Guide*, 318.
17. Van Hyning, 133.
18. *1991 Cleveland Indians Media Guide*, 14.
19. Jim Souhan, "Merullo Is Trying to Make the Most of Big Opportunity," *Star Tribune* (Minneapolis), May 6, 1995: 7C.
20. *2011 Arizona Diamondbacks Media Guide*, 49.
21. Sheldon Ocker, "Alomar Looks Like Pure Gold," *Washington Post*, April 12, 1990: B6.
22. Chuck Finder, "It's a Start," *Pittsburgh Post-Gazette*, July 6, 1990: 15, 17.
23. Mark Whicker, "Alomar Brothers Hope to Reunite on All-Star Night," *Indianapolis Star*, July 4, 1990: C-2.
24. Ocker, "Alomar Looks Like Pure Gold."
25. *1991 Cleveland Indians Media Guide*, 14.
26. "Notebook," *Akron* (Ohio) *Beacon Journal*, October 8, 1987: D6.
27. Jean Rhodes and Shawn Boburg, *Becoming Manny: Inside the Life of Baseball's Most Enigmatic Slugger* (New York: Scribner, 2009), 145.
28. "The Best Jokes We Can Tell in *Sports Illustrated*," *Sports Illustrated*, May 30, 2005: 46. Westbrook's joke was: "Two antennae got married. The wedding was terrible, but the reception was great." For an example of Isaac's sense of humor in action, see clevelandtribeblog.blogspot.com/2006/08/.
29. Gabrielle Paese, "Remembering the '95 'Dream Team,'" espn.com/mlb/story/_/id/12263157/remembering-puerto-rico-1995-caribbean-series-dream-team, February 1, 2015.
30. Paul Hoynes, "Divison Title 30 Years in Making for Isaac," *Cleveland Plain Dealer*, September 10, 1995: 11D
31. "Indians Face Adversity," *News-Press* (Fort Myers, Florida), May 5, 1996, 8B.
32. "O'Donnell out, Testaverde In?" *Elyria* (Ohio) *Chronicle-Telegram*, June 24, 1998: B2. Hargrove also took four of Cleveland's coaches when he managed the AL All-Star Team two years earlier but Isaac wasn't among them.
33. Sheldon Ocker, "Wright's Twinge Draws a Crowd," *Ashtabula* (Ohio) *Star Beacon*, March 11, 2002: B4.
34. "Indians Fire Bullpen Coach," *Sandusky* (Ohio) *Register*, October 1, 2008: B1.
35. Ibid.
36. Ibid.

37 Patrick McManamon, "AFC North Has Rough Times Ahead," *Ashtabula* (Ohio) *Star Beacon*, October 5, 2008: C7.

38 Bill Livingston, "Aha, the Bullpen Coach Is to Blame," *Plain Dealer* (Cleveland), October 2, 2008: D1. The version online at cleveland.com/livingston/index.ssf/2008/10/isaacs_dismissal_a_stain_on_in.html has Jamie Turner's byline atop it, though Livingston is also credited partway down.

CHARLIE MANUEL

BY ANDY STURGILL

We're told from a young age not to judge a book by its cover. We're also told you never get a second chance to make a first impression. With Charlie Manuel, outward presentation and first impressions often prove misleading.

"You hear his country accent, and you think he's a little bit slow," longtime Phillies shortstop Jimmy Rollins once said. "But he's sharp as a tack."[1]

Charles Fuqua Manuel was born on January 4, 1944, somewhere in southern West Virginia or the western part of Virginia. His official birthplace is listed as North Fork, West Virginia, but this is not quite accurate. "Evidently, I was born in a car and they took me to the doctor in North Fork," Manuel said. "I never actually lived there, but, if you go online, I'm listed somewhere as their most prominent citizen."[2]

Charlie was the third of 11 children (and first boy) born to Charles Fuqua Manuel Sr. and June Manuel. Charles Sr. was a Pentecostal preacher given his unique middle name by his mother after the doctor who delivered him.[3] The Manuels settled into Buena Vista, Virginia, in the western portion of the state, where they struggled to get by. The family of 13 lived in a house with only three bedrooms. Despite young Charlie's love of baseball, the Manuels couldn't afford proper equipment, so he made his own. "I used to cut my own bat out from a stick," he said. "I wanted something better than just a broomstick. I wanted to round it up top and make a handle."[4]

Manuel was a four-sport star (baseball, football, basketball, and track) at Perry-McCluer High School in Buena Vista. He was recruited to play basketball by several colleges, including the University of Pennsylvania. Charlie probably would have taken Penn's offer until his life changed dramatically two months before graduation. Manuel's father took his own life inside the family's home. He left Charlie, the oldest son, a note charging him with providing for the family. "I felt like all of a sudden I had a lot of responsibility on my hands," Manuel said. "I felt like that someone had to work, someone had to provide for them, someone had to feed them, someone had to take care of them."[5]

Feeling the need to provide, Manuel bypassed college and signed with the Minnesota Twins organization in 1963 for $20,000. He continued to send money home during the season and worked offseason jobs back home.

Manuel, then sometimes known as Chuck, began his professional career in 1963 near his home with the Wytheville (Virginia) Twins of the Appalachian League, hitting .358 with seven home runs in 58 games. From 1964 through 1966 he continued through the Twins organization, splitting time between Orlando and Wilson (North Carolina), hitting no higher than .265 with a total of 11 home runs over the three seasons.

As a 23-year-old in 1967, the powerful 6-foot4, left-handed-hitting Manuel established himself as a legitimate prospect. Playing for Wisconsin Rapids of the Midwestern League, Manuel surpassed the magic .300/.400/.500 mark (.313 batting average/.403 on-base percentage/.514 slugging percentage). After a successful campaign for Double-A Charlotte in 1968 (.283, 13 home runs, 79 RBIs) that saw him named a Southern League All-Star, Manuel was invited to spring training with the Twins in 1969.

Manuel was the star of the Twins' 1969 spring training. Manager Billy Martin had no choice but to keep him on the team when it headed north for the season. The 25-year old made his major-league debut in the Twins' 4-3 Opening Day loss at Kansas City on April 8, grounding out to second in the 12th inning against Moe Drabowsky. He got his first major-league hit in his first start, a double off the California Angels' Tom Murphy, and cracked his first home run a week later against the White Sox' Don Secrist.

At the end of May, Manuel was hitting .311 with a pair of home runs and was receiving regular playing time as a platoon player in the outfield. However, his production regressed in June, and his playing time did likewise in July. He hit a double against the Seattle Pilots on July 19, which turned out to be Manuel's last hit of the season. From July 20 through the end of the season on October 1, he improbably went 0-for-36 and saw his respectable average of .258 crater to a final mark of .207 for the season.

As bad as his season was, it was the one in which he played in the most games and set career highs in virtually every counting stat.

Manuel played in 59 games for the Twins in 1970, but again found himself in the minors, seeing action in 21 games for Triple-A Evansville. Despite spending most of the season with the Twins, he started only six games all season, a startling departure from his more frequent playing time as a rookie in 1969.

After splitting time between the majors and Triple-A and playing in only 18 games for Minnesota in 1971, Manuel again spent the entire 1972 season with the Twins. He started 27 games, played in 63 overall, and scuffled his way to a .205 batting average and one home run in 129 plate appearances. He would never again spend significant time in the major leagues as a player.

Manuel spent the entire 1973 season with Triple-A Tacoma, then was part of a four-player deal that sent him to the Los Angeles Dodgers. He spent most of the next two seasons at Triple-A Albuquerque, batting better than .300, and topping .400 in on-base percentage and .600 in slugging percentage in each season. He finished in the top 11 of the Pacific Coast League in all three categories during both seasons, and his .601 slugging percentage led the league in 1975. He got into 19 games for the Dodgers in 1974-75, never starting a game. At age 31, he had played in his last major-league game.

Though his career as a player in the major leagues was over, Manuel was not done playing. He was just entering the most prominent phase of his playing career, not in the United States but in Japan.

He signed with the Yakult Swallows of Tokyo for the 1976 season. The team flew him into town, gave him an interpreter, and called a press conference – hardly the welcome expected for a .198 hitter in the major leagues. "I was kinda petrified," Manuel said of the welcome. "They had my [jersey] number. I was already a star before I ever got there. They were talking about how good I was. I thought, 'You gotta be kidding me.'"[6]

Despite his foreboding, between 1976 and 1981, Manuel terrorized pitching in Japan's Central League, hitting .303 with 189 home runs and 491 RBIs for the Swallows and the Kintetsu Buffaloes. His .324 average, 37 home runs, and 94 RBIs for Kintetsu in 1979 earned him the league MVP, the first American player to be so honored. He followed up his MVP season by slugging 48 home runs for the Buffaloes in 1980, which long stood as a record for an American player in Japan. Manuel played for two pennant-winning teams in his six seasons in Japan. His power at the plate and his reddish hair earned Manuel the nickname Aki Ono (Red Devil) among the fans and players in Japan.

Manuel's playing career ended after the 1981 season, and he wasted little time getting involved in the game on the other side of the white lines. He spent the 1982 season as a scout for the Twins. In 1983 Manuel was back on the field, taking over as the manager of Wisconsin Rapids, the Twins' entry in the Class A Midwest League, and one of the teams he had played for on the way up to the majors. Just as he had done as a player in the '60s, Manuel began climbing up the Twins organization as a manager. He managed Double-A Orlando in 1984 and '85, then took over the Twins' Triple-A outposts in Toledo and Portland in 1986 and 1987.

Manuel joined the Cleveland organization in 1988 as the Indians' hitting coach. He held this role for two seasons before returning to the minors as a manager in 1990, just as the team was building the nucleus that would power it to two World Series appearances in the 1990s. The Indians of the '90s were paced by a powerful offense, and the principal members of the attack – Albert Belle, Carlos Baerga, Manny Ramirez, Jim Thome, et al. – all played for Manuel in his four seasons as manager of Cleveland's Triple-A teams at Colorado Springs and Charlotte. In 1992 Colorado Springs won the Pacific Coast League title, and Manuel took home the league's Manager of the Year honors. He followed that up in 1993 by leading Charlotte, the Indians new Triple-A affiliate, to the International League crown.

In 1994 Manuel returned to the majors for his second stint as Cleveland's hitting coach. By now these Indians were talented and ready to win. After finishing one game out of the division lead in the strike-shortened 1994 season, the team won five straight AL Central titles from 1995 to 1999, posting three of the top five-win totals in team history. The run was highlighted by 100 wins in 144 games in 1995, when Cleveland won the Central Division crown by 30 games. The 1995 and 1997 editions both captured the American League pennant before falling in the World Series.

Manuel oversaw a powerful offense that bludgeoned teams with its run-scoring prowess. The top three run-scoring teams and the top six home-run-hitting teams in Indians history all came under Manuel's watch as hitting coach and his subsequent run as manager.

While watching your powerful lineup pound opposing pitching is fun, not everything was fun during Manuel's time in Northeast Ohio. After suffering a heart attack in 1990, he had another in 1998 that necessitated a quadruple bypass. In 2000 Manuel was diagnosed with diverticulitis, which caused a pouch in his colon to rupture. During the ensuing surgery, doctors discovered that he had kidney cancer. He ended up managing from the bench with a colostomy bag under his uniform for about a month. "That might have been the lowest point I've ever been in my life," he recalled years later. "I was pretty much sick that whole summer."[7] Then early in the 2001 season Manuel grew ill while throwing batting practice. Scar tissue had grown over his small intestine, his gall bladder needed to be removed, and his body had filled with infected fluid. The incident required Manuel to remain on IV fluids for nearly four months to allow the fluid to continue draining.

"(His health history is) one of the reasons why his tolerance for people to go on the DL is not very high," said Ruben Amaro Jr., who was assistant general manager and then GM during Manuel's time in Philadelphia.[8]

Manuel replaced Mike Hargrove as Indians manager in 2000. The Indians continued to score runs but could not match the overall success of the Hargrove years. A Central Division title in 2001 was bracketed by playoff misses in 2000 and 2002. Unable to come to terms with him on a contract extension, the Indians fired Manuel as manager in July of 2002.

After the 2002 season, one of Manuel's prized protégés, Jim Thome, left the Indians and signed as a free agent with the Phillies. Unattached after more than a decade with the Cleveland organization, Manuel followed Thome to Philadelphia, taking a job as a special assistant to Phillies GM Ed Wade.

The signing of Thome raised expectations in Philadelphia higher than they had been in a decade. After consecutive nonplayoff seasons in

2003 and 2004, manager Larry Bowa was fired and Manuel succeeded him.

Perhaps born of its tendency to be overlooked halfway between New York City and Washington, Philadelphia boasts a rougher edge than its sophisticated mid-Atlantic neighbors. It may lack the financial power of New York or the political power of Washington, but one thing no city can top is Philadelphia's embrace of its four major sports teams. The day after the Phillies announced Manuel's hiring, Rob Maadi of the Associated Press presciently wrote, "Charlie Manuel's thick Southern drawl, down-home charm and folksy nature make him an odd fit for gritty Philadelphia. He'll be a perfect choice as manager if he leads the Phillies to the playoffs."[9]

"I came here to do a job," Manuel said at his introductory press conference. "It's a we, not an I. And we're going to get the job done. Our goal is to get to the World Series and win it. That's what we're going to do."[10]

The fans were unsure what to make of Manuel. His stuttering and malaprops left them uninspired. His occasional mistake in executing a double switch left the fans confused. The team again narrowly missing the playoffs in 2005 and 2006 left the fans frustrated, and the folksy manager was an easy target. Many in the fan base and media called for Manuel's ouster.

Lost in the disappointment of 2006 was a changing of the guard in Philadelphia. Longtime stalwarts like Bobby Abreu, Mike Lieberthal, and David Bell were either shipped out or saw their roles diminished. Ryan Howard, Jimmy Rollins, and Chase Utley emerged as three of the elite players in the National League, and ace left-handed pitcher Cole Hamels made his debut. The team was given a winning attitude and hard-nosed grit in the acquisition of World Series champion center fielder (2005 White Sox) Aaron Rowand, who, in contrast to the timid fielding Abreu, literally broke his face chasing down a fly ball in a May game. The complacent, good but not good enough attitudes and players that dominated the Phillies for years had been replaced by a group of gritty gamers. The passion of the group on the field matched the passion in the stands, and the common thread among these players was that they loved playing for Charlie Manuel. "He not only brought the best out of myself, but he brought the best out of a lot of players," Utley said.[11]

The Phillies' young core of stars bore a striking resemblance to the 1990s Indians teams Manuel had been a part of, and the 2006, 2007, and 2009 editions led the NL in runs scored, while the 2008 team tied for second.

Before the 2007 season Jimmy Rollins declared his team the team to beat in the National League East. The Phillies hadn't been to the playoffs since 1993. Things did not start well. By April 20 the Phils were already 6½ games out of first place and Manuel had gotten into a heated postgame verbal altercation with a local media personality. The pitching staff struggled, but the offense kept the Phillies in view of a playoff spot. The Phillies trailed the New York Mets by six games in the East in late August when the two teams squared off in a four-game series in Philadelphia. The Phillies swept the four-game set, including two walk-off wins, the finale a wild 11–10 triumph that shrank the Phillies' deficit to two games.

A cold streak after the Mets series left the Phillies seven games behind with 17 to play. But they beat the Colorado Rockies and then swept the Mets over the next four games. They finished on a 13-4 tear while the Mets never recovered from their second consecutive sweep by the Phillies and stumbled to a 5-12 finish that allowed the Phillies to win the NL East on the last day of the season. Even though the Phillies were swept out of the National League Division Series, the team had gotten over the hump and the core of young stars provided hope to a fan base that hadn't seen a major championship in nearly 25 years.

The 2008 season followed a pattern similar to 2007. The team struggled out of the gate, hung around first place on the strength of a powerful offense, and found itself 2½ games behind the Mets with 17 left to play. The Phillies once again finished 13-4 and finished three games ahead of the Mets to win their second straight division title. After dispatching the Milwaukee Brewers in four games in the NLDS, Philadelphia defeated the Los Angeles Dodgers in five games in the NL Championship Series to win its first pennant since 1993. The victory was bittersweet for Manuel, whose mother, June, died before Game Two of the NLCS. He stayed with the team through the end of the series before traveling to Virginia for her service. Manuel later told reporters that his mother was a huge fan of his team and that he put a Phillies hat in her casket.[12]

Just as in their first two postseason series, the Phillies lost only once in clinching their first World Series since 1980, a defeat of the Tampa Bay Rays. Weather became a prevailing storyline in the series, delaying the start of Game Three for several hours and causing a two-day stoppage in the middle of Game Five. But when Phillies closer Brad Lidge struck out Tampa Bay's Eric Hinske to end it, Manuel's declaration that the Phillies were going to win the World Series under his watch came true.

As the on-field party celebrating the victory unfolded, Manuel was interviewed on the field by Fox Sports. As he answered questions, the ballpark chanted a chorus of "Charlie! Charlie!" Grabbing the microphone from interviewer Jeanne Zelasko, Manuel addressed Phillies fans everywhere, bellowing in his Southern drawl "Hey listen! ... This is for Philadelphia! ... This is for our fans! ... Hey! ... Who's the world champions!?!"

The bumbling manager had become a folk hero to the fans of Philadelphia.

As an encore, the 2009 team again won the National League pennant but could not overcome the New York Yankees in the World Series. The 2010 and 2011 seasons saw two more division titles, running the Phillies' streak, echoing the Indians of the '90s, to five in a row. Injuries and age kept the Phillies from competing in 2012 and 2013, and in mid-August of 2013 Manuel was fired. He managed his last game knowing that he was about to be removed.

Manuel left the Phillies with exactly 1,000 wins as a major-league manager, two pennants, and a World Series title. As of 2018 he was the winningest manager in the Phillies' long history; his 780 wins were more than 130 ahead of second-place Gene Mauch. Of the 49 postseason wins the Phillies registered between 1883 and 2011, 27 of them came under Manuel's stewardship.

Manuel has two adult children from a previous marriage and considers the three children of his longtime girlfriend Missy Martin as his own as well. After living near his roots in Virginia for many years, as of 2015 he made his home in Winter Haven, Florida.

After leaving the Phillies dugout, Manuel was given the title of senior advisor to the general manager. In 2014 he inducted into the Phillies Wall of Fame.

"I know how lucky I've been, how fortunate about how long I've gotten to be in the game that I love," he said of his career in baseball. "All the people that I've met, all the places that I've been. I look at that, and I can't even put into words how I feel about it."[13]

NOTES

1. Editorial, "Charlie Manuel: An Appreciation." *Philadelphia Inquirer*, August 23, 2013.
2. Doug Doughty, "Favorite Son Returns Home," Roanoke.com, October 24, 2013.
3. Victor Fiorillo, "One of Us: Charlie Manuel," *Philadelphia Magazine*, May 2014.
4. Mandy Housenick, "No Easy Journey: Charlie Manuel Overcame Myriad of Challenges in Reaching Pinnacle of Career," *Allentown* (Pennsylvania) *Morning Call*, October 16, 2010.
5. Ibid.
6. Ibid.
7. Ibid.
8. Ibid.
9. Rob Maadi, "Manuel Hired to Manage Phillies," USAToday.com, November 3, 2004.
10. Ibid.
11. Editorial, "Charlie Manuel: An Appreciation," *Philadelphia Inquirer*, August 23, 2013.
12. Joe Juliano, "Manuel's Mother Knew the Phillies," *Philadelphia Inquirer*, October 19, 2008.
13. Bob Ford, "For Phillies' Charlie Manuel, Another Year Begins in a Long Baseball Career," *Philadelphia Inquirer*, February 11, 2013.

DAVE NELSON

BY RICK SCHABOWSKI

David Earl Nelson was born on June 20, 1944, in Fort Sill, Oklahoma. He loved sports and played in the Little League, the Babe Ruth League and Connie Mack ball. Basketball was also a favorite sport. Nelson's idols growing up were Oscar Robertson and Jackie Robinson. Nelson graduated from Junipero Serra High in Gardena, California, in 1963. He had an outstanding athletic career, playing baseball, basketball, and football, and running track. Nelson was on the baseball and track teams at the same time. One day he had a baseball game followed by a track meet in which he competed in the 100-yard dash. He wasn't too fatigued after the baseball game, winning his event with a time of 9.6 seconds.

Commenting about his football skills, Nelson remarked, "A lot of people don't know about my football career. I have kept it a secret. I played a lot of football in high school and had a lot of success with it. I had more success with it than I did baseball. I had all kinds of football scholarship offers. I had scholarships from Notre Dame, Brown University, Oregon State, and a number of other schools, but I wanted to stay close to home."[1]

Nelson attended Compton (California) Junior College for one year. His parents were going through a divorce, and he wanted to stay close to his mother. He played football and was selected as a back on the 1963 Junior College All-American football team. From Compton Nelson accepted a baseball scholarship to Los Angeles State College (now Cal State LA). After his two years in college, Nelson decided that he wanted to pursue a professional baseball career. At a tryout he caught the eye of Cleveland Indians scout Bob Mattick and signed a contract. Assigned to the Dubuque Packers of the Class A Midwest League in 1964, Nelson batted .253, was second in stolen bases with 53, and was the league's All-Star second baseman. In 1965 Nelson played for the Salinas Indians and led the Class A California League in stolen bases with 41. He was promoted to the Pawtucket Indians of the Double-A Eastern League, again led his league in stolen bases (57) and earned a spot on the league all-star team. Promoted to the Triple-A Portland Beavers in 1965, Nelson led his league in stolen bases (29) for the third time in a row, and in a poll of managers was voted the league's fastest baserunner.

The Indians new manager Alvin Dark liked Nelson because of his speed, and a great spring training, in which he was voted the most outstanding player by writers and broadcasters covering the team, resulted in Nelson making the move to the major leagues for the 1968 season. On April 11, 1968, he made his major-league debut when he ran for catcher Duke Sims in the eighth inning. In his first major-league start, on April 20 at Fenway Park in Boston, playing second base and leading off, Nelson made his presence known. He walked to open the game and promptly stole second base. In the third inning he had his first hit, a single off Jerry Stephenson. An injury to starting second baseman Vern Fuller gave Nelson more playing time. He finished the season batting .233 in 189 at-bats and stealing 23 bases, and was chosen to the Topps Major League Rookie All-Star Team at second base.

A confident Nelson arrived for spring training in 1969. "I'm just trying to win a job," he said. "Last season, even though I was in the big leagues, I didn't know myself if I belonged here or not. Now I feel like I fit into the picture. Now I feel so confident I could play any place except catcher or pitcher – and it's a great feeling."[2] A torn hamstring muscle, suffered in the next to last spring training game, bothered Nelson all season, and he batted .203 in 123 at-bats, stealing four bases. After the season, the Indians traded Nelson, Horacio Pina, and Ron Law to the Washington Senators for Dennis Higgins and Barry Moore.

Senators' manager Ted Williams remembered Nelson from an at-bat against his team the previous summer. Nelson pulled a Casey Cox slider for a hit, prompting Williams to say, "Anybody who can handle a pitch like that can play for me."[3] There was a lot of competition for the starter's job at second base, but Nelson hit around .400 in spring training and won the job. Williams said of Nelson, "He has done everything expected of him and more. He is a most pleasant development."[4] But Nelson had a tough season, batting .159 in 107 at-bats, and in May was sent to Triple-A Denver, where he batted .369 in 236 at-bats. Nelson bore no animosity toward Williams, saying, "Whenever I got a chance, I always sat near him on the bench and listened. I really learned a lot that way. He teaches you a lot about confidence, attacking the ball and picking on your pitch. I told him I'd work hard and come back a better ballplayer."[5]

Going into the 1971 season, Nelson was confident about winning back the second-base job, but after a few exhibition games he was shipped to Denver. "That was the biggest disappointment of my career," he said. "Ted kept saying he had to have a long look at Richie Scheinblum because he had the best credentials on the club with his .337 batting average. I kept hearing that and reading that. I batted .369!"[6] At Denver, Nelson batted .307 and was recalled on June 15. He started at third base the next night. Three days later, on June 18, Nelson hit his first major-league home run off Boston's Sonny Siebert at Washington's RFK Stadium. He went on a tear and a month later on July 15, he was batting .327 with three home runs, after having 419 times at bat over 2½ seasons without one. He finished the season batting .280 with 5 home runs and 17 stolen bases.

The transition to third base wasn't easy for Nelson, but he worked hard. "It didn't come naturally to me as it does to some people," he said. "I had to work at it. I still have to. I don't feel that I'm overconfident or lazy, but I can't take my mind off what I'm doing. There's no such thing as a reflex play for me with the glove."[7]

In 1972 the Senators moved from Washington to the Dallas-Fort Worth, Texas, area, becoming the Texas Rangers, and Nelson made sure they got off to a running start by stealing seven bases in eight attempts in the first 13 games of the season. Rangers TV broadcaster Don Drysdale observed, "Nelson studies the pitchers, and for the first two or three steps he has tremendous explosion. That's what Maury (Wills) had in his prime. He didn't have blazing speed, but he could get into high gear quickly."[8]

Manager Ted Williams respected Nelson's ability on the base paths, commenting, "This year I gave him his head on the bases. He has the go-ahead anytime he feels he's ready. He's not a glory hog and he won't go unless he thinks it will help us. I'm not surprised he's off to a good start hitting and stealing bases. That's the way he ended up last year."[9] Speed is an obvious factor for base stealing, but there are some intangibles also. Nelson elaborated, "You got to know your pace and the catchers and pitchers. You get the feel of it. You can figure your odds pretty well before you take off."[10]

Nelson's batting average hovered in the .280 range for the first two months of the season, then fell off, dropping to .235 by the All-Star break. He finished the season with a .226 batting average and 51 stolen bases, one behind league leader Bert Campaneris.

After the season Nelson moved from Los Angeles to Texas and helped the Rangers with promotions. He also would be playing for a new manager, Whitey Herzog, and returning to second base in 1973. Herzog wanted to try Joe Lovitto at third base, with Nelson going back to his old position. The move wasn't easy for Nelson, who said, "When I first moved back this spring, nothing felt right. I was butchering plays I should have made easily. It was tough, but everything feels natural again. I like it."[11] Rangers' third-base coach Chuck Hiller was amazed at Nelson's transition, saying, "I never saw a guy so handcuffed find himself so fast."[12]

The 1973 season proved to be the best of Nelson's career. He batted .286 with 43 stolen bases, and was selected to play in the All-Star game in Kansas City, an honor that Nelson called his greatest baseball thrill. Among the highlights of the season were homering twice off the White Sox' Eddie Fisher on April 17, becoming the first Rangers player to hit two homers in a game, and being selected in a vote by the media covering the Rangers as their Most Valuable Player. At least two clubs approached the Rangers seeking to acquire Nelson, but the Rangers weren't interested.

Billy Martin managed the Rangers in 1974. On April 14 he drove in six runs against the Athletics with a three-run homer, a single, and a sacrifice. But injuries were a big part of his season. In a game against the Chicago White Sox on May 10, Nelson and Lenny Randle collided on a short fly ball off the bat of Ron Santo. Nelson was knocked unconscious and carried off the field with a broken nose, sprained ankle, and a whiplash injury. He was in the hospital for five days. (Randle suffered a severe shoulder sprain.) Nelson didn't return to the playing field until June 12. On July 21 he injured a knee against the Red Sox when Rick Miller slid into him trying to break up a double play.

Things were back to normal on August 30 when Nelson stole second, third, and home in the same inning. Nelson was happy, "It was very satisfying. It proved that, at long last, I can move again," he said.[13] He stole 25 bases during the season but batted only .236.

Nelson pulled an unusual hidden ball trick against the Brewers' Bob Coluccio on June 14. Teammate Tom Grieve recalled it a few years later: "Dave was playing second base, he takes the throw and Coluccio is safe. So Dave tells him, 'Step off the bag for a second, I want to kick the dirt off it.' So Coluccio steps off the bag and Dave tags him out, pulls the hidden ball trick on him."[14] Remembering the play Nelson said, "At first he just laughed about it. Then he went into the dugout and his manger, Del Crandall, just chews him out. So the next inning, he comes running out of the dugout and mad and he says, 'You embarrassed me and you embarrassed my team.' I said, 'I didn't embarrass your team, you did.' He said, 'I'm going to get you back. You watch out, one day you're going to be playing second base and I'm going to get you.' I said, 'Why wait, let's get it on right now!'"[15]

After his injury-plagued 1974 season, the Rangers wanted Nelson to prove without a doubt that he was the starter at second base. Nelson responded with one of the best spring trainings of his career in 1975, both at bat and in the field, and kept his starting position.

Nelson got off to a great start, stealing six bases in the first 11 games, but on April 19 he reinjured his ankle sliding into second base in a game against the Royals. After conferring with Martin, Nelson decided to have another surgery.

Dr. Harvey O'Phelan, the Minnesota Twins physician and a close friend of Martin's performed the surgery on April 29. Nelson remained on crutches until May 19, and was in a walking cast until early June. After therapy and a conditioning program, it was hoped Nelson would be as good as new. On August 15 he returned to the active roster, but started only 10 games the rest of the season, batting only 39 times. He finished the season with a .213 batting average. Reflecting on the 1975 season Nelson said, "Last season was a lost one for me. When I finally was ready to play, I didn't get to. I started so well in '74, but the injury messed me up."[16]

After the season Nelson was traded to the Kansas City Royals for pitcher Nelson Briles. "Dave is going to be a great addition to our club," said manager Whitey Herzog, who had been his skipper in Texas. "He goes all out all of the time. Not only will he give us more maneuverability, but he can hit and steal bases. I won't be afraid to use him leading off as the designated hitter."[17]

Nelson was elated to be reunited with Herzog, reflecting after his career, "Whitey Herzog was without a doubt the best manager I ever played for. He did all phases of the game well. As a manager he was a great communicator. He was able to let everybody know what their roles were, and they played hard for him."[18]

Before 1976 spring training, Nelson met with Royals general manager Joe Burke and, according to Burke, said he wouldn't complain if he wasn't a regular. "... I'm confident he can help us," Burke said.[19] An injured leg muscle put Nelson on the disabled list early in the season. While he was on the DL, he joined the Royals' TV crew as a color man.

Back in action, he had a big game on June 15 in a 21-7 victory over the Tigers at Tiger Stadium. He went 3-for-4 and drove in four runs. He finished the season with a .235 average and 15 stolen bases.

The Royals were playoff-bound. Nelson recalled, "It was exciting. I felt we had one of the best teams in baseball that year. We struggled at the end to win the Western Division. We ended up playing the Yankees in the playoffs, and it was one of the most exciting playoff series I have ever been involved in."[20] The Royals lost to the Yankees when Chris Chambliss hit a walk-off homer in Game Five.

Injuries again limited Nelson's playing time in 1977, limiting him to 55 plate appearances in 27 games. He suffered a pulled leg muscle early in the season and a pulled groin muscle in midseason. On September 27 he doubled off Oakland's Matt Keough in what turned out to be his last major-league at-bat. After winning the AL West again, the Royals faced the Yankees in the 1977 ALCS. Because of injuries, Nelson was not on the playoff roster.

After the season, the Royals offered Nelson a job managing their rookie-league team in Fort Myers, Florida, but he wanted to try to play one more season with the Royals. The Royals gave Nelson his release on April 1, 1978. Nelson turned down an offer to play in Japan, and sought a non-baseball career. Through friends in Washington he landed a job with the Department of Housing and Urban Development helping redevelop low-income homes. The job was interesting and fun, but not what he wanted to do for the rest of his life. Nelson joined the Royals TV booth for the 1979 season, then after the season he took a job as an assistant coach for Texas Christian University near his offseason home in Fort Worth. He liked coaching, but he yearned to return to the majors in that capacity.

Good fortune came Nelson's way. A baseball's winter meetings in Dallas, former teammate Tom Grieve asked Nelson if he could fill in for Dick Howser who was scheduled to do a speech on infield play. Nelson did such a great job talking about not infield play, baserunning, and stealing; that he got a number of job offers to coach. Nelson signed with the White Sox as a minor league infield and baserunning instructor. Chicago manager Tony LaRussa was so impressed with Nelson's work during spring training that he used him with the White Sox from 1981 to 1984.

In 1985 Nelson left to work as minor-league coordinator for the Oakland Athletics for two years. He returned to the broadcast booth with the Chicago Cubs for two years, in 1988-1989. He missed the playing field and served as the Montreal Expos minor-league baserunning instructor for two seasons.

In 1992 Nelson returned to the majors as a coach for the Cleveland Indians, a position he held through the 1997 season. Longtime Indians announcer Herb Score retired, so the Indians moved Nelson to the broadcast booth, working with Mike Hegan and Tom Hamilton. Nelson missed the playing field. "Working with the players, being in uniform, down on the field – that's my first love," he said. "Working with Tom and Mike was tremendous fun, as was being involved in the media side of baseball. But my heart is on the field."[21]

Nelson spent the 2001 and 2002 seasons as an outfield instructor in the minors for the Milwaukee Brewers before working as the Brewers' first-base coach from 2003 to 2006. He returned to the broadcast booth in 2007, serving as an analyst for Brewers games for Fox Sports, a position he still held in 2018.

Outside of the broadcast booth, Nelson stayed busy as the director of Brewers alumni relations, and joined the board of directors of Open Arms Home for Children, which provides homes to orphaned children affected by the AIDS pandemic in South Africa.

NOTES

1. Chuck Greenwood, "Licensed to Steal: Nelson Stole Three Bases in One Inning." *Sports Collectors Digest,* October 28, 1994.
2. Russell Schneider, "Nelson Puts Headlock on Second Sack," *The Sporting News,* April 5, 1969: 10.
3. Merrell Whittlesey, "Nelson Gives Nats a Solid Midway Lift," *The Sporting News,* April 11, 1970: 37.
4. Ibid.
5. Frank Haraway, "Nelson's Big Bat, Glove Brought on the Spurt of the Grizzlies," *The Sporting News,* September 5, 1970: 33.
6. Merrell Whittlesey, "Nats Rejoice Over Nelson Bat Revival," *The Sporting News,* July 7, 1971: 11.
7. Merle Heryford, "Nelson's Flying Feet, Hot Bat Win Plaudits of Ranger Fans," *The Sporting News,* June 10, 1972: 33.
8. Major Flashes: "Nelson a New Wills?" *The Sporting News,* July 8, 1972: 30.
9. "Nelson's Flying Feet."
10. Ibid.
11. Merle Heryford, "Nelson's Quick Shift Ends Ranger Keystone Problem," *The Sporting News,* April 21, 1973: 22.
12. Ibid.
13. Merle Heryford, "Triple Theft Signals Return," *The Sporting News,* September 21, 1974: 19.
14. T.R. Sullivan. "Ex-Ranger Nelson Embodies Spirit of Robinson," *"Texas Rangers.com,"* April 13, 2012.
15. Ibid.
16. Joe McGuff, "Royals Pad Their Keystone With 'Full' Nelson," *The Sporting News,* November 29, 1975: 53
17. Ibid.
18. Greenwood.
19. Joe McGuff, "K.C. Cools Toward Cleon, But Warms to Nelson," *The Sporting News,* February 11, 1976: 39.
20. Greenwood.
21. "Tribe's pitching Coach Regan Resigns; Nelson Quits," *Cleveland Plain Dealer,* October 14, 1999: 6D.

JEFF NEWMAN

BY GARY LIVACARI

Jeff Newman had a long career in professional baseball, spanning 36 years from 1970 to 2006. After six years in the Cleveland Indians' minor-league system, he played nine years in the major leagues, mostly as a catcher for the Oakland Athletics and the Boston Red Sox. After his playing days, he was a coach for four teams and had a short stint working in the commissioner's office. One of the highlights of Newman's career was serving as interim manager for the A's for 10 games in 1986 between the firing of Jackie Moore and the hiring of Tony La Russa.

An unselfish player who was always a positive voice in the clubhouse, Newman was known for his versatility and toughness. He is best remembered as an outstanding defensive catcher and a fine handler of pitchers. Through his years of experience behind the plate, he accumulated a vast knowledge of hitters' weaknesses – knowledge he readily shared with his pitchers. He was also proud of his success in developing young pitching arms while catching for Oakland.

Jeffrey Lynn Newman was born in Fort Worth, Texas, on September 11, 1948, the third child of Thomas Clayton Newman and Birdie Brooks. He picked up the nickname "NuNu" sometime in the minor leagues, but its origin is not known. Newman came from an athletic family. His mother was a big influence in his baseball development. While he was growing up, Birdie often threw him batting practice and regularly served as his catcher whenever he wanted to practice pitching. Jeff had two siblings: a sister, Wilma, eight years his senior, who was known in the Newman family as the "pre-war baby," and a brother, Thomas, four years his senior, who was the "war baby," while Jeff was known in the family as the "postwar baby." Both siblings were also athletic, playing tennis, baseball, and basketball in high school. Jeff benefited from having an older brother, as he was allowed to play sports with his brother and his brother's friends. Being able to play with "the big kids" greatly influenced his athletic development.[1]

Neman attended Greenbrier grade school and Paschal High School, both in Fort Worth, where he played baseball and basketball. He attended Texas Christian University as a history major and graduated with a bachelor's degree in education in 1970. Playing first base, third base, and the outfield on the TCU baseball team, he was one of the most accomplished players in the school's history and later was honored with induction into the Texas Christian University Sports Hall of Fame.

Honors included All-Southwest Conference and NCAA All-District Six first team and NCAA College All-American first team. He set TCU records for the longest hitting streak in conference play, and the most RBIs and the most runs scored in Southwest Conference play; and tied the record for most hits. Newman married high-school sweetheart Diane Rosen in 1969. They became the parents of two children, Thomas (45 in 2018) and Ryan (36) and have four grandsons.

Newman was drafted by the Indians in the 26th round of the June 1970 amateur draft and was signed by scout Bobby Goff. As a 6-foot-2, 215-pound utility infielder and outfielder, he was assigned to the Sarasota Indians in the Gulf Coast Rookie League for the 1970 season. He led the league in RBIs (53), tied for the lead in home runs (6), and was sixth in batting (.313), earning an All-Star selection. He played his first full season as a catcher in 1972 while playing for the Reno Silver Sox in the Class-A California League. His inexperience at the new position showed as he set a league record for passed balls in one season (51). His defense improved markedly in 1973 with San Antonio of the Double-A Texas League, leading the league in assists (72), chances (750), and double plays (10), earning him another All-Star selection. Later minor-league stops included Oklahoma City in the Triple-A American Association (1974), Salt Lake City in the Triple-A Pacific Coast League (1974), Toledo in the Triple-A International League (1975), and Tacoma in the Pacific Coast League (1976). Over his six-year minor-league career, he batted .260 with 78 home runs and 370 RBIs.

After the Oakland Athletics purchased Newman's contract in October 1975, and with his improved defense noticed by Oakland manager Chuck Tanner, the 28-year-old Newman finally got the call to the major leagues in June 1976. He got his first major-league hit on July 1 against the Kansas City Royals' Mark Littell. Pinch-hitting in the top of the ninth, he hit a two-run single in a 5-2 Oakland victory. He spent most of his rookie season as backup catcher to Gene Tenace and Larry Haney, playing in 43 games and hitting .195. The highlight of his season was a game against the Yankees in which he threw out three potential base stealers. Newman backed up Manny Sanguillen in 1977, and then platooned with Jim Essian behind the plate from 1978 through 1980, while also backing up at first base.

Newman's best year in the majors came in 1979; he set personal highs with 22 home runs and 71 RBIs and earned a selection to the All-Star Game as Oakland's sole representative. At the All-Star break he was second to Ted Simmons for the most home runs by a major-league catcher. He outhomered Dave Duncan, who held the A's record of 19 homers by a catcher in a season. But of Newman's 22 homers, six came while he was playing first base, so that particular record remained intact. Newman's last home run in 1979, hit in Arlington Texas, was described by some in the press box as the second longest home run ever hit to the left-field bleachers in that ballpark.[2]

Well-spoken with a degree in education, Newman became the A's player representative in 1980. He became involved in civic activities during the offseason, making public appearances, visiting patients in children's hospitals, accepting speaking engagements, and participating in fundraisers and signings for the team whenever asked. He also started a golf tournament to benefit a local school founded to care for extremely challenged children. Newman said at the time, "I'll do charity work for as much time as I have. I'll do anything. When I see those kids I thank the Lord I've got two beautiful children."[3]

The A's returned to the postseason in 1981 for the first time since 1975, winning the first half of the strike-shortened season with a 37-23 record. In his only trip to the postseason as a player, Newman went hitless in eight at-bats in the American League Division Series and Championship Series. During the 1982 offseason, the A's sent Newman and outfielder Tony Armas to the Boston Red Sox for Carney Lansford, Garry Hancock, and minor-leaguer Jerry King. The Red Sox intended for Newman to be the backup to catcher Rich Gedman. His defensive skills and knowledge of hitters around the league were expected to be assets. In addition, he had hit well in Fenway Park, with four homers in only 37 at-bats. However, he fell to third on the depth chart behind both Gedman and Gary Allenson and after being seldom used for two seasons, was released during spring training in 1985. At age 35, his playing career had come to an end. In his nine years in the majors, Newman played in 735 games with 2,123 plate appearances, hitting .224 with 63 home runs, 233 RBIs, and 189 runs scored. He had his most success against Wayne Garland, going 13-for-18 (.722) with two home runs. He made the only pitching appearance of his career on September 14, 1977, throwing a scoreless inning, although he hit Hal McRae, the first batter he faced.

Toward the end of his career, Newman commented on what was considered his greatest asset: his ability to handle pitchers.

"It's a matter of experience. I know hitters because I've been around a long time but a lot of catchers are in the same position. The key to working well with pitchers is to know them well enough to be able to get in sync with them. You have to establish a rhythm with each pitch. You have to sense his rhythm on a given day and stay in sync with him, which will help his frame of mind."[4]

Shortly after his playing career ended, Newman returned to the A's, serving as manager Jackie Moore's bullpen coach. When Moore was fired on June 28, 1986, general manager Sandy Alderson selected Newman as the interim manager. With no prior managing experience at any level, and with other experienced candidates available, no one was expecting the job to go to Newman. He seemed as surprised as anyone.

"It was a major shock ... and a thrill," Newman said. "It's the biggest thing to happen to me since I was released from Boston. I was very much surprised. I was sort of asking 'Why me?' I figured if they ask me I'll do the best job I can. You won't see anything different. With the injuries we have, and the people on the bench, there aren't many changes I can make. We need to get a winning attitude. That's no reflection on Jackie; it's just losing makes you stale. Winning makes you fresh."[5]

The A's went 2-8 in Neman's short tenure as interim manager. He remained as a manager in the Athletics' organization at the minor-league level through 1991. Managerial stops included Modesto in the California League (1988); Huntsville in the Southern League (1989-90) where he was named Manager of the Year for 1989; and Tacoma in the Pacific Coast League (1991). In 1992 he was hired by the Cleveland Indians as manager Mike Hargrove's third-base coach. He remained with the Indians through the 1999 season, including the pennant-winning years of 1995 and 1997. Newman served under Hargrove again as the Baltimore Orioles' bench coach in 2000.

Neman traded in his baseball uniform for a suit in 2002 when he, Bill Madlock and Tom Lawless were named field assistants for the commissioner's office. Reporting to MLB Vice President Bob Watson, they handled duties including monitoring the pace of major-league games and overseeing on-field operations in the major-league ballparks. Newman was given responsibility for covering the Western United States. He resigned this petition after three years. His last stop in baseball came in 2005 when he was hired by Seattle Mariners' general manager Bill Bavasi to serve once more as manager Mike Hargrove's third-base coach. Hargrove was pleased with Newman's selection, saying: "I've known Jeff for a long time. We played against each other and we became close friends over the years. I had him with me all those winning years in Cleveland and one year in Baltimore. He does a tremendous job as a catching instructor and in his days with the Indians, he had the reputation of being the best third-base coach in the American League. He's a good solid addition to our staff."[6]

Newman said he had vivid memories of the 1995 Indians team, which he recalled as one of his most enjoyable years in baseball.

"This was a team with a lot of professionals, like Eddie Murray, Sandy Alomar Jr., Kenny Lofton, Albert Belle, Carlos Baerga, Omar Vizquel, Charles Nagy, Orel Hershiser, Dennis Martinez, just to name a few," he said. "Every night somebody always came through, they never gave up. And it wasn't always the stars either, although we had a lot of them. If we were losing after the seventh inning, I almost felt sorry for the other team. I knew we'd almost always find a way to win."⁷

An Achilles injury requiring surgery prematurely ended Newman's coaching career in Seattle and brought his 36-year career in baseball to an end. As of 2018, Newman and his wife, Diane, resided in Scottsdale, Arizona. Fully retired since 2006, he said in a 2014 telephone conversation that he spent much of his time golfing, playing three to four times a week (with a six handicap). Other hobbies included occasional fishing and traveling with his wife to places they had never been before. Newman said his favorite activity was spending time with his family, especially with his four grandsons, Trey, Luke, William, and Jax, and following their baseball development. The Newman's' older son, Tom, is a district manager for the pharmaceutical company Astra Zeneca, while younger son Ryan followed his father's footsteps into professional baseball. He was an infielder for three years in the Pittsburgh Pirates organization before becoming a coach for the 2005 Gulf Coast League Pirates. From 2008 to 2018 he has managed in the minor leagues. He won a league championship with Great Falls of the Pioneer League in 2011. Currently, Newman is the manager of the Birmingham Barons of the Class AA Southern League.

SOURCES

"A's Win Record 11th Straight, Then Lose," *Milwaukee Journal*, April 20, 1981.

"A's Fire Moore, Name Newman Interim Manager," *Palm Beach Post*, June 27, 1986.

"Winter Meeting Opens With Trade Talks, Speech," *Spartanburg* (South Carolina) *Herald-Journal*, December 7, 1982.

ONLINE SOURCES

MLB.com, "Jeff Newman Named Seattle Mariners Third Base Coach, Carlos Garcia Named First Base Coach," November 16, 2004.

MLB.com, "M's Price, Baylor Won't Return Next Season," October 5, 2005.

Baseballgauge.com.

OTHER

Baseball Hall of Fame Library, player file for Jeff Newman.

Phone conversation with Jeff Newman, November 9, 2014.

NOTES

1 Phone conversation with Jeff Newman, November 9, 2014.
2 From the Jeff Newman Hall of Fame player clip file.
3 Ibid.
4 Ibid.
5 Ibid.
6 Ibid.
7 Phone conversation with Jeff Newman, November 9, 2014.

MARK WILEY

BY JOEL RIPPEL

In his high-school yearbook, Mark Wiley said his ambition was to play professional baseball.

"It's funny," Wiley said. *"(Kids) laughed at me over that."*[1]

But Wiley, who began his 49th season in professional baseball in 2018, understood the reaction.

He didn't letter in baseball until his senior season for Helix Charter High School in La Mesa, California. His modest 3-1 record didn't result in much scrutiny from college recruiters.

"We had four senior pitchers," Wiley said, "so playing only two or three games a week, you might go 10 days without pitching. But all four of us went on to pitch in college."

While he wasn't heavily recruited, Wiley managed to find an ideal place to play college baseball.

"Cal Poly Pomona was the perfect place for me," said Wiley, who was born in National City, California, on February 28, 1948, to Harry Wiley, a postmaster, and Miriam Wiley, an elementary-school teacher.

As a college junior in 1969, Wiley had a team-leading 2.08 ERA for the Broncos, who finished with a 26-21 record. As a senior in 1970, he blossomed.

On February 21, Wiley earned his first victory of the season by pitching 10 shutout innings with 17 strikeouts in a 1-0 victory over Stanford in the first game of a doubleheader at Palo Alto, California. (In the second game, Stanford pitcher [and future major leaguer] Steve Dunning pitched a five-hit shutout in a 3-0 victory over the Broncos.)[2]

After going 4-4 in his first eight decisions, Wiley finished the season with 11 consecutive victories. On April 28 he outdueled future major leaguer Brent Strom in the Broncos' 3-2, 10-inning victory over number-1 USC. Wiley allowed just six hits and struck out 16 in the complete-game effort for his seventh consecutive victory.

"What a competitor. I'll tell ya, he's a great one," said Cal Poly Pomona coach John Scolinos.[3]

"Scolinos has said all along that his senior right-hander is his best against the toughest competition. He proved it Tuesday."[4]

Wiley's 15 victories (Pomona was 31-24 in 1970) were tied for the most (with Florida State's Gene Ammann) in major-college baseball in 1970. His 170 strikeouts set a school single-season record. Wiley finished his career with 20 victories, 232 strikeouts, and a 2.39 ERA.

Wiley's senior year had started out with the news that he had been selected by the Oakland Athletics in the sixth round of the regular phase of the January draft. But the selection was voided by major-league baseball because Wiley wasn't eligible to be taken in the January draft. The January draft was for high-school and college players who graduated in the winter. Wiley hadn't graduated yet.

After the 1970 season, Wiley was taken in the second round of the June amateur draft by the Minnesota Twins. Four days after the draft, he signed with the Twins for what the Twins termed "a substantial bonus."[5]

Wiley was assigned to the Twins' Auburn (New York) farm team in the rookie New York-Penn League, where he continued his successful year. Wiley went 10-3 with a 1.49 ERA and a league-leading 144 strikeouts in 15 starts. He completed 14 of 15 of his starts and had six shutouts. In 127 innings he allowed just 87 hits and helped Auburn win the New York-Penn title with a 43-26-1 record.

He was named to the league's all-star team, and was selected as the Topps-George M. Trautman Minor League Player of the Year for the New York-Penn League and the top player in the Twins farm system.[6]

Wiley's mound success for 1970 wasn't completed yet. He reported to the Twins team in the Florida Instructional League, where he was instrumental in the Twins winning a second consecutive Florida Instructional League Northern Division title.

The Sporting News described the thrilling race: "The Twins, bidding for back-to-back league titles, had pulled off the almost improbable. They won nine of their last 10 games to overcome a Philadelphia power which needed only one victory or one Twins defeat during the last two days to gain its first league crown.

"Heroes of the Twins final day victory were pitcher Mark Wiley, who pitched a six-hitter with only two days rest to bring his innings-pitched total for the year to a whopping 368, and left-fielder Steve Brye, who belted a two-run homer as the Twins defeated Baltimore. Meanwhile, the Phils were bowing to the Mets."[7]

According to Wiley, "The instructional league was different back then. The coaches wanted to win really bad, and I don't know why. Steve Barber, Ray Corbin, and I, the three of us, each pitched on two days' rest twice down the stretch. After the league ended, the Twins told me there was a team in Venezuela that wanted me to pitch. I said, 'If the Twins want me to go, I'll go. But I've already thrown 370 innings this year.' The Twins said, 'Never mind.' They had no idea I had thrown that many innings."

Wiley's outstanding rookie season earned him an invitation to spring training in the Twins' big-league camp. The Twins, coming off back-to-back AL West Division titles, went into camp looking for starting pitching depth.

Wiley was called one of the candidates for the role: "A trade may yet develop, but veterans like (Dave) Boswell, (Luis) Tiant and (Jim) Kaat and youngsters like Steve Luebber and Mark Wiley will receive first shots at the job."[8]

Wiley remained in the big-league camp until the final week of March before being sent to the minor-league camp. He opened the 1971 season with Portland of the Triple-A Pacific Coast League. In the first month of the season, there were a couple of quality starts – a 2-1 victory over Hawaii on April 17 and a 1-0 loss to Tacoma (and future Twins teammate Joe Decker) on May 13. A complete-game, 5-1 victory over Hawaii improved his record to 3-6, but he lost his next four decisions to become the first 10-game loser of the PCL season.

In mid-June Wiley was sent to Charlotte of the Double-A Dixie Association. After going 3-10 with a 7.77 ERA in 15 starts for Portland, he regrouped to go 5-2 with a 2.72 ERA in 14 starts for Charlotte. The Dixie Association, in its only season, was a merger of the Southern and Texas Leagues. Charlotte won the Eastern Division title and defeated Asheville in the first round of the playoffs. In the finals, Charlotte swept Arkansas (Cardinals), 3-0, to win the league title.

In the opening game of the finals, Wiley had a perfect game through four innings but left in the fifth inning because of a sore arm. Vic Albury took over and finished Charlotte's 2-0, one-hit victory. Charlotte finished the season with a 97-51 record – 92-50 in the regular season and 5-1 in the playoffs – for the best winning percentage in professional baseball.

"Warming up before my last start in the instructional league (in 1970), I felt a pain I had never felt before," said Wiley. "But I went ahead and pitched. In January (of 1971) when I started to throw again, my arm was sore. For about a year and a half, it was sore. I was finally told that I had tendinitis."

Wiley returned to Charlotte (now in the Southern League) to start the 1972 season. In early July he pitched back-to-back shutouts to improve his record to 7-6 and earn a promotion to Tacoma of the PCL. In 11 games at Tacoma, he went 4-6 with a 3.63 ERA.[9]

In 1973 Wiley again opened the season at Double A. He got off to a rough start with Orlando before settling down.

The Sporting News explained: "Manager Jackie Warner's decision to stick with Mark Wiley in Orlando's rotation was paying off with victories for the Twins. The 24-year old right-hander, who won only three of his first 10 decisions, balanced his record with his fourth straight victory June 7, when he shut out Knoxville, 5-0, Wiley scattered eight hits and struck out six. 'The most pleasing thing,' said Warner, 'is that he didn't walk a batter.'"[10]

After another victory, Wiley was promoted to Tacoma. In his first start after the promotion, he pitched a two-hit shutout. In early August, he pitched a complete-game seven-hitter in a 5-1 victory over Spokane to help Tacoma stop a seven-game losing streak. He was 4-5 in 10 starts with Tacoma.

Wiley spent the entire 1974 season at Tacoma in a new role. After being a starter in his first four seasons, he pitched in 56 games as a reliever. He was 8-5 with a 5.26 ERA. After the season he was added to the Twins' 40-man roster.

Wiley returned to Tacoma in 1975 and opened the season as a reliever. A month into the season, he reverted to a starting role. He was 9-1 with a 2.15 ERA in 17 appearances (nine starts) when he was recalled by the Twins in mid-June.

Wiley made his major-league debut on June 17, when he pitched 2⅔ innings of relief in the second game of a doubleheader against the Oakland Athletics at Metropolitan Stadium. He allowed three earned runs in Oakland's eight-run fifth inning.

Over the next 13 days, Wiley made three short relief appearances, pitching 2⅔ shutout innings. On July 1, in the second game of a doubleheader against the California Angels at Metropolitan Stadium, Wiley made his first major-league start. He went the distance, allowing just one earned run and eight hits in the Twins' 12-3 victory over the Angels. Wiley was supported by Rod Carew, who drove in five runs.

On August 3, Wiley saved both Twins victories in a doubleheader sweep of the Chicago White Sox at Metropolitan Stadium. In the opener, he entered in the ninth inning with two runners on base and one run in. He got a double-play and groundout to seal the Twins' 7-4 victory. In the nightcap, he allowed just one run in 3⅓ innings to secure the Twins' 12-9 victory.

In 15 appearances with the Twins, which included three starts, Wiley was 1-3 with two saves and a 6.05 ERA.

Wiley was with the Twins in spring training in 1976, but was returned to Tacoma. He spent the entire season with Tacoma, going 15-15 with a 3.70 ERA in 34 games (and a career-high 31 starts) and 219 innings. In spring training with the Twins in 1977, he pitched in only two exhibition games, going 0-1 with a 12.00 ERA in 3⅓ innings. He was released by the Twins on March 30. A week later, Wiley agreed to terms with the San Diego Padres and was assigned to Triple-A Hawaii.

Wiley was the Islanders' most consistent starter all season. On July 9 he pitched 12 shutout innings in the Islanders' 3-0 victory over visiting Salt Lake City. On August 8 he went 13 innings in the Islanders' 4-3 victory over visiting San Jose in the second game of a doubleheader.

Wiley went 16-7 with a 4.33 ERA in 28 appearances to help the Islanders win the PCL West Division. In the playoffs, the Islanders lost to East Division champion Phoenix. Wiley had one victory in the series, pitching a complete game – scattering 14 hits – in the Islanders' 15-4 victory in Phoenix.

Wiley went to spring training with the Padres in 1978 and went down to the final cut, when the Padres kept Dave Wehrmeister for the 10th (and final) pitching spot on the roster. He was 6-7 with a 4.40 ERA when he was recalled by the Padres from Hawaii on June 22.

On June 27 at San Diego Stadium, Wiley made his NL debut with 1⅔ innings of scoreless relief in the Padres' 9-1 loss to the San Francisco Giants.

Four days later, Wiley made his first NL start. He allowed one earned run and four hits in five innings in the Padres' 9-3 victory over the Houston Astros in the second game of a doubleheader at the Astrodome. The doubleheader was the third in seven days for the Padres.

On July 6 Wiley pitched a scoreless third of an inning in the Padres' 5-4 loss to the San Francisco Giants at Candlestick Park. The next night in Atlanta, he gave up four runs in two-thirds of an inning in an 11-3 loss to the Braves.

A week later, Wiley was sent back to Hawaii. In his second stint with the Islanders, he was 5-4. Included in that stretch, was a 3-2 victory over Vancouver on August 13, his 100th professional victory.[11] He finished with an 11-11 record, 10 complete games and a 4.36 ERA. On September 12, a week after the PCL season ended, Wiley was traded by the Padres to the Toronto Blue Jays in exchange for outfielder Andy Dyes.

Wiley joined the Blue Jays, mired in last place in the AL East standings, and made two appearances over the final three weeks of the season.

He pitched two shutout innings in the Blue Jays' 5-1 loss to the Yankees (and Catfish Hunter) in New York on September 27. Two days later, he allowed two runs in two-thirds of an inning in an 11-0 loss to the Red Sox in Boston. It was his final major-league appearance as a player.

After going to camp with the Blue Jays in 1979, Wiley spent the 1979 season with Syracuse of the International League. He was 12-11 with 15 complete games and a 3.65 ERA in 27 starts. On July 25, he pitched a 7-hitter in Syracuse's 11-2 victory over Tidewater. It was fifth victory of the season over the Tides. At that point, he was 3-10 against the rest of the league.[12]

In March of 1980, the Blue Jays traded Wiley to the California Angels for pitcher Mike Barlow. After a brief time in the Angels camp, Wiley was reassigned to Salt Lake City before being sent to the Orioles' organization. Wiley spent the 1980 season with Rochester of the International League, going 8-7 with a 4.05 ERA in 35 appearances (11 starts).

During the 1980-81 offseason, the Orioles offered Wiley an opportunity to manage in their farm system.

"Frank Robinson (an Orioles coach in 1980) became the manager of the Giants. Jimy Williams (who managed Charlotte in 1980) was promoted," Wiley said. "They told me if I didn't want to do it, I'd still be on the Triple-A roster and I'd come to camp. I accepted the job."

Wiley's playing career was over. In 11 minor-league seasons (all or part of 10 at the Triple-A level), he was 120-96 with a 3.89 ERA in 321 appearances. At Triple A, he was 90-78 with a 4.14 ERA. In two seasons in the big leagues, Wiley was 2-3 with two saves in 21 appearances.

At 33, Wiley managed the Charlotte O's in 1981 to a 74-69 record and a second-place finish in the Southern League East Division.

He spent the next six seasons in the Baltimore minor-league chain as either a manager or a coach. "I was happy in Charlotte," said Wiley, "working with young players. Sure, I wanted to be in the big leagues, it was the furthest thing from my mind."

In 1987, at the age of 39, Wiley became the Orioles pitching coach under manager Cal Ripken Sr. At the time, he was the youngest pitching coach in the major leagues.

The Orioles went 67-95 and Wiley was fired after the season. The next season he was hired as the pitching coach of the Cleveland Indians under manager Doc Edwards. Under Wiley's direction, the Indians pitching staff, which had the worst ERA in the AL in 1987, improved to the fifth-best in 1989.

In 1992 Wiley became a special assignment scout for the Indians and spent three seasons in that role. In 1995 he returned to the Indians coaching staff. In 1995 and 1996, the Indians had the lowest ERA in the AL.

"The 1995 team had a strong bullpen and lineup, good defense and was a complete team," said Wiley. "As long as our starters got far enough into the game, we knew we could win with our bullpen. We beat every team's top closer multiple times. (Bench coach) Buddy Bell and I sat next to each other and I don't know how many times in the ninth, we'd say to each other, 'You've got to be kidding me.'"

The much-traveled Wiley went to the Kansas City Royals as the pitching coach in 1999. He spent the 2000 season as the Colorado Rockies director of player personnel.

From 2001 to 2004, Wiley was back with the Orioles as pitching coach. He spent the 2005 season as the Florida Marlins pitching coach. He returned to the Rockies in 2006 as a special assistant for player development.

Wiley returned to the Marlins in 2008 and 2009 as pitching coach. In 2010, he became a special assistant to the Marlins general manager. In 2013 he returned to the Rockies as director of pitching operations. He was still with the Rockies in 2018.

"I have a lot to do with preparing for the draft each year," said Wiley. "We're very protective of our pitchers. It's totally different from when I was a player. Part of my philosophy is based on my experiences as a player. Back then, nobody tracked a college pitcher's innings. To prepare for the draft, we track a pitcher's innings going back to the previous summer."

Wiley credited his college coach, John Scolinos, for much of his professional philosophy. "I can say that 90 percent of my philosophy comes from what I learned from John," he said. "At the core of those teachings is the fact that coaching is about the players, not about yourself."

Wiley was elected to the Cal Poly Pomona Athletic Hall of Fame in 2016. He and his wife, Jo Ann, have a son, Clinton, and a daughter, Kristen.

"When I talk to kids' groups, I tell them, 'Don't be afraid to set goals,'" said Wiley. "My career couldn't have turned out any better than it did."

SOURCES

Besides the sources cited in the Notes, the author also consulted Baseball-Reference.com, Broncoathletics.com, Mlb.com/Rockies, and Retrosheet.org. All quotes from Mark Wiley are from a phone interview on January 13, 2018.

NOTES

1 Author interview with Mark Wiley on January 13, 2018. Unless otherwise indicated, all of Wiley's quotations are from this interview.

2 "Broncos Visit Cal State Seeking Win," *Pomona Progress Bulletin*, February 23, 1970: B5.

3 Jerry Miles, "Another Wiley Story," *Pomona Progress-Bulletin*, April 29, 1970: 52.

4 Ibid.

5 Tom Briere, "Twins Bid High for Hasbrouck," *Minneapolis Tribune*, June 9, 1970: 26.

6 *The Sporting News*, December 19, 1970: 39.

7 Jack Ellison, "Chisox' FIL title – An Omen of Better Things to Come?" *The Sporting News*, December 5, 1970: 55.

8 Bob Fowler, "The Killer Feels Great; It's Harm-ful News to Hurlers," *The Sporting News*, March 27, 1971: 32.

9 *The Sporting News*, August 5, 1972: 41.

10 "Southern League," *The Sporting News*, July 28, 1973: 52.

11 Ferd Borsch, "Wiley the Workhorse," *Honolulu Advertiser*, August 14, 1977: B-10.

12 *The Sporting News*, August 18, 1979: 40.

THE BROADCASTERS

JACK CORRIGAN

BY JOSEPH WANCHO

At an early age Jack Corrigan had his sights set on being a sports broadcaster. As a youngster, he played wiffle ball in his neighborhood with his friends, imitating their favorite players. Whoever was at bat provided the call when the ball left the cul-de-sac where Corrigan lived and the games were played. It was here where Corrigan uttered his signature home-run call for the first time. "It's touch 'em all time for Woodie Held," Corrigan exclaimed.

Corrigan, along with his neighbor and friend, Joe Coreno, attended Indians games with tape recorder in hand, trying to find the right pitch and style that one day would serve him well as a broadcaster. It may not have been the perfect way to learn his trade, but Corrigan nonetheless was determined to one day call major-league action.

John Joseph Corrigan was born on September 12, 1952, in Cleveland. He was the second oldest of seven children of the Honorable John V. and Eileen Corrigan. Judge Corrigan served on the bench for over 40 years, primarily as a jurist for the Common Pleas and Appellate Courts in Cuyahoga County. While Judge Corrigan was handing down jurisprudence in his courtroom, Eileen was a homemaker, providing guidance for her seven children at their home in the West Park area on the west side of Cleveland.

Corrigan enrolled at St. Ignatius High School on Cleveland's near west side. He was a three-sport star (football, basketball, and track) at the college preparatory school. After he graduated from St. Ignatius in 1970, he continued his education at Cornell University. Corrigan, who was a history major, played wide receiver on the football team and lettered three years for the Big Red.

Corrigan was signed as a free agent by the Dallas Cowboys but he was released after a short tryout. He enrolled at Kent State University and obtained his master's degree in communications.

The long climb up the sports broadcasting ladder began in Youngstown, Ohio, at WFMJ-TV/AM. He did the sports on the 6 and 11 o'clock news for television, and covered high-school and Youngstown State football, basketball, and baseball games on the radio. On one of his first radio play-by-play assignments, the star of the game was a Cardinal Mooney player, Bob Stoops, who went on to a tremendous coaching career in college football. In, 1980, a move to WTVR-TV in Richmond, Virginia saw him continue similar duties there, with special attention toward the University of Richmond, the University of Virginia – during the Ralph Sampson era – and the

Richmond Braves, the Atlanta Braves' Triple-A affiliate at the time. During his time covering the R-Braves, future Indians players Brett Butler and Brook Jacoby were on the Richmond roster. Corrigan returned to Cleveland in 1983. He joined WUAB-TV as the voice of the Cleveland Force of the Major Indoor Soccer League (MISL) and the Cleveland Cavaliers of the National Basketball Association (NBA). He was paired with the late Nev Chandler on both assignments. Chandler, like Corrigan, was locally born and raised and his voice was a familiar one to sports fans. Chandler served as a sports anchor on WEWS TV but he was also the radio voice of the Indians (1980-1984) and the Cleveland Browns (1985-1993).

In 1985 Corrigan teamed with Joe Tait to call Indians games on television. It was the beginning of a long relationship for Corrigan with major-league baseball. For three years he was partnered with Tait, a legendary announcer for his radio work with the Cavaliers. Tait also did radio for the Indians in the 1970s.

For Corrigan, the education he received from working with both Chandler and Tait was immeasurable. He was a good student, soaking up the process the veteran announcers used for their preparation and the use of fundamentals for each broadcast.

In his first season, when Corrigan tried out his home run call of "touch 'em all time," Tait said it sounded pretty good and that he might want to hang on to the call. Who was Corrigan to ignore the advice of a legend? Like most of the notable baseball announcers, the home-run call has become a part of him.

The 1985, 1987, and 1991 Indians teams lost more than 100 games. The Indians had only one winning season in Corrigan's first nine with the club, finishing the 1986 season with a record of 84-78. No matter how talented a broadcaster may be, if the team is losing year after year, the motivation may start to wane. Corrigan asked longtime Indians radio man Herb Score about keeping the motivation alive in the grind that is a major-league baseball schedule. Score, the former left-handed hurler for the Indians, may have seen the most non-winning baseball in major-league history, according to Corrigan.

Score outlined three points to Corrigan:

Something will happen during the course of the game that you have never seen before.

There will be a play made, on either side, that will make you exclaim, "Wow."

The team will win at least 60 games a season (in most cases). Treat each game individually. If the club loses, well, it still will probably win at least 60, and now the odds have improved.

Of course, the ultimate judge is the fan. They are tuning in to listen to the ballgame. They want their announcers to describe the action in passionate and knowledgeable tones. For many fans, baseball is a release from the work day. Just as easily as they tuned in to listen/watch, they can turn to a different station just as quickly.

These are basics that Corrigan has kept in mind through his long career. And he shows up at the park for each game mindful of the insight that Score shared with him many decades earlier.

Corrigan believes that being a broadcaster of a perennially losing franchise made him much better at his trade. For he was not only the voice of the team on TV, but he was a fan as well. It takes a special kind of mettle to follow a losing team, year after year. The same can be said of a broadcaster who cannot get up and leave but must entertain for a full nine innings.

In 1989 Corrigan was paired with another former major-league player, Mike Hegan. The son of Indians catcher Jim Hegan (1942-1957), Mike Hegan played parts of 12 seasons in the major leagues with the New York Yankees, Seattle Pilots, the Oakland A's, and the Milwaukee Brewers. A terrific defensive player, Hegan had a front seat to the glory years of Indians baseball and what many consider their glory years in the late 1940s to the mid-1950s. Hegan also served as a television broadcaster for the Brewers from 1978 to 1980 and again from 1982 through 1988.

Like many who are fans of the game of baseball, Corrigan thought he knew all there was to know.

But he was mistaken. For the next 13 seasons, Hegan (also a graduate of St. Ignatius) pointed out so many nuances of the game that many fans miss. It was not uncommon, said Corrigan, for the two broadcasters to play a round of golf and talk baseball through all 18 holes.

Corrigan volunteered his time at his alma mater, working as a receivers coach for the varsity football team at St. Ignatius. Corrigan was part of a true dynasty in high-school sports. (The Wildcats won nine state championships during his tenure, a state record in Ohio.) That relationship was especially gratifying, working with future NFL players like Anthony Gonzalez, Brian Hoyer, and Drew Haddad, and because he got to spend those winning years with his close friend Chuck Kyle, the Wildcats' longtime head coach, as well as his brother, Dan, a 30-plus-years teacher and coach at the school.

Corrigan kept busy in the offseason. In part because of the contacts he made while he was working in Richmond. Corrigan worked Atlantic Coast Conference (ACC) football games in the fall. He worked both color with Brad Nessler and play-by-play with former Washington Redskins tight end Doc Walker. It was not uncommon for Corrigan to finish his broadcasting duties for the ACC on a Saturday afternoon, hop a plane, and arrive at the ballpark back in Cleveland to coach the Wildcats' wide receivers.

Corrigan also kept busy calling college basketball for ESPN and other broadcast groups, teaming with some of the true giants of the college hardwood. Corrigan worked games with Billy Packer, Al McGuire, Dan Bonner, and Sean McDonough.

The tide was turning in Cleveland, as the Indians moved into their new ballpark, Jacobs Field, for the 1994 season. Finally, there was a young, winning team in Cleveland and for many folks, Corrigan included, it was a feeling that was brand-new. Of course, the rug was pulled out from them when the players struck on August 12, 1994, eventually forcing the cancellation of the rest of the regular season and the playoffs. Cleveland finished the season with a record of 66-47, just one game behind first-place Chicago in the newly formed AL Central Division.

The strike carried over to the beginning of the 1995 season, which did not get underway until April 27. Corrigan knew the 1995 Indians were special. They were a powerful team, and as Corrigan remembers, it was not if they were going to win, but how they were going to win. Who would be the hero tonight? The camaraderie and friendships in the clubhouse were the catalysts for this talented team.

One of Corrigan's greatest memories of the season came on July 18. The California Angels were leading the Tribe, 5-3, in the bottom of the ninth inning. The Angels closer, Lee Smith, was facing Albert Belle with the bases loaded. It was a fierce battle between the two, but Belle won out, smashing a grand slam to center field and giving the Indians a 7-5 walk-off win.

The Indians were in the postseason for the first time in 41 years. And Corrigan went along for the ride, providing commentary for home and away games on WUAB's coverage of the playoffs and World Series.

The Indians provided excitement in northeast Ohio the next few years, winning their division from 1995 to 1999 and again in 2001. Unfortunately for Corrigan, the 2001 season was his last calling Indians baseball. The Indians formed their own station, Sportstime Ohio (STO). This essentially gave them a free path to broadcast their own games. WUAB and FOX (the Indians' cable home) were left out. Mike Hegan and the FOX announcers, Rick Manning and John Sanders, were still under contract, but Corrigan was not. He was the odd man out as the Indians went to rotational broadcasting teams.

In 2002 Corrigan took the year off and turned to writing. He began work on a novel about baseball, *Warning Track* (Peakview Press, 2005). The book details a player's rise to fame while under the suspicion that he was using illegal substances. It gave readers an honest insight into the problem that plagues major-league baseball.

During the 2002 season, legendary broadcaster Jack Buck passed away. The voice of the St. Louis Cardinals had been at the mic for decades and he was considered one of the top broadcasters in baseball. Corrigan applied for the opening, and the decision came down to him and Wayne Hagin. Hagin, a Denver native, was a veteran play-by-play-man. After years working for various clubs, Hagin returned home to Denver and called Colorado Rockies games from 1993 to 2002.

The Cardinals, who had the final decision, chose Hagin over Corrigan. But that left a job opening in Denver. Corrigan then set his sights on the Rocky Mountains. KMOX, the Cardinals flagship station, spoke well of Corrigan's audition to KOA, the station that carried the Rockies games. Dan O'Dowd, who was once the assistant general manager in Cleveland, was now the top man in Denver. Although Corrigan and O'Dowd had a strong relationship, ultimately it was his work with the Indians, and the prodding of KMOX, that landed Corrigan in Denver beginning with the 2003 season.

Corrigan, whose whole career had been in the American League, was now in new territory, dealing with new venues and the absence of the designated hitter. On his first visit to Dodger Stadium, Vin Scully greeted Corrigan: "Welcome to the league where we play real baseball." Corrigan now is a convert of sorts, admiring the strategies and unforeseen occurrences that are common in the style the NL plays.

Another change for Corrigan was moving from the television booth to the radio broadcast team. Professional and Collegiate sports, especially those on TV, embraced the information age. Baseball was right there with them, as now when a player steps into the batter's box, you not only get the ball and strike count and the score of the game, but the viewer can also see the batter's statistics in any given situation, the speed of the pitch, the pitch count, and in many cases, a ball/strike chart depicting the hitter's strengths and weaknesses. In some instances, a scrolling scoreboard will be displayed at the bottom of the TV screen. All of these visuals were added to enhance the viewing experience.

But it has been said that baseball is a game made for radio, and Corrigan is partial to this belief. He enjoys painting the picture and describing the many nuances that are a big part of major league baseball games. TV cameras cannot pick up everything that is going on during a game, and Corrigan relishes being able to bring the action on the diamond to the fans, and he has the innate ability to put them in the middle of the action.

In 2007 the Rockies won 13 of 14 games to close the season and finished with a 90-72 record. They finished in second place in the NL West, behind Arizona. But their hot finish carried over to the playoffs, and the Rockies swept Philadelphia in three games in the NLDS and then swept Arizona in the NLCS in four games.

But the sweep in the NLCS did them no favors in the end. Their sweep against the Diamondbacks was completed on October 15. They had to wait around for nine days for Boston and Cleveland to slug it out in the ALCS. Boston won out in seven games, and then swept the Rockies in the World Series. Although Boston had a strong team, Corrigan felt that the long layoff played a part in the Rockies getting swept.

Corrigan has continued as the Rockies play-by-play man on KOA as of the 2018 season, his 16th. He resides in the Denver area with his wife, Lisa (nee Pawlak). They have been married for 41 years. Their two children, Megan and Michael, have gone on to carve out their own lives, leaving Jack and Lisa as empty-nesters. But Corrigan stays busy after the Rockies season, serving as an assistant football coach for the varsity team at Regis Jesuit High School. Jack and Lisa also keep busy supporting several charities in the Denver area.

Corrigan took on another writing project in 2014. The title, *Night of Destiny, December 24, 1944* (Jack Corrigan/FaithHappenings Publishers, 2014), is based on events surrounding his father's service in World War II. Jack's father served in the European Theater and provided Jack with many of the details used in the book. Included was a 12-page letter he wrote to his mother while he was in the service, but due to wartime censorship was never mailed.

In 2016 Corrigan was diagnosed with prostate cancer. His prognosis is excellent because he caught the disease early on. Prostate cancer occurred in his family, so Corrigan was vigilant about getting tested regularly. His message is one of encouragement, warning men to get tested, keep ahead of the cancer, because it can be cured. It's a message that he delivers after each broadcast, and one that he feels is vital to share.

In 2018 he completed a sequel to his first book, tentatively titled *Hit and Run.*

Jack Corrigan shows no signs of slowing down, as he looks forward to every game with the same passion he had when he began. Many of those who have come into contact with Corrigan would agree that he has hit a home run in life, not just as a baseball broadcaster.

Indeed, it is "touch 'em all time" for Jack Corrigan.

SOURCES

Author interview with Jack Corrigan, July 11, 2018.

mlb.com/rockies.

mlb.com/indians.

https://www.retrosheet.org/boxesetc/1995/B07180CLE1995.htm

TOM HAMILTON

BY KELLY BOYER SAGERT

Tom "Hammy" Hamilton was well known as the "Voice of the Tribe," broadcasting games on the radio for the Cleveland Indians since 1990 and serving as the chief radio announcer since 1998. He was well loved for his enthusiasm for baseball; for his ability to help listeners picture exactly what was happening in the game; and for his quirky catchphrases. During his first 28 years with the Indians, Hamilton called all 89 postseason games, including all the 1995, 1997, and 2016 World Series games.[1]

This includes games throughout the highs and lows of the 2017 season, when the team won a record-breaking 22 consecutive games for a 102-victory season. Entering the postseason with "justifiably high expectations," they lost three in a row in postseason play, including the season-ending Game Five of the American League Division Series.[2]

Hamilton was scheduled to announce the 2018 season with Jim "Rosie" Rosenhaus, including any postseason play. The games were to be broadcast on WTAM 1100, 100.7 FM WMMS, and ALT 99.1.

Growing Up Years

Hamilton was born on August 19, 1954, with most sources saying he was born in Waterloo, Wisconsin. However, his family didn't move into Waterloo (population 2,000) until he was in the eighth grade. Prior to that, Tom lived on a 150-acre dairy farm in an even more rural location than Waterloo. In *Glory Days in Tribe Town: The Cleveland Indians and Jacobs Field 1994-1997*, Hamilton recalled being so isolated on the farm that he was frequently talking to himself, milking cows before dawn broke and "half" hating his three brothers and sisters because they were so cooped up together.[3]

When Hamilton was in the eighth grade, his father, Frank, got a job at the Perry Printing Company, which was a more stable lifestyle than trying to make it at farming. After moving to Waterloo, they were now only half an hour from Madison, Wisconsin, bringing them much closer to what he perceived as civilization.

There, Hamilton listened to Earl Gillespie call Milwaukee Braves games on the radio. He also listened to Chicago Cubs games and, for basketball, the Milwaukee Bucks. He played amateur ball himself and dreamed of becoming a major-league baseball player. When it became clear that this dream was not coming to fruition, he formed a new goal while still in high school – to become a sports announcer. Although broadcasting "seemed so beyond me," he attended Brown College in Minneapolis to learn the trade.

A college professor, Dr. Walker helped him to develop his broadcasting skills and he attended local high-school games and sat by himself, recording how he would call those games. He'd then turn the tape into his professor to receive critiques.[4]

Early Career

Hamilton began broadcasting in Appleton, Wisconsin, where he read the news, played music, and called sports, including local high-school competitions and Lawrence University games. He also gave a few reports on the Green Bay Packers and called Class-A Appleton Foxes baseball games (25 a year). While he worked at the Appleton station (1977-1981), he put in 10 to 12 hours a day before bartending – and still didn't make $20,000 a year. He also worked in other fairly remote locations – Shell Lake, Wisconsin, and Watertown, Wisconsin – applying for better jobs and hoping for a break in the competitive industry of broadcasting.

Hamilton moved up the ladder when he began calling University of Wisconsin-Madison football games with Earl Gillespie, who was known for hollering "Holy cow!" when someone hit a home run during a Milwaukee Braves game he was calling. During one winter, Hamilton also flew to Colorado to call University of Colorado basketball games. But in 1984, he was laid off from the Madison radio station, a blow to his career plans.

He next did some part-time radio broadcasting and some part-time voiceovers for commercials, hating the latter work. In 1986 a Columbus. Ohio, station where he had interviewed before going to Madison called. They had remembered his tryout and hired him for morning drive sports, plus Ohio State University football pregame, halftime, and postgame reporting. Hamilton offered to relieve Terry Smith, who was calling Triple-A Columbus Clippers baseball games (the Clippers were the New York Yankees' top farm club); because Hamilton offered to do so for free, they took him up on his offer and this is what he did from 1987 to 1989. During the football season, Hamilton was working 80-hour weeks, but he had time to meet his future wife, Wendy, who was reporting morning news.

In 1989 Paul Olden left his job as the radio announcer for the Cleveland Indians games (second to Herb Score), but Hamilton didn't apply, not feeling qualified. When he saw a news story saying the Indians were down to the four final candidates. He thought it was probably too late to apply, but Wendy talked him into making a tape and sending it to the Indians. The Indians offered him the job for $40,000 a year. It was less than he was making, but it was also a dream come true: a major-league broadcasting job.

Hired by Cleveland

Hamilton was hired by the Indians in 1990, the same year his first child was born. "Without question," Hamilton told sportswriter Jim Haynes in 2014, "1990 is the best. It was my first year in the big leagues and it was the impossible dream becoming a reality. Nothing will ever top that."[5]

During the offseason, Hamilton started broadcasting Big Ten football games on television, mostly for Ohio State University; he did this as a backup in case his baseball job didn't pan out. And, just in case, he and his wife bought a house in nearby Bay Village, choosing it because it had "good resale value." He was well aware that off mike he doesn't have much of a filter about what he says – and it's all too easy for a broadcaster to think he's off air and say something he shouldn't.

In other words, Hamilton didn't really expect this great gig to last.

Hamilton called the Indians games with Herb Score, a man he called an "icon." When he first met Score, he asked if they should do a trial run show, but Score declined – and also shared three rules: Hamilton was not to ask about Score's family on air; he was not to say something like "Isn't that right, Herb?" because Score might not agree; and he needed to have fun. The first game he called was against the Giants and he recalled talking a lot on the two-hour ride from Tucson to Scottsdale because he was so nervous.

The biggest lesson Hamilton learned from Score, he said, is that the game is the most important thing because, for many people, it's a three-hour respite from whatever challenges they may be facing in their lives.

Although Hamilton wasn't sure how long he'd last in this job, he had high hopes for the 1990 Indians, assuming they'd be a playoff team – that is, until Score set him straight. That year, the Indians' record was 77-85. The next year they plunged to a dreadful 57-105, one of the worst in a long and checkered franchise history – and the next two years didn't go well for the team, either. But, from 1994 to 2001, the team boasted eight consecutive winning records with six AL Central titles and two World Series teams.

Catchphrases

Sometime during the 1990s, Hamilton developed his signature home-run call, one that sounds something like this: "Swing and a drive ... going back ... waaaay back ... gone! A home run!"

Hamilton told Haynes he did not recall when he started calling home runs that way, although he didn't remember doing it in the minor leagues. He credited the excitement of the 1990s for the development of his home-run-calling style. "I don't call all the home runs the same," he said, "and I think the worst thing you can do is say to yourself, 'I have this home-run call and I'm going to use it every time' because quite frankly it doesn't sound natural."[6]

During his tenure with the Cleveland Indians, other fan-favorite catchphrases have included:

And we're underway at the corner of Carnegie and Ontario (at the start of home games; he often tailors this opening to acknowledge something about the location of the other teams at away games).

Swung on and belted!

Strike. Three. Called.

How about that?

A mobbing at home plate!

Mmm ... mmm ... mmm (indicating a mistake).

So long, everybody.

Fans like to collect some of Hamilton's most enthusiastic calls to replay them later.[7]

More about the 1990s

One of the most painful events of Hamilton's career happened during– in 1993, when Indians pitcher Steve Olin died in a boating accident in Winter Haven, Florida, during spring training. Hamilton and his wife were close friends with Olin and his wife; pitcher Tim Crews was also killed in the accident, and pitcher Bob Ojeda was badly injured. Although Hamilton was clearly shaken up by this tragedy, he continued to broadcast Indians games at a professional level.

And, of course, Hamilton was the voice of the Tribe when Cleveland's baseball franchise went from being a national joke to one where proud Cleveland fans streamed into sold-out ballparks eagerly awaiting an October to remember.

Hamilton said some of his best memories of the Indians championship era include Kenny Lofton's borderline-insane run from second base to home plate on a passed ball in Game Six of the 1995 ALCS. This run, described as a "mad dash" by a sportswriter, seemed to change the momentum in favor of Cleveland, and Hamilton said he could remember Lofton rounding the bases as if it happened just yesterday.

Terry Pluto summed up what that entire era was like and the central role played by Hamilton:

Close your eyes and think back to the middle 1990s. Those weren't baseball seasons, they were yearlong celebrations. It was the end of baseball's darkest decades in Cleveland. It was Jacobs Field packed with fans wearing Wahoo red, white, and blue. It was horns blaring from the cars of East 9th and Ontario Avenue. It was a late-night symphony of toots after yet another Indians victory.

It was Tom Hamilton screaming one word that said so much. BALLGAME!

The Tribe radio voice uttered that word on the final out of every Tribe victory.

BALLGAME!⁸

Score retired after the 1997 season. (He died in 2008.) In 1998, Hamilton took the lead role in broadcasting the games, initially partnering with Mike Hegan, a man for whom he had great respect.

Post-1990s

Hamilton continued to partner with Hegan through 2011. From In 1998 and 1999, Dave Nelson worked in a three-man setup with Hamilton and Hegan; from 2000 to 2006, Matt Underwood played the third role, until the Indians returned to a two-person team. After Hegan retired, Jim Rosenhaus has teamed up with Hamilton in broadcasting the games.

Although Hamilton brings a high level of enthusiasm to the game, he typically maintains control over what he says and how he says it, but this is perhaps the most notable exception.

In March 2013 Hamilton injured his knee while in Arizona for spring training. He planned to wait until October to address the medical issue but needed to take a couple weeks off from broadcasting during the All-Star break in July to repair a torn meniscus.

On May 27, 2013, the Indians played the Cincinnati Reds. During that game, Aroldis Chapman threw a couple of fastballs at Nick Swisher in the ninth inning, probably intentionally; one went over Swisher's head while the other was near it. The situation became tense and Hamilton's controversial words included: "What you'd love to see Swisher do here is knock it right off the temple of Chapman and see how much fun it is to have a ball coming at your head. That is bush league." Hamilton also predicted retaliation later in the series but when asked about his comments, he said he did not want to be the focus of the story.⁹

Family

As of 2018 Hamilton resided in Avon Lake, a suburb on the west side of Cleveland, with his wife, Wendy. They have four children: sons Nicholas and Bradley, and daughters Kelsey and Katie.

Nick is a graduate of Kent State University, where he played an important role on the 2012 College World Series Golden Flashes team. In June 2012, he was drafted by the Indians in the 35th round, with his switch-hitting ability being praised. Tom Hamilton was quoted as saying that, when he first learned the good news, it didn't immediately sink in.¹⁰

But on March 24, 2014, tears flowed freely. The Indians and Reds were to play a preseason game. The Reds, as the home team, chose to not use the designated hitter, so Nick Swisher – the planned DH – was sent home. Shortly before the first pitch, though, the Reds decided to allow the DH and so manager Terry Francona chose to use Nick Hamilton, an extra in the lineup.

This game was not scheduled for radio broadcast, so Hamilton was free to watch – and to cry happy tears as his son came up to bat, while Jim Rosenhaus provided play-by-play coverage on the team's webcast. "You couldn't script it any better than that," Hamilton said. "We'll never forget Tito and the Indians for making that happen."¹¹

Meanwhile, in 2015, Brad became a freshman catcher for Kent State University.

As of 2018 Hamilton was a seven-time winner of the National Sportscasters and Sportswriters Association Ohio Sportscaster of the Year Award: 1997, 2000, 2001, 2004, 2006, 2013, and 2016.¹² In 2008 the Indians honored him with a Tom Hamilton talking bobblehead and, on July 31, 2009, the team celebrated his 20th season with the Tribe with a postgame fireworks show that featured some of his most memorable calls.

In 2009 Hamilton was inducted into the Cleveland Association of Broadcasters Hall of Fame. He celebrated his 25th year with the Indians in 2014, making him the Indians broadcaster with the second longest tenure, next to Herb Score; the Indians honored him in a pregame ceremony.

Hamilton coauthored *Glory Days in Tribe Town: The Cleveland Indians and Jacobs Field 1994-1997* with Terry Pluto. In 2015 Hamilton received the 2015 Lifetime Achievement Award from Greater Cleveland Sports Awards.

NOTES

1. Cleveland Indians, "Broadcasters." No date. Retrieved from cleveland.indians.mlb.com/team/broadcasters.jsp?c_id=cle.

2. David Waldstein, "What Happened to the Cleveland Indians?" *New York Times,* October 12, 2017. Retrieved from nytimes.com/2017/10/12/sports/baseball/cleveland-indians-playoffs.html.

3. . Terry Pluto and Tom Hamilton, *Glory Days in Tribe Town: The Cleveland Indians and Jacobs Field 1994-1997* (Cleveland: Gray and Company, Publishers, 2014), 297.

4. Jim Haynes, "A Big League Voice: Exclusive Interview with Tom Hamilton," *New Philadelphia* (Ohio) TimesReporter, February 20, 2014. Retrieved from timesreporter.com/article/20140220/Sports/140229952.

5. Ibid.

6. Ibid.

7. JLTRAIN233. "Voice of the Cleveland Indians: Tom Hamilton," YouTube.com, May 7, 2012. Retrieved from youtube.com/watch?v=cmE6P3H5PZ4.

8. Pluto and Hamilton, 13.

9. Craig Calcaterra, "Indians Broadcaster Tom Hamilton Got a Little Too Into the Aroldis Chapman-Nick Swisher Beanball Incident," NBC Hardball Talk. May 28, 2013. Retrieved from hardballtalk.nbcsports.com/2013/05/28/indians-broadcaster-tom-hamilton-got-a-little-too-into-the-aroldis-chapman-nick-swisher-beanball-incident/. Associated Press, "Tom Hamilton: What's Said Is Said," ESPN.com, May 28, 2013. Retrieved from espn.go.com/mlb/story/_/id/9319766/cleveland-indians-broadcaster-tom-hamilton-not-backing-criticism-cincinnati-reds-aroldis-chapman.

10. Paul Hoynes, "Tribe Draft Includes Tom Hamilton's Son; Nick Hamilton of Kent State," Cleveland.com. June 7, 2012. Retrieved from cleveland.com/tribe/index.ssf/2012/06/johnny_damon_knows_he_has_to_g.html.

11. Jordan Bastian, "With Dad Watching, Nick Hamilton Makes Debut." MLB.com, March 24, 2014. Retrieved from mlb.com/news/indians-broadcaster-tom-hamilton-watches-son-debut-vs-reds/c-70053664; Zack Meisel, "For Tom Hamilton, the Voice of the Cleveland Indians, 'the Impossible Dream Came True,'" Cleveland.com, August 1, 2014. Retrieved from cleveland.com/tribe/index.ssf/2014/08/cleveland_indians_tom_hamilton.html.

12. HSMA, "Ohio," No date. Retrieved from nationalsportsmedia.org/awards/state-awards/ohio

MIKE HEGAN

BY JOSEPH WANCHO

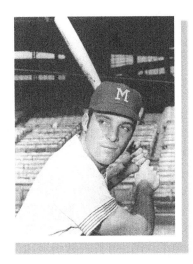

During the summer of 1954 the Cleveland Indians visited New York to play a three-game series against the Yankees with both teams in contention for the American League pennant. The story of the second game wasn't the Yankees' 4-1 victory, or Eddie Lopat outdueling Mike Garcia, but the 12-year-old batboy in the Cleveland dugout, Mike Hegan. Mike, the son of Indians starting catcher Jim Hegan, was pressed into service because the normal visiting team batboy, Mike Morton, was absent. The Little Leaguer became a celebrity when Red Barber interviewed him on his pregame TV show. The Yankees' batboy, 18-year-old Joe Carrieri, heaped praise on his younger counterpart, saying, "Considering his lack of experience, Mike showed some real promise."[1] Little did Mike Hegan know that he would make his major-league debut 10 years later in the same stadium.

James Michael Hegan was born on July 21, 1942, in Cleveland, the son of Jim and Clare Hegan. Jim Hegan, a five-time All-Star, played on Cleveland's last world championship team, in 1948. One of the best defensive catchers ever, he was a fan favorite in Cleveland for his all-out play and professionalism. His career lasted 17 years, 14 of them with the Indians.

During Mike's early years, the Hegan family made their offseason home in Lynn, Massachusetts, Jim's hometown. In the summer it was common to see Mike hanging around the clubhouse or shagging fly balls in the outfield at Cleveland Stadium.

In 1954 Jim and Clare Hegan relocated their family of three children (Mike, Patrick, and Catharine) to Lakewood, Ohio, after Jim entered a business venture with Cleveland Browns quarterback Otto Graham. Their business was called Hegan-Graham Inc., and later became Hegan-Graham Appliance, a store in downtown Cleveland that sold appliances, sporting goods, luggage, and jewelry and urged customers to "get the right pitch, before you buy."

In 1956 Mike enrolled at St. Ignatius High School in Cleveland. He excelled in football, basketball, and baseball. On the baseball team he pitched and played first base and made several local and state all-star teams. (In 1989 he was elected to the St. Ignatius High School Athletic Hall of Fame.)

After high school Hegan accepted a football and baseball scholarship from Holy Cross College in Worcester, Massachusetts. He passed up offers from Notre Dame, Stanford, Syracuse, Maryland, and Wisconsin to play for Holy Cross's legendary baseball coach, Jack Barry, who had been a shortstop for the Philadelphia Athletics from 1908 to 1915 and started in Connie Mack's famed "$100,000 Infield." As a freshman Hegan played freshman football and baseball, and hit .510 while playing first base for a baseball team that finished 6-10.

In August 1961 Hegan was offered contracts by 15 major-league clubs and signed with scout Bill Skiff of the New York Yankees even though two other teams offered more money. He felt the short distance down the right-field line at Yankee Stadium would be to his advantage since he was a left-handed pull hitter, so he accepted the Yankees' offer of a minor-league contract with "a substantial bonus." The following year, he was off with the rest of the Yankees for spring training in Fort Lauderdale, Florida. General manager Roy Hamey said of Hegan, "We'll play him as high as we can."[2]

As Hegan's playing baseball career was beginning, his fathers had just ended. After 14 years with the Indians and short spells with four other teams, Jim Hegan was hired as the bullpen and catchers coach for the Yankees. "I felt I had to be better to justify being the coach's kid," Mike said. "But Dad treated me just like any other player."[3]

Mike returned to Cleveland to continue his college education and enrolled at John Carroll University. "My father and mother told me that when you take that step to play professional baseball, you'd better have something to fall back upon," he said. "One of their stipulations was that I finish my college education."[4]

Mike thought of his father as a disciplinarian, but fair. "He didn't yell or scream, but when he gave you that look, you didn't go any further." Mike was living at home when he came in one morning at 2:30. "When I pulled into the driveway, I saw a light on in the kitchen," Mike said. "My father was sitting at the table." Jim was not happy and let Mike know it. "You've got your whole career in front of you, and I don't want to see you start screwing up," Jim said. "I don't want to see you coming home this late again."[5] Mike understood his father's message.

Playing first base in his first pro season, with Fort Lauderdale in the Class-D Florida State League in 1962, Hegan hit .306 and walked 100 times in 121 games. Said Yankees assistant general manager Dan Topping, Jr., "He's got terrific determination and great coordination." Everybody who saw him in his first year as a pro agrees he's a big-league fielder right now."[6]

In 1963 Hegan was promoted to Idaho Falls of the Class-C Pioneer League. In 126 games, he hit .323, smacked 28 home runs, had 98 RBIs, and had a league-leading 123 runs scored. He was named to the league's All-Star team. Idaho Falls won the league title, besting Billings two games to one in the final series. After the season, on October 12, he and Nancy McNeill were married at St. Pius Church in Lynn.

The next season Hegan played for Double-A Columbus (Southern League) and was a late-season call-up to the Yankees. He made his major-league debut on September 13, 1964, against the Minnesota Twins as a pinch-hitter for Whitey Ford and flied out to right field. He was 0-for-5 with one walk in five games and was added to the Yankees' World Series roster when Tony Kubek suffered a sprained wrist. In Game One against the St. Louis Cardinals in St. Louis, Hegan ran for Johnny Blanchard at second base in the eighth inning and scored on a Bobby Richardson single. The Yankees lost, 9-5, and eventually lost the Series in seven games. Hegan had the distinction of scoring a run in a World Series game before getting his first regular-season major-league hit.

Hegan returned to Columbus in 1965 and earned a midseason promotion to the Triple-A Toledo Mudhens. He returned to Toledo in 1966, led the International league in triples and walks, and was a late season call-up by the Yankees. He collected his first major-league hit on September 15, 1966, two years and two days after his debut with the Yankees. Batting leadoff against the Washington Senators, Hegan singled in the fifth inning and eventually scored on Clete Boyer's hit. In the seventh inning he singled and scored on a hit by Joe Pepitone.

When the 1967 season began, Hegan was completing his active duty with the Army National

Guard and did not join the Yankees until May 12. He hit his first major-league home run on September 1 off of Dick Lines of the Washington Senators in the 12th inning to provide the Yankees with a 2-1 win.

On February 23, 1968, Mike and Nancy welcomed their first son, Shawn Patrick, three days before Mike was to report for spring training. First base was becoming crowded with Mickey Mantle starting and Andy Kosco and Joe Pepitone backing him. At the end of spring training the Yankees assigned Hegan to Syracuse, where he hit .304 with 11 homers and 39 RBIs, while mostly stationed in right field. He was selected to play in the International League All-Star Game, but he was unable to play because of military reserve commitments. On June 14 the Yankees sold Hegan to the expansion Seattle Pilots for $25,000. The one caveat to the deal was that Hegan finish out the year in Syracuse.

Hegan was the first player to sign with the Pilots, who would begin play one year later in 1969 in Seattle's Sick's Stadium. He was thrilled to join the expansion Pilots. "It's a mental lift to be with the Pilots," Hegan told *The Sporting News*. "While I was with the Yanks, I put a lot of time into the service and couldn't get rolling. And then I always had to back another first baseman. When I came up, they had Moose Skowron. Then they had Joe Pepitone. Then I was a fill-in when they shifted Mickey Mantle to first. What if Mantle retires? Then I would have to back Pepitone again. Here I may be in a similar situation with [Don] Mincher on first. But I played more outfield than first in Syracuse, so right field would suit me fine."[7]

Hegan found familiar faces in Seattle. Also coming over to the Pilots from the Yankees were pitchers Jim Bouton, Steve Barber, Dooley Womack, and Fred Talbot, infielder John Kennedy, and outfielder Steve Whitaker. Garry Roggenburk, also from St. Ignatius High School, was on the Pilots' pitching staff. Scout Bill Skiff, who had originally signed Hegan, was now a scout with the Pilots. Former Cleveland broadcaster Jimmy Dudley was the radio voice of the Pilots.

Managing the Pilots was Joe Schultz, who came to Seattle from the St. Louis Cardinals, where he had been the third-base coach for the 1968 National League pennant winners. Schultz emphasized a running style with the Pilots, who led the American League in 1969 with 167 stolen bases. Unfortunately for the expansion club, the team batted .234, grounded into 111 double plays, and led the American League with 1,015 strikeouts. The pitching staff yielded 172 home runs.

But Hegan had his finest year to date in the major leagues. He hit the first home run for the Pilots on Opening Day off Jim McGlothlin of the California Angels. He led the Pilots in batting average (.292), slugging percentage (461), and on-base percentage (427), and was chosen for the All-Star Game, but had to withdraw in favor of Don Mincher because of a hamstring injury. Hegan missed 67 Pilots games, partly due to injuries.

Just before the 1970 season the Pilots were sold to Milwaukee car dealer Bud Selig, who moved the club to his hometown, where they became the Milwaukee Brewers.

On September 24, 1970, Hegan began a streak of playing in 178 consecutive games at first base without making an error, and the streak went into 1973, when he was a member of the Oakland Athletics. The record stood as the major-league mark for 12 years and was the high-water mark in the American League until 2010, when it was broken by Seattle's Casey Kotchman.

Also in 1970 Hegan got a glimpse of his career after baseball. During the offseason he began doing drivetime sports reporting and TV interviews for WTMJ-TV in Milwaukee.

On June 14, 1971, Hegan was sold to the Oakland Athletics. A month before, on May 18, Nancy gave birth to their second son, James Joseph (known as JJ).

It was a break of sorts for Hegan to go from the struggling Brewers to the A's, who won their first of five consecutive AL West Division crowns in 1971.

In 1972, the A's adopted the moniker "The Mustache Gang." Reggie Jackson reported to spring training with a full-grown mustache. Although no official rule banned players from wearing facial hair, it was more or less an unwritten rule. A's owner Charlie Finley didn't like the look of Jackson's mustache, but instead of making him shave it off, he told a couple of other players to start growing mustaches. It was Finley's hope that Jackson would not feel like an individualist, and would shave his whiskers. Instead, the strategy backfired, and all the players grew mustaches. Finley began to like the idea and offered a cash incentive to any player who grew a mustache by Father's Day, or "Mustache Day." True to his word, the players found $300 apiece in their lockboxes after the game. In addition, Finley extended his idea to the fans, and any fan bearing a mustache was admitted free on Father's Day.

Hegan shaved his mustache off shortly thereafter, giving into a higher authority than Finley: his wife Nancy. "My wife didn't like it," he admitted.[8]

On the field the Athletics stormed through the American League West, winning 101 games despite 49 players going through a revolving door on the roster. After they defeated Detroit in the American League Championship Series, the National League champion Cincinnati Reds awaited them in the World Series. Hegan played in six of the seven games, mostly as a defensive replacement for first baseman Mike Epstein. At the plate he got a single in Game Five, his only hit of the Series, won by the A's in seven games. It was the first of three straight world championships for Oakland.

Jim and Mike Hegan claimed a first by becoming the first father-and-son combination to each win a World Series. There have been six other such combinations since.

As the 1973 season commenced, Hegan was again a backup at first base, this time to Gene Tenace. On June 3 Hegan's streak of consecutive errorless games at first base ended. The error occurred in the eighth inning against the Boston Red Sox on a groundball by Carl Yastrzemski to Hegan, who threw late to pitcher Vida Blue covering first base.

On July 18 in Baltimore, a glimpse of Mike Hegan's future was on display. A's radio announcer Jim Woods was ailing, and Oakland manager Dick Williams instructed Hegan to report to the radio booth to call three innings. After three innings, he went to the clubhouse, put on his uniform, and reported to the dugout.

On August 18 Hegan was reunited with his father when the Yankees purchased his contract. Jim was still the Yankees' bullpen coach. Mike, a lefthanded hitter, batted mostly against right-handed pitchers, and hit .275, with 6 homers, 14 RBIs, and 36 runs scored. On September 30 he became a bit of Yankee trivia as the last batter in Old Yankee Stadium when he flied out to center field in an 8-5 loss to the Tigers.

Hegan opened the 1974 season platooning at first base with Bill Sudakis until April 26, when the Yankees acquired first baseman Chris Chambliss from the Cleveland Indians. Chambliss commanded most of the playing time, and Hegan asked the Yankees to move him to one of three teams: Boston, where Nancy's family lived; Milwaukee, where they made their offseason home; or Detroit, where his father had become the Tigers' bullpen coach. The Yankees granted Hegan's request and sold him to the Brewers, where George Scott was getting most of the playing time at first base.

In 1975 and 1976, Hegan split his time between first base, designated hitter, and the outfield. He became only the sixth player (all left-handed batters) to pinch-hit for Hank Aaron, on July 8, 1975, against Kansas City at Royals Stadium. On September 3, 1976, Hegan became the first Brewer to hit for the cycle by going 4-for-5 with six RBIs against Detroit's Mark Fidrych, at Tiger Stadium.

As the 1977 season unfolded, Hegan was dissatisfied with his diminished playing time, and with the direction of the team under manager Alex Grammas. On July 8 he played in his last major-league game, getting his release from the Brewers a week later.

Hegan had done the sports news at WTMJ-TV during the offseason in 1976 and had decided to stay in broadcasting. Ten days after his release, he was in the broadcasting booth with sportscaster Ray Scott, providing color commentary for Brewers games, and the next season he started doing some play-by-play. In all, he handled Brewers games for 11 seasons.

Broadcasting major-league baseball was not all that kept Mike Hegan busy. For 15 years he owned Grand Slam USA in suburban Milwaukee, which housed indoor baseball and softball batting cages, and pitching machines. Grand Slam USA also offered instruction in hitting, pitching, and fielding.

In 1989 Hegan returned to Cleveland to broadcast Indians games on WUAB-TV. A generation of Tribe fans grew up listening to him describe the action for the Indians. Later he moved to the radio broadcast team. He called play-by-play and color on both television and radio. Hegan retired from broadcasting after the 2011 season.

Hegan died of heart problems on December 25, 2013. He was survived by his wife of 50 years, Nancy; their sons, Shawn and JJ; and four grandchildren.

This article originally appeared in Mustaches and Mayhem: Charlie O>s Three Time Champions: The Oakland Athletics: 1972-74 (SABR, 2015), edited by Chip Greene.

SOURCES

In addition to the sources cited in the Notes, the author also consulted baseball-reference.com, ignatius.edu, Retrosheet.org, thebaseballcube.com, and:

Rosen, Byron, *Washington Post*, July 13 and July 16, 1977.

Shippy, Dick, "Hegan Returning as an Established Pro," *Akron Beacon Journal*, April 2, 1989.

Author interviews with Mike Hegan on May 19 and August 1, 2007

NOTES

1. "Hegan's Son, a Little Leaguer, Drafted as Tribe Relief Batboy," *New York Times*, September 2, 1954: 27.
2. "Yankees Give Big Bonus to Coach Hegan's Son, 19," *New York Times*, August 10, 1961: 20.
3. Bob Dolgan, *Heroes, Scamps and Good Guys* (Cleveland: Gray and Company, 2003), 35-36.
4. Ibid.
5. Ibid
6. Til Ferdenzi, "Bombers Eye Hot-Shot Hegan as No. 1 Nifty on '63 Camp List," *The Sporting News*, December 1, 1962: 10.
7. Hy Zimmerman, "Pilots Gleeful Over Hot Swinger Hegan," *The Sporting News*, March 29, 1969: 26.
8. Bruce Markusen, "Thirty Years Ago… Birth of the Mustache Gang," Respect Our Legacy: Keep the A's in Oakland, March 14, 2002, http://oaklandfans.com/columns/markusen/markusen134.html. Accessed September 28, 2018

RICK MANNING

BY KELLY BOYER SAGERT

Rick Manning, to quote journalist Steve Eby, "just might be the ultimate Cleveland Indian."[1] He was drafted by the Indians in 1972 and played center field for them from 1975 to 1983, when he was traded during the season to the Milwaukee Brewers. He played for the Brewers through 1987. Manning returned to Cleveland to work as the color commentator for the Indians cable network in 1990. It is a position he still maintained as of the 2018 season. This is the longest tenure of any television broadcaster for the franchise – and this also means that he broadcast games throughout the entire glory days period of the 1990s. It should be noted that Tom Hamilton has been the radio broadcaster for the Tribe since 1990, becoming the chief radio announcer in 1998.

When you listen to broadcasts, you may hear Manning referred to as "Arch" or "Archie." This became his nickname because of another professional athlete who also has the name of Manning: former New Orleans Saints quarterback Archie Manning. The only other Indians player who has been associated with the team for as long as Manning is Herb Score (38 years as a pitcher, then announcer); Manning recently surpassed Mel Harder's time with the club (37 years as a pitcher, then coach). Overall, as a player, Manning earned a lifetime batting average of .257, with 56 home runs and 458 runs batted in.

Richard Eugene Manning was born to Roy and Doris (Bartlett) Manning on September 2, 1954, in Niagara Falls, New York. An older brother (July 14, 1951-September 12, 2015)[2] was named Glenn. A brother named Kevin was known as "Gopher" (February 6, 1956-December 13, 2017) and other siblings were Gary, Terry, and Gwyn. Rick attended LaSalle High School[3] in Niagara Falls. He was a fan of the National League and because his father was from St. Louis, he rooted for the Cardinals, even though other people from his hometown would travel to see the Indians play.[4]

Manning, who played shortstop in high school,[5] has been quoted as saying he was scouted by multiple teams and, in 1972, he was drafted by the Indians as the second pick of the first round of the draft – with Manning believing the Indians to be one of the least likely teams to draft him.[6]

Manning, who threw right-handed and batted left-handed, spent less than three full seasons in the minor leagues. After drafting him, the Indians sent him to Reno of the Class A California League. In his second year there, 1973, he smacked 14 triples and had 24 stolen bases. He was promoted to Triple-A Oklahoma City in 1974 and after 30 games there in 1975, he was called up to the Indians in May.

The 20-year-old, 6-foot-1 inch, 180-pound Manning played his first game for the Indians on May 23, 1975,[7] starting against the Oakland Athletics. Batting against Sonny Siebert in the first inning, he flied to right field in his first major-league at-bat. In the seventh, he got his first big-league hit, a single to center off Jim Todd.

In 120 games, Manning batted .285 and stole 19 bases. Of his debut major-league season, he said, "I was just happy to get to the big leagues. It was a dream come true. I was only 20 years old and back then there were no expectations – you just get to the big leagues and that's what you wanted to do."[8] In 1976 the team moved All-Star George Hendrick to left field, making Manning their main center fielder and leadoff hitter. Manning proceeded to win a Gold Glove.[9]

Some major-league highlights include his head-first slide into second base on June 4, 1977. Manning finished the game against the Seattle Mariners in the Kingdome (and in fact played for three more games before it became too challenging for him to play) but required a back brace for several weeks thereafter. A second set of x-rays, taken about a month later, showed a fractured vertebra that nearly ended his season (he played in only 68 games); he never batted as well after that, with some analysts, including Cleveland sports journalist Terry Pluto, blaming this injury.[10]

The following year, 1978, Manning recovered from his back injury at the home of Dennis Eckersley, one of his close friends. While he stayed at the Eckersley home, Manning became involved with his friend's wife, Denise. To resolve the tensions that arose, the Indians knew they needed to trade one of the players and chose to trade Eckersley, along with Fred Kendall, on March 30, shortly before Opening Day.[11]

In return for Eckersley and Kendall, the Indians got Ted Cox, Bo Diaz, Mike Paxton, and Rick Wise from the Boston Red Sox. After the Eckersleys divorced, Manning married Denise, but they later divorced.

On May 15, 1981, Len Barker needed one more out to pitch a perfect game against the Toronto Blue Jays. The 27th batter was Ernie Whitt, and he hit a ball to left-center field. Manning caught the ball to clinch both the win (3-0) and Barker's place in history. Manning told journalist Steve Eby that he wanted the ball hit to him. "He [Barker] was cruising," Manning said, "and mentally it didn't matter where that ball was hit, I felt I was going to catch it."[12]

On June 6, 1983, the Indians traded Manning, by now an eight-year veteran, along with Rick Waits to the Milwaukee Brewers for Ernie Camacho, Jamie Easterly, and Gorman Thomas.[13] Manning began playing fewer games in 1986 when Robin Yount was moved to center field. But he did get caught up in one more memorable moment before his career ended in 1987.

On August 26, 1987, the Brewers were playing the Indians, and the Brewers' Paul Molitor was hoping to extend his 39-game hitting streak, the longest streak since 1900. By the 10th inning, the game was scoreless and Molitor had gone 0-for-4. Cue the moment. Manning comes up to pinch-hit, with Paul Molitor on deck and runners on first and second. Doug Jones of the Indians throws a strike. The fans cheered, confusing Manning since a win was close at hand.

"When I heard the cheers after the first strike," Manning said, "I had to step out of the batter's box and collect myself. I wondered if I'd gotten traded back to Cleveland between innings or something. But I checked my uniform and it was still a Milwaukee one."[14]

He then realized that the fans actually wanted him to make an out – to give Molitor another chance to bat – but he hit a walk-off single. Fans booed Manning, even though he'd just clinched the victory for the Brewers. Molitor, meanwhile, was the first to give Manning a hug.

In 1990, Manning began providing color commentary for the Cleveland Indians regional cable network and he has also announced games on Fox.

Journalist Marc Bona summed up Manning's broadcasting style and ability this way: "Manning has an ability to break down the nuances of a game. He'll explain why something happened, offers praise when he thinks it's deserved, and he doesn't withhold criticism. He knows the league, and he allows frustration to sometimes boil over into his commentary – not necessarily a bad thing. He doesn't feel a need to fill in every gap in conversation, and he respects the past. But he sometimes repeats Underwood and lets his guard down on clichés every now and then. ('Back in the day' is common.) And while not a joke-a-minute guy, he can be funny."[15]

Manning and his wife Sue have two children, Kyle and Jessica, as well as six grandchildren. They live in Scottsdale, Arizona.[16]

In 1980 Manning won the Baseball Writers' Association of America "Good Guy" Award.[17] In 1999 he was inducted into the Greater Buffalo Sports Hall of Fame.[18] In 2014 he was awarded the Cleveland Association of Broadcasters Excellence in Broadcasting Award.[19] In 2017 he was inducted into the Greater Cleveland Sports Hall of Fame. The Cleveland Indians include Manning in their all-time top 100 list for the ballclub.[20]

NOTES

1. Steve Eby, "Catching Up With Rick Manning." Did the Tribe Win Last Night? December 11, 2013. Retrieved from didthetribewinlastnight.com/blog/2013/12/11/catching-up-with-rick-manning/.
2. "Mr. Glenn E. Manning," Hooper Funeral Home. No date. Retrieved from hooperfuneralhome.com/obituaries/Glenn-Manning-3/#!/ Obituary.
3. "Rick Manning: Professional Baseball Player." Greater Buffalo Sports Hall of Fame. No date. Retrieved from buffalosportshallfame.com/member/rick-manning/.
4. Eby.
5. Greater Buffalo Sports Hall of Fame.
6. Eby.
7. "Indians to Honor STO Analyst Rick Manning May 23, 40th Anniversary of MLB Debut," Fox Sports. May 15, 2015. Retrieved from foxsports.com/ohio/story/cleveland-indians-sportstime-ohio-rick-manning-051515
8. Eby.
9. Eby.
10. W. Laurence Coker, M.D., *Baseball Injuries: Case Studies, by Type, in the Major Leagues* (Jefferson, North Carolina" McFarland, 2013), 162.
11. Kris Kaiser, "Today in Cleveland Indians History: Tribe Trades Eckersley to Boston," Fansided. 2018. Retrieved from believelandball.com/2018/03/30/cleveland-indians-history-tribe-trades-eckersley-boston/.
12. Eby.
13. "Top 100 Indians: #90 Rick Waits," SB Nation, July 3, 2012. Retrieved from https://www.letsgotribe.com/2012/7/3/3133709/top-100-indians-90-rick-waits
14. Richard Riis, "August 26, 1987: Rick Manning's Walk-Off Single Preserves Teddy Higuera's 10-Inning Shutout." *Society for American Baseball Research*, 2016. https://sabr.org/gamesproj/game/august-26-1987-pinch-hitter-rick-manning-s-walk-single-preserves-teddy-higuera-s-10
15. Marc Bona, "Cleveland Indians' Rick Manning: Analyzing the Team's Color Analyst," *Cleveland.com*, August 12, 2013. Retrieved from http://www.cleveland.com/tv/index.ssf/2013/08/rick_manning_analyzing_the_col.html
16. Cleveland Indians. [What is this?]
17. Ibid.
18. Greater Buffalo Sports Hall of Fame.
19. "Rick Manning Honored by Cleveland Association of Broadcasting," *Cleveland Indians*, May 2, 2014. Retrieved from https://tribevibe.mlblogs.com/rick-manning-honored-by-cleveland-association-of-broadcasting-be2a047f42cc
20. "Rick Manning." *Greater Cleveland Sports Hall of Fame*, 2017. Retrieved from http://www.clevelandsportshall.com/manning-rick/ and "Top 100 Greatest Indians," *Cleveland Indians*. No date. Retrieved from http://cleveland.indians.mlb.com/cle/history/greatest_100.jsp

HERB SCORE

BY JOSEPH WANCHO

"It's going to be a tough act for the kid to follow," said Cleveland pitcher Bob Feller.[1] Indeed, it would be. Feller had just thrown the 12th one-hitter of his fabulous career, blanking Boston, 2-0, in the first game of a doubleheader at Cleveland on May 1, 1955. Boston catcher Sammy White singled to center field in the seventh inning for the only Red Sox safety. He had been kept alive at the plate when Tribe catcher Jim Hegan could not corral a foul tip on a 2-2 count. The 36-year-old Feller, who had not been given a starting assignment by the Indians in the previous season's World Series, reminded those who had written him off that he could still contribute in a big way to arguably the best pitching staff in baseball, even in his 17th season in the major leagues.

"The kid" Feller referred to was a tall, left-handed rookie from Lake Worth, Florida, Herb Score. Score was making his third start of the season. After witnessing Feller's mastery of the Red Sox, Score sat in front of his locker thinking, "This is gonna be great . . . me coming in after *that* performance."[2] But if he was concerned about measuring up to Feller, his anxiety was quickly eased. Score struck out nine batters in the first three innings and 16 for the game in a 2-1 Cleveland victory. He came within two strikeouts of equaling the record at the time for strikeouts in a game held by Feller. Score credited Indians' pitching coach Mel Harder for his recent success. "Mel Harder has been working with me and one day he found I was gripping my curveball improperly," said Score. "I was gripping it too much with one finger -instead of getting a good, full grip with two. That's why it was breaking better today."[3]

But the promise of future greatness that shined so brightly in that game was not to be fulfilled. After Score pitched two outstanding seasons for the Tribe, in 1955 and 1956, his career was curtailed by a line drive that struck him in the face on May 7, 1957. Score returned to pitch the following year, and always denied that the ball hit by New York's Gil McDougald cut short a productive career. But Cleveland fans will always ponder what kind of a career Score could have had after posting a won-loss record of 38-20 before the injury, as opposed to his record of 17-26 after it.

Herbert Jude Score was born June 7, 1933, in Rosedale, a neighborhood in the Queens section of New York City. He was the oldest of three children – the others were sisters Helen and Anna Mae -- born to Herbert A. Score, a New York City police officer, and Anne Score. Herbert worked traffic duty in

Manhattan. As a child, young Herb was stricken with many injuries and ailments. When he was 3, he was run over by a truck that crushed both legs just below his pelvis. Doctors were worried that he might never walk normal again, but the bones settled back into place on their own. Herb was stricken with rheumatic fever a few years later and was bedridden for ten months. As a freshman in high school, he fractured his ankle while playing basketball, and while the cast was still in place, he suffered through an emergency appendectomy. Anne Score was a devout Catholic and gave her son the middle name of Jude, in honor of St. Jude, the patron saint of hopeless causes. Both Score and his mother believed that his many recoveries were due to devoted prayer.

At Holy Name of Mary School, he was playing the outfield when the team needed a pitcher. Score volunteered to step in. After the game the team's coach, Father Tom Kelly, informed Herb that his outfield days were over. His days at Holy Name were over as well when Anne Score, who was separated from her husband for several years, relocated the family to Lake Worth, Florida, so she could take a job at a bank. Lake Worth, a suburb of West Palm Beach, was a small town, and word about young Score's pitching ability spread fast. Cleveland scout Cy Slapnicka, who had signed Feller in 1936, lived in Lake Worth. On a tip from a local policeman, Slapnicka scouted Score, and liked him instantly. Score averaged two strikeouts per inning in his high-school career. He also pitched a half-dozen no-hitters. Although he threw very fast, he was also very wild. In one instance, Score threw a no-hitter against rival Fort Pierce in 1952, striking out 14 batters while walking nine in the 5-1 victory.

Because of Score's ailments back in New York and the loss of his transcripts, he was behind his classmates and did not graduate with his class in 1952. Major-league baseball forbids its teams to negotiate with high-school players until they graduate or reach their 19th birthday. So, on June 7, 1952, when Score turned 19, he signed a contract (which had a $60,000 bonus attached to it) with Slapnicka and the Indians. Score was sent to Indianapolis of the American Association, where he made 10 starts, posting a 2-5 won-loss record. He allowed only 37 hits in 62 innings, but walked 62.

In 1953, Score was moved down to Cleveland's Class-A affiliate, Reading (Pennsylvania) of the Eastern League. There he met Rocky Colavito, who was from the Bronx, New York. Score and Colavito formed what became a lifetime friendship, serving as roommates for their time together in both the minors and the major leagues, and forever referring to each other as "roomie."

Score won 7 games and lost 3 at Reading, giving up only 64 hits in 98 innings but walking 126, when an injury curtailed his season. He was in the outfield chasing fungoes when one sailed over his head. As he leaped to catch it, he fell on his left shoulder. X-rays revealed that the collarbone had separated from the shoulder. Score was shelved for the rest of the season and did not throw again until the first of the year. The time off was not a total loss for Score; he was able to complete the needed credits to receive his diploma from Lake Worth High School.

For the 1954 season, Score and Colavito, along with Reading manager Kerby Farrell, were promoted to Triple-A Indianapolis. While the Indians were setting an American League record for wins in 1954, with 111 victories, Score was also having a record-setting year. He had a lethal fastball to go with a solid curve and changeup. In his delivery, Score took a big windup, turning his body away from the batter, uncoiled, and threw the ball to the plate. He barely glanced at the batter or the plate, and when he concluded his delivery, he was in a defenseless position on the mound.

Score was named the American Association>s Most Valuable Player after finishing with a stunning record of 22-5. He gave up only 140 hits in 251 innings, set an American Association record with 330 strikeouts, and had the league's lowest earned-run average, 2.62. While his walks in his first two seasons averaged at least one an inning, this season he cut that ratio almost in half, giving up 140 walks in his 251 innings. Score was named the Sporting News Minor League Player of the Year. Humble and self-deprecating by nature, he passed the credit to his pitching coach, Ted Wilks. "You should have seen him work last year with Ted Wilks, our pitching coach at Indianapolis," said Indians catcher Hank Foiles. "They worked together-a lot every day. And at the start of spring training this year, he was three months advanced as a pitcher-over what he was at the end of last season. Wilks taught him his curve, his change-up and his control-which is 90 percent of pitching."4

Even though the Indians set a league record for victories in 1954, they went into 1955 spring training feeling a little unsatisfied; they had been swept in the World Series by the New York Giants, four games to none. Still, their pitching staff was considered to be the best in the league. It was led by 23-game winners Early Wynn and Bob Lemon. Mike Garcia captured 19 victories, Art Houtteman had 15, and Bob Feller had 13. Feller was coming to the end of his brilliant career, and most felt that Score could be slotted right into the rotation. He was already being referred to as a "left-handed Bob Feller." *The Sporting News* picked the Indians to repeat as kings of the American League, based on their strong pitching.

Two weeks after his 16-strikeout effort against Boston on May 1, Cleveland visited Fenway Park for a two-game series. Many teams avoided starting a left-handed pitcher, much less a rookie, at Fenway Park because Boston could stack its lineup with right-handed hitters. The Red Sox would try to take advantage of the left-field wall and the short distance for a home run. A reporter asked Cleveland manager Al Lopez if he was afraid to start Score in this situation. Lopez grinned and replied that he was not afraid to start his rookie hurler any place or against any other team. The Señor knew his pitcher: Score threw a three-hit shutout, striking out nine. His early success put Score on the cover of the May 30 issue of *Sports Illustrated*. The article was about Score and "Bullet" Bob Turley, a young, promising right-handed pitcher of the New York Yankees.

The Indians were nip and tuck with New York all season, pulling ahead by two games after sweeping a doubleheader from Washington on September 13. But the Indians went 3-6 to close out the season, while New York thundered home with a 9-2 record to capture the pennant. The Indians finished three games behind the Yankees with a record of 93-61.

As for Score, his inaugural season was one for the record books. He led both leagues with 245 strikeouts, shattering the rookie record of 227 set by the Phillies' Grover Cleveland Alexander in 1911. Score's record stood for 29 years when Dwight Gooden of the New York Mets struck out 276 batters in 1984.

Score finished with a record of 16-10 and a 2.85 ERA. Manager Lopez named Score to the American League roster for the All-Star Game, but the pitcher did not make an appearance. He was named *The Sporting News* Rookie of the Year in the American League. "I was surprised being chosen for *The Sporting News* rookie award," said Score in his usual humble way. "I thought of several others who were more deserving. I guess I got it because of my strikeout record."5

There was no sophomore jinx for Score in 1956. He won seven of his final eight starts to post a 20-9 record, sharing the team lead in victories with Lemon (20-14) and Wynn (20-9). Score led the league in strikeouts (263) and the team in ERA (2.53). His strikeout total was the most since Feller struck out 348 in 1946. Score became the first pitcher in modern baseball history to strike out more than 200 in his first two seasons. He was again named to the American League roster for the All-Star Game and pitched one scoreless inning.

Cleveland had again been a pennant favorite in 1956, but again the Tribe lost out to the Yankees. The Indians finished in second place with an 88-66 record, nine games back. Lopez resigned at the end of the season. He denied rumors that he had had differences with general manager Hank Greenberg. Lopez had built a solid record as the Tribe's head man, but he felt it was just not enough to keep going.

Kerby Farrell assumed the reins of the Indians for the 1957 campaign. Farrell was reunited with Score and Colavito a third time, having managed both players at Reading in 1953 and Indianapolis in 1954. Both teams had won the pennant. Farrell may not have had Score on his pitching staff if Joe Cronin had his way. The Boston general manager and former Red Sox great let it be known that he had offered Greenberg a million dollars for Score. (That sum was the equivalent of more than $7 million in 2009 dollars.) Cronin insisted that the offer was no joke. "If Greenberg had shaken hands on the deal", he said. "I would have called Yawkey (Boston Red Sox owner Tom Yawkey) for approval"[6]. What was Score's reaction to all of this? "I wonder what Nancy will think when she reads that I am supposed to be worth a million dollars."[7] Nancy MacNamara was Herb's fiancée, whom he had met at Lake Worth High School. She was attending St. Mary's College in South Bend, Indiana.

For Score, his career took a tragic turn when on May 7, 1957, he was struck in the eye by a batted ball. He was pitching the first inning of a home game against New York when Yankee shortstop Gil McDougald, the second batter he faced, smashed a line drive back towards Score. The ball hit Score in the right eye and ricocheted to third baseman Al Smith, who threw to first base for the out. But McDougald was not running down the first-base line. Instead he ran to the pitching mound, where Score was lying with his glove covering his eye. Because of Score's delivery, he was defenseless against a batted ball after he threw.

Score remembered the play. "A fast ball, probably just below the belt, "said Score. "I threw it straight, and he hit it just as straight. I didn't see the ball until it was on me. I threw up my glove and I think I just nicked it. All I know is the ball got big fast."[8]

Score was taken to Lakeside Hospital. He had suffered a broken nose, a lacerated right eyelid, damage to the right cheekbone and damage to the right eye. Score kept his thoughts to St. Jude, praying and appealing to the saint to be by his side once more. McDougald was an emotional mess after the incident. He was put at ease somewhat after a long conversation with Anne Score, Herb's mother. Nancy, his fiancée, rushed to Cleveland when she heard the news. Score was hospitalized for three weeks, until May 28. Although he looked fit and fully recovered, Score was months away from the playing field. He sympathized with McDougald: "I talked to Gil and told him it was something that could happen to anyone. It's just like a pitcher beaning a batter. He didn't mean it."[9] McDougald lost his desire to play baseball and retired after the 1960 season. Whether or not the incident with Score was responsible, the Yankee's average dropped from .289 in the seven years before 1957 to .253 from 1957 through 1960.

Herb and Nancy had become engaged earlier in the year and planned for an October wedding. Since Herb was on the shelf as far as baseball was concerned, they moved their wedding day up to July 10 in Boynton Beach, Florida. Score's old baseball coach, Father Kelly, officiated at St. Mark's Catholic Church.

Score did return to the team before the season ended to take some batting practice and shag fly balls in the outfield. He was still quite a way from pitching. His eyesight had improved greatly, but he was having difficulty with depth perception and things were blurry up close. He still could not read with his right eye but was encouraged that his eyesight would make a complete recovery, based on his doctors' prognosis. But Score would not pitch again in 1957.

As a team, Cleveland finished with a 76-77 record, in sixth place and 21½ games behind the Yankees. It was the first time the Tribe had finished under .500 since 1946. Not only did they lose Score for the season, but Lemon developed bone chips in his right elbow. He was shelved for the final two months of the season. Farrell was fired at the end of the season. He and Yankees manager Casey Stengel met up at the World Series in 1957. Farrell relayed what Stengel told him, that he lost his job on May 7, the front office just retained you after that. General manager Hank Greenberg was also relieved of his duties after the season.

Bobby Bragan was the new manager for 1958, chosen by Frank Lane, who succeeded Greenberg. Bragan had managed previously in Pittsburgh. Lane had also served as GM for the St. Louis

Cardinals and Chicago White Sox. "Trader" Lane loved to make deals. And he had his critics. "I'm afraid to trade with him," said Stengel. "He trades ballplayers and then tells you they're no good."[10] With the Indians, he wasted no time in making trades. In the offseason, Wynn and Smith were dealt to the White Sox and Hegan went to the Tigers. During the season, Garcia was released in May, Roger Maris was traded to Kansas City in June, and Lemon was released in July.

As for Score, he was pitching like his old self when 1958 spring training rolled around. He reported early to the Indians' camp in Tucson, Arizona, and appeared not to have lost any speed on his pitches. Some were concerned that he might change his delivery, but Score nixed that notion. "If you get to the point where you feel cowardly towards criticism, you'll never make a deal,"[11] said Lane.

Indeed, Score looked like himself when he beat Billy Pierce and the White Sox, 2-0, on April 23. Score surrendered three hits and struck out 13 to raise his record to 2-1. A week later on a damp night in Washington, Score was pitching in a close game. His left arm began to get sore in the fourth inning. In the seventh inning he threw a pitch that bounced in front of home plate by about ten feet. He threw another pitch but got the same result. He had torn a tendon in his left elbow and was sidelined for a month before he could start throwing again.

When Score returned on June 14, in Washington, he relieved Cal McLish in the seventh inning with the Indians leading 10-2. In the ninth inning he felt the pain in his elbow again; the elbow felt as if it had been stabbed with a knife. "I thought Herbie slipped as he threw the ball," said teammate Mudcat Grant. "I was in the dugout and I swore that I heard something pop in his arm."[12] Score made only seven more appearances (one start), the rest of the year, and finished the season with a 2-3 record.

It became apparent during the season that Lane did not like to keep his managers intact, either. Bragan was fired after 67 games and was replaced by former Yankees and Indians great Joe Gordon. Gordon piloted the Tribe to a 46-40 record the rest of the way and a fourth-place finish.

Score seemed recovered in spring training for the 1959 campaign. He was throwing the ball well. In a game against Boston, he threw a strike past Ted Williams, who turned to catcher Russ Nixon and said, "Herbie's got it again. And I'm glad."[13]

It did seem as though Score was back. He pitched his way to a 9-5 mark in the first half of the season. In three of those wins he had double-digit strikeout totals. But in nine starts in the second half of the season, he was 0-6. The Indians battled Chicago all season long, holding a two-game lead at the All-Star break. Cleveland was riding an eight-game winning streak and trailed Chicago by 1½ games on August 27. Chicago visited for a four-game series that weekend and swept the Indians, virtually putting the pennant out of the Indians' grasp.

Cleveland broke camp in 1960 and headed north to begin another season. Optimism was high for the Tribe even though 1959 had ended with a loud thud. The real thud was about to hit Indians fans square in the head. On Sunday, April 17, Cleveland and the White Sox met for their final preseason tuneup, in Memphis, Tennessee. During the game, Gordon informed Colavito he had been traded to Detroit for Harvey Kuenn. The home-run king was traded for the batting average champion. Colavito was the face of the Tribe, the idol for all Indians fans. "Don't Knock the Rock" was the mantra of many of Colavito's followers. GM Lane had coveted Kuenn for a long time and thought that the home-run ball was overrated. It was rumored that Lane was jealous of Colavito's popularity with the fans. Whatever Lane's motive was, it is still considered the worst trade in Indians history. Lane just did not understand that not only was Colavito the heart of the team, but he put people in the stadium seats. Many people called in to the papers complaining of the trade, vilifying Lane, and threatening never to go to another home game. It was a black day for Cleveland.

Score, Colavito's roommate, was given his ticket out of town to Chicago the next day. Lane was living up to his slogan on dealing players which was not to brood about a bad trade, move on to the next one. Lopez had taken the reins in Chicago after he left Cleveland. White Sox owner Bill Veeck, no stranger to rolling the dice via the trade himself, sent pitcher Barry Latman to Cleveland for Score. "I've never seen Al want a player as badly as he wanted Score," said Veeck. With Colavito and Score traded, that left infielder George Strickland and Nixon as the only Indians remaining from when Lane took over the club at the end of the 1957 season

Score was a very popular player in his own right, both with his teammates and the Tribe faithful. Had he been dealt a week earlier, it may have made more of an impact, "a stop the presses" kind of story. But coming on the heels of the Colavito trade, it was almost like a footnote. "We simply reached the point were we felt that Herb could not win for the Indians," Lane said. "We would not have traded him if we felt otherwise. The condition of his arm is questionable, but it certainly would not surprise me if goes over there and wins for the White Sox. That's the risk we had to take."[14] Lane also commented that Score's troubles were "more psychological than physical, though I've got to admit he complained of aches and pains when he was a 20-game winner."[15]

Going to Chicago was like a homecoming for Herb, with Garcia, Wynn, and Al Smith being on the White Sox roster. Dick Brown, a backup catcher with the White Sox, was Score's batterymate at Lake Worth High School, and had also played briefly in Cleveland. "Frank gave Al permission to talk to me and I told Al I'd like to be traded to the White Sox," said Score. "And after the deal was completed, I thanked Frank."[16] But he was most satisfied at being reunited with Lopez. "I have wanted Score on our side for some time," Lopez said. "We tried to get him during the winter meetings in Florida. I think he's still a fine pitcher. I am hoping that we can get him straightened out."[17]

Score started 22 games for the White Sox in 1960, going 5-10 with a 3.72 ERA. There were some bright days, but for the most part he couldn't regain the speed on his fastball. Also, he lost the movement on the ball. It went straight as an arrow. In June 1961, he was optioned to San Diego of the Pacific Coast League. "We had a long talk with Herb and he was agreeable to the move," Lopez said. "There's nothing wrong with his arm. He can throw hard on the sidelines for 45 minutes solid. If there was anything wrong with his arm, he couldn't do that. What he needs most is control." Score went 7-6 for the Padres, but his ERA ballooned to 5.10.

Lopez brought him back to the White Sox for the 1962 season, but after four relief appearances, Score was optioned to Indianapolis of the American Association. Score was 10-7 for the Indians, but still posted a high ERA of 4.82. He returned to Indianapolis in 1963 and posted a 0-6 record with a 7.66 ERA. He asked White Sox general manager Ed Short to place him on the voluntary retirement list. "People asked me why I went to the minors to pitch," said Score. "I still believed my arm might come back. I was only 30. I didn't want to be sitting somewhere when I was 60 and wondering, 'What if I pitched one more year, would I have found it?' Now I know. I have no doubts."[18]

For his career, Score was 55-46 with a 3.36 ERA. Before being struck by the line drive in 1957, he was 39-20 with an ERA of 2.46, and struck out 547 batters in 512 2/3 innings. After 1957, Score was 17-26 with an ERA of 4.70 in 345 2/3 innings. To his credit, he never used the accident as an excuse. He did not blame anyone, and always claimed that his pitching problems had more to do with his arm troubles in 1958 than his damaged eye in 1957.

Lane left Cleveland after the 1960 season to assume the same responsibilities in Kansas City. Gabe Paul came over from Houston to become the Indians' new general manager. n 1964, Paul hired Score to provide color commentary on the Indians' TV broadcasts. After four years in the TV booth, he moved over to the radio side and spent the next 30 years describing the action to generations of Tribe fans. Initially, Score was partnered with veteran broadcaster Bob Neal. "Bob Neal was the difference in my career," Score said. "If the professional broadcaster doesn't like the ex-athlete, he can make you look bad, and you have no chance. It happens a lot in this business. But Bob Neal never showed any resentment toward me."[19]

Score was passionate about baseball. He didn't pretend to be interested or speak in an exaggerated voice the way some broadcasters have done. Score was genuine. He was beloved by fans all over, but especially those in Cleveland. Many did not know that he had a playing career, and that included some of the younger players. But that was OK with Score. Broadcasting baseball was his career; playing it was in the rear-view mirror. He was not highly polished; at times he may have given the wrong venue where the team was playing, or he did not give the score or the inning of the game often enough. But that was OK, because Score was real, and the fans adored him, even if he didn't always understand why. To Herb, the players were the stars, not the broadcaster. He didn't feel the need to give expertise on every play, or dwell on a bad play. He was seldom critical of a player or a manager, trying to be objective at all times. He always felt that fans should remember what happens on the field, not what is said in the booth.

The Indians' flagship station, WWWE, was a powerful, 50,000-watt station. It covered over two-thirds of the country, giving Score the audience, he deserved. The radio station had a slogan that it could be heard in "38 states and half of Canada." While some local listeners may have doubted the accuracy of this claim, Score's broadcast partner, Joe Tait, remembered a story that exemplified it: "In Kansas City, the Indians and Royals were playing a twi-night doubleheader. The first game went extra innings and was delayed by rain several times. It was Cleveland's final visit to KC and the Royals were in a pennant chase. The second game was played and more rain. During a delay at about 1:45 A.M. (EDT), we decided to have a contest to see if anyone was still listening. We offered an Indians press guide and a baseball to the person living the farthest from Cleveland. All they had to do was put their name and address on a postcard and the time 1:45 A.M. We only mentioned it once and resumed the broadcast, which eventually concluded in a full nine innings. The team went on to Texas and Oakland, and so did we. In Oakland, WWWE's program director called because of the load of postcards. Herb and I decided to declare co-winners because we couldn't figure out which was further from Cleveland, St. John's or St. Croix, both in the Virgin Islands. We had cards from Mexico, Canada, and about 20 states." [20]

But while Score learned a lot about broadcasting from Neal, others learned a lot about baseball from Herb. "If I ran the Indians, Herb Score would be my general manager, and I'd give him carte blanche to do whatever he wanted," said Tait. "He is the smartest baseball man I've ever met."[21]

For the first 30 years of Score's broadcasting career, the Indians were for the most part a horrible team. They never seriously contended for the playoffs, finishing at .500 or higher only six times in those 30 years. "Herb Score has probably watched more bad baseball than anyone in the history of the game," Tait said.[22]

But times changed and the Indians improved. In 1995 and 1997, they made it to the World Series, losing both times. Score announced his retirement from the broadcast booth in 1997, and called his last game at Game Seven of the World Series, a 3-2, 11-inning victory by the Florida Marlins. Wrapping up the game – his last addressing Indians fans as a broadcaster – Score signed off by saying, "And so that is the season for 1997. And there's very little else we can say except to tell you it's been a pleasure. I would like to thank all the fans for their kindness over the years. You've been very good to me. And we hope that whoever sits in this chair next, you'll be as kind to them as you have been to me. The final score in 11 innings, it's the Marlins 3, the Indians 2. The Florida Marlins are the world champions."[23]

In 1998, Score was involved in a traffic accident near New Philadelphia, Ohio. His car pulled out in front of a tractor-trailer. He suffered hip, head, and pelvic injuries. He recovered from the injuries to make a handful of public appearances, but he suffered a stroke in 2002. He then had bouts with a staph infection and pneumonia. After a lengthy hospital stay, Score died on November 11, 2008. He was 75 years old. He was survived by his wife, Nancy, and three children, David, Mary, and Judy. He was preceded in death by his daughter Susan in 1994.

Score was the connection to baseball generations of Indians fans, first as a player then as a broadcaster. In the early 1990s, he said, "People will tell me I was unlucky. Me? Unlucky? I started with a great team in the Indians and played under a great manager in Al Lopez. Then I went from the field to the broadcasting booth, at the age of 30, and 30 years later I'm still doing the games. If you ask me, that's not unlucky. That's a guy who has been in the right place at the right time."[24]

That was Herb Score. Positive at all times. A gentleman at all times. He was a man who always saw the glass as half-full.

NOTES

1. Hal Lebovitz, "Tribe's Terrific Twosome: Mr. Robert, Master Herbie," *Cleveland News*, May 2, 1955: 33.
2. Ibid.
3. Roger Birtwell. "Better Grip on Curve Helped Score Blow Down Bosox Hitters," *The Sporting News*, May 11, 1955: 9
4. Ibid
5. Jimmy Burns, "'55 Just Long Surprise for Herb Score," *The Sporting News*, November 23, 1955: 11.
6. Bob Holbrook, "Cronin and Greenberg 'Cook' Deal That Develops O.B. Stomach Ache," *The Sporting News*, March 27, 1957: 6.
7. Hal Lebovitz, "'Flattered' Score Ribbed on Million-Dollar Baby," *The Sporting News,* March 27, 1957: 6.
8. Hal Lebovitz, "'St. Jude, Stay With Me', Plea of Score When Hurt," *The Sporting News*, May 15, 1957: 8.
9. Terry Pluto, *The Curse of Rocky Colavito* (New York: Simon & Schuster, 1994), 28-29.
10. Shirley Povich, "Quotes," *The Sporting News*, April 29, 1959: 16.
11. Harry Jones, "Tribe Gets Kuenn in Colavito Trade," *Cleveland Plain Dealer*, April 18, 1960: 33.
12. Terry Pluto: 52.
13. Hal Lebovitz, "Training Tidbits," *The Sporting News*, March 25, 1959: 25
14. Harry Jones, "Score is Traded; Bell Hurls Today," *Cleveland Plain Dealer*, April 19, 1960: 1A.
15. Ibid
16. Cooper Rollow, "Happy Score Thanks Lane," *Chicago Tribune*, April 19, 1960: F-1.
17. Edward Prell, "Sox Get Herb Score: Trade Latman," *Chicago Tribune*, April 19, 1960: F-1;
18. Pluto, 52.
19. Pluto, 182.
20. Correspondence with Joe Tait, April, 2009.
21. Pluto, 187.
22. Pluto, 177.
23. *USA Today*, October 26, 1997, Herb Score player file, National Baseball Baseball Hall of Fame.
24. Unidentified newspaper clipping, Herb Score player file, National Baseball Baseball Hall of Fame.

THE FRONT OFFICE

RICHARD JACOBS

BY CLAYTON TRUTOR

Richard E. "Dick" Jacobs was the majority owner of the Cleveland Indians from December 1986 until February 2000. He purchased the team with his older brother, David H. Jacobs (1921-1992), from the estate of the late F.J. "Steve" O'Neill in December 1986 for $35.5 million. Jacobs oversaw the restoration of the Indians to on-the-field and at-the-box-office success following three decades of mediocrity.

Before purchasing the Indians, Jacobs became one of the richest men in the United States in the real-estate development business. He played a prominent role in the revitalization of downtown Cleveland during the 1980s and 1990s through his work as a developer as well as his support for the Gateway Project, which culminated in the construction of Jacobs Field (later renamed Progressive Field), a Cuyahoga County-owned downtown ballpark that hosted the Indians as its primary tenant, as well as the Gund Arena (later the Quicken Loans Arena), an indoor coliseum that lured the Cleveland Cavaliers basketball team back into the city. Jacobs' stewardship of the Indians from a national joke into one of the most profitable and successful franchises in professional sports preserved major-league baseball for Cleveland. "The reason the Indians remain in Cleveland," wrote Terry Pluto soon after Jacobs' death, "is because Dick Jacobs bought the franchise in 1986."[1]

Richard Jacobs was born on June 16, 1925, in Akron, Ohio. His parents, Vivian and Adeline (Yeiter) Jacobs, were of German extraction and natives of Michigan. Richard's older brother, David, was his only sibling. The Jacobses were pious Methodists. Vivian "V.R." Jacobs, Richard and David's father, had relocated from Michigan after serving in the Coast Guard during World War I to work in the marketing department at Goodyear. V.R. climbed the corporate ladder quickly, reaching the corporation's executive ranks while his sons were teenagers.[2] Richard grew up in the Goodyear Heights neighborhood on the east side of Akron. The family lived close enough to the Goodyear tire plant to smell burning rubber throughout the day.[3]

An industrious young man, Richard began working at an early age, doing odd jobs around the neighborhood. The most formative of his early jobs came when he worked at Swenson's, the regionally famous drive-in car hop near his home. Jacobs began working at Swenson's at age 12 as a potato peeler. A year later, he was promoted to car hop, a job he held throughout his adolescence.[4] Jacobs graduated from Buchtel High School in Akron in 1943. At the height of World War II, he was accepted into the US Army Officer Candidate School, where he was trained in the artillery. Second Lieutenant Jacobs served in the Philippines, where he commanded an artillery company. After V-J Day he commanded a company in the occupation force in Osaka, Japan.[5] Jacobs attended several colleges during the late 1940s, including Albion College (Michigan), Kent State University (Ohio), and the University of Akron. He completed his bachelor's degree in business administration at Indiana University in 1949.[6]

After college, Jacobs worked in sales for several years. He showed great ability as a salesman and soon joined his brother David in the real-estate business. In 1955 Richard and David established the real-estate development firm of Jacobs Visconsi Jacobs (JVJ) with pioneering suburban shopping-center developer Dominic Visconsi. Based in Cleveland, JVJ built and leased shopping malls, office buildings, hotels, and mixed-use urban and suburban developments. When Richard and David Jacobs purchased the Indians, JVJ was the nation's fourth largest shopping-mall management company.[7] The success of JVJ enabled all three partners to become wealthy. When Richard Jacobs purchased the Indians, he was estimated by *Forbes* to be worth $500 million and was listed by the magazine as one of the 400 richest Americans in 1986.[8] The leadership triumvirate at JVJ remained intact for decades until the Jacobs brothers bought out Visconsi in 1988 and renamed the company the Richard and David Jacobs Group. Richard was the chairman and CEO of JVJ for decades while David was vice chairman and oversaw construction projects.[9] (After David's death, Richard renamed the company the Richard E. Jacobs Group in 1992.)

In a 1987 profile of Richard Jacobs for *Cleveland Magazine*, Edward Whalen wrote that JVJ was able to "capitalize on one of the greatest demographic changes in modern America – the growth and malling of the suburbs in the 1960s and 1970s."[10] During the 1960s, JVJ emerged as one of the nation's leading developers of suburban shopping centers. Its first major successes came in the Columbus (Ohio) metropolitan area. Working closely with Sears, JVJ developed the Northland Mall north of downtown Columbus. Opened in 1964, the Sears-anchored mall was the first in the Columbus area. Northland was an immediate hit with area shoppers. It prompted the development of several other JVJ-designed and -operated malls in the Columbus area over the next decade: Eastland (1967), Westland (1969), and Southland (1975). Sears was one of the anchor stores at all four of JVJ's Columbus area developments. The relationship that JVJ and Sears developed in Columbus inaugurated a highly profitable series of partnerships between the real-estate development firm and the department store. More than 30 JVJ properties included Sears stores as one of their anchors.[11]

Building on its success in Columbus, JVJ expanded its empire across Ohio and eventually across the Midwest, Northeast, West Coast, and Southeast. By the time of David Jacobs' death in 1992, the Richard and David Jacobs Group, JVJ's successor firm, owned 40 properties in 15 states.[12] Beyond suburban shopping centers, JVJ played a major role in the redevelopment of downtown Cleveland. In 1986, JVJ purchased the 40-story Erieview Tower in downtown Cleveland for $45 million. The following year, JVJ opened the $43 million, two-story Galleria Mall at Erieview, the first enclosed mall in downtown Cleveland. The mall helped lure suburban shoppers back into the longtime shopping desert of downtown Cleveland for the first time in years.[13] In 1991 JVJ opened the Society Center (later renamed the Key Tower), a 57-story mixed-use development on Public Square in downtown Cleveland and the largest building between New York and Chicago.[14]

JVJ and its successor firms also developed office parks around the country, including the Chagrin Highlands Office and Research Park in Beachwood, Ohio, which opened in 1999.[15] JVJ's other investments included stakes in Marriott hotels in several Midwestern cities as well as the Pier House Hotel in Key West, Florida. The Jacobs brothers also owned 25 Wendy's franchises in the New York metropolitan area.[16]

When the Jacobs brothers purchased the Indians in 1986, Pat O'Neill, the nephew of deceased

Indians owner Steve O'Neill (1899-1983), was operating the franchise on behalf of the former owner's estate. Pat O'Neill took his time finding a new owner for the Indians. He was set on finding a Northeast Ohio-based owner for the club to ensure that it would stay in Cleveland.[17] Additionally, he wanted to get a good price for the team since most of the money was to go to Steve O'Neill's favorite charity, the Catholic Diocese of Cleveland.[18] Numerous individuals and ownership groups from out of town made generous offers for the team.Several underfunded local investor groups also tried to buy the club.[19] The Jacobs brothers met both criteria.They were well-heeled and they were local. Foreshadowing their conduct as owners, the brothers remained aloof from the press during their negotiations with the O'Neill estate.[20] After a half-year of quiet negotiations, the Jacobs brothers agreed to purchase the Indians for $ 35.5 million in December 1986. Richard agreed to buy 75 percent of the Indians while David purchased the remaining 25 percent.[21]

Outside of business circles, Richard Jacobs's name was not well-known in Cleveland at the time he purchased the Indians.[22] He became famous by buying the Indians, but he shunned that fame during the 14 years he owned the team, preferring instead to work behind the scenes. Jacobs sat in his loge behind home plate at most home games, but he rarely agreed to interviews and appeared in public infrequently. Jacobs hired a cadre of baseball experts to run his franchise. He kept his hands off the on-the-field product and allowed his experts to build a winning team. He made his ample resources available to them so that they could rebuild a strong foundation for the Indians franchise. "He never told them what to do, only that they keep him informed, operate within the budget and be successful," his obituary in the *Cleveland Plain Dealer* said of Jacobs' relationship with his personnel.[23]

The Jacobs-era Indians invested heavily in their farm system. Jacobs hired Baltimore Orioles general manager Hank Peters, an expert on developing minor-league talent, to serve as president of the Indians. Peters (1987-1991) and his successor, John Hart (1991-2001), built the Indians from the ground up, developing one of baseball's premier minor-league systems.[24] Jacobs showed patience while Peters and Hart built this base of future success. The Indians struggled on the field in the early years of the Jacobs era, continuing a dubious legacy that dated back to 1959, the last time the Indians had finished above third place. The Indians' sixth-place finish in the American League East in 1993 was the franchise's 34th consecutive finish in third place or lower in the standings. In the words of *Cleveland Plain Dealer* sportswriter Bill Livingston, the Indians had the "national profile of a bump in the road" when the Jacobs brothers bought the team.[25]

The Indians finally finished above third place in 1994, posting a 66-47 record and a second-place finish in that strike-shortened season. The Tribe would have qualified for the inaugural wild-card bid had the postseason been played. In 1995 the Indians won the first of five consecutive American League Central Division titles (1995-1999) under the Jacobs ownership. The 1995 division championship was the Indians' first postseason appearance since they won the 1954 American League pennant. The Indians won two pennants under the Jacobs ownership, in 1995 and 1997. The Indians lost the World Series on both occasions. In 1995 the 100-44 Indians, who owned the best record in baseball that season, lost in six games to the Atlanta Braves. The 1997 Indians came within two outs of capturing Cleveland's first World Series in five decades. A ninth-inning rally in Game Seven by the Florida Marlins off Cleveland's previously lights-out closer Jose Mesa tied the game and sent it to extra innings, and the Marlins won in 11 innings.

The success the Indians enjoyed during the late 1990s was a product of the minor-league system that the Jacobs organization built and the free agents the organization brought in, beginning in 1994. Products of the minor-league organization who became stars for the team during the 1990s included Jim Thome, Albert Belle, Charles Nagy, and Manny Ramirez. Prospects acquired by the Jacobs-era Indians early in their careers including Kenny Lofton, Carlos Baerga, Omar Vizquel, Sandy Alomar, and Jose Mesa. High-profile free agents brought in by the Indians during the mid-1990s included Dennis Martinez, Jack Morris,

Eddie Murray, Tony Peña, Orel Hershiser, and Jack McDowell.[26]

The success the Indians enjoyed on the field during Jacobs' tenure as owner was facilitated in large part by the construction of Jacobs Field, which may well have been Jacobs' greatest accomplishment as owner. From the moment the brothers bought the Indians, they were looking for a new stadium. The Indians had been tenants of Browns owner Art Modell since 1973, when Modell bought Cleveland Municipal Stadium, the decaying waterfront playing facility that had been home to the Indians since the Great Depression. The Indians were undoubtedly second-class citizens at the "Mistake by the Lake," the best known of epithets for Cleveland Municipal Stadium. Modell tapped heavily into the meager revenue streams available to the Indians at the ballpark, including parking and concessions. Proposals for a replacement ballpark had been floating around for years.[27] When Modell proposed the construction of a new multipurpose football and baseball stadium in downtown Cleveland during the late 1980s to Jacobs, the Indians owner told Modell that "it's hard for two guys to share the same lunchbox," a statement Jacobs understood all too well from the years he had already spent in a shared venue with the Browns.[28]

Jacobs supported the Gateway Project, a county-wide effort to build a new baseball park and basketball arena in downtown Cleveland. The project aimed to revitalize downtown Cleveland by making the ballpark and arena its centerpiece. Simultaneously, the Gateway Project sought to bring professional basketball back to the city from the suburbs.[29] In May 1990 a slim majority of Cuyahoga County residents voted to approve the project. Richard Jacobs expressed his public support for the Gateway Project, both because of its positive impact on the Indians and his belief that the new ballpark would continue the momentum he helped kick-start for the redevelopment of downtown Cleveland.[30]

Jacobs was intimately involved with the planning of fan-friendly, nostalgia-laden Jacobs Field, the second of the retro-ballparks that proved popular with fans during the 1990s.[31] The $175 million facility, which bore Jacobs' name during its first 15 seasons of operation, drew record crowds to watch the Indians play. On Opening Day 1994, President Bill Clinton threw out the first pitch, helping to foster the national media buzz surrounding the ballpark's debut. By that summer, the Indians' success on the field and the positive reviews the ballpark received in the media helped transform it into a national hot-spot where celebrity sightings were common.[32] The Indians' financial success at Jacobs Field enabled them to keep reloading their roster with high-priced free agents and helped them continue to compete for a world championship for the remainder of Jacobs' ownership.[33] From June 12, 1995, until April 4, 2001, the Indians sold out 455 consecutive games at Jacobs Field.[34] This was a record number of sellouts until the Red Sox surpassed the streak at Fenway Park in 2008 with a streak that reached 820 games (2003-2013).[35]

Jacobs sold his controlling interest in the Indians to Larry Dolan for $323 million in February 2000, an almost tenfold return on the original investment of the Jacobs brothers. Additionally, Jacobs earned $50 million in a public stock sale of a minority interest in the Indians in 1998. Jacobs told Terry Pluto that he lost $40 million on the Indians between 1986 and 1993. Additionally, he paid $13 million for the naming rights to Jacobs Field for the first 15 years of the ballpark's existence. Public documents released after the stock sale revealed that Jacobs made $55 million on the team between 1994 and 1999.[36]

In 1952 Jacobs married Helen Chaney, a college classmate originally from New Jersey. They divorced in 1983. The couple had three children, Jeff, Marilyn, and Nancy. Jeff Jacobs became a noted developer and Republican politician in Ohio.[37] In addition to his home in Lakewood, Ohio, Jacobs maintained a residence in New York City, where he often conducted business and became an art collector of renown.[38] Jacobs died on June 5, 2009, at his home in Lakewood, 11 days short of his 84th birthday.

SOURCES

In addition to those cited in the notes,

The Sporting News.

Websites:

Cleveland Indians Website: Indians.com.

ESPN.com.

ESPNBoston.com.

Richard E. Jacobs Group Website: rejacobs.com.

NOTES

1. Terry Pluto, "Bottom Line? Dick Jacobs Gave Cleveland Indian Fans a Lot to Be Thankful For," *Cleveland Plain Dealer*, June 5, 2009. Accessed on November 19, 2014: cleveland.com/pluto/blog/index.ssf/2009/06/bottom_line_dick_jacobs_gave_c.html.
2. Edward Whalen, "Top Gun," *Cleveland Magazine*, March 1987. Accessed on November 19, 2014: clevelandmagazine.com/ME2/dirmod.asp?sid=E73ABD6180B44874871A91F6BA5C249C&nm=&type=Publishing&mod=Publications::Article&mid=1578600D80804596A222593669321019&tier=4&id=F1C8A394BCF64BB4924CD7100FBEFEE5.
3. Ibid.; Bill Livingston, "Dick Jacobs Gave the Cleveland Indians the Gift of Renewed Pride, and So Much More," *Cleveland Plain Dealer*, June 5, 2009. Accessed on November 19, 2014: cleveland.com/livingston/index.ssf/2009/06/dick_jacobs_gave_the_cleveland.html.
4. Terry Pluto, "Bottom Line?"; Edward Whalen, "Top Gun."; Bill Livingston, "Dick Jacobs."
5. Edward Whalen, "Top Gun."
6. Ibid.
7. "David H. Jacobs, 71, a Developer and Owner of the Cleveland Indians," *New York Times*, September 19, 1992, 47; "The Richard E. Jacobs Group History," Richard E. Jacobs Group Website. Accessed on November 19, 2014: rejacobs.com/index.aspx/?id=34/.
8. Edward Whalen, "Top Gun"; Terry Pluto, "Bottom Line?"
9. "David H. Jacobs, 71," *New York Times*, September 19, 1992, 47; "The Richard E. Jacobs Group History," Richard E. Jacobs Group Website; Edward Whalen, "Top Gun."
10. Edward Whalen, "Top Gun.."
11. Ibid.
12. David H. Jacobs, 71," *New York Times*, September 19, 1992, 47; Edward Whalen, "Top Gun."
13. Peter Zacari, "Indians Former Owner, Developer Dick Jacobs dies at 83," *Cleveland Plain Dealer*, June 5, 2009. Accessed on November 19, 2014: cleveland.com/tribe/index.ssf/2009/06/dick_jacobs_dies_at_84.html; Edward Whalen, "Top Gun."
14. David H. Jacobs, 71," *New York Times*, September 19, 1992, 47.
15. Peter Zacari, "Indians Former Owner."
16. Terry Pluto, "Bottom Line?"; Edward Whalen, "Top Gun."
17. Terry Pluto, "Bottom Line?"
18. Ibid.
19. "Former Indians Owner Dies at 83," ESPN.com, June 5, 2009. Accessed on November 19, 2014: sports.espn.go.com/mlb/news/story?id=4233383; Edward Whalen, "Top Gun."
20. Edward Whalen, "Top Gun."
21. David H. Jacobs, 71," *New York Times*, September 19, 1992, 47.
22. Edward Whalen, "Top Gun."
23. Peter Zacari, "Indians Former Owner."
24. Bill Livingston, "Dick Jacobs."
25. Ibid.
26. Ibid.
27. Ibid.
28. Terry Pluto, "Bottom Line?"
29. Tom Verducci, "Grand Opening With a New Stadium as Backdrop, Cleveland Ushered in an Era of Optimism With a Win Over Seattle," *Sports Illustrated*, April 11, 1994. Accessed on November 19, 2014: si.com/vault/1994/04/11/130838/grand-opening-with-a-new-stadium-as-backdrop-cleveland-ushered-in-an-era-of-optimism-with-a-win-over-seattle
30. Tom Verducci, "Grand Opening"; Verducci, "Good Home Cookin' by Eating Foes Before Raucous Crowds at New Jacobs Field, The Indians Streaked into First Place," *Sports Illustrated*, July 4, 1994. Accessed on November 19, 1994: si.com/vault/1994/07/04/131578/good-home-cookin-by-eating-up-foes-before-raucous-crowds-at-new-jacobs-field-the-indians-streaked-into-first-place
31. Bill Livingston, "Dick Jacobs."
32. Tom Verducci, "Good Home Cookin'."
33. Bill Livingston, "Dick Jacobs."
34. Anthony Castrovince, "Sellout Streak Etched in Tribe Lore," Indians.com, September 4, 2008. Accessed on November 19, 2014: m.indians.mlb.com/news/article/3418249/.
35. Gordon Edes, "Boston Red Sox's 820-game Sellout Streak Ends," ESPNBoston.com, April 11, 2013. Accessed on November 19, 2014: espn.go.com/boston/mlb/story/_/id/9158007/boston-red-sox-820-game-sellout-streak-ends.
36. "Former Indians Owner"; Terry Pluto, "Bottom Line?"
37. Edward Whalen, "Top Gun."
38. Ibid.

JOHN HART

BY RICK BALAZS

The Cleveland Indians' return to prominence in the mid-1990s is well known. So is the plan that general manager John Hart used to orchestrate it. The plan focused on developing young players and signing them to long-term contracts before they became eligible for arbitration and free agency.

What perhaps is not so well known is the story of Hart's own ascent to becoming the Tribe's general manager, and that the story is founded on refreshing ideals like hard work and following one's own heart.

John Henry Hart was born in Tampa, Florida, on July 21, 1948, to John Hart Sr. and Anne (Reen) Hart. From a young age, his life was centered on sports, and he played baseball, basketball, and football at Winter Park (Florida) High School. He also moved quite a bit in his early years. He spent time in Europe and Turkey living with his mother and stepfather, who was a colonel in the Air Force. Hart didn't enjoy living overseas, however, and went to live with his grandmother when he was a sophomore in high school. Two years later, he moved in with his father.[1]

After graduating from high school, Hart received a baseball scholarship from Eastern Tennessee State, but quit halfway through his freshman year.[2]

"They told me I wasn't going to start, and I said, 'I'll see ya,'" said Hart.[3]

Hart then attended Seminole Junior College (now known as Seminole State College of Florida), in Sanford, Florida. He played baseball for two years at Seminole State, which is where he met his future wife, Sandi DeVorak.

"I was going out with one of the cheerleaders and Sandi was a cheerleader too," said Hart. "I played with Greg Pryor, who played in the big leagues. His brother Jeff was a can't-miss prospect with the Angels. He came into town and asked me if I could get him a date. I asked Sandi and we double-dated. About 10 days after that, I called Sandi."[4]

The Montreal Expos signed Hart as a catcher and assigned him to their Class-A club in West Palm Beach in 1969. Hart played three seasons in the Expos' organization, two in West Palm Beach and one with Quebec City in the Double-A Eastern League. Over the three seasons, he hit .223 with two home runs. Hart knew that if he was ever going to make it to the big leagues, it wasn't going to be as a player.

"I was the kind of player coaches and managers loved," he said. "If they told me to run 10 miles, I'd run 12. I was a damn good high-school player and junior college All-American. But when I got to the pros, I didn't hit. I was a good defensive catcher. I did a lot of the little things right – I was a good leader and called a good game. But I knew I wasn't major-league caliber. I knew I'd probably end up a coach or manager."[5]

Knowing his professional playing days were over, Hart had to decide what his next step would be. His father told him to follow his heart. John Hart Sr. did not have a career in professional baseball; he was the president and general manager of Associated Grocers of Florida, a grocery wholesaler. But his father's advice significantly influenced John's future career path in baseball.

"After I stopped playing, I bounced around a little," Hart said. "I didn't have a lot of money. He never told me to do this or that or to come work with him. He said, 'Do what your heart is telling you to do and you'll be all right.'"[6]

Hart graduated from the Florida Technological University (now the University of Central Florida) in 1973, majoring in history and physical education. He finished a six-year stretch in the US Army Reserve, earning the rank of sergeant first class. He opened the Hart Athletic Center, the first fitness center in Orlando to use Nautilus equipment.[7]

He even started the John Hart Baseball School, which Hart later said "was like Bingo Long's Traveling Circus."[8] The instructional facility initially consisted of Hart, some bats and balls, a pitching machine, and an old Plymouth truck.[9] The baseball school eventually grew to be a well-known baseball camp, and Hart continued to return home and operate the camp even after he achieved success as the Indians' general manager.[10]

"No matter where I live, this is still my home, my community," Hart said in 1997, referring to his home base of Central Florida and the Orlando metropolitan area.[11] In addition to instruction in baseball-playing skills, the camp offered students advice on the draft process, including what to expect from scouts and what questions to ask.[12]

Hart limited enrollment in the camp to around 100 students. That way, he believed, with about 25 instructors on staff, including college and pro coaches and scouts, he could provide proper and meaningful instruction to the students.

One of the students was A.J. Pierzynski, who attended the camp in high school and then returned as an instructor after he was drafted as a catcher by the Minnesota Twins.

"I can't tell you how much this camp helped me," Pierzynski said in 1997. "I loved it here. So when John asked me to come and help, I was glad to do it. He really cares about the kids."[13]

Hart's first coaching job with an actual team, however, wasn't in baseball. He led a junior-high football team that had lost every game the previous year to an undefeated season and a victory in a game called the Kumquat Bowl.

"That was really the start for me," Hart said. "When I coached these kids in football, I realized that I really loved teaching. And I really loved winning."[14]

These modest beginnings in baseball didn't exactly scream "future major-league GM," making Hart's rise to prominence all the more impressive.

"John has gone on to do everything pretty well for a guy who just wanted to be a middle-school teacher," said Lee Driggers, one of Hart's classmates at Florida Technological University, who himself become a longtime collegiate baseball coach. "He was just happy doing the John Hart Baseball School and teaching at Westridge Junior High. We had to talk him into applying for the Boone [High School] job."[15]

Driggers was referring to William R. Boone High School in Orlando. Taking the job as Boone's head baseball coach turned out to be fortuitous. Hart was quite successful coaching there, guiding the team to a state championship in 1981.

"That was one of the greatest things I'd ever been through," Hart said in 1985. "Championships come and go, but that one will never go away. I had a super group of kids."[16]

Boone was also where Hart was "discovered" as a prospective major-league manager and executive. Tom Giordano was a longtime colleague of Hank Peters with Baltimore, serving as the Orioles' director of scouting and player development. Giordano visited Boone in 1982 to scout the team's star catcher, Ron Karkovice, who went on to a major-league career with the Chicago White Sox.[17]

Giordano came away from the scouting trip more impressed with Hart than Karkovice. He noticed how Hart had his players look, act, and practice like professionals. Giordano invited Hart to lunch the next day, and offered him a two-year contract to join the Orioles as a scout.[18]

Hart thought about taking the offer but declined, deciding not to uproot his wife, Sandi, and daughter, Shannon, and move them to Baltimore, nearly 1,000 miles away. But he stayed in touch with Giordano's scout in the Orlando area, Jack Sanford, and attended games with Sanford to evaluate other players. Later, when the Orioles had an opening for a manager with their rookie team, the Bluefield (West Virginia) Orioles, they offered the job to Hart. He accepted, and his career in professional baseball began.[19]

Hart achieved considerable success as a minor-league manager, guiding teams in the Orioles' organization for six seasons. In his first season, Bluefield won the Appalachian League title, its first since 1971, and Hart was named the league's Manager of the Year. He later managed teams in Class A, Double A, and Triple A, achieving a record of 436-334 (.566) for his minor-league managing career. He earned International League Manager of the Year honors while with Triple-A Rochester in 1986.

"Every team I had either won a championship or made the playoffs," Hart said. "That was my course. I wanted to be a major-league manager."[20]

Hart reached Baltimore as third-base coach in 1988. By that time, the Orioles were in full rebuilding mode. The team's owner, lawyer Edward Bennett Williams, fired Peters as the team's general manager after the 1987 season. Peters joined the Indians and wanted Hart with him in Cleveland, but Williams, eyeing Hart as the next Orioles manager, denied him permission to interview with the Indians. But Williams's death in 1988 cleared the path for Hart to join the Indians for the 1989 season.

Hart managed the Indians briefly in 1989, but Peters had something else in mind.

"Hank told me, 'John, part of my job is to take care of the future of this club,'" said Hart. "I want you to be the guy to replace me."[21]

Hart was surprised, given that his experience had been on the field as a minor-league catcher, manager, and major-league coach. His goal had been to manage in the big leagues. "I'd never thought about the front office," he said. … "Hank told me, 'John, I think you'll manage in the big leagues, but sometimes you don't get the team you want and other people are making the decisions,'" said Hart. "I think (being the general manager) would be a better way to go."[22]

Hart did not spend much of his early time with the Indians sitting in an office. Instead, Peters told him to go out, see and scout players, and talk to scouts and other decision-makers. "Hank said, 'This way you're going to see players from a different perspective,' said Hart. 'It's going to help you in your decisions as you go forward.'"[23]

Hart spent much of the 1989 season doing exactly what Peters had told him to do: scouting, networking, and planning for the Tribe's future. That was until, with 19 games left in the season, Peters named him the interim manager after firing Doc Edwards.

"I was at Wrigley Field in September and Hank called and said, 'I want you to take the club over for the last three or four weeks and help me make some decisions,'" said Hart. "Hank made it real clear that I wasn't being considered for the manager's job. He said this was part of the experience I needed to help him make decisions. So that's what we did."[24]

The Indians named Hart their director of baseball operations in January of 1990. At the time Hart said, "I'm really looking forward to doing this, because I'm going to have a chance to be involved in all phases of the game. I think it's going to be a tremendous challenge."25

And what a challenge it was. The Indians had not played in the postseason since 1954, when they set an American League record (since broken) with 111 wins but were swept by the Giants in the World Series. After finishing second in the American League in 1959, the Indians finished as high as third only once, in 1968, and by the time Hart joined the organization in 1989, the Indians had had only seven seasons over .500 (out of 29 total). Add the cold Cleveland weather in April, and the decrepit old Cleveland Stadium, and the franchise was not exactly primed for an immediate turnaround.

"It was the most maligned organization in professional sports," said Mark Shapiro, who later replaced Hart as the Indians GM. "The only thing the Indians were known for was the movie *Major League*."26

Hart basically served as Peters' right-hand man during the 1990 and 1991 seasons. The Indians finished 77-85, fourth in the AL East, in 1990. The team's future fixture at catcher, Sandy Alomar Jr., won the AL Rookie of the Year Award and Gold Glove at catcher. Carlos Baerga hit .260 as a 21-year-old rookie. Peters acquired both players from San Diego after the 1989 season in exchange for Joe Carter, Cleveland's star outfielder.

The team bottomed out in 1991, losing a team-record 105 games, the third time in seven seasons the team had lost more than 100 games. Still, more of the foundation of the future was laid during that season. Surly outfielder Albert Belle managed to stay on the field most of the season and hit 28 home runs. Future All-Star pitcher Charles Nagy made 33 starts and won a team-high 10 games.

Hart assumed the general manager's duties after that 1991 season, and soon thereafter made what arguably turned out to be his signature trade. On December 10, Hart traded promising catcher Eddie Taubensee and pitcher Willie Blair to Houston for pitcher Dave Rhode and a young outfielder named Kenny Lofton.

We project him as an impact-type player who has a chance to help us in 1992," Hart said prophetically after making the trade. "We see him as the prototype leadoff hitter/center fielder."27 Lofton hit .285 in 1992, led the American League with 66 stolen bases, and was considered by many to be the top rookie in the AL that season. (The Rookie of the Year Award went to Milwaukee's Pat Listach). Lofton went on to win four Gold Gloves, make six all-star teams, and lead the American League in stolen bases for five consecutive seasons.

The Indians muddled through losing seasons in 1992 and 1993, finishing 76-86 each season. But Hart set the precedent for which he is became noted, signing the team's young, talented players to multiyear contracts before they were eligible for arbitration. Hart knew that if he could not sign his top young players to long-term contracts, history would continue to repeat itself for the Indians: They would develop talented players into successful big leaguers, but pay them below-market salaries. When the players gained free agency, they had no interest in re-signing. Either the player departed or the Indians were forced to trade him in order to receive value in return. As a result, the Indians had great difficulty keeping a nucleus together.

That was what happened to the likes of Joe Carter, Tom Candiotti, and Greg Swindell. In Carter's case, Peters traded him for Alomar and Baerga. But not every trade is a home run. Some are duds. Hart knew this, and he knew that he had to lock up his young players to ensure that the team could benefit from at least some of the players' prime years. For the players, they gave up their arbitration rights, from which they might or might not make more money, in exchange for more certainty.

"There is an inherent risk on both sides," Hart said. "Players give up potential dollars for security. Our risk comes if some of the players we've signed don't live up to our expectations. But I believe the upside of this is far greater."28

Alomar, Baerga, and Nagy were the three most notable players who signed long-term deals before the start of the 1992 season. Belle, perhaps as a sign of things to come, did not sign a deal at that time, but did in 1993.[29]

"If it's about making the last dollar, then you'll play in New York," Hart told his players. You won't get that in Cleveland. But you'll get more money than you'll ever need in your lifetime."[30]

Hart and his assistant, Dan O'Dowd, developed the plan when they traveled to the arbitration hearings for Swindell and Candiotti in 1991. "We've got to find a better way," Hart told O'Dowd.[31]

Not everyone was a fan of the Indians' plan. Gene Orza, then the associate general counsel of the Major League Baseball Players Association, threatened litigation against the team, claiming that the deals "could be illegal" because of the team dealing "directly with the players instead of going through their agents."[32]

But even super-agent Scott Boras applauded the Tribe's business acumen. "It was good business on the Indians' part," Boras said. "The club knew at what point the player couldn't say no."[33]

The spring of 1992 was an intense time for Hart and O'Dowd.

"Dan and I never came up for air," said Hart. "That's as intense a four-month period as I've ever been through."[34]

Throughout his career, but particularly at this time, Hart forged friendships and mentorships with his younger colleagues in the front office. In his early days as general manager, he and his assistants would arrive each day early in the morning, work out, and then work 16-hour days.[35] Hart loved giving his assistants projects and then sitting down with them for brainstorming sessions, referred to as "couch time."[36]

"You could always walk into John's office, plop down on the couch and look up three hours later and say, 'I have to get back to what I was doing,'" said Josh Byrnes, who started with the Indians as an intern in 1994 and later became the GM of the Diamondbacks and Padres. "He liked the camaraderie of the group and encouraged us to be involved and interact with him."[37]

Said Mark Shapiro, "When I reflect now on the amount of encouragement, empowerment and leadership opportunities that he gave me at 24 or 25 years old, I'm blown away. He was just a guy who found people he believed in. John is just the consummate talent evaluator, in uniform and out of uniform."[38]

Ultimately, Hart was smart enough to surround himself with smart people who had different skill sets and viewpoints than his. Many of his assistants and colleagues proceeded to become general managers, including O'Dowd (Colorado), Shapiro (Cleveland), Neal Huntington (Pittsburgh), and Byrnes (Arizona and San Diego), among others.

"He was secure and confident enough to say, 'There are good people out there who can make us better. I'm going to empower them to do it,'" Shapiro said.[39]

Hart and his front-office team, entering the 1994 season with its core of young players signed, were full of new hope and promise, especially with the opening of Jacobs Field. The Indians won their first game at "The Jake" on April 4 in front of a sold-out crowd of 41,459. The fans were re-energized, and Hart credited signing the core of young players as part of the reason.

"Signing the young players we signed was important in getting the city to believe in us," Hart said. "If we'd shown up here without doing that, we're an empty shell. But the fans have bought in to our players, believe in our players."[40]

In addition to the foundation of young players signed to long-term deals, the Indians signed future Hall of Famer Eddie Murray and veteran starting pitcher Dennis Martinez, and traded for shortstop Omar Vizquel.

The Tribe finished the 1994 season with a 66-47 record before it was cut short by the players' strike. Owner Dick Jacobs was so impressed by the turnaround that he gave Hart a new five-year contract in October 1994.

"John has earned this," Jacobs said of the contract. "What he and his staff have done for this organization is remarkable. We all want that ring on our finger and, in my opinion, we'll have it shortly."[41]

In addition to receiving the new contract, Hart was named Executive of the Year by *The Sporting News*.[42] Since the award was established in 1936, only three other Tribe executives were so honored: Bill Veeck in 1948, Mark Shapiro in 2005 and Chris Antonetti in 2017.

Unlike the rest of baseball, which was recovering from the strike, the Tribe entered the 1995 season with more optimism than ever. Hart signed Orel Hershiser to bolster the starting rotation, and lefty Paul Assenmacher to plug a hole in the bullpen. Both performed admirably. Ultimately, in addition to locking up multiple young players to deals, Hart struck gold on veterans like Martinez, Murray, and Hershiser.

After the Indians won 100 games and advanced to the 1995 World Series, only to lose to the Atlanta Braves, Hart's next challenge was to get the Tribe back to the World Series and win. To do that, Hart needed to maintain the Indians' status as an elite team. He proved adept at building the Indians into a front-runner, but maintaining a contender was a new task for the GM.

As Indians fans unfortunately know, winning a World Series proved elusive for Hart and the Indians. The team came closest in 1997, coming within two outs in Game Seven against Florida before losing to the Marlins. Hart managed to maintain the team's status as a contender, however, as the Indians won the Central Division five of the next six seasons (1996-2001).

Hart announced in April 2001 that he would step down as the GM at the end of the season. He said it was "his decision" to step down and that he was not "burned out."[43] On the other hand, the Indians missed the playoffs the previous season and lost two of its stars, Manny Ramirez and Sandy Alomar, to free agency. The team's long sellout streak also was set to end in 2001, and Larry Dolan, the Indians' new owner, allowed the team to deficit-spend in 2001 to try to remain in contention. Hart knew that such deficit spending was not going to continue, saying he saw "no scenario where it could happen again."[44]

The Indians won the Central Division again in 2001 with a 91-71 record but lost to the Seattle Mariners in the Division Series. The plan was for Hart to remain with the Indians as an adviser to their new GM, Mark Shapiro, but Hart was soon courted by Texas owner Tom Hicks to be the Rangers' general manager.

Hart signed a three-year, $6 million contract with the Rangers in 2001, becoming the highest-paid general manager in the big leagues at the time. With that new contract, a huge payroll, and Alex Rodriguez came much higher expectations. But those expectations went largely unfulfilled. Hart was the Rangers' GM for four seasons, and the team went 311-337 over that span, without any playoff appearances.

After stepping down as GM, Hart remained with the Rangers as a senior adviser for several seasons. He also became an analyst with the new MLB television network. After his contract with the Rangers expired at the end of the 2013 season, Hart joined the Atlanta Braves as a senior adviser. After the Braves fired general manager Frank Wren, Hart stepped in as the interim GM. Named the president of baseball operations on October 23, 2014, he became the Braves' de-facto general manager.

At first, Hart did not intend to become the general manager. But longtime Braves' executive John Schuerholz, a friend, talked him into it. The proximity of the Braves' spring-training site at Lake Buena Vista, Florida, to his home in Windermere, where he and Sandi lived near their two grandchildren, didn't hurt either.[45]

At the start of the 2015 season, the Braves under Hart mirrored his Indians of the early 1990s. In 2017 the Braves were to move to a new stadium in suburban Atlanta. In his first offseason as the team's president, Hart traded three of the team's top hitters, Justin Upton, Jason Heyward, and Evan Gattis. Upton and Heyward had only one year left on their contracts, and Hart felt it was imperative to get something in return for both players and revive a flagging minor-league system that was among the worst in the game.[46]

Hart was unable to duplicate in Atlanta the success he achieved in Cleveland, however. After finishing 67-95 in 2015, the Braves promoted Hart's protégé, young executive John Coppolella, to general manager. Two years later, Coppolella was at the center of arguably the largest amateur free agent signing scandal in MLB history. In November 2017, MLB announced that the Braves had violated international free agent signing rules in the three preceding signing periods, primarily due to the team misrepresenting to MLB signing bonus amounts for several of their international free agent prospects.[47]

MLB imposed several penalties on the Braves, which included nullifying the contracts for 13 of the team's international prospects and restrictions on future international signings.[48] More significantly, Coppolella was banned from MLB for life for his role in leading the wrongdoing. Hart was not punished by MLB amidst the scandal. Nonetheless, as the team's president of baseball operations, he presumably supervised Coppolella and all front office personnel.[49] Hart ultimately resigned just days before MLB announced its penalties.[50]

Ironically, while the Indians' revival under Hart in the 1990s was largely attributable to a successful turnaround of the team's player development system, it was the Braves' illegitimate efforts to do the same that effectively ended Hart's time in Atlanta. After an ill-fated run in Atlanta, Hart's success in Cleveland undoubtedly is the highlight of his career as a front office executive, which he, and Indians fans, will surely recall fondly for years to come.

"One of the things that I think everybody should look for in their life is that time when you're young and full of energy and have a chance to build something from the ground up," he said when he was inducted into the Indians' Distinguished Hall of Fame. "That was really the joyful part of it for me. The World Series and the winning were great. That was all fantastic. But it was seeing where that franchise came, the respect that franchise got, the great years in Cleveland for the city. It may sound corny, but it meant a lot to me."[51]

NOTES

1. Paul Hoynes, "Restless Hart – General Manager Never Stops Looking for Ways to Make Indians a Winner," *Cleveland Plain Dealer*, March 20, 1994: 2D.
2. Ibid.
3. Ibid.
4. Ibid.
5. Ibid.
6. Ibid.
7. Ibid.
8. Dan McGraw, "John Hart Hates Losers," *D Magazine*, April 2002. dmagazine.com/publications/d-magazine/2002/april/john-hart-hates-losers.
9. Ibid.
10. Andy Lee, "Florida Is Home Base for Hart," *Orlando Sentinel*, January 5, 1997. articles.orlandosentinel.com/1997-01-05/news/9701021455_1_john-hart-matt-hardy-hart-baseball.
11. Ibid.
12. Ibid.
13. Ibid.
14. Dan McGraw, "John Hart Hates Losers.".
15. Bill Buchalter, "2 Coaches Reminisce, But Share New Honors as Well," *Orlando Sentinel*, June 21, 1998. articles.orlandosentinel.com/1998-06-21/news/9806190925_1_driggers-college-baseball-baseball-coaching.
16. Paula J. Finocchio, "Boone's Class of '81 Still Champions; State Baseball Title Started Several Players Toward Bigger, Better Things," *Orlando Sentinel*, May 29, 1985. articles.orlandosentinel.com/1985-05-29/sports/0300250059_1_pleicones-boone-baseball-championship.
17. George Christian Pappas, *A Tribe Reborn How the Cleveland Indians of the '90s Went from Cellar Dwellers to Playoff Contenders* (New York: Sports Publishing, 2014), 42-43.
18. Pappas, 43-44.
19. Pappas, 44.
20. Hoynes, "Restless Hart."
21. Ibid.
22. Ibid.
23. Ibid.
24. Ibid.
25. Tim Povtak, "Indians Make Hart Chief of Operations," *Orlando Sentinel*, January 12, 1990. articles.orlandosentinel.com/1990-01-12/sports/9001124885_1_john-hart-cleveland-indians-manager-and-coach.
26. Jerry Crasnick, "The Disciples of John Hart," ESPN.com. sports.espn.go.com/mlb/playoffs2007/columns/story?id=3057755.
27. Paul Hoynes, "Indians Get 'Impact-Type' Center Fielder," *Cleveland Plain Dealer*, December 11, 1991: 1E.

28. Paul Hoynes, "Tribe Signs 11 Players to Multiyear Contracts," *Cleveland Plain Dealer*, March 11, 1992: 1F.

29. Belle left the Indians as a free agent after the 1996 season, signing a five-year, $55 million contract with the Chicago White Sox, then the largest contract ever in Major League Baseball.

30. Jack Torry, *Endless Summers: The Fall and Rise of the Cleveland Indians* (South Bend, Indiana: Diamond Communications, Inc.,1995), 238.

31. Ibid.

32. Paul Hoynes, "Union Might Contest Contracts," *Cleveland Plain Dealer*, March 11, 1992: 5F.

33. Ibid.

34. Paul Hoynes, "The Leader of a Baseball Revival/John Hart's Bold Plan Built a Downtrodden Team Into a Thriving Franchise," *Cleveland Plain Dealer*, April 8, 2001: 1C.

35. Crasnick, "The Disciples of John Hart."

36. Ibid.

37. Ibid.

38. Anthony Castrovince, "Hart of a Champion: Tribe GM Drew Up Resurgence," MLB.com, June 21, 2013. m.indians.mlb.com/news/article/51279712/.

39. Crasnick, "The Disciples of John Hart."

40. Bud Shaw, "Just Perfect! A Beautiful Day, A Gorgeous Park, A Thrilling Victory," *Cleveland Plain Dealer*, April 5, 1994: 1A.

41. Paul Hoynes, "Indians Secure Their Hart," *Cleveland Plain Dealer*, October 21, 1994: 1D.

42. Hart won the award again in 1995 after the Indians won 100 out of only 144 games.

43. Paul Hoynes, "GM to Step Down in November," *Cleveland Plain Dealer*, April 6, 2001: 1A.

44. Paul Hoynes, "A Foundation Built on the Mound, *Cleveland Plain Dealer*, April 1, 2001: 8S.

45. Tyler Kepner, "Pioneering G.M. Is Eager to Mold Another Winner in Atlanta," *New York Times*, March 1, 2015: Sports Sunday, 4.

46. Associated Press, "John Hart Says Braves Will Contend," ESPN.com, January 15, 2015. espn.go.com/mlb/story/_/id/12173446/atlanta-braves-john-hart-says-team-contender.

47. Mark Bowman, "Braves penalized for int'l signing violations," MLB.com, November 21, 2017. https://www.mlb.com/news/mlb-hands-braves-penalties-for-signings/c-262279086.

48. Ibid.

49. David O'Brien and Gabriel Burns, "Coppolella, Braves Face Hard Penalties," *Atlanta Journal-Constitution*, November 22, 2017: C5.

50. Mark Bowman, "Longtime exec Hart leaves Braves," MLB.com, November 17, 2017. https://www.mlb.com/braves/news/john-hart-leaves-atlanta-braves/c-262091232.

51. Castrovince, "Hart of a Champion."

DAN O'DOWD

BY CHRISTOPHER WILLIAMSON

Dan O'Dowd was a baseball man from the beginning. Born in Morristown, New Jersey, on September 6, 1959, Dan grew up working on his parents' (Marty and Anna Mae) dairy farm and in O'Dowd's Milk Bar on Route 46 in Pine Brook. As it is for most, his love of baseball was cultivated from playing the game throughout childhood and young adulthood. As a high-school freshman, he was the starter at third base on the 1974 Morris County, New Jersey Tournament championship team. During senior year, his high-school coach, John Gallucci, had the "what do you want to do with your life" conversation with Dan. "He said he wanted to be in sports management," Gallucci recalled. "He knew right from the very beginning. You don't see that very often."[1]

O'Dowd went on to play college ball at Rollins College in Florida but recognized early on that he was an average ballplayer without a professional future. A nose-shattering line drive during his sophomore year virtually ended his playing days and by his senior year he had transitioned into a coaching position assisting Rollins coach Boyd Coffie and soaking up every ounce of baseball knowledge and nuance available.[2]

After graduation, O'Dowd was accepted into the executive development program with Major League Baseball and from there secured employment in the Baltimore Orioles' front office in 1983 and more importantly with his baseball mentor, Orioles general manager Hank Peters.[3] He instantly got to savor the sweet taste of victory as the Orioles won the 1983 World Series. Over the next few years he was rotated through several positions within the organization and became versed in both the baseball and business sides of the game.

By October of 1987, the relationship between Orioles owner Edward Bennett Williams and Hank Peters had soured to the point that Williams decided to clean house in his front office. Both Peters and O'Dowd were out of a job – but not for long. The Jacobs brothers had bought the Cleveland Indians in 1986 and had been interested in bringing in Hank Peters as their general manager and president of baseball operations to lead a turnaround effort for the decades-long American League doormat team. Peters, who was known as a very loyal man, brought on many of his former associates who that had been casualties during the purge in Baltimore, including the now 28-year-old Dan O'Dowd as his farm director.

The Cleveland media viewed the hiring of Dowd skeptically in view of his relative inexperience. Peters acknowledged O'Dowd's greenness and commented, "We are going to train him. I was trained. He has some interesting qualifications. And I think with time and guidance, he will grow into a very competent baseball executive."[4]

A few of the noteworthy changes Peters instituted were a return to the policy of developing from within, rebuilding through the farm system to create a sustainable fount of continuous talent for the Indians. He also drastically improved the organization's relationship with its current players by offering some multiyear contracts prior to free agency and agreeing to generous one-year deals to avoid arbitration with star players such as Joe Carter. Rebuilding the farm system and making the team's current players happy were sound and logical first steps toward getting the organization on a path to relevance.

The first six years of the rebuild were slow and O'Dowd's farm did not bear much fruit initially. The philosophy put into place by O'Dowd, Peters, and Tom Giordano (special assistant to Peters) heavily favored drafting high-school over college players. In spring training of 1990, O'Dowd noted, "It's not that there aren't some good college coaches, but with most college players, you have to spend time trying to overcome all the bad habits they've learned."[5] That same spring, the Indians' hottest young prospect was 20-year-old shortstop Mark Lewis of Hamilton, Ohio, whom they drafted in the first round and second overall in the June 1988 draft. (Charles Nagy was drafted 17th overall with their second first-round pick in 1988.) O'Dowd said of Lewis, "Defensively, he's a major league shortstop…I won't tell you he's now a major-league hitter, or possibly even a Triple-A hitter…Right now, he's a fastball hitter. What he's got to work on is hitting the breaking ball and the changeup."[6]

O'Dowd's lack of hyperbole was prescient. Lewis debuted with the Indians in 1991 and started 78 games at shortstop and second base but made virtually no impact at the plate. His 1992 season was very similar: He played in 122 games with an OPS under .700, and his 25 errors tied for the most in the American League. Lewis was traded to the Cincinnati Reds in 1994 and bounced around the National League until 2001 as a low-impact, glove-first utility infielder who had some nice seasons defensively.

Near the end of the 1991 season, John Hart was promoted from director of baseball operations to general manager and executive vice president, replacing Peters. O'Dowd became Hart's right-hand man as the assistant GM. This helped set the stage for Indians to become a powerhouse during the mid/late-'90s. The organization endured two more losing seasons in 1992 and 1993 but the farm system began to strengthen under the dual management of O'Dowd and Hart. Manny Ramirez was drafted in the first round in 1991 and quickly blossomed into a superstar.

The 1994-1998 Opening Day lineups:

Batting Order	1994	1995	1996	1997	1998
1)	Kenny Lofton, CF	Kenny Lofton, CF	Kenny Lofton, CF	Marquis Grissom, CF	Kenny Lofton, CF
2)	Omar Vizquel, SS	Omar Vizquel, SS	Julio Franco, 1B	Omar Vizquel, SS	Omar Vizquel, SS
3)	Carlos Baerga, 2B	Carlos Baerga, 2B	Carlos Baerga, 2B	Jim Thome, 1B	Shawon Dunston, DH
4)	Albert Belle, LF	Albert Belle, LF	Albert Belle, LF	Matt Williams, 3B	Manny Ramirez, RF
5)	Eddie Murray, 1B	Eddie Murray, 1B	Eddie Murray, DH	David Justice, LF	Geronimo Berroa, LF
6)	Candy Maldonado, DH	Jim Thome, 3B	Jim Thome, 3B	Manny Ramirez, RF	Travis Fryman, 3B
7)	Sandy Alomar Jr, C	Manny Ramirez, RF	Manny Ramirez, RF	Julio Franco, 2B	Sandy Alomar Jr, C
8)	Manny Ramirez, RF	Paul Sorrento, 1B	Sandy Alomar Jr, C	Kevin Mitchell, DH	Jeff Manto, 1B
9)	Mark Lewis, 3B	Tony Pena, C	Omar Vizquel, SS	Sandy Alomar Jr, C	Enrique Wilson, 2B
10	Dennis Martinez, P	Dennis Martinez, P	Dennis Martinez, P	Charles Nagy, P	Charles Nagy, P

For the Indians' minor-league system, 1993 was a banner year. From the rookie leagues up through

Triple A, all six of the organization's affiliates made the playoffs. O'Dowd said, "I know wins and losses don't always indicate the success of your system, but we've never even had five teams in the playoffs, and this year we could have six. I really believe this is an indication that our scouts are doing the job of bringing the right kids in our system."[7] Several future major leaguers were in the system in 1993, including Brian Giles, Kelly Stinnett, David Bell, Mitch Meluskey, Chad Ogea, Albie Lopez, and Paul Shuey.

By 1994, the Indians were ready to move out of decrepit Municipal Stadium and into beautiful new Jacobs Field. The major-league clubs put together by Hart and O'Dowd over the next five years were formidable and won the division every year until O'Dowd's departure after the 1998 season (not including strike-shortened 1994).

After decades of futility, the Indians won five straight division titles (1995-1998) and made World Series appearances in 1995 and 1997. The star power on the field during those years was clearly evident. However, the star power off the field was almost equally impressive. During or immediately after the 1998 season the Indians' front office was loaded:

- John Hart, general manager
- Dan O'Dowd, assistant GM
- Mark Shapiro, player development Director
- Josh Byrnes, scouting director
- Paul DePodesta, advance scout
- Ben Cherington, advance scout
- Neal Huntington, assistant director of minor-league operations
- Chris Antonetti, baseball operations assistant

Every one of those eight went on to become a general manager. Three became club presidents, and one became an NFL chief strategic officer. O'Dowd and Shapiro were the visionaries who originally came up with the idea to sign young players to contract extensions before arbitration. This created a sustainable model for small-market clubs to achieve long-term cost certainty and gave young players financial security early in their careers and before reaching free agency. The Indians were the first clubs to create personalized player-development plans and not fall victim to the one-size-fits-all mentality; early on they embraced advanced statistics like OPS (On Base + Slugging Percentage) and data analytics. "I don't know what it was like to work at Apple or any of the tech firms in their heyday," said O'Dowd, "but I'd imagine it was a lot like that. It was a creative think tank, and it was invigorating."[8]

After the 1998 season, O'Dowd was a hot commodity on the open market to fill general-manager vacancies. He had created quite a name for himself as the assistant general manager of the American League's model organization and both Hart and Dick Jacobs were getting calls for permission to interview the 39-year-old hot shot. With Pat Gillick retiring, the Orioles were in the market and were given permission to speak to O'Dowd with the stipulation that if he was hired, no other members of the Cleveland front office would follow him. But the GM position never materialized for O'Dowd and he decided to take the 1999 season off to fully pursue other GM positions around baseball.

After a year of pursuit, O'Dowd was hired in September 1999 as general manager of the Colorado Rockies. "Dealin' Dan" didn't waste any time overhauling the roster in preparation for the franchise's eighth season. Sixteen new players were added to the club's 25-man roster and only Todd Helton, Mike Lansing, and Neifi Perez were in both the 1999 and 2000 Opening Day lineups. O'Dowd's goals were for the team to become younger and more athletic with the intent of improving defensively and on the basepaths. He made six trades, and a bevy of other roster moves before the 2000 season. Notable departures were Vinny Castilla, Dante Bichette, Darryl Kile, and Dave Veres. Notable arrivals included Jeff Cirillo, Tom Goodwin, and Julian Tavarez. The Denver media and the fan base were taken aback by the sheer quantity of roster turnover and the departures of fan favorites like Castilla and Bichette. O'Dowd's response: "I don't know what the downside is. We lost 90 games last year. Any time you trade away marquee players for guys who may not be as well known, it's tough for the fans to swallow. But we definitely have a plan here. I think it's going to take some time when you make this many changes. But maybe change can create a better environment. I trust that Buddy (Bell) and his staff can create that."9

After a surprise 82-win season in 2000, Dealin' Dan was at it again in the offseason and made the two most scrutinized free-agent signings of his career. O'Dowd inked two big-name left-handed free-agent pitchers to long-term contracts. Denny Neagle was signed to a $51 million, five-year contract and Mike Hampton was signed for $121 million spread over eight years. To say these deals were a disaster is an understatement. Hampton pitched to a 6.15 ERA in 2002 and was shipped out of town after two years (with the Rockies eating most of the remaining $90 million on his deal), and Neagle was equally ineffective; injuries ended his career in 2003. Needless to say, these two contracts were very detrimental to the Rockies' payroll flexibility and made it very difficult for the organization to make free-agent signings over the next few years.

The Rockies were cellar dwellers in the NL West with seven straight fourth- and fifth-place finishes from 2000 through 2006 until a shocking 90-win, wild-card postseason berth and World Series appearance in 2007. The key contributors to the 2007 team included superstar Todd Helton, Matt Holiday, Brad Hawpe (11th round, 2000 draft), Garrett Atkins (fifth round, 2000 draft), Troy Tulowitzki (first round, 2005 draft), Ryan Spilborghs (seventh round, 2002 draft), Willy Taveras (international free-agent signing), Kaz Matsui (international free-agent signing), Jeff Francis (first round, 2002 draft), and the entire bullpen that was either drafted or acquired by O'Dowd and his front office. The 2007 campaign was an absolute dream season for the organization and its fans. Despite being swept by the Red Sox in the World Series, fans and Denver got to witness a Cinderella story: reaching the playoffs for the second time in franchise history; making an incredible run with an offensive juggernaut, a questionable-at-best starting rotation, and an overachieving bullpen that was masterfully built by O'Dowd's front office. One could infer that O'Dowd learned his lesson after the failures of Hampton and Neagle. Those contracts hamstrung the organization for years and forced the front office to focus on player evaluation and development combined with shrewd short-term free-agent deals. This lower risk/lower reward strategy bore fruit in 2007.

The 2008 season ended in disappointment as the club mustered only a 74-win season. Matt Holiday was sent to Oakland for Huston Street, Greg Smith, and Carlos Gonzalez, and several changes were made to the coaching staff as the front office attempted to retool for the 2009 season. Without taking big risks in free agency, the 2008 squad didn't have enough to repeat their 2007 successes.

The 2009 Rockies season featured an exciting run in the second half that coincided with Jim Tracy being brought on as manager to replace Clint Hurdle. The 2009 Rockies set a team record with 92 wins, but lost to the Philadelphia Phillies in the NLDS three games to one. The next five years until O'Dowd resigned on October 8, 2014, are considered an all-around disappointment. However, O'Dowd and his staff did set up the Rockies for future success by drafting virtually all of the Rockies' near-term major contributors including Nolan Arenado, Charlie Blackmon, Kyle Freeland, Ryan Castellani, Ryan McMahon, Pat Valaika, Jon Gray, Mike Tauchman, David Dahl, Tom Murphy, Scott Oberg, Tyler Anderson, Trevor Story, Chad Bettis, and Dustin Garneau. That is a stunning run of draft success over a seven-year period and the organization was left in tremendous standing for incoming GM Jeff Bridich.

Dan O'Dowd's foundation was built in Baltimore, where he learned the business and sales functions of a major-league organization before moving into the baseball operations/player development side of the house. Moving to the Cleveland Indians with his mentor Hank Peters, his career blossomed; he gained acclaim as one of the top baseball operations minds as part of the historic Indians teams of the '90s. Success in Cleveland allowed O'Dowd to leverage his substantial reputation into a 15-year stint as the general manager and eventually president of the Colorado Rockies. The overall body of work can be scrutinized by detractors but the 2007 World Series appearance and 2009's incredible second-half run can be noted as key highlights. In the end, Dan O'Dowd's analytical mind and opinionated persona found a great fit at the MLB Network as he became a top analyst who speaks his mind and draws upon his life as a baseball man to provide wonderfully insightful commentary.

SOURCES

In addition to the sources cited in the Notes, the author also consulted Baseball-Reference.com and MLB.com.

NOTES

1. Mark Kitchin, "Rockies," *Morristown* (New Jersey) *Daily Record,* October 25, 2017: A6.
2. Ibid.
3. Ibid.
4. "Hank Peters Running the Whole Show in Cleveland, and Couldn't Be Happier," *Baltimore Sun,* April 10, 1988: 24B.
5. Hal Lebovitz, "Bonus for Fans Who Attend Tribe Opener," *Mansfield* (Ohio) *News-Journal*, April 1, 1990: 3C.
6. Ibid.
7. Sheldon Ocker, "Adair, of Course! He Had to Be at Fault All Along," *Akron Beacon Journal,* September 5, 1993: E9.
8. Anthony Castrovince, "Cleveland's 'Dream Team' Front Office," January 7, 2016. sportsonearth.com/article/161217636/1998-indians-front-office-executives-tree.
9. John Mossman, "Dealin' Dan O'Dowd Overhauls the Rockies," *Hazelton* (Pennsylvania) *Standard-Speaker,* January 23, 2000: B16.

THE BALLPARK

JACOBS FIELD, JEWEL OF BASEBALL

BY STEPHANIE LISCIO

The first regular-season game at Jacobs Field was played on April 4, 1994. Through seven innings the Indians were down 2-0, and it looked as though the storyline would center on Randy Johnson's dominant pitching performance. The Indians finally got to the lanky southpaw in the bottom of the eighth, when Manny Ramirez doubled to tie the game. The Indians won, 4-3, on a walk-off single by Wayne Kirby in the bottom of the 11th inning. The exciting and emotional finish seemed to signify the changes that were about to take place for the Indians. Gone were the dreary, sparsely attended games at Cleveland Municipal Stadium; the Jacobs Field era had begun.

After years of planning, the Indians were finally able to leave the less-than-optimal confines of Municipal Stadium for the brand-new Jacobs Field. Unfortunately for the Tribe, the 1994 season came to a disappointing end in August with a strike that even canceled the World Series. The Indians had looked likely for the playoffs that season, but finally ended their 40-year-plus postseason drought in 1995.

It's no secret that the Indians were on the lookout for a new home as far back as the early 1980s. One of the early plans centered on a domed stadium for both the Indians and the Browns, paid for by tax dollars. A ballot initiative for a property-tax increase to be put toward funding the ballpark went down to a crushing defeat on May 8, 1984, by an almost 2-to-1 vote. It appeared that the citizens of Cuyahoga County had made their opinion clear, but Governor Richard Celeste refused to call it a defeat for the dome itself, just for the tax increase (likely meaning new stadium plans would continue, with other financing sources than a property-tax increase).[1]

Even though it was considered a relatively low-turnout election, there appeared to be a lot of interest in the potential dome. Precincts ran low on nonpartisan ballots that bore just the ballot initiatives and not the primary candidates. Extra ballots had to be flown in from their printing plant in Dayton to replenish the dwindling supply.[2] The next year, architect Robert Corna proposed another covered stadium, which he called the "Hexatron." This project never got past the rendering phase, so it didn't even make it as far as a public vote.[3] Despite all of the uncertainty on funding, the city began to acquire property to house new sports facilities in December 1985. By April of 1986, the teams had agreed on the design objectives. Demolition of the buildings on the site, now being referred to as "Gateway," began in June of 1987.[4]

While the property acquisition represented a major hurdle conquered, financing the project was something that still had to be solved. This would be managed by a "sin tax" on alcohol and cigarettes, an issue that came to vote in a ballot initiative on May 8, 1990. The initiative passed, exactly six years after voters vetoed the property-tax increase. It wasn't an overwhelming win, at 51.7 percent for and 48.3 percent against, but it meant that the money would be used toward the $344 million Gateway plan. The 15-year tax was supposed to generate $275 million, and would take effect on August 1, 1990. Voter turnout was considered high for a primary election, with a lot of interest toward the potential new stadiums. Opponents of the ballot initiative thought the money could go to better use in other areas of the city, rather than to help finance sports facilities for millionaire owners.[5]

Ground was broken at the Gateway property in 1992, with plans to house new facilities for both the Indians and the NBA Cavaliers. The excavation was called the "most monumental" in Cleveland since the excavation of the site of the Terminal Tower in the 1920s. The Gateway land was once home to the Central Market or the Haymarket district. Archaeologists who excavated at the site before construction began found a soggy baseball that was at least 100 years old among the broken bottles, cisterns, and false teeth that were uncovered at the site.[6]

The architects, Hellmuth, Obata, and Kassabaum of Kansas City, Missouri, had a $161 million budget for Jacobs Field.[7] The entire 28.5-acre project had a $360 million budget and represented the first significant construction in that area of the city in more than 20 years.[8] (The dollar total was a bit higher than the original $344 million projected cost). Taxpayers would fund about half of the bill, while the rest would be covered by the private sector and the Indians and Cavs. Gateway Development Corporation planned to raise some money by selling $20 million worth of 10-year leases for luxury boxes at the ballpark. Investors could also purchase stadium revenue bonds.[9]

By the end of 1992, more than 1,850 pieces of structural steel were in place, and the upper deck in right field was already standing. Down the left-field line, the steel structure for the Indians' offices were in place, and the entire framework was supposed to be finished by the end of December 1992.[10] By February 1993, 60 percent of the steelwork was complete, even though the site was essentially a parking lot just over a year earlier. There was even a 25-foot-high observation deck installed where fans could come and watch the progress three days a week.[11] Fans got an up-close look at the new ballpark before Opening Day, in the form of an exhibition game against the Pittsburgh Pirates on April 2.

During the game, fans gave the ballpark high praise. One told the *Cleveland Plain Dealer* that it didn't feel like Cleveland and was reminiscent of classic parks like Wrigley Field, Tiger Stadium, and Fenway Park. Of the fan proximity to the field, a fan said, "We're so close, it's almost like you can call a player a name and he'll run over at you."[12] Sight lines were to be much better than those of Municipal Stadium. Thomas V. Chema, executive director of the Gateway Economic Development Corp. of Cleveland, speaking of the support poles that impeded views at Municipal Stadium, said during construction, "The only Poles in this ballpark will be of the ethnic variety."[13]

The praise continued after President Bill Clinton took the mound to throw out the first pitch on Opening Day, against Seattle on April 4, 1994. Even despite the feeling of close proximity to the field, some said the steel and brick façade of the park gave it an aura of strength. A *Plain Dealer* writer, pointing out the ballpark's connection to the city's working-class roots, wrote, "It's a beer-drinker's kind of place more than a white wine-sipper's."[14] One of the few groups that didn't seem eager to lavish praise on the new ballpark were cigarette smokers. Since a major part of the funding came from the "sin tax," smokers felt they should be able to smoke wherever they wanted. But smoking was banned from all of the seats, much to their displeasure.[15]

The Indians decided to make a fairly clean break from Municipal Stadium. They planned to leave the past in the past, and not transfer items from Municipal to the new ballpark, specifically the giant lighted Chief Wahoo. The club kept the Wahoo logo on uniforms, but the lighted Chief went to a new home at the Western Reserve Historical Society. The Indians also left a number of seats behind; Municipal seated close to 80,000, while the new ballpark seated about half that. One of the features of the new ballpark was a statue of Bob Feller, paid for by the sale of engraved bricks. Even though the building and its contents represented a break from the past, the team that played at Jacobs Field was a mix of new and old players, in terms of both youth vs. veterans, and players new to the Indians.

The Tribe had a core of young players in place, ready to take the field in 1994. Players Sandy Alomar Jr., Albert Belle, Jim Thome, Manny Ramirez, Kenny Lofton, Carlos Baerga, Omar Vizquel, and Charlie Nagy were complemented by veterans like Eddie Murray and Dennis Martinez. The *Plain Dealer* noted in a 1993 article that teams entering new ballparks typically enjoyed success after their move. Eleven ballparks had opened around baseball since 1960, and 9 of the 11 teams improved during their first year in the new park. Three teams even won their division in their park's inaugural season – the Pittsburgh Pirates in 1970 with Three Rivers Stadium, the Cincinnati Reds in 1970 with Riverfront Stadium, and the Toronto Blue Jays in 1989 with SkyDome. Three teams won the pennant or a World Series within the first two years of its new park's existence during– the San Francisco Giants won the pennant in 1962 (Candlestick Park opened in 1960); the Los Angeles Dodgers won the World Series in 1963 (Dodger Stadium opened in 1962); and the St. Louis Cardinals won the World Series in 1967 (Busch Stadium opened in 1966).[16] The Indians were hoping the enthusiasm engendered by the new ballpark, coupled with their blossoming young players and experienced vets, would amount to a winning equation.

And boy, did it work. The Indians had a 66-47 record, in second place in the AL Central, at the time of the strike in 1994. By 1995 they dominated the division with a record of 100-44, and finished 30 games ahead of second-place Kansas City. They had the division locked up by September 8, and eventually won the pennant, only to be defeated in the World Series by the Atlanta Braves in six games. The Indians added several more veterans before the 1995 season – Tony Pena, Dave Winfield, and Orel Hershiser – and saw many of their young hitters enjoy an incredible year offensively. Albert Belle finished the season with a 1.091 OPS and 50 home runs; Jim Thome a .996 OPS and 25 home runs; Manny Ramirez a .960 OPS and 31 home runs; Sandy Alomar a .810 OPS; and Carlos Baerga an .807 OPS. All of them, as well as Kenny Lofton, hit better at Jacobs Field than on the road.

The Indians' success continued throughout the 1990s. In 1996 they again made the playoffs, but lost in the Division Series to the Baltimore Orioles. The 1997 Indians, despite winning just 86 games during the regular season, came heartbreakingly close to winning it all – they lost in the 11th inning of Game Seven to the Florida Marlins. In 1998 the Tribe lost to the New York Yankees in the American League Championship Series, and in 1999 they lost the Division Series to the Boston Red Sox. The end of the 1999 season represented the end of an era – Dick Jacobs, owner of the Indians since 1986, sold the team to Larry Dolan for a record (at the time) $320 million. The Indians narrowly missed the playoffs in 2000, but returned in 2001 and lost in the Division Series to the Seattle Mariners. From June 12, 1995, until April 4, 2001, the Indians enjoyed a 455-game sellout streak as fans embraced the first winning baseball they'd seen in the city for more than 40 years. After the 2001 season, the Tribe started a rebuilding phase that all but ended an era.

By the time the Indians returned to the postseason in 2007, the roster looked quite different from those '90s era teams. However, the Indians got a bit of that old Jacobs Field magic on October 5, 2007, in Game Two of the ALDS against the New York Yankees. The Indians were down 1-0 going into the eighth inning, shut down for most of the game by starter Andy Pettitte. Joba Chamberlain, the young reliever who recorded the final two outs in the seventh inning, was about to start the eighth against Indians outfielder Grady Sizemore. Joining the Indians and Yankees on the field were thousands of tiny bugs called midges; and no matter what Chamberlain seemed to do, he couldn't escape the swarming insects. Flustered, he walked Sizemore on four pitches. His first pitch to Asdrubal Cabrera was wild, and Sizemore advanced to second base. Cabrera sacrificed Sizemore to third, and Chamberlain got Travis Hafner to line out for the second out. Was it possible that he could escape from this jam unscathed? Unfortunately for him and the Yankees, his first pitch to Victor Martinez was wild, allowing Sizemore to score the tying run. The Indians won the game in the 11th on a walk-off single by Hafner off Yankees reliever Luis Vizcaino.

Despite going up three games to one on the Boston Red Sox in the ALCS, the Indians ended up losing the series in seven games. The offseason would lead to more changes for Jacobs Field, (and soon the Indians in general). In January 2008, Progressive Insurance bought the naming rights to the ballpark for about $3.6 million per year for 16 years. It was disappointing for fans who had grown to love the name Jacobs Field, and who associated the team's renaissance with the construction of the ballpark. (The original Jacobs Field name had ended up being an almost last-minute deal. Less than two months from Opening Day in 1994, Jacobs purchased the naming rights for $10 million. It had just been referred to mostly as "Indians Ballpark" before that, and several local corporations had some level of interest in putting their name on the park. At one point in 1993, some fans started a drive to name the field after Ray Chapman, the Indians infielder killed by a pitch in 1920.[17] In the end, the building took the name of the man who had helped to shape those 1990s teams and pushed for a new baseball facility in Cleveland.)

The Indians extensively renovated the park between the 2014 and 2016 seasons. The first major overhaul of the ballpark, it lowered the seating capacity from just over 40,000 to around 35,000. During the first phase of renovations, the Indians added a number of new food concession places and areas in which children could play, and opened up the Gate C entry to better views of the city. The home and visitors bullpens were moved together, one tiered above the other, while a portion of upper deck seating was removed and replaced with standing room areas. In the right field corner, the Indians opened a two story bar entitled "The Corner" that includes rows of standing rails in front of it, replacing seating. In 2014 a statue of future Hall-of-Famer Jim Thome was added outside of Gate C at the ballpark, joining the statue of Bob Feller. A statue of Larry Doby, the first African American to play in the American League, was dedicated during the summer of 2015. A statue of Lou Boudreau joined those three in 2017, while a statue of Frank Robinson, the first African American manager, was added to Heritage Park in 2017. During the second phase of renovations, walls and seats were removed behind home plate and the third base line to open the area to the concourse. The Indians also added a bar entitled "The Homeplate Club" with exclusive access to the season ticket holders in the diamond and field box seats. With the closure of the Bob Feller Museum in Van Meter, Iowa, some of the museum's items were installed in the Terrace Club, and there was exhibit space added in "The Corner" bar as well. In 2016 Jacobs/Progressive Field hosted its third World Series as the Chicago Cubs broke their 108-year championship drought after a dramatic Game Seven victory in extra innings. Even though the park may look different than it did at its opening in 1994, the goal remained the same – to bring Cleveland its first World Series title since 1948. There would be no better place to celebrate one than the ballpark at the corner of Carnegie and Ontario.

NOTES

1. Gary R. Clark, "Dome Loses by 2-1 Vote; Hart Scores Ohio Upset: Proponents agree to try other plans," *Cleveland Plain Dealer*, May 9, 1984.

2. Jim Parker, "Dim Night for the Dome," *Cleveland Plain Dealer*, May 9, 1984.

3. "The biggest unbuilt projects of the last 30 years," *Crain's Cleveland Business*. crainscleveland.com/article/20100301/30THANNIVERSARY/100229858 Accessed January 8, 2015.

4. Indians 2009 media guide. cleveland.indians.mlb.com/cle/downloads/y2009/progressive_field.pdf.

5. Catherine L. Kissling, "Gateway Project Takes First Big Step," *Cleveland Plain Dealer*, May 9, 1990.

6. Elizabeth Sullivan, "20 Feet Down to History," *Cleveland Plain Dealer*, May 3, 1992.

7. Steven Litt, "Analysis: Gateway Architects Mindful of Budget in Ballpark Planning," *Cleveland Plain Dealer*, April 24, 1992.

8. Kevin Harter, "Gateway to Boost City, Chema Says," *Cleveland Plain Dealer*, February 25, 1992.

9. James M. Biggar, "Gateway: The Bigger Picture," *Cleveland Plain Dealer*, January 10, 1992.

10. Paul Hoynes, "Right-Field Stands Already in Place at Gateway," *Cleveland Plain Dealer*, December 1, 1992.

11. Steven Litt, "From the Upper Deck at Gateway Construction a Riveting Panorama," *Cleveland Plain Dealer*, February 21, 1993.

12. James F. McCarty, "Dress Rehearsal a Hit With Cleveland Fans," *Cleveland Plain Dealer*, April 3, 1994.

13. Harter, "Gateway to Boost City."

14. Joe Dirck, "New Ballpark's Best Game in Town," *Cleveland Plain Dealer*, April 5, 1994.

15. A number of articles and letters to the editor in the *Cleveland Plain Dealer* discussed fans' annoyance with any potential smoking bans or limitations. For examples, see Catherine L. Kissling, "Gateway Smokers May Get the Gate," *Cleveland Plain Dealer*, August 18, 1993; Joe Dirck, "Geez! Here's Response to Touchy Issues," *Cleveland Plain Dealer*, August 31, 1993; and Bruce Hooley, "Smokers are Getting Blown out of Stadiums," *Cleveland Plain Dealer*, August 29, 1993.

16. Rich Exner, "New Parks Usually Bring Winning Baseball Teams," *Cleveland Plain Dealer*, November 3, 1993.

17. "Fans Speak Out for New Park to be Named Chapman Field," *Cleveland Plain Dealer*, February 21, 1993.

SELECTED GAMES

INDIANS AND TWINS BOTH MAKE TEAM HISTORY IN 17-INNING MARATHON

MAY 7, 1995: CLEVELAND INDIANS 10, MINNESOTA TWINS 9, AT JACOBS FIELD

BY RICHARD CUICCHI

The Cleveland Indians and Minnesota Twins might have been trying to make up for the 18 regular-season games removed from the schedule because of the players strike when they endured a 17-inning game at Jacobs Field on May 7, 1995. In their 10th game into the shortened season that began on April 27, the Indians outlasted the Twins in the longest game (by time) for either franchise.

The afternoon game – in which 47 players took part – lasted 6 hours and 36 minutes. The Indians' previous time record was 6 hours and 30 minutes in a game against Boston that lasted 19 innings on Opening Day on April 11, 1992. Minnesota's previous record was 6 hours and 17 minutes against Cleveland on August 31, 1993, in the Twins' Metrodome. That game lasted 22 innings, which was also the longest by innings in the Indians' history.[1]

Both teams scored freely during the first eight innings, which ended with a 9-9 tie. And then the game went scoreless for the next eight innings before the Indians scored in the bottom of the 17th.

The Twins' Kevin Tapani and the Indians' Dennis Martinez were the starting pitchers for the contest. Forty-year-old Martinez had won his first two games of the season, holding opponents to two earned runs in 13 innings pitched, while Tapani had one losing decision in his two starts and had yielded six earned runs in 13 innings.

The Indians scored first in the bottom of the first inning when Kenny Lofton led off with a double and Eddie Murray drove him home with a single. In the top of the second, Martinez served up a two-out solo home run to Bernardo Brito to tie the score.

The Twins took a 2-1 lead in the top of the third as Alex Cole singled to score Pat Mears, who had tripled. In the bottom half of the inning, the Indians wreaked havoc on Tapani with five runs on an RBI single by Carlos Baerga, a double by Albert Belle, a three-run home run by Murray, and a solo home run by Manny Ramirez (his fifth of the young season). The homer chased Tapani from the game.

Behind 6-2, the Twins tried to mount a rally in the top of the fourth. Martinez gave up two doubles and hit two batters, but managed to escape with only one run scored on Scott Leius's double. The Twins had the bases loaded when Martinez retired the side with the score 6-3.

Martinez continued to struggle in the fifth inning, yielding two singles before being replaced by reliever Dennis Cook. Cook walked Dave McCarty to load the bases. Jason Grimsley replaced Cook and struck out two batters to retire the side.

Eddie Guardado, who had relieved Tapani in the third, kept the Indians from scoring in the fourth and fifth innings. But he ran into trouble in the sixth and was replaced by Kevin Campbell after the first two batters reached base. (Omar Vizquel singled and Baerga walked.) Belle's single scored Vizquel, and Ramirez followed with a single to score Belle. The Indians now led 8-3.

The Twins weren't packing their bat bags just yet, as they rebounded with their own five-run inning in the top of the seventh. Cole led off the inning with a single to center field. Kirby Puckett followed with his second homer of the year. Marty Cordova walked and McCarty smacked a two-bagger. A two-out double by Matt Walbeck resulted in two more runs. Right-hander Julian Tavarez relieved Grimsley and gave up a run-scoring single to Pat Meares. The inning ended in an 8-8 tie.

In the top of the eighth, Cordova broke the tie with a two-out solo home run to deep left field. The Indians came back in the bottom of the inning with their own solo home run by Murray off Dave Stevens.

Eric Plunk, the Indians' sixth pitcher, who had entered the game in the eighth inning, retired the Twins in order in the top of the ninth, and Stevens got the Indians out in their half allowing only one hit.

The Twins squandered a chance in the 10th inning when Marty Cordova struck out to end the inning with two men on base. In the top of the 13th, the Twins mounted a threat on a hit and two walks, but were unable to push across a run when third baseman Jim Thome and first baseman Paul Sorrento made great fielding plays.[2]

Indians reliever Jim Poole entered the game in the top of the 14th inning and struck out the side, then went three more innings and held the Twins to one hit.

Mark Guthrie, making his seventh relief appearance of the season, came into the game in the 16th as the Twins' ninth pitcher. He held the Indians scoreless, and Poole retired the Twins in order in the top of the 17th inning. In the bottom of the inning, Guthrie gave up a single to Ramirez. He struck out Alvaro Espinoza, and Ramirez stole second base on Guthrie's first pitch to Jesse Levis. On the next pitch Levis cued a roller off the end of his bat. Twins third baseman Leius fielded it cleanly but Levis beat out his throw to first, as Ramirez advanced to third. The Twins' infielders moved up for a possible play at the plate, but on Guthrie's first pitch to Kenny Lofton, in the center fielder's 10th at-bat, Lofton hit Guthrie's fastball up the middle against a to score Ramirez with the walk-off tally of the 10-9 game. Afterward, Lofton said about his game-winning hit, "When I got the hit, I felt relief. I was so tired, I didn't even want to run to first."[3]

Twins manager Tom Kelly lamented the loss: "Those games aren't good for anybody, or anything. People say they're good for the fans, or good for the game, but they're just awful. The hitters lose their focus and the game just falls apart."[4]

Poole got credit for his first win of the season, while Guthrie took his first loss. The teams used a total of 17 pitchers. They collected 44 hits and 14 walks between them, and left 39 runners on base. The Twins tied a team record by having four batters hit by pitches.[5] The Twins were led by Cordova with four hits and Cole with three. Lofton, Murray, and Belle each had four hits for the Indians, while Baerga and Ramirez each had three.

Murray's two homers gave him 462 for his career, one behind teammate Dave Winfield, who was 19th on the all-time home-run list.[6]

Four days later, when the Indians defeated the Baltimore Orioles, they moved into first place in in the AL Central Division and never relinquished the lead the rest of the season. The Indians wound up winning the division by 30 games over the Royals. They swept the Boston Red Sox in the Division Series and defeated the Seattle Mariners in six games to take their first American League pennant since 1954. The Indians lost to the Atlanta Braves in the World Series.

SOURCES

In addition to the references cited in the Notes, the author also consulted:

Baseball-Reference.com.

1996 Cleveland Indians Media Guide.

1996 Minnesota Twins Media Guide.

NOTES

1   Dennis Manoloff, "Long Day's Journey Ends in Win," *Cleveland Plain Dealer,* May 8, 1995: 1D.

2   Jim Souhan, "The Longest Day: Twins Lose in 17," *Minneapolis Star Tribune,* May 8, 1995: 5C.

3   Manoloff.

4   Souhan, 1C.

5   Ibid.

6   Manoloff.

SORRENTO'S TWO-RUN BLAST LIFTS THE TRIBE

JUNE 4, 1995: CLEVELAND INDIANS 9, TORONTO BLUE JAYS 8, AT JACOBS FIELD, CLEVELAND

BY JOSEPH WANCHO

The Cleveland Indians were feeling pretty good about themselves. They had won six of their last seven games and were atop the American League's Central Division, five games ahead of Kansas City. Among those six victories was a sweep over Chicago. The White Sox were thought to be the Indians' biggest obstacle to a division crown in 1995. But at the moment, Chicago was 10 games off the pace.

Cleveland and Toronto split the first two games of the three-game set at Jacobs Field. Al Leiter shut out the Indians, 5-0. Dennis Martinez came back the next day to raise his record to 5-0, shutting out the Jays, 3-0.

Toeing the rubber for the visitors in the third game was David Cone, the reigning Cy Young Award winner in 1994. Pitching for his hometown team, the Royals, Cone posted a 16-5 record with a 2.94 ERA in the strike-shortened season. But on April 6, 1995, just after the strike was settled, Cone was dealt north to the Blue Jays. Moving Cone and his $5 million salary was not a surprise. The Royals were dumping high salaries; a day before trading Cone, they sent center fielder Brian McRae to the Chicago Cubs. The Cone deal was a lopsided one for sure, as it brought utilityman Chris Stynes and two players who never made it to the big leagues to K.C. The change in scenery did not deter Cone, who was 4-3 with a 3.12 ERA in the rather young season.

Cleveland countered with Jason Grimsley. Grimsley, who was from, of all places, Cleveland, Texas, was a spot starter who had bounced between the Indians and their affiliates over the last few years. Grimsley might be best known for deception, and not while he was on the mound. On July 15, 1994, White Sox manager Gene Lamont was tipped off that Indians slugger Albert Belle was using a corked bat. In the first inning, plate umpire Dave Phillips confiscated Belle's bat and it was placed in Phillips' locker in the umpires' dressing room. Since all of Belle's bats had cork in them, Grimsley grabbed a Paul Sorrento model, doctored it some and crawled his way above the ceiling tile from the Indians' clubhouse to the umpires' room. Grimsley crawled around the cinder block, through a maze of air-conditioning units, and wires using a flashlight to make the switch. It took him over an hour and a half and 5½ innings to make the round trip. The break-in and the heist were immediately detected by the White Sox officials. Eventually, the Indians handed Belle's bat over to the umpires. Belle's bat was taken, x-rayed, cut open, and cork was found. Belle was suspended seven games for his actions. Grimsley was not fined or suspended, and it was five years before his caper came to light.

Toronto, which had won back-to-back world championships in 1992 and 1993, was indeed a formidable outfit. The 41,688 folks who crammed into Jacobs Field that day were believers from the get-go. Grimsley walked the first three Blue Jays he faced in the first inning and Toronto sent 11 men to the plate, scoring seven runs. Former Indian Joe Carter drove in a pair and Shawn Green followed with a three-run round-tripper. Grimsley lasted a mere third of an inning as the Jays kicked sand in the Indians' faces. "If I had gone around and taken a poll with Cone on the mound for the Blue Jays, I would've said the game was over," said Tribe skipper Mike Hargrove.[1]

Chad Ogea relieved Grimsley. The teams each scored a run in the third inning, and Toronto led 8-1. The tally by the Jays was the only blemish on Ogea's stat line for the afternoon.

The Tribe started to mount a comeback in the fourth and fifth innings. Kenny Lofton singled home two runs in the fourth, while Eddie Murray hit a two-run homer, his seventh of the season, in the fifth.

Belle singled home another run in the sixth, and with the score 8-6, Cone was done for the day. He was relieved by Tony Castillo, who shut the Tribe down over the next 2⅔ innings. "I just couldn't stop the bleeding," said Cone. "There were a couple of turning points to the game. Lofton's two-out hit and Murray's two-run homer got them back in the game. I couldn't really negotiate my split-finger, and I threw a lot in the dirt. … It's a shame to waste that lead."[2]

Toronto's 8-6 lead held until the bottom of the ninth, when Carlos Baerga led off for Cleveland. He was thrown out on a bunt attempt by Castillo. Jays skipper Cito Gaston then summoned right-hander Darren Hall into the game. Hall had led the Blue Jays in saves with 17 in 1994, and he was expected to pick up where Castillo had left off. It was not to be.

Belle singled and took third base on Murray's hit to right field. Alvaro Espinoza ran for Murray, but was erased on a fielder's choice, Belle scoring on the grounder by Jim Thome. On a first-pitch fastball by Hall, Paul Sorrento smacked a home run to right field, the baseball landing several rows deep. The Indians dugout emptied out on to the field in celebration. It was Sorrento's 12th home run of the season and capped the comeback by the Tribe, their seventh such victory so far in the season. "Someday, the comebacks are going to stop," said Hargrove. "But this has been going on for a year and a half."[3]

Sorrento was the hero of the hour, but it was Ogea holding the Blue Jays at bay for 6⅔ innings that allowed the Indians to creep back into the game. He was followed by Julian Tavarez, who pitched two innings of one-hit ball to claim the win. "When I first hit it, I thought it was way out," said Sorrento. "But the wind kind of swirls. It's kind of weird. I looked out, and I had to start running a bit."[4]

The win catapulted the Indians to win their next five games, and nine of their next ten. They were on their way.

NOTES

1 Amy Rosewater, "Deep Hole, Long Climb, Sorrento's Home Run Caps 9-Run Comeback," *Cleveland Plain Dealer*, June 5, 1995: 1D.

2 Amy Rosewater, "Cone Lets Big Lead Get Away," *Cleveland Plain Dealer*, June 5, 1995: 5D.

3 Rosewater, "Deep Hole."

4 Ibid.

HERSHISER STRIKES OUT 10, LOFTON HOMERS TWICE IN SHUTOUT OF DETROIT

JUNE 5, 1995: CLEVELAND INDIANS 8, DETROIT TIGERS 0

AT JACOBS FIELD, CLEVELAND

BY GREGORY H. WOLF

"We were a rock star baseball team," said right-hander Orel Hershiser about the 1995 Cleveland Indians. "You'd drive around and see Wahoo signs in almost every front yard. You'd walk into restaurants, and there were pictures of the players on the walls. I'd never quite seen anything like it. I get the chills just to think about it."[1] Little did Hershiser know that he'd play one of the many starring roles on Cleveland's thundering US tour.

Hershiser's career was at a crossroads in 1995. Two years after winning 23 games, tossing a big-league-record 59 scoreless innings, and leading the Los Angeles Dodgers to the World Series championship in 1988, Hershiser underwent rotator-cuff surgery on his right shoulder in late April 1990. His road to recovery was agonizingly slow. After four mediocre seasons and no longer being considered one of the NL's elite starters, Hershiser became a free agent after the strike-shortened 1994 season, in which he won just six times. Only the San Francisco Giants and the Cleveland Indians showed interest in the 36-year-old former Cy Young Award recipient with 134 career victories. "I looked at Cleveland's roster," Hershiser recalled in an interview with sportswriter Terry Pluto, "and it looked like those guys would score seven runs a game. And they had a good bullpen."[2] Less than three weeks before Opening Day, Hershiser signed with the Indians, on April 8, 1995, for about half his salary from the previous year; however, little was expected of the free-agent acquisition.

When the Indians and Detroit Tigers headed to Cleveland's Jacobs Field to play the first contest of a three-game series, on Monday, June 6, the teams were going in opposite directions. Skipper Mike Hargrove's Tribe had won seven of its last eight games and was firmly ensconced in first place (24-10), five games in front of the Kansas City Royals. Sparky Anderson, in his 16th and final campaign as Detroit's pilot, had his club in second place, but the Tigers had lost six of their last eight games, and had fallen to 16-20.

The pitching matchup featured age versus experience. Hershiser, who had been slated as a possible fourth or fifth starter, revived his career in 1995. The 13-year veteran with 310 career starts had won his last four decisions in May. "[My] shoulder is doing more naturally what I want it to do," he said in an attempt to explain his unexpected success.[3] Rugged, 6-foot-4 right-hander Sean Bergman, in his first full season in the majors, was making his 18th career start for the Tigers.

On a warm, 71-degree evening, the "Jake" held 34,615 spectators, about 7,000 fewer than capacity. The three-game set with the Tigers marked the last time fans could casually buy tickets at the ballpark's box office for a long time. Beginning on June 12, 1995, Cleveland sold out every game until April 4, 2001. Hershiser, nicknamed "Bulldog," set the tone of the game by striking out the side in the first inning. His competitive mound presence belied his tall and lanky, altar-boyish appearance. In a scoreless game, the potent Indians offense erupted in the bottom of the third inning. Center fielder Kenny Lofton led off by blasting a home run to deep right field. After a two-out walk to cleanup slugger/left fielder Albert Belle, 39-year-old DH Eddie Murray, who began the game just 24 hits shy of 3,000, smashed the 466th round-tripper of his career to make it 3-0. With runners on first and third, first baseman Paul Sorrento singled to deep center field, driving in Jim Thome. Lofton increased Cleveland's lead to 5-0 in the fifth inning with his second home run.

Relying on pinpoint control and ball movement, Hershiser rekindled memories of 1988. He used an assortment of sinking fastballs, cutters, curves, sliders, and changeups to keep Tigers hitters guessing, whiffing 10 batters for the first time since 1989. (It was the sixth and final time he reached double figures in K's in his career.) "[D]ifferent locations, different speeds and slightly different arm angles on all those pitches gave me a pretty wide palette of choice," Hershiser once said about his varied pitching arsenal.[4] He surrendered just six hits, did not issue a walk, and was never in trouble. Detroit managed two baserunners in an inning only once, when Bobby Higginson connected for his third hit followed by Danny Bautista's single with two outs in the seventh. With runners on the corners, Hershiser induced Chris Gomez to fly out to Lofton.

The Indians tacked on three more runs in the sixth inning off John Doherty, who had relieved Bergman the previous inning and hurled the final four frames of the game. Demonstrating that they could also play small ball, Cleveland had two doubles, two singles, and a walk. Shortstop Omar Vizquel, second sacker Carlos Baerga, and Belle each drove in a run.

Hershiser set down the side in order in both the eighth and ninth innings to record his first shutout in two years and the 25th and last in his career. "The last four or five outings, there hasn't been much difference [from 1988]," he said after the game. "Maybe a mile or two an hour on the fastball. But the movement is almost completely back, and the breaking ball is almost completely back."[5] He threw 107 pitches, including 72 strikes, and finished the game in 2 hours and 43 minutes.

The victory was a team effort, with seven of the nine starters (everyone except Baerga and catcher Tony Pena) recording at least one hit; six players drove in at least one run. The Indians improved their record to 25-10, marking their best start since 1966. "It was like being on one big hot streak," reminisced Hershiser about the Indians' pennant-winning season and 100 victories in 144 games.[6]

SOURCES

In addition to the sources included in the Notes, the author also relied on Baseballreference.com and Retrosheet.org

NOTES

1   Terry Pluto, "Cleveland Indians Still Special to Orel Hershiser, Who Remembers a Rock Star Baseball Team," Cleveland.Com, May 2, 2014. cleveland.com/pluto/index.ssf/2014/05/cleveland_indians_still_mean_a.html.

2   Ibid.

3   "Indians Win Behind Hershiser's Shutout," *Washington Post*, June 6, 1995.

4   Quoted from Bill James and Rob Neyer, *Neyer/James Guide to Pitchers* (New York: Fireside, 2004), 241.

5   "Indians Win."

6   Pluto.

EDDIE MURRAY JOINS 3,000 HIT CLUB

JUNE 30, 1995: CLEVELAND INDIANS 4, MINNESOTA TWINS 1, AT HUBERT H. HUMPHREY METRODOME, MINNEAPOLIS

BY JOSEPH WANCHO

It is one of the gold standards of major-league baseball: the 3,000-hit club. More than 16,500 players have participated in at least one major-league game. Of those, only 19 players had exceeded more than 3,000 hits in their career. On June 30, 1995, Eddie Murray became the 20th member to become immortalized on that coveted list. (As of 2018, the list has grown to 32 players.)

Murray was as accomplished a player as there was in major-league history. Beginning in 1977, when he was named AL Rookie of Year while with Baltimore, Murray was the epitome of both greatness and class in his 17-year career before joining the Cleveland Indians in 1994. His defense was flawless; he won the Gold Glove Award three years in a row (1982-1984). Murray's durability was his calling card: He played in more games at first base (2,413) than any other player in the major leagues. He was recognized twice by *The Sporting News* as its first baseman on their post-season All-Star Teams (1983, 1990). Murray was the power that drove the Baltimore Orioles to a world championship in 1983. He led the team in homers (33) and RBIs (111). You won't find his name among the yearly league leaders in offensive categories too often. Yet, when Murray retired after the 1997 season, he was second all-time to Pete Rose in hits (3,255) by a switch-hitter, and one of only three players to total 500 home runs and 3,000 RBIs (Willie Mays, Hank Aaron).

But he was a leader between the lines and in the clubhouse. The Indians signed Murray and his former Baltimore teammate, pitcher Dennis Martinez, in late 1993 to instill some leadership in the young Tribe players. In 1995 they signed Dave Winfield and Orel Hershiser, again emphasizing what it takes to win from two more proven stars.

For the Cleveland Indians, they were enjoying life in the penthouse. They sported a 19-7 record in the month of May and coming into the last day of June, they were 19-8 for the month. They led the majors with a 40-17 record and led the Kansas City Royals by nine games in the American League Central Division. There were no serious contenders to challenge them for the division title. The Indians were playing downhill on most evenings, surely a different sight for Cleveland fans.

As the countdown began to the magical number of 3,000, the Indians were catching the fever. Murray, who had little to say to the media, did not comment on the streak as it built to a climax. That didn't stop his teammates from marveling at his accomplishment. "This is exciting," said Charles Nagy. "It's something you'll remember being a part of for a long time. With the exception of Dave Winfield, probably none of us have seen this. And it's neat because Eddie is such a good guy, and a good team guy."[1]

As Cleveland and Minnesota got ready to tangle in the second game of a four-game set at the Hubert H. Humphrey Metrodome, the focus naturally shifted to Murray. The Indians' designated hitter for the evening was sitting at 2,999 hits. It was only a matter of time before he joined two Indians legends who had each attained their 3,000th hit in an Indians uniform, Nap Lajoie (1914) and Tris Speaker (1925).

Cleveland and Minnesota each scored a run in the third inning. Martinez, the Cleveland starter, was off to a great start in the season with a record of 6-0. Minnesota starter Mike Trombley was at the opposite end of the spectrum; he came into the game with a 0-2 record. But both pitchers battled to a 1-1 tie through five innings.

Albert Belle led off the sixth inning with a double to left field. Into the batter's box stepped Murray. He had walked and lined out to center field in two previous plate appearances. On a 0-and-1 fastball from Trombley, Murray lined a single between first and second base into right field. He had his 3,000th hit. The Indians dugout emptied as Murray's teammates rushed to first base to congratulate him. The Metrodome scoreboard showed a video of his career. Murray tipped his batting helmet and cap to the crowd of 27,416, who cheered wildly.

When the game resumed, Jim Thome struck out. Manny Ramirez's grounder forced Murray at second base, but Belle scored on the play for a 2-1 lead. Wayne Kirby added a run with his first home run of the season in the seventh inning and Cleveland won, 4-1. Martinez raised his record to 7-0, striking out seven in eight innings. José Mesa came on in the ninth to save his 20th game in as many opportunities.

"I enjoyed it," said Murray. "We've had a lot of fun in Cleveland. This is the wildest group of guys I've ever played with. The music in the locker room, the jokes we play on each other, the reporters who come into our locker room must think we're crazy."[2]

Murray met with the media after the game. When he returned to the locker room, most of the players were on the bus waiting to return to the hotel.

"I'm happy for him," said Omar Vizquel. "I think it was a lot of pressure on him. I think all this publicity bothered him a little bit and I'm pretty sure he wanted to have that over."[3]

The Indians went on to win the Central Division and snap a 41-year postseason drought. They marched through the AL playoffs but lost to Atlanta in the World Series.

Eddie Murray played two more seasons. He was elected to the National Baseball Hall of Fame in 2003. "He was the best clutch hitter during the decade that we played together, not only on our team, but in all of baseball," said Mike Flanagan.[4]

NOTES

1 Paul Hoynes, "2,999 … And Counting. Murray Has Two Hits as Tribe Wins," *Cleveland Plain Dealer*, June 30, 1995: 1D.

2 Paul Hoynes, "3,000! Murray Hits Milestone in Victory," *Cleveland Plain Dealer*, July 1, 1995: 1D.

3 Tim Warsinskey, "Murray Is Calm in Spotlight," *Cleveland Plain Dealer*, July 1, 1995: 1D.

4 National Baseball Hall of Fame website, player page, accessed June 18, 2016.

DENNIS MARTINEZ DEFIES AGE, GETS 9TH CONSECUTIVE WIN

JULY 21, 1995: CLEVELAND INDIANS 6, OAKLAND A'S 1, AT OAKLAND-ALAMEDA COUNTY COLISEUM

BY RICHARD CUICCHI

Someone forgot to tell Dennis Martinez that he should be winding down his major-league career at his age of 41. Instead, it was as if he had found a fountain of youth and become invincible since the start of the 1995 season, as he remained undefeated in nine decisions after his complete-game win against Oakland on July 21. Martinez was a key contributor with the Cleveland Indians, who were the runaway leader in the American League Central Division in July and eventually captured the AL pennant.

Going into the first game of a three-game series at Oakland, Cleveland had a 53-22 record and a 14½-game lead over the Milwaukee Brewers. The Indians had been in sole possession of first place in their division since May 12, while the A's were currently in last place in the West Division.

The right-handed Martinez, who had pitched two innings in the All-Star Game on July 11, was making his 16th start of the season. To date, he had a 2.47 ERA and had walked only 17 batters in 102 innings pitched.

The Indians featured a potent offense led by 1995 All-Stars Albert Belle, Manny Ramirez, Carlos Baerga, and Kenny Lofton. The team also included veteran stars Eddie Murray, Dave Winfield, Sandy Alomar Jr., and Tony Peña, as well as up-and-coming players Jim Thome and Omar Vizquel.

The A's countered with Todd Stottlemyre as their starter. He was the leader of the A's staff, having posted an 8-2 record and an ERA of 3.72. The righty had pitched five games with double-digit strikeouts in his 16 starts, including 15 in a game on June 16 against the Kansas City Royals. The A's lineup was without first baseman Mark McGwire and outfielder Rickey Henderson, who were nursing nagging injuries, while outfielder Ruben Sierra was on the disabled list.[1]

The Indians' Belle got the scoring started in the top of the second inning when he hit a solo home run at the 400-foot mark in center field. It was his 17th of the season and fifth in the last 20 games.

Retiring seven of the next eight batters, Stottlemyre held the Indians in check until he faced Belle again in the fourth inning. Belle and Thome both singled before the 23-year-old Ramirez cleared the bases with his 22nd home run of the season. Ramirez picked up where he left off the week before, when he homered three times in the Indians' four-game sweep of the A's.

Meanwhile, Martinez held the A's scoreless until the fourth. That's when Geronimo Berroa singled to lead off the home half of the inning and Mike Aldrete doubled off the fence in right. Brent Gates then hit a fly to deep right-center field which

Ramirez caught, but it scored Berroa from third to make the score 4-1. After walking Mike Bordick, Martinez retired Stan Javier, who represented the tying run at the plate, on a groundout.

In the top of the fifth inning, Cleveland extended its lead when Stottlemyre served up his third homer, to Peña, making the score 5-1.

The Indians scored their final run in the sixth on Herbert Perry's single that scored Thome, who had singled and advanced on a wild pitch.

Don Wengert replaced Stottlemyre in the top of the seventh and threw three perfect innings. Martinez retired 13 of the last 14 batters he faced, yielding only a double to Scott Brosius.

Martinez picked up his ninth win while hurling his third complete game of the season. He yielded six hits, struck out six and walked three. He had not lost a game since July 31, 1994. Indians GM John Hart commented, "For two years he's been the anchor of our staff. He's been as good as anybody in the league since May of last year."[2]

Stottlemyre was tagged with his third loss, giving up all six runs on six hits and two walks.

The Indians' three homers put them at 118 for the season in 76 games played. The *Plain Dealer* noted that the Indians were on pace to belt 224 in the 144-game strike-shortened season, which would easily surpass their club record of 187 in 1987.[3] The Indians wound up breaking their record with 207 home runs.

Belle finished the season with 50 home runs, the most in the American League. He led the league in runs (121), doubles (52), RBIs (tied with 126), and slugging (.690). He was the first major leaguer to collect 50 doubles and 50 home runs in a season and just the eighth to get 100 or more extra-base hits in a season (and the first since Stan Musial in 1948).[4]

Martinez was the first Indians pitcher since Barry Latman in 1961 to start a season 9-0. Johnny Allen held the franchise record by starting the 1937 season with a 15-0 record.[5] Martinez's streak was broken when he took the loss in his next outing, on July 26, against the California Angels. In his 12 games from July 26 to the end of the season, Martinez wasn't nearly as effective as he was in his earlier nine-game winning streak: He posted a 3-5 record and 4.14 ERA. However, he had an excellent outing in the deciding sixth game of the ALCS against the Seattle Mariners.

Martinez, the first Nicaraguan to play in the major leagues, played three more seasons in the majors. In his 23 seasons, he compiled a 245-193 record and a 3.70 ERA, and was selected to four All-Star teams.

The Indians maintained their winning ways for the remainder of the year to win the Central Division by 30 games and beat Seattle to end a 41-year drought for an AL pennant, only to lose in the World Series to Atlanta.

SOURCES

In addition to the references cited in the Notes, the author also consulted:

Baseball-Reference.com.

retrosheet.org/boxesetc/1995/B07210OAK1995.htm.

baseball-reference.com/boxes/OAK/OAK199507210.shtml.

NOTES

1 Paul Hoynes, "Bang by the Bay. Tribe Rides Homer Power, *Cleveland Plain Dealer*, July 22, 1995: 1D.

2 Sheldon Ocker, "A.L. Central: Cleveland Indians," *The Sporting News*, August 21, 1995: 30.

3 Hoynes.

4 1996 Cleveland Indians Media Guide, 247. Other players to have 100 or more extra-base hits in a season were Babe Ruth (1921), Lou Gehrig (1927, 1930), Chuck Klein (1930, 1932), Hank Greenberg (1937), Jimmie Foxx (1932), and Rogers Hornsby (1922).

5 Hoynes.

THE CLINCHER

SEPTEMBER 8, 1995: CLEVELAND INDIANS 3, BALTIMORE ORIOLES 2, AT JACOBS FIELD, CLEVELAND

BY JOSEPH WANCHO

It had been 41 years since the Cleveland Indians were in the postseason. Of course, back in 1954, there was just the World Series. There was no Division Series or Championship Series, just two eight-team leagues, with the respective winners facing off in the fall classic. Expansion over the years, from those eight clubs to the 28 teams in 1995, made it necessary to add layers of playoffs. The Division Series, or LDS as it became known, was to be brand-new in 1994. But there was no postseason in 1994 because a player strike wiped out the end of the season after August 10, and even part of 1995.

But Tribe fans could care less what the level of playoffs were ahead. It was only a matter of time before their team clinched one of the four spots in postseason play. They had opened up a 22½-game lead on the Kansas City Royals, and had been coasting for some time. They had been playing before sellouts since June, and baseball was at a fever pitch in Cleveland.

There was another attraction present at the ballyard that evening. Cal Ripken was baseball's new ironman, having eclipsed Lou Gehrig's streak of 2,130 consecutive games played. Ripken set the new record of 2,131 on September 6, and the next day a parade was held through the streets of Baltimore in his honor. "After having gone through the parade and everything I can't ever remember being this tired," said Ripken. "Mentally it has been draining and physically exhausting. But there is a certain sense of relief."[1]

The sellout crowd of 41,656 at Jacobs Field gave Ripken a standing ovation at the beginning of the game, and in the bottom of the fifth inning, when consecutive game 2,132 became official. Each time, the classy Ripken acknowledged the crowd by doffing his cap.

The starters for the game were two right-handers. Orel Hershiser in his debut season for the Indians was as advertised. "Bulldog" provided veteran leadership and together with Dennis Martinez, Charles Nagy, and Ken Hill made up a formidable rotation for the Tribe. He was 12-6 so far and answered the call even though his 37th birthday was just a handful of days away.

Hershiser's opposition was Kevin Brown, a hard-throwing, oft-injured pitcher who had led the AL in wins (21) in 1992. But he was 7-8 for the Orioles, and at season's end would depart the Charm City for the Florida Marlins.

The Indians broke through first in the bottom of the third inning. The big hit was a two-out single by Eddie Murray that plated two runs. The Indians were up 3-0 after three.

The Orioles answered with a single tally in the top of the fourth when Curtis Goodwin scored on a double-play ball hit by Bobby Bonilla. They scored again in the seventh on doubles by Harold Baines and Jeff Huson, chasing Hershiser from the game. Cleveland's lead was sliced to 3-2.

But the Indians bullpen held the Orioles the rest of the way. In the ninth inning, José Mesa came on to earn his 40th save. Mesa walked Chris Hoiles with two outs, and the crowd grew a bit anxious. It was not until third baseman Jim Thome caught a pop fly off Huson's bat that delirium set in. Hershiser got the win to raise his record to 13-6, while Brown was tagged with the loss, his record on the year dropping to 7-9.

The team headed out as one to center field, wearing AL Central Division Champion shirts and caps to raise the banner that proclaimed their first championship of any kind since 1954. "I cried watching it go up," said Sandy Alomar Jr. "That's the first banner we've had here. I never saw the one in 1954. I wasn't born yet."[2]

As the banner was being raised, the song "The Dance," by Garth Brooks, was blaring from the ballpark's speakers. The song was in remembrance of Indians pitcher Steve Olin, who had died two years earlier with fellow pitcher Tim Crews in a spring-training boating accident. It was Olin's favorite song. Cleveland manager Mike Hargrove requested that the song be played over the public-address system. "I thought it would mean a lot to anyone who was there (with the Indians at the time of the accident in 1993)," said Hargrove. "For those who weren't there, it had no significance, but it was still a good song. It was a tribute to those guys, to their families. It was part of our promise to never forget them. We didn't tell anyone that we were going to do it. For those who knew, there wasn't a dry eye to be seen. I saw Charlie Nagy, tears rolling down his face."[3]

It would not be until October 4 that the Indians would play their first playoff game. The wait for the postseason to begin was nearly unbearable as the Indians played out the rest of the season without consequence. It was to be a memorable playoff run at that. As former Indians President Gabe Paul once said, "Cleveland is a sleeping giant. Give the fans a winning team and they'll flock to the stadium as they did in the past."[4]

Fittingly, Gabe Paul was able to see his proclamation come true in 1995.

NOTES

1 L.C. Johnson, "Ripken Wants Hoopla to Wind Down," *Cleveland Plain Dealer*, September 9, 1995: 4C.

2 Paul Hoynes, "The Wait Is Over: Indians Are Champions for the First Time Since 1954," *Cleveland Plain Dealer*, September 9, 1995: 1D.

3 Tim Kurkjian, ESPN.com, March 21, 2003.

4 Russell Schneider, *Tales from the Tribe Dugout* (New York: Sports Publishing LLC, 2002), 173.

NAGY SHUTS OUT YANKEES ON THREE HITS

SEPTEMBER 13, 1995: CLEVELAND INDIANS 5, NEW YORK YANKEES 0, AT JACOBS FIELD, CLEVELAND

BY GREGORY H. WOLF

It was a foregone conclusion that the Cleveland Indians were headed to the postseason for the first time since 1954 when they faced the New York Yankees on Wednesday evening, September 13, 1995, at Jacobs Field. The Indians owned the best record in baseball (88-39) and enjoyed a 24-game lead over the Kansas City Royals in the American League Central Division. Manager Mike Hargrove's squad had played especially well at the "Jake" as the two-year-old park was affectionately called, winning 48 of 64 games; however, they were coming off losses in the first two games of the three-game set with the Yankees, the first and only time all season that the Indians lost consecutive games at home. The New York Yankees were playing their best ball of the season. After a miserable stretch in August (4-14), skipper Buck Showalter's team had won 12 of their last 14 games to improve their record to 66-61, good for second place in the AL East. More importantly, they began the evening with a half-game lead over the Seattle Mariners for the AL wild-card spot. A victory would also mark the Yankees' first three-game sweep of the Indians in Cleveland since 1982.

Taking the mound for the Indians was 28-year-old right-hander Charles Nagy, practitioner of sinkers, slow curves, and split-fingered fastballs. A six-year veteran who came up through the Indians organization, Nagy had won nine of his last 10 decisions to improve his record to 13-5 and move over the .500 mark for his career (54-48). His opponent was the reigning AL Cy Young Award winner, 32-year-old David Cone, whom

the Yankees had acquired about six weeks earlier in a trade with the Toronto Blue Jays. The 10-year veteran, with 126 wins to his credit, had won five of six decisions for the Yankees, but had been roughed up in his last three starts, surrendering seven home runs and 16 earned runs in just 22⅓ innings. "Cone had one of the best repertoires I've ever seen a pitcher possess," said former Indians knuckleballer Tom Candiotti.[1] Cone's legitimate six-pitch arsenal included a fastball, splitter, slider, overhand curve, side-arm curve, and changeup.

The game, delayed 77 minutes by rain, finally got underway at 8:52 P.M. on a warm, 68-degree and humid night on Lake Erie. Despite the weather, a sellout crowd of 41,707 packed Jacobs Field for the 46th consecutive game since the streak started on June 12. (The streak ended on April 4, 2001, after a then big-league record 455 games.)

The last time Nagy faced the Yankees, in the second game of a doubleheader on August 10 in the

Bronx, he was roughed up for 11 hits and seven runs in just 5⅔ innings, but avoided the loss when the Indians scored five runs in the ninth to win, 10-9. Nagy crafted a different narrative in this game, one of the best in his career. He erased Yankees leadoff hitter Wade Boggs, who was hitting .398 (37-for-93) in his last 24 games, on a weak grounder to second baseman Carlos Baerga. In his only rough stretch the entire game, Nagy walked two of the next three batters before ending the inning by striking out outfielder Daryl Strawberry. Nagy tossed 23 pitches, and allowed two baserunners in one inning for the only time in the game.

The Indians struck quickly in the first inning. All-Star center fielder Kenny Lofton, who had taken Rickey Henderson's mantle as arguably the game's most dangerous and disruptive leadoff hitter, drew a walk, stole second and third, and then scored on shortstop Omar Vizquel's double to right field. Cone retired third baseman Jim Thome (whose grounder moved Vizquel to third) and left fielder Albert Belle before walking DH Eddie Murray on four pitches. With runners on the corners, right fielder Manny Ramirez singled to drive in Vizquel for a 2-0 lead. By the time Cone induced first sacker Paul Sorrento ground out to his counterpart, Don Mattingly, for the third out, he had thrown 34 pitches.

Nagy cruised in the second and third innings, needing only 16 pitches to register six outs. Right fielder Paul O'Neil led off the fourth inning with the Yankees' first hit of the game, a seeing-eye single between Baerga and Vizquel. Undeterred, Nagy set down the next three hitters to end the inning. In the fifth frame, he surrendered another leadoff single, to left fielder Dion James. The next batter, shortstop Tony Fernandez, hit a grounder back to the mound which Nagy fielded to start the Indians' only double play (1-6-3) in the game.

Cone labored to hold the Indians scoreless in the second through fourth innings. In the second, he yielded a one-out double to catcher Tony Peña, who moved to third on Lofton's single. En route to leading the AL in stolen bases for the fourth of five consecutive seasons, Lofton swiped second. Cone got out of the jam by striking out Vizquel and Thome swinging on full counts. The Indians threatened again in the fourth when Peña connected for a two-out single and then stole second (it was his 80th and final swipe in his 18-year big-league career). Lofton walked to reach base for the third consecutive time before Vizquel grounded out.

Albert Belle, who led the AL in homers (50) and RBIs (126) in 1995, ended a six-game homerless streak by launching, in the words of Jack Curry of the *New York Times*, "a prodigious" home run to deep right-center field.[2] It was his 37th blast of the season and marked the beginning of one of the biggest power surges in Cleveland's history: In his last 16 games, Belle walloped 14 round-trippers and drove in 21 runs. Seemingly in trouble every inning, Cone surrendered three consecutive hits in the sixth, but only one run (on Vizquel's single, driving in Peña) to make it 5-0.

In total command of his pitches, Nagy retired 12 of 13 batters from the sixth inning through the ninth. His only blemish was Don Mattingly's double in the seventh. The game ended after 2 hours and 29 minutes when Nagy struck out catcher Mike Stanley swinging.

Nagy threw 115 pitches and fanned five to register his first shutout since his only career one-hitter, a 6-0 victory over the Baltimore Orioles at Camden Yards on August 8, 1992, and recorded his fifth of sixth career shutouts. Both the Indians and Yankees finished the strike-shortened season strongly and ended long playoff droughts. While Cleveland won 12 of its last 17 games to finish 100-44 and capture the AL Central crown, New York went 13-4 to secure the wild-card spot and secure their first postseason berth since 1981.

SOURCES

In addition to the sources listed in the Notes, the author also relied on Baseball-Reference.com, Retrosheet.org, SABR.org, and *The Sporting News*

NOTES

1 Quoted from Bill James and Rob Neyer, *The Neyer/James Guide to Pitchers* (New York: Fireside, 2004), 169.

2 Jack Curry, "Yankees Bash and Jacobs Field Finally Is Broken Up," *New York Times*, September 14, 1995: B17.

OTHER FEATURES

1995 AMERICAN LEAGUE DIVISION SERIES

OCTOBER 3-4, 1995: CLEVELAND INDIANS 5, BOSTON RED SOX 4, AT JACOBS FIELD

BY MARK S. STERNMAN

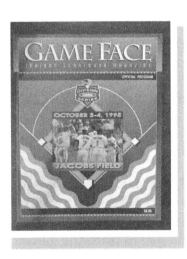

Cleveland backup catcher Tony Peña's 13th-inning home run off Boston's Zane Smith gave the Indians a thrilling 5-4 win over the Red Sox in Cleveland's first postseason victory since Game Six of the 1948 World Series over the Boston Braves.

Starting pitchers Dennis Martinez and Roger Clemens both began strongly. After retiring the first four batters, Martinez yielded a single to Boston's Mike Greenwell before stranding him. Clemens retired the first nine Cleveland batters.

In the top of the third, Boston second baseman Luis Alicea, the ninth-place hitter with a regular-season average of .270 but the Red Sox hitting star of Game One, singled with one out. Right fielder Dwayne Hosey hit a grounder to shortstop for a force play, then scored on shortstop John Valentin's home run to deep right. Valentin had hit 27 home runs and driven in 102 runs in what would prove to be by far the best season of his 11-year career.

In the bottom of the fourth, Cleveland got singles by Kenny Lofton and Carlos Baerga, but Clemens struck out Albert Belle and got Eddie Murray to ground to Alicea to end the threat.

In the fifth, Alicea reached on a one-out infield hit and stole second, but Martinez induced a lineout from Hosey and a pop from Valentin to strand Alicea.

The Indians scored three runs with two outs in the sixth to take the lead. After Omar Vizquel walked, Cleveland put on a hit-and-run. "Valentin broke to cover the bag, Baerga angled a bouncer through the vacated hole at short to put runners on first and third for Belle," wrote one sports scribe.[1] "Belle ropes an RBI double to the gap in left-center. Valentin goes to the plate with a perfect throw, but Mike Macfarlane, his mask on, drops the ball. Baerga is safe, Belle winds up at third, and the game is tied, 2-2," wrote another.[2] Then Murray scored Belle with a single to put Cleveland up 3-2.

With the lead, Manager Mike Hargrove hooked Martinez, who had thrown just 86 pitches, and replaced him with Julian Tavarez, who retired the Red Sox in order in the seventh, culminated with swinging strikeouts of center fielder Lee Tinsley and Macfarlane.

After Clemens set down Cleveland in order in the home half of the seventh, Alicea, the most unlikely of Boston power hitters who homered only six times in 1995 and slightly more than one out of 100 at-bats over his career, homered off Tavarez to tie the game. The Indians almost unraveled after that. Lefty Paul Assenmacher replaced Tavarez after Valentin's one-out single to face Mo Vaughn, the Red Sox' best left-handed hitter and the eventual 1995 AL MVP. Assenmacher struck out Vaughn, who would struggle throughout the ALDS. Righty Eric Plunk came in to face Boston DH Jose Canseco and had Valentin picked off, but errors by Murray and Lofton allowed Valentin to advance to third base. Plunk got Canseco to fly to right to end the threat and keep the score tied.

With Clemens at 103 pitches, Red Sox manager Kevin Kennedy turned to his bullpen, tapping lefty Rheal Cormier. After fanning Lofton, Cormier walked Vizquel and hit Baerga before exiting in favor of righty Stan Belinda. Belinda got Belle to pop out before leaving for Mike Stanton, who induced a fly from Murray to end the eighth.

Plunk stayed in for the ninth and got into trouble right away. Greenwell singled and advanced to second on a sacrifice by Red Sox third baseman Tim Naehring. Plunk intentionally walked Tinsley to face Macfarlane, but Kennedy called on his best pinch-hitter, Matt Stairs, who had made the ALDS roster only because of a late injury to Troy O'Leary.[3] Plunk struck out Stairs and got Alicea to line out (the only time Alicea failed to reach all game) to end the frame.

Stanton got Cleveland in order in the ninth. With no possible save situation remaining, Hargrove turned to closer Jose Mesa in a tie game in the top of the 10th. After having walked just 15 batters unintentionally all season, Mesa passed Hosey and Valentin before giving up consecutive line drives to Vaughn and Canseco. The Indians caught both, and the second went as a 5-4-5-4 double play to allow Mesa to escape.

Stanton finally faltered in the bottom of the 10th when Cleveland catcher Sandy Alomar Jr. beat out a bunt. Wayne Kirby ran for Alomar. Lofton struck out, and Vizquel reached on a fielder's choice that retired Kirby. Vizquel stole second, but Baerga struck out. Stanton had retired seven of eight batters, four by strikeout.

Cleveland brought in a new battery for the 11th, replacing Plunk with Jim Poole and Alomar with Peña. After getting Greenwell to line out, Poole gave up a home run to Naehring before retiring the next two hitters, so Boston led 4-3 going into the bottom of the 11th.

With the lead, "Kennedy had the Tribe right where he wanted 'em. He had a one-run lead and his closer ready to come in to the game."[4] Rick Aguilera had to face the best power hitters of the Indians in Belle, Murray, and Jim Thome. Belle, who before the ALDS had expressed doubts about the continuation of "his incredible pace – 31 homers in 217 at-bats since Aug. 1."[5] retied the game with his second clutch extra-base RBI hit of the game, a line-drive home run to deep left, after which Kennedy got the umpires to confiscate Belle's bat to test it for corking.

The test proved negative, and even the Boston press mocked Kennedy, with columnist Dan Shaughnessy writing, "Somehow this doesn't seem fair. Belle loses a Wonder Boy bat and the Sox are not penalized for their challenge. Shouldn't there be some penalty if the challenge is invalid – like in Scrabble?"[6]

Seemingly unbothered, Cleveland got two more on via singles by Thome and Paul Sorrento. "Then Aguilera injured himself in the process of pitching to Manny Ramirez, and had to leave the game."[7] Mike Maddux got Peña to ground out to end the inning. Aguilera's failure to seal Game One for the Red Sox turned the tide of the entire ALDS.

Boston had a prime chance to recapture the lead in the top of the 12th. Alicea doubled, but Hosey did not bunt him over and struck out. The lefty Poole walked the righty Valentin to face the lefty Vaughn and struck out Mo. Righty Ken Hill, who had just one relief appearance for Cleveland in 1995 and loomed as the Game Four starter,[8] came on to get Canseco looking to end the top of the 12th.

The Indians almost won the game in the bottom of the inning. Maddux hit Lofton, and Alicea mishandled Vizquel's sacrifice, sending Lofton to third with none out. Baerga could not get the winning run in as he popped to Valentin. Maddux walked Belle to load the bases with one out, and

Kennedy called on the lefty Zane Smith to face Murray. Smith excelled, getting Murray to ground into a 5-2 force and likewise getting Thome to ground to Vaughn to escape the nasty threat.

After giving up a leadoff single to Greenwell, Hill took care of the rest of the top of the 13th himself, striking out Naehring and getting back-to-back comebackers from Tinsley and catcher Bill Haselman, who had replaced Macfarlane after Stairs' pinch-hitting appearance.

On this day, Cleveland had a better-hitting backup catcher than Boston, and that difference proved decisive when Peña, the former Red Sox catcher, hit a two-out walk-off home run on a 3-and-0 meatball from Smith to end what at that time was "the longest night playoff game in major league history."[9]

Cleveland Indians 4, Boston Red Sox 0 – October 4, 1995, at Jacobs Field

Making his first postseason start in seven years, Cleveland starter Orel Hershiser extended his streak of outstanding October pitching by three-hitting Boston over 7⅓ innings as the Indians blanked the Red Sox 4-0 to take a commanding two-games-to-none lead in the best-of-five American League Division Series.

Cleveland started sloppy with two errors and a wild pitch beginning the game. Belle misplayed a Hosey drive into a two-base error, and Paul Sorrento dropped a throw from Vizquel, allowing Valentin to reach. But Boston ran itself out of the inning. Hosey tried to advance on Sorrento's miscue but went out 6-3-5. Rather than putting runners at second and third with no out, Hershiser's wild pitch merely advanced Valentin to second with one out. Hershiser escaped by fanning Vaughn and getting Canseco to fly to Belle, who this time made the play.

Valentin returned the favor to the Indians by kicking a Vizquel grounder. With two outs, Belle singled Vizquel to third and took second on the throw, but Red Sox starter Erik Hanson, who had made his lone All-Star Game appearance at midseason, struck out Murray swinging to end an eventful but scoreless first frame.

After retiring Greenwell and Naehring, Hershiser got into an even bigger jam in the top of the second. In this game, Kennedy started Willie McGee in right field, shifted Hosey from right to center, and benched Tinsley. McGee made the move look wise by singling, Macfarlane singled, and Hershiser walked the pesky Alicea to load the bases with two outs for Hosey. Hershiser got Hosey to ground to second "and was never remotely in trouble the rest of the way."[10]

Neither team threatened again until the bottom of the fourth, when Murray, who had no triples in 480 regular-season plate appearances in 1995, tripled to left with one out. But Hanson pitched himself out of trouble by striking out Thome swinging and Ramirez looking.

Macfarlane singled to lead off the fifth, his second hit of the game and the third by the Red Sox, who would have no more hits in the game. With one out, Hosey replaced Macfarlane on a fielder's choice and stole second, but Valentin struck out swinging to end the inning.

"Hanson, who had been pitching marvelously for four innings, lost it in the fifth, a bizarre inning," noted a Boston sportswriter.[11] The patient Indians took the lead for good in the bottom of the fifth. Sorrento walked and went to second on Alomar's sacrifice. "Macfarlane signaled for a fastball, but Hanson threw a curve. The pitch crossed up his catcher, hit him in the groin and knocked him down. Sorrento took advantage and scooted to third. For the first time, Hanson appeared rattled."[12] He walked Lofton. Vizquel's double scored both runners. After Baerga popped out, Hansen passed Belle intentionally before getting Murray to ground out to Vaughn. Cleveland led 2-0 after five.

Both teams went down in order in the sixth and the seventh. In the eighth, Hershiser walked Alicea again and got Hosey to hit into a fielder's choice. Hargrove replaced Hershiser, who had "good movement on his fastball and a breaking pitch that fell off the plate"[13] in throwing "a near-flawless game,"[14] walking two and striking out seven. Tavarez got Valentin to pop to Baerga, and Assenmacher came on to face Vaughn. "He took the first pitch for a called strike, then swung and missed at a ball that was far outside. After taking a ball, Vaughn swung and missed badly again."[15] Assenmacher had struck out Vaughn for the second straight game, ending the eighth.

Cleveland broke the game open in the bottom of the eighth. With one out, Belle walked, Hanson's fourth walk of the game. "Murray's two-run homer on a Hanson changeup … sealed the verdict,"[16] making the score 4-0. Hanson got the final two batters, but Kennedy may have stayed with his starter too long. Unlike Hargrove, who had hooked his pitcher after an eighth-inning walk, Kennedy, in the same situation, left his hurler in with disastrous results.

"The fireworks and dancing and music and car horns began after Jose Mesa threw four pitches and got three outs,"[17] easily retiring Canseco, Greenwell, and Naehring in the ninth, leaving Cleveland in prime position to close out the ALDS if the Indians could capture a game in Boston.

Cleveland Indians 8, Boston Red Sox 2 – October 6, 1995 at Fenway Park

Charles Nagy gave up one run in seven innings, Jim Thome drove in Cleveland's first three runs, and the Indians swept the Red Sox with an 8-2 win in Boston, the Red Sox' 13th consecutive postseason loss.

Boston starter Tim Wakefield, who would finish third in the 1995 Cy Young race and 13th in the MVP balloting, retired the first four batters. Nagy, a New Englander from Connecticut who had faced Vaughn in high school,[18] struggled with his control in the first inning and throughout the game, walking two in the first but getting Greenwell to hit into a Vizquel-to-Baerga force.

Cleveland got on the board in the second. Wakefield, also wild, walked Murray with one out before Thome hit "a two-run homer around the foul pole in right field to stake Cleveland to a 2-0 lead in the second inning."[19] Nagy retired the side in order in the bottom of the second, and Wakefield got the first two in the top of the third. But Baerga's single followed by consecutive walks to Belle and Murray again loaded the bases for Thome. He, too, walked, scoring Baerga with what would turn out to be the winning run.

"The bottom of the third typified the Sox' frustration in this series. Boston had runners on second and third with one out and Mo Vaughn and Jose Canseco due up. Vaughn struck out swinging, extending his slump to 0 for 12, then Canseco lined to left to end the inning and give Jose a line of 0 for 11."[20]

After the Indians went down in order in the top of the fourth, Boston put together three straight singles and Macfarlane's sacrifice fly to make the score 3-1. With two on and two out, "leadoff man Dwayne Hosey hit a would-be double inside first base. Sorrento somehow tumbled down and stopped it, scrabbling to his knees to throw to Nagy for the final out of the inning."[21]

Wakefield "looked as if he were finding himself again,"[22] getting Cleveland out easily in the top of the fifth and working on a streak of retiring seven straight. Baerga's error and a walk to Canseco (one of only two times he would reach base in the ALCS) put two on with one out, but Nagy struck out Greenwell and got designated hitter Reggie Jefferson, who played just this game in the ALDS as Canseco moved to right field, to ground to Baerga to escape.

The Indians broke the game wide open in the top of the sixth to put the contest and series out of reach. Murray singled to reach for the third straight time. After Thome flied out to Greenwell, Ramirez walked. Sorrento "lined a single just over second baseman Luis Alicea's glove"[23]; Murray "had to hold up while leading off second … [but] still scored, challenging Jose Canseco's arm, while Manny Ramirez lumbered into third."[24] Alomar doubled in Ramirez to make the score 5-1 and knock out Wakefield. Rheal Cormier came on to strike out Lofton, but Vizquel singled in a pair, and Baerga doubled in Omar. Cleveland led 8-1 in the top of the sixth, and sold-out Fenway grew as quiet as a library.[25]

Nagy, who "was in command for most of seven innings,"[26] got through his final two unscathed, getting the bottom of the order easily in the sixth and pitching around an error and his fifth walk in the seventh. Tavarez took over in the eighth and gave up a meaningless run on a groundout after three straight singles. Assenmacher again struck out Vaughn in the ninth swinging "at a pitch over his head"[27] and stayed on to get Canseco and Greenwell. Belle caught Greenwell's fly to end the game and the series, closing a fitting sweet cycle of revenge on a "cheesy"[28] Red Sox team that had accused him in Game One of cheating with his bat.

Cleveland would face the winner of the New York–Seattle series in the ALCS, while Boston would mourn a sudden end to a surprising season that just earlier in the week had seemed so promising.

NOTES

1. Mike Sullivan, "Indians Top Red Sox in 13 – Pena's Homer Puts an End to Marathon Playoff Opener, 5-4," *Columbus Dispatch*, October 4, 1995.

2. Jackie MacMullan, "The Opener Definitely Was a Game for All Time," *Boston Globe*, October 5, 1995: 85.

3. Nick Cafardo, "A Protective Measure by Vaughn," *Boston Globe*, October 3, 1995: 29. Mike Sullivan, "Loss of O'Leary Hits Boston Outfield Depth – Back Injury to Keep Him Out of Series," *Columbus Dispatch*, October 4, 1995.

4. Dan Shaughnessy, "Boston Sent into Mourning after Long Night," *Boston Globe*, October 4, 1995: 85.

5. Mike Sullivan, "Martinez Relishes Third Chance," *Columbus Dispatch*, October 3, 1995.

6. Dan Shaughnessy, "Their Opening Act Almost Never Closed," *Boston Globe*, October 5, 1995: 81.

7. Paul Hoynes, "Indians Win in 13; Pena Ends It with Home Run," *Cleveland Plain Dealer*, October 4, 1995.

8. Paul Hoynes, "For Tribe, It's a New Ballgame; Despite Game's Best Record, Indians Must Start Fresh in Postseason," *Cleveland Plain Dealer*, October 3, 1995.

9. Nick Cafardo, "Pena Ends a Corker in 13th; His Home Run Finishes Off Red Sox," *Boston Globe*, October 4, 1995: 85.

10. Peter May, "Hershiser Has Put His Mind to It," *Boston Globe*, October 5, 1995: 82.

11. Nick Cafardo, "Hershiser Has Sox's Number; Indians Righthander Helps Leave Vaughn, Canseco and Boston in a Huge Hole," *Boston Globe*, October 5, 1995: 81.

12. Jackie MacMullan, "Hanson Gets No Dividends; Pitcher Is Lacking a Supporting Cast," *Boston Globe*, October 5, 1995: 82.

13. George Willis, "Hershiser Still Has the Stuff for Success," *New York Times*, October 5, 1995.

14. Susan Vinella, "Hershiser Shuts Out Red Sox," *Dayton Daily News*, October 5, 1995.

15. Dan Shaughnessy, "Erstwhile Sluggers Zeroing In on Futility," *Boston Globe*, October 5, 1995: 81.

16. Paul Sullivan, "Hershiser Lifts Indians to 2-0 Lead," *Chicago Tribune*, October 5, 1995: 1.

17. Michael Holley, "Indians Are Up-Tempo; The Music Is Sweet as Cleveland Eyes a Sweep," *Boston Globe*, October 5, 1995: 83.

18. Nick Cafardo, "Bottom Line for Sox: Wake or a Funeral? Knuckleballer Is Their Last Hope," *Boston Globe*, October 6, 1995: 37.

19. Mike Sullivan, "Indians Finish Off Red Sox; Nagy Pitches a Beauty as Tribe Completes Sweep with 8-2 Win," *Columbus Dispatch*, October 7, 1995.

20. Dan Shaughnessy, "And That's All, Folks; Red Sox End It with a Whimper, Indians Roll, 8-2," *Boston Globe*, October 7, 1995: 1.

21. Bill Livingston, "The Indians Clinch the AL Something," *Cleveland Plain Dealer*, October 7, 1995.

22. Nick Cafardo, "It's a 1-2-3 Outing for Red Sox; Indians Make Still Another Sweeping Playoff Statement," *Boston Globe*, October 7, 1995: 71.

23. Paul Hoynes, "Sorrento's Play Cited as a Key in Game 3," *Cleveland Plain Dealer*, October 8, 1995.

24. Harvey Araton, "Fenway Is Anything but Friendly to the Red Sox," *New York Times*, October 8, 1995.

25. The author, a fan of the New York Yankees, had moved to Massachusetts in the spring of 1995 and attended 13 regular-season games at Fenway Park before buying a bleacher seat to Game Three at the box office the morning of the game. The silence in the ballpark for the second half of Game Three proved lasting.

26. Frank Dell'Apa, "All Things Considered, Total Package Was Too Much," *Boston Globe*, October 7, 1995: 76.

27. Michael Madden, "Vaughn and Canseco Simply Lost Contact," *Boston Globe*, October 7, 1995: 71.

28. Dan Shaughnessy, "They're Slump Lords Now; Sox Couldn't Be in Worse Neighborhood," *Boston Globe*, October 6, 1995: 37.

1995 AMERICAN LEAGUE CHAMPIONSHIP SERIES

BY STEVE WEST

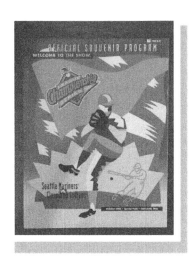

Game One: Tuesday, October 10, 1995 at the Kindome / Seattle 3, Cleveland 2

The 1995 American League Championship Series featured two teams with a long history of failure. The Cleveland Indians hadn't been in the playoffs since the 1954 World Series, and the Seattle Mariners were in their first-ever postseason. Even their recent history hadn't given much room for optimism: "Three years ago, this would have been nobody's idea of the dream American League playoff series," wrote Jayson Stark.[1]

The Indians had cruised for the last month, having won their division by 30 games, and sweeping the Red Sox in the Division Series. This gave them an extra couple of days of rest, and allowed them to line up their rotation, but even though they were heavy favorites, they weren't counting their wins. "This team is not the champion of the American League yet," Orel Hershiser said. "What we've accomplished is just to qualify to have a shot at that."[2]

The Mariners had been fighting though, battling through a one-game playoff to break the AL West tie against the Angels, and then a tough Division Series, losing the first two games to the Yankees before winning the last three. The last of those games was an 11-inning finale in Seattle that had exhausted the team. Mariners manager Lou Piniella had used ace Randy Johnson in Friday's game, and Johnson threw 117 pitches; and again on Sunday for three innings in relief, winning both games. This put Piniella in a bind, not sure how his rotation would line up against the Indians. "You can tell me one and you might be closer to the right one than I am right now," he said.[3] Piniella ended up surprising everyone by adding rookie Bob Wolcott to the ALCS roster and announcing him as the Game One starter. Wolcott had pitched in Double A and Triple A most of the season, making just six starts for Seattle during the year. He hadn't pitched in 10 days, and hadn't started in 23 days.

The one thing the Mariners did have was home-field advantage, which they had used to beat the Yankees. Major League Baseball had decided before the season that the AL East and West champs would have home-field advantage, which led to the odd situation in which the Indians, with by far the best record in the regular season (14 games better than the Red Sox, and 21 games ahead of the Mariners), would have no advantage. The Mariners had a very good record at home – they were 19-3 in their last 22 games in the Kingdome, including the playoffs – and hoped to use that to propel them to the World Series. But the Mariners were still underdogs, so much so that Jim Litke wrote, "Anything beyond a five-game series against Cleveland would be a moral victory."[4]

The day before the first game the Mariners held a rally for their fans, who waved signs with the motto the team had adopted: "Refuse to Lose." At the rally Piniella spoke to the crowd. "When it's all said and done, we're going to go to the World Series," he said, and talked about the crowd noise in the Kingdome. Indians starter Dennis Martinez replied by saying, "The best way to keep the crowd quiet is to win the game."[5]

The game started badly for the rookie Wolcott, as he walked the first three batters, throwing just one strike. Piniella came to the mound to calm him down, and had Bob Wells get up in the bullpen. Wolcott got out of the jam, though, striking out Albert Belle, getting Eddie Murray to pop foul to third on the first pitch and Jim Thome to ground out to second baseman Joey Cora, who made a diving stop to save a couple of runs. "That probably was the tale of the game right there," Indians manager Mike Hargrove said. "That set the tone. I wouldn't say we were down after that, but we lost a golden opportunity."[6]

It was Indians starter Martinez who broke first, in the second inning walking Jay Buhner, then giving up a two-run home run to Mike Blowers, who had struggled so far in the playoffs. The Indians struck back in the third, Thome driving in Carlos Baerga on a single, but Paul Sorrento hit into a double play with the bases loaded to end another threat. The two pitchers then settled down, and although Wolcott was allowing at least one baserunner every inning, the score remained 2-1 through six innings, with Martinez getting out of his own jam, a double play ending the sixth with runners at the corners.

It took Belle in the top of the seventh to tie the game on a 441-foot solo shot, but Luis Sojo untied it again in the bottom of the inning, doubling Buhner home after Thome throwing error. That got Martinez out of the game, and at the top of the eighth Wolcott came out as well, having performed far above expectations for his team. The Mariners loaded the bases in the bottom of the eighth with one out, but Eric Plunk came in and struck out Buhner and got Blowers to ground out, to keep the score close. Closer Norm Charlton came in for the ninth, struck out two and had Eddie Murray ground to short to end the game. The Mariners won 3-2, and the home field advantage had worked.

The Indians struggled all night with the bat, stranding 12 runners, one shy of the ALCS record set in 1971 and 1993. "I think as much as anything, we got a little impatient," Hargrove said.[7] But the story of the day was Wolcott, who was nervous at the start but settled down to take the plaudits: "I have to admit, I had my doubts in the first inning. But it all worked out."[8]

Game Two: Wednesday, October 11, 1995, at the Kingdome / Cleveland 5, Seattle 2

On the road, down a game in the series and with Randy Johnson scheduled to start Game Three, the Indians found their backs against the wall. "They have to win the next one and they know it," Mariners infielder Luis Sojo said.[9] The Indians were feeling the pressure for perhaps the first time in the whole season, while the Mariners felt a weight lifted off their shoulders by the winning performance of rookie Bob Wolcott in Game One.

Game Two would feature two former Dodgers teammates pitching against each other. Orel Hershiser and Tim Belcher had been starters in 1988, when each had won three games in the postseason as the Dodgers won the World Series. Now they would face each other, Belcher hoping to give the Mariners a big lead in this series, while Hershiser just wanted to keep his team alive.

A huge crowd, at 58,144 the largest ever to see the

Mariners play in the Kingdome, was excited to get things going. Stomping and yelling throughout Game One, they had clearly had an impact on the game, with several Indians talking about the crowd noise afterward. But Hershiser was used to the noise, indeed he said he often fed off it even when it was coming from the other side.

Just as in Game One, both sides threatened in the first inning of Game Two. Each left runners on first and second to end the inning, with Eddie Murray hitting a fly to deep left to end the top of the inning on a sliding catch by Ken Griffey Jr. But the pitchers settled down, allowing scattered hits until the fifth inning. In the top of the fifth, Manny Ramirez singled, and when Paul Sorrento grounded to first, Tino Martinez threw to second to get Ramirez out, but Luis Sojo dropped the ball when he tried to throw back to first. This opened the door for the Indians, as after Sandy Alomar Jr. flied out, Kenny Lofton singled and Omar Vizquel walked to load the bases. Carlos Baerga came up and singled up the middle, scoring two runs, and all of a sudden the pressure that had been on the Indians since the start of the series seemed to lift.

In the top of the sixth Belcher again got two quick outs, but this time Ramirez homered to right, then a single and a screaming line-drive triple by Alomar past Vince Coleman in left added another run to make it 4-0, Indians. Griffey led off the bottom of the sixth with a home run, tying a record with his sixth home run in a single postseason, but Ramirez hit his second home run of the game in the top of the eighth to put the lead back to four runs. Jay Buhner's home run off Jose Mesa in the bottom of the ninth did little damage, as the game ended with a 5-2 Indians win and the series was tied 1-1 as they returned to Cleveland.

Hershiser got the win with an outstanding performance, going eight innings and allowing just four hits. His only walk was intentional, and the only runner to pass second base was Griffey on the home run. From a hit by pitch with one out in the third to a Griffey single with two out in the eighth, he allowed just two baserunners, Coleman reaching on a strikeout/wild pitch and the Griffey home run. Hershiser could hardly have been better for his team. Even his former teammate was impressed: "That was the best pitching you're ever going to see on the planet," said Belcher.[10]

The other star of the game was Manny Ramirez. He came into this game 1-for-16 in the playoffs, feeling out of sorts and struggling to get things going. Working with hitting coach Charlie Manuel, he adjusted his batting stance, spreading his feet so he could get a little lower in the box. It paid off this night, his 4-for-4 game with two home runs giving him his first home runs since September 6, and the first multi-homer postseason game in Indians history.

For both teams, the result felt pivotal in the series. "Tonight, as far as we were concerned, we had to win this game. I can't emphasize that enough. If this was a test of our character, we passed," said Hargrove.[11] Lou Piniella said, "When you win the first one, naturally you get a little greedy. It just didn't happen."[12] The Indians returned home feeling much better about themselves, while Ken Griffey Jr. summed it up for many people: "It's still early, man. ... We've still got a lot of games left in this series."[13]

Game Three: Friday, October 13, 1995 at Jacobs Field / Seattle 5, Cleveland 2

The series now moved to Cleveland, where the Mariners were able to get Randy Johnson up for the first time, having rested him since the end of the Division Series. "I'm strong and ready to go. I haven't had any discomfort," he said.[14] Lou Piniella was feeling confident: "We pitched a rookie in the first game and we haven't even used our best pitcher (Randy Johnson) yet. Looking at it from that aspect, we're not in bad shape."[15] On the other side of the field, Mike Hargrove was expecting his team to battle as they always did. "I don't think anyone has told Randy that if you throw your glove out there that you're going to win," Hargrove said.[16]

Meanwhile, the governor of Washington, Mike Lowry, and state legislators were working on plans to fund a new ballpark for the Mariners. An election in September had defeated a sales tax to pay for a new ballpark. Mariners ownership had indicated that if they didn't get a new ballpark, they would look to move the franchise. As discussions went back and forth, the knowledge that the Mariners were still playing baseball while they debated was certainly helping the push for the new ballpark. The state legislature went into emergency session on Thursday to discuss the issue, and continued on Friday. On Friday evening the members took breaks in their deliberations to watch the Mariners game, and continued their negotiations afterward.

The Indians changed their lineup to face Johnson, switching to an almost all-right-handed lineup. Herbert Perry replaced Paul Sorrento at first and Alvaro Espinoza was at third instead of Jim Thome. The only left-handed batter was leadoff man Kenny Lofton. On the mound for Cleveland was Charles Nagy.

Jay Buhner followed up his home run on Friday night with a solo shot to lead off the second inning. In the top of the third, Ken Griffey singled with two out, then stole second and went to third on a wild throw by catcher Sandy Alomar, with the ball sailing into center field. An error by Espinoza allowed Griffey to score and made it 2-0, Mariners. In the bottom of the fourth, the Indians pulled a run back when Lofton tripled just over left fielder Vince Coleman's glove, and scored on Omar Vizquel's sacrifice fly. From then until the eighth inning, the pitchers began to control the game, although the Indians stranded the tying run at third in the fifth.

In the eighth it all began to go wrong for the Mariners. Espinoza lifted a fly to deep left, and Buhner misjudged it as he backpedaled, his error allowing Espinoza to reach second. Wayne Kirby pinch-ran, and when Lofton singled he scored the tying run. The two managers then got busy earning their keep, making a flurry of changes. In the ninth Piniella let Johnson go to the mound before coming out to pull him, which allowed Norm Charlton some extra time to warm up. The biggest cheer of the night came when Johnson was pulled, as the Indians crowd now thought they would get to the Mariners.

Charlton came into the tied game, and in the bottom of the ninth hit Albert Belle, who twisted his ankle trying to jump out of the way. The Indians couldn't take advantage of the leadoff runner, though, and the score stayed tied until the 11th. With two out, Tino Martinez worked a 3-and-1 count off Eric Plunk, and Mike Hargrove decided to walk him, setting up the righty-righty matchup on Jay Buhner. His error had allowed the Indians to tie the game in the eighth, but he took care of that with a three-run homer to make the score 5-2. "Now you've done it," Griffey yelled at Plunk. "You gave us three instead of one."[17] After the game the intentional walk was questioned, but Hargrove had no doubt. "That's a no-decision as far as I'm concerned," Hargrove said. "You put the lefty on and go with the odds."[18]

In the bottom of the 11th, Piniella left Charlton in, even though he'd already thrown two innings. Charlton got Baerga, Belle, and Ruben Amaro (who had earlier run for Eddie Murray) out to end the game, but whether the pitcher would be available for the next couple of days was now in question. "I don't believe in trying to save too much for the next day. You get what you can and move forward," said Piniella.[19]

With the Indians' first loss in 15 extra-inning games this season, the Mariners took a 2-to-1 series lead and knew that at worst they'd be finishing the series in their own ballpark. As for Buhner, he'd gone from goat to hero in the space of a few innings, and all the talk was about his turnaround. "How's that for redemption?" said Piniella. "Guy misjudges a fly ball and then redeems himself with a home run. Can't do better than that."[20]

Game Four: Saturday, October 14, 1995 at Jacobs Field / Cleveland 7, Seattle 0

On Saturday Albert Belle walked into the clubhouse on crutches, nearly giving manager Mike Hargrove a heart attack. "I thought he was joking," said Wayne Kirby when Belle walked in,[21] but the injury sustained when he was hit by Norm Charlton on Friday night was serious. X-rays were negative, but he was going to miss at least one game. Worse followed for the Indians when starting catcher Sandy Alomar showed up with a stiff neck, which he had slept on badly in the night. Now Hargrove had two starters out of the lineup, and he also decided that Dennis Martinez wouldn't be ready on three days' rest, so Ken Hill was sent to the mound to face Andy Benes.

Back in Washington state, the House of Representatives passed a stadium bill and sent it to the Senate, and later on Saturday the Mariners got the good news that the Senate had also passed it, meaning the Mariners would get a new $320 million ballpark. It was contingent on the King County Council passing a sales tax, and although that was going to be a tough sell it was also expected to pass.

Cold weather had come in overnight, with a game-time temperature of 53 compared with 79 the night before, and it was windy and drizzling. In the first Kenny Lofton sparked things again, a leadoff single followed by a steal of second and a throwing error by catcher Dan Wilson allowed Lofton to go to third. With Omar Vizquel up, Lofton kept bluffing to steal home, which so unnerved Benes that he walked Vizquel, who was 0-for-14 in the series. The next batter, Carlos Baerga, grounded to second, allowing Lofton to score the first run of the game. And the batter after that, Eddie Murray, homered to deep right to make it 3-0, and the Indians were rolling.

In the second inning, backup catcher Tony Peña singled. Wayne Kirby hit a chopper to the hole between third and short. Mike Blowers fielded it and threw out Kirby, but as Peña rounded second, he saw that no one was covering third, and beat Blowers to the bag in a footrace. Lofton then hit a sacrifice fly to right and the heads-up baserunning had cost the Mariners a run.

In the top of the third, the Mariners got runners to second and third after Hill had walked two, but Edgar Martinez couldn't come through. The Indians once more took advantage, a Baerga single to third followed by Jim Thome's home run, and at 6-0 the home crowd was going crazy. Again and again the Mariners gave themselves chances, and each time they failed to capitalize. In the second, third, and fourth innings they stranded two runners. In the fourth they had a single and a double to make it second and third with nobody out, but Hill came through to strike out Blowers and Luis Sojo, then got Wilson to ground out. "I was fortunate to get out of that inning. That gave me even more confidence," Hill said.[22]

In the bottom of the fifth inning, as Baerga was batting, the Indians mascot, Slider, fell off the center-field wall while attempting a somersault. He landed on the warning track unnoticed, and as Baerga stroked a single to left field Slider crawled to the bullpen door. He turned out to have torn ligaments in his knee and would miss the rest of the postseason, although someone else donned the mascot costume and appeared at later games wearing a bandage on their knee and using crutches.

After that the Indians missed a chance in the fifth, leaving the bases loaded, but in the sixth they tacked on a run as Kirby singled and Vizquel doubled him home to make the score 7-0. It would remain that way the rest of the game, despite another flurry of changes in the late innings. The game ended with pinch-hitter Alex Rodriguez making his first ALCS appearance (after one at-bat in the ALDS). He struck out against Alan Embree to end the game and tie the series at two games apiece.

After the game all the talk was about the pitching. Benes had struggled badly, giving up six runs in 2⅓ innings. "I was only ahead of one batter. They took advantage," he said. "I have no excuses."[23] His manager wasn't feeling any more charitable, noting that Benes didn't have a physical problem, it was just bad pitching: "We didn't notice anything mechanically wrong. ... He got a few pitches up, and they hit 'em."[24] Piniella didn't even seem to be concerned about hitting star Edgar Martinez, who had hit .356 during the regular season and .571 during the ALDS. "His timing seems to be a bit off," said Piniella about the player who was just 1-for-15 in the series.[25]

The Indians felt that the tide had turned in their favor. Hill had thrown seven shutout innings in his first postseason start, keeping the Mariners off-balance all night. With the top three starters now available for the Indians and Randy Johnson likely available for only one game, they felt that even though the series would definitely go back to Seattle, they were now in the driving seat.

Meanwhile the NLCS ended as the Atlanta Braves completed a sweep of the Cincinnati Reds, giving them several extra days of rest before the World Series began the following Saturday.

Game Five: Sunday, October 15, 1995, at Jacobs Field / Cleveland 3, Seattle 2

The fifth game of the series began with the Indians attempting to reverse their curse by having Rocky Colavito throw out the first pitch. It was a cold day, with a swirling wind making everything feel colder. "The wind was a factor in everything," said Omar Vizquel.[26]

Mike Hargrove decided to start Orel Hershiser, moving him up ahead of Dennis Martinez because of the weather and because Martinez had a stiff shoulder. Even so, Hershiser was not expected to go more than five or six innings on short rest.

Lou Piniella changed his lineup, hoping to find the right combination to spark his team. He benched Vince Coleman, 1-for-16 in the series, and Mike Blowers, shifted Joey Cora to leadoff and moved Edgar Martinez from cleanup to the second spot. He then moved the hot-hitting Jay Buhner to cleanup to try to take advantage of his streak. With not many options in his pitching staff, he turned to Chris Bosio to start the game.

Things started quickly for the Indians, Vizquel reaching base in the home first when Tino Martinez let the ball go through his legs for an error, taking second on Baerga's single, stealing third, and scoring on Eddie Murray's single. In the top of the third Hershiser had three strikeouts, but wrapped them around a single by Joey Cora, a stolen base, and a ground-rule double by Ken Griffey, which tied the game at 1-1.

The weather bothered everyone all night long, and in the fifth inning a windblown Griffey fly ball glanced off Albert Belle's glove in left for an error. Cora, running hard from first, came around to score when Belle's throw home bounced and hit him in the back, giving Belle a second error on the play as Griffey went to second base.

Back came the Indians. With Eddie Murray on base in the bottom of the sixth, Bosio threw a sinker that didn't sink and Jim Thome hit it 440 feet into the second deck in right field, and the Indians took a 3-2 lead. Bosio was done, but the Mariners were still trying. In the seventh, back-to-back errors by first baseman Paul Sorrento put two runners on base. After a fielder's choice, the Mariners had first and third with one out, but Hargrove turned to his bullpen. Paul Assenmacher came in and struck out Griffey on three pitches, then got Buhner on a 2-and-2 count. "I just looked stupid trying to hit a couple of pitches I never should have swung at," said Buhner.[27]

Through the rest of the game both sides had their chances. "We missed the opportunity this time and others, and you can't do that at this time in the season," Griffey said.[28] In the bottom of the seventh, the Indians had the bases loaded with one out, but Bill Risley struck out Thome, then got Manny Ramirez to fly to right. In the eighth with runners on first and second and one out, Luis Sojo lined into a double play. The Mariners had sent their runners, which made Vizquel move to cover second base, where he had an easy catch of the line drive and tag of Alex Diaz coming down from first. Had the runners not been moving, Vizquel would never have caught the ball and it might have gone all the way to the wall. A game of inches.

The Mariners' final opportunity came with two out in the ninth and Edgar Martinez facing Jose Mesa. Martinez hit a deep fly down the right field line but in the gusting wind it curved foul. Finally, on the 10th pitch of the at-bat, he lined a ball to the center-field warning track but Lofton raced back and made the catch, ending the game with a 3-2 Indians win and a 3-games-to-2 Indians series lead.

"That was a big, huge win for us," said Hershiser,[29] who in earning his seventh career postseason win, broke Lefty Gomez's record for the most postseason wins without a loss. In the other clubhouse, Bosio was disappointed in the outcome but not in his effort. "I kept us in the game," he said. "I gave it all I had."[30] Piniella was still pushing his team's chances, saying, "Believe me, we've been in this position before, and like I said after the two games in New York, we're down but not out yet."[31]

Game Six: Tuesday, October 17, 1995, at the Kingdome / Cleveland 4, Seattle 0

The series now returned to Seattle, where the Mariners were confident they could repeat their result from the ALDS. "We were down two games against New York (in the first round) and we came home and swept them," said Randy Johnson.[32] They were running out of pitchers though, and Lou Piniella changed his rotation once again. Johnson was tired, and the plan had been that if they had the lead in the series they would save him for a seventh game. But without the lead, Piniella was forced to bring him back in game six, and figure out what to do in a possible game seven later. Johnson would be pitching for the fifth time in 16 days. Piniella also changed his lineup back to what it had been, since the changes he made in game five had not worked.

The Mariners did get some good news during the day, with Washington Governor Mike Lowry signing the bill the Legislature had approved to fund a new ballpark for the team. They still had a major hurdle to get over, with the King County Council balking at paying as much money as the bill required them to. The political negotiations would continue.

The Indians had pushed Dennis Martinez back to get him extra rest. With a sore arm and a sore leg (he was planning offseason surgery to repair the knee), he needed the extra time, and being able to pitch in the warmer Kingdome instead of the cold Jake would also help him. Before the game Martinez talked to Mike Hargrove, who then announced that Sandy Alomar was scratched due to his sore neck, and Tony Peña would start. Peña had been Martinez's favorite catcher during the season, catching all but four of his starts, and Martinez may have wanted the comfort of the catcher he knew best. It would be another game in the series where the starting pitchers were former teammates, Martinez and Johnson having been together in Montreal a few years earlier.

Albert Belle had come out of the fifth game in the seventh inning because his sore ankle had stiffened up, and skipped batting practice on Monday to rest it further. The Indians changed their lineup, putting the right-handers Herbert Perry and Alvaro Espinoza back in to face the left-handed Johnson.

Before the game, Cleveland complained about the height of the pitching mound. After measuring, the umpires made the grounds crew reduce the height of the mound by half an inch. Anything to reduce the advantage the 6-foot-10 Johnson would have. The fans would try to help with that advantage though; with 58,489 in the ballpark, a record was set again for the Kingdome.

The danger man for the Indians was Kenny Lofton, who had been sparking them all series long. Johnson knew it, and in the first at-bat of the game he threw a fastball at Lofton's head, knocking him down and setting the tone. Lofton struck out and went back to the bench scared, and struck out again in the third before teammates on the bench talked to him and calmed him down. Otherwise there was little action in the early part of the game, both pitchers mostly dominating, but in the fifth Espinoza reached on a groundball to the hole between first and second, when Joey Cora fielded the ball but threw behind Johnson who was covering first. The error allowed Espinoza to reach second, and Lofton, now calm and looking for payback after the earlier brushback, singled to left, scoring Espinoza with the first run of the game.

The Mariners could not get much working on offense, Martinez keeping them off-balance all night long. They wasted an opportunity in the seventh, getting runners to second and third before stranding them. And that proved to be a turning point, because in the top of the eighth the Indians broke things open. Peña doubled to open the inning (Ruben Amaro pinch-ran), then Lofton got a bunt single and stole second. With the next batter up, a pitch tipped off catcher Dan Wilson's mitt for a passed ball toward the Cleveland dugout. Amaro ran down from third to score, and as Wilson trotted after the ball, Lofton rounded third and kept running. Too late, both

Wilson and Johnson realized that Lofton hadn't stopped, and he slid in to easily score. "I was trying to bluff and run real hard and see how they reacted off me. And they never reacted, so I just kept running," said Lofton.[33] "Kenny scoring from second base on that play probably was the biggest in that it really did seem to take the wind out of their sails and pump us up," said Hargrove. "I thought it was the determining factor in the game."[34] Two batters later, Carlos Baerga hit a home run to make it 4-0, driving Johnson from the game. "I'm not making any excuses, but I was getting tired. I wasn't overpowering anybody tonight," Johnson said.[35]

The Mariners couldn't do anything the rest of the way against the Indians bullpen, and the Indians completed the win and a 4-2 series victory. After such a long career Martinez was ecstatic to have earned his first postseason win, becoming at 40 the oldest pitcher to win an LCS game. He had excelled throughout the night, giving up just four hits in seven innings. Even Piniella was impressed, saying, "He changed speeds. He threw to spots. He was like a surgeon out there."[36] The Indians celebrated on the field and in the clubhouse, and when their flight returned to Cleveland in the early hours of the morning they were greeted by thousands of fans at the airport, cheering their team's first World Series appearance in 41 years.

Although many felt that Lofton deserved the MVP of the series, it went to Orel Hershiser. He had won two critical games, shutting the Mariners down both times when a switch in the result could have turned the entire series in the other direction. Hershiser earned a $50,000 bonus for winning ALCS MVP honors. Lofton had sparked the team all the way, hitting .458, stealing five bases in the series, taking the extra base in game six, and making some great fielding plays.

For the Mariners, they were defeated but not down. The fans had given Johnson a standing ovation when he left the game, and they stayed and cheered the team at the end, until players came out for a curtain call. Some of the players wandered about the field, throwing souvenirs into the crowd. The Mariners had scored just 12 runs in the series, the fewest ever in a six-game ALCS, beating the previous record of 23 scored by the White Sox in 1993. Despite Ken Griffey Jr. hitting .333 and Jay Buhner .304, as a team the Mariners hit just .184, with Edgar and Tino Martinez combining to go 5-for-45 in the middle of the lineup. A disappointing end for the hitters, who had been dominated throughout by the Cleveland staff.

The following Monday the King County Council finally approved an ordinance that would ensure that the Mariners new ballpark would be built. It essentially accepted the plan that had come out of the legislature, putting taxes on restaurants, car rentals, and ballpark tickets to pay for the new ballpark. The team's performance in the last month was a key factor in getting the plan through the political minefields. "To be brutally frank, this has a great deal to do with the team's success on the field and that indefinable feeling of public oneness they created in this community," said Mariners Chairman John Ellis.[37] "It was a season where baseball in Seattle was saved," said Piniella.[38]

NOTES

1 Jayson Stark, "A Series With Everything," *Elyria* (Ohio) *Chronicle-Telegram*, October 10, 1995: B2.

2 "Indians Having Fun Playing Waiting Game," *Intelligencer Record*, October 9, 1995: B-1.

3 Jim Cour, "Seattle Staff in Jumble," *Elyria Chronicle-Telegram*, October 9, 1995: B5.

4 Jim Litke (Associated Press), "Difficult to Come Back Against Indians," *Walla Walla* (Washington) *Union-Bulletin*, October 10, 1995: 14.

5 Steve Herrick, "Tribe Out to Prove Kingdome Noise Is Just Hot Air," *Elyria Chronicle-Telegram*, October 10, 1995: 1.

6 Steve Herrick, "Indians Strand 12, Fall 3-2," *Elyria Chronicle-Telegram*, October 11, 1995: B1.

7 Bill Knight, "Indians Missed Opportunities," *Syracuse Herald-Journal*, October 11, 1995: C4.

8 Ben Walker (Associated Press), "Mariners, Braves Prevail in Openers," *Altoona* (Pennsylvania) *Mirror*, October 11, 1995: D2.

9 "Rookie Gives M's a Winning Start," *Daily Sitka* (Alaska) *Sentinel*, October 11, 1995: 8.

10 "Reds Blow Scoring Chances," *Wisconsin State Journal* (Madison), October 12, 1995: 5C.

11 "Indians Get Even with Mariners," *Valley Independent* (Monessen, Pennsylvania), October 12, 1995: 1B.

12 "M's Fall Victim to Hershiser Pitches," *Daily Sitka Sentinel*, October

12, 1995: 6.

13 Bart Hubbuch, "Mariners Love Jacobs Field," *Elyria Chronicle-Telegram*, October 13, 1995: B3.

14 Tom Boswell (*Washington Post*), "Indian Summer or Early Fall?" *Elyria Chronicle-Telegram*, October 13, 1995: B1.

15 Terry Pluto, "The Real Test Comes Tonight," *Elyria Chronicle-Telegram*, October 13, 1995: B3.

16 Paul Sullivan, "Tribe's Mr. October Cools Off Mariners," *Chicago Tribune*, October 12, 1995.

17 Mark Whicker, "Buhner Swings at Infamy – and Connects," *Orange County Register* (Anaheim, California), October 14, 1995: 4.

18 Steve Marantz, "Know Decisions," *The Sporting News*, October 23, 1995: 11.

19 Ibid.

20 Jerome Holtzman, "As Series Turns, Indians Turn to Hershiser," *Chicago Tribune*, October 15, 1995.

21 Steve Herrick, "Indians Even Series Without Belle, Alomar," *Elyria Chronicle*, October 15, 1995: C1.

22 Todd Stumpf, "Hill Fills His Role Well," *Elyria Chronicle-Telegram*, October 15, 1995: C5.

23 Jerry Romback, "Seattle Still Confident," *Elyria Chronicle-Telegram*, October 15, 1995: C5.

24 Chuck Melvin, "Thome, Murray Propel Indians to Win," *Valley Morning Star*, October 15, 1995: B8.

25 Paul Sullivan, "Rest Easy, Cleveland, Indians Tie ALCS," *Chicago Tribune*, October 15, 1995.

26 "Maybe the Postman Would've Enjoyed It," *Elyria Chronicle-Telegram*, October 16, 1995: B4.

27 Bob Finnigan *(Seattle Times)*, "3-2 Loss Sends M's Home in 3-2 Hole," *Walla-Walla Union Bulletin*, October 16, 1995: 13.

28 Ibid.

29 "Hershiser Keeps His Perfection in Prime Time," *Orange County Register*, October 16, 1995: 10.

30 "Mariners Hit with Cold Reality," *Orange County Register*, October 16, 1995: 10.

31 Chuck Melvin, "Cleveland Moves to Brink of Title with 3-2 Victory," *Indiana* (Pennsylvania) *Gazette*, October 16, 1995: 12.

32 "Cleveland Takes 3-2 Lead Over Mariners," *Daily Sitka Sentinel*, October 16, 1995: 7.

33 "Lofton Hero in Long Run," *Orange County Register*, October 18, 1995: 10.

34 Ibid.

35 "Johnson Fatigued but Proud," *Orange County Register*, October 18, 1995: 10.

36 Terry Pluto, "You Better Believe It: A Dream Come True," *Elyria Chronicle-Telegram*, October 18, 1995: B3.

37 "Play Ball! Council OKs Stadium," *Walla-Walla Union-Bulletin*, October 24, 1995: 1.

38 Art Thiel *(Seattle Post-Intelligencer)*, "Mariners Win Back City in Defeat," *Pacific Stars and Stripes*, October 20, 1995: 24.

1995 WORLD SERIES

BY JEANNE M. MALLETT

The 1995 major-league baseball season began late, still under the shadow of 1994. That year marked the first time in its history that the World Series was canceled. What two world wars could not stop, a labor dispute over caps on players' salaries did. Throughout the country baseball fans were angry and showed it. They loudly damned baseball owners and players on sports talk shows, in letters to newspapers, and, where they could, on the still-new Internet. Fantasy baseball leagues disbanded. Most importantly, to team owners and players who wanted more pay, 1995 preseason ticket sales dropped precipitously. Everywhere – except in Cleveland.

The anger of Indians fans was dramatically different. In 1994, for the first time in 40 years, they had had a contending team that could win it all, just as Akron native Dick Jacobs had promised when he became Indians owner in 1986. And in 1994, they finally had their field of dreams, Jacobs Field, which had opened to rave reviews in April. Fans packed the ballpark and loved the team they saw, a combination of seasoned vets and talented, exciting youngsters, all focused on bringing baseball's World Series championship back to Cleveland. This was no *Major League*. This was the real thing. Indians fans were ecstatic. So when the 1994 season came to a screeching halt on August 12 with their Indians' record at 66-47 and the team only a game out of first place in its division, Indians fans were angry. They'd been cheated out of a champion. And unlike the rest of the baseball world, in Cleveland the minute 1995 single-game ticket sales were announced to start in February 1995, at reduced prices, no less (because of the possibility of replacement players), fans started buying. Season ticket sales rose too. By the Indians' home opener on May 5, with the strike over and the players fans had come to know and love in 1994 on hand, not only was that game sold out but almost every future game. From June 12 on every game was a complete sellout, the beginning of a 455-game sellout record.

The 1995 Indians did not disappoint. They came out of the gate fast, moved into sole possession of first place in the Central Division by May 11 and never relinquished that spot, powering their way to a 100-44 record, topping their closest competitors, the Kansas City Royals, by 30 games, the best record in major-league baseball.

A new postseason alignment forced the Indians to hurdle two rounds of playoffs instead of one before they could get to the World Series. The Tribe swept through the American League Division Series, beating Boston in three straight with the combination of good pitching, speed, and timely hitting that had characterized the team throughout the season. They faced a tougher opponent in the American League Championship Series, the Seattle Mariners. In a dramatic Game Six on the road, the Indians' Dennis Martinez outpitched the Mariners' young superstar Randy Johnson for the win. The victory gave the Tribe their first American League championship in 41 years. And when the Indians' normally stoic and long-suffering manager, Mike Hargrove, screamed into Herb Score's microphone during postgame interviews, "Hey, Herbie, we're going to the Series!," Indians fans throughout the world screamed with him.[1] At last, fans believed, their Indians, so long a butt of jokes, and were now winners, destined to win it all. At a Cleveland steakhouse filled with jubilant diners, owner George Dixon III exclaimed, "We're fated to be champions this year. ... We'll go to Atlanta, and our bats will explode. ... The city is on such a roll, and this is a cherry on top."[2] The day before Game One against the Atlanta Braves, more than 30,000 fans formed a rally in Public Square in downtown. Even the dour bronze statue of Moses Cleaveland sported an Indians batting helmet.

The euphoria of Indians fans was met with the wary hopes of Braves fans. Unlike the Indians, the Braves had been to the World Series recently. After a 33-year drought and a change of home cities from Milwaukee to Atlanta, the Braves had reached the World Series in 1991, the same year the Indians lost a record 105 games. The Braves lost that Series to the Minnesota Twins. As the Indians began their climb to respectability, the Braves went to the Series again in 1992, and lost again, this time to the Toronto Blue Jays. They just missed winning the National League pennant in 1993 and were in position to win at least a wild-card spot in 1994 when the strike ended their quest. The Braves seemed able to win everything but the "Big One." Still, in 1995, the Braves seemed more dominant than in prior championship runs. They finished 21 games ahead of the Mets and the Phillies in the National League East. They won 90 games in the shortened regular season, second in the major leagues only to the Indians, who had won 100. And they swept through their postseason series against the Colorado Rockies and the Cincinnati Reds, both hard-hitting teams. Braves manager Bobby Cox, who like Indians manager Hargrove had skippered his team in bad times as well as good, summed up is team's feelings heading into the Series: "I and my coaches and everyone connected with the Atlanta Braves want to win very, very badly."[3]

Without a doubt the 1995 World Series would feature the two best teams in baseball. Oddsmakers made the Indians only slight underdogs heading into the Series. And sportswriters' predictions were almost evenly split. Invariably writers who picked the Braves did so because of their pitching, relying on the old baseball adage "Good pitching beats good hitting." One might add that, since their last World Series loss in 1992, the Braves had acquired Greg Maddux, generally assumed to be the best pitcher of the day, to join Tom Glavine and John Smoltz in future Hall of Fame rotation. Early in 1995 the Braves also installed Mark Wohlers as their closer, and further solidified their bullpen by reacquiring Alejandro Pena late in the season as setup man and relying on former Indian farmhand Greg McMichael in middle relief. In the Braves' NLCS sweep of the Reds, the bullpen allowed only one run in 11 innings and the starters allowed only four runs in 28 innings. And, while the Braves' .250 team batting average was the second-worst in the National League, they won 25 regular-season games in their last at-bat and added four more such wins in the playoffs

Still, those who picked Cleveland were best represented by Dale Hoffman of the *Milwaukee Journal Sentinel*, who picked the Indians in seven: "Their pitching is closer to the Braves' pitching than the Braves' hitting is to the Indians' hitting."4 The Tribe's rotation was led by veteran and proven postseason winners, 37-year-old Orel Hershiser and 40-year-old Dennis Martinez. Added to complete the rotation were younger stars: Steady, hard-working Charles Nagy, who had come up through the Indians' system, and Ken Hill, a late-season addition with National League experience. The Indians, too, had a great closer in Jose Mesa, who had an American League-leading 46 saves and a microscopic 1.13 ERA. Paul Assenmacher solidified the middle relief. And the Indians pitchers were supported by one of the most dominant offenses ever assembled. Tribe batters were among the leaders in every offensive category in 1995. Albert Belle finished first in home runs (50), extra-base hits (103), and slugging percentage (.690) and tied for first in runs batted in (126). Kenny Lofton led the league in stolen bases (54). Four regulars batted better than .300 and the Indians had a .291 team batting average. While the Indians' offense did not dominate in the postseason as it had in the regular season, batting only .219 against Boston and .257 against Seattle, the Indians' pitching rotation produced a record almost matching the Braves', going 6-1 with a 1.29 ERA.

Game One – Saturday, October 21 – Atlanta-Fulton County Stadium – Maddux is Masterful

Even before the first pitch the Indians were thrown a curve. Without the 1994 strike the American League winner would have had home-field advantage in a 1995 World Series according to the MLB rule under which the leagues alternated home-field advantage. But since the last Series was in 1993, when the American League had home-field advantage, the advantage went to the National League instead. Still the Indians were confident. They had their ace, Orel Hershiser (19-6), who had never lost in seven postseason starts including World Series experience with the Los Angeles Dodgers. He would face the Braves'

Greg Maddux (21-1), who was appearing in his first World Series after posting a so-so record in this postseason of 3-2 with a 5.57 ERA.

Things started out well for the Indians as the leadoff man, center fielder Kenny Lofton, who had batted .458 in postseason play thus far with five steals and three RBIs, grounded to short, but ended up at first when Braves shortstop Rafael Belliard misplayed the ball for an error. The next batter, shortstop Omar Vizquel, struck out swinging, but Lofton stole second. During second baseman Carlos Baerga's at-bat, Lofton helped himself to third base and when Maddux got Baerga to ground out to short, Lofton sped home with the Indians' first run.

In the bottom of the first inning the Braves' leadoff man, center fielder Marquis Grissom, smacked a line-drive single and advanced to second when second baseman Mark Lemke grounded out. But rookie third baseman Chipper Jones hit a line drive to short that Vizquel turned into a double play, catching Grissom off second to end the inning.

In the bottom of the second, Braves first baseman Fred McGriff, another addition since Atlanta lost the 1992 World Series, led off with a home run to deep center field to tie the game at 1-1.

Both starting pitchers were masterful throughout the middle innings. Strikeouts and groundouts were the order of the day with only the Indians even hitting the ball to the outfield, Albert Belle's fly to deep right in the fourth inning being the hardest-hit ball.

Then came the bottom of the seventh inning. Hershiser, who like Maddux, had been cruising through the Atlanta lineup, giving up only two hits to Maddux's one, suddenly could not find the strike zone, missing high. He opened the inning by walking McGriff. When he walked the next batter, outfielder David Justice, pitching coach Mark Wiley came to the mound intending to give Hershiser a brief break. He was, after all, facing the heart of the Braves' lineup the third time around and had thrown 101 pitches. But Hershiser surprised Wiley by taking himself out of the game. Hershiser later said that while he was fine physically, he couldn't "execute." So when Wiley asked him how he felt, the veteran righty answered, "I can't make the adjustment." Hershiser said later, "I knew the mistakes I was making were right where [the next hitter Ryan] Klesko likes to hit it."[5] Given that analysis, Hershiser thought the lefty reliever Assenmacher would have a better chance of getting the left-handed Klesko out.

But when Hargrove brought in Assenmacher, Bobby Cox countered with right-handed pinch-hitter Mike Devereaux and Assenmacher walked him to load the bases. The managerial chess match continued as Hargrove, in a double switch, brought in first baseman Paul Sorrento for Assenmacher and right-handed reliever Julian Tavares for Eddie Murray, who had been playing first. Cox then replaced his right-handed batter, catcher Charlie O'Brien, with lefty-swinging Luis Polonia. In a critical decision Hargrove chose to play the infield back at double-play depth, conceding a run to keep the inning from getting out of hand. And Polonia obliged, hitting a sure double-play ball to shortstop Vizquel. But then the unthinkable happened. The usually sure-handed Vizquel bobbled the ball and got only a force at second while McGriff scored from third, putting Atlanta in the lead, 2-1. Although Cox argued that Vizquel had not even had control when he touched second, the ruling stood and Cox was ready with his next move, one that effectively put the game in the bag for the Braves. With Justice on third and Polonia on first, Rafael Belliard made up for his first-inning error by executing a perfect suicide squeeze bunt that scored Justice with what turned out to be the winning run.

After grounding out to end the seventh, Maddux returned to the mound and continued his mastery over the Indians. The daring Kenny Lofton gave Tribe fans some hope in the ninth inning when he singled with one out, raced from first to third on Vizquel's groundout to second, and scored when first baseman McGriff threw wildly to third to try to get him. But Maddux got the next batter, Baerga, on a foul pop, only his 95th pitch, and the Indians' hopes were dashed. Maddux had held the best-hitting lineup in the majors to two singles.

Braves 3, Indians 2

Game Two – Sunday, October 22 – Atlanta-Fulton County Stadium – Javy Lopez Catches Indians by Surprise

With all-time home-run king Hank Aaron throwing out the ceremonial first pitch and the weather (65 degrees and dry at game time) something the large contingent of Clevelanders who had followed their heroes to Atlanta could really appreciate, Sunday evening was an almost perfect night for baseball. Tribe fans everywhere hoped for perfection on the field as well. After all, they reasoned, their team had been behind in the ALCS twice to the Mariners before beating them on the road in Seattle in six games. And whose masterful pitching had finished off the Mariners? "El Presidente" Dennis Martinez, the same Dennis Martinez who was starting for the Tribe in Game Two. Even though he was working on four days' rest instead of the six he'd had before the Seattle game and he was 40 years old, the third oldest pitcher ever to appear in a World Series, Tribe fans had faith.

But Martinez's struggles started early. After Braves' starter Tom Glavine set down the Indians in order in the top of the first inning. Martinez loaded the bases in the bottom of the first before getting slugger Ryan Klesko to pop to third. Martinez got support in the top of the second inning when the Indians again scored first, this time on a two-run homer by Eddie Murray, driving in Albert Belle, who had singled. Martinez followed by getting the Braves in order in the bottom of the second, but ran into trouble again in the third inning. He hit leadoff hitter Grissom with a pitch, then compounded his problem by trying to pick Grissom off second after the next batter, Lemke, had singled him there. Grissom moved to third on the errant throw and the next batter, Chipper Jones, drove him in with a fly ball. After Martinez got McGriff on a groundout, Justice singled to bring Lemke in from second and tie the score at 2-2.

Martinez stayed out of further trouble in the fourth and fifth innings while Glavine, a finesse pitcher like Maddux, allowed only one more hit after the home run to Murray. But after Glavine took care of the Indians in order in the top of the sixth, Martinez made a crucial mistake again. Facing the Braves' hard-hitting young catcher Javier Lopez with David Justice on base and one out, Martinez had Lopez down 1-and-2 in the count, and then threw him a fastball, which Lopez hammered to deep center field. Unlike his fourth-inning blast to right field, which Albert Belle caught against the wall, this one went well over the 402-foot sign where even the great center fielder Kenny Lofton couldn't reach it without a helicopter. Later Martinez said he'd tried to "go away" with the fastball but it had ended up in the middle of the plate. Lopez agreed it was a fastball, but it was "away" in the same spot as the changeup away he'd hit to right in the fourth. Either way, the Braves now led 4-2. Martinez struck out Belliard for the second out. But Bobby Cox then had Dwight Smith pinch-hit for Glavine. Smith singled and, after Grissom followed with another single, Hargrove pulled Martinez for Alan Embree, who got the final out.

The Indians got one run back in the top of the seventh, striking at Greg McMichael, who had replaced Glavine on the mound. Again it was not the power-hitting Indians fans had come to expect during the season. Instead speedster Kenny Lofton jumped into the breach. After McMichael got two quick outs, Lofton singled, stole second, and scored when left fielder Mike Devereaux, who had just come in to replace Klesko, over-ran Omar Vizquel's line drive, turning it into a two-base error. McMichael then walked Carlos Baerga. With two men on and Albert Belle coming up, Tribe fans were loudly welcoming the man who had hit 50 home runs and driven in 126 runs during the shortened season. But Bobby Cox brought in Alejandro Pena, who immediately dampened fans' hopes by getting Belle on a foul pop to catcher Lopez.

Still, the rest of the heat of the Indians' lineup was due up in the eighth and the Braves were pitching from their bullpen. Pena started the eighth by getting Eddie Murray to fly out. Then Manny Ramirez singled. With power-hitting Jim Thome at bat, the real drama ended up being the faceoff between two young players, Ramirez on first and Lopez behind the plate, each only in his second full major-league season. With a 2-and-2 count on Thome, Ramirez was the one who made the youthful error, taking a huge lead off first base. Catcher Lopez watched him carefully, remembering that his first baseman, McGriff, had said that the first time Ramirez singled, he took a big lead. After Manny took his lead this time, Lopez gave McGriff the sign, took the ball three Pena had thrown and in one motion threw a strike to McGriff, nailing Ramirez before he could get back. Lopez, who had already used his bat to put the Braves in the lead, used his brain and arm to snuff out the Indians' last real hope. Thome ended up walking, which would have put Ramirez at second had he not been picked off. Cox then brought in fire-balling closer Mark Wohlers, who finished the inning by getting Paul Sorrento to fly to center, then mowed down the Indians in the ninth, allowing only a two-out single to Vizquel.

Braves 4, Indians 3

Game Three – Tuesday, October 24 – Jacobs Field – Home Cooking Warms Indians' Bats and Crowd

After their two best pitchers lost in Atlanta and the vaunted Tribe power offense never got on track, many in the Cleveland media made comparisons to Game Three in 1954, when the Indians also returned home 0-2 after their two best pitchers failed to tame the New York Giants. But 1995 was as different from 1954 as night from day.

With a day off after flying back to Cleveland, Indians players were able to enjoy all the comforts of home cooking and sleep in their own beds as well as get in a full practice session the day before the next game, which would be in their beloved Jacobs Field. And Carlos Baerga, who had been playing with a sore left ankle and was 0-for-8 thus far in the Series, got to receive treatment. Baerga echoed the thoughts of his teammates when he said: "This is do-or-die for us. We've got to go out and win it right away. We can't even talk about playing Games Four or Five in Jacobs Field."[6] As a team, the Indians, after posting a .291 batting average in the regular season, were hitting .235 overall in 11 postseason games and only .125 in the Series.

Instead of facing a day game in heat and oppressive humidity hours after they arrived home by train as the 1954 team had done, the 1995 Indians had a night game after that restful night at home and another day to get ready. And on this Tuesday night, the weather was real Cleveland late-October weather, 49 degrees at game time with a 25-mph wind blowing out to right field making it feel like 29 degrees, which was more of a shock to the Braves players than to the Indians. And the sellout crowd of 41,877 may have been bundled in coats and clapping with their mittens on, but they came to cheer loudly for their Tribe.

Another plus for Indians hitters was that instead of a third finesse pitcher in a row, they were facing the fastball pitcher John Smoltz. And starting for the Tribe was the workmanlike Charles Nagy, who during the regular season had inspired the greatest run support from his teammates. But clubhouse man Tom Foster and his staff left nothing to chance. Channeling *Major League,* they brought out of hiding Joeboo, the Chia-pet version of the Indians' voodoo doll mascot in that film. They'd stationed him on a perch on a pole next to the Tribe's dugout during the season, but he'd been damaged. Now, restored to green-haired and two-eyed glory, he'd watched batting practice on Monday and, just before Game Three, he got two buckets of fried chicken donated by the Bay Village Jaycees sacrificed to him in the traditional *Major League* ceremony.

Kenny Lofton, the one Tribe star of this Series so far, had an even better idea. He called a pregame meeting with his teammates. In it the players talked about what they weren't doing right, like focusing at the plate and swinging only at good pitches. Every one of them realized that each one had to do something. Together they pledged that, if they were going down, they'd go down fighting. The Indians were ready to do battle. Mickey Mantle's widow, Mervyn, with her sons beside her, threw out the ceremonial first pitch and an inspired choice in the opening ceremonies only helped the players' determination – black and white film clips of their predecessors, the 1948 and 1954 Indians, were shown on the replay screen while "Circle of Life" from *The Lion King* thundered over the sound system.

This time the Braves took the early lead, scoring a run in the top of the first on a double by Chipper Jones followed by a single by Fred McGriff. But in the bottom of the inning the Indians struck right back. Kenny Lofton singled to lead off. Vizquel followed with a triple to deep right field, scoring Lofton. Then Carlos Baerga's groundout to first scored Vizquel.

In the bottom of the third the Tribe struck again, knocking Smoltz out of the game. Lofton, again leading off, doubled to center. Vizquel followed with a bunt single, moving Lofton to third. Baerga, with his first hit of the Series, drove in Lofton with a single to left. Albert Belle then sent a ball through the hole to center field, scoring Vizquel and moving Baerga to second. Although Smoltz struck out Eddie Murray, he walked the next batter, Jim Thome, loading the bases with one out. Bobby Cox had seen enough. He pulled Smoltz for Brad Clontz, who got Manny Ramirez to ground out into a 6-4-3 double play, ending the threat.

Meanwhile sturdy Charley Nagy mastered the Braves until the sixth inning, when he gave up a solo homer to Fred McGriff. When he gave up another home run to slugger Ryan Klesko in the top of the seventh, the crowd began to worry. The Indians' lead was slowly slipping away. But, after a stretch and a rousing "Take Me Out to the Ball Game," the Indians got an insurance run, with Kenny Lofton leading the way again. With one out, he worked a walk off lefty reliever Kent Mercker, moved to second when Vizquel grounded out, and stole third with Baerga at the plate. When Baerga singled, Lofton scored with the Tribe's fifth run. The Indians had a chance for more when the next batter, Albert Belle, walked. But Bobby Cox went to his bullpen again, dipping into what seemed an endless supply of quality relief pitchers for all situations. This time he picked Greg McMichael, who came in to strike out Eddie Murray for the third out.

Unlike Cox, Mike Hargrove had been criticized for leaving his starters in too long and, in some critics' opinions, costing the Tribe two close games. This time, though, with the Indians adding that insurance run in the bottom of the seventh and Nagy having thrown only 81 pitches, Hargrove's choice to leave him in seemed reasonable despite the two solo homers Nagy had surrendered in the prior two innings. Unfortunately for Hargrove, his faith was not rewarded. Facing the top of the Braves order, Nagy gave up a double on the first pitch to Grissom, then a run-scoring single to Luis Polonia. Hargrove brought in the lefty Assenmacher, but things did not get better. With Chipper Jones at bat, Polonia stole second. Assenmacher then walked Jones. McGriff flied out to center, moving the runners up to second and third with only one out. Assenmacher might have got out of the inning without further damage when he induced David Justice to hit a groundball to second. But Baerga booted it. Polonia scored, tying the game. Managerial maneuvers continued as Hargrove replaced Assenmacher with righty Julian Tavares and Cox countered by pinch-hitting for DH Ryan Klesko with Mike Devereaux. Devereaux responded by lashing a single to right field, scoring Jones, to put the Braves in the lead. With Justice now on second, Tavares was able to avoid further damage by getting catcher Javy Lopez to hit into a 4-6-3 double play. But the Braves were now leading and the Indians had only two innings to come back.

And come back they did, as the Tribe tied the game again in the bottom of the eighth. Sandy Alomar doubled off the Braves' premier closer, Mark Wohlers, scoring Manny Ramirez. From that point on it was a duel between two of the best closers in baseball, Wohlers and the Indians' Jose Mesa, each stretching his abilities beyond the normal one inning through the ninth and 10th. Mesa made things a bit too interesting for Tribe fans by getting into jams in both the ninth and 10th, counting on his fielders to deliver sterling plays to get him out. Rookie first baseman Herbert Perry came to his rescue in the ninth and Baerga bailed him out in the 10th. But in the top of the 11th, Mesa set down the Braves in order.

For the bottom of the 11th, Bobby Cox, figuring that Wohlers had reached his limit by pitching the equivalent of three innings since he came on to close out the eighth, replaced him with Alejandro Peña. For once Cox's move proved to be wrong. The first man Peña faced was Carlos Baerga, whose error in the eighth had led to the Braves' go-ahead run. Baerga worked Pena to a 3-and-2 count, and then lined a double to deep center. Alvaro Espinoza ran for him. Peña intentionally walked the dangerous Albert Belle and took on the venerable Eddie Murray instead. But Murray lined the first pitch to center, scoring Espinoza and giving the Indians their first World Series win in 47 years.

It was 12:42 A.M. Wednesday when the game ended, 4 hours and 9 minutes after it started, the longest night game in World Series history and the third longest of all World Series games to date. But the cold, bleary-eyed Tribe fans who remained danced their way toward the exits to the tune of Bruce Springsteen's "Glory Days," which blared from the sound system while fireworks burst into the frigid air.

Indians 7, Braves 6 (11 innings)

Game Four – Wednesday, October 25 – Jacobs Field – Battle of the Bullpens

For the second time on this Wednesday, the Indians would be playing a World Series game. They and their fans hoped the result would be the same this night as it was at 12:42 A.M., when they ended a long night of baseball by securing an 11-inning victory over Atlanta in Game Three. The Indians' prodigious hitting seemed finally back on track with 12 hits in Game Three. They'd won in their last at-bat as they'd done 28 times already this year. Jacobs Field Magic was back. And, to the relief of Tribe fans, Bobby Cox decided not to start the virtually unhittable Greg Maddux in Game Four. He chose instead the young lefty Steve Avery, who had a 7-13 record with a 4.67 earned-run average during the regular season, although his ERA in the postseason was 1.36. Mike Hargrove countered with right-hander Ken Hill, who had been picked up late in the season specifically to bolster the starting pitching in the postseason and who only the season before had finished second to Maddux in the National League Cy Young Award voting. Hill already had two playoff victories for the Tribe, one in relief and one as a starter, while pitching shutout ball.

Indians all-time great pitcher Bob Feller, a veteran of both the 1948 and 1954 American League champion teams, threw out the ceremonial first pitch. Pitching dominated the game for the first five innings, both pitchers justifying the faith their managers placed in them. The game was scoreless after five. The Braves had four hits; the Indians, two.

In the top of the sixth, however, the Braves again scored first on a one-out solo homer belted 400 feet to right field by Ryan Klesko. But Hill set down the next two batters to end the inning. In the bottom of the sixth, as they had in Game Three, the Indians immediately came back when Albert Belle homered to right. Although Belle hit his homer with two men out, the Tribe had a chance for a bigger inning as Avery gave up his fifth walk to the next hitter, Eddie Murray. Then, with Manny Ramirez at the plate and the count already 2-and-0, Avery was called for a balk and Murray went to second. Avery put Ramirez on with an intentional walk. But rookie Herbert Perry, starting in his first Series game at first base after his defensive heroics the previous night, struck out swinging.

In the top of the seventh, Hill started well, striking out Belliard. But then he walked Grissom and the next batter, Polonia, laced Hill's first pitch to deep right field for a double, scoring the speedy Grissom from first and putting the Braves back in the lead. That ended Hill's night as Hargrove brought in Assenmacher to face the heart of the Braves' lineup. But the Indians' troubles continued. Assenmacher intentionally walked Chipper Jones. Then, with Fred McGriff at bat, a passed ball put Polonia on third and Jones on second. Assenmacher struck out McGriff for the second out. But David Justice lined a single to center field, driving in both runners. Assenmacher struck out Klesko for the final out, but the damage was done; the Braves led 4-1.

Greg McMichael came on to protect Atlanta's lead in the bottom of the seventh. After giving up a leadoff double to Jim Thome, McMichael easily handled the Tribe, getting six straight ground-outs in the seventh and eighth, while Cleveland relievers struggled. Julian Tavares gave up two hits and a walk in the eighth before Alan Embree replaced him to get the final out with the bases loaded when Chipper Jones flied to deep right. In the ninth, however, it was Embree in trouble. He gave up two hits, the second a line-drive double by Javy Lopez that drove in Fred McGriff for the Braves' fifth run.

Once again the Tribe was down to its last chance and fans could only hope that what happened so many times before could happen again. Cox brought in his closer, Wohlers, despite his extended outing the night before. When the first batter, Manny Ramirez, homered to deep left field and pinch-hitter Paul Sorrento doubled to left, Tribe fans took heart. But then Cox brought forth from the bullpen yet another reliever Tribe hitters had not yet seen in the Series: Pedro Borbon. He quickly struck out Thome and Alomar. Then he faced Kenny Lofton who, for the first time in the Series, had not got on base in this game. Lofton lined a sharp drive to right, but right fielder Justice made a fine running backhanded catch near the warning track to end the game.

Braves 5, Indians 2

THE SLEEPING GIANT AWAKES 391

Game Five – Thursday, October 27 – Jacobs Field – Happy Birthday, Grover!

With the Indians down three games to one and the feared Greg Maddux again on the mound, Tribe fans packed Jacobs Field one last time, the sellout crowd inside and the hundreds outside peering through the iron gates. Win or lose, this would be the last contest in this season of dreams at Cleveland's field of dreams. And after a full night's sleep this time, fans were set to cheer their lungs out for their Tribe. They brought optimistic signs – "There is no fat lady in Cleveland"; "Not here – Not tonight." They brought streamers and balloons to help celebrate manager Mike Hargrove's 46th birthday.

Grover himself opted for a short pregame talk reminding his players that they had won the American League championship and deserved to be in this World Series. He asked them to play this game as they'd played throughout the year. To do that against Maddux, the Indians knew they had to make adjustments. The hitters would try to crowd the plate more and swing at the first two pitches. For his part, Orel Hershiser thought of adjusting his release point and thought of Sandy Koufax's advice to him when he was with the Dodgers that if he wanted the ball to go down he had to stand tall.

The team was ready to do their best. The fans were charged up. And if heavenly intervention was needed to beat Maddux, they got at least a semblance of that in the opening ceremonies. For the first time the ceremonial first pitch was thrown from outer space by Commander Ken Bowersox, on board the space shuttle Columbia, surrounded by the crew members. The ceremony was transmitted from the shuttle via satellite and played on the Jacobs Field scoreboard. Through animation the ball made its way through space to downtown Cleveland. Then the crowd saw a ball appear to fly in and land in center field near the Indians' mascot, Slider. The crowd cheered.

The cheers continued from the first pitch Hershiser threw and never stopped. And Hershiser did not disappoint. With the exception of a two-out double by Chipper Jones, he handled the top of the Braves' lineup easily. Then in the bottom of the first came ignition and liftoff for the Tribe batters against Maddux. Maddux walked the second man he faced, Vizquel. He then got Baerga on a groundout, which moved Vizquel to second. With two outs, Albert Belle came up and did what he'd done so often this year, hit the first pitch to deep right field off the top of the wall and bouncing into the crowd for a home run. For the first time, the Indians had scored earned runs off Maddux and now held a two-run lead.

Indian fans were already cheering wildly, but the inning held more drama. Maddux followed up with a first-pitch strike to the next batter, Eddie Murray. Then he threw a high, tight fastball that Murray just barely dodged. The usually quiet Murray had words with the umpire and Braves catcher O'Brien, then angrily stalked toward the mound. Both benches and bullpens emptied, with Indians players surrounding Murray to avoid a full-scale brawl. Even Hershiser came out and spoke briefly to Maddux. Maddux told him he wasn't trying to hit Murray, just "jam" him. Hershiser replied: "You can do better than that."[7] Maddux, the master of control, said nothing in reply. When the dust settled, Maddux walked Murray, but catcher O'Brien picked him off first to end the inning.

Both starting pitchers mastered the hitters through the second, third, and fourth innings, with Hershiser giving up only a leadoff homer to Polonia in the fourth. In the top of the fifth, however, Klesko singled to open the inning. The next batter, Lemke, grounded to Hershiser, who threw to second to try to get the lead runner. The throw was wild and both runners were safe. y O'Brien bunted the runners to second and third. Hershiser gave an intentional walk to pinch-hitter Dwight Smith to load the bases. Marquis Grissom then drove in the tying run with an infield single. With still only one out, Tribe fans anxiously waited. The next batter, Polonia, a key force in other games, drilled a hard grounder up the middle and the sure-handed Vizquel grabbed it and quickly turned it into an inning-ending double play. The crowd cheered in relief.

Tribe batters didn't get to Maddux again until the bottom of the sixth. With one out, Baerga doubled to left. Maddux intentionally walked his first-inning nemesis Belle. Murray's fly to right moved Baerga to third. Then, with two outs, Jim Thome, who'd had only two hits so far in the Series, singled sharply up the middle to drive in Baerga. Manny Ramirez followed with another single to right to drive in Belle. The Indians had pulled ahead, 4-2.

Hershiser added two more masterful innings, closing his eight innings of work with a flourish. Mike Mordecai, now playing short for the Braves, led off the eighth with a single and Grissom followed with a line shot at Hershiser, who snared the ball and doubled Mordecai off first. Hershiser pumped his fist, and then returned to the mound to strike out Polonia swinging. Jim Thome added an insurance solo homer in the bottom of the eighth off Brad Clontz, who had replaced Maddux in the eighth.

The Indians led 5-2 with only three outs left for the Braves. Hargrove brought in closer Jose Mesa to do the honors. Once again Mesa made the inning more interesting than Tribe fans wanted. Chipper Jones, leading off, lined deep to right, a sign of things to come. The next batter, McGriff, lined a double to right and went to third on Justice's groundout to second. But balls were being hit hard. Tribe fans could not relax. Klesko justified their worst fears when he launched a home run to deep right, cutting the Indians' lead to 5-4. Finally Mesa, as he had done 46 times during the season, turned up the heat and struck out Mark Lemke to salvage the win for the Tribe.

"Glory Days" played one last time as the Indians left the field to go on to Atlanta with their fans' deafening cheers still ringing in their ears.

Indians 5, Braves 4

Game Six – Saturday, October 28 – Atlanta-Fulton County Stadium – Justice Backs Mouth With Bat

Atlanta city officials had been so confident that Maddux would bring the Braves home a winner that they planned a victory parade for Saturday to celebrate the Braves' finally winning a World Series. Instead they got to host the Indians for Game Six and Braves fans were feeling insecure now that their ace was beaten and the Braves would face Dennis Martinez, who had pitched a Game Six gem on the road to bring the Tribe the American League championship. Would the World Series championship slip away a third time? A soaking rain Friday further dampened Atlantans' mood.

The rain washed out both teams' Friday workouts at Atlanta's ballpark as well. The Braves hitters got in some practice at the batting cage under the stands. Tribe hitters went to their videotapes of Tom Glavine, who had allowed them only two runs on three hits in Game Two. They wanted to make the right adjustments against him as they had against Maddux. The rain didn't keep Braves outfielder David Justice from sounding off. After cursing Orel Hershiser for saying Thursday that the pressure was on the Braves now, Justice ripped into Atlanta fans for not having the same boundless love for the their team as Cleveland fans did for theirs. He compared Tribe fans giving their team a steady ovation even when they were three runs down in the ninth inning of Game Four with Atlanta fans who, he said, would boo the Braves out of their own ballpark if they got behind and who hadn't seen the Braves off at the airport when they'd left for Cleveland.

The rain cleared up for Saturday night's game, although at 56 degrees with the wind blowing to right field at 15 mph, it seemed the Indians had brought their weather with them. It wasn't too cold for 51,875 fans to pack the ballpark, some with their own choice words for David Justice. "Hope your bat is as big as your mouth," read one fan's sign. Justice had struggled through the entire postseason, with a .214 batting average and no extra-base hits in 42 at-bats.

With the same starters facing each other, the game developed into even more of a pitchers' duel than Game Two. Neither side scored in the first five innings. The Tribe's 40-year-old starter, Martinez, who had allowed only two hits before the fourth, began to tire in that inning, allowing a double to Justice after two were out, then, after intentionally walking Klesko, using 12 pitches before walking Javy Lopez to load the bases. He got Belliard on a short fly to center to end the inning. In the fifth Martinez again got the first two batters out. But after a seven-pitch walk to Lemke and a single by Chipper Jones and the heavy-hitting part of the order coming up, Mike Hargrove had seen enough. He replaced Martinez after his 82nd pitch with the fresh arm of lefty Jim Poole. Poole struck out McGriff to end the threat.

In the top of the sixth, Indians catcher Tony Peña led off with a single, the first and only hit off Glavine, but Poole, batting for himself, couldn't move him to second, popping up his bunt attempt. Peña was forced out at second when Kenny Lofton hit a grounder to Glavine. Lofton stole second, but Glavine easily retired Vizquel on a foul pop to first.

Poole returned to the mound for the bottom of the sixth and David Justice, who had been on deck when McGriff struck out, stepped in. With something to prove to himself as well as Braves fans, he homered to deep right field, giving the Braves a 1-0 lead. Braves batters did no more damage to Poole in the sixth. But after another quick top of the seventh by Glavine, the Braves mounted another threat. Ken Hill started the bottom of the seventh and gave up a single to his former Expos teammate Grissom on a 3-and-1 pitch. Alan Embree relieved Hill and got the first out when Lemke sacrificed Grissom to second. Embree intentionally walked Chipper Jones. Fred McGriff then sent a liner to deep left but Albert Belle grabbed it at the wall, deflating the hopes of Braves fans. Embree had to pitch next to Justice, whose bat had suddenly awakened in this game with a walk and two hits, including the go-ahead homer. With Embree pitching carefully, Grissom stole third. Embree then walked Justice to load the bases. The Braves couldn't add to their lead, however, as the next batter, Mike Devereaux, hit a pop fly to second to end the inning. Glavine breezed through the eighth as did Indians relievers, Tavares and Assenmacher, in the bottom of the inning.

The Indians were now only three outs from the end of their season and suddenly they had to face the fireballing closer, Mark Wohlers, whom Cox brought in to start the ninth after consulting with Glavine. Glavine told his manager his back had stiffened in the eighth and, as much as he would have liked to finish the game, Wohlers was the man for the situation. With Kenny Lofton set to lead off, Indians fans hoped for one last Lofton Special miracle. It was not to be. Throwing fastballs approaching 100 mph, Wohlers got Lofton on a foul pop, then made quick work of pinch-hitter Paul Sorrento and Carlos Baerga on two fly balls to center, giving the Braves their first World Series championship in three tries. The victory parade was back on.

Braves 1, Indians 0

Series Lost, but Not the Dream

Good pitching doesn't always beat good hitting. But truly great pitching can stymie even the best hitting. The Indians, most of whom had never played in postseason games let alone the World Series, faced three future Hall of Fame pitchers and still beat two of them. Every game was close. Manager Mike Hargrove, who had also been an Indians player and coach, accentuated the positive. "This was a good season," he said. "The only thing we didn't do this year was win this thing. But we played like champions. I really feel we did."[8]

Tribe fans felt the same. Their feelings even right after the loss were, "They're still our Tribe." The fans would be ready for next year. Despite their disappointment, the players, too, sounded optimistic about the future. Carlos Baerga spoke for all when he said: "We've got to learn from our mistakes and be ready the next time we get here."[9] This was no idle boast because the foundation of this winning team was a plan that general manager John Hart and his assistant Dan O'Dowd had devised in the early '90s – sign young players to long-term contracts before they were eligible for free agency. That way a team could keep a core together for a number of years. At the time it was a revolutionary thought and it certainly didn't set well with superagent Scott Boras, who advised his clients to hold out for free agency. But two of his clients, Sandy Alomar and Carlos Baerga, were the first to sign the long-term contracts Hart offered and then led others to do so. The Indians had given them their first real chance to play and they appreciated that as well as the feel of the team. As a result the nucleus of this championship team would be Indians in 1996 and beyond.

The good feeling of all of Cleveland about the future showed in the *Cleveland Plain Dealer* editorial the following Monday, which thanked the Indians for a great season, recounted the great memories, and reminded Indians' fans: "So let there be no whining about not winning it all on the first try. The 1995 Indians were as legitimate as an uncorked bat. They'll be back. There's no 'maybe' about next year."[10]

NOTES

1. Terry Pluto and Tom Hamilton, *Glory Days in Tribe Town, The Cleveland Indians and Jacobs Field 1994-97* (Cleveland: Gray and Company, 2014), 83.

2. Grant Segall, "Fans Explode: We Did It! We Did It!," *Cleveland Plain Dealer*, October 18, 1995: 1A.

3. Murray Chass, "Braves' Unfinished Business Is Indians' Unchartered Water," *New York Times*, October 21, 1995: 31.

4. Burt Graeff, "Opinions Are Split on Series," *Cleveland Plain Dealer*, October 21, 1995: 9D.

5. Bonnie DiSimone, "Hershiser Chooses to Leave Game," *Cleveland Plain Dealer*, October 22, 1995: 3S.

6. Paul Hoynes, "Indians Players Ready to Turn It Up; Players Toughen Under Pressure of 0-2 Deficit," *Cleveland Plain Dealer*, October 24, 1995: 1D.

7. Liz Robbins, "Bench-Clearing Spark; Maddux-Murray Altercation Gives Indians Incentive to Win," *Cleveland Plain Dealer*, October 27, 1995: 3S.

8. Paul Hoynes, "Glavine Stifles Tribe; Oh So Close," *Cleveland Plain Dealer*, October 29, 1995: 1S.

9. Paul Hoynes, "Braves' Pitchers Derailed Tribe's Offensive Machine," *Cleveland Plain Dealer*, October 30, 1995: 1C.

10. Editorial, "Thanks for Everything; The Indians Have Nothing to Be Ashamed of, Because Losers Don't Get to the World Series," *Cleveland Plain Dealer*, October 30, 1995: 8B.

1995 INDIANS BY THE NUMBERS

BY DAN FIELDS

1.176
WHIP of Dennis Martinez, third-best in the AL. Orel Hershiser (1.207) was seventh in the league.

1.311
WHIP of the 1995 Indians, best in the AL.

2
Players on the 1995 Indians who won Gold Glove Awards: Kenny Lofton (outfield) and Omar Vizquel (shortstop). Lofton won four consecutive Gold Gloves with the Indians from 1993 through 1996, and Vizquel won eight straight with the Indians from 1994 through 2001.

2.08
Ratio of strikeouts to walks by Cleveland pitchers, best in the AL.

3
Wild pitches by Jason Grimsley in 1 1/3 innings on May 24 against the Milwaukee Brewers.

3
Doubles by Albert Belle in a June 11 game against the Brewers. He also hit a single.

3.08
ERA of Dennis Martinez, third-lowest in the AL.

3.83
ERA of the 1995 Indians, lowest in the AL.

4
Runs scored by Albert Belle on May 16 and by Kenny Lofton on May 19 and June 9.

5
Hits (including a double) in six at-bats by Carlos Baerga in a 12-inning game against the Oakland Athletics on July 16.

5
Home runs by Albert Belle over two consecutive games, on September 18 and 19 against the Chicago White Sox, to tie a major-league record. In the latter game, he homered in three consecutive plate appearances.

5
Players on the 1995 Indians with at least 20 home runs: Albert Belle (50), Manny Ramirez (31), Paul Sorrento (25), Jim Thome (25), and Eddie Murray (21).

6
RBIs by Paul Sorrento, batting eighth, on May 3 against the Detroit Tigers. He hit a two-run double in the second inning and a three-run

homer in the third inning and also drove in a run on a sacrifice fly in the sixth inning.

6

Players on the 1995 Indians in the All-Star Game on July 11 in Arlington, Texas. The AL starting lineup included center fielder Kenny Lofton (batting first), second baseman Carlos Baerga (batting second), and left fielder Albert Belle (batting fifth). Baerga had a double and two singles in three at-bats and scored the game's first run, but Belle and Lofton were each hitless in three at-bats. Also playing were Dennis Martinez (who gave up one hit — a solo home run by Craig Biggio — in two innings), Manny Ramirez (who drew two walks), and Jose Mesa (who pitched a perfect ninth).

6

Players on the 1995 Indians with a batting average of at least .300: Eddie Murray (.323, fifth in the AL), Albert Belle (.317), Carlos Baerga (.314), Jim Thome (.314), Kenny Lofton (.310), and Manny Ramirez (.308).

8

Runs scored by the Indians before an out was recorded in the first inning on May 9 against the Kansas City Royals. The Indians won 10-0.

8

Games that the 1995 Indians won by at least 10 runs.

9

Consecutive games won by the 1995 Indians from August 23 to September 1.

10

Wins in relief by Julian Tavarez, against only two losses (.833 winning percentage).

11

Assists as a center fielder by Kenny Lofton, tied for most in the majors.

13

Triples by Kenny Lofton, most in the majors. He hit two triples on July 8, August 2, and August 16

13-0

Record of the 1995 Indians in extra-inning games.

16-6

Record each of Orel Hershiser and Charles Nagy. They tied for third in the AL in winning percentage (.727) and fifth in the league in wins.

17

Home runs by Albert Belle in September, to tie Babe Ruth's 1927 record for most homers in September.

18.0

At-bats per strikeout by Carlos Baerga, second best in the AL.

24

Double plays grounded into by Albert Belle, second in the majors.

27

Games won by the 1995 Indians in their final at-bat.

30

Games by which the 1995 Indians won the AL Central over the second-place Royals, the largest margin in major-league history. The Indians clinched the division title on September 8, in their 123rd game of the season.

43

Age of Dave Winfield, who played 46 games with the Indians during his final season. In his 22-year career, he amassed 3,110 hits, 465 home runs, 1,833 RBIs, and 5,221 total bases.

46

Saves by Jose Mesa, most in the majors in 1995 and still a Cleveland record (through 2014). On August 20, he set a major-league record with 37 consecutive saves without a blown opportunity.

50 AND 52

Home runs and doubles, respectively, by Albert Belle. He is the only player in major-league history (through 2018) to hit 50 home runs and 50 doubles in the same season. Belle led the majors in home runs in 1995 (no one else had more than 40) and tied with Edgar Martinez of the Seattle Mariners for most doubles. Belle shattered Al Rosen's team record of 43 home runs, set in 1953, and had the most doubles by a Cleveland player since 1926 (George Burns-64).

54

Stolen bases by Kenny Lofton, most in the AL. He led the league in stolen bases for five consecutive years from 1992 through 1996.

54-18

Record of the 1995 Indians at Jacobs Field. The .750 home winning percentage was the highest in the majors since the 1975 Cincinnati Reds.

97

Walks drawn by Jim Thome, fifth in the AL.

100

Wins by the 1995 Indians, against only 44 losses. The .694 winning percentage was the highest in the major leagues since 1954, when the Indians went 111-43 (.721).

103

Extra-base hits by Albert Belle, most in the majors since 1948. He broke Hal Trosky's team record of 96 extra-base hits, set in 1936.

121

Runs scored by Albert Belle, tied (with Edgar Martinez) for most in the AL. It was the most runs by a Cleveland player since 1955 (Al Smith-123).

126

RBIs by Albert Belle, tied (with AL MVP Mo Vaughn of the Boston Red Sox) for most in the AL. Manny Ramirez had 107 RBIs and tied for seventh in the league.

132

Stolen bases by the 1995 Indians, most in the AL.

175

Hits by Carlos Baerga, fifth in the AL. Albert Belle had 173 hits and tied for seventh in the league.

207

Home runs by the 1995 Indians, most in the majors and a new record for the team.

.291

Batting average of the 1995 Indians, highest in the majors since the 1950 Red Sox.

.361

On-base percentage of the 1995 Indians, highest in the majors.

380

Total bases by Albert Belle, most in the majors in 1995 and most by a Cleveland player since 1936. (Hal Trosky-501)

.438

On-base percentage of Jim Thome, third in the majors.

444

Assists by second baseman Carlos Baerga, the most by any fielder in the majors.

445

Walks allowed by Cleveland pitchers, fewest in the AL.

.479

Slugging average of the 1995 Indians, highest in the majors.

.690
Slugging average of Albert Belle, highest in the majors. Manny Ramirez and Jim Thome (both .558) finished in the top 10 in the AL.

766
Strikeouts by Cleveland batters, fewest in the majors.

.839
OPS of the 1995 Indians, highest in the majors.

840
Runs scored by the 1995 Indians, most in the majors. It was the most runs by the team since 1938 (847).

1.091
OPS of Albert Belle, second in the majors. Jim Thome (.996) and Manny Ramirez (.960) finished in the top 10 in the AL.

3,000TH
Career hit by Eddie Murray on June 30, with a single off Mike Trombley of the Minnesota Twins. He become the third player (after Nap Lajoie and Tris Speaker) to join the 3,000-hit club with Cleveland.

2,842,745
Regular-season attendance of the 1995 Indians at Jacobs Field, second highest in the AL and a new team record.

AL Division Series: Indians over Red Sox (3 games to 0). Eddie Murray had a triple and a home run in Game Two and went 5 for 13 (.385) during the series.

AL Championship Series: Indians over Mariners (4 games to 2). Orel Hershiser won Game Two and Game Five, allowing two earned runs in 14 innings, and was named the ALCS MVP. Kenny Lofton batted .458 (11 for 24) and stole five bases, and Carlos Baerga batted .400 (10 for 25).

World Series: Braves over Indians (four games to two)

0
Hits in 16 at-bats by Rafael Belliard of the Braves.

1ST
Team to win a World Series representing three cities: the Braves. They won as the Boston Braves in 1914, the Milwaukee Braves in 1957, and the Atlanta Braves in 1995.

2-0
Record of Tom Glavine, who won Game Two and Game Six. He allowed only four hits and two earned runs over 14 innings and was named the World Series MVP.

2.67
ERA of the Braves. The Indians had an ERA of 3.57.

3
Consecutive games in which Ryan Klesko of the Braves hit a home run (Game Three, Game Four, and Game Five).

3
Decades in which Eddie Murray hit a World Series home run (in 1979 and 1983 with the Baltimore Orioles and in 1995 with the Indians).

5
Games in the 1995 World Series decided by one run.

6
Runs scored and bases stolen by Kenny Lofton, the most by any player on either team.

.179
Batting average of the Indians. The Braves batted .244.

Around the Majors in 1995

0
Hits allowed in a 7-0 complete-game win by Ramon Martinez of the Los Angeles Dodgers on

July 14 against the Florida Marlins. He retired the first 23 batters before walking Tommy Gregg in the eighth inning. Ramon's younger brother, Pedro Martinez of the Montreal Expos, pitched nine perfect innings on June 3 against the San Diego Padres but gave up a double in the 10th.

0.811

WHIP of Greg Maddux of the Braves, lowest in the majors since Walter Johnson in 1913. Randy Johnson of the Mariners was best in the AL, with a WHIP of 1.045.

1ST

Career hit by Derek Jeter of the New York Yankees, a single off Tim Belcher of the Mariners on May 30. His 3,465th and final hit was a single off Clay Buchholz of the Red Sox on September 28, 2014.

1ST

Forfeited game in the major leagues in 16 years, on August 10, 1995. At Dodger Stadium, the visiting St. Louis Cardinals were awarded a 2–1 forfeit with one out in the bottom of the ninth after promotional giveaway baseballs were thrown onto the field.

1ST

Shortstop to win the NL MVP Award since Maury Wills in 1962: Barry Larkin of the Reds. He was second in the league in stolen bases (51), fifth in runs scored (98), and sixth in batting average (.319). In addition, he won his second Gold Glove Award.

1.63

ERA of Greg Maddux, who had the lowest ERA in the majors for the third consecutive year. Randy Johnson's ERA of 2.48 was best in the AL.

2

Home runs by Jeff King of the Pittsburgh Pirates in the second inning on August 8 against the San Francisco Giants.

2

Grand slams in consecutive innings (fourth and fifth) by Robin Ventura of the White Sox on September 4 against the Texas Rangers.

2

Players with at least 30 home runs and 30 stolen bases in 1995: Barry Bonds of the Giants (33 homers and 31 steals) and Sammy Sosa of the Chicago Cubs (36 homers and 34 steals).

3

Pinch-hit home runs in a May 6 game between the Dodgers and the Colorado Rockies, tying a major-league record.

3

Consecutive innings in which Andres Galarraga of the Rockies hit a home run on June 25 against the Padres. He connected in the sixth, seventh, and eighth innings off three pitchers.

3

Games in a four-day period in which Ken Caminiti of the Padres hit home runs from both sides of the plate, on September 16 and 17 against the Cubs and September 19 against the Rockies.

3

Players who hit for the cycle in 1995: Rondell White of the Expos on June 11 (13-inning game), Gregg Jefferies of the Philadelphia Phillies on August 25, and Tony Fernandez of the Yankees on September 3 (10-inning game).

4

Home runs in consecutive at-bats by Jeff Manto of the Orioles, over three games from June 8 to 10. He walked twice during the June 9 game.

4

Consecutive walks allowed by Brian Boehringer of the Yankees on July 5 against the White Sox before retiring a single batter. Then he gave up a grand slam.

4

Home runs allowed by Brian Anderson of the California Angels in the second inning of a September 5 game against the Orioles.

4

Extra-inning home runs in 1995 by Ron Gant of the Reds, to tie the NL record set by Willie Mays in 1955.

4

Shutouts by Mike Mussina of Orioles, most in the majors. Greg Maddux of the Braves and NL Rookie of the Year Hideo Nomo of the Dodgers tied for most in the NL with three shutouts.

4

Players on the Rockies with at least 30 home runs: Dante Bichette (40, most in the NL), Larry Walker (36), Vinny Castilla (32), and Andres Galarraga (31). Bichette hit 31 homers at home and nine on the road. He had nearly twice as many home runs as walks (22).

4TH

Consecutive NL Cy Young Award won by Greg Maddux. Randy Johnson won the AL Cy Young Award.

5

Home runs by Mark McGwire of the Athletics in consecutive games on June 10 (two home runs) and June 11 (three home runs) against the Red Sox.

5

Consecutive games with a home run by AL Rookie of the Year Marty Cordova of the Twins, from May 16 through 20, and Jose Canseco of Red Sox, from August 21 through 25.

5

Consecutive shutouts thrown by the Baltimore Orioles in the last five games of the season (September 26 through October 1).

5TH

Consecutive year in which Frank Thomas of the White Sox hit .300 or higher with at least 20 home runs, 100 RBIs, 100 runs, and 100 walks. He ran the string to seven years in 1997.

6

Deficits that the Cubs overcame to beat the Houston Astros 12–11 in 11 innings on September 28.

7.87

Ratio of strikeouts to walks by Greg Maddux, best in the majors. Randy Johnson led the AL with a 4.52 ratio.

9

Consecutive hits by Lance Johnson of the White Sox from September 22 to 24 against the Twins. He hit three triples on September 23 to tie the post-1900 single-game record and led off the next game with a triple.

9

Triples by Brett Butler (seven with the New York Mets and two with the Dodgers) and Eric Young of the Rockies, tied for most in the NL.

10

Complete games by Greg Maddux, most in the majors. Jack McDowell of the Yankees led the AL with eight complete games.

10TH

Player to hit a home run in his first All-Star Game at-bat: Jeff Conine of the Marlins. His pinch-hit homer in the eighth inning off Steve Ontiveros of the Athletics was the deciding run in the NL's 3–2 win over the AL, and Conine was named the game's MVP.

12

Errors in a May 12 game between the Cardinals and the Dodgers. Third basemen Scott Cooper of the Cardinals and Garey Ingram of the Dodgers each had three errors.

12
Home runs by the Tigers (7) and White Sox (5) in a May 28 game, to set a major-league record. The teams also hit a total of nine doubles; the 21 extra-base hits in the game set an AL record. The White Sox won 14-12.

14
Hits by Mike Benjamin of the Giants in three consecutive games (June 11 to 14) while filling in for injured third baseman Matt Williams. Benjamin matched the three-game record set by Willie Keeler in 1897.

16
Losses by Paul Wagner of the Pirates, most in the majors. Three pitchers tied for most in the AL with 15 losses: Jason Bere of the White Sox, Kevin Gross of the Rangers, and Mike Moore of the Tigers.

18
Consecutive road wins by Greg Maddux from July 2, 1994, to September 27, 1995.

19
Wins each by Greg Maddux and Mike Mussina, tied for most in the majors.

23
Consecutive games with a base hit by Dante Bichette of the Rockies (May 22 to June 18) and Jim Edmonds of the Angels (June 4 to June 29), the longest hitting streaks in 1995.

28
Pinch hits by John Vander Wal of the Rockies, to set a major-league single-season record. He had four pinch-hit homers.

35.7
At-bats per strikeout by Tony Gwynn of the Padres, best in the majors since 1979. Gwynn struck out only 15 times in 535 at-bats.

38
Saves by Randy Myers of the Cubs, most in the NL.

40
Consecutive stolen bases by Tim Raines of the White Sox without getting caught, from July 23, 1993, to August 4, 1995. He was caught stealing in his next attempt, on September 2.

40 1/3
Consecutive scoreless innings pitched by Kenny Rogers of the Rangers from May 6 to June 1.

51
Doubles by Mark Grace of the Cubs, most in the NL.

56
Stolen bases by Quilvio Veras of the Marlins, most in the majors.

76
Games by Curt Leskanic of the Rockies, the most by any pitcher in the majors. Jesse Orosco of the Orioles led the AL with 65 games.

108
Walks thrown by Al Leiter of the Toronto Blue Jays, most in the majors. Ramon Martinez led the NL with 81 walks.

123
Runs scored by Craig Biggio of the Astros, most in the majors. He scored five runs on July 4 and September 28 (11-inning game).

128
RBIs by Dante Bichette, most in the majors.

136
Walks drawn by Frank Thomas, most in the majors. Barry Bonds led the NL with 120 walks.

150
Strikeouts by Mo Vaughn, most in the majors. Andres Galarraga led the NL with 146.

197

Hits by Dante Bichette and Tony Gwynn, tied for most in the majors. Lance Johnson led the AL with 186 hits.

229 1/3

Innings pitched by David Cones, most in the majors. He pitched 130 1/3 innings with the Blue Jays and 99 innings with the Yankees. Greg Maddux of the Braves and Denny Neagle of the Pirates tied for most in the NL with 209 2/3 innings.

232

Days that 1994-95 strike and subsequent lockout lasted (August 12, 1994, to April 2, 1995), resulting in the cancellation of 938 regular-season games and the entire 1994 postseason. The 1995 season began on April 25 and was shortened to 144 games. Owing to fan anger about the strike, attendance in 1995 was down 20% from 1994.

294

Strikeouts by Randy Johnson, most in the majors. His rate of 12.35 strikeouts per nine innings pitched set a major-league record. Hideo Nomo led the NL with 236 strikeouts.

.318

Career batting average of Kirby Puckett, whose final season was 1995. He averaged 192 hits a year during his 12 seasons with the Twins. Loss of vision in his right eye owing to glaucoma forced him to retire in 1996.

359

Total bases by Dante Bichette, most in the NL.

.368

Batting average of Tony Gwynn, highest in the majors. Edgar Martinez led the AL with a .356 average, becoming the first designated hitter to win a batting title.

.479

On-base percentage of Edgar Martinez, highest in the majors. Barry Bonds led the NL with a .431 mark.

607

At-bats by Lance Johnson, most in the majors. Brian McCrae of the Cubs led the NL with 580 at-bats.

.620

Slugging average of Dante Bichette, highest in the NL.

673

Plate appearances by Craig Biggio, most in the majors. Chad Curtis of the Tigers led the AL with 670 appearances.

.905

Winning percentage of Greg Maddux, highest in the majors. Randy Johnson led the AL with a .900 mark.

1.107

OPS of Edgar Martinez, highest in the majors. Barry Bonds led the NL with 1.009.

1,915TH

Game together as teammates by Alan Trammell and Lou Whitaker of the Tigers, on September 13 against the Brewers, to break the AL record set by George Brett and Frank White of the Royals. Both Trammell and Whitaker made their major-league debut on September 9, 1977, in the second game of a doubleheader against the Red Sox.

2,131ST

Consecutive game played by Cal Ripken of the Orioles on September 6 against the Angels, to break Lou Gehrig's long-standing record. The crowd of more than 46,000 at Camden Yards included President Bill Clinton, Vice President Al Gore, and Hall of Famers Joe DiMaggio and Frank Robinson. When the game became official (after 4 1/2 innings had been completed), Ripken took a lap around the ballpark to greet fans. His streak began on May 30, 1982.

2,194

Career wins by Sparky Anderson, who managed the Reds from 1970 to 1978 and the Detroit Tigers from 1979 to 1995. He won two World Series titles with the Reds in 1975 and 1976 and another with the Tigers in 1984. Anderson was the first manager to win the World Series in both leagues.

5,280

Feet (exactly one mile) above sea level of the upper deck's purple-painted 20th row in Denver's Coors Field, which opened in 1995.

SOURCES

Nemec, David, ed. *The Baseball Chronicle: Year-by-Year History of Major League Baseball* (Lincolnwood, Illinois: Publications International, 2003).

Society for American Baseball Research. *The SABR Baseball List and Record Book* (New York: Scribner, 2007).

Solomon, Burt. *The Baseball Timeline* (New York: DK Publishing, 2001).

Sugar, Burt Randolph, ed. *The Baseball Maniac's Almanac* (third edition) (New York: Skyhorse Publishing, 2012).

baseball-almanac.com

baseballlibrary.com/chronology/byyear.php?year=1995

baseball-reference.com

retrosheet.org

thisgreatgame.com/1995-baseball-history.html

ACKNOWLEDGMENTS

I never felt that Mike Hargrove received the credit he was due in his time as manager of the Cleveland Indians. Mostly because he never received the Manager of the Year Award from the Baseball Writers' Association of America (BWAA). Perhaps the sportswriters who make up the BWAA thought Grover had it too easy. With an All-Star at every position, he was said to have a "push-button" lineup, his managerial skills shrouded by an overwhelming amount of talent. It's a harsh assessment, but one that even Grover might give credence to.

I may be able to understand a bit how Hargrove feels. I too had an All-Star, at every position on my editing team. We brought the band back together from my last venture as an editor when in 2014 the team collaborated on *Pitching to the Pennant: the 1954 Cleveland Indians*. I am nobody's fool: Stick with what works.

It would seem likely that any conversation with regard to the BioProject begins and ends with Bill Nowlin and Len Levin. Bill has written more bios than any other SABR member, with the total approaching 700. In addition, Bill is often the first reader of the bios for the book projects. He offers sound critiques and keen insight on how each article could be written tighter and more clearly.

Len has edited more bios for the BioProject then anyone. He is often the copywriter for most book projects and he has easily surpassed 1,000 bios edited. In addition, Len also serves as the first reader of the stories that are submitted to the Games Project.

Rick Huhn rounds out the triumvirate as he once again served as the fact-checker for every article. I shudder to think what errors might show up in each article if it were not for Rick's keen attention to detail.

With Bill, Len, and Rick on the editing team, there is never a reason for concern. The tasks will be completed and in a timely fashion. I am greatly appreciative for all of their efforts, and I probably don't tell them that often enough.

Of course, this book would not even be remotely possible without the work of the contributing authors. There were 36 writers in all who unselfishly gave their time and their talents to put together one remarkable volume. It was a delight to work with each, and I am indebted to each one of them.

My thanks to John Horne at the National Baseball Hall of Fame, who assisted in sending me images from the photo archives at the HOF. Special thanks to Chuck Guerrieri, Lou Boyd, Bill Gagliano, Larry Phillips, Jack Corrigan of the Colorado Rockies and Curtis Danburg of the Cleveland Indians for submitting images that were used in this book.

I would also like to extend a big thank-you to Gregory H. Wolf and Rory Costello. Not only did they both submit articles, but both Gregory and Rory serve as co-chairs for the BioProject Committee at SABR. They do an outstanding job and I am obliged for their support of this project.

Finally, a note of remembrance. Jeanne M. Mallett and Charles Faber both contributed articles to this project, but unfortunately both passed away before it's publication. I never had the pleasure of meeting either individual in person, but I was fortunate enough to get to know them through various projects like this one. I enjoyed working with them and they will both be missed. Jeanne, who split her allegiances between the Indians and Tigers, commiserated with me on the Tribe's loss in Game Seven of the 2016 World Series. We decided to take the high road and not pout or whine about the outcome.

But that's another book for another day.

- Joseph Wancho

CONTRIBUTORS

Rick Balazs is an attorney and CPA and lives in Columbus, Ohio with his wife, Laurie. He grew up in Greater Cleveland and is an avid Indians fan. He has been a SABR member over 10 years and wrote the biography of Jim Hegan in SABR's *Pitching to the Pennant: The 1954 Cleveland Indians*.

Richard Bogovich is the author of *Kid Nichols: A Biography of the Hall of Fame Pitcher* and *The Who: A Who's Who*, both published by McFarland & Co. He has contributed to various SABR books, including *Bittersweet Goodbye: The Black Barons, the Grays, and the 1948 Negro League World Series* and biographies of Freddie Sanchez and Dewon Brazelton for *Overcoming Adversity: Baseball's Tony Conigliaro Award*. He works for the Wendland Utz law firm in Rochester, Minnesota.

Augusto Cárdenas lives in Maracaibo, Venezuela, and is the author of *My story: Luis Aparicio*, the authorized biography of the only Venezuelan inducted into the Hall of Fame, and also was from 2002 to 2016 the baseball beat writer of *Diario Panorama*, a local newspaper with more than 100 years of experience. He has covered the Venezuelan Winter League since 2000 and has been a special correspondent to cover Major League Baseball games, MLB Spring Trainings, All-Star Games, the World Baseball Classic, the Nippon Professional Baseball and the Caribbean Series. Cárdenas is a SABR member who loves to write about the Venezuelan players who saw playing when he was a just a kid, and is the founder of Cárdenas Sports Media, a Venezuelan media outlet and a PR sports department for Venezuelan athletes.

Alan Cohen serves as Vice President-Treasurer of the Connecticut Smoky Joe Wood Chapter, and is a datacaster for the Hartford Yard Goats, the Double-A affiliate of the Rockies. He has written more than 40 biographies for SABR's bio-project. He has expanded his research into the Hearst Sandlot Classic (1946-1965), which launched the careers of 88 major-league players. He has four children and six grandchildren and resides in Connecticut with wife Frances, cat (Morty), and dog (Sam).

Philip A. Cola is an Associate Professor of Management at Case Western Reserve University in Cleveland, Ohio. He obtained his Master's Degree in Experimental Psychology from Cleveland State University and his PhD in Management from Case Western Reserve University. He lives in Middleburg Hts., Ohio with his wife Diane and their two children Adam and Samantha. They are big fans of the Cleveland Indians.

Rory Costello enjoyed taking part in this project because it allowed him to write about the third generation of Amaro ballplayers as well as the first and second. He lives in Brooklyn, New York, with his wife Noriko and son Kai.

Richard Cuicchi joined SABR in 1983 and is an active member of the Schott-Pelican Chapter. Since his retirement as an information technology executive, Richard authored *Family Ties: A Comprehensive Collection of Facts and Trivia about Baseball's Relatives* and contributed to numerous SABR BioProject and Games publications. He does freelance writing and blogging about a variety of baseball topics on his website TheTenthInning.com. Richard lives in New Orleans with his wife, Mary.

Charles F. Faber was a native of Iowa who lived in Lexington, Kentucky, until his passing in August 2016. He held degrees from Coe College, Columbia University, and the University of Chicago. A retired public school and university teacher and administrator, he contributed to numerous SABR projects, including editing *The 1934 St. Louis Cardinals: The World Champion Gas House Gang*. Among his publications are dozens of professional journal articles, encyclopedia entries, and research reports in fields such as school administration, education law, and country music. In addition to textbooks, he wrote 10 books (mostly on baseball) published by McFarland. His last book, co-authored with his grandson Zachariah Webb, was *The Hunt for a Reds October*, published by McFarland in 2015.

Dan Fields is a senior manuscript editor at the New England Journal of Medicine. He loves baseball trivia, and he enjoys attending Boston Red Sox and Pawtucket Red Sox games with his teenage son. Dan lives in Framingham, Massachusetts, and can be reached at dfields820@gmail.com

A SABR member since 2006, **Chip Greene** is a regular contributor to the BioProject. In the 2015 he edited SABR's *Mustaches and Mayhem, the story of the 1972-74 Oakland A's*. Chip lives with his wife, Elaine, in Waynesboro, PA.

Edward Gruver has been a contributing writer to SABR for several years. An award-winning sportswriter for 34 years, he has written seven books on sports and has been a contributing writer to seven additional sports books. He writes for several online sports sites. A native of north Jersey, he lives in Lancaster, Pennsylvania with his wife Michelle.

Mark Hodermarsky's latest book, *The Animals: True Rock Royalty* (New Haven Publishing) is his seventh. A retired English teacher, Hodermarsky's love of baseball and baseball writing remain passionate. He lives in Olmsted Falls, Ohio.

A SABR Member since 2001, **Paul Hofmann** is the Associate Vice President for International Programs at Sacramento State University. He is a native of Detroit, Michigan and lifelong Detroit Tigers fan. During his free time, he enjoys reading, writing and collecting baseball cards. Paul currently resides in Folsom, California.

Rick Huhn is the author of full-length biographies of Hall of Famers Eddie Collins and George Sisler. His latest book, The *Chalmers Race* (University of Nebraska Press, 2014), analyzes the controversial 1910 American League batting race. He is a founding member and co-coordinator of the Hank Gowdy Columbus (OH) Chapter of SABR.

Jay Hurd, is a librarian and museum educator. He retired from Harvard University where he worked as the Preservation Review Librarian for Widener Library. He studies, writes, and presents on baseball history, including the Negro Leagues, women in baseball, and baseball literature for children and young adults. A long-time member of SABR, he recently relocated from Medford, Massachusetts to Bristol, Rhode Island.

Jimmy Keenan has been a SABR member since 2001. His grandfather, Jimmy Lyston, and four other members were all professional baseball players. A frequent contributor to SABR publications, Keenan is the author of the following books; *The Lystons: A Story of One Baltimore Family* and *Our National Pastime -The Life, Times and Tragic Death of Pitcher Win Mercer- The Lyston Brothers: A Journey Through 19th Century Baseball.* Keenan is a 2010 inductee into the Old-timers Baseball Association of Maryland's Hall of Fame and a 2012 inductee into the Baltimore's Boys of Summer Hall of Fame.

Ted Leavengood worked for the federal government in Washington, DC for many years and in retirement has written extensively about Washington baseball history, including numerous books. He lives in Chevy Chase, MD with his wife Donna.

Bob LeMoine grew up in Maine, following the Red Sox on the radio or black and white TV. He joined SABR in 2013 and rarely finds a book project he doesn't like. His works include co-editing with Bill Nowlin, *Boston's First Nine: the 1871-75 Boston Red Stockings*. A future project will explore the Boston Beaneaters of the 1890s. Bob lives in Rochester, New Hampshire, and works as a high school librarian and adjunct professor.

Len Levin, a retired newspaper editor, is the grammarian and copyeditor for the Rhode Island Supreme Court. He has been the copyeditor for most of SABR's recent books. He lives in Providence, R.I.

Stephanie Liscio is the author of *Integrating Cleveland Baseball: Media Activism, the Integration of the Indians, and the Demise of the Negro League Buckeyes*. She is a member of the leadership team in Cleveland's Jack Graney chapter of SABR, and a board member of SABR's Negro League committee. Stephanie has contributed essays to a number of SABR publications, and to the *Black Ball Journal*. She just completed her Ph.D. in history at Case Western Reserve University, where she wrote a dissertation on stadiums and community after World War II.

Gary Livacari is a baseball historian and SABR member. He is the co-editor of the Old-Time Baseball Photos Facebook page (with over 73K followers), and administrator of the Baseball History Comes Alive! web page. He was an editor for the Boston Public Library Leslie Jones Baseball Collection project, helping to identify ball players in almost 3,000 photos from the 1930s and 1940s. He has also written biographies for the SABR BioProject, plus numerous articles and book reviews. He resides in Park Ridge, Illinois and can be contacted at: Livac2@aol.com

John McMurray is Chair of both the Deadball Era Committee and the Oral History Committee for SABR. He is a member of the Editorial Board of *Base Ball: New Research on the Early Game*.

Jeanne M. Mallett was a writer and an attorney who resided in Washington D.C. before passing away in November, 2017. Thanks to her father, she was a lifelong baseball fan who appreciated the glory and tragedy of America's grand game, especially for Cleveland fans. Although she was not allowed to play Major League Baseball, she often wrote about it. This was her fifth baseball-themed publication.

Wynn Montgomery served as co-editor of SABR's 2010 Atlanta convention journal. His baseball interests include the art and history of the game, minor league and college baseball, and the Negro Leagues. His annual "B-4" Road Trip with two other SABRites feeds his passion for Baseball, Battlefields, Burial Grounds (historic cemeteries), and Barbeque. He has seen every MLB team play a home game and has visited more than 100 minor league and college ballparks.

Bill Nowlin has been active in SABR for many years now, particularly involved in helping edit many of SABR's books. A former political science professor, he is a co-founder of Rounder Records and honored in the International Bluegrass Music Hall of Fame. He lives in Cambridge, Massachusetts with his son Emmet.

Gregg Omoth A SABR member since 2000 he is a lifelong Minnesota Twins fan. Gregg and his wife Dianne live in Maple Grove, MN with their three children, Amelia, Nolan and Emma.

Anna Pohlod is an SEO content writer and ghostwriter creating blog posts, e-books, SEO strategies, and more for clients all over the internet. She also provides marketing support for the Ohio State University Press and judges fiction competitions for NYC Midnight. Anna has a BA in English literature from Ohio University and an inbound marketing certification from HubSpot Academy. Learn more about her work at annapohlod.com.

Joel Rippel, a Minnesota native and graduate of the University of Minnesota, is the author or co-author of nine books on Minnesota sports history and has contributed to several SABR publications.

Kelly Boyer Sagert is a full-time freelance writer and the author of 15 books, most of them history-related. One of her books was a biography of Shoeless Joe Jackson, which led to Sagert appearing on an ESPN documentary about the Black Sox. She also writes historical plays. One of them served as the basis of an Emmy-nominated documentary appearing on PBS (Trail Magic: The Grandma Gatewood Story). Sagert received full writing credits for that documentary.

Rick Schabowski has been a SABR member since 1995. He is a retired machinist from Harley-Davidson Company, is currently an instructor at Wisconsin Regional Training Partnership in the Manufacturing Program and is a certified Manufacturing Skills Standards Council instructor. He is President of the Ken Keltner Badger State Chapter of SABR, President of the Wisconsin Old-time Ballplayers Association, Treasurer of the Milwaukee Braves Historical Association, a member of the Hoop Historians, and the Pro Football Research Association. He lives in St. Francis, Wisconsin.

Harry Schoger counts his blessings that in his lifetime, he has seen both the Chicago Cubs and the Cleveland Indians win a World Series. In the latter case (1948) he was a ten-year old fifth grader in Anderson, Indiana, when the series pitted the Indians vs the Boston Braves. His teacher, Mr. Sluder, brought a radio to class so the students could listen to the broadcasts of the games with Mel Allen and Jim Britt on the mike. As the series unfolded he adopted the Indians as his team.

Blake W. Sherry is a lifelong Pittsburgh Pirates fan who resides in Dublin, Ohio. A retired Chief Operations Officer of a public retirement system, he has been a member of SABR since 1997. He co-leads the Hank Gowdy SABR Chapter in Central Ohio, and currently runs that chapter's quarterly baseball book club. He contributed to the SABR book *Moments of Joy and Heartbreak: 66 Significant Episodes in the History of the Pittsburgh Pirates*.

From an early age **David E. Skelton** developed a lifelong love of baseball when the lights from Philadelphia's Connie Mack Stadium shone through his bedroom window. Long removed from Philly, he resides with his family in central Texas where he is employed in the oil & gas industry. An avid collector, he joined SABR in 2012.

Doug Skipper first joined SABR in 1982. A member and former president of the Halsey Hall (Minnesota) Chapter, Doug has written a number of Biographies and Game Project summaries for SABR publications and websites. He serves as chairperson for the Larry Ritter Award Committee and has been a member for several years. A native of Texas, who grew up in Colorado, lived in Wyoming and North Dakota, and now Minnesota, Doug has been an avid Red Sox fan since his maternal grandfather took him and his two brothers to see their first major league game, on Thursday, August 3, 1967 at Fenway Park (a 5-3 win). Doug and his wife Kathy have two daughters, MacKenzie and Shannon. He is a marketing research, customer satisfaction and public opinion consultant who reads and writes about baseball.

Mark S. Sternman roots for the Yankees and, since he has lived in Massachusetts since May 1995, for whichever team plays the Red Sox. In this book, he writes about the first of many playoff games that he has seen in Boston, which took place on October 6, 1995. Having watched the game from the bleachers, Sternman still recalls how quiet the Fenway faithful got as Cleveland completed its sweep of the ALDS.

Andy Sturgill lives in suburban Philadelphia with his wife, Carrie, and son, Ray. A lifelong Phillies fan, he enjoys visiting ballparks and reading about baseball and US Presidents.

Clayton Trutor is the chair of the Gardner-Waterman (Vermont) chapter. He has made more than 20 contributions to the SABR Biography Project. He is the co-editor of Overcoming Adversity: Baseball's Tony Conigliaro Award. You can follow him on Twitter: @ClaytonTrutor.

Nick Waddell is a graduate of Wayne State University and DePaul University College of Law. He's a lifelong Tigers fan, and previously wrote the biography on Al Kaline for Sock It To 'Em Tigers. He thinks a good baseball game involves peanuts, keeping score, and trying to decode the other team's signs.

The Sleeping Giant Awakes is the second BioProject book that **Joseph Wancho** has served as editor. In 2014, he was at the helm of *Pitching to the Pennant: The 1954 Cleveland Indians* (University of Nebraska Press). In 2018, he authored *So You Think You Are a Cleveland Indians Fan?* (Skyhorse Publishing).

Wancho has been a member of SABR since 2005 and he currently serves as the Vice Chair for the Baseball Index Committee.

Tom Wancho grew up rooting for the Indians in the West Side Cleveland hamlet of Brooklyn. He is a graduate of St. Edward High School, John Carroll University (BA), and Northwestern State University (MA). He currently works as a curator for the Bullock Texas State History Museum in Austin, Texas.

Steve West joined SABR in 2006. He has written several articles for the BioProject.

Christopher Williamson joined the Rocky Mountain Chapter of SABR in 2017. He works in software implementation but writes about prospects for dynasty fantasy baseball owners on his website – makeprospectsgreatagain.com and will be a contributor for baseball-farm.com during the upcoming 2018 season and beyond. His loyalty lies with the White Sox but he has become an adopted Rockies fan since moving to Denver in 2015.

A lifelong Pirates fan, **Gregory H. Wolf** was born in Pittsburgh, but now resides in the Chicagoland area with his wife, Margaret, and daughter, Gabriela. A professor of German studies and holder of the Dennis and Jean Bauman Endowed Chair in the Humanities at North Central College in Naperville, Illinois, he has edited eight books for SABR. He is currently working on projects about Wrigley Field and Comiskey Park in Chicago, and the 1982 Milwaukee Brewers. As of January 2017, he serves as co-director of SABR's BioProject, which you can follow on Facebook and Twitter.

Made in the USA
Columbia, SC
25 March 2019